VATICAN COUNCIL NOTEBOOKS
I

HENRI CARDINAL DE LUBAC

VATICAN COUNCIL NOTEBOOKS
I

Introduced and annotated by
LOÏC FIGOUREUX

Foreword by
FRANÇOIS-XAVIER DUMORTIER, S.J.
and JACQUES DE LAROSIÈRE

Preface by JACQUES PRÉVOTAT

Translated by Andrew Stefanelli
and Anne Englund Nash

IGNATIUS PRESS   SAN FRANCISCO

Original French edition:
Carnets du concile I
© 2007 by Éditions du Cerf, Paris

Cover designed by Roxanne Mei Lum

CONTENTS

FOREWORD

The publication of Father Henri de Lubac's *Council Notebooks* has been long and carefully considered. In fact, although we have a typewritten text corrected by Father de Lubac, the original manuscripts of the *Council Notebooks* seem now to have disappeared. The reasons for this have been the subject of conjecture, all the more complex given the fact that the opinion of Father de Lubac regarding the publication of these *Notebooks* seems to have changed over the course of the years and led him to write one day, in his own hand, in an undated text: "These pages must not be published." He justified this wish by the limitations of his notes, "simple reference points for my own use, noted in the day-to-day course of events and copied out cleanly"; he indicated these same limitations in a second series of preliminary notes in which he places greater emphasis on the evolution of the conciliar situation, of which he was not able to take account, and on the partial nature of his information. These notes come from an author who, in thinking about what he has written, sees their limitations. That is the explicit reason for the wish expressed in this regard by Cardinal de Lubac. So the desire to publish this typewritten text cannot be attributed to Cardinal de Lubac himself.

Because these *Council Notebooks* were known to exist and quotations from them had been published and because they could contribute to a better understanding of the work of the council, it seemed to the Cardinal de Lubac International Association and to the French provincial of the Society of Jesus that the publication of this text of the *Council Notebooks* should be authorized, while at the same time drawing the reader's attention to what was expressed by Cardinal de Lubac while alive.

Father François-Xavoer Dumortier,
French Provincial of the Society
of Jesus Internationale

Jacques de Larosière,
President of the Association
Cardinal Henri de Lubac

PREFACE

In the rich historiography associated with the Second Vatican Council, there has been no lack of syntheses and local studies or of testimony from participants, bishops, experts, observers, and witnesses from all over the world. The French actors in this drama have not been outdone. The *Notes quotidiennes au Concile* (Daily notes from the council) by Father Chenu (1995) were followed by *Mon Journal du Concile (My Journal of the Council)* by Father Congar (2002), who had wished his work to be published, on the condition that the publication be delayed until after the year 2000. Now at last we have Henri de Lubac's *Council Notebooks (Carnets du Concile)*, long awaited and also an indispensable source for understanding this event.

Apart from *Entretien autour de Vatican II* (Conversation about Vatican II), an interview given to Angelo Scola that appeared in the Italian magazine *30 Giorni* (June 1985) and was reprinted in July 1985 by the publishing house Éditions du Cerf,[1] Henri de Lubac kept a low profile. Was this due to a reluctance to open up, to the painful memory of what he suffered during the 1950s, or to the desire to preserve the discretion and distance of one closely involved in the council's work? Or to the fear of exploitation by the media of remarks intended to remain on the plane of the sole competence he acknowledged: that of a theologian? So many factors explain the reserve shown, up until his final years, by one of the principal thinkers and inspirers of the council about consenting to make public these *Notebooks*, written day by day in the course of the sessions and subsequently recopied and amended with that care and precision, that scrupulous regard for accuracy and for the *mot juste* so characteristic of what he conceived to be the manner and requirements of his task as an expert at the council.

From the time of his nomination as a consultor to the Preparatory Theological Commission in July 1960, then as an expert on the

---

[1] Henri Cardinal de Lubac, *Entretien autour de Vatican II* (France catholique-Éd. du Cerf, September 25, 1985).

Doctrinal Commission, Father de Lubac was an active participant in or a witness to all the diverse aspects of the council: the general congregations, the Doctrinal Commission (which met in the afternoons during the sessions but continued its work during the intersessions as well), meetings of the French bishops, private encounters between French and foreign bishops on the fundamental questions, various conversations, preparation and clarification of interventions at the council at the request of numerous bishops, lectures in front of audiences of bishops or of seminarians studying in Rome. Father de Lubac was always present, except for a brief interruption due to illness at the beginning of the second session.

All aspects of the council are recalled; first of all, the slow and laborious fine-tuning of the definitive texts, in the course of interventions in Latin by the council Fathers in the *aula*, scrupulously reproduced from day to day and punctuated with commentaries, at times sharp and vivid; next, the numerous opportunities for encounters encouraged by the extraordinary theological and cultural ferment that prevailed in Rome during the council. Notable among these were encounters with observers from other confessions, such as Cullmann or Boegner, who were constantly present. Other aspects not without interest included discussions in bars, where friendships were formed and rare exchanges took place, as well as behind-the-scene maneuvers fomented by one group or another, by which he was not fooled. Nor did Henri de Lubac overlook minor, everyday incidental details, like the deafening racket made in the basilica when heavy carts loaded with printed amendments to be distributed to the Fathers would enter from behind Bernini's baldachino!

European influence was still dominant, but there were personalities from outside Europe that were able to make their presence felt, for example the Melchite patriarch Maximos IV, advocate of a sister Church founded by the apostles, warm defender of ecumenism, fervent opponent of the Holy Office, whose remarks were hardly ever repeated, or Helder Câmara, presented with a lively sympathy though not without reservations. The presence of other Churches, particularly the African Church, united around her leaders – Gantin, Rugambwa, Sangaré, Zoa – and very much alive, brought out in a striking manner the universality of the Church, her catholicity.

On the essential points, the theologian did not give way: wherever the opportunity was presented to him – and the occasions were not

lacking – he firmly defended his ideas, particularly one on which he
insisted: the orthodoxy of the Catholic faith of Father Teilhard de Chardin. The struggle was severe, and the moments of leisure few. Nevertheless, strolls in Rome or the surrounding country stirred up secret
memories and reflections that remind one how much the author of the
Drame de l'humanisme athée (*The Drama of Atheistic Humanism*) remained
a humanist and true poet.

Besides information about the numerous aspects of the conciliar
assembly, what makes the testimony of these notebooks so captivating
is the strongly rendered presence of men and their psychology. The
author excels in sketching the portrait of the actors with only a few
words. Thus, the masters of the Holy Office, confident of possessing
the truth – Ottaviani, Browne, Parente, Tromp – who made the painful
discovery that they were not the masters of the council, are depicted
with a sense of nuance and an understanding that help to recreate the
relationship between the forces and to grasp why the majority were
reluctant to put forward their views. On the side of the majority, hostile
to the schemas prepared by the Curia, were the cardinals from various countries, particularly of central Europe – Döpfner, Frings, König,
Léger (from Montreal) – supported by Bea, who finally in the course
of the first session proved to be the dominant figure. The clarity of
their remarks, their calm aptitude for going back to and clarifying what
was essential, conferred on them an authority in the assembly that was
(with some exceptions) not enjoyed to the same degree by the French
episcopate, which was an insufficiently consistent group. De Lubac has
the gift of spotting nascent talent. In the course of the elaboration, rich
in new developments, of the constitution *De Ecclesia*, he deepened his
acquaintance with "Dr." Joseph Ratzinger, whom he describes as a
"theologian as peaceable and kindly as he is competent". In the same
way, during the long discussion over the drafting of the constitution
Gaudium et spes, he observed the assertiveness of Archbishop Wojtyła,
whose interventions struck him because of the seriousness, the rigor,
and the solidity of his faith and created in him a lively flow of fellow
feeling, which was reciprocated.

The criteria he uses in his judgments and assessments are quite naturally those of a theologian, hence his almost constant distrust of journalists. The contamination of theological questions by political ideology or
propaganda never ceased to trouble him. De Lubac does not conceal his
opinions. That makes this document valuable. The judgments he makes

concerning the remarks of some seemingly well-qualified religious figures are sometimes surprising. For example, in the course of the discussion about *De revelatione* (the constitution *Dei Verbum*), he observes: "I
note, in all these discussions, the nearly equal ignorance of the theologians and the exegetes, bishops or not, of the traditional doctrine on
Scripture. Some excellent formulae, completely traditional, are set aside
without being understood."

If we had to define the principal axis of this consistency in high spiritual standards and theological rigor, we would need to come back to
the central conception of his religious thought: the close link between
the natural and the supernatural. Loïc Figoureux quite rightly points
out the importance of this idea at the beginning of his introduction.
One could cite numerous examples that reveal, in the judgments as well
as in the doctrinal choices of Father de Lubac, the fundamental character of this criterion. Thus, to give one example, dated November 1964,
during the third session, observe in what terms he defines his method
to some close associates: "I try to bring the problems back to their most
simple expression and in terms of faith. I also seek to show how much
the questions we are debating today need to be fundamentally clarified
by a coherent doctrine of nature and the supernatural." Again, during
the discussion of schema 13 (*Gaudium et spes*), he recalls (September 25,
1964): "If we are not convinced a priori, through the view of faith,
that there is a certain preestablished harmony between the revelation
of Christ, grasped in its fullness, and the secret expectation planted by
God in the depths of men of all times, we will lack the apostolic daring that alone has a chance of reaching the men of our time." Making due allowances and distinguishing between levels, is there not also
a connection here between this criterion and his explicit reservations
about the abandonment by the CFTC [Confédération française des travailleurs chrétiens, a French trade union] of its Christian label? But,
above all, is this not the profound reason that caused him to second the
remarks of Bishop Volk and Archbishop Wojtyła during the discussion
of *Gaudium et spes*? We should continue this line of questioning and ask
ourselves if the importance that he attached to the question of collegiality and of the famous *Nota explicativa praevia*, relative to the discussion
of chapter 3 of the constitution *De Ecclesia*, an importance greater than
Father Congar, no less vigilant himself on this topic, seems to have
granted it, is not a product of these same deep reasons. Nor has it been
ruled out (the question remains unresolved) that a certain theological

and ecclesiological proximity to Don Dossetti might be due to similar considerations.[2]

These *Notebooks* bear witness to the difficulties Father de Lubac experienced in the years following the publication of *Surnaturel* (*Supernatural*, 1946), very much in evidence within the Theological Commission, in the preparatory period (1961–1962) during which the theologian, just recently named to the commission by John XXIII, was confronted with future conciliar schemas prepared by his adversaries. Nevertheless, it was his theology that prevailed in *Lumen gentium* as also in *Dei Verbum*. The approval that Étienne Gilson showed him, shortly before the last session of the council (June 24, 1965), delighted him. All in all, a major turning point had occurred, with tremendous consequences.[3]

This monumental work could not have been accomplished without the conjunction of fortunate circumstances: the new edition of the *Œuvres complètes* (*Complete Works*) of Henri de Lubac on the initiative of the Association Internationale Cardinal Henri de Lubac and the publisher Éditions du Cerf; then the opportunity that was offered, in order to complete the difficult task of editing and annotating this work, to benefit from the aid of Loïc Figoureux, a young professor of history who, in addition to his talents as a researcher and skills as a historian, has the rare capacity to seek, wherever it might be found, the information and expertise available. How can one not pay tribute to the judicious choice he made in having recourse to Father Leo Declerck, the author of numerous works on the council, an internationally recognized expert, whose experience, discreet knowledge, and competence offered on a daily basis contributed to the remarkable work of the young historian.

JACQUES PRÉVOTAT,
Professor of modern history, University of Lille-III

---

[2] Guillaume Cuchet, "À propos de quelques parutions récentes sur le concile Vatican II", *Revue d'histoire de l'Église de France*, vol. 88, no. 221 (July–December 2002), p. 465, no. 4.

[3] For developments in the area of missions, see Ilaria Morali, *La salvezza dei non cristiani: L'influsso di Henri de Lubac sulla dottrina del Vaticano II* (Editrice missionaria italiana, 1999). The author emphasizes the influence of Father de Lubac on no. 16 of the constitution *Lumen gentium*.

INTRODUCTION

It was on the chance reading of a newspaper,[1] in July 1960, that Father Henri de Lubac[2] learned that he had been called to participate in the preparation of Vatican Council II. His *Notebooks* take their beginning from this point. These retrace, over the course of five and a half years, his participation in the preparation and then in the four sessions of the council. However, his nomination as a consultor to the Preparatory Theological Commission, in the summer of 1960, was hardly expected, and Father de Lubac even appears astonished by it. How does one explain this reaction? What importance would it have for the journal he was then beginning? Can one, finally, attempt a first approach toward answering the question of what Father de Lubac's role was at the council?

An "Astonishing Piece of News"[3]

These few words, recorded by Father de Lubac in his *Notebooks* at the announcement of his official nomination as consultor to the Preparatory

---

[1] Henri de Lubac, *Mémoire sur l'occasion de mes écrits* (1st ed., Namur: Culture et vérité, 1989; 2nd ed., 1992), in *Œuvres complètes*, vol. 33 (Paris: Éd. du Cerf, 2006), 117; trans. by Anne Elizabeth Englund as *At the Service of the Church: Henri de Lubac Reflects on the Circumstances That Occasioned His Writings* [ASC] (Communio Books; San Francisco: Ignatius Press, 1993), 116.

[2] Henri Sonier de Lubac was born on February 20, 1896, in Cambrai. Soon thereafter, the de Lubacs returned to Lyon, after a few years spent in Bourg-en-Bresse. He entered the Society of Jesus in October 1913, but his formation was interrupted by World War I, during which he experienced, as did so many others, the horror of the trenches. As a result of having been wounded in 1917, at Ville-sur-Tourbe (Marne), he suffered, from 1922 on, from violent headaches that permitted him to do hardly any sort of work other than reading during these attacks. He was ordained a priest on August 22, 1927, and he was named a professor of theology at the Catholic Faculties of Lyon in October 1929. He taught fundamental theology there and, from 1930 on, the history of religion. In 1938, his first important book, *Catholicisme*, was published. When the Second World War broke out, he got involved in the spiritual resistance and the *Cahiers du Témoignage chrétien* (Notebooks of Christian witness). Forced to leave Fourvière in 1950, he returned there in 1960. He was named as a consultor to the Preparatory Theological Commission in 1960 and a council expert (*peritus*) in 1962. Father de Lubac was created cardinal on February 2, 1983, and died on September 4, 1991.

[3] *Notebooks*, July 25, 1960.

Theological Commission, say a great deal about the suspicion in which he was held, principally after the Second World War, by one group within the Society of Jesus, the "Roman" theologians, but also, sometimes, by the pope himself.[4] In fact, one cannot understand Father de Lubac's astonishment without going back to the theological controversy of the late 1940s, from which he suffered grave consequences. Without going into all the details of a study already thoroughly carried out elsewhere,[5] it is advisable to recall this background, the echoes of which will be found in the *Notebooks*.

There were sharp tensions within French Catholicism in the period after the war. They were rooted, but only in part, in the differences that emerged in the course of the black years.[6] In Thomist circles, the climate was troubled principally because of several Jesuit initiatives that seemed to call scholastic theology into question, whereas this theology represented for the Thomists "the truly scientific state of Christian thought".[7] Two book series symbolize the initiatives of the priests of the Society of Jesus: "Sources chrétiennes"[8] (Christian sources), a series of patristic texts whose first volumes had appeared in 1942, and "Théologie", sponsored by the faculty of theology at Fourvière,[9] the first volume of which, *Conversion et grâce chez saint Thomas d'Aquin* (Conversion and grace in Saint Thomas Aquinas, 1944), by Father Henri Bouillard, S.J., was vigorously debated.[10] When an article by Father Daniélou devoted to the "Orientations présentes de la pensée religieuse" (Current directions in

---

[4] In a letter to his superior André Ravier on March 30, 1957, published in the November 2006 *Bulletin* of the Association Internationale Cardinal Henri de Lubac, Father de Lubac, recounting the "Fourvière affair", wrote: "In an audience in the course of which Cardinal Gerlier wanted to plead my cause, the Holy Father [Pius XII] said to him: 'But with this priest, what is alarming is that one never knows if he says what he thinks.'" Let us note, however, that in 1958 Father de Lubac received the confidence of the same Pius XII through his confessor, A. Bea.

[5] We are following here the work of É. Fouilloux, "Dialogue théologique? (1946–1948)", in *Saint Thomas au XXᵉ siècle* (Paris: Éd. Saint-Paul, 1994), 153–95.

[6] On this phase of the [Nazi] occupation and the Vichy regime in France, besides the essay by Fouilloux, 166–67, see H. de Lubac, *Entretien autour de Vatican II* (Paris: France catholique-Éd. du Cerf, 1985), 15. Also see the Fouilloux's work *Une Église en quête de liberté: La Pensée catholique française entre modernisme et Vatican II, 1914–1962* (Paris: Desclée de Brouwer, 1998), esp. chap. 7.

[7] M. M. Labourdette, "La Théologie et ses sources", *Revue thomiste* 46 (1946): 353–71.

[8] A series founded by Fathers de Lubac, Daniélou, and Mondésert, from a project of Father Fontoynont. See É. Fouilloux, *La Collection "Sources chrétiennes": Éditer les Pères de l'Église au XXᵉ siècle* (Paris: Éd. du Cerf, 1995).

[9] This refers to the Jesuit Scholasticate, located on Fourvière Hill in Lyon.

[10] We note that the book had been approved by Father Charles Boyer.

religious thought) appeared in the French Jesuit magazine *Études* in April 1946, the fears of the Thomists were confirmed, helped by the sharpness of Father Daniélou's expressions. He did in fact condemn "a progressive desiccation of theology" and judged that "Neo-Thomism still stresses theological rationalism." He recalled "categories that are those of contemporary thought and that scholastic theology had lost". The article was regarded as an attack and provoked the reaction, in measured terms, of the Dominican Labourdette in the journal *Revue thomiste*,[11] which he edited. In his eyes, the disparagement of scholasticism presented the risk of an abandonment of the claim to universal truth, in short, a risk of relativism. The Jesuit response, composed by Father de Lubac, appeared in a journal of the Society, *Recherches de science religieuse*, in February 1947.[12] The article was interpreted as a "point blank rejection".[13] The publication, in the fall of 1946, of *Surnaturel: Études historiques*[14] (*Supernatural: Historical Studies*) only reinforced the mistrust felt for what some were calling the "Fourvière school", from the name of the hill in Lyon that sheltered the Jesuit scholasticate where Father de Lubac resided but where he did very little teaching. His questioning in this work of scholastic teaching since the sixteenth century on the question of the relationship between nature and the supernatural was the subject of keen debate. Father de Lubac intended in particular to dispute the notion of pure nature, which resulted, in his view, in an extremely harmful dualism: if there exist two "strata" in man, nature and the supernatural, each foreign to the other, there would seem to be a great risk of seeing them studied separately, by philosophy and theology respectively, as if the latter had nothing to say about the whole, living man. If the work was hailed by several journals as a particularly important study on the supernatural,[15] critics were no less numerous, reproaching him especially for calling into question the gratuitous character of the supernatural: if there exists in human nature a desire to see God, is man then not able to demand to see God and thus compel him? Henri de Lubac believed that he had been misunderstood. Indeed, he did not intend to question the

---

[11] Labourdette, "Théologie et ses sources", 353–71.

[12] October–December 1946 issue, 385–401.

[13] Letter from Marie-Dominique Philippe, O.P., to Labourdette, February 7, 1947, quoted by Fouilloux, "Dialogue théologique?", 174.

[14] H. de Lubac, *Surnaturel: Études historiques* (Paris: Aubier-Montaigne, 1946).

[15] In ASC 203–23, Father de Lubac reproduces several reviews that, while sometimes mentioning a few reservations, recognize the importance of his book.

gratuity of the supernatural. To insist on the profound unity of man, in opposition to dualism, did not imply that man could attain to the knowledge of God by himself.[16] Nevertheless, "critics abounded everywhere. 'Refutations' of *Surnaturel* increased. The most sinister news, apostasy included, circulated. Every country brought its own contribution to the campaign. Some *Semaines religieuses* warned the faithful against the 'wolves in sheep's clothing'."[17]

In Rome, concerns about these French affairs were coming to light. Father Garrigou-Lagrange, O.P., a professor of theology at the Angelicum and a major figure in Roman Thomism, published a violent attack in the journal *Angelicum*,[18] "La nouvelle théologie où va-t-elle?" (Where is the new theology going?), in which he judged that the latter "amounted to modernism". Henri de Lubac, who obviously could not accept such an accusation, also rejected the label of new theology used by his Dominican opponent. In part, because it grouped together under a single heading theologians who, in his opinion, in no way formed one school of thought; and also because he judged that his theology was in no respect a novelty but was, on the contrary, a return to the sources, he who recalled that "it is necessary to go back to the farthest past – which will reveal itself to be the nearest present."[19] Thus, in the controversy surrounding *Surnaturel*, Father de Lubac reckoned that he had returned to the sources of Thomism and was more of a Thomist than some of its defenders, who were proving to be more faithful to the commentators on Saint Thomas, Cajetan in particular, than to the

---

[16] For a succinct presentation by Father de Lubac himself, refer to *Entretien autour de Vatican II*, 28–32.

[17] ASC 62. Among the criticisms, Father de Lubac mentions most particularly the article by Father Garrigou-Lagrange, "La Nouvelle Théologie où va-t-elle?", *Angelicum*, October–December 1946, 126–45, that of Father Boyer, "Nature pure et surnaturel dans le 'Surnaturel' du P. de Lubac", *Gregorianum* 28 (1947): 379–95, that of Father Jacques de Blic in *Mélanges de science religieuse 1947*, and the relevant pages of Father de Broglie's *De Fine ultimo humanae vitae* (Paris: Beauchesne, 1948). See ASC 272–73, the letter to the Father Provincial of March 16, 1948.

[18] "Nouvelle Théologie où va-t-elle?" However, the article was not made public until the beginning of 1947. We should note that there was no coordination between the French Dominicans and Father Garrigou-Lagrange, as Fouilloux points out. The *Revue thomiste* had even refused to publish the latter's article, judging it too violent.

[19] H. de Lubac, *Paradoxes*, 1946, republished in *Œuvres complètes*, vol. 31 (Paris: Éd. du Cerf, 1999), 11; trans. Paul Simon and Sadie Kreilkamp as *Paradoxes* and included in *Paradoxes of Faith* (San Francisco: Ignatius Press, 1987), 20. We note, however, that Fouilloux, in his book *Une Église en quête de liberté*, judged, without trying to be controversial, that the appellation "new theology" was well deserved. See chap. 6.

Angelic Doctor himself. Among the Jesuits, the attitude of the Superior General, Jean-Baptiste Janssens, elected in 1946, changed.[20] At first he had shown confidence in Father de Lubac, entrusting to him the editorship of the journal *Recherches de science religieuse*.[21] Rather quickly, however, when the controversy swelled, he took a cautious approach: so in March 1948 he asked that Father de Lubac's responses to the objections made against him be submitted not only to the censor of his province, which was normal, but also to the Jesuit censor in Rome.[22] It would, however, be going too far to speak of a repudiation, although Father de Lubac wrote to his provincial: "The exceptional rule to which it [the double censorship] submits me (and which does not apply to any of my detractors) shows me clearly, despite the paternal assurances you have given me, that I am considered suspect."[23] But the attacks against *Surnaturel* did not cease, even from within the Society of Jesus: "The main charge was drawn up by Father Guy de Broglie.[24] It was spread throughout the world, thanks to the relations of the Gregorian with all countries. The fact that Father Charles Boyer (and, no doubt, a few others) is in Rome allows him to reach and disturb the most influential members of the Church's government."[25] The confidence of the Superior General weakened as a consequence: "In 1950, on receipt of an outrageous dossier, full of calumnies as incredible as they were appalling, Father General, badly advised by Father Dhanis,[26] who had no fear at the time of playing the role of false witness, virtually signed off on that dossier without making the least beginning of an inquiry."[27]

The consequences of this were very serious. At the beginning of 1950, Father de Lubac received a secret letter[28] from the Superior General of the Jesuits. He informed him that he would have to cease teaching at the faculty of theology, from that summer onward, and that he would have to

---

[20] We are relying here on Father de Lubac's documents, without having been able to consult the archives of the Holy See or those of the General Curia of the Society of Jesus, still closed for this period.

[21] Father de Lubac learned of this decision on January 22, 1947: see ASC 62, n. 6.

[22] ASC 274.

[23] Letter from H. de Lubac to his provincial, March 25, 1948, quoted in ASC 274.

[24] In his book *De Fine ultimo humanae vitae* (Paris: Beauchesne, 1948).

[25] Letter from H. de Lubac to his povincial, André Ravier, March 30, 1957, in the November 2006 *Bulletin* of the Association Internationale Cardinal Henri de Lubac.

[26] The latter had been the apostolic visitor in France in 1949.

[27] Letter from H. de Lubac to his provincial, André Ravier, March 30, 1957.

[28] ASC 64.

step down from his post as editor of *Recherches de science religieuse*. Official notification, again from the Superior General, was not slow in coming. Several professors who resided at Fourvière were relieved of their duties: Fathers Émile Delaye, Henri Bouillard, Alexandre Durand, Pierre Ganne, and Henri de Lubac, for "pernicious errors on essential points of dogma".[29] Furthermore, they had to leave Fourvière for new accommodations. For Father de Lubac, these were in Paris, on Rue de Sèvres. According to his testimony, it was, moreover, on the very day of his arrival in Paris that Pius XII's encyclical *Humani generis* was published in the newspaper *La Croix*. The encyclical was understood to be a condemnation of the "new theology", although Henri de Lubac always insisted on the fact that he found nothing in the document that could affect him doctrinally. Not in the sense that no passage in the encyclical was directed at him, but in the sense that his doctrine, clearly understood, was not in contradiction with it.[30] Even so, his works *Surnaturel, Corpus mysticum, De la connaissance de Dieu* (*The Discovery of God*), and his article in *Recherches de science religieuse* on "Le mystère du surnaturel"[31] (The mystery of the supernatural) were withdrawn from all Jesuit houses of formation the world over, on the decision of the Superior General dated October 25, 1950. From this time forward he was forbidden to publish any works of theology.

"From 1955–1956 on, a certain relaxation in official severity began to manifest itself."[32] Already in 1953, however, his work *Méditation sur l'Église* (*The Splendor of the Church*) was able to appear in print, but that was, in the opinion of the Superior General himself, "quite by chance".[33] In 1956, as a sign of détente, Father de Lubac was able to publish *Sur les chemins de Dieu* (*On God's Paths*), a much enlarged version of the second

---

[29] ASC 68.

[30] He wrote as follows on September 22, 1960, in his notebooks regarding the "Fourvière affair": "I reread some passages of the encyclical *Humani generis* that chanced to fall beneath my eyes. I am sickened by the stupidity and baseness of the calumnies that resulted in certain paragraphs of this text. How can so much meanness be possible in the center of Catholicity? And such an absence of discernment? What is most cruel is that this comes from the Society of Jesus itself, from false reports made by brothers and solemnly ratified by Father [General], and, more than ten years later, despite the evidence, still maintained in full."

[31] H. de Lubac, *Corpus mysticum: L'Eucharistie et l'Église au Moyen Âge, étude historique*, Théologie (Paris: Aubier-Montaigne, 1944; 2nd ed., 1949), and *De la connaissance de Dieu* (Paris: Éd. du Témoignage chrétien, 1945; 2nd ed., 1948), trans. by Alexander Dru as *The Discovery of God* (Grand Rapids: Eerdmans, 1996). "Le Mystère du surnaturel", *Recherches de science religieuse* 36 (1949): 80–121. The article had been approved by the Jesuit superior general.

[32] ASC 80.

[33] ASC 75.

edition of *De la connaissance de Dieu*, and, in November 1959, after an interruption of nine years during which time he had been supported by Cardinal Gerlier, he was able to resume teaching at the Catholic Faculties in Lyon. This background is indispensable for a proper understanding of the *Notebooks*, but the fundamental question remains. Why, despite all these signs of abatement, did Henri de Lubac in fact regard the news of his nomination as consultor to the Preparatory Theological Commission to be "astonishing"? Did this not seem to be in line with the rehabilitation that had been in progress since the mid-1950s? In reality, Father de Lubac judged, with good reason, moreover, as will be seen in these *Notebooks*, that not all opposition was extinguished. The Superior General had not entirely recovered from his mistrust toward him and had never acknowledged the least error of judgment in the measures taken with regard to the priests of Fourvière. In May 1959, Father de Lubac wrote the following in a report prepared for an interview with his provincial:[34] "Even just recently, Father General opposed with all his power the steps he knew would be successful in assuring the regular resumption of my teaching duties; it was only a few days ago that he caused me to understand once more that he would not authorize any doctrinal publication from me." Although testimonies of friendship and esteem were not lacking, Father de Lubac considered the accusations of 1950 to have discredited in part what he said. This is what he explained to the provincial, Blaise Arminjon, in January 1960, that is, only a few months before his nomination as consultor: "The less-than-mediocre men who are the supreme authorities in the view of our Father General are blind – and, what is more, moved by passions that are infinitely petty. Until my death I will be regarded as being at least among the suspect. And this is what compels me to keep quiet. For more than twelve years, I have been present, in silence (as far as essential matters go), at the Tragedy of the Faith that is playing out in our time. The lies solemnly ratified by Father General in 1950 have killed me."[35] The words of this letter and of the report are obviously very harsh, but they must be understood in the same sense as the letter to Father Ravier in 1957:[36] in

---

[34] Archives of the Jesuit Province of France, Henri de Lubac, dossier 28, report dated May 23, 1959.

[35] Ibid., dossier 29, 1960, folder, letter from H. de Lubac to Father Arminjon, dated January 21, 1960.

[36] One can refer for this to the presentation of this letter by Father Georges Chantraine, in the November 2006 *Bulletin* of the Association Internationale Cardinal Henri de Lubac.

these excerpts, Father de Lubac speaks openly to his superior, as, for that matter, the functioning of the Society of Jesus expects. He does not conceal from him what he judges to be dishonest tactics. Father de Lubac cannot accept the substance of the accusations, because they appear to him simply false, without that calling into question the obedience and respect owed to his superiors. It should be noted that these clarifications, implacable as they may be, are limited to the relation between the Jesuit and his superior, and an excerpt from the letter to Father Ravier is significant in this regard: "I will never say anything outside; but every time this matter comes up between my superiors and me, I will say to them again: in the accusation brought against me there is not a single atom of truth."[37]

So Father de Lubac's astonishment is explained by the harshness endured and the persistent distrust. His nomination thus appeared to be a sign of appeasement. Gaston Fessard, moreover, wrote to him on August 1, 1960: "I have learned of your nomination as theological "consultor" to the future council ... beside Congar, Labourdette, and others. Hearty congratulations. It is a small and late reparation."[38] Father de Lubac likewise saw in this a change in the climate, since he answered his confrere: "They wanted to give a symbolic reassurance to the two religious orders[39] that were shaken up in France under the former regime."[40] Moreover, this interpretation was not limited only to the man concerned or to the circle of his friends, since the *Informations catholiques internationales* wrote in the issue for January 1, 1961, dedicated to the council: "One point merits being raised. John XXIII has called upon the expertise of two theologians deeply controversial among some in Rome, isolated for a time from the debates, and who thus are making a conspicuous comeback: Fathers Congar and de Lubac."[41] However, the doubts concerning his orthodoxy were not limited to a few Jesuits surrounding the Superior General and, especially, had not suddenly disappeared at the announcement of his nomination. The council, announced by John XXIII on January 25, 1959,

---

[37] Letter to Father Ravier of March 30, 1957.

[38] Fessard–de Lubac correspondence, consulted in its typewritten version at the Henri de Lubac Center in Namur.

[39] The Jesuits and the Dominicans. This was still Father de Lubac's interpretation in his *Entretien autour de Vatican II*, 16.

[40] Letter to Gaston Fessard, August 4, 1960.

[41] Page 11.

had begun with a phase termed "antepreparatory" (from May 17, 1959, to May 30, 1960), intended for the collection, perusal, and classification of the *vota*[42] of the future council Fathers, as well as those from the faculties of theology and canon law. Now the *vota* issuing from the Lateran, the Gregorian, and the Angelicum[43] carried the trace of past quarrels. The one from the theology faculty of the Lateran, composed by A. Piolanti, named the incriminated theologians, quoting extracts from their works in order to illustrate and underline their errors. Henri de Lubac was cited three times, at the head of the authors criticized. Some names already seen above, such as that of Henri Bouillard, are also found there. The works from which the quotes were drawn included, of course, *Surnaturel* and *Corpus mysticum*, to which must be added the article that appeared in the journal *Recherches de science religieuse*.[44] Once again, it was a question of defending against any form of relativism, which the writings of Henri de Lubac were said to imply, particularly on the question of dogmatic and theological progress. Father Dhanis, S.J., had been given the task of drafting the *votum* of the theology faculty of the Gregorian, and, even at the time of the preparatory phase of the council, Father de Lubac saw in it serious attacks aimed at himself.[45] Ten years after *Humani generis* and at the dawn of the council, the controversy surrounding the "new theology" was not yet extinguished.

A Journal of the Council

It was in this somewhat tense context that Father de Lubac arrived in Rome and took part in the preparation for the council. His *Notebooks* allow us to follow him during this preparatory phase, then throughout the four sessions (from 1962 to 1965). Before wondering what interest these notes might have for the contemporary reader, let us listen to Father de Lubac himself:

> These pages must not be published. They are personal recollections, simple reference points for my own use, jotted down from day to day and then written up. Sometimes they repeat mere gossip or jokes. Various

---

[42] Wishes regarding the subjects t be treated at the council.

[43] This refers to the pontifical universities or the Roman ecclesiastical faculties. The Dominicans run the Angelicum, and the Jesuits the Gregorian.

[44] "Le Mystère du surnaturel", 80–121.

[45] See especially the entry dated September 28, 1961, in the *Notebooks*.

names are misspelled. I have often noted, not what was most important, but what I was able to hear, whether in the general congregations in Saint Peter's or in the meetings of the Doctrinal Commission or in various chance conversations. The days when I had the most work were also the days when I lacked the time to take notes. And many papers were lost before everything could be gathered together and put in order.

a. On various points, in the course of these six years (1960–1965), my opinions have sometimes changed, either because certain situations evolved or because I found myself better informed about the men or circumstances by subsequent events.

b. There is obviously no question here of a report that intends to be complete and always balanced. It is a series of notes taken from day to day according to what I was able to see and hear from my window. Even when I was a direct witness, many things escaped me, and many elements were lacking for me to form a judgment. When, for example, I talk about a general congregation in Saint Peter's, I only mean that part of it which I heard or understood from my seat, according to my capacity to pay attention at any given moment.[46]

The Redaction of the "Notebooks"

Father de Lubac indicates that his *Notebooks* were written up from notes taken on the spot that are no longer available to us. A question arises for the historian: How much time passed between the events and their new transcription in the *Notebooks*? Beneath this question, which might appear somewhat trifling, resides a subtle problem: Did the delay between taking the notes on the spot and their final rewriting lead Father de Lubac to correct his first impressions? We can only suggest some partial answers. The final version of the *Notebooks* was at times composed at least several months after the fact. This is certain for the first session. In fact, in the entry for October 4, 1962, that is, just before his departure for the council, Father de Lubac wrote: "This morning, in Marseilles, I kissed mama for the last time." Since Gabrielle de Lubac did

---

[46] This undated document is part of a dossier entitled "Cahiers du Concile" (council notebooks) consulted at Namur, at the Henri de Lubac Center, itself part of the Molette collection. It is possible, however, that this note dates from the 1980s, for it is certain that H. de Lubac reread his *Notebooks* for his book *Entretien autour de Vatican II*, as p. 34 of that work attests: "According to a note I made on September 19, 1964, on that date, Paul VI had already agreed with the four 'moderators' to make the decision." One will observe that this note does indeed appear under that date in the *Notebooks*.

not die until March 15, 1963, it is evident that all the pages dedicated to this first session were put in final form after March 15, 1963.[47] That does not necessarily imply, however, that Father de Lubac corrected his first impressions in the final version.

To detect such amendment of the notes taken on the spot is made rather difficult by the absence of those notes from the archives. Nevertheless, we have been able to avail ourselves of Father de Lubac's correspondence, which gives us a snapshot of his immediate reactions. After consulting several sizable collections of letters, we have found only one obvious discrepancy, concerning the black week during the third session of the council, between his impressions at the time and their transcription in the *Notebooks*. The black week was characterized by a great deal of emotion in the council *aula* due to three events: the addition to the schema *De Ecclesia* of the *Nota praevia*, which explained, on the pope's initiative, the doctrine of collegiality and responded to the concerns of the minority at the council; the postponement of the vote on religious liberty, even though the vote was eagerly expected; the addition of *modi* to the decree on ecumenism "in a sense that was felt as a blow to ecumenical amity".[48] On all these points, the level-headedness of Father de Lubac in his *Notebooks* is remarkable. He endeavors to gather the reactions of various people, seeks to inform himself accurately, but he is scarcely moved, or, rather, he does not allow it to show. He only notes that he confided his sorrow to Carlo Colombo, a close friend of Paul VI, and wished that a little light might be shed on all these decisions, since the lack of information was giving rise to comments of every sort.[49] A close comparison of his correspondence with the *Notebooks* is illuminating here, for it reveals the evolution of Father de Lubac's thought. In a letter to Father Bernard de Guibert on November 23, 1963, he writes:

---

[47] The theory according to which the words "for the last time" could have been added later does not hold, for it is the only private note in the *Notebooks*, which is justified only by its exceptional character. One can discover another sign of this chronological gap between the time the events occurred and the time they were recorded: twice during the first session (on November 29 and December 7, 1962), Father de Lubac speaks of Jean Villot as Cardinal Villot, although he was not created a cardinal until February 1965. That would lead one to think that the definitive composition of the manuscript version took place only after that date and, without doubt, after the council, but one ought to be cautious, given the rarity of these clues, even if an error on this point at the time of the events related seems surprising, for Archbishop Villot, Coadjutor Archbishop of Lyon, was not unknown to Father de Lubac.

[48] R. Laurentin, *Bilan du concile* (Paris: Éd. du Seuil, 1966), 19.

[49] *Notebooks*, November 19 and 20, 1964.

November 19, 20, and 21 will remain for a long time, I fear, days of
mourning for the Church. It no longer does any good to get indignant over
what must well be called a "robbery";[50] the wrong has been done, with
incalculable consequences. One could see in Saint Peter's a cardinal, one
of the most solid members of the council, shedding tears. And I would not
dare to report the reflections of certain observers. A few men (a handful),
knowing exactly what they were doing, have set out to ruin any sort of
aggiornamento, to abolish any chance for ecumenism, to send the bishops
of the entire world back to the condition of valets, and everything was
accomplished in three days. The Holy Father, without yielding to them
in everything (far from it!), has yielded sufficiently to put the bishops now
in a false position, reduced to impotence. The incidents of decadence are
going to gather pace, and perhaps in reaction anarchic revolts will spring
up. Catholicity has been completely mocked. One had to have been present at the tragedy from the inside to understand its significance. Let us pray.

The contrast with the *Notebooks* is striking. In fact, on the subject of the
Nota praevia one reads: "Moreover, the most reasonable people must see
very well that the insertion of the *Nota praevia* changes nothing essential
and that this document retains its character whether it is put into the
section or not", and this is noted under the date of November 19. On
November 20, regarding the decree on ecumenism:

> The majority of these corrections are in fact insignificant. But one or two
> of them were the subject of caustic criticism this morning. In particular,
> the next-to-last one. Some saw it as offensive to Protestants. The text of
> the decree says: "In ipsis Sacris Scripturis Deum inquirunt et inveniunt
> sibi loquentem."[51] The new text has: "... Deum inquirunt quasi sibi
> loquentem."[52] So, one asks, has a Christian never been able to find God
> by meditating on Scripture? So the good that he believes he has found in
> his reading has never been more than an illusion (*quasi*)? So the intention
> is to instruct the bishops either to utter this insult or to reject *De œcu-
> menismo?*... However, a question begins to arise, well suited to restore
> calm, at least in this area of ecumenism: Would one go to war over a
> word taken in the wrong sense?

Finally, on the text devoted to religious liberty: "No one, however,
seems to allude to the actual fact that the text of *De libertate* presented

---

[50] An allusion to the "Robber Council of Ephesus", a name given to the Second Council of
Ephesus (449).

[51] In Holy Scripture, they seek and find God, who speaks to them.

[52] They seek God as the one who speaks to them.

by Bishop De Smedt is really a revised text, a point that gave a reason (for some, a pretext) to call for a postponement", in the note for November 21.

This discrepancy between the correspondence and the *Notebooks* is easily explained, not by any hypothesis of double speak, Father de Lubac being far too attached to the truth for that, but by the period of time that elapsed between the notes taken on the spot and their final, rewritten form. Here again, we do not know how much later the definitive version was composed, but a few days were sufficient, in this case of the black week, for Father de Lubac, better informed, to recover his serenity. In fact, in his letter of December 28, 1964, to the same Father de Guibert, the tone is quite different:

> Yes, it is true, the last few days of this conciliar year have been painful, and there is some risk of "trauma" remaining as a result. But, as regards what is basic, that has not brought about any notable change. On the subject of ecumenism, there are two regrettable modifications – but these are only details in a text of which all the substance remains.... And we have to be very glad that, in the end, Paul VI has approved this Note [the *Nota praevia*] in the form that the Theological Commission had finalized it in the last redaction after a great deal of back and forth discussion and many necessary modifications.

Thus the *Notebooks* do not always provide a snapshot of reactions taken from real life but, rather, constitute a text that has sometimes been reworked and amended according to what Father de Lubac later learned.

Finally, these *Notebooks* have been the object of several stages of redaction. As we have said, the first was the taking of notes on the spot, in Saint Peter's during the general congregations or in committee or subcommittee, from which six notebooks were drafted. This manuscript was then typed up at an unknown date. Comparison of the manuscript and typewritten versions reveals some small changes, essentially in the form of short additions intended to clarify Father de Lubac's thought. The fact that the author declared to Philippe Levillain, when he gave him the manuscript version of his *Notebooks* for the latter's thesis[53] in 1972, that he had never reread them permits us to think that these modifications were made after this date, and doubtless even after 1975, the year that Levillain's thesis was published. Indeed, Father de Lubac was

---

[53] *La Mécanique politique de Vatican II: La Majorité et l'unanimité dans un concile* (Paris: Beauchesne, 1975).

alarmed to read some of the judgments[54] he had made; perhaps that was what prompted him to take up his *Notebooks* again. Finally, a third version consists of additions, sometimes voluminous, especially concerning the preparatory phase, and based on the typewritten version. In this case, too, we have no date.[55] It is certain, however, that Father de Lubac referred to his *Notebooks* at the beginning of the 1980s for his book *Entretien autour de Vatican II* (1985), as the work itself and the archives of the French Province of the Society of Jesus at Vanves[56] prove. We cannot deduce from this, however, that all the additions date from the same period.

Might these different versions and the difference in tone observed between the *Notebooks* and the letters not also reveal a difference in the nature of the sources? Let us note immediately that here we are entering the realm of hypothesis. If the *Notebooks* were purely for private use, why not retranscribe the evolution of his thinking on the subject of the black week, an evolution, moreover, that would be completely understandable (the total absence of information allowed one to imagine secret machinations of the worst kind aimed at sabotaging the council, since very few knew what had really happened). Perhaps it was because Father de Lubac thought his *Notebooks* might be used,[57] and he did not wish to inflate incidents and aggravate disagreements that turned out, after more was learned, to be unfounded or at least exaggerated, whereas the letters were written in the grip of emotion. So, in what concerns himself at least – for he notes clearly and accurately the reactions of those around him – Father de Lubac did not wish, on every occasion, to retranscribe the different stages of his reactions but preferred, at least for this episode, to come directly to the conclusions he reached, conclusions that were restrained and better founded, out of concern for the truth but also for appeasement. Father de Lubac was not doing the work of a historian, and one can well believe that transcribing his transient emotions mattered much less to him than showing the debates at issue and their importance for the faith.

---

[54] The author's correspondence with Philippe Levillain, August 2006. Levillain used the *Note-books* in his thesis, without however mentioning them explicitly (he spoke of unpublished documents), in conformity with Father de Lubac's wishes when he gave them to him.

[55] All these additions, deletions, and modifications have been indicated in the notes.

[56] In fact, in box 7 of the Henri de Lubac collection, there is a sort of table of contents of the *Notebooks*, written in Father de Lubac's hand, on the back of printed leaves mentioning among others a book published in 1983.

[57] It is, moreover, significant that some of the corrections are minor ones, matters of pure style: What is the point of that in a purely private document?

The Journal's Interest

In the note quoted at the beginning of this section, Father de Lubac insists, as he often does, on the caution with which his work must be considered. Who would be surprised that these *Notebooks* ought not to be taken as an official, exhaustive, and absolutely sure source of information? Henri de Lubac, qualified as he might be to understand what is going on at the council, is nevertheless only a man, with moments of fatigue, inattention, difficulty in understanding because of static interference or various accents. If this note must not be ignored, insofar as it puts Father de Lubac's text into historical and theological perspective, it remains no less true that the *Notebooks* offer us a particularly interesting account of a fundamental event of the Church. Father de Lubac's research had since the 1930s helped to prepare this *aggiornamento* of the Church that was Vatican II. His *Notebooks* thus prove to be invaluable for those who wish to grasp the crux of the problems under discussion, the issues in the debates, all the more so since Father de Lubac shows himself to be most often remarkably accurate in quoting the speakers and sometimes accompanying their interventions with short comments or more developed passages that permit the reader to share his analyses. The *Notebooks* thus allow one to grasp, in the course of the debates but also in Father de Lubac's informal meetings, correspondence, and readings, the intellectual climate that surrounded him: that of the Roman theologians during the preparatory phase,[58] for whose work he had little esteem, then the abandonment of this theology (even if it retained some supporters), judged too juridical, too inclined toward definitions to the point of stifling the mystery. Finally, even if they never made him lose confidence in the council, Father de Lubac recorded his fears, which were more frequent starting with the third session, about tendencies and expressions he judged to be rash[59] and about a spirit he considered too little concerned with the respect owed to doctrine, tradition, and superiors.[60] In short, the reader is invited to immerse himself in the theological ferment that was the council, in the company of a guide capable of pointing out the principal issues. Obviously, this journal is not sufficient on its own; it must be compared with and completed by others, but it constitutes an invaluable source for understanding the council and the history of Catholicism.

[58] *Notebooks*, September 19 and 20, 1961.
[59] Ibid., November 11, 1964, for example.
[60] Ibid., July 28, 1964.

These *Notebooks* also permit us to become better acquainted with Father de Lubac himself. To be sure, this is not an intimate journal, and the note of October 4, 1962, already mentioned, stating that he kissed his mother for the last time, is the only really private one in the *Notebooks*. But his analyses, his sympathies, his agreements, and his disapprovals teach us a great deal about the manner in which he experienced the council. The *Notebooks* also put into writing the life of an expert at Rome, made up of numerous meetings, encounters with bishops and priests from all over the world, discussions about the schemas or about unverifiable rumors, advice given to the council Fathers, conferences, study of texts. Besides this work, which was that of every expert, much of Father de Lubac's time and energy was taken up with defending his own orthodoxy, principally during the preparatory phase, and, during the whole council, that of his colleague Teilhard de Chardin, who holds a noteworthy place in this journal. Thus, these *Notebooks* constitute a particularly interesting witness for anyone who wishes to be better acquainted with the council, the history of Catholicism, and Father de Lubac himself. The author shows prudence, is concerned above all with the truth, and introduces us with remarkable precision into debates that are sometimes still current.

Henri de Lubac and the Council

We do not claim to be carrying out an in-depth study here but simply wish to give a few points of reference.

During the preparatory phase, in the course of which, let us remember, he was named a consultor to the Preparatory Theological Commission, Father de Lubac found himself in a delicate situation, to say the least. Even at the time of his nomination, moreover, he showed caution: "You will have learned that I am now a 'consultor' to the Theological Commission of the council! I received a fine piece of paper to that effect, signed Tardini. It occurs to me that these 'consultors' are hardly ever consulted; and besides, you will have seen the other names ..."[61] Father de Lubac was in fact going to be seated beside men who had played a part in the rigors he had experienced for the last ten years or who had even drafted *vota* aimed at having his theses condemned by the council (one thinks here of É. Dhanis and A. Piolanti). To be

---

[61] Letter to Henri Bouillard of July 28, 1960, in the archives of the Jesuit Province of France.

sure, the commission included many other men, members and consultors (such as Yves Congar), who were in no way hostile to Father
de Lubac or who were scarcely familiar with the facts of the whole
controversy. It is no less true, though, that throughout the preparatory
phase, Father de Lubac had to struggle to defend his orthodoxy, which
he judged to be directly, although anonymously, called into question
by the texts of the commission to which he belonged. Constrained by
the secrecy demanded of the members and consultors, and so unable to
reveal anything to those outside, neither could he hope for an effective
clarification in committee, since the consultors could only intervene at
the invitation of a member. The position seemed so hopelessly entan-
gled that at one point he thought of resigning from the commission.[62]
Dominated as it was by the Holy Office and the "Roman" theologians, the commission was still marked by the climate of suspicion that
prevailed in the 1940s and 1950s toward Father de Lubac and others,
including his confrere Pierre Teilhard de Chardin. This explains why
the Jesuit from Lyon could afterward consider himself to have been
something of a hostage, even a defendant.[63] To be sure, he sometimes
intervened during the meetings, and he drafted a memorandum on the
knowledge of God, but the impact of such interventions was minor,
and he was very severe regarding the result of the commission's work.
In fact, the schemas prepared seemed to him far too little concerned to
present the Church to the world, to return to the sources of Christianity, to show its power and importance for the present world, overly
preoccupied as they were with pursuing error and reducing the faith to
formulae that were ever more precise but, in Father de Lubac's view,
ever more foreign to its very essence.[64] Hence the question that comes
almost as the conclusion of this period in the Notebooks: "What will this
council be?"[65]

Father de Lubac was not, at first, certain of attending the council.
Since no French bishop had called on him to serve as an adviser during
the sessions, the provincial, who wished his presence in Rome, looked
for a bishop likely to accept him as a theologian. He found one in Bishop
Gilbert Ramanantoanina, S.J., a Madagascan bishop from Fianarantsoa.
This precaution, however, proved unnecessary, since Father de Lubac

---

[62] Notebooks, September 28, 1961.
[63] ASC 117.
[64] Notebooks, September 29, 1961, for example.
[65] Ibid., March 12, 1962.

was named an expert (*peritus*) of the council.[66] In October 1962, he was able to embark for Rome. The first session of the council is, by far, the one to which he devotes the most pages, like many Fathers and experts who kept a journal during the council. No doubt the effect of novelty played some part in this: while everyone experienced this extraordinary event with enthusiasm, some time was undoubtedly needed to prioritize, to distinguish what was important from what was secondary, and to give up transcribing everything. For the reader, it is also the opportunity to observe the profound disagreements between the majority of the Fathers and the spirit that had presided over the drafting of most of the preparatory schemas. The meticulousness of Father de Lubac's transcription of the interventions of this period thus permits one to have a clear picture of the debates at that time and the issues of the *aggiornamento* desired by John XXIII. In fact, on the liturgy, revelation, or the Church, the reader is able to grasp the diversity of theological positions at a time when it became apparent that the Holy Office did not represent the majority of the council Fathers. But Father de Lubac was not content to attend the general congregations in Saint Peter's, during which these debates were held. Admittedly, during this first session, he did not participate in any conciliar commission, a fact that necessarily limited the possible impact of his actions, for it was in the commissions that the texts were drawn up, proposed corrections were examined and amended, and so on. This is not very surprising, moreover, since only the Liturgical Commission did any important work during the first session. Father de Lubac's activity was nonetheless intense: following the general congregations in the morning were numerous visits, lunches, meetings, conferences on Teilhard but also on the schemas under discussion or to come, dinners at the various houses that welcomed the council Fathers and the experts, personal study of the conciliar texts, and so on. The dogmatic schemas left him deeply unsatisfied, and he was anxious to contribute to their replacement by participating in meetings,[67] by disseminating his own remarks (or those of his confrere Father Martelet), by means of writing or during the conferences, like the one on October 27, during which he responded to questions from 150 bishops, priests, and seminarians.

---

[66] The rules of the council make clear that the experts (*periti*), named by the pope, attend the general congregations but do not speak there unless they are questioned. At the request of the presidents of the conciliar commissions (doctrinal, of the liturgy, and so on) they work on the drafting and amendment of the schemas.

[67] *Carnets*, November 18, 1962.

A letter addressed to Father Henri Bouillard bears witness to his activity: "I cannot find a single moment to write or, of course, to work or to read – and sometimes even to sleep. I am caught up in an immense whirlwind, with long sessions of four hours running in Saint Peter's, almost every morning. Anyway, all that is not without interest; one more or less gets caught up in what is going on, and one is fascinated by what is at issue."[68]

Nevertheless, we would do well to keep a measured tone: we do not see, in fact, Father de Lubac forging steady working relationships, throughout the session, in a structured group with the task of proposing a replacement text or a modification of a conciliar document, which makes difficult any direct influence on the work of the council. His relations with the French episcopate remained rather loose[69] (that would be a cause of complaint for Father de Lubac throughout the council), in spite of some meetings and lectures, sometimes before an important audience. Thus it is amusing to note that when Cardinal Liénart met Father de Lubac at the end of the first session, he asked him what he was doing in Rome![70]

In December 1962, when the first session of the council ended, a session marked in particular by the rejection of the schema on the sources of revelation and, so, foreshadowing the refusal to allow a takeover of the council by the Holy Office and the "Roman" theologians,[71] Father de Lubac displayed a cautious optimism, founded on a twofold experience: that of the catholicity of the Church, experienced during the general congregations and in the numerous encounters made possible by the council, and that of the action of the Spirit.[72] A letter addressed to Msgr. Bruno de Solages bears witness to this: "Yes, I believe that something

---

[68] Letter of November 1, 1962, in the archives of the Henri de Lubac Center, Namur, where all the correspondence referred to on the following pages was consulted.

[69] Among the French episcopate were some who were not Father de Lubac's supporters. Even during the fourth session of the council, on October 25, 1965, he wrote: "Bishop Gouyon recently told me that he had proposed to have me invited by the French bishops for a conference on Teilhard, but he had come up against a veto from some of them." The opposition of certain bishops to Teilhard could also account in part for this veto.

[70] Notebooks, December 4, 1962.

[71] Although these men did not form a united group on every occasion. Thus, we see that, after the council, Archbishop P. Parente, assessor of the Holy Office, was in favor of collegiality.

[72] Father Michel Sales, who knew Father de Lubac well and who had numerous very specific conversations with him regarding the council, especially between 1968 and 1971 and between 1974 and 1986, insisted on this aspect relative to the final text, voted on and promulgated, of Lumen gentium, during an interview with the author.

extraordinary has taken place during these first two months of the council. It would be too much to say a 'revolution', since nothing has yet been accomplished.... However, an evangelical breath has passed over the council, the breath of the Spirit of Christ."[73]

It was during the first intersession that Cardinal Ottaviani, as president of the Doctrinal Commission, invited Henri de Lubac to Rome to participate in its work. The latter, however, believing himself to be too tired,[74] had himself excused. Moreover, one month later, he was hospitalized for a double operation, for appendicitis and prostate problems. Although far from Rome, he did not lose interest in the council. The intersession allowed him, in fact, to work on the schemas dedicated to revelation and to the Church and to meet with bishops. Even in the hospital, his interest did not flag, as Henri Rondet, S.J., attests in a letter to Msgr. de Solages, in which he brings up Father de Lubac's state of health: "Yesterday, on the contrary, he spoke a great deal and told me that he could not manage to refrain from doing so; he was even surprised that he was able to give a long discourse in Latin relating to the council!"[75] So it was starting from the second conciliar session that Father de Lubac participated in the work of the Doctrinal Commission, and this change is very important for the *Notebooks*. In fact, that very circumstance introduces us to the immense work of redrafting the texts made necessary by the rejection of the preparatory schemas. These passages are invaluable, for, unlike the debates held in the general congregations, those of the commissions and subcommissions have not been made the subject of official publications. For the Doctrinal Commission, we have at our disposal the *Relatio*[76] of Father Tromp, the secretary of the commission, and some private accounts, including this one, which thus assume great importance for understanding the council.

During this session, the *Notebooks* carry the trace of Father de Lubac's recent hospitalization. In fact, he was only able to come to Rome at the end of October 1963, thus one month after the beginning of the session,

---

[73] Letter of December 20, 1962.

[74] Letter to Gaston Fessard, May 12, 1963.

[75] Letter of June 23, 1963. However, Father de Lubac thought at the time that he would not return to the council, as a letter to Father Fessard, dated August 11, 1963, attests: "There is no longer any question of Rome or the council. Moreover, there is such a campaign organized against me among the integrist clans (a campaign in part clear-sighted, in part originating from the ridiculous legend forged in 1950), that I would be much too uncomfortable there."

[76] This can be consulted at Louvain (Belgium), in the archives of Monsignor Gérard Philips, among other places.

since his two operations necessitated a lengthy convalescence, which he continued in Rome. Thus, his conciliar activity was less intense than during the first session, and, if we take his word for it, he was almost a tourist visiting the council:

> During this time, I set out for Rome at the wish of our superiors; everything was settled in a few hours, and I left. And it has been twenty days already that I have been here, convalescing under the beautiful Roman sky, installed at the Holy See's expense in a hotel where I find a level of comfort that no house of the Society could offer me. But as soon as I want to get a bit closer to the council, I quickly become exhausted, and my correspondence suffers.... In any case, I am happy to be attending some memorable sessions, and I am gathering information on a great many things. [77]

A passage like this will not surprise those who are accustomed to read the Jesuit from Lyon, always inclined to downplay the importance of the work he was able to conduct. The reader of the *Notebooks* will qualify this statement slightly, since Father de Lubac carried on many meetings, was consulted, and attended the sessions of the Doctrinal Commission. Nevertheless, it is certain that his activity was much less feverish than it had been in 1962,[78] even in writing his *Notebooks*, which are much less extensive for this session. While no fewer than 270 pages are devoted to the first session (in the typewritten version), the second is treated in only thirty-five pages![79]

The *Notebooks* resume a greater fullness beginning with the second intersession. Father de Lubac attended very important meetings of the Doctrinal Commission, from the first week of June 1964 on, and offers us a detailed report. In fact, he devotes almost as many pages to this week alone as he did to the whole of the second session. Even if these few days represent only a part of the work carried on during the intersession,[80] this testimony proves very interesting, for it introduces us into the work of

---

[77] Letter to Gaston Fessard, November 18, 1963.

[78] Father de Lubac is thus not mentioned among the experts of the seven subcommittees constituted to review *De Ecclesia*. See G. Alberigo, *Histoire du concile Vatican II* (Paris: Éd. du Cerf, 2000), 3:131.

[79] One could certainly argue against this deduction the words of Father de Lubac himself: "The days when there was the most work were also the days when I had no time to take notes", but his correspondence confirms a less important activity during this session.

[80] Father de Lubac does not provide us with a complete survey of the work of the Doctrinal Committee during this period, since he was not present at the meetings in January-February, then in March 1964, devoted to *De Ecclesia*, or at those in April on *De revelatione*.

the commission on *De Beata* (a chapter of the text *De Ecclesia*) and on *De revelatione* and also relates the episode of the thirteen suggestions of Paul VI concerning collegiality. With a great deal of precision, especially on the thirteen suggestions, which were the subject of intense discussions, well transcribed here, Father de Lubac plunges us into the heart of the commissions' work, permitting us to understand another side of conciliar activity, those debates turning on one word, one phrase, behind which there are often a whole theology and conception of the faith being expressed. This testimony also allows the reader to see the conciliar texts as the products of history, of long discussions and necessary compromises, in short, it allows us to be introduced to a greater understanding of what the council and its texts were. Finally, the intersession was also the occasion for Father de Lubac to participate in a new task, that of revising schema 13, devoted to the Church in the modern world, by a mixed committee (the Doctrinal Commission and the Commission for the Lay Apostolate). If his direct influence remained weak, Father de Lubac occasionally advised one or another council Father: Bishop Ancel, auxiliary bishop of Lyon, or Bishop McGrath, auxiliary bishop of Panama City until March 1964, then bishop of Santiago de Veraguas, whom he had met during the first session.

Henri de Lubac takes up once again during the third session (170 pages in the typed version) a much more sustained activity. Added to his personal work on the texts were his explanations of them and advice to various council Fathers. In particular, Father de Lubac addressed a group of bishops, mainly African, at the hotel *Giotto*, where he resided with Father Martelet (for example, he gave a talk on the first two chapters of *De revelatione*),[81] without this, of course, hindering him from working with others, including Bishop Muñoz-Vega, with whom he held a work meeting devoted to the study of *De revelatione* and to the chapter of *De Ecclesia* on collegiality, and the Melchite Élie Nijmé, who asked him for a note after an intervention by Archbishop Marty "that compromises the transcendence of revelation".[82]

In the counsel he gave and in his interventions, Father de Lubac shows himself to be anxious for a clear affirmation of Christian doctrine, especially in the work on schema 13 and the work of the Secretariat for Non-Christians, created by Paul VI on Pentecost 1964 and to which he

---

[81] *Notebooks*, September 28, 1964.

[82] Ibid., September 19, 1964, and October 2, 1964.

had been called. He recalls the necessity, in his view, of speaking to men as a Christian, and thus he is opposed to a tendency, which he regarded as dangerous, to dissociate Catholicism and "real life", as if the former had nothing to say to the latter, a tendency he found, for example, in an article by Henri Fesquet.[83] Certainly, Father de Lubac's concerns about the religious situation of his time are not new (as early as February 1961, he had a conversation with Father de Peretti concerning "the decline of the spirit of faith and of prayer among the French clergy, secular and regular"),[84] but they become more frequent from this session on; satisfaction and concern mingle. He himself wrote, in September 1964, that he had observed since the winter of 1963–1964 a "growing anarchy".[85] Thus he looked unfavorably on the direction taken by the journal *Concilium*,[86] on whose directorial committee he sat, primarily on account of an article by E. Schillebeeckx.

It is nonetheless true that the council always seemed to him to bring a healthy renewal. A letter to Father Bouillard shows us this: "On the council, impressions vary from day to day. As a whole, it is a marvelous adventure, a real thaw. There are shadows, of course, and there are dangers. But what a difference from what we have known, even just yesterday!"[87] Even more, Henri de Lubac hoped that the council would permit a way out of a religious situation that troubled him: "It is very true, in any case, that the current religious situation worries me, and, as you know, has for a long time. . . . We find ourselves caught between two factions to which the council (misunderstood by both) has given the opportunity to aggravate each other. . . . But I am very hopeful, all the same, that once the council is over, the main lines will be brought out, which will allow us to rally people of goodwill."[88] So the importance he places on the explanation of the council, his major concern, is understandable. His warnings against false interpretations (he confided this, for example, to Cardinal Léger, to whom he addressed a letter on this subject and who expressed a desire to use it for a coming intervention)[89] led Archbishop Marty to call him, maliciously, "the guardian angel of the council".[90]

---

[83] Ibid., November 11, 1964.

[84] Ibid., February 11, 1961.

[85] Ibid., September 10, 1964.

[86] Ibid., November 17, 1964.

[87] Letter of October 4, 1964.

[88] Letter to Father Ravier, December 18, 1964.

[89] *Notebooks*, October 17 and 19, 1964.

[90] Ibid., October 28, 1964.

During the third intersession, Father de Lubac went to Rome twice, for the mixed commission charged with the preparation of schema 13 and for the Secretariat for Non-Christians. If, during the intersession, Father de Lubac did not take part in the meetings of the mixed commission that were organized in February 1965 at Ariccia, for the purpose of drafting a new schema 13 (the ancestor of *Gaudium et spes*), he was certainly in Rome for those that took place from the end of March to the first week in April. It was there that he was in close contact with Archbishop Wojtyła, who made a strong impression on him and with whom he felt a profound common understanding. Moreover, the impression was mutual: it was Father de Lubac who wrote the preface to the French edition of *Amour et responsabilité* (*Love and Responsibility*), which the archbishop of Kraków brought out in 1965. During this intersession, Father de Lubac, who was lodging with the Fathers of the Holy Cross on via Aurelia Antica, was, at the same time, a part of an informal work group around Bishop McGrath. This little group attended the sessions of the mixed commission for the revision of the schema on the Church in the modern world and also organized work meetings intended to improve the schema under discussion, which Father de Lubac judged too superficial and not authentically Christian enough. The debates, not grasping the problems they addressed sufficiently to satisfy the Jesuit from Lyon, are transcribed here, moreover, with less precision than is customary with him, a sign no doubt of a lesser interest in debates judged disappointing, despite the interventions he found valuable, those of Bishop Volk of Mainz and Archbishop Wojtyła.

During the last session (sixty-four pages in the typed version), Father de Lubac continued to attend the sessions of the Doctrinal Commission, of the mixed commission for the revision of schema 13, of the Secretariat for Non-Christians, but also of the Secretariat for Non-Believers.[91] The worries that had become more acute during the preceding session were confirmed. Thus Father de Lubac was troubled to see the work of the council poorly understood, through faulty liturgical translations or through the agitation (something he called the "paracouncil") kept up by various journals and priests more anxious, so it seemed to him, to set parties at odds and to stir up controversy than to inform themselves calmly and accurately. Consequently, he called on the bishops to guide the faithful, and he himself went to great lengths to do so by means of

---

[91] These last two were not conciliar organs.

various conferences. In his mind, it was a matter of carefully distinguishing between true and false *aggiornamento* and of speaking to the men of his times while remaining faithful to tradition.[92] His concern with regard to secularizing tendencies was just as marked: he insisted, a number of times, notably on the occasion of the text on atheism, a theme that particularly preoccupied him, on the need for clear doctrinal reminders.[93] He himself surprised some of his listeners, during a conference at the Belgian college, when he declared that atheism was an evil and that it had to be combated,[94] convinced as he was that "the 'understanding' of atheists and their atheism that was being sought and preached risked developing an inferiority complex among the faithful – and encouraging a worldly progressivism that made everything turn to the disparagement of believers."[95]

The context had at that time changed significantly. If Father de Lubac could feel like an accused person during the preparatory phase, if there were rumors circulating during the first session about his eviction from the council, during the last one he received the honor of concelebrating with the pope,[96] and it was then that another rumor began to circulate, one that he went to great lengths to deny: that he would soon be made a cardinal![97] Even so, it would be wrong to oversimplify and make of the council the period of Father de Lubac's sudden rehabilitation, passing from the state of an exile to that of a respected "great theologian".

---

[92] The testimony of Bishop Léonard of Namur, is revealing: "We welcomed Father de Lubac to the Belgian college for a conference. We were all on fire about the idea that it was necessary to translate the Christian faith into a new language. We had to find an innovative way in which to address the world.... But Cardinal de Lubac, equipped with a formidable knowledge of history told us: 'One does not invent a language that way: one must draw inspiration from tradition, from Scripture, from the Fathers of the Church. One can be creative, but on the condition that one remains truly faithful to the sources. The use of a new language is not something that can be decided on in an office.' In short, he tempered our ardor" (*Monseigneur Léonard: Entretiens avec Louis Mathoux* [Paris: Parole et silence; Brussels: Mols, 2006], p. 109).

[93] *Notebooks*, September 23, 1965, for example.

[94] Note 241 of the *Journal* of Albert Prignon, rector of the Belgian college, edited by L. Declerck and A. Haquin, p. 95.

[95] *Notebooks*, September 21, 1965.

[96] Ibid., November 18, 1965.

[97] Let us recall that H. de Lubac was indeed created a cardinal ... but by John Paul II, in 1983, eight years before his death. On this rumor, see, for example, the letter to H. de Lubac from Father Fessard on December 4, 1965. Father de Lubac vigorously denied this rumor. However, according to the testimony of René Brouillet, French ambassador to the Holy See, referring to the words of Cardinal Villot, secretary of state, Paul VI had hesitated for a long time between Father de Lubac and Father Daniélou for the Consistory of 1969 (testimony of René Brouillet received by Philippe Levillain).

First of all, because the suspicions of which he was the object involved only a few men, sufficiently influential nonetheless to constrain him to silence for a time, while many others showed him esteem. Next, because all hostility toward him had not suddenly disappeared. The *Notebooks* give several examples of this, coming principally from the "Roman" milieu. Thus the publication of an article favorable to Father de Lubac[98] in a small Assisi journal, *Rocca*, elicited a letter of protest from Cardinal Ottaviani, asking the bishop of Assisi that the magazine be subject to an ecclesiastical censor from that time on. But Father de Lubac judged that he was also the object of another hostility, coming from within the Society of Jesus itself: "The Roman milieu always hostile and impenetrable (despite the pope), the French episcopate keeping away from me (for four years, for example, I was constantly in the same room as Archbishop Garrone, on the Theological Commission, and he never spoke a single word to me about the council), and violently rejected by the so-called progressive wing of the Society, today in favor."[99] Father de Lubac is seen here caught between what he called the "two integrisms".[100] On one side, the integrism of certain Romans, already mentioned; on the other, a secularizing way of thinking that poorly misunderstood, according to Father de Lubac, the dialogue with the world, in whose train it seemed to want to find a place, reinterpreting revelation and tradition in a not very traditional sense. He saw in this the danger of a dualist conception of man, one that totally separated nature and the supernatural. Indeed, it is not without interest that Father de Lubac published in 1965 *Le Mystère du surnaturel* (*The Mystery of the Supernatural*), which, in a sign of change, was well received. In the preface he wrote:

> Though the dualist – or, perhaps better, separatist – thesis has finished its course, it may be only just beginning to bear its bitterest fruit. As fast as professional theology moves away from it, it becomes so much more widespread in the sphere of practical action. While wishing to protect the supernatural from any contamination, people had in fact exiled it altogether – both from intellectual and from social life – leaving the field free to be taken over by secularism. Today that secularism, following its course, is beginning to enter the minds even of Christians. They too seek to find a harmony with all things based upon an idea of nature which might be acceptable to a deist or an atheist: everything that comes from Christ, everything that should lead to him, is pushed so far into the

---

[98] "Incontri all' ora del Concilio Henri de Lubac", *Rocca* 23 (May 15, 1964).
[99] Letter to Father Ravier, November 8, 1965.
[100] *Notebooks*, October 3, 1965.

background as to look like disappearing for good. The last word in Christian progress and the entry into adulthood would then appear to consist in a total secularization which would expel God not merely from the life of society, but from culture and even from personal relationships.[101]

At the end of the council, what balance sheet can be drawn up? In what concerns his conciliar activity, let us listen to Father de Lubac himself: "This will be the end of a large parenthesis, within which I have led a life less active than usual: no real work, comings and goings, visits, impromptu meetings, lunches in restaurants, and then, long sessions of the general congregations, and especially of the subcommissions and commissions."[102] Readers of the *Notebooks* will be in a position to qualify this judgment. It is certainly true that we would be hard pressed to draw up a list comparable to the one made by Yves Congar, enumerating the conciliar texts that were from his pen or that were based on one of his texts,[103] and it is obvious that Father de Lubac did not have the same level of activity as the Dominican, to take the example of a man who was in a similar situation to his at the opening of the council. But we should appreciate the true value of Father de Lubac's activity: through the advice he lavished on numerous Fathers, through the many meetings that he attended, through the defense of his fellow Jesuit Teilhard de Chardin (the growing success of which seemed to him potentially dangerous since it distorted his thought), he put a great deal of effort into the work of the council. If his direct influence, that is, the influence he was able to exert directly on the drafting of the conciliar texts, was slight, that should not make us forget the importance of a more diffuse influence. Many had read his works on the Church, on exegesis, on the supernatural, on Teilhard; their impact is admittedly difficult to measure precisely,[104] but it is important, since Father de Lubac, along with others, of course, has contributed so much to the theological renewal of the twentieth century.

---

[101] *Le Mystère du surnaturel* (Paris: Aubier Montaigne, 1965); republished in *Œuvres complètes*, vol. 12 (Paris: Éd. du Cerf, 2000), 15; trans. Rosemary Sheed as *The Mystery of the Supernatural* (New York: Herder and Herder, 1967), xi–xii.

[102] Letter to Father Bouillard of November 24, 1965.

[103] See Y. Congar, *Mon Journal du concile* (Paris: Éd. du Cerf, 2002), 2:511; trans. Mary John Ronayne, O.P., and Mary Cecily Boulding, O.P, as *My Journal of the Council* (Hindmarsh: ATF Press, 2012), 919–28.

[104] Jean-François Chiron shows in "La Naissance eucharistique de l'Église", in *La Rencontre au cœur de l'Église* (Paris: Éd. du Cerf, 2006), pp. 133–47, that *Lumen gentium* 26 follows *Méditation sur l'Église*, where Father de Lubac speaks of the Eucharist that makes the Church. In this connection one can also quote Father de Lubac himself, who, in the foreword to the fifth edition of *Méditation*

It must be remembered that Father de Lubac was not a council Father, and his role as expert was really to advise the Fathers, not to impose on them (something, moreover, of which Congar was equally convinced). He also felt the limits of his action in a conciliar mechanism that consisted, for an expert, of slipping a brief note to a bishop or an influential secretary in the hope of modifying a word, a sentence, without any expectation of a complete revision. Father Martelet, who associated a great deal with Father de Lubac during the council, emphasizes this point. According to him, in fact, Father de Lubac was a "fish out of water",[105] a writer and not a teacher, not well suited to stepping into the conciliar mechanism. Although Father de Lubac felt close to certain Fathers, he did not have continuous links to a formally constituted work group. No doubt, too, the persistent suspicions about his orthodoxy did not encourage him to intervene. However, it would be wrong to think of Father de Lubac as a timid man,[106] and several times we see him providing advice to a bishop, encouraging a speaker (and especially Karol Wojtyła during the revision of schema 13) whose intervention seemed to him particularly important, which is another kind of possible influence. He judged, not without pain, that the religious situation of the time presented a good number of dangers and that it was necessary to face that fact. Thus we see him concerned after Archbishop Marty's speech *in aula* on atheism, during the fourth session,[107] and anxious to explain to him the implications of his intervention.

---

sur l'Église (1968), wrote the following: "Since [this book] was written, an ecumenical council has been held, a dogmatic constitution on the Church has been promulgated. If nothing in it shows any disagreement with the work of the council, *if it even is found to have anticipated it in more than one regard*, it nevertheless requires a few adjustments to correspond better to the aim of *Lumen Gentium*" (italics not in the original). As for his book *Surnaturel*, one can cite an excerpt from *Entretien autour de Vatican II*, 27–28. Father de Lubac, in response to the question: "Does the orientation of the council not owe something all the same to a certain theologian of the 'Supernatural'?", judged that he, along with many others, might have had a very general influence and added: "What I grant you is that I feel very comfortable with the orientations of the council that are able to find a foundation in the traditional position: that of Saint Thomas, among others, which I had tried to revive.... One can say without exaggeration that the council put an end to extrinsicism." Finally, there can be no doubt that Father de Lubac's influence can be seen on chapter 1 of *Gaudium et spes*.

[105] Interview, August 2005.

[106] One thinks especially of his intervention of October 11, 1965, on the sidelines of the council, to defend his confrere Teilhard de Chardin, harshly attacked by Henri Rambaud. One will observe on that occasion that Father de Lubac did not put himself forward in his *Notebooks*, simply writing: "In the end, I asked to speak. In a few sentences, I reestablished the truth." His correspondence bears witness in a more vivid manner to the spirited nature of Father de Lubac's opposition to Rambaud. In fact, he wrote, in a letter to Father Ravier on October 21, 1965: "I took the floor and demolished him in eight minutes."

[107] *Notebooks*, September 28, 1965.

At the conclusion of the council, Father de Lubac's general assessment was divided between satisfaction with the work carried out at the council (with some reservations with regard to schema 13) and with the first acts of Paul VI, whom he never ceased to defend, and a growing concern in the face of secularizing tendencies. This is what is sometimes presented as a "stiffening" of Father de Lubac's views, while others preferred to see in it a fidelity that a shifting context made to appear as a more conservative tendency. He explained his state of mind in a letter to Bernard de Guibert: "Although happy on the whole, I am unable to refrain from some melancholy thoughts. Will all these conciliar texts be strong enough to resist an interpretation of the Christian faith that is weakening and secularizing? Too many people, as you know, are inclined in that direction today, and they have had an opportunity, in the atmosphere created by the council, to push their point of view. Will the desired renewal happen? Are we ready to preach it? I have seen Father Arrupe, a very likeable man. With him, with Paul VI, Providence has provided us with good guides."[108] So he called on the bishops to devote themselves right from the time of the council to an accurate, straightforward explanation of the conciliar texts. This seemed to him to have priority, at which task, moreover, he himself would work by means of several publications.[109]

LOÏC FIGOUREUX
Professor of History, Université Lille-III

---

[108] Letter of November 3, 1965.

[109] One can only indicate a few benchmarks here, without aiming to be exhaustive. In the period immediately after the council, Father de Lubac, in spite of the concerns already set forth, manifested a certain serenity and set to work on the explication of the council. The characteristic texts from this point of view are found in *Paradoxe et mystère de l'Église* (Paris: Aubier, 1967), trans. James R. Dunne as *The Church: Paradox and Mystery* (New York: Ecclesia Press, 1969), *La Révélation divine* (Paris: Éd. du Cerf, 1968, where there is a commentary on the *Prooemium* and chapter 1 of *Dei Verbum*), and *Athéisme et sens de l'homme: Une double requête de "Gaudium et spes"* (Paris: Éd. du Cerf, 1968); the last two works have been reprinted by Éd. du Cerf, *Révélation divine, Affrontements mystiques, Athéisme et sens de l'homme*, in *Œuvres complètes*, vol. 4 (Paris, 2006). Father de Lubac later became more and more troubled by trends of growing importance that interpreted the Second Vatican Council as a transformation, and he published *L'Église dans la crise actuelle* (Paris: Éd. du Cerf, 1969) and *Les Églises particulières dans l'Église universelle* (Paris: Aubier, 1971), trans. by Sr. Sergia Englund, O.C.D., as "Particular Churches in the Universal Church", in *The Motherhood of the Church* (San Francisco: Ignatius Press, 1982), in order to fight against what seemed to him to be false interpretations of the council. Finally, always in this desire to be faithful to *aggiornamento*, he published *Entretien autour de Vatican II*, on the occasion of the synod of 1985, and gave a talk at the plenary session of the Sacred College: "Sur la collégialité épiscopale et la primauté du successeur de Pierre" (On episcopal collegiality and the primacy of the successor of Peter), published in Michel Sales, *Le Corps de l'Église: Études sur l'Église une, sainte, catholique et apostolique* (Paris: Fayard, 1989), 229–30.

LIST OF ABBREVIATIONS

Religious Orders

A.A.	Assumptionist
B.A.	Basilian Alepian
B.S.	Basilian Salvatorian
C.I.C.M.	Congregation of the Immaculate Heart of Mary
C.M.	Lazarist
C.M.F.	Claretian
C.PP.S.	Missionary of the Precious Blood
C.S.C.	Holy Cross Father
C.S.Sp.	Spiritan
C.Ss.R.	Redemptorist
M.E.P.	Foreign Missions of Paris
M.S.	Missionary of La Salette
M.S.C.	Missionary of the Sacred Heart
M.S.F.	Missionary of the Holy Family
M.S.F.S.	Missionary of Saint Francis de Sales
O.C.D.	Discalced Carmelite
O.C.S.O.	Cistercian of the Strict Observance (Trappist)
O.F.M.	Franciscan
O.F.M.Cap.	Capuchin
O.F.M.Conv.	Friar Minor Conventual
O.M.I.	Oblate of Mary Immaculate
O.P.	Dominican
O.S.B.	Benedictine
O.S.B.M.	Basilian of Saint Josaphat
O.S.A.	Augustinian
O.S.M.	Servant of Mary (Servant Friar)
O.S.U.	Ursuline
P.B.	White Father
P.S.S.	Sulpician
S.D.B.	Salesian of Don Bosco

S.J.   Jesuit
S.M.   Marist or Marianist
S.M.M.   Montfort Missionary
S.V.D.   Divine Word Missionary (Verbite)

Other Abbreviations
AAS   *Acta Apostolice Sedis*
ACA   Assembly of Cardinal and Archbishops
ACO   Action catholique ouvrière
AS   *Acta synodalia sacrosancti concilii oecumenici Vaticani II*
B.I.   Biblical Institute
Card.   Cardinal
CELAM   Latin American Episcopal Conference
CFTC   Confédération française des travailleurs chrétiens
Msgr.   Monsignor
DH   Heinrich Denzinger, *Compendium of Creeds, Defini-
                  tions, and Declarations on Matter of Faith and Morals*, ed.
                  Peter Hünermann, 43rd ed. (San Francisco: Ignatius
                  Press, 2012)

NOTE ON THE TEXT

The version of Father de Lubac's *Notebooks* published here is the result of different stages of redaction. The text taken as a reference for this edition is the manuscript text produced from notes taken day to day at Saint Peter's or in committee. We are familiar with this text thanks to photocopies of the six original notebooks made as documentation by Philippe Levillain, with the assent of Father de Lubac, for the former's thesis *La Mécanique politique de Vatican II: La Majorité et l'unanimité dans un concile* (Paris: Beauchesne, 1975). The notebooks themselves have been lost. This text was then typed out, but it is not known precisely when[1] or by whom. It is nevertheless possible that it was the work of Brother Mouton, S.J., given the fact that he had done typing for Father de Lubac on other occasions. Whatever the case, this typewritten version presents some slight modifications in relation to the manuscript version. Most often this involves brief pieces of information or judgments on some particular intervention or Father or expert. We have indicated these additions or changes in a note, preceded by an asterisk. An asterisk also marks its place in the body of the text. Finally, we have found, at Namur and at Vanves, a third stage of redaction. In fact, in the Molette collection then on deposit at the Henri de Lubac Archives Center, there is the typewritten version augmented, for the preparatory period only, with important additions, undated, in Father de Lubac's own hand and with the title changed from *Cahiers* to *Carnets*.[2] These sometimes involve simple, very short details, but Father de Lubac also produces the text of letters to which he refers, following a procedure not unlike the voluminous notes of his *Mémoire sur l'occasion de mes écrits* (*At the Service of the Church*). In a few rare cases, some passages are deleted. Here also, we have kept the manuscript text as our basis and have indicated the additions or deletions in a note with an asterisk. At Vanves rare additions were found to

---

[1] See the introduction for theories about this.

[2] The words are synonymous, and both are translated here as "notebooks". – TRANS.

the typewritten version, this time concerning the conciliar period itself and appearing here in the notes.

The numerous people cited by Father de Lubac are almost all the subject of a short biographical note where they are first mentioned. These notes are confined to the conciliar period, except when the people in question later occupied positions of particular importance. Mistakes in proper names have been corrected, without indicating the error in a note, if there was no doubt about the identity of the person in question. On the other hand, we have chosen to keep the incorrect name in the body of the text when it departs significantly from the true name, or what we suppose to be the true name, with a note indicating this.

Other notes attempt to explain allusions, help in the comprehension of the operation of the council, and sometimes correct errors, due in particular to a lack of distance.

The appendices are intended to provide various aids to a better understanding of this conciliar journal. Thus we have indicated the subject of the paragraphs under discussion during the council sessions or intersessions, of which Father de Lubac sometimes mentions only the number. One should take particular care, when consulting these references, to check the date of discussion of the texts, since these sometimes underwent very important modifications in the course of the sessions and intersessions. A list of members of the Preparatory Theological Commission and of the conciliar commissions, a presentation of the different governing bodies of the council and of the course followed by a conciliar text, a glossary, and some chronological benchmarks try to make the consultation easier.

We could not have accomplished this work alone, and we would like to thank all those who contributed to the present publication. First of all, this book would not have been possible without Father Dumortier, S.J., provincial of France and beneficiary of Father de Lubac, and Father Nicolas-Jean Sèd, O.P., managing director of Éditions du Cerf. Numerous archivists willingly answered our questions, notably Father Robert Bonfils, S.J., archivist of the French Province, and Madame Gosset, archivist of the Province of Southern Belgium. We have also been able to count on the warm encouragement, wise advice, and answers of Jacques Prévotat, professor of modern history at the University of Lille-III, of Father Georges Chantraine, S.J., and of Father Michel Sales, S.J. Anne showed great patience when it was necessary to compare the typed and manuscript versions. Éric Mahieu, whose work on Congar[3] was a valuable resource, graciously reread a part of this work. Finally, last but not least, we would like very particularly to thank Father Leo Declerck, fine connoisseur of the council, whose help was as constant as it was indispensable. It goes without saying that we are solely responsible for any errors or inaccuracies that might be found in this edition.

Loïc FIGOUREUX

---

[3] Yves Congar, *Mon Journal du Concile*, ed. Éric Mahieu, 2 vols. (Paris: Éd. du Cerf, 2002), trans. Mary John Ronayne, O.P., and Mary Cecily Boulding, O.P., as *My Journal of the Council* (Hindmarsh: ATF Press, 2012).

SIX "COUNCIL NOTEBOOKS"

1960

July 25, 1960. – At Fourvière, where I settled in again a few days ago,[1] I received an official notice, signed: Tardini,[2] that names me as a consultor for the Preparatory Theological Commission[3] at the council. I had heard about this some time earlier, through an issue of *La Croix*, read in the parlor of a convent, but I wondered if this astonishing piece of news could be correct.

August 6, 1960. – I received a letter from Cardinal Ottaviani,[1] explaining the role of the consultors on this commission and enjoining me to secrecy from now on.

November 11, 1960. – Arrived in Rome. I am lodging at the Biblical Institute, where I saw Frs. Haulotte,[1] Lyonnet,[2] des Places,[3] and Philip[4] (who had come from the Gregorian).[5] In the afternoon, Dom

---

July 25

[1] This refers to the Jesuit scholasticate in Lyon from which H. de Lubac had been removed back in 1950. Since 1954, however, he had divided his time between rue Sala, in Lyon, and Paris.

[2] Domenico Tardini (1888–1961), Italian, ordained in 1912. Pro-secretary of state for Pius XII from 1952, he became secretary of state for John XXIII in December 1958, a position he occupied until his death on July 30, 1961.

[3] This was one of the eleven commissions that, together with the three secretariats, were at work during the preparatory phase of the council, opened by John XXIII on June 5, 1960. They prepared the texts that were to be submitted to the council Fathers. These commissions and the secretariats were headed by a Central Preparatory Commission.

August 6

[1] Alfredo Ottaviani (1890–1979), Italian, ordained in 1916. Assessor of the Holy Office in 1935, he was created cardinal in 1953, then named secretary of the Holy Office in 1959. He presided over the Preparatory Theological Commission, then over the Doctrinal Commission. In 1966, he became pro-prefect of the new Congregation for the Doctrine of the Faith.

November 11

[1] Edgar Haulotte, S.J. (1920–1989), French. Professor of exegesis.

[2] Stanislas Lyonnet, S.J. (1902–1986), French, ordained in 1934. He taught Sacred Scripture at Fourvière beginning in 1938. Then he was professor of exegesis and theology at the Biblical Institute. He had to cease teaching, however, at the request of the Holy Office, at the end of the academic year 1961–1962, until July 1964.

[3] Édouard Barbou des Places, S.J. (1900–2000), French, ordained in 1931. A specialist in Greek studies, from 1948 on he taught Greek religion and philosophy in their relation to the New Testament at the Biblical Institute.

[4] Octave Philip, S.J. (1893–1971), French, ordained in 1922. Bursar at the Gregorian from 1955 to 1967.

[5] The Pontifical Gregorian University was founded by Ignatius of Loyola and Francis Borgia in 1553. Pius XI in 1928 associated it with the Biblical Institute, founded by Pius X on May 7, 1909. Both were entrusted to the Jesuits.

Jean Leclercq[6] brought me to the house of the Cistercians of the Common Observance, on the Aventine; young monks from every country are assembled there: Cistercians, Trappists, Benedictines; conversed first of all with a small group of thesis students, then with the whole group (around thirty).

November 12. – This morning saw Fr. Donatien Mollat,[1] Fr. Pin,[2] Fr. Évode Beaucamp, O.F.M.[3] Fr. Lyonnet showed me his mimeographed response to an attack that appeared in May in *Divinitas*, the journal of the Lateran.[4] Fr. Leclercq told me about the death of Erik Peterson,[5] a few days ago; since our first meeting in 1953, in the church of St. Louis des Français, and our common prayer at Saint-Eustache, I greatly loved the man. In the afternoon, visited Fr. Philippe de la Trinité[6] (whom I knew long ago as a student of philosophy at Mongré,[7] in 1923–1924) at San Pancrazio; his Spanish confreres have persuaded him of the authenticity of Canticle B of St. John of the Cross. In my free moments, read in the

---

[6] Dom Jean Leclercq, French Benedictine (1911–1993) of St. Maurice Abbey in Clervaux (Luxembourg). A specialist in the monastic history and spirituality of the Middle Ages, author of, in particular, *L'Amour des lettres et le désir de Dieu* (Paris: Éd. du Cerf, 1957); trans. Catharine Misrahi as *The Love of Learning and the Desire for God* (New York: Fordham Univ. Press, 1961).

November 12

[1] Donatien Mollat, S.J. (1904–1977), French, ordained in 1935. Exegete, professor of Sacred Scripture at Fourvière, then at the Gregorian from 1959 on, he was a specialist in the Johannine writings.

[2] Émile Pin, S.J., born in 1921, French. Professor of general and religious sociology at the Gregorian.

[3] Évode Beaucamp, O.F.M. (1917–1997), French. Professor of Sacred Scripture at the Lateran University.

[4] Quarterly journal, published since 1957, of the Lateran University. The origin of the university goes back to 1773, when Clement XIV entrusted the faculty of philosophy and theology of the Roman college to the clergy of Rome. It became a pontifical university by decision of John XXIII, in May 1959.

[5] Erik Peterson (1890–1960), German, converted to Catholicism in 1930. A friend of Karl Barth, theologian and historian of religions, he was hostile to Nazism and took refuge in Rome in 1933. He is famous for his book *Le Monothéisme comme problème politique* (Leipzig: Jakob Hegner, 1935). He died on October 26.

[6] Philippe de la Trinité (Jean Rambaud), O.C.D. (1908–1977), French, ordained in 1934. He entered the Holy Office in 1952, and, starting the next year, he also presided over the Roman theology faculty of the order [Discalced Carmelites]. He ceased teaching, however, in 1960.

[7] Notre Dame de Mongré, an establishment run by the Jesuits, at Villefranche-sur-Saône, that H. de Lubac attended as a student from 1909–1911. In 1923–1924 he spent the regency period of his Jesuit formation there, between his years of philosophy and theology, and became an aide to the prefect of studies of the college.

library of the B.I.:[8] Farrar,[9] on the history of exegesis; Buteonus,[10] on Noah's Ark, etc.

November 13. – At the Abbey of St. Jerome.[1] High Mass. Conversation with Father Grégoire,[2] a Belgian, who is preparing a thesis on St. Bruno of Segni; conversed also with Frs. Leclercq, Gribomont,[3] Thibaut,[4] etc. After lunch, recreation in the living room of the abbot, Dom Salmon;[5] made the acquaintance of Msgr. Jacqueline,[6] chaplain of the Chateaubriand school, who is finishing a thesis on Saint Bernard and Roman pontifical law;[7] and of Leonardi,[8] scriptor at the Vatican and a member of the Italian Historical Institute for the Middle Ages. At the

---

[8] Biblical Institute.

[9] Frederic W. Farrar (1831–1903), British. A well-known writer and Anglican preacher, he wrote several works of fiction as well as important philological and theological studies, including *History of Interpretation* (1884) and *The Life of Christ* (1884).

[10] Pseudonym of Jean Borrel, author of the *Opera geometrica*, published at Lyon in 1554. In this work he studies many subjects, among them the construction of Noah's ark.

November 13

[1] Benedictine abbey in Rome, instituted in 1933 by Pius XI for the revision of the Vulgate.

[2] Réginald Grégoire, O.S.B., born in 1935, Belgian. He worked in the service of the Holy See from 1957 to 1983, collaborating on the critical edition of the Vulgate. His thesis, *Bruno de Segni: Exégète médiéval et théologien monastique* (Spoleto, Centro di studi sull'alto medioevo), was published in 1965.

[3] Jean Gribomont, O.S.B. (1920–1986), Belgian, a monk of Clervaux (Luxemburg). Editor of the critical edition of the Vulgate. Specialist in patristics, he was also open to ecumenical questions.

[4] Michel Thibaut, O.S.B. (1877–1962), Belgian, ordained in 1902, with the name Raymond in religion. A monk of the Benedictine abbey of Saint-Benoît de Maredsous (Belgium). Former editor of the *Revue bénédictine* from 1905 to 1914. He was the disciple of Dom Columba Marmion, abbot of Maredsous from 1900 to 1923 and spiritual master.

[5] Pierre Salmon, O.S.B. (1896–1982), French, ordained in 1924. Abbot of Saint-Jérôme, expert at the council during the first two sessions, he was named titular bishop in June 1964.

[6] Bernard Jacqueline (1918–2007), French, ordained in 1944, *minutante* [a kind of secretary] for the Congregation of Propaganda and chaplain of the Chateaubriand school in Rome, a school created at the beginning of the twentieth century at the instigation of the French ambassador to the Holy See to permit French or foreign children in Rome to receive their education in French.

[7] Bernard Jacqueline had already defended, in 1949, a thesis on "Pontifical Law according to Saint Bernard of Clairvaux: An Essay on Ecclesiastical Law in the Middle Ages", at the Institut catholique in Paris, but he was continuing his research on "Episcopate and Papacy in Saint Bernard of Clairvaux", a thesis that he defended at Paris-IV in 1971.

[8] Claudio Leonardi, born in 1926, Italian. Scientific secretary at the Istituto storico italiano per il medioevo (Italian Historical Institute for the Middle Ages); founded in 1883 to "unify the publication of national historical sources", it became the Istituto storico italiano per il medioevo in 1934; scriptor (a member of the scientific body of the Vatican Library charged with the production of catalogues, inventories, and bibliographic instruments) for the Latin manuscripts in the Vatican Library.

end of the afternoon, reception at the Villa Buonaparte[9] (the embassy close to the Vatican); there I saw again Archbishop Perrin[10] (Carthage)* [11] and Archbishop Veuillot (Angers).[12] Saw Bishop Mercier (Sahara).[13] Msgr. Girard,[14] superior general of the Sulpicians, introduced me to his friend and former student*[15] Father Gagnebet, O.P.[16] – The Assistant[17] (de Gorostarzu)[18] caught sight of me (I was sitting); he came up to me, flanked by two tall men whose arms he was holding: "Ah, hello! I want to present these two journalists to you, they are very dear friends of mine", and then he went away, leaving me with L'Hopital, from *Le Monde*, and a correspondent from *Paris-Soir*.[19]

November 14. – Ceremony at Saint Peter's, where I was driven by Father Georges Jarlot,[1,*2] in the right-hand gallery in the apse. The pope arrived to the chanting of the Credo. On the throne, underneath the chair of Bernini, he read his speech, with an appearance as tranquil as a nice old grandfather reading his newspaper after dinner. A chant. And

---

[9] Since 1950, the French embassy to the Holy See has been located in this building, erected in 1750 by Cardinal Silvio Valenti Gonzaga, secretary of state for Benedict XIV.

[10] Paul Marie Perrin (1904–1994), French, ordained in 1936. Auxiliary bishop, then archbishop of Carthage from 1947 to 1964, he was named apostolic delegate to Iraq in July 1964, then archbishop of Baghdad in August 1965. Member of the Commission for the Missions.

[11] * "Who had given me such a kind reception in Tunis at the time of Archbishop Gounot."

[12] Pierre Veuillot (1913–1968), French, ordained in 1939. Bishop of Angers since 1959, he was named coadjutor of the archbishop of Paris in July 1961. He became archbishop of Paris in 1966 and remained so until his death. He was created cardinal in 1967. Member of the Commission for Bishops and the Government of Dioceses.

[13] Georges Mercier, P.B. [Père Blanc, a member of the White Fathers] (1902–1991), French, ordained in 1928. Bishop of Laghouat (Algeria) from 1955 to 1968.

[14] Pierre Girard, P.S.S. [a Sulpician] (1892–1974), French. Superior of the university seminary in Lyon from 1934 to 1945, then of the Seminary of Saint Irenaeus from 1945 to 1952, he was superior general of the Society of Saint Sulpice from 1952 to 1966. Expert at the council beginning with the second session.

[15] * "Seminary of Clermont-Ferrand".

[16] Rosaire Gagnebet, O.P. (1904–1983), French, taught theology at the Angelicum. He was a qualificator, then, in 1964, consultor to the Congregation of the Holy Office. Member of the Preparatory Theological Commission, he was named an expert in 1962.

[17] Adviser to the Jesuit superior general for an Assistancy (a country or group of countries of the Society).

[18] Bernard de Gorostarzu, S.J. (1890–1970), French. Assistant for France from 1944 to 1963.

[19] There must be confusion here with *France-Soir*, whose correspondent was Jean Neuvecelle.

November 14

[1] Georges Jarlot, S.J. (1894–1980), French, ordained in 1925. Professor of social doctrine at the Gregorian from 1950 to 1974, he is the author of *Doctrine pontificale et histoire*, 2 vols. (1964 and 1973), on social teaching from Leo XIII to Benedict XV and on Pius XI. He was a member of the Preparatory Commission for the Lay Apostolate.

[2] * "An old friend from the Jersey novitiate".

John XXIII,[3] after having shaken the hands of all the cardinals, departed on the Sedia, hailed by applause. A banal and empty ceremony. I did not understand the speech, in Italian; I was told it contained nothing very particular.

Saw Fr. Leloir,[4] from St. Jerome, again, who had come to work at the Biblical Institute; he gave me some details about the mixed committee (Jesuits and Benedictines) charged with correcting the new Psalter; the directives given by Cardinal Bea,[5] the president, were: 1/ the new text is to be taken as the base; 2/ return to the language of Augustine and Jerome; 3/ consider the chant; 4/ consider its liturgical usage. It does not seem like the committee is going to be very active.

Saw Fr. Dumeige[6] and Fr. Alfaro[7] at the Gregorian; the latter has little respect for his compatriot Fr. Alonso, C.M.F. [a Claretian], as a theologian.

Met Father Salaverri,[8] accompanied by a young Spanish priest, under the cloister of the Biblico [the Pontifical Biblical Institute]. After greeting him, I told him that he had been mistaken, or rather that he had been misled, in the campaign he made against Fourvière in 1949–1951. Then I congratulated him on the fine collection that he had just brought out and that had appeared very recently in the publications of Comillas. We are to see each other again tomorrow morning at the Holy Office.

November 15. – At 8:45 A.M., I entered the Holy Office.[1] (I had come there once before, in September 1946, to visit Msgr. Ottaviani, to

---

[3] Angelo Giuseppe Roncalli (1881–1963), Italian, ordained in 1904. Nuncio in France from 1944 to 1953, he was created cardinal in 1953 and became patriarch of Venice. Elected pope on October 28, 1958, he was beatified in September 2000.

[4] Dom Louis Leloir, O.S.B. (1911–1992), Belgian, from the abbey of Clervaux (Luxembourg), ordained in 1935. He was working at the time on a doctorate in theology.

[5] Augustin Bea, S.J. (1881–1968), German, ordained in 1912. Confessor of Pius XII, rector of the Biblical Institute from 1930–1949. He was created cardinal in 1959. President of the Secretariat for Promoting Christian Unity in June 1960.

[6] Gervais Dumeige, S.J. (1913–1996), French, ordained in 1946. Professor of ecclesiastical history and prefect of studies for the theologates at Enghien (Belgium) and at Chantilly, he taught at the Gregorian from 1960 on.

[7] Juan Alfaro, S.J. (1914–1993), Spanish. Professor of dogmatics at the Gregorian, where he was general prefect of studies from 1964 on.

[8] Joaquín Salaverri, S.J. (1892–1979), Spanish, professor of theology at the Pontifical University of Comillas (Spain). Consultor to the Preparatory Theological Commission, then named council expert in 1962.

November 15

[1] Roman congregation, descended from the Inquisition and charged with examining doctrinal questions. The prefect of the congregation was the pope himself. Also called Suprema Congregatio, it became the Congregation for the Doctrine of the Faith in 1965.

whom I had offered the last two volumes that had then been published of *Sources Chrétiennes*,[2] and who had given me in return his treatise on the Public Law of the Church,[3] with a beautiful inscription). In the little waiting room, where I was the second to arrive, I found myself face to face with Father Labourdette, O.P.,[4] who had arrived first.[*5] At 9 A.M., opening meeting of the commission. Cardinal Ottaviani told me that he remembered my visit in 1946. Some explanations in Latin were given in turn by the cardinal president[6] and Father Sébastien Tromp, S.J.,[7] the secretary. I greeted Fr. Van den Eynde, O.F.M.,[8] Msgr. Schmaus[9] (Munich), etc. Don Carlo Colombo,[10] superior of the seminary in Milan, has a friendly, smiling face. I was driven back to the Biblical Institute by Father Philippe, O.P.,[11] who also took along his confreres Labourdette and Gagnebet.

I swore an oath on the Gospel[12] that Cardinal Ottaviani held on his knees.

---

[2] A series of patristic texts, started by Fathers Claude Mondésert, S.J., Daniélou, S.J., and de Lubac, S.J., the first volumes of which appeared in 1942. On this subject, reference can be made to the book by É. Fouilloux, *La Collection "Sources chrétiennes": Éditer les Pères de l'Église au XXᵉ siècle* (Paris: Éd. du Cerf, 1995).

[3] A. Ottaviani, *Institutiones juris publici ecclesiastici* (Rome: TPV, 1947–1948).

[4] Michel Labourdette, O.P. (1908–1990), French. Professor of moral theology at the Dominican *studium* in Toulouse. Consultor to the Preparatory Theological Commission, then named as an expert to the council in 1962. Member of the Pontifical Commission for the Study of Population, the Family, and Birth. According to H. de Lubac, this was their first meeting. Father Labourdette had been at the origin of a theological controversy with the Jesuits, particularly on the subject of the place of Scholasticism, in 1946.

[5] * "Brief exchange, cordial".

[6] This was Alfredo Ottaviani.

[7] Sebastiaan Tromp, S.J. (1889–1975), Dutch, professor of theology at the Gregorian from 1929 to 1967. Secretary of the Preparatory Theological Commission, then of the Doctrinal Commission. He was also a consultor to the Congregation of the Holy Office. Expert at the council.

[8] Damien Van den Eynde, O.F.M. (1902–1969), Belgian. Rector of the Antonianum, member of the Preparatory Theological Commission, named an expert to the council in 1962. He contributed in particular to the drafting of the preparatory schema *De fontibus revelationis* and to the liturgical constitution *Sacrosanctum concilium*.

[9] Michael Schmaus (1897–1993), Austrian. Professor of theology at the University of Munich until 1966. Member of the Preparatory Theological Commission, he was named an expert in 1962.

[10] Carlo Colombo (1909–1991), Italian, ordained in 1931. Professor of dogmatic theology at the Seminary of Milan. Member of the Preparatory Theological Commission, expert at the council during the first two sessions. He was also Giovanni Battista Montini's private expert. He became auxiliary bishop of Milan, a position he held from 1964 to 1985.

[11] Paul Philippe, O.P. (1905–1984), French, ordained in 1932. Commissioner of the Holy Office from 1955 to 1959, then secretary of the Congregation for Religious. He was a member of the antepreparatory commission. He became titular bishop in August 1962 and was named a member of the Commission for Religious at the time of the first session. Created cardinal in 1973, he was prefect of the Congregation for the Oriental Churches from 1973 to 1980.

[12] He is referring to the oath of secrecy regarding the work undertaken by the Preparatory Theological Commission.

At the Gregorian, I saw Frs. Philip, Blet,[13] Lonergan.[14] Saw at the Biblical Institute several young priests and old Father Alberto Vaccari,[15] happy to tell me his memories of Beirut.

Visited Cardinal Paolo Marella,[16], *[17] on via della Conciliazione; he showed me in detail his beautiful library of Far-Eastern religions, as well as, in a large alcove, a library made up exclusively of Japanese works: many were ancient, magnificently illustrated, laid out in rolls or in sheets, the latter in boxes. We were admiring them at full speed when someone came to announce Archbishop Guerry[18] of Cambrai; the cardinal made him wait so that he could finish showing me his treasures.

November 16. – This morning once again at the Holy Office. I saw Fr. Leclercq,[1] Oblate of M.I., a very likeable man. He is Fr. Tromp's secretary for the Theological Commission, at the same time as he is working at the Holy Office. We talked about Teilhard,[2] etc. Then he led me into the library, where I was welcomed by Fr. Hendrix,[3] one of the German

---

[13] Pierre Blet, S.J., born in 1918, French, ordained in 1950. Professor of modern history at the Gregorian from 1959 on, he revived in particular the history of pontifical diplomacy. He was one of the group of four Jesuits to whom Paul VI opened the Vatican's secret archives to permit them to study the actions of the Catholic Church during the Second World War and to publish the volumes of the *Actes et documents du Saint-Siège relatifs à la Seconde Guerre mondiale*, 11 vols. (1965–1981).

[14] Bernard Lonergan, S.J. (1904–1984), Canadian, ordained in 1936. Theologian, philosopher, he was professor of theology at the Gregorian from 1953 to 1965. An expert at the council beginning with the third session.

[15] Alberto Vaccari, S.J. (1875–1965), Italian, ordained in 1905. Professor of Old Testament exegesis at the Biblical Institute from 1912 to 1959, he was also a professor at Saint Joseph University in Beirut. Member of the Preparatory Theological Commission, expert at the council.

[16] Paolo Marella (1895–1984), Italian, ordained in 1918. Apostolic nuncio to France from 1953 until February 1960. He was president of the preparatory commission, then of the conciliar Commission for Bishops and the Government of Dioceses. A member of the Secretariat for Unity from 1963 on. President of the Secretariat for Non-Christians. For a long time he was apostolic delegate to Tokyo (1933–1948), which enabled him to build up this rich library on Far-Eastern religions.

[17] * "Former nuncio in Paris, who had been very good to me there".

[18] Émile Guerry (1891–1969), French, ordained in 1923. Archbishop of Cambrai from 1952 to 1966. Member of the Commission for Bishops and the Government of Dioceses.

November 16

[1] Michel Leclercq, O.M.I., born in 1926, French, ordained in 1951. From 1959 until 1962, he was a *scrittore* at the Holy Office for work in the French language. *Minutante* [a kind of secretary] for the Preparatory Theological Commission.

[2] Pierre Teilhard de Chardin, S.J. (1881–1955), French, ordained in 1911. Intensely interested in the sciences, he thought that the Christian tradition did not contradict them but that the two could be combined in a harmonious synthesis. In particular, he believed that Christian faith and evolution were compatible. The Holy Office, however, was disturbed by his positions and his influence, and the majority of his non-scientific writings were not published during his lifetime.

[3] He is actually referring to Wilhelm Hentrich, S.J. (1887–1972), German, ordained in 1917. Private librarian of Pius XII from 1942 until his death. A consultor to the Holy Office from 1955 on. (Information communicated by the Congregation for the Doctrine of the Faith).

Jesuits on familiar terms with Pius XII.[4] It was on the ground floor; the window looks out on the courtyard of the Inquisition; in the prison, they tell me, they now store potatoes. I can guess the clever secrecy in the lay-out of the chambers.

At noon, at the Ursuline Sisters' on via Nomentana, I had lunch with Fr. Stanislas Lyonnet. A certain number of Mothers passed by. Chatted with the elderly Mother Saint-Jean,[5] who seems more robust than ever.*[6]

In the afternoon, a visit with the mother abbess of Rabat,[7] a woman from Lyon, spiritual daughter of Father Monchanin.[8] She founded a religious community at Nazareth. With the support of Msgr. Baron[9] in Rome, she, along with her entire monastery of Poor Clares in Rabat, went over to the Eastern rite. Cardinal Bea drove me to his house, on via Aurelia (the Brazilian College); a good and simple man, he spoke to me about Taizé, etc. His secretariat for Christian unity doubles as a secretariat for the Jews.[10]

November 17. – This morning, at the Gregorian, consulted some journals. Spoke with Fr. Gathier,[1] who has just been named a consultor to the Commission for Studies; he gave me his recent book on Hindu thought.*[2] Also saw the Rev. Fr. René Arnou,[3] who is making at this

---

[4] Eugenio Pacelli (1876–1958), Italian, ordained in 1899. Secretary of the Congregation for Extraordinary Ecclesiastical Affairs from 1914 to 1917, then nuncio to Germany, he was created cardinal in 1929 and became secretary of state in 1930. He was elected pope on March 2, 1939.

[5] Marie de Saint-Jean Martin, O.S.U. (1876–1965), French. Prioress General of her order from 1926 to 1959.

[6] * "She had taken me in with great courtesy and care in 1953."

[7] Mother Véronique of the Holy Face (Clotilde Vacheron) (1909–1981), French. Superior of the Poor Clares of Rabat in 1936. In 1958, she founded the first Poor Clare monastery in the Greek Melchite Church, at Nazareth. She had been profoundly affected by Father de Lubac's book *Catholicism*.

[8] Jules Monchanin (1895–1957), French, ordained in 1922. He was strongly interested in the ecumenical, scientific, and philosophical activities of his time. In 1939, he left for India, where he founded a small contemplative hermitage with Father Le Saux. After the council, Henri de Lubac wrote *Images de l'abbé Monchanin* (Paris: Aubier-Montaigne, 1967). Also see the works of Françoise Jacquin, especially *Jules Monchanin, prêtre: 1895–1957* (Paris: Éd. du Cerf, 1996).

[9] André Baron (1893–1981), French, ordained in 1930. Rector of Saint-Louis-des-Français from 1949 to 1962. In 1960 named a consultor to the Preparatory Commission for Religious.

[10] The Secretariat for Promoting Christian Unity, created on June 5, 1960, by John XXIII, was charged with strengthening relations with non-Catholic Christians but also with Judaism.

November 17

[1] Émile Gathier, S.J. (1892–1963), French. Professor of Hindu philosophy at the Gregorian. He was the author of *La Pensée hindoue: Étude suivie d'un choix de textes* (Paris: Éd. du Seuil, 1960).

[2] * "He knew Abbot Monchanin well in India."

[3] René Arnou, S.J. (1884–1972), French, ordained in 1915. Professor of philosophy from 1926, then of dogmatic theology from 1932 on, at the Gregorian. In 1958, he became major superior of the interprovincial Jesuit houses in Rome up until 1964.

time a visitation at the Gregorian. He strongly desires an internation-
alization of the Curia. Like me, he had noticed the pope's speech *in
Italian*, Monday, at St. Peter's.

Had lunch at the embassy, invited by Mr. de la Tournelle.[4] Cardinals
Liénart[5] and Bea were also present. Saw Count d'Harcourt,[6] nephew
of the one I used to know. Mr. de Sayve,[7] adviser to the ambassador,
exhorted me to prepare a "revolutionary" council; I asked him what he
meant by that. At the table, I sat beside Fr. Delos, O.P.,[8] ecclesiastical
adviser;*[9] we talked about Fr. Fessard's[10] last book (which he did not
accept – although he was moderate in his remarks). Chatted also with
Msgr. Girard*[11] and with two young priests from Lille,[12] who were preparing their theses and living at St.-Louis des Français.

At 4 P.M., at the Reformed Cistercians'. I first of all admired, in the
hollow of the small valley, the beautiful church of Three Fountains,
which dates from the origins of the Order. Nearby, on the hill, a new
monastery houses the abbot general of the Trappists (Dom Sortais)[13] and
the students. Chatted a moment with Bishop Suhr[14] of Copenhagen,
a Benedictine, former prior of Saint-Jérôme; he spoke to me about

---

[4] Guy Le Roy de la Tournelle (1898–1982), French diplomat. French ambassador to the Holy
See from 1959 to 1964.

[5] Achille Liénart (1884–1973), French, ordained in 1907. Bishop of Lille from 1928 to 1968,
created cardinal in 1930, president of the ACA [Assembly of Cardinals and Archbishops] in 1949.
He was a member of the Central Preparatory Commission, then, during the council, a member of
the Board of Presidency and the Coordinating Commission.

[6] Bernard d'Harcourt (1905–1966), representative of the French Association of the Order of
Malta to the Grand Master of the Order of Malta in Rome. He was the nephew of Robert d'Har-
court (1881–1965), French, former professor of German language and literature, member of the
Académie française, and himself the nephew of Albert de Mun.

[7] Olivier de Sayve, adviser to the French Embassy to the Holy See from 1958 to 1961.

[8] Thomas Delos, O.P. (1891–1975), French, ordained in 1922. Adviser of the French Embassy
to the Holy See and professor of public law at the Angelicum.

[9] * "In contact with Bruno de Solages: social studies groups in Fribourg".

[10] Gaston Fessard, S.J. (1897–1978), French, ordained in 1928. Philosopher, editor of the journal
Études, in 1941 he wrote *France, prends garde de perdre ton âme* , the first installment of *Témoignage
chrétien*, then *France, prends garde de perdre ta liberté* in 1945, faced with the rise of Marxism. He was
the "philosopher of human liberty created by God and called forth by him". His last book was *De
l'actualité historique* (Paris: Desclée, 1960).

[11] * "Who had so often received me at Lyon long ago, the superior of the university seminary".

[12] One of them was Gérard Nottebaere, born in 1932, French, ordained in 1956. He had been
studying at Rome since 1957.

[13] Gabriel Sortais, O.C.S.O. (1902–1963), French. Abbot of Bellefontaine from 1936 to 1951, he
became general of the Trappists in 1951 and remained so until his death.

[14] Johannes Theodor Suhr, O.S.B. (1896–1997), Danish, ordained in 1933. Bishop of Copenhagen from 1953 to 1964. Member of the Central Preparatory Commission.

Father Roos, S.J.,[15] whom I know; he was not happy about being summoned to Rome for no other reason, he told me, than to hear a speech
from the pope; there had not been a single meeting of his commission
(Central Commission?). I gave a talk in front of about thirty young
monks. Interventions from Dom Jean Leclercq and from Dom Olivier
Rousseau[16] (from the Benedictine priory of Chevetogne).[17] The atmosphere was fervent, very pleasant. As we were beginning to speak about
the study of the Church Fathers, an American, no doubt a student at the
Angelicum,[18] stood up and said to me: "But the Church tells us to study
the doctrine of Saint Thomas!" Clarifications from Dom Leclercq, Dom
Rousseau, and myself. Next we went to Vespers, in the new church,
which resembles the one at Sept-Fons in its present state.

November 18. – This morning, worked. (I am noting down nothing
that relates to the Theological Commission.) Saw Fr. Donatien Mollat
again. Father R. Araud,[1] who is at the Bellarmino,[2] came to see me; he
had asked Father Boyer,[3] the rector, to invite me, but his suggestion was
not accepted. After lunch, meeting in my room with some professors
of the Biblical Institute, who were wondering about the doctrinal and
pastoral repercussions of their science. In the afternoon, caught sight of
Fr. Labourdette, who had come to see Fr. Lyonnet, to speak with him
about original sin in Scripture and in St. Thomas.

---

[15] Heinrich Roos, S.J. (1904–1977), Danish. Professor of philosophy at the University of
Copenhagen.

[16] Olivier Rousseau, O.S.B. (1898–1984), Belgian. Monk of Chevetogne, editor of the journal
Irénikon, his particular interests were liturgy, ecumenism, and monastic life.

[17] It was founded at the end of 1925 by Dom Lambert Beauduin (1873–1960), who wished to
found a monastery dedicated to Christian unity. Installed first at Amay-sur-Meuse, the community
moved to Chevetogne (in the diocese of Namur) in 1939. The priory was raised to the rank of
abbey in 1990.

[18] Saint Thomas Aquinas College, held by the Dominicans, which received pontifical title in
1906 and became a pontifical university in March 1963.

November 18

[1] Régis Araud, S.J. (1925–1993), French, ordained in 1957. At the time he was completing a
two-year program in moral theology in Rome and in 1962 became professor of moral theology at
Fourvière.

[2] Jesuit college in Rome, where, among others, Jesuits studying in the various Roman universities reside.

[3] Charles Boyer, S.J. (1884–1980), French, ordained in 1916. Professor of theology at the Gregorian until 1962, he was the founder of the Unitas center and of the journal of the same name, created
in 1946, official bodies of the Vatican's unionism. Also rector of the Bellarmino from 1955 to 1961,
he organized many Thomist conferences in Rome. He was named a member of the Secretariat for
Unity in 1960, then an expert to the council in 1962.

At 6 P.M. I gave a lecture in the great hall of the Biblical Institute on "the study of the Bible in the twelfth century". Numerous students from just about everywhere. At the end, I exchanged views with some of those present.

November 19. – This morning, for the first time during this stay, I ventured into Rome. The Church of Saint Pudentiana and Saint Mary Major. At the Oriental Institute,[1] visited with Frs. Hausherr[2] and Goubert;[3] at the Russicum,[4] visited Fr. Tyszkiewicz.[5] Fr. Hausherr had me read a recent article by Fr. Louis Bouyer,[6] published in *Contacts*,[7] a French Orthodox journal. He promised me that he would very shortly write the chapter that I had asked from him for the collective work being edited by Fr. Ravier.[8] He spoke to me very highly of J. A. Cuttat.[9]

At the end of the morning, saw Fr. Magrassi, O.S.B.,[10] from the abbey in Genoa, presently in Rome, vice-rector of the Maronite college.[11] He

---

November 19

[1] Institute founded by Benedict XV on September 15, 1917, and incorporated into the Gregorian University by Pius XI in September 1928.

[2] Irénée Hausherr, S.J. (1891–1978), French, ordained in 1923. Philologist and theologian, he taught at the Oriental Institute of Rome from 1927. In 1934, he occupied the chair of spiritual theology.

[3] Paul Goubert, S.J. (1901–1967), French. Specialist in Byzantine history, he was a professor at the Institut catholique of Lyon.

[4] Pontifical college of Rome, entrusted to the Jesuits, founded in 1929 by Pius XI for the formation of clergy destined for Russia.

[5] Stanisław Tyszkiewicz, S.J. (1887–1962), Ukrainian, belonging to the Austrian Province, ordained in 1915. He had been teaching at the Russicum since 1931, dealing especially with young ecclesiastics of the Byzantine rite.

[6] Louis Bouyer (1913–2004), French. Theologian, Lutheran pastor until the Second World War, he became a priest of the Oratory in 1944 and taught at the Institut catholique of Paris until 1963, then in England, Spain, and the United States. Consultor to the Preparatory Commission for Studies and Seminaries at Vatican II, he was a consultor for the liturgy, the Congregation for Worship, and the Secretariat for Promoting Christian Unity. He was one of the figures of the biblical and liturgical movements and a co-founder of the journal *Communio*.

[7] *Contacts: Revue française de l'orthodoxie*, founded in 1949 by Jean Balzon; a journal of theology and spirituality.

[8] André Ravier, S.J. (1905–1999), French, ordained in 1937. Superior of the Jesuit Province of Lyon from 1951 to 1957, he was then editor of *Études* and dedicated himself especially to works on spirituality (on Francis de Sales in particular). The collective work that he edited was *La Mystique et les Mystiques* (Paris and Tournai: Desclée De Brouwer, 1965). In this book, Father Hausherr wrote the chapter "Les Premières générations chrétiennes".

[9] Jacques Albert Cuttat (1909–1989), Swiss, diplomat and orientalist, he was a specialist in the study of religions.

[10] Andrea Magrassi, O.S.B. (1930–2004), Italian, ordained in 1953.

[11] College founded by Gregory XIII in 1584. It is one of the many colleges of Rome for the formation of clerics.

is the author of a thesis on Rupert de Deutz[12] which should soon be translated (adapted) into French. He is going to hasten the completion of the first volume on Rupert to appear in our *Sources*.

Lunched at the Gregorian. In the cafe, with Fr. Arnou (delegato)[13] and the rector (Muñoz-Vega).[14] After the break, Fr. Henri Vignon[15] showed me, with a good deal of commentary, the Gregorian's *Vota*[16] for the council. It was insane. These good Fathers would each like to canonize in solemn fashion their own little obsessions. Sectarianism and puerility. Fr. Édouard Dhanis[17] composed in particular a *votum* on revelation and the formulae of dogma. No sense of the simple grandeur of the Church's faith that is to be proclaimed. A strange diminishment (to say nothing more) of faith in Christ. Another *votum* would like to see condemned those who hope that God might have an ordinary means of saving infants who have died without baptism, etc. These are the kinds of things that are going round and round in many*[18] Roman heads since the announcement of the council!

Msgr. Piolanti,[19] rector of the Lateran, gave a vehement speech yesterday in the great hall of his university. It was the final meeting of a week of conferences on the councils. He is supposed to have declared that the council will condemn all modern errors, in particular those

---

[12] Rupert of Deutz (circa 1075–1129). Benedictine monk, born in Liège, he accomplished a monumental work. Abbot of Deutz, near Cologne, and a theologian, he was, in H. de Lubac's view, "a giant on the threshold of the twelfth century". The first volume of Rupert to appear in the series Sources chrétiennes was *Les Œuvres du Saint Esprit*, Sources chrétiennes (Paris: Éd. du Cerf, 1967).

[13] The Delegato is the delegate of the superior general for the houses in Rome that depend directly on him.

[14] Pablo Muñoz Vega, S.J. (1903–1994), Ecuadorian, ordained in 1933. He was rector of the Gregorian from 1958 to 1963 and named an expert to the council in 1962. Named coadjutor bishop of Quito in February 1964, he attended the last sessions of the council as a council Father. He was created cardinal in 1969.

[15] Henri Vignon, S.J. (1894–1963), French. Professor of theology at the Gregorian.

[16] This refers to the wishes of the conciliar Fathers and of the faculties of canon law and theology, collected during the period prior to the preparatory phase (May 17, 1959–May 30, 1960), regarding the subjects to be treated at the council.

[17] Édouard Dhanis, S.J. (1902–1978), Belgian, ordained in 1929. In 1949, he was charged by Father Janssens with visiting the Jesuit houses of higher learning in France. Professor of fundamental theology at the Gregorian, where he was prefect of studies, then rector from 1963 to 1964. That same year, he also became a consultor to the Holy Office. Member of the Preparatory Theological Commission, he was named an expert in 1962.

[18] * Father de Lubac changed "many" to "some" and added this sentence: "Besides, it seems that these *Vota* do not really represent the opinion of the competent teachers at the Gregorian."

[19] Antonio Piolanti (1901–2001), Italian. Rector of the Lateran and consultor to the Holy Office. Member of the Preparatory Theological Commission, he was named an expert in 1962.

mentioned in *Humani generis*[20] and most especially the "new theology"[21] (according to Fr. Paul Goubert, who was there and who judged that this week at the Lateran was a success). At the opening session, Archbishop Parente,[22] assessor of the Holy Office,[23] had made a similar speech; he had gone back as far as Descartes, Kant, and Hegel in his condemnations. (According to Dom Jean Leclercq, who attended the session and who heard that he had been awarded the title of professor at the Pontifical Lateran University, without having heard anything about it beforehand.)

In the afternoon, a visit from Fr. Balducci[24] from Florence (*Testimonianze*), currently in Rome, and also Msgr. Baron, rector of St.-Louis des Français. He spoke to me about his recent trip to Israel, about Maritain,[25] etc.; I spoke to him about Msgr. Journet[26] with regard to Teilhard.

At 6 P.M., Fr. Leclercq came to get me, to take me to the scholasticate of his brother Oblates of Mary Immaculate. Warm reception. I gave nearly the same lecture as yesterday, in front of more than a hundred theology students. Dined with the small community of future professors, who are preparing their theses. The rectors of the two communities were very friendly. Father Bélanger[27] was there, having come from Ottawa for the preparation of the council; he would like, it seems to me, to push

---

[20] Encyclical of Pius XII of August 12, 1950, "Concerning some false opinions threatening to undermine the foundations of Catholic doctrine". Henri de Lubac's adversaries thought that the encyclical had condemned his positions on the supernatural, although he always denied that.

[21] This expression was popularized especially by Father Garrigou-Lagrange in an article in 1946, "La Théologie nouvelle, où va-t-elle?" *Angelicum*, October-December 1946, 126–45. De Lubac objected to this expression applied to the "Fourvière group", another just as mythical entity, in his view.

[22] Pietro Parente (1891–1986), Italian, ordained in 1916. Assessor of the Holy Office from 1959, then secretary of the Congregation for the Doctrine of the Faith from 1965 to 1967. He was created cardinal in 1967. Member of the Doctrinal Commission.

[23] The person who has the second highest rank after the secretary in the Holy Office. His functions correspond more or less to those of the secretary of the other congregations. In 1965, when the Holy Office became the Congregation for the Doctrine of the Faith, the assessor became secretary.

[24] Ernesto Balducci (1922–1992), Italian priest, he founded, in 1958, *Testimonianze*, a journal that, along with some others in Italy, wished to initiate a theological, spiritual, and ecclesial renewal.

[25] Jacques Maritain (1882–1973), French. A philosopher, he contributed to the renewal of Thomist studies by showing the modernity of St. Thomas Aquinas' philosophy.

[26] Charles Journet (1891–1975), Swiss, ordained in 1917. Professor at the Seminary of Fribourg, friend of Jacques Maritain, he edited the journal *Nova et vetera* that he founded with François Charrière. In February 1965, he was created cardinal. He opposed Teilhard in the name of the defense of Thomism.

[27] Marcel Bélanger, O.M.I., Canadian, vice-rector of the Catholic University of Ottawa. Consultor to the Preparatory Theological Commission, he was named as an expert to the council.

for a definition concerning the Virgin Mary; he is preparing, with Fr. Balić, O.F.M., [28] the international Marian congress in Ottawa for 1962 (certain Mariologists seem to be placing their hope in this congress to put pressure on the council). After dinner, more cordial conversation; the thesis students asked me all kinds of questions. I had the opportunity to speak for rather a long time about Fr. Teilhard.

Sunday, November 20. – Last day in Rome. I said yesterday to our secretary, Fr. Leclercq,[1] that several people were surprised at the absence of Fr. Karl Rahner[2] from the commission; he answered that there had been a roadblock. Chatted with Father Moran[3] about the two Testaments, the preparation for the council, etc. Said goodbye to the rector of the Biblical Institute,[4] who is defending his Institute to the best of his ability in the face of certain critics; spoke with him about the work of Miss Jaubert on the date of the Last Supper.[5] A walk in the Forum, accompanied by Fr. Haulotte, saw the Crucifixion fresco in the church of Santa Maria Antica and the mosaic at Saints Cosmas and Damian. In the evening, the manuscript for Fr. Lyonnet's next article, for *Biblica*. Saw Frs. Jarlot, Philip, and Mollat again. Fr. Haulotte accompanied me to the station. Left at 10 P.M.*[6]

---

[28] Carlo Balić, O.F.M. (1899–1977), Yugoslavian. Theologian, Mariologist, professor of dogmatic and Marian theology at the Antonianum and, from 1959, at the Lateran. He was a consultor to the Congregation of the Holy Office and founding president of the Pontifical International Marian Academy. Member of the Preparatory Theological Commission, he was named as an expert in 1962.

November 20

[1] Michel Leclercq, O.M.I.

[2] Karl Rahner, S.J. (1904–1984), German, ordained in 1932. A theologian, he exerted a very great influence on Catholic thought. Consultor to the Preparatory Commission for the Discipline of the Sacraments, he was named an expert in 1962. He was one of the founders of the journal *Concilium* in 1965.

[3] William L. Moran, S.J. (1921–2000), American. Specialist in Assyriology and professor of exegesis of the Pentateuch at the Biblical Institute from 1958 to 1966.

[4] Ernst Vogt, S.J. (1903–1984), Swiss, ordained in 1933. Rector of the Pontifical Biblical Institute from 1949 to 1963. He was named as a consultor to the Preparatory Theological Commission at the beginning of 1961.

[5] Annie Jaubert, *La Date de la Cène: Calendrier biblique et liturgie chrétienne* (Paris: J. Gabalda, 1957).

[6] * At this point there are several inserted additions. First of all, a handwritten letter from Father de Lubac, dated November 19, 1960: "Very dear friend [unidentified]. Our letters crossed in the mail; yours reached me this morning; I have passed on to Father Philip that which was for him. My stay in Rome is over; I leave tomorrow evening and will be in Lyon Monday at 1:00 P.M. I hope that next Thursday the result will be satisfactory. Let us know immediately at Lyon. Here, everything went smoothly. But, and this will not surprise you, I will not leave very comforted. The state

of mind of all the personnel in charge as far as theology is concerned is always the same. No understanding, a great deal of pettiness, ignorance of the world to which the Gospel must be preached, lack of spiritual life, a cast of mind that is incurably polemical and negative. At the Lateran, the rector (Monsignor Piolanti) and the Master of the Sacred Palace (an Italian Dominican) gave a speech at the beginning of the new term. Their great objective, according to what I was told (I was not there): to have the "new theology" condemned and to strengthen the encyclical *Humani generis*. I will relate to you some other matters (among those that are not *sub secreto*!). Today I had lunch at the Gregorian, where I saw some Frenchmen. Here, yesterday, a lecture: on the Bible in the twelfth century. It did not go badly. The atmosphere of the Biblical Institute is friendly. Goodbye! *Frater in Christo.*" Next comes a typewritten sheet: "On my return to Lyon, reread some passages from the great 'Letter' of Father General to the Assistancy of France [cf. the note on this letter dated September 23, 1961], which threatens to become news again in the preparation for the council. There are some truly appalling passages in it: the expressions of the authors that one wants to condemn are broken up, mixed together, deformed, changed from the meaning that the context makes clear, in order to make error come forth. By means of procedures like these, one could just as well cause exactly the opposite error to emerge. For in these matters, everything rests on a delicate balance. This determined will to make their own children appear heterodox or even gravely culpable would be incredible, if one were to suppose that the person who signed this letter knew what it contained. One would not find a single other example in our history. And this still persists; it is impossible to explain anything about it to Father General, who would himself be alarmed if he saw it."

January 16, 1961. Sent to Father Tromp in Rome the essay he had asked for from me on the natural knowledge of God.

January 20. Read the "*Philosophie de l'histoire des conciles tenus en France*" by Abbot Cacheux (1884, Paris). Some excerpts, chosen at random: "The search that the council of Aix conducted into the Empress Judith cleared her of any suspicion of adultery." "In order to refresh the lawns of discipline with a sheet of flowing water in these scorching days, the meeting took place at Attigny." "Amoléon gave a sweetness to the idealism of the Christian philosophy." "The councils were struck with sadness to see the terrain of virtue littered with debris." "As the majestic figure of Christianity advanced on the road of time, she made the forces of history shine." "The torrents of disorder were dried up at the council of Auch" . . ., etc.

January 26. Wrote to Father Séb. Tromp to thank him for his volumes 2 and 3 on the *Corpus Christi quod est Ecclesia* that he recently sent me (I had sent him the first two volumes of *Exégèse médiévale*). "Propter reformationem universalis Ecclesiae", "pro universali Ecclesia reformanda": formulae of Innocent III, sermon to the Lateran Council [For the reform of the universal Church, for the universal Church to be reformed].

Saturday, February 11, 1961. – Arrived in Rome in the morning. Once again, I am staying at the Biblical Institute. At lunch there were two of us as guests: we were seated beside Fr. Rector, with me the second of the two. Fr. Rector explained to our neighbor that I had arrived for the preconciliar commission, and he told me the name of the other man, who had arrived from Sicily: Father Spedalieri.[1] This man (who had written a violent piece against me)[*2] did not seem in any way ill at ease; we shook hands and chatted amiably; he told me I should come to Sicily, etc., etc. Toward the middle of the meal, however, he asked me in a slightly confused manner: "Isn't there still another person who is supposed to be coming from France for this commission?" – Not that I knew of. – But yes, a certain de Lubac? – But that is I ..." Spedalieri was stunned. I shook his hand again, made him laugh, and we continued chatting. At the start of the meal, he had not heard my name when Fr. Rector said it.

In the afternoon, I went to Monte Verde Vecchio to see Fr. L. de Peretti,[3] superior general of the Canons Regular of the I. C. (Dom Grea).[4, *5] He spoke to me about Cardinal Ottaviani, whom he knew well; about the power of the Holy Office in Italy, about Archbishop Parente, etc. According to him, the commissary of the Holy Office,[6] a Dominican, as the occupant of this position always is, was of the opinion that I should be chosen for the Theological Commission; he is supposed to have argued that my name be proposed by various people; no doubt this was a response to some others, who wanted to exclude me; the opinion of the commissary was supposedly "inspired" by someone higher up. Fr. de Peretti praised John XXIII for his simplicity. He was

---

February 11

[1] Francesco Spedalieri, S.J. The piece of writing in question is "Selectae et breviores philosophiae ac theologiae controversiae" (Rome: Officium libri catholici, 1950).

[2]* "Addressed directly to the pope, who had been a schoolmate of his, something he boasted about to Father Frédéric Bertrand."

[3] Louis de Peretti, C.R.I.C. (1906–1987), French, ordained in 1930. Superior general of the Canons Regular of the Immaculate Conception from 1957 to 1976.

[4] Dom Adrien Gréa (1828–1917), French. As a priest, he founded the Canons Regular of the Immaculate Conception in 1871, a men's religious congregation of diocesan right. His research prepared for the renewal of ecclesiology in the twentieth century.

[5]* "Who had received me at the seminary of Gap".

[6] After March 1959, the successor of Paul Philippe was Father Raimundo Verardo, O.P.

troubled by the decline in the spirit of faith and of prayer among the French clergy, secular and regular, and he wondered if the future council would be able to provide a remedy for this profound ill. We spoke for a long time on that subject.

According to Fr. de Peretti, Cardinal Ruffini[7] read in manuscript and approved the article by Msgr. Romeo[8] that appeared in *Divinitas*, directed expressly against Father Alonso Schökel[9] and the whole of the current Biblical Institute and also taking aim at Cardinal Bea and Pius XII's encyclical *Divino afflante*.[10] Msgr. Piolanti, rector of the Lateran, publicly supported Romeo; both of them, opposed as they are to this encyclical, have*[11] tried several times since to obtain a condemnation of the Bible scholars who have made it their charter: an offensive against Mr. Gélin[12] (Lyon) – the business of the Introduction to the Bible[13] – criticism of the Italian biblical series sponsored by Fr. S. Lyonnet – an attack in *Divinitas* against Fr. Lyonnet's doctrine on original sin, etc. – The scale and the violence of the new article by Romeo shows that the discussion will be brought to the council. It is also necessary to take account of the ambition and jealousy of the Lateran, which, having become a pontifical university, would like to have its own Biblical Institute; what's more, the Parente-Piolanti-Romeo circle continues the "integrist" tradition of Benigni,[14] Canali,[15] etc., a tendency that still finds more than one sympathizer in Rome.[16]

---

[7] Ernesto Ruffini (1888–1967), Italian, ordained in 1910. Archbishop of Palermo from 1945 until his death, created cardinal in 1946. A member of the Board of Presidency of the council.

[8] Antonio Romeo (1902–1974), Italian. Professor of Sacred Scripture at the Lateran, he also worked at the Congregation for Seminaries and Universities. His article is "L'enciclica 'Divino afflante Spiritu' e le 'Opiniones Novae' ", *Divinitas* 4 (1960): 387–456.

[9] Luis Alonso Schökel, S.J. (1920–1998), Spanish. Professor of Sacred Scripture, a specialist on the Old Testament, he taught at the Biblical Institute beginning in 1957.

[10] Encyclical of Pius XII, dated September 30, 1943, on Sacred Scripture and its interpretation. It promoted biblical studies.

[11] * "Have" was changed to "were said to have".

[12] Albert Gélin, P.S.S. (1902–1960), French, a professor at the faculty of theology in Lyon.

[13] A. Robert and A. Feuillet, eds., *Introduction à la Bible* (Tournai: Desclée & Cie, 1957–1959). Volume 1, referred to the Holy Office, reappeared in 1959 with some minor alterations but no fundamental change. Volume 2 came out without difficulty in 1959.

[14] Umberto Benigni (1862–1934), Italian. Professor of ecclesiastical history, prelate at the Secretariat of State, he put in place an international network of denunciation, the Sodalitium Pianum (called "la Sapinière" in French) (1909–1921), to fight against modernism. See É. Poulat, *Intégrisme et catholicisme intégral, un réseau secret international antimoderniste, La Sapinière, 1909–1921* (Tournai: Casterman, 1969), and *Catholicisme, démocratie et socialisme: Le Mouvement catholique et Mgr Benigni, de la naissance du socialisme à la victoire du fascisme* (Casterman, 1977).

According to Fr. Donatien Mollat, whom I met at the end of the afternoon, this Romeo-Alonso affair is rather serious, because in similar cases, many people let themselves be intimidated. One sees here, he told me, the same process occurring as in the "Fourvière affair": suspicions, insinuations, concerns expressed, collective accusations, improper comparisons, etc.: in this way a mythical monster is created. At the present time there is supposedly still, in Rome and in the Society, much distrust with regard to Fourvière. This might be the case to some extent with the rector of the Gregorian.[17] Hardly surprising, after the official statements and the conversations that the rector must have had with Frs. Boyer, Dhanis, Hürth,[18] etc.

However, Fr. Alonso Schökel is well defended. At a meeting with the Marist superior,[19] who asked him if he could continue in good conscience to send students to the B. I., Cardinal Bea responded with a vigorous letter, expressing his indignation at Romeo's article. Father Tromp, who is secretary of both the Holy Office and the preconciliar Theological Commission, complained that people were likely to think that the commission and the Holy Office had something to do with the affair, since Msgr. Piolanti was a member of both. An intervention of the pope was reported, though in various ways; according to some, he had a word of rebuke for the tone of Romeo's article; others said, but without being able to vouch for it, that John XXIII had telephoned the Father editor[20]

---

[15] Nicola Canali (1874–1961), Italian, ordained in 1900. Assessor of the Holy Office in 1926, he was created cardinal in 1935. In 1939, he was named president of the Pontifical Commission for the Vatican State.

[16] Rome at the time was experiencing a great controversy about biblical studies; some, particularly in the Holy Office and the Congregation for Seminaries and Universities, were worried about the direction of those studies. In his article, A. Romeo accused "the Pontifical Biblical Institute of having abandoned the positions of the magisterium and of taking part in what the intransigence of Romeo considered to be a vast campaign to replace the faith of the Church with a new Christianity inspired by Teilhard de Chardin and reminiscent of freemasonry". Cf. G. Alberigo, *Histoire du Concile Vatican II*, vol. 1 (Paris: Éd. du Cerf, 1997), 311.

[17] Father Pablo Muñoz-Vega.

[18] Franz Hürth, S.J. (1880–1963), German, ordained in 1911. A moralist, he was one of the counselors of Pius XII. A teacher at the Gregorian, he was a member of the Preparatory Theological Commission and was named an expert in 1962.

[19] Alcime Cyr, S.M. (1882–1973), American. Elected superior general for life in September 1947, he retired in August 1961.

[20] Roberto Tucci, S.J., born in 1921, Italian, ordained in 1950. He was the editor, from 1959 to 1973, of this bimonthly journal published by the Italian Jesuits and launched in 1850. Roberto Tucci, named an expert to the council, led the daily press conferences for the accredited journalists during the last three sessions. He was created cardinal in 2001.

of the *Civiltà cattolica* (where the article by Fr. Alonso that was under attack appeared) to reassure him. Both accounts in their own way are pieces of gossip.

I found an enormous envelope here, containing a report of the work accomplished by the Theological Commission in the course of these last few months. A letter from Fr. Tromp summons me to the meetings of the plenary session that are supposed to take place at the Vatican on February 13, 14, 15, and 16.

Msgr. Spadafora,[21] professor of Sacred Scripture at the Lateran, a friend of Msgr. Romeo, was supposed to have made very sharp remarks, so I was told, about Pius XII and Cardinal Bea.*[22] According to Fr. Zerwick,[23] professor at the Biblical Institute, the goal of the Romeo-Piolanti party is to have the Jesuits thanked for their services by the pope and to take their place at the Biblical Institute. Moreover, it is understandable that some people find abnormal the nearly absolute monopoly of the Jesuits with regard to higher education in Bible studies. Fr. Simon,[24] also a professor at the Biblical Institute, recently said: "I have been in Rome for more than thirty years, and I have never seen a member of the Roman Curia undertaking a matter of this sort not to achieve his aim." But the perspective of the council might bring something new. Others think that the matter could be settled through administrative channels: the Lateran would be invited to let Spadafora return to his native land (Sicily?), and the Biblical Institute to let Spain take back Father Alonso. But there are fundamental questions that would keep the disagreement going.

The rector of the Biblical Institute wrote a memorandum, long, precise, forceful.*[25] The memorandum was presented to the pope; he is supposed to have expressed the desire that it be given to all the cardinals.

Msgr. Piolanti is alleged to have said: "If we are defeated in this affair, Msgr. Romeo will have no other option than to become a country priest, and as for me, I will be able to realize the dream of my youth; I

---

[21] Francesco Spadafora (1913–1997), Italian. Professor of exegesis at the theology faculty of the Lateran. Member of the Preparatory Commission for Studies and Seminaries.

[22] * "And the Biblical Institute".

[23] Maximilian Zerwick, S.J. (1901–1975), German, ordained in 1931. Exegete and specialist in Biblical Greek. He was forced, along with Stanislas Lyonnet, to give up teaching at the end of the 1961–1962 academic year, at the request of the Holy Office, until July 1964.

[24] Jean Simon, S.J. (1897–1968), Belgian, professor of Ethiopian and Coptic.

[25] * "He showed it to me."

will become a Dominican." Several people have told me that Romeo's zeal, although badly informed, is very genuine.

It was the young Father Coste,[26] from the General Curia of the Marists, who came to speak to Fr. Lyonnet about this matter, asking him for news. On Fr. Lyonnet's suggestion, he persuaded his assistant general, Fr. Lambert,[27] to write to Cardinal Bea in order to ask him what he ought to do: If the reproaches were justified, was it not advisable for him to withdraw the young Marists taking courses at the Institute? Hence Cardinal Bea's response, which made no claim to be confidential.

February 12, 1961. – At the end of the afternoon, a visit from Fr. Dhanis. He came about a detail concerning our commission. We came to speak of more serious matters. If he is to be believed, he had almost nothing to do with the Fourvière business, he had neither read the texts of Fr. General[1] nor censured my books, etc. Perhaps only "once or twice" he had been called on to "give an opinion", etc. This is his way of keeping the secrets to which he doubtless feels himself bound. Following his visit, I wrote him a letter reminding him of some indisputable facts, telling him his present duty, explaining to him also my position in matters of faith, and drawing his attention to the spiritual ruins that result from certain attitudes. On reflection, I did not send my letter.

February 13 and 14. – Commission, meetings.

February 15. – This morning, at 9:30, in the Pauline chapel,[1] the imposition of ashes by the bishop of Vatican City:[2] Cardinal Ottaviani presided, some bishops, some members attended. Then, the usual meeting,

---

[26]Jean Coste, S.M. (1926–1994), French, ordained in 1951. From 1955, he collaborated on the project launched by the general administration to conduct a scientific study on the origins of the Marists.

[27]James Lambert, S.M. (1913–1992), American, ordained in 1937. Assistant general of the Marists from 1954 to 1969.

February 12

[1]Jean-Baptiste Janssens, S.J. (1889–1964), Belgian, ordained in 1919. He was superior general of the Society of Jesus from 1946 until his death. Member of the council's Commission for Religious named by the pope.

February 15

[1]At the Vatican, the private chapel of Paul III, decorated by Michelangelo, among others.

[2]Bishop Pierre Van Lierde, O.S.A. (1907–1995), Belgian, ordained in 1931. He entered the Curia in 1951 and retired from it in 1991.

lasting 3 hours, much like yesterday and the day before. A number of things would have been worth noting, interesting, amusing, or serious things. But I have written nothing about them because of my vow of secrecy. At the end of a few hours, of a few meetings, the character of each person becomes visible; his doctrinal tendencies, the quality of his knowledge or thought, the authority he enjoys.

Yesterday morning, the Holy Father came to follow, for nearly 2 hours, the discussions of our session. In excusing himself, he said a few words, in poor Latin – without leaving any personal impression.

After renewed reflection, I added a postscript to my letter to Fr. Dhanis, and I intend to give it to him tomorrow: "My good Father, here is the letter that I wrote to you three days ago. I was hesitant to give it to you because I feared to cause you further distress – a distress that is echoed in me, I can assure you ... My conviction is growing that I must do everything possible, in my very small sphere of action, to remedy the ills of the Church, and it is out of faithfulness to this program that I have decided to send you this letter ... I would like to assure you of my entirely fraternal sentiments in Xto Jesu."[3]

February 16. – The last day of this *Sessio plenaria.*[1] In the morning, in subcommittee in the premises of the Holy Office. In the middle of the meeting, a coffee break. Then I withstood a hard combat (against Msgr. Piolanti and Fr. Dhanis, who want the condemnation of Fr. Teilhard at all costs). In the afternoon, the last meeting of the commission at the Vatican. The next plenary session is to take place in September.

February 17. – In the morning, met with Frs. Mollat, Lyonnet, Philip. A Dutch biennist[1] from the Bellarmino came to see me; he told me that a thick book[2] had just come out, in Italian, on "the Supernatural", a collective work edited by Msgr. Piolanti. One whole chapter of the work, he said, was directed against me, placing my opinions among the most serious errors of our time against the faith. The author of the chapter is

---

[3] "In Jesus Christ".

February 16

[1] "Plenary session".

February 17

[1] A Jesuit student completing a two-year cycle of studies, most often in philosophy and theology.

[2] A. Piolanti, ed., *Il Soprannaturale* (Turin: Marietti, 1960).

Father Perego, S.J., who has already on several occasions over the last ten years indicated his opposition to me. Four days ago, *L'Osservatore Romano* published a laudatory article on this book.

Departed from Rome at 1:40 P.M. Fr. Haulotte accompanied me to the Termini. Arrived in Paris on the morning of the 18th. I brought back from Rome the long mimeographed response of Fr. Vogt, rector of the Biblical Institute, to the Romeo article. It has been given to all the cardinals present in Rome, as well as some others (including Cardinal Gerlier).[3]

September 12, 1961. – I am preparing to leave again for Rome. Since February, I have had to do some work for our Theological Commission (concerning the knowledge of God).*[1]

In the course of the year, Cardinal Ottaviani published a collection of writings and speeches under the title: *Le boulevard*;[2] translated into French: *Le Rempart* [The rampart]. Too defensive. I fear that the real translation should be: "The Maginot Line".

September 16. – The 13th, in Milan: Saint Ambrose. The 14th and 15th: Florence; the inside of Santa Croce, in the evening. The 16th: Arezzo, Rome. I am staying at the Gregorian.

September 17. – Sunday. Conversations with Fr. Tromp, Fr. Philip, Fr. Congar, O.P.[1] – Fr. Lyonnet spoke to me about the next biblical congress on Saint Paul, which he is currently preparing. In the mail that was waiting for me, I found a letter from a student who was helped by *Chemins de Dieu* and *Paradoxes*.[2]

---

[3] Pierre Marie Gerlier (1880–1965), French, ordained in 1921. Archbishop of Lyon from 1937 until his death, created cardinal in 1937.

September 12

[1] * "This work served no purpose, it never came under discussion. It was no doubt a test to judge my orthodoxy."

[2] This refers to *Il Baluardo*, translated into French as *L'Église et la Cité* (Rome, 1963).

September 17

[1] Yves Congar, O.P. (1905–1995), French. Theologian, consultor to the Preparatory Theological Commission, named an expert in 1962. He worked in particular on the Church and ecumenism. Co-founder of the journal *Concilium*. Created cardinal in 1994.

[2] H. de Lubac, *Paradoxes* (Paris, Éd. du Seuil, 1946), trans. Paule Simon and Sadie Kreilkamp as *Paradoxes of Faith* (San Francisco: Ignatius Press, 1987), and *Sur les chemins de Dieu* (Paris: Aubier-Montaigne, 1956), trans. Alexander Dru as *The Discovery of God* (Grand Rapids: Eerdmans, 1996).

September 18. – This morning, the first meeting for this plenary session of the Theological Commission. The room at the Vatican being
under repair, we met at the Palace of the Chancellery,[1] in the hall called
"of the one hundred days", decorated by the frescoes of Vasari.[2]

This afternoon, at the General Curia, I saw Frs. de Gorostarzu and
Bottereau.[3] The one*[4] is superficial, the other*[5] is a great administrator.
The real questions do not seem to interest them; no idea of making
inquiries, of questioning.

September 19 and 20. – Every morning, plenary session. Every afternoon, at the Angelicum, meetings of the *De Ecclesia*[1] subcommittee, in
which I take part, with Fr. Gagnebet, O.P., presiding.

On the evening of the 20th, at the Gregorian, in getting up from the
table, Father Tromp told me: "In the constitution *De ordine morali*,[2] we
dropped those things about Fr. Teilhard." I had fought for that. The
members and consultors had received a brief memorandum, duplicated
through the efforts of Father Leclercq, clarifying more than one matter.
But it was still necessary that Fr. Tromp's wise decision be adopted in a
plenary session.

The beauty of Rome, which has captured me again. The Quirinal
square, the Trevi Fountain, the little Piazza della Pilotta, as seen from
the terrace of the Gregorian ... and the cupola of Saint Peter's, floating
in the air at sunset.*[3]

September 18

[1] Building constructed by Cardinal Riario at the end of the fifteenth and beginning of the
sixteenth century and confiscated by Leo X. The structure houses the Chancellery, charged with
writing up the acts of the popes.

[2] Giorgio Vasari (1511–1574), Italian writer, painter, and architect, famous for his biographies of
artists of the Italian Renaissance.

[3] Georges Bottereau, S.J. (1912–1985), French, ordained in 1942. A great Latinist, he was, in
Rome, deputy to the Assistant of France until 1962, then superior of the house of the General
Curia.

[4] * "Very amiable".

[5] * "Friendly, but discreet".

September 19 and 20

[1] "On the Church".

[2] "On the moral order".

[3] * Here is inserted a typewritten page, although the facts are slightly later (see the entry for
Tuesday, September 26): "In the chapter *De Deo*, the author finished, in a truly comical fashion,
with an exhortation addressed to all the faithful to place increasing emphasis on the proofs of God's
existence. I pointed out that there was also a supernatural revelation about God, that God had made
himself known in his innermost life, that he had revealed himself to be Love, that he was calling

Everything essential, in this Theological Commission, is done by a small group of Roman theologians. Sometimes they argue among themselves, but on the basis of a common mentality, common reflexes. They know their field, but little more. One senses among them a certain indifference toward Scripture, the Fathers, the Eastern Church; a lack of interest and of concern regarding current doctrines and spiritual trends contrary to the Christian faith.*[4] They are, it seems, too sure of their superiority; their habit of judging does not encourage them to work. This is the milieu of the Holy Office. The observations, the work, the *vota* of theologians who have come from somewhere else (except those of a few friends and spokesmen) scarcely hold their attention – even in reference to bishops.

The result is a small academic system, ultra-intellectualist without any great intellectuality; the Gospel is forced to fit this system, which is the constant a priori. Father Dhani, who plays an important role, seems to want to minimize in every respect the Person of Jesus Christ: the latter is no longer*[5] anything more than one of the "legatores divini"; he is designated thus, in anonymous fashion, in the chapter on revelation. Christ the teacher does not possess "the treasures of wisdom and knowledge"[6] (he*[7] had this Pauline text deleted from this same chapter). The whole of his revelation is reduced to the proclamation of a few formal propositions, added to those that are found in the Old Testament, analogous to those of the prophets and apostles; from these propositions, the Church (= the group of Roman theologians) draws new propositions in order to impose them on everyone. Several times, formulae are put forward that are intended to make equivalent the progress of revelation up to Christ and dogmatic progress within the Christian revelation.

It is this little system, pushed to the point of madness, that for the past twelve years some have wanted to impose on us as the only orthodox

---

us in Jesus Christ to be no longer only his creatures and his servants but his sons; I recalled some texts from Saint Paul and Saint John that are central, fundamental to our faith; finally, I proposed in writing a text where this fundamental truth concerning the truth of God would be stated. They appeared to accede to my request. But my text, examined in subcommittee, with me absent, was completely changed, and all mention of our divine filiation by means of grace was removed, as if there were something dangerous in the doctrine. Our theologians love diminished truths, ones that they think are surer, easier to delimit conceptually."

4 * "They are unaware of them."

5 * "Primarily".

6 Col 2:3.

7 * "Dhanis".

one. Because I will not bow to this, everything I write is distorted. By his personal *Votum* (wrongly said to be the wish of the Gregorian, despite the protestations of more than one professor), by the composition of several passages of the preconciliar schemas that have been entrusted to him, by his many oral interventions in the commission, F. D.[8] is seeking to make this system prevail and to have those in the Church condemned who resist this in some way. In the Society, Fr. General continues to place blind confidence in him. In the Church, his influence at the present time is all the greater for the fact that he is not generally known and consequently not discussed: he has never produced a single publication, no matter how unimportant. Even within the commission, many people do not realize the situation. Certain bishops are in this respect remarkably naïve.

One does not sense, among the group of theologians assembled here, any concern for what would be necessary to nourish and guide the Christian people or to call the world to the Gospel. All that, they say, is "pastoral", it is not "dogmatic", it is not our business; that sort of thing, to their way of thinking, is only a matter of practical applications and popularizations … In that way they firmly entrench a rather dangerous dichotomy, and they make the Pastors subordinate. Their "dogmatics" itself seems to lose interest in the great central dogmas; it refuses to recognize the Christian Mystery in its profound unity; it is transformed more and more into an ideology of pulverized assertions. Observing them in a group, in their disdainful thoughtlessness, in the accord that shows through their disputes, one sometimes has the impression of elderly children to whom powerful means of destruction have been imprudently entrusted.

For example: The text of a profession of faith was being studied: Paragraph on the Redemption: "Christ satisfied the justice of God." It is proposed (by Philippe de la Trinité) that the adverb "misericordite"[9] be added. Refusal. Why? – Because that is evident, it goes without saying, no one denies it, etc. – So, neither by this adverb nor in any other manner will this text on the redemption make allusion to the divine mercy. It will speak only of justice. Anyone who then wants to speak of mercy will be accused of wishing to contradict or at the very least weaken the solemn text.

---

[8] Father Dhanis.

[9] "Mercifully".

Cardinal Ottaviani presides over everything very actively, with much presence of mind. His attention sometimes appears to become casual, but that is only in appearance. At the right time he will intervene or give the floor to someone he has chosen. Inevitably, he is intimidating. Because of that, certain candid explanations are prevented. There is a climate of opportunism and distrust. Besides, on important points, it would be very difficult to make oneself understood.

Father Schmidt, S.J.,[10] a member of the Liturgical Commission, told me that only the Theological Commission is bound by a rigorous secrecy – contrary, he told me, to the intentions of the pope. It is true that this is the commission that deals with the most serious and the most delicate matters. Fr. Schmidt also told me that, nevertheless, people in Rome know something of what goes on in the debates of our commission, through some bishops who are unhappy and are complaining. In session, however, these bishops hardly ever intervene, and none of them seems to be either willing or able to play a truly effective role. We miss Archbishop Stohr[11] of Mainz; he died a few months ago; he was a man of few words, but firm; he was the one who intervened in a terse way last February, in the subcommission on *De deposito fidei*[12] gathered at the Holy Office, to support me against the anti-Teilhardian offensive led by Fr. Dhanis and Msgr. Piolanti: he simply said, in a severe, slow voice and with gravity, looking right into the faces of those leading the attack: "Ne quid nimis! ne quid nimis!"[13]

September 23. – Yesterday afternoon, a new session of the subcommission on *De deposito fidei fideliter servando*.[1] Fr. Dhanis proposed his (printed) text on revelation, faith, etc. In two places, this text contains

---

[10] Herman Schmidt, S.J. (1912–1982), Dutch, ordained in 1940. A specialist in the liturgy, he was professor of liturgy at the theological college of Maastricht beginning in 1942 and at the Gregorian from 1950 on. During the council, he was consultor to the *consilium ad exsequendam Constitutionem de Sacra Liturgia*, an organization set up after the adoption of the constitution on the Liturgy to oversee its application.

[11] Albert Stohr (1890–June 1961), German, ordained in 1913. Bishop of Mainz from 1935 until his death.

[12] "On the deposit of the faith".

[13] "Nothing to excess! Nothing to excess!" [A sentence borrowed by the Latins from the Greeks (*Mêden agan*).]

September 23

[1] "On the deposit of the faith to be faithfully guarded".

a passage intended to have me condemned by the council: he picks up some expressions from the encyclical *Humani generis*, mixed with expressions drawn from Fr. General's letter to the French Assistancy,[2] on some points that were applied to my writings with the methods of a forger. – There were 11 or 12 of us gathered. The proposed text was read: "Periculose errant qui etc."[3] Not one person asked to whom it referred. There is weakmindedness here that astounds me. These men, charged with drawing up the doctrinal texts of an ecumenical council, do not demand any evidence, do not verify anything, do not even seek to inform themselves. We were presided over by a Canadian bishop,[4] full of good spirits but giving the impression of vacuousness. Now, among those present, doubtless only one or two understood what and who were at issue. Msgr. Piolanti silently rejoiced and, by his acquiescence, sealed his complicity with Fr. Dhanis. Father Tapiè,[5] who has probably never read those of my writings targeted here, but who is intelligent and rather well-informed about the undercurrents in doctrinal disputes, perhaps kept silence out of pity for me. The others only saw the fire in it. And all, now, will perhaps go the same way, first at the plenary session of the commission, then at the council; and the day after the council ends, some commentaries will be published explaining who was condemned, and the passages that will be quoted from a letter of Fr. General will furnish the proof. These solemn declarations of Father General, cleverly crafted 11 years ago, will still prevail over the authentic texts that hardly anyone knows, to which no one will refer, especially on dogmatic subjects that, alas, today make almost everyone in the Church yawn.

---

[2] This refers to a letter of February 11, 1951, implementing the encyclical *Humani generis*. The Jesuit superior general, in the accompanying letter to the provincials of the Assistancy of France, wrote: "Several refuse to admit that the encyclical aims at and hits professors and writers currently living among us, but whom the Holy Father, in his paternal goodness, refrained from naming. The consequence of this is that the condemned opinions will in fact continue to be supported and taught as if they were not affected."

[3] "Those are dangerously in error who ..." [Father de Lubac thought that he was particularly targeted by no. 22 of chapter 4, on a "recent form of relativism": "periculose etiam a vero discedunt qui sentiunt enuntiationes et conceptus quibus veritates revelatae communicantur, impares esse ad res divinas omnino vere significandas, etsi utique et incomplete" (those people depart dangerously from the truth who think that the concepts and words by which revealed truths are communicated are incapable of expressing divine things, even if incompletely and imperfectly).]

[4] Lionel Audet (1908–1989), Canadian, ordained in 1934. Auxiliary bishop of Quebec from 1952 until his death.

[5] This must be Agostino Trapè (1915–1987), of the Order of Saint Augustine, of which he was the prior general. He was professor of patrology in various Roman universities. A member of the Preparatory Theological Commission, he was named an expert to the council in 1962.

Every morning, the plenary sessions continue to take place at the Palace of the Chancellery. The subcommissions meet at the Holy Office. I have taken part in two of them in the hall of the *Consulta*, under the eye of Torquemada:[6] a large, full-length portrait; he carries a lily in his hand, a symbol, I suppose, of the purity of the doctrine.

This afternoon, September 23, again at the Angelicum, an "extraordinary" (= private) session to examine the chapter of *De Ecclesia* on bishops. Msgr. Fenton[7] (from Washington) wants their power in the temporal order defined; two others want a definition that gives a bishop the right to punish his subjects, in particular with financial penalties. This morning, in connection with mixed marriages, Cardinal Ottaviani intervened in a spirited fashion. He shows in general a solid good sense. But his positions are always negative and defensive. They proceed from a human experience that is only too real and at the same time from a firm attachment to the Catholic tradition. But this experience nevertheless appears a little narrow, and his traditional sense seems insufficiently enlivened by the evangelical spirit. – Several members and consultors are unhappy over the fact that, in the schema of the constitution *De ordine morali*, almost nothing is said about charity, except to condemn those who are always promoting it and distorting it, etc. – At the Dominicans', I was overcome by a bit of fatigue, followed by a long nosebleed, which earned me the attentions of Father Gagnebet.

Sunday, September 24. – According to Father Congar, it was Cardinal Montini[1] who succeeded in imposing Don Carlo Colombo, from the Seminary of Milan, on the Theological Commission. One does, in fact, get the clear impression that he does not make up part of the inner circle.

---

[6] Tomas de Torquemada, O.P. (1420–1498), Spanish, inquisitor. He placed the Inquisition under the authority of the tribunal of the Holy Office, on which he sat.

[7] Joseph Fenton (1906–1969), American. Professor of dogmatic theology at the Catholic University of America (Washington) until 1963. Member of the Preparatory Theological Commission, then an expert at the council beginning in 1962.

September 24

[1] Giovanni Battista Montini (1897–1978), Italian, ordained in 1920. Archbishop of Milan from 1954 to 1963, created cardinal in 1958. He became pope under the name of Paul VI in 1963. Cardinal Montini had indeed addressed a letter to Archbishop Dell'Acqua, at the Secretariat of State, on July 19, 1960, expressing his surprise that the Preparatory Theological Commission did not include any professor from the faculty of theology in Milan and calling for the correction of this oversight. Among the names he listed: Carlo Colombo (Montini Archives, Milan, ENTI–127–554).

I was not able to attend the meeting of the subcommission on *De deposito fidei jure servando* that was concerned with the question of Teilhard on creation. In February, the day after the stormy subcommission meeting where I intervened, supported by Bishop Stohr, an intervention by Msgr. Philips[2] (from Louvain), in plenary session, had obtained a vote deciding that the passage in question would be dropped. And yet, it is still there, just as it was, in the text printed today, contrary to what Father Tromp told me the other day.[3] And I note besides that my written observation, citing some texts from Fr. Teilhard exactly contrary to what they accuse him of, has been rejected. There is no allusion to it in the new mimeographed sheet proposing changes to the draft of *De deposito*.

Tuesday, September 26. – This morning, while waiting for the car that was to bring us, along with the elderly Father Hürth, to the Cancelleria, a brief exchange with Father Dhanis on the steps of the Gregorian. Yesterday, on the same spot, I had simply said to him: "I respect your silence, but I am always ready to speak in a fraternal manner with you, whenever you wish, on the doctrinal reproaches you have made against me." After the customary greetings, he said to me this morning: "I did not understand very well what you wanted to say to me yesterday." I answered him that for nine days we have not exchanged a single word on the subjects of our commission; but that nevertheless he is taking a great deal of interest in me; that I would very much like to have some explanation from him on a certain paragraph of the texts written by him. Then he responded: "I will not answer you." I asked him why. He said to me: "I have my reasons." I said to him: "Father, this is a very serious refusal, and one that is not justified." On that note, Father Hürth arrived, and we put him into the car with us.

Canon Ph. Delhaye,[1] whom I have seen these past days, is very annoyed (his usual attitude). He told me how he and his colleague Msgr.

---

[2] Gérard Philips (1899–1972), Belgian. Professor of dogmatics at the theology faculty of Louvain. Member of the Preparatory Theological Commission, he was named an expert in 1962 and became adjunct secretary of the Doctrinal Commission in 1963. He established himself as the real organizer of the Doctrinal Commission's work and played a considerable role in the drafting of *Lumen gentium*.

[3] Father de Lubac had indeed mentioned, on September 20, that Father Tromp had informed him of the removal of the mention of Teilhard, but in *De ordine morali*. Here, it is a question of *Deposito fidei*. Both texts were indeed critical of Teilhard. See the Philips Collection 286, 330, and 337.

September 26

[1] Philippe Delhaye (1912–1990), Belgian. Professor at the Catholic Faculties of Lille and Louvain (faculty of theology). Consultor to the Preparatory Theological Commission, he became an

Janssen[2] (from Louvain) were introduced almost by breaking and entering into the subcommission on *De ordine morali*. The discussions there
were lively. For some (Hürth, Gillon, O.P.),[3] the moral order must be
defined by the lex naturalis;[4] according to others (including Delhaye),
by charity. Fr. Hürth pointed out that charity occupies a rather small
place in the Gospel; it might even be, he is supposed to have added, that
Jesus would not have spoken of it if he had not been questioned by the
scribes. Fr. Häring,[5] a Redemptorist and a professor in Rome, argued
in favor of charity. Father Gillon claimed that the doctrine he was supporting along with Fr. Hürth was one of the points on which the Holy
Office had given them instructions not to yield. On that, Fr. Tromp,
very annoyed, reproached Fr. Gillon for his indiscretion, etc.

Yesterday, Monday the 25th, I spoke at the microphone, asking that
there be added at least one sentence to the last paragraph of the chapter
de Deo.[6] I pointed out that this paragraph said some good things but
remained entirely in the domain of natural reason. Now since this is a
chapter of *De deposito fidei*, it would therefore be proper to make at least
an allusion to the God of Christian revelation. Cardinal Ottaviani then
invited me to compose a text. This morning, Tuesday, I delivered it to
Father Tromp, the secretary. Three bishops, to whom I showed it, declared that they were very happy with it. I do not know whether it will
be considered.

The thoughtlessness of this assembly of "theologians". What occurred
on September 25 with respect to the text directed secretly against me
happened again in a similar manner with respect to Fr. Teilhard – except
that, this time, people at least knew who the person was. – On the
word of Fr. Dhanis alone, a whole paragraph was adopted condemning
an erroneous doctrine on creation, "such as it is found in some mimeographed papers". No one asked the author of the text to show these

---

expert starting with the second session. He later became secretary of the International Theological
Commission.

[2] Arthur Janssen (1886–1979), Belgian. A professor of moral theology at Louvain from 1918 to
1969. Consultor to the Preparatory Theological Commission.

[3] Louis-Bertrand Gillon, O.P. (1901–1987), French, ordained in 1931. Rector of the Angelicum
until 1961, then dean of the faculty of theology beginning in 1963. Member of the Preparatory
Theological Commission, then named an expert to the council.

[4] "Natural law".

[5] Bernard Häring, C.Ss.R. (1912–1998), German, ordained in 1939. A great moral theologian,
professor at the Alfonsianum in Rome from 1949 to 1987. Consultor to the Preparatory Theological
Commission, he was named an expert in 1962. He was very active in the drafting of *Gaudium et spes*.

[6] "On God".

papers; no one even asked him to quote one line; the text was adopted with eyes closed. Tomorrow, perhaps, on the word of fifty serious men specially chosen from the whole Church for their competence and charged with verifying everything, the council Fathers will pronounce in their turn a condemnation, this one definitive. Every member of the commission has the relator's text in front of him; several no doubt have not even read it (they did not get it in advance, and they are going so quickly ...); others have read it distractedly while listening to something else; no one would be ready to give me the trust that they all give to the relator – although he did not cite a single text and I quoted several that contradict the relator's opinion. Perhaps, too, some think (or do they know?) that the matter has already been secretly decided in advance by the Holy Office, and they are afraid to appear opposed.

According to Fr. Philippe de la Trinité, the superior general of the Carmelites[7] (who is also a consultor and who comes from time to time to the commission's meetings) has noticed the defects in method of which I am complaining; it is clear that some are fabricating arguments that resemble Mr. Prudhomme's saber,[8] in accordance with the needs of the cause.*[9]

This afternoon, Tuesday the 26th, I have time off. I accompanied Father Donatien Mollat as far as the hall of the Cancellaria where the public sessions of the Pauline Congress are being held. Today, it is Dom Christopher Butler,[10] Benedictine abbot of Downside, who is speaking. His topic: faith according to Saint Paul. A printed resume in Latin of his conference was distributed to us. It is exactly the idea of revelation and faith that Fr. Dhanis declares heterodox and that our commission is preparing to condemn. So, in Rome, within the very same walls of the

---

7 Alberto Ballestrero (1913–1998), Anastasius of the Holy Rosary in religion, O.C.D., Italian. Consultor to the Preparatory Theological Commission, member of the Doctrinal Commission on the death of J. Griffiths. Created cardinal in 1979.

8 Joseph Prudhomme is a character created by Henry Monnier in 1852, who promised to use his saber "to defend the Power ... and, if need be, to bring it down".

9 * "In fact, in the space of two days, I have heard from the same lips this observation: 'Several bishops support this opinion', once in order to conclude from this that it was indeed necessary to take this opinion of the bishops into account, a second time in order to conclude that it was indeed necessary to oppose this error since it was winning over even some bishops."

10 Dom Basil Christopher Butler, O.S.B. (1902–1986), English, convert from Anglicanism, ordained in 1933. Abbot of Downside from 1946 to 1966, president of the Congregation of English Benedictines from 1961 to 1966, auxiliary bishop of Westminster from 1966 until his death. Member of the Doctrinal Commission, elected during the second session.

Cancellaria, in the morning a doctrine is explicitly condemned with a view to the coming council, and in the afternoon this doctrine is exalted as being that of Saint Paul. And it concerns the very center of the Christian faith.

Returned to the Biblical Institute in the company of the good Father Jean Levie,[11] who attended the Pauline congress. He spoke to me about his works in preparation. He has suffered and suffers still from the touchy dictatorship of Fr. Dhanis, his former student. – Fr. Lyonnet is recovering from several days of illness; he hopes to be able to give his scheduled talk at the Pauline congress in three days. – This evening, chatted again with Fr. Donatien Mollat, a good and faithful friend. At the beginning of this month, in the west of France, he met a young Italian priest, fresh from the Lateran, who, with great assurance and energy, fulminated against me. Fr. Mollat said to me: "It rarely happens to me, but I got angry." The same young priest, who insisted on being called canon (all of them are in his southern diocese, which has a total of 16 priests), kept up the same refrain with the abbess of the Benedictine convent where they were staying. The abbess also put him in his place.

Wednesday, September 27. – This morning, sessio plenaria [plenary session]. We are studying the last two chapters of the constitution *De deposito fidei*. Chap. 8: "De peccato originali". Chap. 9: "De unitate (et) de communi origine generis humani."[1]

The preliminary draft said with insistence in regard to original sin: "vere et proprie peccatum", "homines reos tenet",[2] etc. It must have caused a great deal of difficulty to have the clarification accepted: "licet diversa ratione ac peccatum personale".[3] Still, in the margin, in this chapter, there appears a biased summary, seven lines long, without any quotation, with the note: "Teilhard de Chardin".[4]

Paragraph 48 states that Rom. 5 contains the doctrine of original sin as it had just been set forth and quotes the words: "... in quo omnes

---

[11]Jean Levie, S.J. (1885–1966), Belgian, ordained in 1917. Former editor of the *Nouvelle revue théologique* (1926–1951), he was professor of New Testament exegesis at the Jesuit theological college in Eegenhoven.

September 27

[1]"On original sin". "On the unity and the common origin of the human race".

[2]"True and authentic sin. It makes mankind guilty."

[3]"However, in a different manner from a personal sin".

[4]The *Acta et documenta concilio Vaticano II apparando* no longer make any mention of Teilhard in this chapter.

peccaverunt".[5] Some would have liked to have this whole passage deleted; others, that at least the quotation: "in quo [omnes] ..." be deleted. Others wanted to keep everything: they gave as a reason the fact that Paul's text was quoted in this sense by the councils of Carthage, Orange, and Trent.[6] Father Dhanis insisted on preserving the whole thing; we do not say, he pointed out, "Sacrosancta Synodus definit",[7] but only: " ... declarat"![8] Father Tromp, wiser, proposed to speak only "in genere"[9] of Rom. 5, without quoting the text. Fr. Dhanis retook the floor in order to oppose this removal. Father Tromp next proposed to say only: "Sacrosancta Synodus firmiter tenet ...",[10] which is supposedly less binding on the council. Fr. Dhanis still rejected this slight amendment as weakening the "declaration" too much. (What a maze of dishonest subtleties!) He was strongly supported against Tromp by Msgr. Piolanti and Fr. Ciappi, O.P.,[11] master of the Sacred Palace.[12] Thanks to those three, they were going to end up by carrying the motion. It was at that point that Fr. Tromp went back to his first proposal: only to cite Rom. 5 in general (after having proposed another solution: to follow the "in quo ..." of the Vulgate with the Greek text in parentheses). The opinion of the secretary of the commission, whom no one takes for a liberal, reassured those who were hesitant. Tromp's proposal was

---

[5] "Propterea sicut per unum hominem in hunc mundum peccatum intravit et per peccatum mors et ita in omnes homines mors pertransiit in quo omnes peccaverunt", following the text of the Vulgate. "Therefore, just as sin came into the world through one man, and death came through sin, and so death spread to all because all have sinned." [The problem linked to this passage is that the Augustinian tradition understood the *in quo* as "the sin of Adam *in whom* all have sinned". So it is thought that through the disobedience of Adam, sin affects all men, apart from the personal sins of each. However, another exegetical tradition, relying on the Greek text, judges that Adam's sin opened a breach and that the power of sin entered this world *from the fact that (eph'ô)* all have sinned. Thus it is through the personal sins of each that the power of original sin affects all men.]

[6] The Councils of Carthage (418), Orange (529), and Trent (1545–1563) used this biblical citation in order to assert that original sin was passed to all mankind through a single man.

[7] "The Very Holy Council defines" [in the sense of a dogmatic definition].

[8] "Declares".

[9] "In general".

[10] "The Very Holy Council firmly upholds".

[11] Mario Luigi Ciappi, O.P. (1909–1996), Italian, ordained in 1932. Master of the Sacred Palace from 1955, consultor to the Congregation of the Holy Office. Member of the Preparatory Theological Commission, named an expert in 1962. Created cardinal in 1977.

[12] The Sacred Palace refers to the usual residence of the pope. The Master of the Sacred Palace is an institution going back to the thirteenth century. This duty, always entrusted to Dominicans, took the name of Master of the Sacred Palace until 1968, when it became "theologian of the Pontifical House". The Master of the Sacred Palace can, in particular, be consulted in doctrinal matters.

adopted, to the despair of the Dhanis-Piolanti-Ciappi trio. Msgr. Garo-falo[13] had made, in the name of exegesis, a long, confused intervention, which was prolonged by a duel with Msgr. Piolanti. Flowing eloquence and theatrical gestures from Piolanti, whom no one could manage to silence. Many were amused by this duel. The scene truly was comical. Several were naïve enough to think that it really was a great theological battle.

Next we began the study of chapter 9. There was talk of preliminary difficulties raised by several people (Philips, Colombo, Philippe de la Trinité, etc.). It was Msgr. Philips who first laid these out with clarity and in a very peaceable manner. He wanted, on the subject of polygen-ism, to keep to what is said about that by the encyclical *Humani generis*.[14] Once again, Msgr. Piolanti stood up; he was indignant at such minimal-ism, and there was another duel. Don Colombo supported Msgr. Philips in his own way. In vain. The most moderate people who dared to speak ended up asking, as a minimal solution, that we content ourselves with repeating the text of the encyclical *H. G.*, while giving it more weight: "solemnius".[15] They were defeated. An entire special chapter against polygenism will be kept. Fr. Dhanis proved a little more moderate here: he thought that the numerous affirmations in the preceding chapter, if they were clearly emphasized, could suffice.

Something to be noted, a clever intervention by Father Ciappi.*[16] Father Congar, he said, had asked that there be a condemnation of rac-ism; but that is impossible, except in a chapter expressly condemning polygenism. That seemed to make an impression. Then once it was adopted to keep this chapter 9, since quite a few were expecting a men-tion of racism, Ciappi took the floor once again to declare: As for rac-ism, that is a question of morality; this is not the place to talk about that; besides, it goes without saying; and it will be dealt with in another schema.

---

[13] Salvatore Garofalo (1911–1998), Italian. Exegete, professor at the Lateran, then rector of the Urbanian (also called the *Propaganda fidei*). Member of the Preparatory Theological Commission, he was named an expert in 1962.

[14] The encyclical stipulates that "the faithful cannot embrace that opinion which maintains that either after Adam there existed on this earth true men who did not take their origin through natural generation from him as from the first parent of all, or that Adam represents a certain number of first parents" (no. 37).

[15] "More solemn".

[16] * In this paragraph, the name of Ciappi has been crossed out and changed to "X".

The whole margin of freedom they agree to leave is that which frames the old school disputes. We are locked into, not the liberating enclosure of the faith, but the narrow halls of the Schoolmen. We seek formulae that might be able to satisfy both Thomists and Scotists,[17] as they would have done in the 14th century.

It is the old Orders that are the largest and at the same time the most traditional. But there is not a Benedictine on our commission. (There is a Claretian!)[18]

Some lackluster interventions by Archbishop Dubois[19] of Besançon, happy to be doing theology.*[20]

On the afternoon of the 27th, saw Fr. Henri Rondet[21] at the General Curia, where the Congregation of Procurators[22] is being held. Met Archbishop Villot,[23] who had also come to Rome for a preconciliar

---

[17] Disciple of John Duns Scotus, O.F.M. (1266–1308), Scottish. Among the most influential philosophers and theologians of the Middle Ages; his thought is at the origin of a Scotist school of Scholastic philosophy.

[18] The congregation of the Claretians was founded only in 1849, and its constitutions approved by the Holy See in 1870. The Claretian in question is Narciso García Garcés (1904–1989), C.M.F., Spanish. Founder of the Spanish mariological society and editor of the journal *Ephemerides mariologicae*. Consultor to the Preparatory Theological Commission, he became the consultor to the Spanish episcopate during the council.

[19] Marcel-Marie Dubois (1896–1967), French, ordained in 1921. Archbishop of Besançon from 1954 to 1966. Member of the Preparatory Theological Commission.

[20] *Inserted here is the following passage, which is repeated nearly verbatim in the entry for September 28: "One of the texts studied on this day said something like 'Sicut semper tenuerunt Patres...'. Someone made the observation that in fact the Fathers never said that (since the theory of satisfaction presupposed by the text came after their time). So without any further examination, the mention of the Fathers was thus deleted, and Father Ciappi agreed to the deletion: he did not intend to oppose historical criticism or sound exegesis. But, since the Fathers and Scripture scarcely come into our schemas except 'ad illustrationem', when it becomes all too clear that the illustration is not 'ad rem', there is nothing to do but delete it. We have previously seen similar examples."

[21] Henri Rondet, S.J. (1898–1979), French, ordained in 1928. Professor of theology at the scholasticate at Fourvière, he was dismissed from teaching from 1951 to 1960, when he became professor of patrology at Fourvière. Theologian of the bishops of Chad at Vatican II.

[22] Convoked by the Jesuit superior general, it assembles the procurators elected by the provincial congregations. This Congregation of Procurators decides on the advisability of a meeting of a general congregation and examines, in general, the affairs of the Society.

[23] Jean Villot (1905–1979), French, ordained in 1930. Coadjutor of the archbishop of Lyon in 1959, then archbishop of Lyon in 1965, he was created cardinal in 1965. He was one of the undersecretaries of the council during its first three sessions. Prefect of the Congregation for the Clergy in 1967, he became secretary of state under Paul VI in 1969. Consultor to the Preparatory Commission for Bishops. See A. Wenger, *Le Cardinal Jean Villot (1905–1979), secrétaire d'État de trois papes* (Paris: Desclée De Brouwer, 1989).

commission. At the Biblical Congress, talks by Dr. Schlier,[24] then by Father Benoit, O.P.,[25] with Cardinal Bea presiding, to whom I said hello at the end. Returned to the Gregorian at night with Father Donatien Mollat (lights of the Capitol).

At the Gregorian, one Father told me jokingly: "Before the congregation of the procurators, people everywhere were saying: Father General is very well, the Assistant [of the Father General] of Italy has made a very good recovery, etc. As soon as the procurators leave again, people everywhere will be saying: poor Father General is very tired; the Assistant of Italy is obviously sick, etc."

September 28. – In this morning's session, we dealt primarily with the question of children who die without baptism. Fr. Xiberta[1] (a discalced Carmelite, an intelligent scholastic), Don Colombo, Fr. Häring, Msgr. Schmaus, Fr. Salaverri made various remarks in the interest of prudence and moderation. Father Dhanis opposed them. He conceded that Schmaus and Häring were "theologi majores"; he treated the others (without giving names) as "theologi minores".[2] Several, as always, have a tendency to think that the role of a council is to make doctrine more "specific", that is to say, in practical terms, to make it narrower, to conceptualize it to an extreme degree, on precisely those points where many put forward new difficulties. This is what they call timely clarifications and condemnations, so as to respond to the errors of our time.

Seven out of nine bishops were against the proposed text on children who die without baptism. Finally, the text was sent back to the subcommission for study.

Cardinal Ottaviani gave the following argument in substance: We have to affirm the principle; otherwise, in practice, the consequences will be dangerous; and, then, "omnia relinquere ad misericordiam Dei".[3] Then Don Colombo intervened to say, in substance: Good, but

---

[24] Heinrich Schlier (1900–1978), German. Protestant who converted to Catholicism, professor of theology.

[25] Pierre Benoit, O.P. (1906–1987), French, ordained in 1930. Member of the Biblical Institute of Jerusalem from 1933, he directed it from 1964 to 1972. Expert starting from the third session.

September 28

[1] Bartolomé Xiberta, O.C.D. (1897–1967), Spanish, ordained in 1919. A theologian, he was a consultor to the Preparatory Theological Commission. Expert at the council.

[2] "Major theologians. Minor theologians".

[3] "To abandon all things to the mercy of God".

I ask that this last point, this recourse to the divine mercy, also figure in our text.

Concerning the Satisfaction made by Christ, the text had something like: "Sicut semper tenuerunt Patres ..."[4] Someone (Salaverri?) then made the remark that the theory of satisfaction[5] came later, after the Fathers. Solution: this mention of the Fathers was deleted. Fr. Ciappi agreed. He is not opposed to historical criticism or to sound exegesis, either; the Fathers and Scripture only come into the texts "ad illustrationem";[6] when it is all too evident that the illustration is not *ad rem*, it can be sacrificed. But the *res* remains unchanged.

Another remark on method, concerning chapter 11, no. 54. They wanted to insert biblical images from the prophets in a dogmatic text that has a logical and rational style, as if these were revealed concepts. Where might you not end up that way!

Fr. Congar showed me a remark that he has written so as to warn the commission against the risk of a new Galileo Affair in connection with polygenism. He still does not know whether he will pass it on to the commission.

One consultor said to me: "It is obvious that Fr. Dh.[7] is Cardinal Ottaviani's right-hand man."

On the morning of September 28, I renewed the request I made to Fr. Dhanis on the morning of the 26th. Would he agree to speak with me about the text written by him for the commission and about the authors that this text intends to condemn? He refused to answer me. I then asked him if he realized that such an attitude toward me was arrogant. Just at that moment, Father Tromp arrived; he rushed over to him and told him: "I was insulted by Fr. de L.!" Fr. Tromp was dumbfounded; a good man, he said to us something like: "You both seem to me to be very agitated; but after all, you are brothers in Christ." In response to this, I said: "Exactly, Father, I was proposing to Fr. Dhanis that we have a fraternal conversation, but from the time I arrived here, he has been evading me. Can a consultor of the Theological Commission not converse with a member of the same commission in order to inform

---

[4] "As the Fathers have always taught".

[5] This refers to the superabundant compensation for all the sins of the human race, made to God through the sacrifice of Christ on the Cross and achieving the reconciliation of men with God.

[6] "As an illustration".

[7] Édouard Dhanis.

himself about the text that member has written? This should be all the easier since we are brothers and are now living in the same house." – "But of course", Father Tromp replied. And he had to get into his car, which was waiting for him. I only had time to say to him: "I will tell you briefly what it is about; I have not done so until now because these past days you have been too busy." – So in light of this changed situation, I wrote a letter to Fr. Tromp in the afternoon, which, under secrecy, I had Fr. Donatien Mollat look over. And in the evening, at dinnertime, I put it into Fr. Tromp's box. This was my only recourse – since I cannot explain the situation to anyone outside, bound as I am by the secrecy of the commission.

Yes or no, am I a man whose doctrine is seriously in error, worthy of being condemned, on several grounds, by an ecumenical council? If yes, I ask to be excluded from the Theological Commission preparing this council; I will hand in my resignation to the Holy Father. Otherwise, I ask at least that a frank explanation put an end to these accusations or that our superiors judge between my accuser and me. (But I know very well I will not get that.)*[8]

---

[8] *There is inserted at this point a handwritten letter from Father de Lubac to Father Tromp, dated September 28, 1961: "Here is the word of explanation that I owe you. I had wished to obtain from Fr. Dhanis some clarifications on several paragraphs of the *Constitutio de deposito fidei* of which he is the author; in particular, on chapter IV, par. 22: *Recens relativismi forma*. My intention was not to raise any sort of objection against the doctrine laid out there; and that is why I have not intervened publicly. But as it says there: "Periculose a vero discedunt qui sentiunt, etc.", I wanted to know who the authors so designated are. Although I have asked several times since my arrival in Rome, Father Dhanis has categorically refused to answer me; when I asked him why, he merely said: "I have my reasons." However, I need to know what this is about. For several other texts, of various types, written over the course of these last ten years (in the Society) insistently attribute to me the error pointed out in this paragraph 22; so that it is difficult for me to be uncertain about the identity of their author. The refusal to respond that I have encountered can only confirm my fears. Since I have not been able to obtain anything from Fr. Dhanis, I must address myself, through you as intermediary, to the Theological Commission, in order to ask: Does the Commission intend to denounce, by this text, an error that is supposed to be mine or at least to include me, in one way or another, in the group of those who "periculose a vero discedunt"? If the answer is no, I will take note of the fact. If it were to be yes, I should submit to the Holy Father my resignation as a consultor: for it would not be appropriate to have even a minimal part in the doctrinal preparation for an ecumenical council entrusted to someone whom this council would be called on to condemn. I dare to ask humbly for an unequivocal response; and, in the case of the second hypothesis, I beg that someone kindly indicate to me what has made it possible to attribute such an error to me. I am not aware of ever having written anything, even long ago, that resembles it or of ever having said or thought any such thing. I ask you, my Reverend Father, to be kind enough to inform those to whom you might wish to speak about this matter of the motives behind the step I have taken, as I have set them forth in this letter. I am, my Reverend Father, in union with your Holy Sacrifices, R^{ae} Vestrae infimus in Christo servus."

At the Gregorian, I recopied the two *Vota* written by Fr. Dhanis, prefect of studies, for the preconciliar Theological Commission. These are *Vota* nos. 3 and 4: "De declaranda indole revelationis" and "De immutabilitate veritatis et progressu dogmatico".[9] These wishes were printed along with others as being those of the Gregorian University; in reality, all the competent professors disapproved of their content and complained to the rector; but it was too late, and no one dared to press the issue.

Once more, I recognize there the methods that have been customary for the past twelve years. These two *vota* were aimed directly against Fr. Lebreton,[10] Fr. de Grandmaison,[11] and myself; of course, they have totally distorted our thought; they reproduce exactly the censures written by Fr. Dhanis against my study on Fr. Lebreton[12] (which had been approved by the latter, as also, later, by my censors in France). They contain the sort of formulae to which I am accustomed and by means of which everything can be made blameworthy: "Hoc votum proponitur quia sententiae similes illis quae in eo reprobantur, hodie ... intraverunt in theologiam quorumdam catholicorum ..."; "Relativismi semina continent"; "Non desunt theologi qui negent aut propensos se praebeant ad negandum quaedam, quae in prima parte voti exponuntur ..."[13] These are models of their kind. The scrupulous conscience of their author seems to find reassurance by expressing itself in hints.

September 29, 1961. – We are examining the plan of the constitution *De Ecclesia.* Msgr. Fenton has a simple theology: Ecclesia catholica =

---

[9] "On the specification of the nature of Revelation". "On the immutability of truth and dogmatic progress".

[10] Jules Lebreton, S.J. (1873–1956), French, ordained in 1903. Professor of theology at the Institut catholique of Paris beginning in 1905, he inaugurated there the chair of "Christian origins". He edited the journal *Recherches de science religieuse* from 1927 to 1945, with the intention of showing that it was possible to be both orthodox and exactingly critical.

[11] Léonce de Grandmaison, S.J. (1868–1927), French, ordained in 1898. A professor of theology, he became editor of *Études*, from 1908 to 1919, and founded, in 1910, *Recherches de science religieuse*, which he edited until his death.

[12] He is referring to a study entitled "La Doctrine du Père Lebreton sur la Révélation et le dogme d'après ses écrits antimodernistes", written in 1951, approved by the Jesuit censor for the province, but rejected by the Jesuit censor in Rome, who thought that the doctrine of the article was false and modernist. The article appeared in *Théologie dans l'histoire* (Paris: Desclée De Brouwer, 1990).

[13] "This proposition was formulated because opinions similar to those that are condemned in it have today penetrated the theology of certain Catholics." "They contain the seeds of relativism." "There is no lack of theologians who deny or show themselves inclined to deny certain of the doctrines that are set forth in the first part of the proposition."

Corpus mysticum = Regnum Dei.[1] A perfect identity. All of which is applied directly to the Church militant. In his intransigence, Fenton went so far as to accuse Father Tromp of being opposed to Pius XII's encyclical *Mystici Corporis*;[2] – that made everyone laugh, for it is well known that that encyclical is Tromp's favorite. – The Mystical Body is so strongly identified with the Roman hierarchical Church that it no longer has anything to do with the interior order of grace and the theological virtues; "The Holy Spirit can give all that outside of the Mystical Body" (sic) – Outside of the Catholic faith, professed by submission to the Roman magisterium, there cannot be, said Fenton again, any real faith, but only *fides falsa*.[3]

Msgr. Piolanti also intervened often, in an integrist, wholly extrinsicist direction.[4] Signs of energetic approval from Fr. Dhanis. There was some wavering in the commission.

The theologians who impose their views in our work, who put their mark on the texts, who are supported by the president, who allow others the right to only a few timid corrections of detail, have no method in the conduct of their thinking. They have not received a true intellectual formation.

One could say, from a certain point of view, that there are two kinds of theologians; some say: let us reread Scripture, Saint Paul, etc.; let us examine tradition; let us listen to the great classical theologians; let us not forget to pay attention to the Greeks; let us not neglect history; let us situate ourselves in this vast context and understand the ecclesiastical texts according to it; let us not fail, either, to inform ourselves about the problems, needs, and difficulties of today, etc. – The others say: let us reread all the ecclesiastical texts of these last hundred years, encyclicals, letters, occasional speeches, decisions made against something or other,

---

September 29

[1] "Catholic Church = Mystical Body = Kingdom of God".

[2] Encyclical of Pius XII, "On the Mystical Body of Jesus Christ and on Our Union in It with Christ", dated June 29, 1943.

[3] "A false faith".

[4] A way of considering things as exterior to each other, without seeing their inherent connections: reciprocal causalities, affinities, relations of all orders. Thus, the extrinsicist conception of dogma thinks of it as a thing in itself, independent of history, and imposed from outside on the believer, without his interior participation. The term is used by Blondel to criticize the integrist positions just after the condemnation of modernism. See *Une Alliance contre nature, catholicisme et intégrisme: La Semaine sociale de Bordeaux* (1910; Brussels: Lessius, 2000).

monita[5] of the Holy Office, etc.; from all that, without either dropping any of it or correcting the least word, let us make a mosaic, let us push the thought a little farther, let us give to each assertion a stronger value; above all, let us not look at anything outside; let us not lose ourselves in the new research on Scripture or tradition or a fortiori on any recent ideas, which might make us relativize our absolute. – Only the theologian of the second type is considered to be "sure" in a certain milieu.

"Hoc non fundatur in documentis":[6] I have heard that more than once. The conclusion to be drawn from it: it is not a sure doctrine; it is a doctrine that it is advisable to dismiss, even if it has the support of Scripture and tradition. Only the ecclesiastical documents count, especially the most recent ones. The least words of these documents are received as absolute. In response to any objection against any particular idea or formula or one-sided phrase: "Ipsa verba desumpta sunt ex documentis; sunt in talibus litteris encyclicis; in tali oratione pontificali."[7] So no one can do anything any longer but submit.

There is in this a very excessive positivism of method and fundamentalism of spirit – which could provoke as a reaction, among some, a contempt for all writing of the magisterium.

This morning, the 29th, Father Tromp, a little embarrassed, avoided greeting me. He must be thinking over his response to yesterday's letter from me.

In the afternoon, I paid a visit to his Excellency Bishop Franić,[8] a Croatian bishop (episcopus Spalatensis). He was the only one who made a proposal that caught my attention. On chapter 4 of the constitution De deposito fidei, he said: "Humiliter propono, ut hoc caput omittatur ..."[9] "In fact, the errors that it pursues are unknown." That encouraged me to go and see him. He is living at the Saint Jerome College for the Croats. I explained to him who is the target in this enigmatic text; I showed him the texts that prove it, among others the two vota "sic dicta" of the

---

[5] A monitum is a warning, unaccompanied by sanctions.

[6] "This is not based on the [ecclesiastical] documents."

[7] "These expressions are taken from the ecclesiastical documents; they figure in some particular encyclical letter or other, in some pontifical discourse or other."

[8] Frane Franić (1912–2007), Yugoslav, ordained in 1936. Bishop, then archbishop of Split from 1960 to 1988. He was a member of the Preparatory Theological Commission and a member of the Doctrinal Commission.

[9] "I humbly propose that this chapter be omitted." [It was in this chapter that Father de Lubac thought he was anonymously targeted.]

Gregorian, as well as my letter to Father Tromp.*[10] Then we spoke about Yugoslavia, the persecutions it has undergone, etc. An educated man, good, of a very conservative tendency in religious matters, open to social problems.

At 6 P.M., at the Palace of the Chancellery, a lecture by Fr. Stanislas Lyonnet: Justification and salvation according to Saint Paul. Clear, well-organized, animated; topical quotes from Luther and from St. Thomas. A fundamental question for the dialogue with the Protestants. Some surprising passages: "... this famous *sola fide*,[11] which Luther has been so criticized for having invented, is there in black and white in Saint Thomas", etc.*[12]

September 30, 1961. – This morning, left for the chancellery in a car driven by Fr. Michel Leclercq, O.M.I. I was with Fr. Tromp, who had offered me a ride. He spoke to me about my letter and told me he would respond in writing if I wished; I told him that, yes, I would be more reassured that way. Then he added insistently that I must know also that I could be mistaken. With that, I understood that he had found the way to write a skillful letter to me. He said to me again: "Even Saint Thomas was quite mistaken." I said to him: "The writer knows very well that he was targeting me in this text." To which he responded: "But no, no one has spoken about you", which does not mean anything. – "You can be sure", I told him, "that I will not exploit your letter. I am not the sort of man to cause trouble; but I had need of some assurance, I felt obliged to ask for it. I wrote to you, you personally, in French – in spite of your crushing work load these past few days, in order to allow you to judge what ought to be done and not to exaggerate this affair." He said to me again, "But it was not Fr. Dhanis who wrote the constitution." Still another effugium.[1] I answered, "No, of course not, not the whole constitution; but this chapter was written by him and him alone, personally." We arrived at our destination.

Discussion, in the session, over the expression "vicarii Christi",[2] which could be applied to the pope and the bishops; it was rejected; Fr.

---

[10] * "The good bishop could not believe it."

[11] "By faith alone".

[12] * "The refutation of the Lutheran interpretation, by the way, is clear and firm."

September 30

[1] Latin for "evasion". – TRANS.

[2] "Vicars of Christ".

Tromp cleverly proposed: "vicarii Domini nostri";[3] everyone smiled. Cardinal Ottaviani granted a full hearing to the words of Msgr. Piolanti, who intervened volubly, carelessly.

In accordance with the wish of some, I had proposed a text to conclude the chapter *De Deo*, in order that at least a little might be said about the God of revelation. I was given a small semblance of satisfaction. (I was not admitted to the subcommission that dealt with it.) The entire aim of Christian revelation is indicated by these words, which punctuate the chapter: "ut Deo ... credant eique serviant".[4] This amounts to diminishing Christian truth once again.

At the end of the session, Cardinal Ottaviani said to us: "Before going our separate ways, let us say a prayer together for the Holy Father." And he started: "Oremus pro Pontifice nostro Pio",[5] – which made everyone laugh. A good sport, he laughed as well.

At 1 P.M., I was at Saint Jerome abbey, to which I was invited for the feast of its patron saint. The abbot, Dom Pierre Salmon, introduced me to a cardinal (I did not catch his name) who, on learning that I came from Fourvière, said to me "Ah! you are from the great school of Fourvière!"

That afternoon, I got the letter that Fr. Tromp had promised me. I will declare myself satisfied. In fact, I can only be grateful to Fr. Tromp. His letter is nonetheless too clever; it could have two meanings.*[6] –

---

[3] "Vicars of our Lord". [It is a matter, no doubt, of avoiding attributing to the bishops the same terminology that is applied to the pope, traditionally called *vicarius Christi*.]

[4] "In order that they might believe in God and serve him".

[5] "Let us pray for our Pope Pius."

[6]* "Or none at all. Here is the letter and my response: Father Tromp's letter: Sept. 30, 1961. 'Ad epistolam tuam respondere mihi liceat in redactione § 22 cap. IV *De Deposito pure custodiendo*, sicut etiam in discussionibus, hac de paragrapho habitis, neminen cogitasse de te vel de uno alterove modo subintellexisse inter eos qui "periculose a vero discedunt". Memineris quoque virum eximium in theologicis errare posse, quin desinat esse magnus theologus et, quod plus est: bonus christianus. Commendo me ...' [Permit me to say in response to your letter that in the drafting of § 22 of chapter IV of *De Deposito pure custodiendo*, as in the discussions that were held on this paragraph, no one thought that you were, in any way, implied to be among those who "depart dangerously from the truth". Remember also that eminent theologians can err, a fact that does not hinder them from being great theologians and, what is more, good Christians. I recommend you ...] My response to Fr. Tromp: 'October 1, 1961. Reverend Father, Pax Christi! I thank you for your letter, which fully reassures me regarding the sentiments of the Commission (although I cannot have any doubt about the author of the paragraph in question). You of course understand that if I addressed myself directly to you, it was done, not to exaggerate this incident, but to avoid complaining openly about a brother (although this brother's conduct toward me was disgraceful). Yes, I know that I am subject to error, like everyone else, and I gladly accept being corrected. The one who has accused his brother is no less subject to it; he should at least have accused me frankly and provided evidence of

That afternoon, at the Gregorian; Fr. Jean Villain,[7] in Rome for the Congregation of Procurators, reported to me that the order to submit Fr. Bouillard's[8] work to Roman censure has been lifted. – Deo gratias! – At St. Jerome, I had chatted with Dom Hesbert.[9] just passing through, and Dom Lemarié,[10] from the Abbaye de la Source[11] (Chromatius of Aquileia), as well as with a young Benedictine who is preparing a thesis on Bruno de Segni.[12] I was at table with Msgr. Pellegrino,[13] professor of ancient Christian literature at Turin.

October 1, 1961. – Greeted Fr. Rector of the Gregorian; I made allusion to the two "vota" said to be from the Gregorian. – At dinner, the young professor of ecclesiastical history at Chieri (Turin) spoke to me about the thesis he is completing here on Lorenzo Valla;[1] Valla's thought, he told me, is Christian, even in its morality; it is very little known. He spoke to me also about Fr. Perego.

In the afternoon of this Sunday, a visit from Fr. Philippe de la Trinité. He spoke to me about the Theological Commission, in which he

---

his accusations, not libels. But I do not wish to trouble Your Reverence further with this matter. I remain grateful to you for the good, straightforward terms you have used toward me. R^{ae} V^{ae} servus et frater in Christo.' "

[7] Jean Villain, S.J. (1892–1982), French, ordained in 1925. He notably exercised his apostolate in the social domain, participating actively in Action populaire from 1930 to 1952 and directing it starting in 1946. In 1952, he became editor of the journal *Études*, following Father d'Ouince, until 1956. He was an adviser on social matters whose opinion was highly valued by the episcopate.

[8] Henri Bouillard, S.J. (1908–1981), French, ordained in 1936. While studying theology at Fourvière, he met H. de Lubac; this was the beginning of a long and deep friendship. He taught theology at Fourvière from 1941 to 1950, on which date he was dismissed like H. de Lubac. Also like the latter, Father Bouillard was subjected to the double censorship of his Province and of the Jesuit General Curia in Rome. From 1965 on, he was professor of theology and philosophy of religion at the Institut catholique of Paris. Father Bouillard did a great deal of work in the field of rapprochement between Catholics and Protestants.

[9] René-Jean Hesbert, O.S.B. (1899–1983), French. A monk of Solesmes, he was ordained in 1929. In 1948 he joined Saint Wandrille Abbey while remaining a monk of Solesmes. His numerous works have as their objective, among other things, the rediscovery of an authentic interpretation of Gregorian chant.

[10] Joseph Lemarié, O.S.B., born in 1917. He published the *Sermons* of Chromatius of Aquileia (335–408), Bishop of Aquileia, in the Sources chrétiennes series in 1969 and 1971.

[11] A Benedictine abbey in Paris, also known as Sainte-Marie de Paris. – TRANS.

[12] Réginald Grégoire.

[13] Michele Pellegrino (1903–1986), Italian, ordained in 1925. Professor at the University of Turin from 1943 to 1965. Archbishop of Turin in 1965, he was created cardinal in 1967. A specialist in the Fathers of the Church and in particular Saint Augustine.

October 1

[1] Lorenzo Valla (1407–1457), Italian humanist and philosopher. Among other things, he praised epicurean pleasure, opposed the dialectic of Scholasticism, and protested against the Church's interference in the affairs of the world.

has noticed certain one-sided tendencies; he intends to write a series of observations on this subject.

At 6 p.m., at the Collegio Bellarmino, I went to see Fr. René Arnou. He was very welcoming and seemed very interested in the news that I gave him. However, I spoke to him only about extraconciliar matters, so as not to break the oath of secrecy regarding the commission's work. I recounted to him the accusations brought against me in the "Vota" supposedly of the Gregorian; he asked me spontaneously: "Have you spoken about all this with Father Tromp?" Then I had to answer him: "I was only telling you what I know independently of the commission; but yes, in fact, I was obliged speak to Fr. Tromp." Fr. Arnou understood that it was a serious matter. Next, we spoke about Fr. Teilhard. He told me that he had lent copies of my lecture on Teilhard to several people, in particular to a Vatican prelate, who was delighted with it, etc. – The affairs of a theological order, he told me, never reach him; he is kept out of the loop. Just as well, I said to him, I did not come to ask you anything. But I was anxious that you know certain things before the council takes place.

Return to Lyon. – Saw the provincial[2] in Lyon on October 4. That same day, at the Faculty of Theology, we elected a new dean, Mr. Maurice Jourjon.[3]

On the 5th, I submitted to the Fr. Socius[4] the manuscript of my "Teilhard".[5]

> ... nihil loquamur subdolum
> Volvamus obscurum nihil.[6]
> (Feria 5a, hymn from Lauds)

---

[2] Blaise Arminjon, S.J. (1917–1998), French, ordained in 1947. Provincial of the Province of Lyon until 1964.

[3] Maurice Jourjon, born in 1919, French. Dean of the theology faculty of the Catholic Faculties of Lyon. An expert in patristics.

[4] The socius is a collaborator of the provincial or the superior general. In this case, it is Robert Isaac.

[5] H. de Lubac had been trying since 1960 to publish a study on the religious thought of his fellow Jesuit Teilhard. In the spring of 1961, he received the support of his provincial, Father Arminjon. In September 1961, the two provincial censors approved it. There remained the Roman censor. The book was published in March 1962 by the publishing house Aubier, *La Pensée religieuse du père Teilhard de Chardin*; trans. René Hague as *The Religion of Father Teilhard de Chardin* (New York: Desclée, 1967).

[6] "Let not our speech be sly / Nor our intention be to obscure."

1962

March 1962: Rome, the last plenary session of the Theological Commission

Friday, March 2, 1962. – Lyon-Turin. Having arrived in Turin early in the afternoon, I went to the Jesuit residence, on via Barbaroux. The Fr. Superior[1] told me about a meeting scheduled for 2:30 P.M. It was Francesco Coppellotti,[2] a student in philosophy, who had organized this meeting with his classmates. They questioned me about all sorts of things: what is theology; how are revealed subjects and human knowledge, historical realities, distinguished; to what extent does the Church need to concern herself with the latter, etc., etc. One student protested fiercely against the "social encyclicals", which, he said, canonized a capitalist, essentially historical, and transitory order, in which man is exploited. (Br. C. explained to me later that this student also works as a laborer to support his family and that he has been influenced by Simone Weil).[3] There was also present one of Msgr. Pellegrino's teaching assistants from the Faculty of Letters; he spoke very pertinently about the Fathers of the Church. These young people have read a lot of French books, especially from our "Théologie" series;[4] they have already read *Le Mystère du temps*, a very recent work by Mr. Mouroux.[5] A young priest from our college, who is chaplain to the students, joined them. – Upon going out, one of them saw, in the vestibule, some posters inviting people to a Lenten lecture, the next Sunday, in the residence church, by a priest from here: "The Opening to the Left";[6] they showed them to me with

---

March 2

[1] Aldo Piloni, S.J. (1909–1989), Italian.

[2] Francesco Coppellotti, born in 1940, Italian, philosophy student.

[3] Simone Weil (1909–1943), French. Graduating in philosophy in 1931, she ceased teaching in 1934 and became a factory worker. She also had mystical experiences consisting of a purification of the soul. She died a refugee in London in 1943.

[4] This refers to the series sponsored by the Jesuit Faculty of Theology at Lyon-Fourvière.

[5] Jean Mouroux (1901–1973), French, ordained in 1926. Theologian, professor of theology at the major seminary of Dijon, he is the author of *Le Mystère du temps, approche théologique* (Paris: Aubier, 1962). He was named as an expert to the council by Paul VI, but he only went to Rome for a few days during the last session, because of his frail health.

[6] The opening to the left designates the politics of rapprochement practised by the Italian Christian Democracy party, around Fanfani and Aldo Moro, and the Italian Socialist Party of Pietro

99

indignation: "Look, this is what the Church concerns herself with! and in a pulpit, at church! and for a Lenten sermon!"

Toward evening, I took a walk with a teaching assistant in philosophy and a student of political economy, who spoke to me about Origen and spiritual exegesis.[7] I went to greet Francesco Coppellotti's mother on the Corso Vittorio Emanuelle: an excellent woman, without any scientific education, but astute, very Christian; she is worried about the health and the faith of her son, who gets into an intellectual fever. Francesco drove me back to the residence.

I was not able to see Msgr. Pellegrino, who had just left for Rome.

Saturday, March 3. – At 8 A.M., I departed for Rome. Greeted in passing the names henceforth inseparable from the name of Nietzsche: Genoa, Rapallo, Santa Margarita, Portofino. – Arrived in Rome late in the afternoon and went to the Biblical Institute; a very cordial reception from Frs. Stanislas Lyonnet and Édouard des Places as well as from the rector, Fr. Vogt, and some others. Fr. Vogt fears that the offensive against the Biblical Institute, momentarily lulled to sleep, might reawaken. He has been waiting a long time for an interview on this subject with Father General: he has great hope.

Sunday, March 4, 1962. – This morning, saw Fr. Donatien Mollat at the Gregorian, who is in the process of correcting several hundred essays. Also saw Fr. Juan Alfaro, professor of dogma; he confided to me that Father Arnou has given him the job of revising my "Teilhard", and he was delighted to learn that the work is being printed; I showed him the plans for the cover, which I found here with the proofs upon my arrival. Fr. Henri Vignon brought me up to date on the latest gossip; from what I was able to verify, he seems to me to be rather well-informed. With regard to the famous "opening to the left", when the pope decided to allow Italian Catholics their liberty, Cardinal Ottaviani was supposed to

---

Nenni. This resulted in a center-left government in 1962, with the "favorable abstention" of the PSI [the Socialists], which entered the cabinet formed by Aldo Moro in December 1963.

[7]Spiritual exegesis, believing that Scripture does not only have a literal sense, looks for another meaning, also willed by God, really existing in the text, even if the human author was not aware of it. H. de Lubac, who wanted to give a new vigor to an ancient form of exegesis that particularly honored the spiritual sense, was the author of *Exégèse médiévale: Les Quatre Sens de l'Écriture*, 4 vols. (Paris: Aubier-Montaigne, 1959–1964); the first three vols. have been trans. as *Medieval Exegesis: The Four Senses of Scripture*, Ressourcement (Grand Rapids, Mich.: Eerdmans; Edinburgh: T. & T. Clark, 1998–2009).

have requested an audience; the pope apparently refused, saying to his secretary: "I am too upset, I do not know what I would say to him, it would be better that I not see him right now." Ottaviani would thus seem to be less powerful. The deaths of Cardinal Tardini and of Cardinal Canali have dealt a harsh blow to the famous "Pentagone".[1] They say that Archbishop Parente himself has become more moderate.

Fr. Vignon spoke to me further about a young Italian priest, Father Charles Boyer's secretary for his journal *Unitas*, who knows Archbishop Parente well; regarding the theological discussions that contrasted Parente with Fr. P. Galtier[2] (Christology) and with Frs. de Broglie[3] and Vignon (faith), the opinion of this priest can be summed up thus: "These priests are doing serious work; – not the other one." There is perhaps here in the account of Fr. Vignon a certain Gregoriano-hagiographic bias.

Finally, he spoke to me at length about the rumors circulating about the preconciliar Central Commission. Cardinal Ottaviani and Fr. Tromp are said to have endured some harsh attacks there. Fr. Tromp is supposed to have cried out one day, on returning to the Gregorian: "It is hopeless! There is nothing left to do but pray to the Holy Spirit." The plans of the Theological Commission seemed to be in peril. But after a little while, Tromp seems serene again. In fact, Ottaviani has supposedly been allowed personally, together with some members of the commission, to revise the criticized texts; these texts would then be submitted to a commission of five cardinals named by the pope. It appears that these 5 cardinals, who are hardly theologians (among them, Micara,[4] known to be useless), will prove to be very accommodating.

March 4

[1] The Pentagone refers to a small group of cardinals, very influential under Pius XII, very conservative on the doctrinal plane and supporters of a preferential alliance with the United States against communism, which explains the name. Cardinals Pizzardo, Canali, Micara, and Ottaviani, among others, belonged to this group. Tardini, though close to these men, was not formally a member. A book that appeared at the time, C. Falconi, *It Pentagono vaticano* (Bari, 1958), had been devoted to it.

[2] Paul Galtier, S.J. (1872–1961), French, ordained in 1904. Professor of theology at the Gregorian beginning in 1938. His disagreement with Archbishop Parente was over the human consciousness of Christ.

[3] Guy de Broglie, S.J. (1889–1983), French, ordained in 1918. He taught fundamental theology at the Institut catholique of Paris from 1923 to 1960 and at the Gregorian from 1947 to 1965. His theology is a form of Thomism rethought in the spirit of Pierre Rousselot.

[4] Clemente Micara (1879–1965), Italian, ordained in 1902. He carried on an important diplomatic career up until the Second World War and was created cardinal in 1946. He became vicar general of the pope for the diocese of Rome beginning in 1951.

At noon, at the Biblical Institute, a conversation with a group of American biennists. In the afternoon, at Monte Verde, at the residence of Fr. L. de Peretti, superior general of the Canons Regular of the Immac. Conception (Dom Gréa). He is of the opinion that "the opening to the left", which seems to some prelates to introduce communism, only allows the implementation of some reforms that have already taken place in almost every country: France, England, the Federal Republic of Germany, etc. In Rome, the plans for the nationalization (or municipalization) of water distribution (currently divided up for the city among 5 private companies) has caused several to raise an uproar; the real reason is said to be because the Vatican is the principal shareholder in 3 of these companies. – On the other hand, Fr. de Peretti is troubled by the present attitude of the French clergy, by their frequent lack of education, in the humanities as well as in theology, by a certain anti-intellectualism that is activist and pretentious, and above all by the disfavor attached to the spiritual life.

Monday, March 5, 1962. – At 9:30 A.M., opening of the plenary session in the great hall of the Vatican on the fourth floor of the courtyard of Saint Damasus. Cardinal Ottaviani was presiding, assisted by Fr. Sébastien Tromp, secretary. Most of the members and consultors were there. The hall for the Central Commission has been renovated since last year; which means that the consultors of the Theological Commission, placed along the walls, are better seated and have a table, like the members, on which to put their papers.

We started by examining the schema of the constitution *De Matre Dei et Matre hominum*.[1] This was at first a simple chapter of the schema *De Ecclesia*. But Fr. Balić, O.F.M., the relator, had composed it in such a way that the chapter plan had become an entire mariological treatise. This was pointed out to him. He therefore managed to have it made into a separate schema, detached from *De Ecclesia*. – I note in passing a reflection made by Fr. Tromp: " . . . Si diceretur: ut docet sacra Scriptura, videretur commissio theologica laborare aliquo complexu inferioritatis erga Protestantes."[2]

March 5

[1] "On the Mother of God and the Mother of Mankind".

[2] "If one were to say: as Scripture teaches, the Theological Commission would give the impression of suffering from some sort of inferiority complex with regard to Protestants."

Father Salaverri, Spanish (Comillas) proposed that one sentence of the schema be deleted, a sentence that was followed by : cf. Gal. 4:4. "Hoc enim neque eruitur ex Gal. 4:4, nec doctrinae Pauli congruere videtur."[3] – The result: the reference to Gal. 4:4 is deleted, and the sentence is retained intact. There is discussion on the formula: "Maria in Christo mediatrix".

We continued with this in the afternoon, then passed on to the chapter of *De Ecclesia*: "De relationibus inter Ecclesiam et Statum necnon de tolerantia religiosa".[4] The relator was Fr. R. Gagnebet, O.P. (Angelicum and the Holy Office). Regarding the "officia religiosa Status" and more precisely its "officium suscipiendi revelationem christianam",[5] Fr. Dhanis intervened. A debate began between him and Fr. Gagnebet. With the approval of Msgr. Philips and Fr. Tromp, Gagnebet, quoting in particular Taparelli d'Azeglio,[6] held that the State cannot officially profess Christian worship unless it represents the moral unanimity of the citizens ("cives fere omnes").[7] To the contrary, Fr. Dhanis, supported by Cardinal Ottaviani and Msgr. Piolanti, thought that the State did not need this near-unanimous consent; it should only need to have the majority; even then, there was here no question of principle, for governments can make use of their authority without consulting those who have elected them. Fr. Dhanis returned to the attack several times; Cardinal Ottaviani continued to support him against the objections of the other party, saying: "Concilium non debet praebere ansam laicistis."[8]

The discussion soon got moving again in regard to the second part of the chapter, concerning the application of the principles "in civitate catholica".[9] The chapter included the statement: "Integre haec doctrina (de officiis Status erga revelationem et Ecclesiam) applicari non potest nisi in civitate in qua cives fere omnes ... fidem catholicam profitentur."[10]

---

[3] "In fact, that cannot be deduced from Gal. 4:4 and does not seem to agree with Paul's doctrine."

[4] "On the relations between the Church and the State and on religious tolerance".

[5] "Religious duties of the State". "The duty to accept the Christian revelation".

[6] Luigi Taparelli d'Azeglio, S.J. (1793–1862), Italian, Thomist Neoscholastic philosopher and theologian. He was one of the principal theoreticians of Catholic international law, and his influence was considerable under the pontificates of Pius IX, Leo XIII, and beyond.

[7] "Almost all the citizens".

[8] "The council must not give an opening to the secularists."

[9] "In the Catholic State".

[10] "This doctrine (on the duties of the State with regard to revelation and the Church) can only be carried out in full in a State in which almost all the citizens ... profess the Catholic faith."

Fr. Dhanis protested : "Haec verba debent tolli, secundum doctrinam catholicam. Haec sunt falsa."[11]

The draft also included this sentence: "Status catholicus aliorum cultuum publicas manifestationes temperare per se potest, et ne falsae doctrinae quibus homines a Deo veraque Ecclesia recedant propagentur impedire."[12] – On that point, I had put forward a written observation: "Sic generaliter expressum, hoc principium videtur implicare gravia pericula. Etenim, ex una parte, norma non est posita, secundum quam 'Status Catholicus' judicabit de falsitate doctrinarum; et ex altera parte, nullus terminus assignatur exercitio talis potestatis. (Quod recte postea dicitur de necessitate procedendi secundum postulata christianae caritatis, nec est norma, nec est terminus juridicus). Atqui, scimus omnes quot abusus in his materiis exhibet historia Statuum sic dictis catholicorum. – Insuper, textus Pii XII citatus in nota, saltem judicio meo, non proponit doctrinam modo tam absoluto. Insuper adhuc, hic fortasse nonsatis attenditur considerationi sequenti scilicet, quod applicatio talis principii ab aliquo Statu catholico, practice fieret invitatio quaedam aliis Statibus, ut eodem modo procederent erga minoritates catholicas."[13]

Fr. Congar and Father René Laurentin[14] presented some analogous remarks. Father Gagnebet made me a "concession" by acknowledging that the text of the draft did not indicate any criteria; he changed (in the name of the subcommission) the words: "et ne falsae doctrinae, etc.,

---

[11] "These words must be removed, in accordance with Catholic doctrine. They are false."

[12] "The Catholic State by its own authority can moderate public manifestations of other forms of worship and prevent false doctrines, by which men are taken away from God and from the true Church, from spreading."

[13] "Expressed thus, in so general a manner, this principle seems to entail grave dangers. In fact, on the one hand, the norm according to which a 'Catholic State' will judge the falsity of doctrines has not been established; on the other hand, no limit has been assigned to the exercise of such a power. (What is said next, quite rightly, on the necessity of proceeding according to the principles of Christian charity is neither a norm nor a juridical limit.) And yet, we all know how many abuses the history of so-called Catholic States presents in this domain. Besides, the text of Pius XII quoted in the note does not present, in my opinion at least, this doctrine in so absolute a fashion. What is more, up until now, no one has perhaps taken sufficient notice of the following consideration: the application of such a principle by some Catholic State would be, in practice, an incitement for other States to proceed in the same manner with regard to their Catholic minorities."

[14] René Laurentin, born in 1917, French. Priest, mariologist, professor of theology at the Catholic University of Angers. Consultor to the Preparatory Theological Commission, he was named an expert to the council in 1962. He was also a religious columnist for *Le Figaro*. He published *L'Enjeu du Concile* (Éd. du Seuil) in 1962, then four volumes of chronicles, still at Éd. du Seuil: *Bilan de la première session* (1963), *Bilan de la deuxième session* (1964), *Bilan de la troisième session* (1965), and *Bilan du Concile* (1966).

... impedire" to the following: "et contra diffusionem falsarum doctrinarum quibus judicio Ecclesiae salus aeterna in periculum vocatur, cives suos defendere".[15] Not everyone seemed to think that there was any real "concession" here. As for Cardinal Ottaviani, he also intervened a number of times to repeat, under various formulations, that one must remember the rights of truth and that error did not have any rights.

That evening, at the Biblical Institute, I had a conversation with Father Ignace de la Potterie,[16] who is finishing his thesis on faith in Saint John this year. He is worried about the habitual lack of theological doctrine among the exegetes; he spoke to me positively and with interest about my *Exégèse médiévale*.[17]

In the session of the commission this afternoon, concerning tolerance, Msgr. Philips had intervened*[18] against Fr. Dhanis. Citing the example of Belgium (both of them are Belgian and Flemish), he had said to him: According to your principles, if a Belgian government obtains a majority of 51%, and if its members are personally Catholics, the government can and must impose Catholicism as the state religion! etc. – After the meeting, I found myself on the bus with Msgr. Philips; he said to me: "I have been discouraged from intervening; doing so makes me seem like a heretic, and the very people who pushed me to it were very careful to say nothing." Then he gave me the names of two members who had strongly complained to him about the "harshness" of the draft and who, in fact, did not open their mouths in the meeting.

Tuesday, March 6, 1962. – This morning, after finishing the discussion about the relations between the Church and the State, we took up the chapter "De Ecclesiae magisterio".[1] Msgr. Ferrari[2] had asked that on

---

[15] "And to protect its citizens against the diffusion of false doctrines through which, according to the judgment of the Church, eternal salvation is threatened".

[16] Ignace de la Potterie, S.J. (1914–2003), Belgian, ordained in 1945. Exegete, specialist in the Gospel of Saint John, he taught at the Biblical Institute from 1959. His thesis is entitled *La Vérité dans saint Jean*, 2 vols. (Press of the Biblical Institute, 1977).

[17] H. de Lubac, *Exégèse médiévale*, 4 vols. (Paris: Aubier-Montaigne, 1959–1964); the first three vols. have been trans. as *Medieval Exegesis: The Four Senses of Scripture*, Ressourcement (Grand Rapids, Mich.: Eerdmans; Edinburgh: T. & T. Clark, 1998–2009).

[18] * "In his calm manner".

March 6

[1] "On the magisterium of the Church".

[2] Agostino Ferrari Toniolo (1917–2004), Italian, ordained in 1941. Involved in the organization Italian Social Weeks, he became auxiliary bishop of Perugia (Italy) in 1967. Member of the Preparatory Theological Commission, then an expert at the council.

the Church and the State, as well as on tolerance, they question the consultors who had not yet been questioned and who might have something to say. Cardinal Ottaviani and Fr. Tromp did not respond.

The relator for *De Magisterio* is Don Carlo Colombo (Milan). Right on the first page, the draft contains the words: "... Hujus indefectibilis veritatis, principium et organum perpetuum constituit Dominus authenticum Ecclesiae magisterium ..."[3] Father Ciappi himself, O.P., master of the sacred palace, found the word "principium"[4] excessive; he asked in which pontifical document it occurs; he proposed in its place: "norma" or "regula".[5] Against "principium", Fr. Congar cited Saint Thomas and Cajetan,[6] and he appealed to Saint John; he also asked how, if the magisterium is the principle, it can also be at the same time the instrument. Fr. Ciappi noted that the encyclical *Humani generis* says "norma".

For my part, I had written: "Vox 'principium' potius Spiritui Christi applicaretur – huic Spiritui sancto cujus magisterium est 'organum'. Sic nihil auferretur auctoritati magisterii, sed melius appareret ipsum Spiritui subjectum, et ita melius objectiones multorum erga catholicam Ecclesiam amoverentur."[7]

But Cardinal Ottaviani, Father Tromp, and the Roman theologians generally were attached to the word "principium". It is necessary, they said, in order to express the causality that one must recognize the magisterium as possessing. So the subcommission decided to say only "proximum principium"; but no mention was made of the "principium remotum",[8] which is the Holy Spirit. Someone observed that this "principium proximum" is too scholastic an expression to figure in a conciliar constitution; but, as they were attached to "principium", we moved on.

From Fr. Tromp: "Spiritus illuminat pastores ut doceant, et fideles ut credant."[9] – From Cardinal Ottaviani, in response to someone who

---

[3] "The Lord instituted the authentic magisterium of the Church, principle and eternal organ of this unshakeable truth."

[4] "Principle".

[5] "Norm or rule".

[6] Cajetan, O.P. (ca. 1469–1534), Italian. Theologian and great diplomat, his influence is especially due to his commentary on the theology of Saint Thomas Aquinas, which contributed to the renewal of Thomism in the sixteenth century.

[7] "The word 'principle' would be better applied to the Spirit of Christ, to the Holy Spirit, whose organ is the magisterium. Thus, nothing would be taken away from the authority of the magisterium, but it would be more apparent that it is itself subject to the Spirit, and in this fashion, the objections of numerous persons with regard to the Catholic Church would be better removed."

[8] "Immediate principle", "remote principle".

[9] "The Spirit illuminates the pastors so that they might teach and the faithful so that they might believe."

made the observation that everyone, pastors and faithful, must "profiteri fidem": "Sufficit ut pastores doceant; fideles debent profiteri fidem."[10]

During a break in the meeting, Msgr. Salvatore Garofalo, Bible scholar, *rector magnificus* of the College of the Propaganda, asked me to sign his copy of *Exégèse médiévale*.

Toward the end of that morning meeting, Archbishop Hermaniuk,[11] metropolitan of the Ruthenian Catholic Church in North America, asked to speak. He deplored the one-sided character of the chapter on the magisterium, its exclusive concern to exalt the pope alone, its tendency to diminish the council, etc. He proposed a new draft, more balanced, taking better account of tradition, better suited to show the Eastern Churches the true Catholic doctrine. He also asked, as several others had done, that it be made clear that when the pope defines a doctrine of the faith, although he should do it "ex sese, etc.",[12] he nevertheless is speaking as the head of the episcopate ("S. Pontifex loquitur ut caput corporis episcoporum, totius episcopatus"),[13] etc. – Father Tromp answered him: "Haec quae dicit Rev. V. sunt verissima quidem, sed prorsus periculosa."[14] One senses a panicked fear of diminishing in any respect the sovereign liberty of the pope, either in relation to the body of bishops ("subjective") or in relation to tradition ("objective"). This last point was set forth at length by Fr. Dhanis: in order to define a dogma, the pope, he said, has no need either to consult the bishops or to examine tradition in any way whatsoever. He can define a dogma for which tradition provides no evidence. If the dogma has been defined, one should conclude from that fact that it is implicitly contained in Scripture, even though no one ever suspected it.

At 1:30 in the afternoon, had lunch with Fr. Stanislas Lyonnet at the convent of the Ursulines of the Roman Union on via Nomentana. I saw Mother Saint-Jean again, in good health. When Fr. Lyonnet left us alone, she told me in confidence that she had recently written to General de Gaulle, telling him that he had a means to consolidate his power and

---

[10] "To profess their faith. It is sufficient that the pastors teach; the faithful must profess the faith."

[11] Maxim Hermaniuk, C.Ss.R. (1911–1996), Ukrainian, ordained in 1938. Archbishop of the Ukrainian Catholics of Winnipeg (Canada) from 1956 to 1992. Member of the Preparatory Theological Commission, he was named a member of the Secretariat for Christian Unity during the second session.

[12] A reference to the constitution *Pastor aeternus* (1870), which attributes infallibility to the pope when he speaks *ex cathedra*. Definitions of this type are irreformable in themselves (*ex sese*) and not by virtue of the consent of the Church (*et non ex consensu Ecclesiae*).

[13] "The Supreme Pontiff speaks as leader of the episcopal body, of all the episcopate."

[14] "What Your Reverence says is certainly very true, but very dangerous."

to gain the unanimous support of the French: to bring Pétain's body back to Verdun. The general answered her that he had carefully read her letter and that he would reflect on it.

Before returning to the Vatican that afternoon, saw Fr. Georges Jarlot, professor of social theology at the Gregorian, for a few minutes. He told me that the recent constitution on Latin, *Scientiarum Dominus*,[15] is considered "the last gasp of the Pentagone". The personal secretary of John XXIII (Capovilla)[16] is said to be inclined in a totally different direction; he, by himself, is supposed to have an influence with John XXIII that equals the combined influence that Father Leiber[17] and Sister Pasqualina[18] had with Pius XII.

Afternoon session at the Vatican: a continuation of the examination of the draft *De Ecclesiae magisterio*. One senses that, for the group of theologians connected with the Holy Office, "unum est necessarium":[19] the power of Rome, which is their power. They sincerely believe that safety lies in this alone. Hence, through all sorts of formulas, with some quibbling from the canon lawyers, their tendency to diminish the doctrinal role of the bishops, in order to magnify that of the Roman congregations and their own. At the end of the meeting, Bishop Griffiths,[20] auxiliary bishop of New York, asked to be allowed to speak; the president made everyone, already standing for the prayer, sit down again; then the bishop made this simple statement:*[21] "Might I be permitted to remark humbly that, on the day of Pentecost, there were bishops in the Upper Room, but there were no Roman theologians."

---

[15] There must be a confusion here with the Apostolic Constitution *Veterum sapientia* of John XXIII, on the promotion of the study of Latin, which came out in February 1962. It sang the praises of Latin as the language of the Church and wanted to restore its usage in the teaching of theology. The constitution *Deus scientiarum Dominus* was issued by Pius XI and dates from 1931.

[16] Loris Capovilla, born in 1915, Italian, ordained in 1940. Personal secretary of John XXIII, bishop of Chieti from 1967 to 1971, then prelate of Loreto. He was named an expert in 1964.

[17] Robert Leiber, S.J. (1887–1967), German, ordained in 1917. Secretary of Pius XII for more than thirty years, from the time of his nunciature in Germany up to his pontificate.

[18] Sister Pasqualina, Josefina Lehnert (1894–1983), German nun in the service of Pius XII from the time he was nuncio in Germany.

[19] "One thing is needful" [Lk 10:42].

[20] James Griffiths (1903–1964), American, ordained in 1927. Auxiliary bishop of New York from 1955 until his death. Member of the Preparatory Theological Commission, then of the Doctrinal Commission.

[21] * "While growing red".

We had a discussion, in the context of the Roman congregations, on the Holy Office. Several people criticized the planned text, which said that the pope "committere solet"[22] certain matters to the congregations. One cannot say that about the Holy Office, they explained; the Holy Office always judges in the name of the pope, it is in the same category as the pope, and not simply charged by him with certain tasks. This torrent of subtleties achieved its end: the text was modified as a consequence. – From this it is clear that the Holy Office, with its theologians, wants to be the supreme power in the Church.

Msgr. Piolanti, who loves diatribes, sharply criticized the young doctors in theology, who, he said, presumptuously assert themselves. Father Gagnebet answered that to attack an entire body that way, in genere,[23] "est calumniosum".[24] Cardinal Ottaviani asked that the text condemn more strongly those theologians who want to draw attention to themselves by inventing novelties. Msgr. Philips intervened next, with a certain courage, in a moderate tone, in order to recall the necessity of theological research. Father Congar intervened in turn to speak about theologians and theology. They listened to him distractedly, and nothing followed from it. It is always that way, whenever it is not a "Roman" who is speaking, when what is said does not immediately relate to a comment on a detail of the text proposed by the subcommission. The consultors, since they are not admitted to the inner workings of the subcommissions, have no chance of getting any sort of revision or addition that carries any weight.

At another time, a member of the commission, Father B. Häring, C.SS.R., made allusion to the Church of the first centuries, which had no temporal supports, etc. Father Tromp responded: Precisely, the propagation of Christian truth and the growth of the Church in the first centuries was a miracle: we no longer have the right to count on miracles.

A formula of the schema said that the ecumenical councils enjoyed the same infallibility, in their definitions, as the pope when he defines a truth "ex cathedra". One member made the observation that the First Vatican Council proceeded in the opposite direction. The president let the remark drop, and the text was left intact.

These days, an allusion to ecumenism has been made several times. The dissidents, they explain, are expecting clear declarations from the

[22] "Is accustomed to entrust".
[23] "In general".
[24] "Is a calumny".

council on the doctrine of the Catholic Church – and on that point they insist more and more on the aspects that can offend Orthodox and Protestants, in a more and more one-sided sense.

Several times, Fr. Philippe de la Trinité was next to me. He was not self-conscious about telling me his feelings, which were very critical, about certain texts and certain discussions. But what exactly his positions and the direction of his thought are, I do not see.

Wednesday, March 7, 1962. – We discussed the chapter *De laicis*, broached yesterday at the end of the afternoon. The report was given by Msgr. Philips (Louvain). Several people praised the schema. Others protested, notably Fr. Balić: "We are giving much too much to the laity", etc. Similar blunt interventions from Msgr. Fenton (Washington); one also from Fr. Garcia.[1]

One sentence said: "Jus habent (laici) a Pastoribus adjumenta ad salutem necessaria accipiendi, ideoque eis necessitates et desideria sua patefaciendi."[2] Fr. Dhanis intervened: "It is not true that the laity has this right; if pastors refuse to receive them or to hear them, they are perhaps lacking in prudence but not at all in justice." As a consequence, the text was slightly modified.

Next came the chapter "De statibus evangelicae adquirendae perfectionis".[3] We made a few changes to it. No serious incident.

At the Biblical Institute, after lunch, chatted again with Fr. de la Potterie on the theology of Scripture, the relations between exegetes and theologians, the Biblical Institute's difficulties, etc. Then I went to the Gregorian to see Fr. Witte,[4] on sick leave with the flu. He is the main author of the chapter *De œcumenismo*;[5] we talked about that. At the subcommission meeting tomorrow, Fr. Lécuyer[6] (C.S.Sp., French seminary) will take his place.

March 7

[1] Narciso Garcia Garcés.

[2] "The laity have the right to receive from their pastors the assistance necessary for salvation and, thus, to reveal to them their needs and their desires."

[3] "The states of evangelical perfection to be acquired".

[4] Jan Witte, S.J. (1907–1989), Dutch, ordained in 1940. Professor of ecumenical theology at the Gregorian from 1955 to 1981. Consultor to the Preparatory Theological Commission, he was named an expert to the council in 1962.

[5] "On ecumenism".

[6] Joseph Lécuyer, C.S.Sp. (1912–1983), French. Director of the French Seminary in Rome, professor at the Lateran. In 1968, he succeeded Marcel Lefebvre at the head of the Congregation of the Fathers of the Holy Spirit. He was a consultor to the Preparatory Theological Commission and was named an expert in 1962.

In the afternoon, I missed the session in which the long chapter *De matrimonio et familia* was examined. Proofreading the book on Fr. Teilhard. Saw Fr. Mollat, with whom I went for a little stroll in the city.

Thursday, March 8. – No plenary session; the subcommissions are working. Tomorrow morning, Fr. Congar will tell me that, at the study meeting on ecumenism, there was a storm. Fr. Lécuyer, replacing Fr. Witte, was calm and smiling. Msgr. Fenton made a statement right at the beginning: This draft, he said, scandalized him, etc. Then he continued to make repeated violent interruptions. Fr. Tromp, although himself opposed to anything that smells of ecumenism, stood up to him several times. As Fenton continued his public demonstrations, Msgr. Philips ended by declaring, in a sweet but firm voice, that he had had enough of being treated like a heretic, and that, given these conditions, he would go. (In fact, he stayed away for about 20 minutes.) Fenton at first calmed down a little, but he soon resumed his obstruction. The assembled members could not succeed in reaching an agreement, and they will have to deliberate again.

During this time, Thursday afternoon, I went to see Father Hausherr at the Oriental Institute. A conversation in the evening with Fr. Moran (USA) at the Biblical Institute. Sent a packet of proofs to Paris.

Friday, March 9, 1962. – At 9:30 A.M., once again on the fourth floor of the Courtyard of Saint Damasus. We are completing the chapter *De matrimonio et familia christiana*.[1]

Upon arriving, under the colonnade of Saint Peter's, met Father Laurentin and Fr. Congar. Laurentin wished that this chapter drew a little less inspiration from the patriarchal system, that it would give greater recognition to the equality between husband and wife; he offered a slogan: "Just as the Church lost the working class in the nineteenth century, so it will lose women in the twentieth." Congar answered him: "At least here, the schema is biblical." It is a question in particular of this sentence: "Auctoritatis autem principium residet in viro ... Naturalem primatum habet in uxorem et liberos ..."[2]

March 9

[1] "On marriage and the Christian family".

[2] "The principle of authority resides in the man. He has a natural primacy over the woman and children."

In the session, a great dispute on the subject of overpopulation. Fr. Gundlach[3] (German, at the Gregorian, friend of Pius XII) was there as a technical adviser. "Theoria 'superpopulationis absolutae' probari nequit, nisi negando indolem spiritualem agendi humani; immo nisi defectus divinae Providentiae ponatur in ordine creationis ab ipso sapientissimo Deo constituto."[4] Several people made objections. Bishop Griffiths wished it to say instead: "Up to the present, this danger of absolute over-population has not been proved." Father Tromp replied: "Non debemus loqui sociologice, sed theologice", and again: "Veritas theologica nullo modo pendet a scientia sociologica."[5] We were at a standstill. Tromp was supported by Gundlach and one or two others. Cardinal Ottaviani came to the rescue: "Per textum Geneseos, 'Crescite et multiplicamini' explicite excluditur possibilitas superpopulationis absolutae."[6] Father Tromp observed, however, that he was arguing not solely on Scripture but also on natural reason and principles of theology: this overpopula-tion, one must say, is a priori impossible. Fr. Gundlach was of the same opinion: "Hoc concluditur ex principiis revelationis et rationis natu-ralis."[7] In the end, Bishop Griffiths intervened again, to say in an insis-tent voice: "Tamen, caute debemus procedere, ne iterum forte dicatur: E pur si muove!"[8]

It was then asked who were those "qui approbant textum prout est".[9] Only ten hands were raised. As the cardinal president and the father secretary did not seem to draw any specific conclusions from this, a member asked that now the number of those who rejected the text be counted. Father Tromp was opposed to this: among that group, he said, not everyone agreed about the content of the text to be substituted for

[3] Gustav Grundlach, S.J. (1892–1963), German, ordained in 1923. He was the man Pius XII relied on when it came to matters of the social teaching of the Church. He was a professor of social ethics at the Gregorian. Consultor to the Preparatory Theological Commission, he died in June 1963.

[4] "The theory of 'absolute overpopulation' cannot be proven without denying the spiritual char-acter of human action, or, rather, without deeming there to have been a failure of divine Provi-dence in the order of creation, established by God himself in his very great wisdom."

[5] "We must not speak sociologically but theologically. Theological truth does not depend in any way on sociological science."

[6] "The possibility of an absolute overpopulation is excluded in explicit fashion by the text of Genesis: 'Increase and multiply.' "

[7] "This follows from the principles of revelation and from natural reason."

[8] "However, we must proceed with care, in order that no one might say a second time: 'And yet, it turns!' " [Allusion to Galileo.]

[9] "Who approve the text as it is".

it; there were at least two categories there, and their votes should not be added together. Balić supported Tromp, saying that those who did not approve of the text should propose a precise positive votum. And the question was left there.

Fr. Congar would say to me on the way out: "It is always the same thing, century after century. Previous experiences teach them nothing, etc."

Once again, here and there, as in other chapters, some texts from Scripture were deleted, based on the critical objections raised by our two principal experts on exegesis: Msgr. Cerfaux[10] (Louvain) and Msgr. Garofalo. With their "principium proximum", which resides solely in the pontifical documents of about the last hundred years, most of the members of the commission have no need to look at Scripture or tradition or to inform themselves about any science at all. It must also be confessed that our exegetes, in commission or outside, withdraw into a philological and critical role; they are pure specialists; they do not know how to bring out the doctrines that stem from the Bible or to show its spirit. As for our theologians, if one brings to their attention a consideration of a more or less scientific order, they respond as Tromp did: "Debemus procedere theologice" – an attitude that does not prevent them, for example, on the subject of human origins, from wanting to decide the degree of certitude or probability of scientific transformism.[11]

Read in Stendhal, *Promenades dans Rome*, vol. 1 (1893 edition), p. 71: "This great man (Raphael) knows how to give grace even to theologians who are arguing."

This Friday afternoon, at 4 P.M., a meeting at the Franciscan house, via Merulana,[12] to finish studying an addition to the chapter on the Blessed Virgin. The text of this addition was composed by Balić. A subcommission began to examine it yesterday, at the Holy Office.

---

[10] Lucien Cerfaux (1883–1968), Belgian exegete. Professor of New Testament exegesis at the Catholic university of Louvain. Member of the Preparatory Theological Commission, he was named an expert in 1962.

[11] Theory that posits the transformation of species into other species, as opposed to creationism.

[12] This refers to the Antonianum, a college directed by the Franciscans and created in 1890. It received the title of Athenaeum in 1933 and pontifical Athenaeum in 1938. It became a pontifical university in 2005.

The character of this new meeting is not clear. I have the impression that, with the tacit agreement of Cardinal Ottaviani, Fr. Balić wants to push his idea of "Maria Mediatrix",[13] in spite of what was decided by the vote approving the Constitution on the Blessed Virgin. Already, in his first draft of the text (which was supposed to have been a chapter of *De Ecclesia* on "Mary and the Church"), Balić, who is clever, had made a sort of summary of "Mariology"; so that, many people having remarked this, he had made sure they would draw the conclusion (foreseen by him): this chapter does not have its proper place in *De Ecclesia*; it ought to become a constitution in its own right. Since then, he has been able to inflate it even more. Now, his explicit objective is to avert the objections of the Protestants with an "ecumenical" intention. But the real goal appears to be otherwise. In fact, Balić is warmly approved of by the most anti-ecumenical Mariologists around. With his joyous consent, those people would insist, in a meeting that lasted over 3 hours, on strengthening his text.

Right at the beginning of the session, questions were posed by Fr. Dhanis and Father Laurentin on the character of the meeting. Since the commission had approved a text, could there be anything else but proposing slight changes or short additions? Moreover, Laurentin claimed to be uneasy, presented with a new, extemporaneous text; he did not have his documentation here, he had no time to make a well-informed decision, etc. I intervened to say that my personal difficulties were greater still, given my lesser competence: on a text that I was seeing for the first time, how could I form a judgment so quickly concerning the doctrine, its timeliness, the way it was written, the authenticity and value of the quoted texts? Besides, by what right were we deliberating in this way, when a complete text on the subject had been definitively approved by the commission? And in the name of what authority were we assembled? Who had selected those to be invited? ...

We had the meeting anyway, and it was a long one. Father Garcia and Fr. X.[14] (Canadian) obtained some "marianizing" modifications; they were supported, more moderately, by Fr. Bertetto[15] and Msgr. Schmaus

[13] "Mary Mediatrix".
[14] He must mean N. Garcia Garcés and Marcel Bélanger, O.M.I., vice rector of the University of Ottawa.
[15] Domenico Bertetto, S.D.B. (1914–1988), Italian, ordained in 1940. Professor of theology at the Salesian Athenaeum. Consultor to the Preparatory Theological Commission.

(Munich); very moderately by Bishop Wright.[16] Father Laurentin had some citations from apocryphal or misinterpreted texts removed. I was amused to see Fr. Balić, with his plumpness, his affability, his cleverness, get around all the obstacles and achieve his goal. Next to me, Msgr. Cerfaux seemed less enchanted.

I forgot to note, at the session this morning, toward the end of the debate on overpopulation, the ridiculous and pathetic intervention of the old archbishop of Agrigento[17] (the one whom Fr. Congar calls "the infant of Agrigento"). Having asked to speak, he solemnly got to his feet, then he said, slowly, in nearly these words: "I must say that certain things have been said here that shocked me, even more, that scandalized me; things unworthy of the Christian faith, things contrary to the Gospel", etc. And he quoted the whole of the sermon on the mount from Saint Matthew, on trust in Providence, etc. When he was silent, Fr. Tromp, embarrassed and gruff, curtly responded: "Everything that the Excellentissimus Dominus recalls, we have said." And we passed on to other matters.

The chapter "De auctoritate et oboedientia in Ecclesia"[18] had not raised any serious difficulties. I intervened at one point to propose a compromise formula, so as to satisfy at the same time Fr. Dhanis and Fr. Tromp, who were arguing; this was in relation to the obedience of judgment.[19] – Msgr. Garofalo once more had a quotation from Saint Paul deleted, as not being *ad rem*.

Saturday, March 10, 1962. – This morning, we started by examining the chapter "De Ecclesiae natura",[1] revised according to the set of notes

[16]John Wright (1909–1979), American, ordained in 1935. Bishop of Pittsburgh from 1959 to 1969, created cardinal in 1969, prefect of the Congregation for the Clergy from 1969 until his death. Member of the Preparatory Theological Commission, then of the Doctrinal Commission.

[17]Giovanni Battista Peruzzo (1878–1963), Italian, ordained in 1901. Bishop of Agrigento beginning in 1932, then archbishop from 1952 until his death. Member of the Preparatory Theological Commission, then of the Doctrinal Commission. *L'Enfant d'Agrigente* is a book by André-Jean Festugière, published by Éd. du Cerf in 1941.

[18]"On authority and obedience in the Church".

[19]This is one of the three forms of obedience, along with the obedience of execution and that of will, that Saint Ignatius describes in his letter on obedience (see *Monumenta Historica Societatis Iesu, Monumenta Ignatiana: Sti Ignatii de Loyola, Societatis Iesu Fundatoris Epistulae et Instructiones* [Madrid, 1903–1911], 4:669–81). The obedience of judgment consists of obeying by having an interior agreement with what the superior asks.

March 10
[1]"On the nature of the Church".

made by Msgr. Lattanzi[2] (Lateran). With the interventions of Fr. Tromp, Msgr. Fenton, etc., we came back to the question of the Church as the body of Christ and of her members. The text of the chapter quoted Galatians 3:28: "Omnes enim vos unus estis in Christo Jesu":[3] this raised new objections regarding its exact sense (intervention of Msgr. Cerfaux). Numerous notes in the schema refer to texts of Saint Paul and Saint John; Fr. Tromp asked that these be replaced, or at least matched, by texts taken from the "ecclesiastical tradition" (that is, essentially, by quotations from the encyclical *Mystici Corporis*, for which he has a paternal weakness).

Next came the schema *De jure et officio Ecclesiae praedicandi evangelium omnibus gentibus*.[4] The relator was Father Gagnebet. He said to me before the meeting that he had taken careful account of my observations. In fact, he started by changing the title, which became: *De necessitate annuntiandi Evangelium*,[5] etc., and from one end to the other, I observed that the juridical point of view of the original schema was softened.

Bishop Griffiths was insistent that we recall the obligation incumbent on the bishops to concern themselves with dissident Christians, in order to bring them back to the Catholic faith. The answer was given to him that this was not the subject of this chapter and that the point is raised elsewhere.

Another discussion. In order to enter into the spirit of my remarks, Fr. Gagnebet introduced a text from the Gospel: "Ignem veni mittere in terram, et quid volo, nisi ut accendatur?"[6] It was pointed out the exegetes today understand this as referring to the Passion and that therefore it is not *ad rem*. Msgr. Cerfaux, consulted, said that it could be cited anyway, taking it in the traditional sense.

After the morning session, the whole commission went to the "Domus Mariae",[7] on via Aurelia (near the Brazilian college, not far from Saint Jerome), for the meal to which Cardinal Ottaviani had invited us. A Pullman coach came right into the interior of the Vatican to pick us up, so that, after exiting the Courtyard of Saint Damasus, we had to pass

---

[2] Ugo Lattanzi (1899–1969), Italian, ordained in 1924. Dean of the theology faculty of the Lateran. Consultor to the Preparatory Theological Commission, he was named an expert in 1962.

[3] "For all of you are one in Christ Jesus."

[4] "On the right and the duty of the Church to preach the Gospel to all peoples".

[5] "On the necessity of proclaiming the Gospel".

[6] Lk 12:49: "I came to cast fire upon the earth; and would that it were already kindled!"

[7] The location of the meeting, a Catholic Action house.

through two very picturesque medieval courtyards with which I was unfamiliar.

Aside from most of the members and consultors of the commission, also present at the meal were: Archbishop Felici,[8] general secretary of the preparation for the council, and Archbishop Parente, assessor of the Holy Office, representative of Cardinal Ottaviani and a member of the Central Commission. Cardinal Ottaviani seated Parente on his right and, at the start of the meal, made a short speech in praise of him. Then we ate. During the meal, I continued to chat (as we had already done many times) with Father Häring, a good, evangelical man, who sees, perhaps to excess, the faults of the Roman milieu. He is upset over the spirit of our draft documents. We need, he said to me, to pray a great deal. He noted that the Roman theologians are motivated, without their even knowing it, by a spirit of power and domination. – Toward the end of the meal, Msgr. Garofalo got up and, half in Latin, half in Italian, made a long toast; everyone laughed; as for myself, I did not understand a word of it. "The Infant of Agrigento" got up in turn and thanked everyone, especially our secretary, Fr. Tromp, whom he decorated with the title of "protomartyr" (Father Tromp's first name is Sébastien).

After the meal, in the middle of the large vestibule, Archbishop Parente amiably rushed up to me. (I had noticed earlier that Cardinal Ottaviani had pointed me out to him.) Seeing that, the cardinal drew near to us. On all sides, people were watching our trio. I said to Archbishop Parente: "Your Excellency, I have not yet had the honor of meeting you; but I already knew you: you have written some nasty things about me. Rest assured, I do not hold it against you." He was rather taken aback; then he poured out a flood of kind remarks about my books, my erudition, my "beautiful *Méditation sur l'Église*",[9] etc. I continued to exchange a few words with him and the cardinal, then our threesome dispersed. Father Gagnebet, in turn, showed himself friendly; he spoke to me about a possible continuation of the preparatory commission during the council itself, etc. (I have noticed, in the course of the sessions, that he has

---

[8] Pericle Felici (1911–1982), Italian, ordained in 1933. Titular archbishop in 1960, made cardinal in 1967, he became president of the Pontifical Council for Legislative Texts in 1967, then prefect of the Supreme Tribunal of the Apostolic Signatura in 1977. Secretary General of the Central Preparatory Commission, he became secretary general of the council.

[9] H. de Lubac, *Méditations sur l'Église* (Paris: Aubier-Montaigne, 1953; new ed. by Éd. du Cerf, 2003); translated by Michael Mason as *The Splendor of the Church* (1956; San Francisco: Ignatius Press, 1999).

extraordinary composure, assurance, consciousness of his role as "great theologian".)

At 4 P.M., we returned to work. This was the last session. We were examining a paragraph proposed by Archbishop Hermaniuk for insertion in the schema *De magisterio Ecclesiae* on the relations between the pope and the council, the pope and the bishops. Father Tromp blocked it. Msgr. Schauf[10] (Trier), the canon lawyer "ut sic", always finds formulas that exalt the pope alone. No decision was made.

We moved on to the study of the new chapter proposed by Fr. Balić to be inserted into the schema on the Virgin. With some changes, it was adopted.

The whole schema of the constitution *De re sociali*[11] remained to be studied. The subcommission that was charged with the task, too few in number, was divided into two irreconcilable parties: the one, "liberalizing", led by Fr. Gundlach; the other, "socializing", led by Msgr. Pavan[12] (the principal author, so Fr. Gagnebet tells me, of the encyclical *Mater et magistra*).[13] There is hope that, by enlarging the subcommission, a compromise might be reached later.

Apart from this social schema, various details will be examined and concluded in the subcommissions formed of the members and consultors residing in Rome. It will be the same for the whole schema *De oecumenismo*, on which the members of the subcommission have not yet succeeded in reaching an agreement. One can judge the difficulties by this observation made by Msgr. Fenton: "Si istud caput a concilio asseretur, prout est, esset calamitas pro Ecclesia Dei. Esset occasio perditionis fidei et apostasiae." And more of the same: "Doctrina in istis lineis ... certo certius non est doctrina Christi. Hoc est, in fine, somnium aliquorum theologorum." And again: "Scandalosa est haec assertio. Haec est doctrina Modernistarum ... Istae sententiae omnino indignae sunt ne Concilio oecumenico tradantur ... Haec non est theologia, sed

---

[10] Heribert Schauf (1910–1988), German priest. He was professor of Canon Law at the seminary at Aix-la-Chapelle and not at Trier. A former student of Tromp, he remained his disciple. There used to be a joke: "What is the superlative of Tromp? Schauf!" Consultor to the Preparatory Theological Commission, he was named an expert in 1962.

[11] "On the social question".

[12] Pietro Pavan (1903–1994), Italian, ordained in 1929. Professor at the Lateran from 1948 to 1969, he became rector of the Lateran in 1969. Created cardinal in 1985. A specialist in the social teaching of the Church, he was a member of the Preparatory Theological Commission and of the Preparatory Commission for the Lay Apostolate. He was named an expert in 1962. He was one of the principal authors of *Mater et magistra*, *Pacem in terris*, and the text on religious liberty.

[13] Encyclical of John XXIII, issued May 5, 1961, on social questions.

vaporizatio poetica ... Ista sententia delenda est, ex eo quod confusionem pessimam insinuat." Again: "Certo certius apud nostros Catholicos maxime scandalosae sunt istae conferentiae 'oecumenicae', in quibus sacerdos Catholicus insimul cum ministro alicujus sectae loquitur. Et, veracitur loquendo, bene scimus tales 'dialogos' non posse esse si sacerdos Catholicus integre dogma catholicum exponit, sc. objective et accurate explicans dogma de necessitate Ecclesiae et de necessitate verae fidei",[14] etc. Msgr. Fenton is a good, big, smiling American fellow; he told me about his heart condition, asked me to pray for him, etc.: but the only Father of the Church as far as he is concerned is Bellarmine;[15] he is a "post-Tridentinist", pure and simple, and he is fanatical.

At this last session, Father Hürth intervened. He spoke with authority, became overly subtle, got confused. One senses that he has had considerable influence (he still has among many), but that he no longer has all of his faculties. He wanted to change something in the chapter on religious life. He argued on the basis of a discourse given by Pius XII that was declared erroneous by Father Larraona[16] and that Pius XII nevertheless had printed in *L'Osservatore Romano*. He insisted on the fact, of great importance in his view, that this discourse was not published until two or three days after, which he felt proved that the pope had had the time to reflect on the objections raised by Larraona; his words in such a circumstance therefore had a special weight, which obliged us to have them ratified by the council, etc., etc. It was decided that Fr. Hürth would compose a votum in writing and that a subcommission would assess it. – A good example of this terribly decadent

---

[14] "If this chapter, as it is, were to be affirmed by the council, it would be a disaster for the Church of God. It would lead to a loss of the faith and to apostasy. The doctrine contained in these lines is certainly not the doctrine of Christ. It is, ultimately, the dream of certain theologians. This affirmation is scandalous. It is the doctrine of the modernists ... These ideas are absolutely unworthy of being transmitted to the ecumenical council ... This is not theology but a poetic dream. This sentence must be removed because it introduces the worst sort of confusion. Assuredly, these 'ecumenical' conferences, in the course of which a Catholic priest speaks along with a minister of some sect, cause a great scandal among our Catholics. And, to speak frankly, we know very well that such 'dialogues' cannot exist if the Catholic priest presents Catholic dogma in a complete fashion, that is to say, by explaining objectively and carefully the dogmas on the necessity of the Church and the necessity of the true faith."

[15] Robert Bellarmine, S.J. (1542–1621), Italian, ordained in 1570. As a theologian, he was one of the principal figures of the Counter-Reformation.

[16] Arcadio Larraona, C.M.F. (1887–1973), Spanish, ordained in 1911. Created cardinal in 1959, he was prefect of the Sacred Congregation of Rites from 1962 to 1968. Member of the Central Preparatory Commission, he was also president of the Preparatory Commission for the Liturgy, then president of the Commission for the Liturgy.

theology of a certain number of Roman theologians, especially of the Gregorian, who were all powerful under Pius XII and whose influence has still carried weight with the preparatory commission. Court theology. One senses among them nostalgia for the time when they could have the pope deliver so many speeches in which they could put their own little ideas. They would still like to reduce all of theology, even more, the faith of the Church herself, proclaimed by an ecumenical council, to something infinitely small and infinitely complex.

Upon leaving the Vatican for the last time, in a downpour, I went to pray in Saint Peter's.

Brief visit to the Curia: Fr. Bottereau, Br. Mouton;[17] the Assistant[18] had gone out. I saw Fr. Jean Lucas,[19] from Radio-Vatican, for a few moments. Returned to the Biblical Institute. The Fathers of the Institute told me that the article on Sacred Scripture published in *L'Osservatore Romano* about 3 months ago, the article whose author was Cardinal Ruffini, has been printed and distributed to all the seminaries in Italy, officially, by the Congregation for Seminaries and Universities.[20] They foresee, like Msgr. Cerfaux, that in the next ten years there will be heated disputes, and perhaps tragic conflicts, on the subject of the historicity of the Gospels, in particular on the subject of the Infancy Narratives.[21]

At 8 P.M., dinner at the Bellarminum. Fr. René Arnou was present. During the recreation, the biennists who understand French went upstairs to a room, where I had to answer their questions (on Cardinal Bea – Taizé – Teilhard – theology in France, etc.). The conversation continued in Fr. Guy's[22] room, with the 4 French biennists, a student from the Congo, and a Canadian.*[23]

---

[17] Stéphane Mouton, S.J. (1894–1983), French, secretary and brother coadjutor at the General Curia, then at Lyon.

[18] Bernard de Gorostarzu.

[19] Jean Lucas, S.J. (1906–1970), French, ordained in 1938. He was director of French programs for Radio Vatican beginning in 1960.

[20] This article is a little older: E. Ruffini, "Generi Letterari e ipotesi di lavoro nei recenti studi biblici", *Osservatore Romano*, August 24, 1961. The article criticizes recourse to literary genres in the interpretation of the Bible.

[21] The part of the Gospels dealing with the infancy and childhood of Jesus.

[22] He must mean Jean-Claude Guy, S.J. (1927–1986), French, who entered the Society in 1944. A great connoisseur of the spirituality of the Desert Fathers.

[23] * This paragraph, along with the following one, was crossed out, and there is a question mark in the margin for each of these paragraphs. However, a letter from Father de Lubac to Henri Bouillard, dated March 14, 1962, recalls the interview, on the initiative of Father Latourelle, with whom the next paragraph is concerned.

Sunday, March 11, 1962. – This morning, at the Gregorian, in the office of the dean of theology, the young Father René Latourelle,[1] a Canadian, who had invited me, a conversation with two other Canadians, a Holy Cross Father and a layman,[2] both of them in Rome for the council, on behalf of Radio Canada. They taped my comments on Frs. Valensin,[3] Teilhard, Fontoynont,[4] de Montcheuil,[5] etc. This was the first time I had allowed myself to be recorded, because of Fr. Latourelle's insistence. (Fr. D. Mollat told me that he had wanted to have me come to the Gregorian to give a lecture but that he could not overcome the opposition of Fr. Dhanis).

In the afternoon, farewell to Rome. I went to the Church of Saint Onuphrius.[6] The place is still preserved. A marble plaque was recently affixed to the exterior wall of the church bearing a few lines from Chateaubriand, mingling his memory with the memory of Tasso.[7] Returned

---

March 11

[1] René Latourelle, S.J., born in 1918, Canadian, ordained in 1950. Professor at the Gregorian and dean of the theology faculty until the summer of 1964.

[2] Father Émile Legault, C.S.C. (1906–1983), Canadian, ordained in 1930. A man of the theater, he wished to use the latter in the service of the faith. He was also engaged in radio evangelization and, during the council, was a correspondent for Radio-Canada. Gérard Lemieux was the coordinator of religious programs at Radio-Canada.

[3] Auguste Valensin, S.J. (1879–1953), French, ordained in 1910. He was professor of philosophy at the Catholic faculties of Lyon from 1920 to 1934. He was closely associated with Maurice Blondel, under whose supervision he had obtained his degree in philosophy. Father de Lubac, who had known him in Lyon, put in a great deal of work on the posthumous edition of his works and his correspondence: *Regards*, 3 vols. (1955–1956), *Correspondance Blondel-Valensin*, 3 vols. (1965).

[4] Victor Fontoynont, S.J. (1880–1958), French, ordained in 1910. A friend of Auguste Valensin, he became, in 1932, prefect of studies at the theology faculty of Fourvière, a post he held for ten years while teaching theology there. As early as 1933, he worked out the plan for the "Sources chrétiennes" series, which did not appear until 1942. He supported the *Cahiers du Témoignage chrétien*.

[5] Yves de Montcheuil, S.J. (1900–1944), French, ordained in 1932. Professor of theology at the Institut catholique of Paris from 1935 to 1944. In 1944 he joined the resistance in Vercors (southern France), where he brought spiritual help to the wounded. He was arrested and executed. At that time, Father de Lubac became involved in the publication of his writings. See B. Sesboüé, *Yves de Montcheuil 1900–1944, précurseur en théologie* (Paris: Éd. du Cerf, 2006).

[6] This refers to a monastery on the Janiculum, mentioned by Stendhal in *Promenades dans Rome*, a work that Father de Lubac quotes *supra* and *infra*. In the entry for August 9, 1827, Stendhal writes: "Today, in order to see the city of Rome and the tomb of Tasso, we climbed up to Saint Onuphrius: magnificent view."

[7] The plaque recalls the wish once made by Chateaubriand to finish his days in Rome, where he was ambassador in 1828–1829. As for Torquato Tasso (1544–1595), one of the most important Italian poets of the Renaissance, he was buried at Saint Onuphrius and always thought that it was "without doubt one of the most beautiful places in the world to die".

by way of Trastevere. At Saint Mark, saw the arrival of the pope, who went in procession from Saint Mark's to the Gesù. From the Biblical Institute, a short walk with Fr. des Places; we contemplated the beautiful palaces in the neighborhood: Doria Pamphili, Palazzo Odescalchi, Colonna ... He showed me, in the Basilica of the Twelve Apostles, the monument of Bessarion;[8] there is a long inscription, where one can read in particular: " ... Graecae pariter et Latinae Ecclesiae concordia inter utraque strenue ac feliciter promota."[9] What would Msgr. Fenton say to that? It is more "modernist" than anything that can be read in the chapter drafted by the excellent Father Witte.

Rome is not elegant. It is beautiful.

I read in Stendhal, *Promenades dans Rome*, vol. 1, p. 105: "The three quarters of Rome to the East and to the South, the Viminal Hill, the Esquiline Hill, the Caelian Hill, the Aventine, are solitary and silent. Fever holds sway there, and the hills are cultivated in vines. It is in the midst of this vast silence that most of the monuments sought after by the curiosity of the traveler are to be found." Things have certainly changed since Stendhal's day. It is less pleasant for a person on foot. But Rome is still admirable.

In the evening, two young priests who are preparing theses at the Biblical Institute accompanied me to the station (Fr. Keil,[10] German-American, whose thesis is on Gnosticism; and a French Canadian[11]). Departed at 10 P.M.

Monday, March 12, Fourvière.

There is a dangerous opposition within a certain current "theology" between safe truths and dangerous truths. It is more than the necessary pedagogy for the intellectual life as for the spiritual life. This comes down in the end to an opposition between truth and safety.

Theology, such as I have seen it operate in Rome, is more and more a speciality that grows complicated and rigid. It is not renewed, it does not

---

[8] Bessarion (1403–1472), Greek and ecclesiastical scholar, he was made cardinal in 1439 and named Latin patriarch of Constantinople in 1463. He worked for the union of the Latin and Eastern Churches.

[9] "The concord of the Church, both Greek and Latin, felicitously and actively promoted between the two".

[10] Nikolaus Kehl, S.J. (1914–2005), German.

[11] Julian Harvey, S.J., Canadian, whose thesis was on "The Prophetic Plea against Israel after the Breaking of the Covenant: Study of a Literary Genre of the Old Testament".

change the old conception of itself as "queen of the sciences": it turns its back on science – without having lost anything of its pretension to rule over the sciences, that is, to dismiss them, in an arrogant and systematic ignorance.

In this kind of theology, the questions that touch on the government of the Church are overdeveloped. They are of exceeding interest; they absorb the forces of a battalion of canon lawyers, whose principal occupation seems always to be to stretch a little further the juridical formulas secreted by their predecessors. Certain of them, considered to be clever theologians, seem not to have reflected for a single instant of their existence on the mystery of faith; such a reflection, moreover, would be incompatible with their work as they understand it.

As for those who devote themselves to the other parts of theology, their concerns all tend toward the requirements (or what are claimed to be the requirements) of academic and primary instruction. They are sometimes reproached for their "rationalism", a very great and very noble word, to designate their verbalism. But the fact that their wild imaginings are as empty of spiritual sense as of any reference to historical reality is only too true.

Whenever anyone asks them to take some note of some particular point of the social sciences, they arrogantly respond that they are proceeding doctrinally, theologically, that they are pronouncing truths in absolute terms; that they have no need to think historically or sociologically or psychologically; they do not consent to descend into the domain of the relative. – That is all well and good. That would have some value, if they occupied themselves with deepening the mystery of the faith. But, in fact, incessantly busy with expanding the field of the "truths" to be imposed on the faithful, they deal with problems that demand some serious scientific knowledge and more humane methods. Without being aware of it, they put in the place of Dogma a theology that usurps its place and that can satisfy neither the scholar nor the believer.

"Natural theology" often interests them more than revealed mystery. It seems to them to be an area more propitious for their hairsplitting method and, on the other hand, to provide a more "secure" base for the government of souls. They are thereby closely akin to their brothers, the canon lawyers. It is very characteristic of their way of proceeding that, in the chapter *De Deo* of the schema *De deposito fidei*, they did not make the least allusion to God's revelation in Christ; and that, having finally decided to make a slight concession to the objections that had been addressed to them, they only mentioned, as the end of this supernatural revelation, the "service" of God. Thus they think to facilitate submission to the leaders of the Church – whom they think to have well in hand through their doctrinal consultations.

On the other hand, they are, each according to his character, good people, and they can be virtuous. Their number, even in Rome, is not great; but they dominate. Without even wishing to (at least not always), they instill fear. An entire system of habits, of rites, of language, makes a frank discussion very difficult; they are "at home", they understand each other, even when they argue. They are unaware of what they lack. Their self-sufficiency is extreme, and their good faith is not in question. There is in this a situation that appears to me disturbing. What will this council be?

The two inscriptions on the elevator in the Vatican, by Cardinal Bacci:[1]

1. In the first vestibule (the Belvedere courtyard):

> Quo commodius et expeditius
> Adeuntes Vaticanas Aedes
> Sursum deorsum vehi possent
> PIUS XII Pont. Max.
> Geminam Anabathrum electrica vi actum
> Quod per ambulacrum autoraedis pervium
> Facile contingitur
> Instruendum curavit A. MCMLVI.[2]

2. In the second vestibule, near the elevator itself:

> Unde lento molimine aquae
> Veteri Scansorio Pegmati dabatur motus,
> Pontificii Palatii fundamentis effossis
> Novoque ad Damasianam usque aulam

March 12

[1] Antonio Bacci (1885–1971), Italian, ordained in 1909. He worked at the Secretariat of State from 1922 to 1931 and became secretary of briefs to princes, a position he held from 1931 to 1960. He was made cardinal in 1960.

[2] "In order that those who come to the Vatican might be able to move up and down more conveniently and quickly, Pius XII, Supreme Pontiff, has taken care to put in place, in the year 1956, this double elevator, moved by electric power and easily approached by means of a level walkway accessible to wheelchairs."

Instructo opere
heic
PIUS XII Pont. Max.
ad Anabathrum electride actum
Quod ab imo ad summum ascendit
Patere jussit adytum.[3]

Thursday, October 4, 1962. – This morning, in Marseilles, I kissed Mama for the last time.[1,*2]

Returned to Fourvière in the evening. I thanked Msgr. Journet for a kind word he sent me regarding the council.

October 6, I departed for Rome.

The Fr. Provincial[1] had had me summoned to Loreto on September 23: unhappy that the archbishop and his auxiliaries[2] had not called on me, he wanted me to go to Rome for the council, as the personal theologian of Bishop Véniat, S.J.,[3] of Fort-Archambault (Chad); Bishop Véniat had agreed to this. But, on September 28, *La Croix* published a list of "experts" named by the pope for the council; my name was on the list. The next day, the 29th, the newspapers were saying that John XXIII was doubtless going to name me as an expert to the council in order to show his unhappiness over the *Monitum*[4] from the Holy Office on

---

[3] "From this place from which movement was given to the mechanism of the old elevator by the tenacious effort of the water, having caused the foundations of the pontifical palaces to be dug out, having caused a new work to be carried out up to the Courtyard of Saint Damasus, in this place, Pius XII, Supreme Pontiff, has ordered that the access to the elevator, moved by electricity, and which ascends from the bottom toward the top, be opened."

October 4

[1] Gabrielle de Lubac died on March 15, 1963.

[2] *This sentence was crossed out by Father de Lubac in his modified version.

October 6

[1] Blaise Arminjon.

[2] The archbishop of Lyon was Pierre-Marie Gerlier. His two auxiliaries were Alfred Ancel and Marius Maziers. Alfred Ancel (1898–1984), French, ordained in 1923, auxiliary bishop of Lyon from 1947 to 1973. He was elected as a member of the Doctrinal Commission during the second session. Marius Maziers (1915–1989), French, ordained in 1938, auxiliary bishop of Lyon from 1959 to 1966, he became archbishop of Bordeaux in 1968 and remained so until 1989. The archbishop of Lyon also had a coadjutor bishop, Jean Villot, in his entourage.

[3] Henri Véniat, S.J. (1917–1998), French, ordained in 1949. Bishop of Sarh (Fort Archambault) in Chad from 1961 to 1987.

[4] This refers to the *Monitum* of June 30, 1962, which warned against "the dangers of the works of Father Teilhard de Chardin and his disciples".

Teilhard and the article*[5] in *L'Osservatore Romano*[6] that explained the *Monitum* by taking a stand against my book on *La Pensée religieuse du Père Teilhard de Chardin*, which some people wanted to put on the Index.

On the other hand, the Fr. Provincial had also sounded out, through Archbishop Thoyer,[7] formerly of Tananarive, Bishop Gilbert Ramanan-toanina[8] of Fianarantsoa (Madagascar). (Bishop Véniat ended up taking Fr. Martelet[9] as his theologian.) On September 30, Archbishop Thoyer brought me a letter from Bishop Gilbert R., setting up a meeting in Rome for October 9.

First Session of the Council

October 7, 1962. – Sunday. I arrived this morning in Rome. Father Boussuge,[1] Substitute of the French Assistancy, was waiting for me at the Borgo S. Spirito.[2] He had had a room reserved for me on the sixth floor, at the same level as the big terrace, next door to Fr. Henri Rondet's room. Mass, served by Brother Mouton. I then greeted Fr. Bottereau, the superior of the house. At coffee, chatted with the Assistant.[3] Before lunch, Fr. Jean Lucas, from the radio station, came to see me.

According to Fr. Lucas, the pope supposedly said recently to Father General, regarding the Biblical Institute and the two professors (Zer-wick, S. Lyonnet) who have been suspended from teaching: "Father

---

5 * "Anonymous".

6 This refers to an article that, though anonymous, was attributed to Philippe de la Trinité, O.C.D., published in *L'Osservatore Romano* of July 1, 1962, following the *Monitum*. The article, while acknowledging the merits of Father de Lubac's book, added: "As for ourselves, frankly and honestly we must declare that we do not agree with the substantially favorable judgment given by Fr. de Lubac."

7 Xavier Thoyer, S.J. (1884–1970), French, ordained in 1914. Apostolic vicar, then bishop and archbishop of Fianarantsoa (Madagascar) from 1936 to March 1962.

8 Gilbert Ramanantoanina, S.J. (1916–1991), Malagasy, ordained in 1948. Auxiliary bishop of Fianarantsoa in 1960, he became its archbishop in 1962 and remained so until 1991. Member of the Secretariat for Unity starting from the second session of the council.

9 Gustave Martelet, S.J., born in 1916, French. Theologian, professor of dogmatics at Four-vière and, later, at the Gregorian. At the council, he came as the expert of Bishop Véniat of Fort Archambault (Chad) and rapidly became secretary of the group of bishops from equatorial Africa and theological consultor of the French-speaking African bishops.

October 7

1 Camille Boussuge, S.J., born in 1921, French, ordained in 1951. Deputy of the Assistant of France.

2 General Curia of the Society of Jesus.

3 Bernard de Gorostarzu.

General, you are right, but, patienza!" With regard to Teilhard, it is
generally agreed, in Rome, that the affair of the *Monitum* put an end
to that, that the party in favor of condemnation has decidedly failed.
Fr. Philippe de la Trinité is thought to have been the main author of the
article in *L'Osservatore*.

The day before yesterday, October 5, the Holy Father received in
private audience L. Senghor,[4] president of Senegal. Fr. Lucas told me
that the conversation was a long one, much longer than he had anticipated. It was because they talked about Teilhard. According to what was
already reported to me in France a few days ago, Senghor supposedly
said recently to one of his friends: "I am going to see the pope, and I
will keep repeating the same refrain on the subject of Teilhard. I will
complain about the *Monitum* from the Holy Office; and I will explain to
him how it is T. who caused me to rediscover the Catholic faith."

I brought with me to Rome one of the tracts distributed in France
against Teilhard: "The Apologetics of Grandpa prostituted by the Science of papa gives birth to a political fossil, the 'Teilhardanthropus pro-
gressivus'. In three stages, one and the same error: Teilhard starts from
a conception of original sin opposed to that of the Church, because
it kills the Liberty of man. Teilhard continues with a conception of
Collectivism opposed to that of the Church, because it kills the Liberty of Man. Teilhard ends with a conception of the End of the World
opposed to that of the Gospel, because it kills the Liberty of Man.
Teilhard sows the error of opposing the Church. He reaps the heresy of
opposing the Gospel. His disciples sow the wind of collectivism. They
will reap the storm of communism! – That is a fact. Look around you:
the Gaullists are more or less Teilhardians, and the reverse is also true,
though this is less easy to see. Why? Could it be that General de Gaulle
conceives of the History of France in the same way Father Teilhard
conceives of the History of the world? And if that is the case? Well,
draw the conclusion!"

According to the Assistant [to the Jesuit Father General], it was the pope
himself who wanted to put me on the list of experts ("periti"). "The

[4] Léopold Sedar Senghor (1906–2001), Senegalese poet and political figure. Professor of literature
and grammar, he entered political life after the Second World War and became député [an elected
representative to the French national assembly] for Senegal. In 1960, he was elected president of the
Republic of Senegal and was reelected four times. He stepped down in 1980.

Holy Father does not want to depend on the Roman Congregations during the council; so he chose some theologians capable of understanding and supporting his thought." The Assistant saw Fr. Philippe de la Trinité (who is again suffering from depression); the latter told him that he was not in agreement with me on the subject of Teilhard; however, the Assistant does not believe that he was the author, or at least not the sole author, of the article in *L'Osservatore*.

When he announced his decision to go to Loreto, John XXIII reportedly said to his close friends: "I will go to pray for the council; and then, the trip will bring me some fresh air, I will be away from here for a few hours."

In the afternoon of this Sunday, October 7, during a procession that was taking place from Saint Mary Major to Saint John Lateran, I began to reread closely the "Schemata constitutionum et decretorum de quibus disceptabitur in Concilii sessionibus, series prima".[5] The volume, magnificently printed, 272 pages long, contains: (1) our four dogmatic schemas of the Preparatory Theological Commission;[6] (2) three other schemas: *De sacra liturgia – De instrumentis communicationis socialis – De Ecclesiae unitate*.[7] Everything according to the text as revised by the Central Preparatory Commission.

A letter signed by Cardinal A. G. Cicognani,[8] dated September 24, 1962, was waiting for me in Rome: it was my nomination as "peritus" to the council. It was accompanied by a booklet by Archbishop P. Felici, general secretary of the council: "Ordo concilii oecumenici Vaticani II celebrandi". Article 10 defines in chapter V the "Peritorum conciliarium officium":

a. Periti conciliares Congregationibus generalibus intersunt et nonnisi interrogati loquuntur. – b. Juxta Commissionum Praesidum designationem et rationem, Periti conciliares cuilibet Commissioni operam navant,

---

[5] "Schemas of the constitutions and decrees that will be dealt with during the sessions of the council, first series."

[6] These were the schemas *De fontibus revelationis, De deposito fidei, De ordine morali*, and *De familia et matrimonio*.

[7] "On the sacred liturgy". "On the means of social communication". "On the unity of the Church".

[8] Amleto Giovanni Cicognani (1883–1973), Italian, ordained in 1905. Made cardinal in December 1958, he was secretary of the Congregation for Oriental Churches from 1959 to 1961 and became secretary of state in August 1961, on the death of Tardini. President of the conciliar Commission for Eastern Churches and of the Coordinating Commission.

adlaborando cum ejus membris in schematibus expendendis atque confi-
ciendis relationibus.[9]

Fr. René Arnou had Fr. Lucas read my remarks on the article in *L'Osservatore Romano* criticizing Teilhard. He was very happy with them. I
suppose that he also gave them to others to read and that he has spoken
to Father General about them. (I had sent my remarks to both of them,
telling them both that.)

Monday, October 8, 1962. – Around 9:30 A.M., Fr. Lucas drove me
to the Secretariat of State, to talk with Father Paul Poupard,[1] who has
been employed there for one year: a former student at the Theology
Faculty of Angers (his thesis was on Bautain),[2] currently working on a
thesis at the Sorbonne on the nunciature of Garibaldi[3] in France; a disciple of Bishop Chappoulie,[4] whom he seems to resemble a great deal,
both in intelligence and cast of mind. I have the impression that, in one
year, he has already been able to make great advances in his knowledge
of the Roman ecclesiastical milieu. Yesterday, Cardinal Tisserant[5] told

---

[9] "Rules to be observed for the ecumenical council Vatican II. Duties of the conciliar *periti*
(experts):

"a. The *periti* of the council are present during the General Congregations and do not express
their opinion unless asked. b. According to the designation of the presidents of the commissions and
the subject under discussion, the conciliar *periti* zealously serve any commission by working with its
members on the schemas to be examined and on the reports to be drafted."

October 8

[1] Paul Poupard, born in 1930, French, ordained in 1954. He worked at the Secretariat of State
from 1959 to 1972. He then became rector of the Institut catholique of Paris (1972–1980), auxiliary
bishop of Paris (1979–1980), pro-president of the Secretariat for Non-Believers (1980–1985). In
1985, he was created cardinal and became president of the Secretariat for Non-Believers (1985–
1993). He has been president of the Pontifical Council for Culture since 1988 and of the Pontifical
Council for Interreligious Dialogue since 2006.

[2] *Un essai de philosophie chrétienne au XIXᵉ siècle: l'abbé Louis Bautain* (Paris: Desclée, 1961). Louis
Bautain (1796–1867), French, ordained in 1828. Philosopher and theologian, he taught theology
in Paris.

[3] Antonio Garibaldi (1797–1853), Italian, ordained in 1819. Interim nuncio to France from 1831
to 1843, then nuncio under the Second Empire.

[4] Henri Chappoulie (1901–1959), French, ordained in 1931. Bishop of Angers from 1950 until
his death.

[5] Eugène Tisserant (1884–1972), French, ordained in 1907. Created cardinal in 1936, he was
secretary of the Congregation for the Oriental Church from 1936 to 1959, prefect of the Congregation of Ceremonies from 1951 to 1967, librarian and archivist of the Holy See from 1957 to 1971.
Member of the Académie française from 1961. He was dean of the Board of Presidency during the
council.

him, even somewhat violently, of his opposition to the plan to have
Pius IX[6] canonized by the council; but it appears that the pope and
Cardinal Ottaviani are united on this; the pope seems very insistent on
it and has made frequent allusions to it; even his trip to Loreto, it is said,
was an allusion to it.[7]

Father Poupard confirmed to me that John XXIII wants reforms in
the Roman congregations. Too much hope on this subject would be
unrealistic; but an attainable reform would consist of implementing at
least what already exists in theory: only, it would be necessary for the
bishops to insist on it. So, for example: Why are foreign cardinals not
even advised of the meetings of the congregations to which they nom-
inally belong? Why are there never any cardinals who are not Italians
at the Holy Office? etc., etc. If the cardinals of the entire world, who
belong to the household of the pope, were effectively associated with
the course of affairs in Rome, that would already be a very important
reform.

Both of us regretted that no French bishop appeared to have chosen
Msgr. Bruno de Solages[8] as his theologian; his help would be invaluable.
We wished that Fr. Karl Rahner, who is on the list of periti, might be
invited to work as such in the Doctrinal Commission ("de doctrina fidei
et morum");[9] but there is a chance that they will keep him isolated, as
they did with the preparatory commission. – The choices that will be
made by the council for the members of the Doctrinal Commission are
of major importance: 8 will be named by the pope (these will no doubt
be Romans); 16 will be elected by the council. Cardinal Ottaviani will
be president. He surely has his list ready for the 16 to be elected, and
thanks to the confusion, with the bishops not having time to consult
with each other, there is a good chance that this list will be adopted. It is
expected that the first session of the council could end around December 5–10. The second would follow, more or less, soon after, according
to whether they parted more or less in agreement. – Father Poupard
attributes the essential points of the article on Teilhard in *L'Osservatore*
to Archbishop Parente.

---

[6] Giovanni Maria Mastai-Ferretti (1792–1878), Italian, ordained in 1819. Elected pope in 1846, beatified in 2000.

[7] Giovanni Maria Mastai-Ferretti had been healed following a pilgrimage to Loreto.

[8] Bruno de Solages (1895–1983), French theologian and exegete. Rector of the Institut catholique of Toulouse from 1931 until his resignation in 1964.

[9] "On the doctrine of the faith and on morals".

At the end of the morning, at the General Curia, two conversations: with the substitute of the Assistancy of India[10] and with Fr. J.-A. Jungmann,[11] who has just arrived; he is on the list of periti. General agreement with Fr. Jungmann on the questions broached. He confirmed to me that the censorship*[12] imposed by the Holy Office on Fr. K. Rahner has been lifted: officially, it has been delegated to Cardinals Döpfner[13] and König,[14] who had written to the pope in his favor. Bishop Volk[15] (Mainz), former professor of dogma at Münster (I saw him there 9 or 10 years ago), is a disciple and friend of Rahner. We hope that he will be selected as a member of the Doctrinal Commission. – Jungmann told me also that, in his circle, many are critical of the doctrinal schemas: they complain that they only set forth a narrow, by-the-book theology, without taking account of anything that has been published in the past century by the best theologians. He would like the council to concern itself first with liturgical questions and other practical matters, postponing the discussion of the doctrinal texts, which would allow time for other ones to be drafted and proposed.

There is, it seems, at the Secretariat of State, an entire service officially dedicated to the writing of "briefs to the Christian princes"; the staff is chosen from among the good Latinists. But there are fewer and fewer princes in the world, the princes are less and less Christian, and when every now and then the pope writes to Princess Grace of Monaco[16] or someone else, he composes his letter in French, the diplomatic language

---

[10] Abraham Adappur, S.J., Indian.

[11] Joseph Andreas Jungmann, S.J. (1889–1975), Austrian. He was one of the major architects of the liturgical movement of the twentieth century. Professor of liturgy and of pastoral theology at the theology faculty in Innsbruck from 1930 to 1956. Member of the Preparatory Commission for the Liturgy, he became an expert in 1962. He was then named consultor to the *consilium ad exsequendam Constitutionem de Sacra Liturgia* [the organization formed to put the Constitution on the Sacred Liturgy into effect – TRANS.].

[12] * "Previous".

[13] Julius Döpfner (1913–1976), German, ordained in 1939. Created cardinal in 1958, archbishop of Munich and Freising from 1961 to 1976. In 1962, he became a member of the Coordinating Commission, and in 1963, moderator of the council.

[14] Franz König (1905–2004), Austrian, ordained in 1933. Archbishop of Vienna from 1956 to 1985. Created cardinal in 1958. President of the Secretariat for Non-Believers in 1965. Member of the Doctrinal Commission.

[15] Hermann Volk (1903–1988), German, ordained in 1927. Theologian, bishop of Mainz from March 1962 to 1982, created cardinal in 1973. Member of the Secretariat for Unity and a member of the Doctrinal Commission.

[16] Grace Kelly (1929–1982), American. An actress, she married Prince Rainier in April 1956, thus becoming Princess Grace of Monaco.

of the Holy See; the Secretaries of State come and go, without anyone thinking to or daring to eliminate these positions. It is true that the personnel have some small, alternative tasks.

In the June 1962 issue of *Divinitas*, pp. 444–55, an Italian translation of an article by Fr. August Brunner, S.J.,[17,*18] published in *Stimmen der Zeit*, in the December 1959 issue, on (against) Teilhard. – In the *Quaderni di Divinitas*, 3 (1962), a booklet of 76 pages by Fr. Philippe de la Trinité, O.C.D.: Teilhard and Teilhardism: 1. Significance of Teilhard according to Fr. Daniélou[19] (5–37); 2. Perspective of Fr. de Lubac on the Religious Thought of Teilhard (38–66). Appendices: 1. Perspective of Mr. Georges Crespy on the Theological Thought of T.; 2. Last page of Fr. T. de Chardin's journal.

At the time of the afternoon siesta, saw Fr. Robert Rouquette,[20] of *Études*,[21] who has come as a journalist for the session of the council. He is staying with other Jesuit journalists at the *Civiltà cattolica*. He tells me that the question of Orthodox observers[22] has not yet been settled; Rome has not yet been notified of the definite refusal, published in the press. Msgr. Willebrands,[23] secretary of the Secretariat for Unity (Card. Bea) has gone to Moscow; it is not known what response he will bring

---

[17] August Brunner, S.J. (1894–1985), German, ordained in 1924. A Neo-Thomist, he taught philosophy and was co-editor of *Stimmen der Zeit* (Munich) beginning in 1946. His article is: "Pierre Teilhard de Chardin", *Stimmen der Zeit* 3, 1959–1960.

[18] *"Whom I got to know at Ore Place". [The theological formation of French Jesuits was moved there until the Society could reopen a scholasticate in France.]

[19] Jean Daniélou, S.J. (1905–1974), French, ordained in 1938. Fascinated by the Bible and the Fathers of the Church, he was one of the architects of the patristic renewal and co-founder of "Sources chrétiennes". He taught at the Institut catholique of Paris, where he was dean of the theology faculty from 1961 to 1969. Named an expert to the council in 1962, he was created cardinal in 1969.

[20] Robert Rouquette, S.J. (1905–1969), French. A contributor to *Études* from 1943, he had a regular column there beginning in 1957, "Chronique d'actualité religieuse", which he continued during the council. The most important columns were collected in two volumes: *Vatican II, la fin d'une chrétienté* (Paris: Éd. du Cerf, 1968).

[21] Journal of the French Jesuits, founded in 1856.

[22] The observers were delegates sent by different Churches and ecclesial communities separated from Rome to witness the workings of the council and to contribute toward an ecumenical opening.

[23] Jan Willebrands (1909–2006), Dutch, ordained in 1934. Rector of the Seminary of Warmond from 1945 to 1960. He was named secretary of the Secretariat for Christian Unity in 1960 and titular bishop in June 1964. In 1969, he became president of the Secretariat for the Unity of Christians and was created cardinal. He was the founder of the Catholic Conference for Ecumenical Questions. An expert at the council.

back. The patriarch of Constantinople, Athenagoras,[24] personally very favorable, does not want to break the union of the patriarchates he has accomplished, which is why he is yielding to the refusal; but at least he will send a personal representative.[25] There will also be some others coming in a personal capacity: thus, someone from the Saint-Serge Institute[26] (Russian Orthodox, in Paris), probably Bishop Cassien[27] (the rector) himself.

According to Fr. Rouquette, the Dutch bishops might not have any influence, because they are too violent. It is also commonly said that in order to neutralize the French, one only needs to get them a little excited; then they speak too sharply and are ruined. Fr. Rouquette regrets that the French episcopate has taken so little interest in the preparation for the council and has made no serious effort to explain it. He also fears that Archbishop Felici, secretary general, does not understand the necessity of keeping the journalists, who have come in great numbers, many of them not Catholic, well informed. Before leaving for Loreto, the pope is supposed to have said in a speech that there had been many difficulties over the origin of this pilgrimage, but that was unimportant: we believe in the incarnation of the Word and his dwelling among us. *L'Osservatore Romano* deleted that passage. In Loreto, John XXIII reportedly never entered the Santa Casa.[28]

At 5 P.M., the profession of faith and the taking of the oath by the periti and the officials in the Pauline chapel. Greeted a number of acquaintances there. Next saw at the Curia the Assistant, who urged me to see Father General and talk to him seriously about conciliar matters.

---

[24] Athenagoras (1886–1972), ecumenical patriarch, elected in 1948, spiritual leader of the Orthodox Church. He worked for the rapprochement of Eastern and Western Christians and met Paul VI, in Jerusalem, in January 1964.

[25] The patriarchate of Constantinople was officially absent, but Bishop Cassian (Bezobrazov) and Father Alexander Schmemann, who were present, were under its authority.

[26] Institute of Orthodox theology, founded in 1925 in Paris. The institute played an important part in the ecumenical movement.

[27] Sergei Bezobrazov, Bishop Cassien (1892–1965), Russian exegete, teacher at the Saint Sergius Institute, whose rector he became in 1947. He was the guest of the Secretariat for Unity at the first three sessions.

[28] According to tradition, the house of the Virgin, in Nazareth, which the angels were supposed to have transported from Galilee to Croatia, then to Loreto, at the end of the thirteenth century. This pilgrimage of the pope to Loreto and Assisi, on October 4, 1962, was the first trip made by a supreme pontiff outside his State in more than a century. The rumor reported here by Father de Lubac, and also appearing in the November 1962 issue of *Études*, is false: John XXIII did indeed enter the Santa Casa.

Visit from Msgr. A. Glorieux.[29] He finds the texts of the Theological Commission rather voluminous; I told him that I found them rather unsuccessful. He too is worried abut the composition of the conciliar commissions, etc.

Fr. Jean Daniélou arrived this afternoon. As the theologian of Bishop Veuillot, coadjutor of Paris, he has already worked with him for a month. Bishop Veuillot is unhappy with the theological schemas. Cardinal Feltin[30] had Fr. Le Blond[31] make a report on them, which Fr. H. Holstein[32] put into Latin.

Tuesday, October 9, 1962. – This morning saw Fr. Zore[1] (Yugoslav, censor at the Curia), in order to give back to him the issue of *Divinitas* borrowed for me by Fr. Davy.[2] – Fr. Henri Rondet arrived in Rome. There are complaints from different sides about a point of order with regard to the council: "Commissionis praeses unum ex conciliaribus theologis seu canonistis expertis eligit, qui secretarii munere fungatur"[3] (art. 6, no. 5). Since the president of each commission is in fact a cardinal of the Roman Curia, that reinforces the domination of the Curia. Cardinal Ottaviani, president of the Commission *De doctrina fidei et morum*, has already chosen Fr. Sébastien Tromp. So, through this, the most important commission, the Holy Office would be able to dominate.

---

[29] Achille Glorieux (1910–1999), French priest, ordained in 1934. Ecclesiastical assistant of COPECIAL (Comité permanent des congrès internationaux pour l'apostolat des laïcs [Permanent committee of international congresses for the lay apostolate]), he became nuncio after the council. At the council, he was secretary of the Preparatory Commission, then of the conciliar Commission for the Lay Apostolate. An expert at the council.

[30] Maurice Feltin (1883–1975), French, ordained in 1909. Archbishop of Paris from 1949 to 1966, created cardinal in 1953.

[31] Jean-Marie Le Blond, S.J. (1899–1973), French, ordained in 1937. From 1952 to 1973 he held the chair of fundamental theology at the Institut catholique of Paris. He was one of the architects of the catechetical movement and was often consulted by the bishops for doctrinal or pastoral notes.

[32] Henri Holstein, S.J. (1906–1980), French, ordained in 1937. Secretary of the editorial staff of *Études*, he was also professor of fundamental theology at the Institut catholique of Paris from 1952 to 1973.

October 9

[1] Ivan Zore, S.J. (1893–1987), Yugoslav, ordained in 1916. Professor of theology at the Gregorian and consultor to the superior general for the Jesuit schools.

[2] Jacques Davy, S.J. (1914–1991), French. Librarian at the Jesuit Curia, then at the Gregorian from 1961 to 1973.

[3] "The president of the commission will choose a person from among the experts in theology or canon law at the council who will perform the function of secretary."

This morning Fr. Daniélou saw Msgr. Willebrands, returned from Moscow. It appears there was extensive coverage of his visit by the Russian newspapers, and it is assumed that observers will be sent. In this way, Moscow aims to become the leader of the Orthodox world.

An American priest showed me an issue of *Time* magazine, with an article: "Council of Renewal". On one page, five photos formed a horizontal band: Ottaviani – Bea – Teilhard de Chardin – Spellman[4] – Léger.[5]

The French embassy to the Vatican has made copies for us of all kinds of information: lists of names, addresses, etc.

In the afternoon, visit from "my" archbishop, Archbishop Gilbert Ramanantoanina, S.J., of Fianarantsoa. He asked me to come on Friday morning to a meeting of the bishops from Madagascar and other African nations: Fr. Chenu, O.P.,[6] will be there, as the theologian of a*[7] bishop from Madagascar.

Chatted with Fr. Jungmann and Fr. Rondet. – The Maronites are, it appears, the only branch of Eastern Christians that does not have an official "peritus". Fr. Khalifé, S.J.,[8] (from Beirut, theologian of Patriarch Meouchi)[9] came to complain to the Assistant [of the Jesuit Father General] about this, a serious insult made to the Maronites, and thus also to all Eastern Catholics ... The Assistant counseled patience.

Fr. Lucas brought me the most recent issue of *Civitas, Nouvelles de chrétienté*, a political-religious integrist bulletin, the inspiration for which comes, alas, from Solesmes (Dom G. Frénaud).[10] "Special number"

---

[4] Francis Spellman (1889–1967), American, ordained in 1916. Archbishop of New York from 1939 until his death, created cardinal in 1946. Member of the Board of Presidency of the council and of the Coordinating Commission.

[5] Paul-Émile Léger, P.S.S. (1904–1991), Canadian, ordained in 1929. Created cardinal in 1953, archbishop of Montreal from 1950 to 1968. Following that, he left for Cameroon as a missionary. Member of the Doctrinal Commission.

[6] Marie-Dominique Chenu, O.P. (1895–1990), French. Professor then regent of the faculties of Le Saulchoir from 1920 to 1942, the date on which his booklet *Une école de théologie: Le Saulchoir* was put on the Index. He was the inspiration for numerous overtures in theology: Catholic Action, priest worker movement, etc. At the council, he was the private expert of Claude Rolland, Bishop of Antsirabe (Madagascar).

[7] * "Another".

[8] Ignace Khalifé, S.J. (1914–1998), Lebanese, ordained in 1943. Expert at the council.

[9] Pierre-Paul Meouchi (1894–1975), Lebanese, ordained in 1917. Maronite Patriarch of Antioch from 1955 until his death, created cardinal in 1965. Member of the Commission for Eastern Churches.

[10] Georges Frénaud, O.S.B. (1903–1967), French, ordained in 1932. Professor of dogmatic theology at the monastery of Solesmes and prior from 1961. He was the theologian of Dom Jean Prou.

(Sept. 27, 1962) on: the *Monitum* of June 30, 1962. The lead piece was a translation of an article by Fr. Cordovani, O.P.,[11] from March 1948, against evolution. Next, quotation of a long passage written by R. Garaudy[12] on Teilhard, etc. 48 pages, in 2 columns. Twice, the anonymous author of the issue speaks of "The Hymn *to* the Universe"[13] by Teilhard. A reminder of all those who have written against Teilhard. My book is criticized. Opposed to T. and evolution: Boule,[14] Piveteau,[15] and ... Salet and Lafont.[16] The article is happy to point out that the mysticism of T. "made Mr. Jean Rostand[17] smile". It says that "the Piltdown ape-man[18] still remained an ape for Fr. T.", etc. Professor Lemoine[19] is quoted at great length. Frs. Le Blond and Fessard are also criticized. The author says that, with the mystical views of T., "the risk is great that in the life of love that should be the Christian life, many will think themselves authorized to choose 'other lovers than the one in the Canticle', as is said regarding the system of Madame Guyon",[20] etc. Quotation

---

[11] Mariano Cordovani, O.P. (1883–1950), Italian. Master of the Sacred Palace from 1936, he was particularly opposed to the theology of Le Saulchoir.

[12] Roger Garaudy, born in 1913. French intellectual, a Stalinist communist, then a Marxist dissident, he was sympathetic to Catholicism, then converted to Islam. He made particular mention of Teilhard in *Perspectives de l'homme, existentialisme, pensée catholique, marxisme* (1959). H. de Lubac made allusion to this work in *La Pensée religieuse du père Pierre Teilhard de Chardin* and spoke of a "complete betrayal" of the work of Teilhard.

[13] This refers to a work by Teilhard, actually entitled *Hymne de l'universe* (hymn *of* the universe) and published in 1961.

[14] Marcellin Boule, French prehistorian who was Teilhard de Chardin's professor. He is known in particular for his study of the Neanderthal man.

[15] Jean Piveteau (1889–1991), French paleontologist, professor at the Sorbonne, he studied the problems of evolution and of human origins.

[16] Georges Salet and Louis Lafont, authors of *L'Évolution régressive* (Èd. franciscaines, 1943).

[17] Jean Rostand (1894–1977), biologist, naturalist, and French writer, he was especially interested in genetics.

[18] Fossil remains that were discovered in 1912 in England, near Piltdown. These remains, put forward as the missing link between apes and men, stirred up lively controversy until scientific analyses proved definitively in 1959 that the remains were a fake, combining a human skull with the jawbone of an ape. Teilhard had participated in some subsequent discoveries with Dawson and Woodward. The person responsible for the hoax was never clearly identified.

[19] Paul Lemoine (1878–1940), French geologist, professor at the Muséum national d'histoire naturelle. He co-edited volume 5 of the French encyclopedia dedicated to living things (1938). Among other things, he wrote there: "Evolution is a sort of dogma that its priests no longer believe but that they maintain for their people."

[20] Jeanne-Marie Bouvier de La Motte, called Madame Guyon (1646–1717), French mystic and follower of quietism, who in particular devoted a work to the Song of Solomon: *Cantique des cantiques de Salomon, interprété selon le sens mystique* (1688).

from an article by Fr. Genevois, O.P.,[21] from the *Courrier de la Mayenne* (the article appeared in various newspapers). In a note, p. 23: "Perhaps one ought to recall here that the Rev. Fr. de Lubac met with some just contradictions precisely on the subject of the gratuity of the supernatural when his work *Surnaturel* was published. Cf. D. Frénaud, *La Pensée catholique*, nos. 5 and 6. (Note from *Civitas* [= Note of Dom Frénaud])."

Wednesday, October 10, 1962. – This morning, wasted a lot of time at the secretariat of the council, trying to pick up the card that would give me the right to enter Saint Peter's. They finally ended up putting me off until the day after tomorrow.

Encountered Archbishop Perrin of Carthage; he also declared himself unhappy with the dogmatic schemas. It was the same story with Bishop Maziers, auxiliary at Saint-Étienne.[1] Met with Archbishop Sartre, S.J.,[2] for a long time. He is interested in the composition of the commissions; for the Commission *De fide*, he would like Bishop Volk, the new bishop of Mainz, former professor of dogma at Münster, to be proposed; he would bring Fr. Rahner with him; and, for France, Archbishop Veuillot, who would bring along Fr. Daniélou. Yesterday, at the Bellarmino, Archbishop Sartre saw Fr. Édouard Dhanis; the latter questioned him about what was thought of the doctrinal schemas, asking him if it would not be advisable to rewrite them completely. I recounted to Archbishop S. various incidents from the preparatory commission, and we talked about the psychology of the Roman theologian, especially of the theologian of the Holy Office. At the Bellarmino yesterday, we celebrated Fr. René Arnou's 60th anniversary in the Society.

Fr. Daniélou, very active, has already organized a small secretariat. I met him again, along with Fr. G. Martelet, who has come as the theologian of Bishop Véniat, S.J. (of Fort Archambault, Chad). Archbishop Dalmais[3] (of Fort-Lamy, Chad), Bishop Véniat, and Fr. Martelet are

[21] Albert Genevois, O.P. (Marie-Albert in religion) (1908–1983), French, ordained in 1933. Chaplain of different movements, including the ACE [a subgroup of French Catholic Action], at the monastery in Bordeaux.

March 10

[1] The diocese of Saint-Étienne was not established until Pentecost 1971, but one of the auxiliaries of Lyon used to reside in Saint-Étienne and was in charge of this archdeaconry.

[2] Victor Sartre, S.J. (1902–2000), French, ordained in 1932. Archbishop of Tananarive (Madagascar) from 1955 to 1960. Vice-president of the conciliar Commission for the Missions.

[3] Paul Dalmais, S.J. (1917–1994), French, ordained in 1949. Bishop, then archbishop of Fort-Lamy (Chad) from 1957 to 1980.

staying at the Albergo Caesar Augustus (on the other side of the Ponte Milvio); their room and board is being paid for by the Holy See – except for the wine.

Before the noon examination,[4] the Father Substitute (Boussuge) drove us (Frs. Rondet, Daniélou, and me) to greet the Fr. General. The latter told us his feelings about the schemas of the preparatory commissions: too long, bookish. He intends to meet with each one of us again, once the first few days have passed.

Oscar Cullmann[5] has come to Rome as a personal guest at the council. He saw the schema *De fontibus revelationis*[6] and told Fr. Daniélou his opinion of it: "It is ridiculous and infantile. If the council were to adopt such a text, it would be the end of any hope for a rapprochement between Catholics and Protestants."

In the parlor, saw the young doctor (in philosophy) from Alessandria, from Don Rossi's[7] association (Assisi, "Civitas Christiana"). He questioned me about the council. I made a few innocuous remarks in reply to him. – Visit from Fr. Octave Philip, from our province of Lyon, bursar of the Gregorian. A few days ago, the rector of the Gregorian[8] received a phone call from a *monsignore* from the Congregation for Seminaries and Universities, complaining that my book on Teilhard was on sale in the bookstore there. Fr. Philip had to remove the book, which is no longer on display.

Fr. Jungmann told me that he is very happy with the visit he just made this morning to Cardinal König. The cardinal had asked him to greet me on his behalf. This afternoon, the German bishops are to meet with their experts. The French bishops have already met, but without calling on their experts to attend (at least not on Fr. Daniélou or on me).

Early in the afternoon, Fr. Hirschmann, S.J.,[9] professor of moral theology at Frankfurt, came to see the two of us, Fr. Daniélou and me. He was charged by the German bishops to ask us about the list that the

---

[4] He is referring to the examination of conscience.

[5] Oscar Cullmann (1902–1999), Lutheran theologian and exegete, particularly interested in the ecumenical movement. Guest of the Secretariat for Unity.

[6] "On the sources of revelation".

[7] Giovanni Rossi (1887–1975), Italian. A Milanese priest, he founded, in Assisi, in 1939, the association whose exact name is *Pro civitate christiana*, which forms young laypeople for ministry.

[8] Pablo Muñoz-Vega.

[9] Johannes Hirschmann, S.J. (1908–1981), German, ordained in 1936. Professor of moral and pastoral theology at the Jesuit scholasticate of Saint George in Frankfurt. An expert at the council.

French bishops had delivered to them through Msgr. Gouet[10] (secretary of the episcopate), a list of the bishops capable of being elected to the various commissions. – Fr. Grillmeier,[11] professor of dogma at Frankfurt, also an expert, arrived yesterday. He showed me the Observations signed by several German bishops on the schemas of the first printed volume. They are extremely harsh on the doctrinal schemas. I made a copy of some of them.

Fr. Daniélou was invited privately by some of the French bishops. It appears that the draft of a sort of manifesto has been submitted to them, to be proclaimed by the council at its opening. According to them, this text was written by Fr. Chenu, Cardinal Liénart approved it, and it has already been proposed to the Holy Father.[12] Fr. Daniélou appeared very reticent; according to what he told me about it, I would be, too. I fear something demagogic, of a naturalistic spirit in its tone – as if the Church, seeing that she can no longer interest people with the message of Christ, the Christian mystery, were looking for an alternative activity in order to survive. Everything must follow from the Faith; it is the Faith that must be explicit and foremost, especially in a council.

A joke is making the rounds in ecclesiastical Rome. Two changes, they say, will soon be made to the *Credo*. Since the "opening to the left" in Italy, we will have to say: "... sedet ad sinistram Patris"; and since the Constitution on Latin: "... qui locutus est latine per prophetas".[13]

This Wednesday evening, during recreation, I chatted with Fr. Grillmeier, who is preparing a report on Fr. Henri Crouzel's[14] two theses on Origen. He is very interested in the large bibliography on Origen that Crouzel has prepared.

---

[10] Julien Gouet (1910–1988), French, ordained in 1937. Director of the general secretariat of the French episcopate. Expert at the council beginning with the second session.

[11] Aloys Grillmeier, S.J. (1910–1998), German, ordained in 1937. Professor of fundamental theology and of dogmatics at the Jesuit scholasticate of Saint George (Frankfurt) from 1950 to 1978. He was created cardinal in 1994. At the council, he served as expert for Wilhelm Kempf, bishop of Limburg, and was a council expert beginning with the second session.

[12] This refers to a message to the world whose outline had been drawn up by Father Chenu, later assisted by Fr. Congar. Cardinal Liénart wished that this message might be taken into account. The message approved by the council on October 20, however, when compared to Father Chenu's draft, had clearly been revised.

[13] "Who is seated at the left hand of the Father; who has spoken in Latin through the prophets" [allusion to the Nicene Creed].

[14] Henri Crouzel, S.J. (1919–2003), French. Professor of moral philosophy, then of patristics at the Institut catholique of Toulouse.

Thursday, October 11, 1962. – This morning, it was raining; but the sun would quickly return. I left with Fr. Daniélou at 7:15 A.M. We entered the Vatican by the bronze door, then went into the basilica. We were led to one of the galleries reserved for the periti and a few other groups: the left nave, second gallery from the transept. There, before and during the ceremony, exchanged a few words with Dom Vagaggini, O.S.B.,[1] from Saint Anselm's Abbey, and Msgr. G. Nabuco,[2] from Brazil. Both of them were members of the Liturgical Commission. They were annoyed because the secretary of their commission has been replaced, and he has even been recently removed from his position as professor at the Lateran. They are referring to Fr. Annibal Bugnini,[3] a Lazarist; some were unhappy with the direction taken by this commission.[*4] – Also met in the gallery the abbot[5] of the Cistercian abbey of Hauterive (near Fribourg, Switzerland) as well as a young Cistercian[6] I had met before, who has just finished his thesis on Saint Bernard and biblical inspiration and who is to leave soon for the United States (Texas), where he will teach theology in a university that in particular gathers together Hungarian refugees.

An impressive ceremony. Sadness, despite it all, thinking about the contrast with the real situation of the Church in the world. Interminable procession of bishops, then the papal retinue, etc. Mass of the Holy Spirit celebrated by Cardinal Tisserant. Gestures of obedience, oaths, professions of faith. The pope, on his knees, was the first to make the profession of faith. The Gospel. Chants in Eastern languages (Greek, Arabic, ...). Fine speech by the pope,[7] very personal, read in a strong

---

October 11

[1] Cipriano Vagaggini, O.S.B. (1909–1999), Italian, ordained in 1934. Theologian, specialist in liturgy, he was one of the figures of the liturgical renewal of the Catholic Church. He was a council expert.

[2] Joaquim Nabuco (1894–1968), ordained in 1918, Brazilian liturgist. Consultor to the Sacred Congregation of Rites for the section concerned with the liturgy. A council expert.

[3] Annibale Bugnini, C.M. (1912–1982), Italian, ordained in 1936. He was secretary of the Congregation for Divine Worship from 1969 to 1976 and apostolic pro-nuncio to Iran from 1976 to 1982. Secretary of the Preparatory Liturgical Commission, he did not continue in that capacity during the conciliar phase but was replaced by Ferdinando Antonelli, though he was a member of the conciliar Liturgical Commission. An expert at the council.

[4] * "Unhappy with the direction that he was giving to this commission".

[5] Dom Bernard Kaul (1919–2001). Superior of Hauterive beginning in 1950 and canonically abbot in 1959.

[6] Denis Farkasfalvy, *L'Inspiration de l'Écriture sainte dans la théologie de saint Bernard* (Rome: Herder, 1964).

[7] *Gaudet Mater Ecclesia*. In this speech, John XXIII rejected the pessimistic visions of the situation of the Church and asked that the council, rather than condemning, might make the Good News

voice. The grouping of the altar under the baldachino, with the papal throne, etc., produced a very fine effect. At the back, the Sedia, with all the men-servants in red, too imperial, almost shocking. John XXIII was well guarded: on his right, Cardinal Ottaviani; in front of him, handling the censer (in one of those ridiculous Roman surplices, pleated and curled), Msgr. Piolanti. – On leaving, in Saint Peter's Square, met Father Paul Chevallier,[8] from Gap, who has come for a few days with his bishop.[9]

The speech of Domenico de Domenichi,[10] as he came into the conclave that was to elect Pius II,[11] August 16, 1458: "Romana curia in multis deformata est, et quis reformabit eam?"[12]

Father Hirschmann, who is very well informed, gave me three pieces of news this afternoon: 1. Different episcopal lists are circulating among the bishops, proposing names for the conciliar commissions; two opposing tendencies can be observed. – 2. A few days ago, the pope apparently was very angry about the measure taken by the Holy Office with regard to Fr. Karl Rahner. – 3. It was Cardinals Bea and Döpfner who supposedly persuaded the pope to indicate clearly, in his opening address, the orientations of the council.

Around 7 P.M., a crowd gathered in St. Peter's Square. John XXIII spoke from his window. He got a laugh; he was applauded. Much vigor and kindness. For example: "Now, you are going to return to your homes, you will hug and kiss your children, and you will tell them that it is a hug and kiss from the pope."

Friday, October 12, 1962. – The whole morning, after a detour through Saint Anselm, where the African bishops were meeting, I was in a meeting at the parish of Saint Chrysogonus, at the Trinitarians' house, with the bishops from Madagascar (there are 15 of them) and the

---

more present to men by means of an *aggiornamento*. For a critical edition, see A. Melloni, "L'allocuzione *Gaudet Mater Ecclesia* (11 ottobre 1962), Sinossi critica dell'allocuzione", in *Fede Tradizione Profezia: Studi su Giovanni XXIII e sul Vaticano II* (Brescia, 1984).

[8] Paul Chevallier (1914–1996), French, ordained in 1938. Former professor of philosophy and theology, he was curate and dean of the cathedral of Gap from 1956 on. In 1965 he became vice-rector of the Catholic Faculties of Lyon.

[9] Georges Jacquot (1904–1970), French, ordained in 1929, bishop of Gap from 1961 to 1966, then archbishop of Marseille until his death.

[10] Domenico de Domenichi (1416–1478), Italian, ordained in 1441. He was named bishop of Torcello in 1448. He stood out as an authority on theological matters, and, during the conclave of 1458, preached firmly about the need for a reform of the Church.

[11] Enea Silvio Piccolomini (1405–1464), Italian, elected pope on August 19, 1458.

[12] "The Roman curia is distorted on numerous points, and who will reform it?"

Apostolic Delegate, Msgr. Pirozzi,[1] whom I knew at the nunciature in Paris. Father Chenu was there. We spent a lot of time making up lists of possible candidates for the elections to the various commissions. Toward noon, Archbishop Sartre arrived from Saint Anselm, with the lists drawn up by the Africans. We got nowhere, for the most part. At 11 A.M., the extraordinary ambassador of Madagascar[2] sent for the opening of the council came to greet the bishops; short speeches were exchanged; there were requests made on each side for prayers, etc. The atmosphere was simple, cordial, rather touching, a little amusing. Photos were taken on the terrace of the monastery. Refreshments. – Lunch at St. Chrysogonus.

The afternoon was very full. Still impossible to get my card allowing entry to the council, for which I have been asking since Monday; the secretariat was closed all afternoon. A visit, at the Borgo, from P. Dubois-Dumée.[3] Visit from a French priest from SAM (Société auxiliaire des missions), sent by a group of Indian bishops who want me to speak at one of their meetings. Fr. Martelet read me a brief report on the faith and the problem of civilizations, rapidly written at the request of some African bishops. Fr. Daniélou, who has seen a lot of people, thinks that tomorrow the bishops could ask for a delay in the elections to the commissions, so as to have the time to clarify their vote. This morning he met for an hour with Cardinal Bea, clear-sighted, open, courageous. Bea told him, regarding the members of the Holy Office: "They would have condemned me a long time ago if I were not a cardinal." That reminds me of something I heard Fr. Tromp say about Bea: "He takes advantage of the fact that he is a cardinal ..."

Still impossible to find the time to write a few remarks on the schemas of the first printed volume. I only have rough notes.

With Frs. Daniélou and Martelet, arrived by taxi at the embassy, Villa Bonaparte (via Piave), at 7 P.M. Saw a number of bishops, prelates, religious, various laymen, journalists. Cardinal Marella expressed to me his very warm satisfaction at seeing me in Rome. Cardinal Tisserant told me that the pope had spoken to him about me and declared to

---

October 12

[1] Felice Pirozzi (1908–1975), Italian, ordained in 1931. Apostolic delegate to Madagascar from 1960 to 1967.

[2] Pierre Razafy Andriamihaingo (1914–1997), Madagascar's ambassador to the Holy See from 1961 to 1965, and head of the Special Mission from Madagascar on the occasion of Vatican Council II.

[3] Jean-Pierre Dubois-Dumée (1918–2001), French journalist, assistant editor of *Informations catholiques internationales* and *La Vie catholique illustrée*.

him his wish that I be an expert. The cardinal himself congratulated me with conviction on my book on Teilhard and told me that he was working actively to protect Teilhard from condemnation. Several other bishops spoke to me with great sympathy about Teilhard and my book. Saw Bishop Collini,[4] recently named coadjutor of Ajaccio, sad to leave Tunis. With Bishop de Courrèges[5] (Montauban) and Bishop Barthe[6] (Fréjus), I spoke about Msgr. Bruno de Solages, whom the bishops*[7] should draw out of his isolation for the general good of the Church, perhaps for the council. – A moment after, I met Cardinal Marella again, accompanied by Roger Schutz[8] and Max Thurian[9] (Taizé), personal guests of John XXIII. Chatted with Oscar Cullmann, who said he was horrified by the schemas that spoke of the Bible; I answered him that many of us were also critical of them. Greeted the Dominicans Gagnebet, Labourdette, Congar, Hamer,[10] Camelot.[11] Fr. Maurice Villain,[12] always sensitive, told me the reactions of the Protestant observers to the opening ceremony (they were placed so as to have a good view of the pope and their backs almost turned to the altar where Cardinal Tisserant was celebrating Mass. But the layout of the choir in St. Peter's makes any other orientation difficult).

---

[4]André Collini (1921–2003), French, ordained in 1947. Coadjutor of Ajaccio from September 1962. He was then bishop of Ajaccio and, from 1978 to 1996, archbishop of Toulouse.

[5]Louis de Courrèges d'Ustou (1894–1979), French, ordained in 1922. Bishop of Montauban from 1947 to 1970.

[6]Gilles de Barthe (1906–1993), French, ordained in 1930. Bishop of Monaco from 1953 to 1962, then of Fréjus-Toulon from 1962 to 1983.

[7]*"French".

[8]Roger Schutz (1915–2005). French pastor, founder of the Taizé ecumenical community and prior of the community. Guest of the Secretariat for Unity at Vatican II.

[9]Max Thurian (1921–1996), Reformed Swiss pastor and theologian, subprior of the Taizé community. Guest of the Secretariat for Unity at Vatican II. He was ordained a priest of the Catholic Church in 1987.

[10]Jérôme Hamer, O.P. (1916–1996), Belgian. Rector of the faculties of Le Saulchoir until 1962, then assistant of the master general for the French-speaking provinces. Secretary of the Secretariat for the Unity of Christians from 1969 to 1973, then of the Congregation for the Doctrine of the Faith from 1973 to 1984, he was created cardinal in 1985 and became prefect of the Congregation for Religious and Secular Institutes, a position he held from 1985 to 1992. At the council, he was the consultor to the Secretariat for Unity and an expert from 1962 on.

[11]Pierre-Thomas Camelot, O.P. (1901–1993), French. Professor of patristics and of the history of doctrines at the faculties of le Saulchoir. Expert at the council.

[12]Maurice Villain, S.M. (1900–1977), French, ordained in 1927. After having been a professor at the seminaries for missions to Oceania, near Lyon, he dedicated himself totally to ecumenical work, in particular through the leadership of the "Dombes group". Personal expert of a Marist bishop from the South Pacific, he also reported on the council for the journal *Rythmes du monde*.

At the embassy, met Numa de Brisis, who invited me to lunch on Sunday.

Fr. Rondet went this afternoon with Archbishop Dalmais to pay a visit to the Melchite patriarch Maximos.[13] The patriarch did not attend the opening ceremony, because they would not accord him precedence over the cardinals; not out of a superficial concern over precedence, it was explained to us, but because the Orthodox have their eyes on the Eastern Churches united to Rome: if they yield their rights, hopes for union will be lost. Moreover, the patriarch has announced that if the Orthodox unite with Rome, he will step down and give place to the leader of the largest community.

The two observers from Moscow[14] arrived this morning.

Wladimir d'Ormesson[15] told me that the issue of *La Croix* that arrived today in Rome contains an article written by him: "What Catholics Expect from the Council". He wrote it at the request of Fr. A. Wenger,[16] on the condition that he have a free hand. He told me that he quoted a text from Fr. Teilhard in it that he took from my book (from a letter to Father Gaudefroy).[17]

This morning, Fr. Chenu explained to the bishops from Madagascar the genesis of the draft of the council's inaugural declaration. He was apparently the author of the first draft; Cardinal Liénart adopted it as his own; several foreign cardinals, including Suenens,[18] rallied behind it.

---

[13] Maximos IV Saigh (1878–1967), Syrian, ordained in 1905. Melchite Patriarch of Antioch from 1947, made cardinal in 1965. Member of the Commission for Eastern Churches.

[14] This refers to the archpriest Vitalij Borovoj, professor of theology, who had been given the task, in 1961, of obtaining membership in the Ecumenical Council of Churches for the patriarchate of Moscow and who represented the patriarchate at Geneva, and to the archimandrite Vladimir Kotliarov, vice-superior of the Russian religious mission of Jerusalem.

[15] Wladimir d'Ormesson (1888–1973), French journalist, writer, and diplomat. He was named ambassador to the Holy See in May 1940, but was removed from the diplomatic corps by Vichy. Nevertheless, he regained his ambassadorship in 1948 and occupied this position until 1956.

[16] Antoine Wenger, born in 1919, French Assumptionist priest, ordained in 1943. After having taught Oriental theology at the Catholic faculties of Lyon, he became editor in chief of *La Croix* in 1962 and reported on the four sessions of the council; four volumes of his chronicles of the council were published by Éd. du Centurion (1963 to 1966).

[17] Christophe Gaudefroy (1878–1971), French priest. A mineralogist, he carried on a correspondence with Teilhard de Chardin.

[18] Léon Joseph Suenens (1904–1996), Belgian, ordained in 1927. Archbishop of Mechelen-Brussels from 1961 to 1979, created cardinal in 1962. Member of the Preparatory Commission for Bishops and of the Central Preparatory Commission. Member of the Secretariat for Extraordinary Affairs. Member of the Coordinating Commission, he was also one of the four moderators of the council named in September 1963.

The pope is supposed to be studying it. One of the goals would be, if I understand correctly, to give to those outside an impression of harmony within the council.*[19]

This afternoon, the German, Austrian, and Swiss bishops all*[20] gathered around Fr. Karl Rahner, whom they had asked to give them a talk. On their side, the French bishops met again; they only, by successive votes, drew up a list of French names that they are proposing for the commissions. One of them is supposed to have said: "We are going to see to it that this council is not the council of experts."

Saturday, October 13, 1962. – Under a pounding rainstorm, at Saint Peter's with Father Jungmann. We sat down in one of the galleries. At 9 A.M., Mass of the Holy Spirit, celebrated by the archbishop of Florence (Florit).[1] Prayer ("Adsumus", of Spanish origin, Saint Isidore of Seville?) by Cardinal Tisserant, president. It was immediately announced that they were going to proceed to the vote on the commissions. Each bishop was asked to put 16 names on each of the 10 sheets of paper he had received, for the 10 commissions. The bishops had already started to fill out their sheets. But Cardinal Liénart, who was at the table with the Board of Presidency, got up; in a very clear, firm voice he said that he at least, and some others, were uneasy, since they had not had time to become better informed. He then asked for a delay. Much applause. He immediately made a positive proposal: that each episcopal commission (conference) draw up a list to propose to the others, etc. He pointed out three advantages of this procedure: 1. The bishops would have time to become better informed; 2. they would give each other proof of their mutual confidence; 3. the vote would be more rapid, and time would be saved. More applause, very hearty. There was an intervention by Cardinals König and Frings,[2] who declared themselves to be in favor of Liénart's proposal. They were applauded. After one or two minutes, Archbishop Felici, general secretary, took the floor to declare that the Board of Presidency (which had just deliberated quickly on the spot)

---

[19]* "(There are also other, slightly different explanations.)"

[20]* "All" has been crossed out.

October 13

[1] Ermenegildo Florit (1901–1985), Italian, ordained in 1925. Coadjutor bishop of Florence from 1954 to 1962, then archbishop of Florence from 1962 to 1977, created cardinal in 1965. Member of the Doctrinal Commission.

[2] Josef Frings (1887–1978), German, ordained in 1910. Archbishop of Cologne from 1942 to 1969, made cardinal in 1946. Member of the Board of Presidency.

supported the proposal and asked that the Fathers come together for the vote on Tuesday morning, the 16th, at 9 A.M. There was more applause, and everyone left.

Canon Martimort[3] (Institut catholique of Toulouse), who was beside me in the gallery, whispered to me that he had himself suggested that procedure to Cardinal Liénart. He was pleased. Another said: "That was imperative; otherwise the bishops would have had to vote haphazardly." On that, a prelate (a relator from the Congregation of Rites), smiling, said: "That was precisely what they wanted." (They = certain Romans, the Holy Office). This dramatic little episode is spoken of as a victory of the bishops over the Holy Office. Other victories will no doubt be more difficult.

Descending from the gallery, I met my former student from the Faculty at Lyon, Bishop Charles de la Brousse,[4] coadjutor of Dijon. He took me to Santa Marta (beside the Basilica), where he is lodging with 7 or 8 French bishops. They met in the parlor. They asked me my opinion on the dogmatic schemas, with which they are unhappy. I gave them some explanations and recommended that they get in touch with the German bishops: it would be pointless to prepare several alternative schemas separately. But they are having a good deal of trouble getting together to work with the other French bishops. They are divided in Rome between 4 principal groups (the French Seminary, Saint-Louis des Français, Procure de Saint Sulpice, Santa Marta) and various other residences. And then again, they sometimes have opposing tendencies ... Bishop Charles de la Brousse passed on to me some observations that Mr. Mouroux, who remained in Dijon, had given to him.

On leaving St. Peter's, I had met Father Balić, O.F.M., who said to me: "These Frenchmen! Come on, children of the Fatherland, the day of glory has arrived!" An allusion to Cardinal Liénart. It seemed to me that Fr. Balić's laughter was a little forced.

An insufficient number of places was prepared for the bishops in Saint Peter's. They had to put a certain number of them in the first row of the galleries.

---

[3] Aimé Georges Martimort (1911–2000), French. Professor of history of the liturgy at the theology faculty of the Institut catholique of Toulouse, co-director of the Centre de pastorale liturgique until 1965. Consultor to the Preparatory Commission for the Liturgy. Expert from 1962.

[4] Charles de la Brousse (1907–1985), French, ordained in 1937. Coadjutor bishop of Dijon from 1962 to 1964, then bishop of Dijon from 1964 to 1974.

In the afternoon, I finished writing some Remarks on the "Constitutio dogmatica de deposito fidei pure custodiendo".[5] Fr. Rondet helped me translate them into Latin. – Cardinal Gerlier (Lyon) showed Fr. Daniélou the letter he is addressing to Cardinal Cicognani, secretary of state, against the schemas of the Theological Commission.

Everyone is wondering what the lists produced by the bishops' conferences will be, what will be the tendencies of the commissions, on what the pope's choices will be based (his personal choices or the choices of the Curia?).

Received a visit from a young Spanish priest, a professor of Church history at the Gregorian. With an ardor that was a bit carried away, he expressed his wish that the council would put an end to the integrism that currently reigns in the Curia; otherwise, he told me, we will be lost for a long time. He thought it very important that it be decided that no one will be able to be condemned without a hearing; that is wise; but the Holy Office has got around that difficulty in advance, by taking or forcing others to take all sorts of measures that are not official condemnations, that do not stir up great collective emotions, and are all the more effective by the fact that their victims are Catholics of the better sort, who spontaneously submit. – The arrogant rut in which a clan of Roman theologians is mired is equalled only by the suffocating system that it tries to make prevail – knowing full well today that it is acting against the desire of the Holy Father.

A priest from Chicago said to me: I was recently on the Rue de Grenelle, in Paris; three times I asked an elderly priest: "Ubinam possum dicere missam?" He did not understand. Finally he said to me, looking me straight in the face: "Si vis loqui latine, forsan potero tibi respondere."[6] Let us hope that the diversity of accents does not make dialogue as difficult for the council Fathers.

Sunday, October 14, 1962. – This morning, typed out my remarks on the second doctrinal schema, *De deposito fidei* on Father Rondet's typewriter ... He is preparing a more complete Latin edition of them.

Around noon, Numa de Brisis came to get me to take me by car into the Sabine hills, near Tivoli, where he lives in what used to be a Franciscan monastery, Saint Antonio, whose foundations were supposed to

---

[5] "Dogmatic Constitution on the Deposit of Faith to Be Preserved in All Its Purity".

[6] "Where can I say Mass? – If you will speak in Latin, perhaps I can answer you."

have been Horace's villa. (Chateaubriand speaks about this in his Letter
to Mr. de Fontanes.)[1] Madame de Brisis is Anglican. At table, there was
an old Italian baroness, who was very well acquainted with all the work
of Teilhard (she had been reading his typewritten works[2] for a long
time), and Msgr. Gaston Courtois,[3] superior of the Sons of Charity. We
spoke about ecumenism and about the council, the missionary bishops,
etc. Anecdotes about the Holy Father. Msgr. Courtois told me that, in
Paris, the nuncio Roncalli had asked him for information on Teilhard
and on me.

I returned to the Borgo S. Spirito around 4 P.M. Finished my typing.
Conversation with Fr. Daniélou; I saw his remarks on the doctrinal
schemas. He is already working on a counter-plan, which perhaps will
be combined with the one we believe Fr. Rahner is preparing. Next I
saw Archbishop Dalmais, who is studying the schemas with Fr. Rondet. He told me how the African bishops were organizing, in view of
Tuesday's vote. He and the group of Africans "cheered" at the session
on Saturday morning, but many of the bishops around them did not
applaud.

I brought my typewritten remarks to Santa Marta (Vatican), to give
them to Bishop Charles de la Brousse or to Bishop Vial.[4] They were
not there. The only French bishop present was Archbishop Martin[5] of
French Congo, a Spiritan; we exchanged a few words; he seemed rather
forbidding. – At Santa Marta, the sisters of Saint Vincent de Paul piously
preserve the memory of Leo XIII:[6] a whole display case of relics, in the
large parlor.

October 14

[1] Louis-Marcelin de Fontanes (1757–1821), a friend of Chateaubriand, French poet and journalist, he was also a political figure, particularly under the Consulate and the Empire. See *Lettre à
Monsieur de Fontanes sur la campagne romaine* of January 10, 1804, by Chateaubriand.

[2] Until his death in 1955, Father Teilhard could not publish the great majority of his writings
that were not strictly scientific. So he bequeathed his manuscripts to Jeanne Mortier, who saw to
their publication by Éd. du Seuil. However, long before these publications, some of his texts had
circulated in typewritten form.

[3] Gaston Courtois (1897–1970), French, procurator general of the Sons of Charity, general chaplain of the International Catholic Child Bureau, and general secretary of the Pontifical Missionary
Union of Clergy. He was also the founder of *Cœurs vaillants* in 1929, a magazine intended for young
people.

[4] Michel Vial (1906–1995), French, ordained in 1935. Coadjutor bishop of Nevers from 1961 to
1963, then bishop of Nevers from 1963 to 1966.

[5] This is obviously a mistake, since there exists neither a Spiritan nor even any bishop of this
name from the Congo.

[6] Gioacchino Raffaele Luigi Pecci (1810–1903), Italian, ordained in 1837. Elected pope in 1878.

Around 7 P.M., on Saint Peter's Square, a massive uproar: shouts, horns, sirens, in one chaotic din, until the pope at last showed himself at his window, in front of the red curtain on which his white silhouette stood out. Acclamations. Present there, awaiting the fateful moment, were men, old women, young couples; many had come on foot; others, in modest vehicles.

I wrote to Archishop Villot: "Father Daniélou told me that Your Eminence has written to Cardinal Cicognani about your concern on the subject of the doctrinal schemas whose printed text we have. This news has delighted me profoundly. For my part, I have given to Bishop Charles de la Brousse, at his request, some remarks limited almost exclusively to the second schema (*De deposito fidei* ...). If I had been able to make more copies, I would have sent you one, but Bishop Ch. de la Brousse can show you these remarks if you wish to see them. – If the council should adopt such drafts without a considerable revision, it would cause an immense disappointment in the Church – and, I fear, a great deal of scorn everywhere."

One gets used to saying: "the terrible Cardinal Ottaviani", "the rigidness of his doctrine", to call him the leader of the integrists, etc. That is an extreme oversimplification; Cardinal Ottaviani appears to me to be a strong personality, one that cannot be reduced to the traits of integrism. On the other hand, these expressions presuppose that one accepts a division that is harmful and not well-founded. There seems to be a belief that integrism is characterized by a greater firmness in the doctrine of the faith, by a refusal of any impoverishing human concessions, etc. This is false. One ought really to say: "the poverty of this doctrine", its ignorance of our great tradition. Building and multiplying barriers around a void: that is how one could almost define the action of certain theologians of the Holy Office and those like them. They hold, they vigorously defend, only:

a) diminished truths. For example, they prefer the "God of nature" to the Christian God; an abstract idea of revelation to the revelation of Christ; they teach that God reveals himself to us "in order that we might serve him", not in order that we might become his children; sin, original or actual, is nothing other than an infraction of the law, not the refusal of our divine vocation, etc.

b) human theories, most often ones that are rather recent, puerile, or outdated, to which they are just as much if not more attached than to dogma, on which they dig in their heels, and which make them forget the essential part of the Christian mystery.

Monday, October 15, 1962. – Father Paul Gauthier,[1] former student of our Faculty in Lyon and former professor at the major seminary of Dijon, currently in Nazareth, has come to Rome for a few days. He will come back here tomorrow afternoon to take me to see Patriarch Maximos. He is under the authority of the Melchite archbishop of Saint John of Acre.[2] – Father Moubarac,[3] a Maronite, has just invited me to dine this evening with Archbishop Khoury[4] of Tyre.

Throughout Rome, a large white poster bearing the initials S.P.Q.R.[5] as the title invites the population to show hospitality to the council Fathers.

A visit from Msgr. Palémon Glorieux,[6] medievalist, former rector of the Catholic Faculties of Lille, friend and theologian of Cardinal Liénart. He told me how he summarizes the text of the dogmatic schemas: inutilis-injuriosus-odiosus.[7]

It has been confirmed that the Curia had its list for the commissions all ready. Cardinal Liénart's intervention ruined their plan. The Spanish were very happy; many of the Italians were unhappy. Among the employees of the Curia, there is talk of a manifestation of "nationalism". Already, one journal article or another says that this is a first thrust from "the progressive minority". I have been told that Cardinal Ottaviani had hoped that in this first hasty vote the majority of bishops

---

October 15

[1] Paul Gauthier (1914–2002), French priest. Initially a professor at the Seminary in Dijon, he sought to share the life of the workers and left in 1957 to found in Nazareth the Companions of Jesus the Carpenter. During the council, he was in Rome, and his testimony and experience agreed closely with the thinking of numerous bishops who were concerned that the Church should be closer to the poorest and be poorer herself. He was thus at the origin of the group "Jesus, the Church and the Poor", which met during the council, without ever obtaining official status, however. He subsequently left the priesthood.

[2] Georges Hakim (1908–2001), born in Egypt, ordained in 1930. Melchite bishop of Saint John of Acre (Israel) from 1943 to 1964, then archbishop of the same place from 1964 to 1967. In 1967, he was elected Melchite patriarch of Antioch and became Maximos V.

[3] Youakim Moubarac (1924–1995), Lebanese. Maronite priest, professor at the Institut catholique of Paris, engaged in the Islamic-Christian dialogue and in the search for unity among the Antiochian Churches.

[4] Joseph Khoury (1919–1992), ordained in 1942. Maronite archbishop of Tyr from 1959 to 1992. Member of the Secretariat for Unity starting from the second session.

[5] *Senatus populusque romanus*: the senate and the Roman people.

[6] Palémon Glorieux (1892–1979), French, ordained in 1915. He was rector of the Catholic faculties in Lille and was a specialist in monastic studies. A theologian, he was one of the intellectual leaders of Action catholique spécialisée. Personal secretary and theological adviser to Cardinal Liénart.

[7] "Useless-offensive-appalling".

would not think that the cardinals were eligible (except for the 10 on the governing council). He is afraid, I am told, that a cardinal might be elected to the Commission on Faith and Morals, for this cardinal would automatically be vice-president. Now, his candidate for this position is Archbishop Parente, who will surely be on the commission: if he were not among the sixteen elected, he would be one of the 8 subsequently named by the pope.[8] Thus, with Ottaviani, Parente, and Tromp, the Holy Office would form the controlling center of the council – for the Commission *De fide et moribus* will insist on supervising everything. Also, without doubt, only a cardinal would have sufficient authority to have Fr. Rahner consulted by the commission; if Cardinal König were elected and became vice-president, he would make it his business to do so.

According to Msgr. P. Glorieux, the draft of the preliminary declaration, thoroughly revised, approved by the pope, will be submitted for the council's approval immediately after the vote on the commissions.

The Holy Father has just named four under-secretaries of the council. Archbishop Villot is one of the four.[9]

Father Paul Chevallier came to see me. He drove me to the Albergo Cesar Augustus inn, where we had lunch with Archbishop Dalmais, Bishop Véniat, Fr. Martelet. Our two bishops from Chad[10] this morning attended the meeting of French bishops at Saint-Louis des Français. They are unhappy with the lack of organization, the hesitation, the waste of time. However, there was a fortunate intervention from Bishop Ancel, criticizing the dogmatic schemas.

In the afternoon, visits to the Gregorian and the Biblical Institute. Fr. Henri Vignon laid out for me once more his position on faith and the signs of revelation. I saw Fr. Guy de Broglie there, who appeared very happy with Liénart's initiative and its success. Fr. Donatien Mollat is to study the Church in the Apocalypse this year with a small group of students. At the Biblical Institute, Fr. Stanislas Lyonnet showed me the booklet that Msgr. Spadafora, professor of exegesis at the Lateran, has just published: it is a reproduction of two review articles; the "rationalism"

---

[8] In each conciliar commission, sixteen members were to be elected by the council Fathers, and eight others named by the pope. That number was raised to nine, however.

[9] In order to assist Archbishop Felici, secretary of the council, four under-secretaries were named: Jean-Marie Villot, French, Casimiro Morcillo, Spanish, John Krol, American, and Wilhelm Kempf, German. A fifth, Philippe Nabaa, Melchite archbishop, Lebanese, was soon added.

[10] Bishop Véniat and Archbishop Dalmais.

of present-day exegetes is vigorously criticized; the author has written on the cover that the booklet is very specially reserved for the Fathers of the council; he has already distributed it to all the Italian bishops.

I am told that Saturday morning, scarcely an hour after the brief meeting of the council at Saint Peter's, Czech radio was broadcasting the story. The only two Czech bishops[11] who came to Rome are said to be closely linked to the Communist regime. – Fr. Martelet told me that, in the draft of his criticism of the schemas, he is taking as his basis the First Vatican Council. – Fr. Courtois sent me this evening a new list of addresses of bishops. – Yesterday, the pope's speech to the non-Catholic observers was very touching.

At the meeting at St. Louis des Français, this morning, Bishop Rupp[12] (Monaco) apparently intervened with some bitterness, reproaching his colleagues for not having followed the directions given by the other episcopal groups. His intervention was apparently rather poorly received.

Tuesday, October 16, 1962. – I was at Saint Peter's before 8:30 A.M. The galleries still almost empty. I took a seat at the front of the nave, in the gallery to the right: that is the best place. A little afterward, Fr. Anastasius of the Holy Rosary arrived, the superior general of the Discalced Carmelites. In Latin, I spoke to him in a friendly fashion about Fr. Philippe de la Trinité (Rambaud), who was a student of philosophy at Mongré in 1923–1924; I lamented the fact that by his booklet on "Teilhard and Teilhardism" he has associated himself with men who are of a different spirit; Fr. Anastasius did not seem unhappy with my remarks.

I saw the cardinals arrive, opposite me: poor Cardinal Gerlier, very tired; Cardinal Feltin, very heavy. – The most striking of all was the black cardinal, Rugambwa Laurean,[1] from Tanganyika; he carried himself in an almost hieratic fashion, hands joined, very erect posture, calm, impassive, with the simple air of a very great lord.

---

[11] František Tomašek (1899–1992), ordained in 1922, auxiliary bishop of Olomouc from 1949 to 1965, future archbishop of Prague, and Eduard Necsey (1892–1968), ordained in 1915, apostolic administrator of Nitra from 1949 to 1968. Member of the Commission for the Lay Apostolate.

[12] Jean Rupp (1905–1983), French, ordained in 1935. Bishop of Monaco from June 1962 to 1974.

October 16

[1] Laurean Rugambwa (1912–1997), Tanzanian, ordained in 1943. Bishop of Bukoba from 1953 to 1968, created cardinal in 1960. Archbishop of Dar-es-Salaam from 1968 to 1992. Member of the Commission for the Missions.

After the Mass, Archbishop P. Felici placed the Gospel on the altar. Cardinal Tisserant, who was presiding, said: "Eminentissimus dominus cardinalis Alfredo Ottaviani postulavit loqui."[2] Cardinal Ottaviani, who was perched up above, on the next-to-last step of the row of cardinals, descended to the microphone. In the course of a rather long intervention, he proposed a method of voting that would have the advantage, he said, of saving a great deal of time; immediately afterward they would be able to begin the "verum laborem".[3] He suggested that we proceed with a single ballot, taking account only of the relative majorities (it would be a question of adding up the votes obtained by each bishop for any commission whatever). Many bishops, he explained, did not wish to linger in Rome; their room and board was expensive; so this would save them money as well as time. He proposed that the meeting now be adjourned for a few minutes so that the Fathers could consult with each other on this subject.

Cardinal Francesco Roberti,[4] canon lawyer, almost immediately took the floor. He rejected Ottaviani's proposal as being contrary to canon law and to the rules of the council (of which Roberti is one of the authors). With such a system, those elected with a relative majority would oust those elected with an absolute majority.

The presidential Board discussed the matter for a few moments. Soon Cardinal Ruffini (who is a member of the Board) rose and declared that the rules of the council could not be changed without the approval of the Holy Father; therefore, it was necessary to submit Ottaviani's proposal to him. In conclusion, Ruffini said that he was speaking in the name of the whole Board. In fact, that was not exactly correct, for one could see Cardinal Tisserant come toward him, and, from their gestures, it seemed clear that Tisserant was reproaching him. Archbishop Felici was present, behind the two of them, at this little scene. Then Cardinal Tisserant returned to the center of the Board's long table and declared that they were going to proceed with the vote; afterward, possible simplifications will be submitted to the pope.

Then Archbishop Felici came to the rostrum. He began by proclaiming the nomination by the pope of four under-secretaries of the

---

[2] "His Eminence Cardinal Alfredo Ottaviani has asked to speak."

[3] "The real work".

[4] Francesco Roberti (1889–1977), Italian, ordained in 1913. Made cardinal in 1958, prefect of the Supreme Tribunal of the Apostolic Signature from 1958 to 1969. Member of the Coordinating Commission and president of the administrative tribunal of the council.

council: Archbishop Villot (Lyon), Bishop Kempf[5] (Limburg), Archbishop Morcillo (Saragossa),[6] and, if I understood correctly, an American.[7] Then he gave some practical advice. The Fathers who had already written out their sheet for the vote and did not wish to change anything were to give their sheet to the officials and leave, if they so wished. The others were to make out their sheets either on the spot or outside, as they wished; but all the sheets were to be handed in directly to the secretariat of the council before 6 P.M. that afternoon. Moreover, the agenda of the congregations would be indicated five days in advance, so that the Fathers would have time to study the subject and to hand in their remarks to the secretariat. The next congregation would take place on Saturday; the examination of the schema on the liturgy would commence at that time.

Cardinal Ottaviani returned to the microphone. He first made the observation that this unsigned vote was contrary to the rules of the council. Next he said that, of course, just like Cardinals Roberti and Ruffini, he thought his proposal should ultimately be submitted to the pope for approval; but, he added, the council could issue an opinion on this matter, which would be an indication for the pope. Why not vote on the matter by a show of hands? One would thus see approximately what the opinion of the Fathers was. He gave a certain impassioned vivacity to his speech. They let him talk. The Board did not intervene. But as soon as he had finished, the translators followed each other to the podium, to repeat in the various languages the instructions that had been given in Latin by Archbishop Felici (Spanish, French, English, German, Italian). Then the bishops departed in small packs, one group after another.

Exiting the basilica by the left transept, I noticed Cardinal Gerlier, standing in the bright sunlight, trying to find and calling in vain for his car. I supported him and kept him company for a few moments. So as not to keep him waiting any longer, another bishop took him in his car. I then met Bishop Vial (Nevers), who was returning to Santa Marta with

[5] Wilhelm Kempf (1906–1982), German, ordained in 1932. Bishop of Limburg from 1949 to 1981, under-secretary of the council.

[6] Casimiro Morcillo Gonzalez (1904–1971), Spanish, ordained in 1926. Archbishop of Saragossa from 1955 to 1964, then of Madrid from 1964 until his death. Member of the Preparatory Commission for Bishops. Under-secretary of the council.

[7] John Krol (1910–1996), American, ordained in 1937. Archbishop of Philadelphia from 1961 to 1988, made cardinal in 1967. Under-secretary of the council.

a few others; we chatted; they want to call on me soon, to speak about
the various schemas. Also saw Bishop ..., a Capuchin from the province
of Savoie, my former student from the Faculty of Lyon, a missionary in
Africa:[8] yet another who is very unhappy with the doctrinal schemas; if
they knew them outside, he said to me, they would make fun of them
or would be grieved about them.

Coming out onto Saint Peter's Square, I was hailed by Fr. Bidagor,[9]
a Spaniard, dean of the Faculty of Canon Law at the Gregorian; he gave
me some canonical explanations and made clear to me why canon law
is against the procedure advocated by Cardinal Ottaviani. He ended by
saying to me: "He had his list all ready."

When Fr. Bidagor left me, I came upon two Marist missionary bishops: Bishop Darmancier,[10] my former student from Lyon, and Bishop
Martin,[11] former superior of their scholasticate at Sainte-Foy. They had
with them as their theologian Fr. de Baciocchi.[12] We promised to get
together. – Returning to the Borgo, I saw Fr. ... there, a German, from
the mission from Copenhagen. He has come to Rome as the theologian
of Bishop Suhr, former Benedictine prior of St. Jerome's Abbey, where
both of them are staying.

Early in the afternoon, an hour's conversation in my room with
Father Raes,[13] former rector of the Oriental Institute, now Vatican
librarian. He gave me some information about how the library functions, then on the Roman Curia: impossible, he thinks, to reform it;
but one can restrict it to its own competence. It is, in law, a simple
organ of administration, of application of the laws. Impetus should be

---

[8] Alphonse Baud, O.F.M. Cap. (1908–1981), French, ordained in 1934. Bishop of Berberati
(Central Africa) from 1955 to 1979.

[9] Ramón Bidagor, S.J. (1894–1977), Spanish, ordained in 1919. A canon lawyer, consultor to
numerous Roman congregations. Secretary of the conciliar Commission for the Sacraments. Expert
at the council.

[10] Michel Darmancier, S.M. (1918–1984), French, ordained in 1946. Apostolic vicar of Wallis
and Futuna from 1961 to 1966.

[11] Pierre Martin, S.M. (1910–1987), French, ordained in 1939. Apostolic vicar of New Caledonia
from 1956 to 1966, then archbishop of Nouméa from 1966 to 1972.

[12] Joseph de Baciocchi-Adorno, S.M., born in 1915, French, ordained in 1940. Professor of
theology at the Catholic faculties of Lyon. Personal expert of the Marist bishops, he was a member
of the Dombes group.

[13] Alphonse Raes, S.J. (1896–1983), Belgian, ordained in 1928. Professor of Oriental ecclesiastical studies at the Oriental Pontifical Institute beginning in 1932, where he was rector from 1957
to 1962; he became prefect of the Vatican library in 1962. Expert in 1962, he became a member of
the Secretariat for Unity in 1963.

given to a body similar to what the Consistory once was, where the cardinals gave their advice to the pope. Today, no one dares to do it; it is no longer anything but a ceremony. As an example: the recent plan to move the vicariate[14] of Rome to the Lateran palace; many thought that incredible expenses would be necessary to reinforce the palace; one of the architects, present at the meeting with the pope, knew that two cardinals were very opposed to the plan: both of them acquiesced without uttering a word.

Fr. Raes has a great deal of respect for the secretary of state, whom he knew closely at the Oriental Congregation. It was Cicognani who obtained the withdrawal by the Holy Office of a measure that had offended Patriarch Maximos (forbidding the use of English in the Melchite services in the United States ...). The personal letter from Maximos to the pope was so harsh against Ottaviani that he was given comments about it without anyone daring to show it to him. The Melchites, Raes told me, are almost the only ones among the Eastern Catholics to realize what they represent. At the Central Preparatory Commission, Maximos asked to express himself in French, not having spoken a word of Latin in 60 years; one wonders how he is going to express himself at the council. – We spoke about Oreste Kéramé.[15,*16] Fr. Raes respects him but judges him to be an extremist, sowing discord; I told him of his presence in Rome. On the liturgy, Fr. Raes thinks that Fr. Jungmann is competent but that his ideas of reform are a little fanciful in their excess. He then told me about the schema on "the unity of the Church", that is to say, on the Eastern Churches. The first part, written by Fr. Benoit, appears excellent to him; for the applications, several people shared the task, according to their specialty. – Next we talked about the dogmatic schemas, their preparation, then about the role, recognized de facto, of the "ecclesiastical conferences" in the preparation of the first vote: Fr. Raes sees in this an encouraging sign of a certain "decentralization", recognizing some autonomy in certain groups of the Western Church: the only means, he believes, capable of preparing for reunion with the Eastern Churches.

A visit from Archbishop Dalmais, who is seeking to know what he could ask for, and how, regarding the adaptation of the liturgy in the African missions.

---

[14] It is charged with the administration of the diocese of Rome.

[15] Oreste Kéramé (1895–1983), Lebanese, ordained in 1925. Archimandrite, personal expert and secretary of the patriarch Maximos at the council, he was particularly interested in ecumenism.

[16]* "(My former fellow novice)".

The third supplement of *Orientations pastorales*, an eighty-page pamphlet, has appeared in Leopoldville: "Le concile œcuménique Vaticanum II", giving the essential information on the preparation of the council: its aims, the principal documents. On p. 8, there is this: "One notes that in the Theological Commission the number of theologians belonging to the circle of Roman theologians, contributors to the journal *Divinitas*, is preponderant, although several other eminent theologians are present as consultors: Laurentin, Congar, de Lubac, Häring, Lécuyer."

Archbishop Dalmais passed on to me a typewritten report, signed by the four bishops from Chad:[17] "Some last-minute reflections suggested to the bishops of Chad by reading the Documents of the Ordinaries of Congo-Leopoldville with a view to the upcoming council." The principal fundamental problems are broached in it. With regard to the Holy Office: "The choice of the members of this Congregation should be made with extreme care. Given the diversity and complexity of the matters submitted to the Fathers of this Congregation for judgment, these venerable judges should really be representative, not only of all the branches of religious knowledge, but also of all the spiritual families that legitimately exist within the Church. That is to say that, here more than anywhere else, it is necessary 'ad pacem et unitatem Ecclesiae'[18] to internationalize and diversify. The very composition of the sovereign tribunal of the Faith will be a guarantee of nobility, truth, and charity in its judgments. The form in which the judgments will be pronounced will no doubt gain by being stamped with a greater mildness. And the Holy Church should especially be vigilant that the official or semi-official newspapers of the Vatican, like for example *L'Osservatore Romano*, do not aggravate or complicate by means of their anonymous commentaries the already at times painful findings of the decisions of the Holy Office."

People have remarked, I have been told, that in the long list drawn up by the Italian episcopate for the conciliar commissions – 160 names – there is not a single French name.[19] – I have not seen this list myself.

Fr. Raes explained to me that the present excessive predominance of the Holy Office derives in part from Pius XII, who was distrustful by

---

[17] Henri Véniat, Paul Dalmais, Honoré Jouneaux, O.M.I., and Samuel Gaumain, O.F.M. Cap.

[18] "For the peace and unity of the Church".

[19] This list, in reality consisting of sixty-two names, did contain one French name: Paul Philippe, member of the Curia. *Acta synodalia sacrosancti concilii oecumenici Vaticani II*, I, 1, 46–47.

nature and relied on the reports and decisions of the Holy Office. Before him, for some time it was the Consistory[20] that dominated with "the terrible Cardinal De Lai".[21]

Visit from Msgr. Maury,[22] apostolic delegate to sub-Saharan Africa (former secretary of Cardinal Gerlier in Lyon, then director of the Pontifical Missionary Works). He informed me on the situation of the Church in Africa. He spoke to me about the visit that Senghor, president of Senegal, made to the pope. At the office of the secretary of state, they told him that John XXIII had been profoundly impressed by what Senghor had told him about Teilhard. In fact, Msgr. Maury observed that the thought of Teilhard has met with extraordinary favor among those in leadership roles in sub-Saharan Africa. – We also talked about the dogmatic schemas. I passed on to him a copy of my Remarks.

Met with Father Paul Chevallier, who is leaving Rome tomorrow. His bishop, Bishop Jacquot, has just taken him for his personal theologian. That permits us to speak more freely.

Wednesday, October 17, 1962. – The French newspapers have particularly picked up on the passage from the pope's opening speech (October 11) that seemed to take aim at the excessive machinations of the Holy Office. – An article by Henri Fesquet[1] in Le Monde sets me in opposition to Father Gagnebet, the principal author of the enormous schema De Ecclesia. That can only hinder me in my relations with Fr. Gagnebet, which I want to be good; he has more than once in the last two years asked for my collaboration, and he has shown himself more moderate than some others.

Today, the first count of yesterday's vote at the secretariat of the council.

This morning, Fr. Rondet finished dictating to me the Latin version of our Remarks on the schema De deposito fidei. Fr. Karl Rahner came to

---

[20] Roman congregation, charged in particular with the nomination of bishops and the establishment and reorganization of dioceses.

[21] Gaetano De Lai (1853–1928), Italian, ordained in 1876. Made cardinal in 1907. Secretary of the consistory from 1908 to 1928.

[22] Émile Maury (1907–1994), French, ordained in 1932. Named apostolic delegate in 1959, apostolic internuncio to Senegal from 1961 to 1965, then nuncio to the former Belgian Congo, Rwanda, Burundi, before becoming archbishop of Reims in 1968, a position he held until 1972.

October 17

[1] Henri Fesquet, French, sent by the newpaper Le Monde, a daily national paper that has been coming out since 1944. His articles were published in Le Journal du Concile (Forcalquier: Robert Morel Éd., 1966).

propose to us a meeting on Friday afternoon intended for a first examination of the counter-plan that he is in the process of drafting.

At the beginning of the afternoon, visits from Father Paul Gauthier
(Nazareth) and from Fr. Maurice Villain, S.M. Various bits of news.
A press bureau has been set up outside of the official bureau, which is
giving out too little information. The initiative came from the Dutch.
Among others, Fr. Wenger (reporting for *La Croix*) and Fr. Tucci (*Ci-
viltà cattolica*) are coming there.

A remark*[2] from Dom Olivier Rousseau: "At Saint Peter's, the Mass
was celebrated in front of the Holy Father exposed."

Father Gauthier drove me to the San Pancrazio district, to where
Patriarch Maximos is staying. A simple, majestic, good old man, with
fixed ideas. He said he is persuaded the Holy Office is condemning itself
by its excesses; in a little while, he thinks, people will speak of it as they
now speak of the Inquisition. He also thinks there will be no difficulty
allowing the use of vernacular languages at the council, with a brief Latin
translation. – Saw, at the patriarch's place, Bishop Hakim of Nazareth
and Archbishop Néophytos Edelby,[3] patriarchal adviser, very intelligent;
he read me the text that he has just written to ask the presidency of
the council that the schema *De episcopis*[4] come under discussion soon;
for several people are afraid that it will be reserved for the end of the
session, when many of the bishops will have left. Now this schema is
bad. Fr. Daniélou took part in a meeting today where Fr. Gagnebet, its
principal author, read it out and defended it; the bishops who were present, especially Archbishop Veuillot, appeared unhappy. At the Melchite
patriarchate it is thought that it will be easy to gather several hundred
signatures for this petition.

Father Gauthier spoke to me about Nazareth and about the booklet
that he has had printed to distribute to a certain number of the Fathers
on the Church and the poor at the present time. The intention is excellent. I am a little afraid that there are some ideology and propaganda in
it that are indiscreet.

---

[2]* "(With a childlike mischievousness)".

[3] Néophytos Edelby, B.A. (Basilian Alepian; 1920–1995), Syrian, ordained in 1941. Titular archbishop in 1961, adviser to the Melchite patriarch of Antioch, Melchite archbishop of Aleppo from
1968 until his death. He was a member of the Commission for Eastern Churches and wrote in
French a journal of the council, published in Italian: *Il Vaticano II nel diario di un vescovo arabo* (Milan,
1996), and later in its original version: *Souvenirs du concile Vatican II (11 octobre 1962 – 8 décembre
1965)* (Raboueh: Centre grec melkite catholique, 2003).

[4] "On bishops".

At 7:30 P.M., there was a meeting at the home of some Polish friends of Father Moubarac (Count Jean Gawronski[5] and his children), with the Maronite Archbishop Khoury of Tyre and Archbishop Luc Sangaré,[6] native African archbishop of Bamako (Mali). I congratulated the latter on the spirit of unity among the African bishops and the speed at which they have organized; they have brought in the bishops of Angola, who up until now were tied to Portugal. Roger Schutz and Max Thurian were present; both were invited to Rome by the pope for the council. Cardinal Bea is charged with having their observations passed on to the secretariat of the council. Perhaps they can even be brought to some of the commissions as observers. Count Gawronski knew Teilhard.

This evening's issue of *L'Osservatore Romano* gave the French text of the fine speech given by Cardinal Bea to welcome the observers. The issue from the day before yesterday gave the French text of the speech, also very fine, addressed to these same observers by the Holy Father.

Fr. Henri Rondet informed me that Cardinal Ottaviani's suggestion concerning the method of voting for the election to the commissions, and possibly for other votes, has been definitely rejected. At the residence of Maximos, I learned a short while ago that Archbishop Parente, in a conference just recently, apparently gave as evidence of the broadmindedness of the Holy Church the fact that she had called to the council even some opponents, such as Fr. de Lubac.

With Frs. Daniélou and Rondet, I have been invited to a meeting that is supposed to take place, no longer at the Germanicum,[7] but at the residence of Bishop Volk, with various bishops and theologians, German and French, to study the counter-plan that Fr. Karl Rahner is going to put forward.

Patriarch Maximos has written to John XXIII to explain to him a fact that seems to cause a major difficulty for the beatification of Pius IX. The pope thanked him for it. The patriarch does not dare to expect that his letter will have any effect. It concerns an incident that supposedly happened at the final ceremony of obedience, at the end of the

---

[5] Jan Gawronski (1892–1983), Polish diplomat and writer.

[6] Luc Sangaré (1925–1998), Malian, ordained in 1954. Archbishop of Bamako (Mali) from 1962 until his death.

[7] Pontificium Collegium germanicum et hungaricum, whose foundation goes back to 1552. Entrusted to the Society of Jesus, since 1580 it has been united with the Hungarian college and is one of the numerous colleges of Rome.

First Vatican Council. The Melchite patriarch[8] had been among the anti-opportunists;[9] he faithfully accepted the decision of the council; when his turn came to pass in front of Pius IX, when he had prostrated himself before him to kiss his slipper, the pope lifted his leg and kicked him in the head, saying: "Testa dura!"[10] The incident, said Maximos, is reported in an archival document, and, up until a little while ago, there was a witness still living.

Thursday, October 18, 1962. – The *Aurore* and *France-Soir*, I am told, have published ridiculous articles on the council. They have gone so far as to talk about the opposition and revolt of the French bishops. Yesterday morning Cardinal Feltin protested before the assembled French bishops; denials were sent to the press by Father Pierre Haubtmann.[1] It seems that these newspapers were repeating some Italian papers that were shocked at the initiative taken by the council as a result of Cardinal Liénart.

It was Father Antonelli,[2] Franciscan, they tell me, who was the author of the note added at the last moment to the heading of the schema on the Liturgy.[3] This note diminishes the import of the schema. It was supposedly Cardinal Ottaviani who inspired him.

This morning, there was a long session at the Trinitarians', at Saint Chrysogonus, with the bishops from Madagascar, to study the schema on the Liturgy. Father Chenu was there. The remarks made by Fr. Jungmann and Archbishop Dalmais were useful to me.

---

[8] Gregory II Youssef, Melchite Patriarch from 1864 until his death in 1897.

[9] This refers to those, also called inopportunists, who accepted the dogma of papal infallibility but who thought its proclamation inopportune in the context of the age.

[10] "Hard head!"

October 18, 1962

[1] Pierre Haubtmann (1912–1971), French priest. Specialist in social matters, former chaplain of the ACO. Beginning in 1961, he taught at the Institut catholique of Paris. He was the assistant director of the general secretariat of the French episcopate. Beginning with the second session, he was called on by the French bishops to conduct a daily press conference in French on the work of the conciliar assembly. Named an expert to the council beginning with the second session, he became one of the primary architects of *Gaudium et spes*.

[2] Ferdinando Antonelli, O.F.M. (1896–1993), Italian, ordained in 1922. Secretary of the Congregation for Divine Worship and the Discipline of the Sacraments from 1965 to 1969. He was created cardinal in 1973. At the council, he was the secretary of the conciliar Commission for the Liturgy and an expert at the council.

[3] The introductory note situated all powers of decision de facto in the hands of the Holy See, something that is in opposition to no. 16 of the schema, according to which the revision of the liturgical books should be carried out by specialists from the world over who would be invited to do so by the Holy See.

Many people were deeply moved and saddened on reading an announcement in *Le Monde*: it was believed that Patriarch Athenagoras of Constantinople had just died. It actually turned out to be an archbishop of the same name, who had died in London.

At the Curia, early in the afternoon, a conversation with Fr. Smulders, S.J.,[4] from Maastricht, a "peritus". He has the impression that the council has started well. He was struck by the importance that was immediately assumed by the Board of Presidency, which seems to him to be well composed. The ten cardinals[5] who compose it will be present at every session. It is thought that Cardinal Tisserant, dean, will continue to preside.

Met Fr. G. Martelet (Fourvière), who brought me the first pages of his critical study of the principal doctrinal schema. He is happy to be of use to the missionary bishops who lodge with him at the Hotel Caesar Augustus.

At 4 P.M., I was at Santa Marta with Bishop Charles de la Brousse, who had invited me. He is organizing privately a meeting for about 25 French bishops and some others, which will take place on Saturday at 4 P.M.: I am supposed to set out my remarks on the first two dogmatic schemas at that time. On returning to the Borgo, visit from Msgr. Nabuco, from Brazil, a peritus, who was a member of the Preparatory Liturgical Commission; from Fr. Bréchet[6] (Geneva), in Rome for the journal *Choisir*; from Fr. Sesboüé,[7] who is beginning a biennium in theology in Rome (at the Bellarmino).

Bishop Cassien, Orthodox rector of Saint-Serge (Paris), has been in Rome since yesterday. – A Swedish Lutheran observer met Msgr. Romeo; the latter criticized at length the current state of Catholic exegesis, riddled as it is with rationalism. The Swede had the impression that he was listening to a man who was well informed and sincere but somewhat lacking in insight.

---

[4] Pieter Smulders, S.J., (1911–2000), Dutch, ordained in 1939. Professor of dogmatic theology and patristics at the Jesuit college of Maastricht. Expert of the Indonesian bishops at the council, he collaborated in particular on the constitution *Dei Verbum*. Expert at the council beginning with the second session.

[5] T. Tappouni, Syro-Catholic patriarch of Antioch, N. Gilroy (Sydney), F. Spellman (New York), A. Caggiano (Buenos Aires), A. Liénart (Lille), E. Pla y Deniel (Toledo), J. Frings (Cologne), B. Alfrink (Utrecht), E. Ruffini (Palermo), E. Tisserant.

[6] Raymond Bréchet, S.J., born in 1923, Swiss, ordained in 1949. Exegete, co-founder of *Choisir*, a journal published beginning in 1959 by the Jesuits in Geneva and for which he reported on the council.

[7] Bernard Sesboüé, S.J., born in 1929, French, ordained in 1960. He developed an important body of work in theology starting in the 1970s.

Friday, October 19, 1962. – This morning, from 11 A.M. until noon, at Father General's. He spoke to me first about my book on Teilhard: the Holy Office, he told me, had been alerted by a denunciation that came from the group at *La Pensée catholique*; it has asked for the manuscript. So after passing the censors of the Society, both in France and in Rome, the text was then submitted to the Holy Office, which has authorized publication! – Next we spoke about the council. Father General told me that he intervened very little in the Central Commission, of which he was a member; but he was able to note that the changes asked for by that body had hardly been made, that the monitoring of the corrections had been insufficient, etc. Before I spoke to him about them, he also told me that the dogmatic schemas were very bad, that they had to be, not corrected, but rejected. He gave me some examples; I provided him with others. He finds them on the whole too long, too "scholastic" in the worst sense of the word, too polemical, containing too many details that a council should not go into. At that point, he criticized an entire way of thinking common in Rome. They confuse, he told me, obedience and flattery; there is also a deplorable habit of entrusting to former nuncios, career diplomats, once they have become old, positions that they are incapable of filling competently and of never obliging anyone to retire once he has become too old, etc. On the "Roman" theologians: I explained to Father General the abuses that result from their idea of the magisterium as "fons proximus".[1] I told him of my two interventions in the preparatory commission so that Christian revelation was mentioned in the chapter on God and so that Jesus Christ was named in the chapter on revelation.

Our good Father General criticized judiciously and forcefully some texts that originated from his advisers, which reproduced the very sentences of his Letter of December 1950 to the French Assistancy.[2] He was not aware of that; I did not tell him. – He was happy to speak freely; after I started to leave, he had me sit down again, and we chatted for another twenty minutes. – Regarding certain paragraphs on Holy Scripture: "These things were taught to me fifty years ago, and here they want to condemn them as heterodox novelties!" An important member of the Central Commission had declared in front of him in a meeting: "I cannot believe that the Church had to wait twenty centuries to learn

---

October 19

[1] "The nearest source".

[2] There must be some confusion here with the letter to the Assistancy of France dated February 1951 already mentioned.

that there are literary genres in Holy Scripture." (On that point he was more correct than he thought, but in a different sense.) Father General found that remark "absurd". He also showed me Spadafora's pamphlet; several people, he confided to me, have pressed him to respond to it; he was loath to lower himself to such a task. He recounted to me the repeated attacks against Fr. Zerwick and Fr. Lyonnet: he has never been able to obtain any specific detailed information against them. He spoke with the pope about this. John XXIII told him that he himself had taught Sacred Scripture for a time and that he had been attacked in a similar manner – and that it had even been a Jesuit who had led the attack. The next day, the pope sent to Father General, for his amusement, the papers concerning that old affair.

Father General also talked to me about bishops who protest against the exemption for religious (I was the one who brought the question up for discussion). Most of them, he said to me, do not know canon law, which gives them tools that are more than sufficient in case of need. It must be acknowledged, he added, that some religious make themselves insufferable – like the Jesuit priest who, while giving the inaugural address at a new university in front of all the bishops of the region, started by declaring that the school was the concern of the Society and that the bishops had no control over it ... But, if the bishops want to insist on keeping the religious in the positions they occupy in their dioceses, how could we respond, for example, to appeals from the Holy See when it asks us for a number of priests for Japan, for South America, etc.?

At 4 P.M., on the northwest slope of the Janiculum, a meeting at the boarding house where Archbishop Volk of Mainz is staying to study the drafting of a positive doctrinal schema and to examine the procedure to follow so as to have it accepted while setting aside the schemas of the preparatory commission. There were 25 of us. Nine bishops: Volk, his auxiliary,[3] the archbishop of Berlin (Bengsch),[4] Garrone[5] (Toulouse),

---

[3] Joseph Reuss (1906–1985), German, ordained in 1930. Auxiliary bishop of Mainz from 1954 to 1978.

[4] Alfred Bengsch (1921–1979), German, ordained in 1950. Bishop of Berlin in 1961, he became archbishop in 1962, was created cardinal in 1967. A member of the Commission for the Discipline of the Clergy and the Christian People.

[5] Gabriel-Marie Garrone (1901–1994), French, ordained in 1925. Archbishop of Toulouse from 1956 to 1966, created cardinal in 1967, pro-prefect then prefect of the Congregation for Seminaries and Universities (which became the Congregation for Catholic Education in 1967) from 1966 to 1980, and president of the pontifical council for culture from 1982 to 1988. Member of the Doctrinal Commission.

Guerry (Cambrai), Ancel (auxiliary of Lyon), Schmitt[6] (Metz), Weber[7] and his coadjutor Elchinger[8] (Strasbourg). Among the theologians: K. Rahner, J. Ratzinger,[9] H. Küng,[10] Msgr. Philips (Louvain), Daniélou, Rondet, Congar, Chenu, Labourdette, a Dutchman[11] ... Very interesting discussion. Bishop Volk presented the broad outlines of a possible schema. Karl Rahner gave some explanations. Then each one gave his opinion, either on the content or on the tactics to adopt. Various possibilities. The German bishops were more scathing than the French. Bishop Elchinger and Bishop Schmitt will serve as liaisons. At the end, they told me that Cardinals König and Léger have been elected to the Commission on the Faith; it will be announced tomorrow morning. Bishop Elchinger told me that Cardinal König had received some time ago a notice from the Holy Office banning him from speaking on ecumenical questions. Other subjects of conversation, after the meeting: the faith and the social milieu – the Theological Commission – the troubles made for Fr. Rahner, Fr. Congar's illness, etc. I had the impression that several were not rising enough above their one-sided concerns.

Saturday, October 20, 1962. – At 8:30 A.M., I arrived at Saint Peter's at the same time as Fr. Labourdette. We sat down in the same gallery and chatted. I showed him the recent book by Fr. Louis Bouyer: *Le rite et l'homme.*[1] This morning, the council Fathers received their definitive

[6]Paul Schmitt (1911–1987), French, ordained in 1935. Bishop of Metz from 1958 to 1987.

[7]Jean-Julien Weber, P.S.S. (1888–1981), French, ordained in 1912. Bishop of Strasbourg beginning in 1945, he became archbishop in 1962, a position he held until 1967.

[8]Léon Arthur Elchinger (1908–1998), French, ordained in 1931. Auxiliary bishop of Strasbourg from 1957 to 1967, then bishop of Strasbourg from 1967 to 1984.

[9]Joseph Ratzinger, born in 1927, German, ordained in 1951. Professor of fundamental theology. Personal expert of Cardinal Frings, he was an expert at the council starting from the second session. He became archbishop of Munich in 1977 and was made cardinal that same year. Prefect of the Congregation for the Doctrine of the Faith from 1981 to 2005. He was elected pope under the name Benedict XVI in 2005.

[10]Hans Küng, born in 1928, Swiss priest and theologian. Professor at the University of Tübingen, where he became director of the Institute for Ecumenical Research in 1963. He was named an expert in 1962. Co-founder of the journal *Concilium*.

[11]According to the testimony of Yves Congar (*Mon Journal du Concile*, vol. 1 [Paris: Éd. du Cerf, 2002], 122–23), he must be referring here to a Belgian: either Piet Fransen, S.J. (1913–1983), Belgian, ordained in 1943, professor of dogmatics at the Jesuit faculty of Louvain, or Edward Schillebeeckx, O.P., born in 1914, Belgian, ordained in 1941, professor of dogmatic theology and hermeneutics at the University of Nijmegen (Netherlands) from 1958 to 1982. Schillebeeckx was the personal expert of the Netherlands' bishops and co-founder of the journal *Concilium*.

October 20

[1]Louis Bouyer, *Le Rite et l'Homme, sacralité naturelle et liturgie* (Paris: Éd. du Cerf, 1962).

places. After Mass, there was an announcement that the only ones allowed to remain were the "Patres, Periti, Officiales et Observatores".[2] We stood up when the Gospel was brought in, carried in procession. The usual prayer. The president announced the decision made by the pope following the request made by the Board of Presidency: for each commission, after those who obtained an absolute majority, those people will be declared elected who have received the most votes. It is a totally different system from the one Cardinal Ottaviani had advocated. Seven out of ten commissions have been filled this way. For the commission on the liturgy, the pope also named without delay the other 8 members, so that the commission can commence its work immediately. – Proclamation of the lists, with the number of votes for each name. On the Commission on Faith and Morals,[3] 3 cardinals: König, Léger and ...;[4] Archbishop Garrone was in second place on the list.

Next Cardinal Tisserant announced that a draft for the address to the world has been presented to the council and that the pope has approved the idea and the content. It was read out. The assembly was given a quarter of an hour to reflect on it. Each person received a copy. When the session was reconvened, there were numerous interventions: I counted 36, in the most diverse directions. Many approved the draft, while asking for corrections, deletions, especially additions. Several pointed out that there were inconsistencies. Some wanted mention to be made of the Blessed Virgin (Bishop Ancel proposed a mention, well placed and biblical, at the beginning: this would be adopted). Some others said: let us not be in too much of a hurry to make such an address; others: let us wait at least until tomorrow to decide, etc., etc. Some said: let us vote immediately on the address as it is. Two excellent observations by Cardinal Döpfner: (1) It was not clear whether the address issued from the pope as well or from the bishops without the pope; (2) one paragraph seemed to say that the council was going to assist in technical progress! – Archbishop Parente was surprised that the "thema doctrinale quasi reticeatur"; today, "multi errores sub specie veritatis" are spreading, and it was necessary to repudiate them right at the start, to protest against the "subversio saniorum principiorum"; besides, "semper mos

---

[2] "The council Fathers, the experts, the *officiales* [service personnel], and the observers".

[3] Doctrinal Commission.

[4] Ruffino J. Santos (1908–1973), from the Philippines, ordained in 1931. Archbishop of Manila from 1953 to 1973, made cardinal in 1960. He became a member of the Doctrinal Commission at the first session.

fuit in conciliis de doctrina fidei loqui in principio",[5] etc. Parente was supported by Archbishop Lefebvre,[6] superior general of the Holy Spirit Fathers: we should take the time to study a more substantial address; the one proposed to us "respicit nimis bona humana, et non supernaturalia".[7] Several were calling for at least a sentence in sympathy and encouragement for "the Church of silence"; one speaker even asked that the council declare its hope to see her soon liberated. Two others, one of whom was Hungarian, pointed out that this would be dangerous, that it would result in more harm than good, both for the Church in general and for persecuted Catholics. An Italian declared that he supported Parente's petition. Others wished to see something on the goal of the council: to prepare for the union of the Churches.

The bishop of Baalbek[8] spoke in French; he asked that the vote be postponed until tomorrow. The patriarch of Egypt and the Sudan[9] expressed himself in Latin: "Beatitudines, Eminentissimi et Excellentissimi Domini, etc." The Melchite patriarch, Maximos, spoke in French: he apologized for his ignorance of Latin; he feared that Arabic would not be understood by the majority; the message seemed excellent to him: let us not draw it out; it is not a question of making it into a theological treatise. Maximos then thanked John XXIII with emotion for this new spirit that he is spreading in the Church and of which this message will be a sign. His tone was firm, filled with emotion; he was applauded.

Finally, the Board of Presidency proposed to vote without further ado on the address such as it was, with one brief addition at the beginning (Ancel's motion) and some slight changes in wording in the last sentence. Voting was by rising or remaining seated. The address was approved with a strong majority. – Next assembly, Monday morning.

---

[5] "The doctrinal theme is passed over in silence, so to speak." "Numerous errors under the appearance of truth." "The subversion of very sound principles." "In the councils, the practice has always been to speak about the doctrine of the faith at the beginning."

[6] Marcel Lefebvre, C.S.Sp. (1905–1991), French, ordained in 1929. Archbishop of Dakar from 1955 to 1962, then of Tulle for several months, before becoming the superior of the Congregation of the Holy Spirit Fathers, a position he held until 1968. He was one of the principal leaders of the *Coetus internationalis Patrum*. Rejecting *aggiornamento*, he founded the Society of Saint Pius X in 1970 and was excommunicated in 1988. He was a member of the Central Preparatory Commission.

[7] "Focuses its attention too much on human goods and not on supernatural things".

[8] Joseph Malouf (1893–1968), Lebanese, ordained in 1925. Melchite bishop of Baalbek (Lebanon) from 1937 until his death.

[9] Elias Zoghby (1912–1988), Egyptian, ordained in 1936. Melchite archbishop, patriarchal vicar for Egypt.

I had come to St. Peter's in the company of Bishop Verwimp, S.J.,[10] former archbishop of Kisantu (Congo), who was a member of the Central Commission. He spoke to me about Ottaviani's plan for the elections to the commissions: "One would not have believed possible the audacity of such a ploy." He also told me (something I had already heard) that, in defending the doctrinal schemas before the Central Commission, Cardinal Ottaviani was citing Frs. Congar and de Lubac as his authority.[11]

Received the October 12 issue of *France Catholique*, sent by Fr. Joseph Guitton,[12] which contains a very moderate article by Jean Daujat[13] on "The Work of Teilhard de Chardin and the Meaning of the Holy Office's *Monitum*".

At 3 P.M., a visit from Fr. Hirschmann, who came to talk to me about the "Rahner affair". It has taken on huge proportions. An address to the pope has been signed by a number of important figures (including, I've been told, Chancellor Adenauer),[14] so that the pope cannot fail to respond. He has already demanded that the matter pass from the Holy Office to Father General, who would undertake Rahner's censorship. (Rahner has supposedly decided not to write any more under such conditions.) But, still according to Hirschmann, the pope must handle the Holy Office tactfully, and Father General must do so even more. So the people at the Secretariat of State think that John XXIII could pass on the German address to Fr. General, asking him to respond in his name. As for Father General, one could advise him to delegate the

---

[10] Alphonse Verwimp, S.J. (1885–1964), Belgian, ordained in 1917. Apostolic vicar beginning in 1931, then bishop of Kisantu (Belgian Congo) from 1959 to 1960. Member of the Central Preparatory Commission.

[11] On January 20, 1962, during his report on the chapter *De Deo* of *De deposito fidei*, A. Ottaviani, after having cited the names of Father de Lubac and Father Marcozzi, pointed out: "Sed non mirabitur quisquis quia ego feci etiam duo nomina, potuissem multa alia nomina facere hominum vere peritorum, sed ideo posui ut videatur, Commissionem Doctrinalem sibi adlegisse viros qui non sunt certe considerandi ut tenebrosi, sicut generatim describitur S. Officium" (*Acta et documenta concilio Vaticano II apparando*, series II, vol. 2, pt. 2, pp. 310–11. ["No one will be surprised that I have cited two names. I could have named many other people, truly competent, but I brought these forward in order that it might be shown that the doctrinal commission has appointed men who are certainly not considered "obscurantists", as the Holy Office is generally described."]

[12] Joseph Guitton, S.J. (1889–1968), French. Priest and bursar at the scholasticate of Fourvière until 1966. He is the uncle of the academician Jean Guitton.

[13] Jean Daujat (1906–1998), French philosopher from a scientific background, he founded, in 1925, and directed the Centre for Religious Studies in Paris, with a neo-Thomist orientation, for the philosophical and theological formation of the laity.

[14] Konrad Adenauer (1876–1967), German statesman, he was the first chancellor of the Federal Republic of Germany, from 1949 to 1963.

provincial for Austria[15] or someone else to carry out the censorship: Fr. Hirschmann intends to give him this advice.

At 4 P.M., in the great parlor in Santa Marta's, there was a meeting with the French bishops. They were more numerous than I was expecting: around fifty, plus three or four Belgian bishops. Bishop Philippe, O.P., was there, which bothered me a little at first, since he is a very important Roman figure, in contact with the Holy Office, to which he used to belong, and a former member of our Preparatory Theological Commission. Cardinals Gerlier and Lefebvre[16] were there. Despite everything, I started. A good two hours of exposition on the first two doctrinal schemas.[17] We will meet again next Saturday, October 27, to discuss it.

While leaving, conversation with Msgr. Etchegaray,[18] second secretary of the French episcopate, former personal secretary of Bishop Terrier[19] in Bayonne. He intends, he told me, to see me again soon. – Next met Father Jorge Mejía,[20] an Argentinian, whom I had seen at Lyon when he used to accompany his patron, Msgr. –,[21] founder and editor of the journal *Criterio* (Buenos Aires). He is now editing *Criterio* and teaching at the Faculty of Theology of Buenos Aires. He is here as secretary of the Argentine bishops, to whom he asked that I come speak sometime soon. – Also a plan to meet with Archbishop Zoa[22] of Yaoundé (Cameroon), who was elected first on the list to the Commission for the Missions.

Fr. Karl Rahner, after Cardinal Liénart's intervention (Saturday, Oct. 13), said in the ear of Fr. Henri Rondet: "Gallus cantavit!" An

---

[15]Johannes Schaching.

[16]Joseph Lefebvre (1892–1973), French, ordained in 1921. Archbishop of Bourges from 1943 to 1969, created cardinal in 1960. President of the French bishops' conference from 1965 to 1969.

[17]*De deposito fidei* and *De fontibus revelationis*.

[18]Roger Etchegaray, born in 1922, French, ordained in 1947. Auxiliary bishop of Paris in 1969, he became archbishop of Marseille from 1970 to 1985, president of the Pontifical Council for Justice and Peace from 1984 to 1998 and of the Pontifical Council *Cor unum* from 1984 to 1995. Created cardinal in 1979. At the time of the council, he was the director of the pastoral secretariat of the French episcopate and provided the secretariat of the conference with delegates from the episcopal conferences, called the "conference of the 22". Expert at the council from the third session.

[19]Léon Terrier (1893–1957), French, ordained in 1922. Bishop of Bayonne from 1944 to 1957.

[20] Jorge M. Mejía, born in 1923, Argentinian, ordained in 1945. Professor of Sacred Scripture in the theology faculty at the Catholic university of Argentina. Editor of *Criterio*, a general Argentinian Catholic journal, from 1955 to 1977, created cardinal in 2001. Expert at the council beginning with the second session.

[21]Gustavo J. Franceschi, editor of *Criterio* from 1932 to 1957; he was not one of the founders.

[22]Jean-Baptiste Zoa (1924–1998), from Cameroon, ordained in 1950. Archbishop of Yaoundé from 1961 until his death. Member of the Commission for the Missions. He was indeed the first elected for this commission with 1,403 votes.

allusion to the hymn from Lauds for that Sunday: "Gallo canente spes redit – Aegris salus refunditur."[23]

People have reported to me some words from Fr. Sébastien Tromp. After a meeting of the Central Commission where his plans had been shaken: "Everything is lost ... There is nothing more to do but pray to the Holy Spirit!" – These last few days, seeing the direction that the council seemed to be taking: "And here are these outsiders who want to impose their ideas on us!"

Sunday, October 21, 1962. – This morning, in the parlor of the Borgo S. Spirito, there was a meeting organized by Bishop Fauvel[1] of Quimper: three French bishops; five Argentinian bishops; a Brazilian, the secretary of the Union of Latin American Bishops ("Celam").

In the afternoon, an outing with Fr. Boussuge, our substitute; visits to a few churches. At the Biblical Institute, saw Fr. Stanislas Lyonnet and, with him, Fr. Pierre Benoit, O.P., from the Biblical Institute of Jerusalem; also saw Fr. Xavier Léon-Dufour,[2] who came as a new consultor of the Biblical Commission.

At the Gregorian, visit to Fr. Donatien Mollat. He assured me that the list distributed by the partisans of the Curia bore the title "Catholic list"! In actual fact, on further investigation, the reality is slightly different. The Italian bishops had first made up a list that contained only Italians; realizing that this was foolish, they hastily composed at night a list that was more varied, which the newspapers named the "Catholic list". As for the list drawn up by the Holy Office, that has circulated only in a confidential way.

Monday, October 22, 1962. – This morning, general congregation. From 8:30 A.M. until 9 A.M., chatted with a religious, an Italian Montfortian, member of the congregation for religious;[1] he spoke French,

---

[23] "The cock has crowed! [This is a pun on the meaning of the Latin word *gallus*: it means cock but also "the Gaul".] At the cry of the cock, hope is reborn / Health returns to the sick."
October 21
[1] André Fauvel (1902–1983), French, ordained in 1925. Bishop of Quimper from 1947 to 1968.
[2] Xavier Léon-Dufour, S.J., born in 1912, French, ordained in 1943. Professor of exegesis at the scholasticate of Fourvière, a specialist in the New Testament, he made a name for himself as the project director of a *Vocabulaire de théologie biblique* (1962); trans. into English under the direction of Joseph Cahill as the *Dictionary of Biblical Theology* (New York: Desclée, 1967). He was a consultor to the Biblical Commission.
October 22
[1] This was undoubtedly Elio Gambari, S.M.M. (1913–1999), Italian, ordained in 1937. Member of the Congregation for Religious from 1946 to 1983, an expert at the council.

an open-minded, practical man full of good sense; we understood each other rather well.

Mass was celebrated by Archbishop Jäger[2] of Paderborn; singing by a choir. – The president-delegate of the day, Cardinal Gilroy,[3] archbishop of Sydney, first announced the death, in Rome, of two bishops, and we recited a *De profundis*. – Archbishop Felici announced the names of those elected to the last commissions. Three Frenchmen to the Sacraments: Renard,[4] Puech,[5] and Lallier;[6] two to Religious: Huyghe[7] and Urtasun;[8] two to Seminaries: Cazaux[9] and Blanchet.[10] – A rescript from the pope was read out, assimilating the Secretariat for Unity to the conciliar commissions; an explanation in four points. Near me, Fr. Gagnebet did not seem very pleased.

Cardinal Larraona took the floor. After a few words on the schema on the Liturgy, he yielded the floor to Father Antonelli (rector of the Antonianum), who summarized the work of the preparatory commission and briefly analyzed the schema. He insisted on the "altiora principia", the "generalia principia"[11] that governed the projected liturgical reform, and said a few words on the "initial note".

Then the interventions began. Today, these were general observations. The cardinals spoke first, then the archbishops, then the bishops.

---

[2] Lorenz Jäger (1892–1975), German, ordained in 1922. Archbishop of Paderborn from 1941 to 1973, created cardinal in 1965. Member of the Secretariat for Unity.

[3] Norman Gilroy (1896–1977), Australian, ordained in 1923. Archbishop of Sydney from 1940 to 1971, created cardinal in 1946. Member of the Board of Presidency.

[4] Alexandre Renard (1906–1983), French, ordained in 1931. Bishop of Versailles from 1953 to 1967, then archbishop of Lyon from 1967 to 1981. Created cardinal in 1967. Member of the Commission for the Discipline of the Sacraments.

[5] Pierre Puech (1906–1995), French, ordained in 1930. Bishop of Carcassonne from 1952 to 1982. Member of the Commission for the Discipline of the Sacraments.

[6] Marc Armand Lallier (1906–1988), French, ordained in 1932. Archbishop of Marseille from 1956 to 1966, then of Besançon from 1966 to 1980. Member of the Commission for the Discipline of the Sacraments.

[7] Gérard Huyghe (1909–2001), French, ordained in 1933. Bishop of Arras from 1961 to 1984, member of the Commission for Religious.

[8] Joseph Urtasun (1894–1980), French, ordained in 1917. Archbishop of Avignon from 1957 to 1970. Member of the Commission for Religious.

[9] Antoine Cazaux (1897–1975), French, ordained in 1922. Bishop of Luçon from 1941 to 1967. Member of the Commission for Seminaries, Studies, and Catholic Education.

[10] Émile Blanchet (1886–1967), French, ordained in 1911. Former bishop of Saint-Dié from 1940 to 1946, titular archbishop, rector of the Institut catholique of Paris. Member of the Preparatory Commission for Studies and Seminaries, then of the conciliar Commission for Seminaries, Studies, and Catholic Education.

[11] "The very lofty principles", "the general principles".

Cardinal Frings: he asked that the Fathers be given the text that had been proposed to the Central Commission; he asked for the deletion of the initial note, belatedly added; on the use of vernacular languages, he wanted the first text to be restored; he wanted an addition to the chapter on sacred music.

Cardinal Ruffini (Palermo): Why was nothing said about the Western rites that are not Roman, especially the Ambrosian rite?

Cardinal Lercaro[12] (Bologna).

Card. Montini (Milan): that we not add anything on the Ambrosian rite, it was pointless. That we recall the text from Paul to the Corinthians, about the *Amen* that one cannot say if one has not understood.[13] A wish for something on the liturgy of the religious orders.

Card. Döpfner (Munich). – Card. Doi[14] (Tokyo): that we delete the introductory note; that a commission for bishops be established to rule on the adaptations, according to the norms set by the council. – Card. Silva Henriquez[15] (Santiago, Chile). – Paul II,[16] patriarch of the Chaldeans: that we apply to the Eastern Churches a large part of the Constitution, which is valid for them as well.

An archbishop[17] criticized the exposition of principle: Pius XII had said it better. – Another[18] declared that there were a number of useless things in it, things that had already been said. – Two opponents who were particularly critical: Archbishop Vagnozzi, apostolic delegate to

---

[12] Giacomo Lercaro (1891–1976), Italian, ordained in 1914. Archbishop of Bologna from 1952 to 1968, created cardinal in 1953. Member of the Commission for the Liturgy. In 1963 Paul VI named him to the Coordinating Commission and made him one of the four moderators of the council.

[13] I Cor 14:16: "Ceterum si benedixeris spiritu qui supplet locum idiotae quomodo dicet amen super tuam benedictionem quoniam quid dicas nescit": "Otherwise, if you say a blessing in the spirit, how can anyone in the position of an outsider say the 'Amen' to your thanksgiving, since the outsider does not know what you are saying?"

[14] Peter Tatsuo Doi (1892–1970), Japanese, ordained in 1921. Archbishop of Tokyo from 1937 to 1970. Created cardinal in 1960. Member of the Commission for Bishops and the Government of Dioceses.

[15] Raúl Silva Henriquez, S.D.B. (1907–1999), Chilean, ordained in 1938. Archbishop of Santiago from 1961 to 1983, created cardinal in March 1962, president of Caritas International. President of the bishops' conference of Chile, he was vice-president of the Commission for the Lay Apostolate.

[16] Paul II Cheikho (1906–1989), ordained in 1930, patriarch of Babylon of the Chaldeans (Iraq) from 1958 to 1979. Member of the Commission for Eastern Churches.

[17] Egidio Vagnozzi (1906–1980), Italian, ordained in 1928. Titular archbishop, apostolic delegate to the United States from 1958 to 1967, created cardinal in 1967. He became prefect of the Prefecture for the Economic Affairs of the Holy See from 1968 until his death.

[18] Fidel García Martínez (1880–1973), Spanish, ordained in 1907. Titular bishop.

the United States; and Archbishop Dante,[19] secretary of the Congregation for Rites, who demolished the schema in 12 points. – Another archbishop[20] asked that a chapter be added on the cult of relics in order to condemn those that excite derision rather than piety (milk of the Virgin, etc.).

Then Cardinal Rugambwa (from Tanganyika) spoke, who had in error been reserved for the time scheduled for the particular remarks; some African bishops had alerted the Board. He was in favor of the draft.

A bishop from Madagascar[21] was delighted that the episcopal commissions would be able to decide on adaptations, with the approval of the pope. A Brazilian[22] was critical of the excessive length of all the schemas. Another bishop went on too long:[23] the president stopped him. A Spaniard[24] found the schema very good, with some corrections.

At noon, the Angelus at top speed, and went out. Some groups of bishops had themselves photographed in front of Saint Peter's.

Around 4 P.M., appointment with three theologians of bishops, who wanted to be informed about the sessions; the meeting was organized by Father Moubarac.

At 5 P.M., Archbishop Zoa of Yaoundé, paid me a visit at the Borgo. He spoke to me about Fr. Alfred de Soras,[25] who has to spend several months each year in Yaoundé, where he gave a fine lecture on the council. Archbishop Zoa next explained to me how the union of African bishops functions in Rome: 9 groups of bishops, each having its own president and secretariat; meeting of the 9 presidents to achieve unity on

---

[19] Enrico Dante (1884–1967), Italian, ordained in 1910. Member of the Antepreparatory Commission, secretary of the Congregation of Rites beginning in 1960, titular archbishop, created cardinal in 1965. Member of the Commission for the Liturgy.

[20] Fidel García Martínez.

[21] In reality it was Laurean Rugambwa, who spoke in the name of the bishops of Africa, Madagascar, and the isles.

[22] Carlos Eduardo de Sabóia Bandeira Melo, O.F.M. (1902–1969), Brazilian, ordained in 1925. Bishop of Palmas (Brazil) from 1958 to 1969.

[23] Afonso Maria Ungarelli, M.S.C. (1897–1988), Italian, ordained in 1928. Prelate of Pinheiro (Brazil). Member of the Commission for the Missions.

[24] Juan Hervás y Benet (1905–1982), Spanish, ordained in 1929. Prelate of Ciudad Real from 1955 to 1976. Member of the Commission for the Discipline of the Sacraments.

[25] Alfred de Soras, S.J. (1899–1966), French. Specialist on Catholic Action, he was a member of Action populaire. In 1962, he left for Africa in order to found a center for religious formation. The approach adopted, however, was different and gave birth to the organization INADES.

all problems; a common secretariat (Fr. Greco, S.J.,[26] is the secretary). Information conferences by language group (Archbishop Zoa wants me to give a presentation on the doctrinal schemas for all the French speakers). Fr. Martelet is the secretary of the group from Equatorial Africa. – Archbishop Zoa told me that he is well acquainted with me, thanks to Archbishop Parente, who was his professor at the Propaganda and who was often opposed to me.

A visit from Fr. Robert Rouquette, who is staying at the *Civiltà*. He asked me to come to the *Civiltà* on Friday afternoon to speak with the group of Jesuit journalists. Father Tucci, editor of the journal, wanted to have me invited to lunch, but it appears that this is impossible, because I have too many "enemies" in the place. Fr. Tucci is active and courageous, but, my visitor told me, it is necessary not to talk about him so as not to put him in a compromising position. In accordance with the desire of the pope and the secretary of state, he had prepared an article on the question of Latin, but, following objections, he has been forbidden to publish it. Fr. Rouquette asked me to invite the French bishops to make contact as soon as possible with the Italian episcopate. He gave me three names: Cardinal Urbani[27] (Venice), a friend of the pope; Cardinal Siri[28] (Genoa), who has a great deal of authority; Archbishop Castelli,[29] secretary of the Italian bishops' conference.

Cardinal Rugambwa supposedly said that he is the target of photographers but that he remains very isolated.

Fr. Rondet met this afternoon with Father General, who criticized the doctrinal schemas in front of him, as he had done in front of me. Fr. Rondet told him that part of them had been written by Fr. Dhanis; "at the instigation of Fr. Tromp", replied Father General.

A decision is said to have been made regarding the *periti*. Those who were on a preconciliar commission would be offered to the corresponding

---

[26]Joseph Greco, S.J. (1911–1987), French. Professor of theology at the Gregorian. At the council, he was the secretary for the French-speaking African bishops and an expert beginning with the third session.

[27]Giovanni Urbani (1900–1969), Italian, ordained in 1922. Patriarch of Venice from 1958 until his death, created cardinal in 1958. Member of the Coordinating Commission.

[28]Giuseppe Siri (1906–1989), Italian, ordained in 1928. Archbishop of Genoa from 1946 to 1987, created cardinal in 1953, president of the Italian Bishops' Conference from 1958 to 1965. He was named a member of the Secretariat for Extraordinary Affairs in 1962 and a member of the Board of Presidency starting from 1963.

[29]Alberto Castelli (1907–1971), Italian, ordained in 1930. Titular archbishop, permanent secretary of the Italian Episcopal Conference. Member of the Commission for Bishops and the Government of Dioceses.

conciliar commission. The others would be evenly allotted among the particular commissions. So I would be on the Commission on the Faith. Where will Father Daniélou be?

On Sunday, Frs. Rahner, Congar, and Daniélou met, following the meeting organized around Bishop Volk. Congar is preparing a totally new schema, as a sort of general prooemium, that they would try to have accepted by the Commission for Extraordinary Affairs. Rahner and Daniélou are preparing a revision of the existing texts, as a fall-back position in case Congar's schema should be rejected on principle.

The newspapers are full of gross inaccuracies, often tendentious.

The pope supposedly said jokingly, while showing some people the first volume of the schemas open on his table to one of the chapters of *De deposito fidei*: "Look, I have just measured it; there are 25 centimeters of condemnations there!"

Tuesday, October 23, 1962. – Before the session, chatted with Fr. Camelot, O.P., and an Italian Redemptorist who seems to be of the so-called "open" trend. The latter told us that the pope would not allow on principle a total rejection of the dogmatic schemas, before any discussion, in favor of a counter-plan.

Cardinal Tappouni[1] is still absent from the Board of Presidency. This morning, it was Cardinal Spellman who presided. The usual Mass. The entry of the Gospel was more solemnized, with chants ("Laudate Dominum", "Christus vincit"). The ritual proclamation: "Exeant omnes".[2] We were reminded that the bishops' procurators[3] could attend only the public sessions.

Archbishop Felici gave some explanations in Latin on how the discussion of the schemas would proceed. His words were then translated into Spanish, French, German, English, Italian, Arabic. – 1. The schema would be presented first by the relator; then the floor would be given to those Fathers who had asked for it at the prescribed time (3 days before); remarks should first concern the whole; next would come the series of interventions on each part, according to the order established by the president. – 2. One should speak distinctly and clearly, without departing

October 23
[1] Ignatius Tappouni (1879–1968), born in Mosul, ordained in 1902. Syrian Patriarch of Antioch from 1929 until his death, created cardinal in 1935. Member of the Board of Presidency.
[2] "Let all depart."
[3] This refers to the representatives of the council Fathers who were absent (whether from illness, lack of a visa, etc.) at the time of the public sessions; the texts were formally promulgated, but it was during the general congregations that they were debated.

from the subject or running over the time; if anyone wished to propose an amendment, he should formulate the text for it with precision; one should not repeat what has been said by others. − 3. The text of the intervention, signed, must be transmitted to the general secretariat. − 4. All proposed remarks and amendments would be directed by the secretariat to the competent commission. − 5. The series of amendments would be printed and distributed to all the Fathers. − 6. On a fixed day, we will proceed to vote on each amendment, interrupting if need be the study of another schema; the vote would be either "placet" or "non placet".[4]

Cardinal Ottaviani opened fire. He asked "ut saltem pars doctrinalis schematis sit subjicienda aliquibus Patribus bonis theologis",[5] to make the text clearer and more exact; such as it was, it contained certain things that could be open to misinterpretation. Then, "recognoscatur textus".[6] The cardinal gave 2 or 3 examples; so, in the first chapter (p. 159, ll. 12−16), it says that Christ accomplished the work of our redemption "praecipue per suae beatae Passionis, ab inferis Resurrectionis et gloriosae Ascensionis paschale mysterium":[7] that is not correct, there was no need of the Resurrection and the Ascension, since our Lord said to the good thief on the cross: "*Hodie*, mecum eris in paradiso."[8] (Sic). What is more, the schema contains some exaggerations. "Ego quoque amo liturgiam, sed cum moderatione justa." The practical conclusion: "Emendatio facienda est a commissione theologica."[9]

Cardinal Joseph Ritter[10] (St. Louis, USA) insisted on the need for a liturgical reform. The schema seemed to him "admirabile pro sua rectitudine, accommodatione et prudentia".[11]

Archbishop Armando Farès[12] of Catanzaro and Squillace observed that this text is intended to be the "magna charta"; so it is necessary to

---

[4]"I approve", "I disapprove".

[5]"That at least the doctrinal part of the schema be submitted to some Fathers who are good theologians".

[6]"That we revise the text".

[7]"Especially through the Paschal mystery of his blessed Passion, his Resurrection from the dead, and his glorious Ascension".

[8]"Today, you will be with me in Paradise" [Lk 23:43].

[9]"I also love the liturgy, but with the appropriate moderation." "Emendation is to be made by the theological commission."

[10]Joseph Ritter (1892−1967), American, ordained in 1917. Archbishop of Saint Louis from 1946 until his death, created cardinal in 1961. Member of the Commission for the Discipline of the Clergy and the Christian People.

[11]"Admirable in its rectitude, its spirit of accommodation, and its wisdom".

[12]Armando Farès (1904−1980), Italian, ordained in 1927. Archbishop of Catanzaro from 1956 to 1980. Member of the Commission for the Discipline of the Sacraments.

explain the connection "inter fidem et liturgiam" and to pay careful attention to liturgical unity for the sake of the unity of the faith. "Sit una lingua, sc. latina."[13] Furthermore, the rites should be simple, intelligible to everyone. We should revise the scriptural texts of the schema.

Bishop Argaya,[14] Spanish, expressed a wish "de solemnibus ... formis simplificandis". The norms should be: pietas, simplicitas, et dignitas. Let everything be brought back to the spirit of the Gospel, especially in the Pontifical. We should eliminate everything that in dress and ceremonies resembles "alicui pompae humanae et mundanae".[15]

Bishop Volk (Mainz) approved of the schema, with some corrections.

Bishop Méndez[16] (Arceo Sergio) of Cuernavaca (Mexico) would like concern for the unity of Christians to be more marked. However, the schema "in genere placet".[17] He asked that the original schema be distributed to the Fathers.

Archbishop Giuseppe d'Avack[18] of Camerino would like some doctrinal clarifications on the Mass and the cross, the priesthood of priests and of the faithful, etc.

An Eastern bishop[19] supported the request of Cardinal Ruffini and Patriarch Paul II that a mixed commission make the link between the Liturgical Commission and the Commission "de rebus orientalibus",[20] so as to apply the schema to the Eastern rites.

A Franciscan bishop from Ecuador:[21] "Non manifestavi intentionem loquendi; nescio qua de causa sim nominatus."[22] Everyone laughed. It was a moment that eased the tension.

We moved on to the examination of the Prooemium and chap. 1. – Cardinal Ruffini made 12 criticisms, some of which I give here. – "Male

---

[13] "Between faith and liturgy". "Let there be only one language, namely, Latin."

[14] Jacinto Argaya Goicoechea (1903–1993), Spanish, ordained in 1928. Bishop of Mondoñedo-Ferrol from 1957 to 1968.

[15] "Concerning the solemn forms to be simplified. Piety, simplicity, and dignity". "Some human and worldly pomp".

[16] Sergio Méndez Arceo (1907–1992), Mexican, ordained in 1934. Bishop of Cuernavaca (Mexico) from 1952 to 1982.

[17] "Pleased, generally speaking".

[18] Giuseppe D'Avack (1899–1979), Italian, ordained in 1923. Archbishop of Camerino (Italy) from 1946 to 1964.

[19] Garabed Amadouni (1900–1984), Turk, ordained in 1925. Apostolic vicar to France for Christians of Armenian rite from 1960 to 1971.

[20] This refers to the Commission for Eastern Churches.

[21] Bernard Echeverria Ruiz, O.F.M. (1912–2000), Ecuadorian, ordained in 1937. Bishop of Ambato from 1949 to 1969, created cardinal in 1994. Member of the Commission for Religious.

[22] "I did not indicate any intention to speak. I do not know why I was called."

mihi sonant vocabula":[23] it would seem that the council wants to change everything. Several paragraphs in chap. 1 are unclear: the encyclical of Pius XII[24] was much better. – Chap. 1, no. 6: "... ut qui receperunt fidem et paenitentiam egerunt filii Dei fiant per baptismum";[25] that is not correct, since children are baptized without performing any act of repentance. – P. 161, ll. 35ff.: this is full of ambiguities and is contrary to a *motu proprio* of Pius XII. – P. 163, ll. 30–31 and the footnote: in the constitution of Pius XII it was not a question solely of the liturgy but of other things as well. – P. 166, no. 22: with strong insistence: this is not enough to give the pope. – P. 166, ll. 27ff.: the text should be changed; in particular, "cultus publicus" should be substituted for "adoratio". – P. 167, ll. 13ff.: "Cautissime procedendum est";[26] there is a great danger here, and it is not in conformity with the teachings of Pius XII. – ll. 25–31, on the sermon: this should be deleted. – P. 168: "a sancta Sede approbatis"[27] should be added.

Another cardinal[28] (in opposition to Ottaviani and Ruffini): The text of the Prooemium should remain as it is.

Card. Feltin: Latin remains the language of the Church. Attamen,[29] pastoral urgency (developed with ardor). Most people do not know one word of Latin. We must extend the concessions that have already been made by the popes for the use of vernacular languages. He suggested that we keep the missa solemnis[30] in Latin as well as the essential formulas of the sacraments.

Cardinal James L. McIntyre[31] (Los Angeles): words of praise for Latin. It is a thing "plus quam humanum".[32] He appealed to history.

---

[23] "These terms cause pain to my ears."

[24] *Mediator Dei*, the encyclical of Pius XII on the liturgy, November 1947.

[25] "In order that those who have received the faith and done penance might become children of God through baptism".

[26] "Public worship" for "adoration". "It is necessary to proceed with the greatest caution."

[27] "Approved by the Holy See".

[28] Jaime de Barros Câmara (1884–1971), Brazilian, ordained in 1920, created cardinal in 1946. Archbishop of São Sebastião de Rio de Janeiro (Brazil) from 1943 until his death. President of the Brazilian Bishops' Conference from 1958 to 1963. Vice-president of the conciliar Commission for Seminaries, Studies, and Catholic Education.

[29] "Nevertheless".

[30] "Solemn Mass".

[31] James Louis McIntyre (1886–1979), American, ordained in 1921. Archbishop of Los Angeles from 1948 to 1970, created cardinal in 1953. Vice-president of the Commission for Bishops and the Government of Dioceses.

[32] "More than human".

To attack the Latin language is in some way to impugn the immutability of dogmas. Latin is not only necessary from the ecclesiastical point of view, it is so from the scientific and civil points of view. It is the Catholic language: Protestants do not use it. "Missa debet remanere ut est."[33]

Card. Léger (Montreal). He approved of the schema "magno corde". "Liturgia est natura sua pastoralis" and "propter homines sunt sacramenta".[34] For many, the liturgy is the only path that leads them to Christ; it is necessary to do everything to make it understandable to them. This does not relate only to mission lands. (The same insistence as with Card. Feltin, but warmer and more emphatic). – He offered four remarks: 1. He joined Card. Döpfner in asking that a commission start work immediately after the council (art. 16): otherwise, there will be no practical application or there will be endless discussions. – 2. Regarding article 22 (p. 166, l. 10), in place of "in quibusdam regionibus", write: "in plerisque regionibus".[35] – 3. Art. 24 (p. 167, l. 19), instead of the simple "proposal" to the Holy See, restore the formula that had been approved by the Central Commission (in this there was an implicit criticism of those who changed the text). – 4. Another small modification to art. 25 (ll. 29–30).

Cardinal John D'Alton[36] (Armagh, Ireland). "Schema generatim placet." "Placet omnino quod dicitur de lingua latina",[37] the language of the Church; but we must resist those who would like to eliminate Latin altogether. That would cause confusion. Let the pope decide, and then "fiat tranquillitas magna".[38] Some say that in our liturgy there is too much rite and not enough speaking; however, in Ireland, Catholics hear the reading of the Gospel and the homily every Sunday. The golden rule: be content with the judgment of the Holy See. – P. 168, no. 28: should be deleted.

Card. Juan Landázuri Ricketts[39] (Lima, Peru): "in genere placet". Let us take care, however, not to favor variety too much. – P. 166, no. 21:

---

[33] "The Mass must remain as it is."

[34] "Wholeheartedly". "The liturgy is pastoral by its nature", and "the sacraments are for men."

[35] "In some regions". "In most regions".

[36] John D'Alton: he really means William Godfrey (1899–1963), Briton, ordained in 1916. Archbishop of Westminster from 1956 until his death, created cardinal in 1958.

[37] "I entirely approve of what has been said about the Latin language."

[38] "Let there be great tranquility."

[39] Juan Landázuri Ricketts, O.F.M. (1913–1997), Peruvian, ordained in 1939. Archbishop of Lima from 1955 to 1989, created cardinal in 1962. Member of the Commission for Religious.

the limits that need to be respected are not clear enough; on the other hand, no. 22 is very good.

Card. Browne:[40] he will not repeat many of the things that have already been said. In the Prooemium, l. 4, "cum Ecclesia" should be written instead of "in". – Chap. 1, p. 161, ll. 27ff., add a mention of the "sacrificium divinum". – Chap. 1, p. 166, ll. 4–8: delete "major",[41] etc.

Patriarch Maximos: "Venerable and beloved friends". This schema is concerned primarily with the Latin Church; however, he was happy to say that on the whole it appeared excellent to him, and he took this opportunity to testify to his admiration for the current liturgical movement. However, the first sentence of no. 24 seemed to him too absolute; instead of "Latinae linguae usus in Liturgia occidentali servetur", he proposed: "Latina lingua est lingua originalis et officialis Ecclesiae latinae".[42] We must remember that Jesus Christ not only preached but celebrated the Last Supper in Aramaic. Then, in Rome, the celebration was in Greek, because that was the common language at that time, which was replaced by Latin, etc. In the East, very early on: Coptic, Aramaic, etc., then Arabic. And all the arguments brought forward in favor of keeping Latin inviolable are powerless against the authority of the apostle. – "Latin is dead, the Church is living." Likewise, the bishops' conferences must have more than the right to propose: this right belongs to every one of the faithful; let them decide, subject to the approval of the Holy See. – Returning to the question of Latin, Maximos observed that it was not only a question of the liturgy; he regretted that simultaneous translation had not been adopted for the council, something that is done in all great international assemblies; finally, he asked the Board of Presidency that the council's decrees be composed in Latin, English, and French, so that the bishops who had to sign them could all perform "a human act".

We left Saint Peter's at five past noon.

Through Fr. Jean Lucas, who knows a few Italian bishops, I learned that they are all rather unhappy that they are not more strongly represented on the commissions.

---

[40] Michael Browne, O.P. (1887–1971), Irish, ordained in 1910. Created cardinal in March 1962, titular archbishop in 1962. M. Browne, former professor at the Angelicum, former master of the Sacred Palace, was the Master General of the Dominican Order from 1955 until March 1962. Member of the Holy Office, he was named to the Doctrinal Commission, where he occupied the post of vice-president starting from the end of the first session.

[41] "With the Church" instead of "in". "Divine sacrifice". "Major".

[42] "The use of the Latin language is to be retained in the Western liturgy." "The Latin language is the original and official language of the Latin Church."

Father Héjja,[43] a Hungarian, from the Curia, informed me about the (only) two Hungarian bishops[44] who came to the council. Apparently one of them is incompetent; the other, very much the vassal of the regime. They were supposedly given the task of getting the Holy See to accept a scheme for the nomination of bishops: the government would recognize three bishops named a long time ago by Rome, who have not yet been able to occupy their seats, and Rome would accept from now on the government's choices. Now one of the government's first candidates is said to be a man without morals, and the others, parish priests of no real worth.

At 4 P.M., visit from Father Michel Leclercq, Oblate of Mary Immaculate. He walked out on the Theological Commission, where he was secretary under the orders of Fr. Tromp. He is keeping his post at the Holy Office. I spoke frankly to him about the weakness of our schemas. He confided to me that Fr. Gagnebet, O.P. (*De Ecclesia*) and Fr. Lio, O.F.M.[45] (moral doctrine) have given the secretaries a lot of trouble with their numerous inaccurate references, second-hand citations, etc. Fr. Gagnebet now has only a few classes at the Angelicum; he has many political connections with whom he enjoys warm relations. Fr. Tromp has managed everything authoritatively; he now senses opposition, but he is ready to fight and expects to win. Archbishop Parente surpasses those around him in his theological knowledge, he shows himself friendly in his relations, but he has a compulsive urge to condemn. Cardinal Ottaviani is not strong on doctrine; he is an opportunist and generally clever; but he is making mistakes by going too far. – I showed Fr. Leclercq the letter that Father General addressed to me on the subject of my book on Teilhard,[46] as well as the anti-Teilhardian pamphlet of Action-Fatima that Fr. Joseph Guitton has just sent me from Lyon.

---

[43] Gyula Héjja, S.J. (1923–1999), Hungarian. Secretary of the Jesuit Curia for the Marian Congregations.

[44] He is referring to Endre Hamvas (1890–1970), Hungarian, ordained in 1913, Bishop of Csanád (Hungary) from 1944 to 1964, then archbishop of Kalocsa (1964–1969), and Sándor Kováks (1893–1972), Hungarian, ordained in 1915, Bishop of Szombathely (Hungary) from 1944 to 1972.

[45] Ermenegildo Lio, O.F.M., Italian, professor of moral theology at the Antonianum. He worked at the Congregation of the Holy Office as a consultor. Consultor to the Preparatory Theological Commission, named an expert in 1962.

[46] Here is an excerpt from the letter, dated September 1, 1962, according to a letter sent from Father de Lubac to Father Bouillard on September 4, 1962: "I am fully in agreement with you: your book constitutes a very important first elucidation of Father Teilhard's work and, in the spirit of the Monitum itself, a 'warning' against possible extrapolations of his thought that are not in conformity with the Church's doctrine."

At the Angelicum, I missed Fr. Congar; I saw Frs. Dumeige and Jarlot at the Gregorian; also conversed with Fr. Allard,[47] who is moving from Lyon to Beirut.

Wednesday, October 24, 1962. – In last evening's *L'Osservatore Romano* (dated the 24th), an article taking note of the council's "message" to the world, recalling the rights of truth and demanding that the doctrinal schemas be given priority.

In the gallery at St. Peter's, I made the acquaintance of Msgr.... from the diocese of Sens, a professor of canon law at the Institut catholique of Paris,[1] and of Msgr. Caloyera, O.P.,[2] a Greek, apostolic administrator in Constantinople, who gave me some news about Father Pasty.[3] – At 9 A.M., Mass, according to the Melchite rite, in Greek and Arabic; liturgy of Saint John Chrysostom; singing by the Greek College of Rome. – Beforehand, I chatted with Archbishop Blanchet, who spoke to me about my book on Teilhard with his customary sensitivity and kindness.

Cardinal Pla y Deniel,[4] primate of Spain (Toledo) was presiding. He announced the death of Archbishop Chichester,[5] this morning, in the atrium of the basilica. Archbishop Ch., S.J., had been staying at the Curia; every morning I said Mass immediately after he did; we had just gone out together, and I had gone a few steps ahead of him when I entered Saint Peter's. He was 85 years old.

We continued the remarks on the Prooemium and chapter 1 of the schema on the liturgy.

Cardinal Eugène Tisserant: a ten-minute dissertation, terse, precise, erudite, without a word wasted; a history of the various translations of

---

[47]Michel Allard, S.J. (1924–1976), French, ordained in 1955. A specialist in the study of Islam, he studied Arabic in Lebanon. Returning to Lebanon in 1962, he became chancellor of the French Institute of Oriental Literature at Saint Joseph's University in Beirut in 1963, a position he held until his death. He sought to promote dialogue between Christians and Muslims.

October 24

[1]Jacques Denis, priest of the diocese of Sens, canon, and vicar general. He was a professor of canon law at the Institut catholique of Paris. Expert at the council.

[2]Domenico Caloyera, born in 1915, Greek, ordained in 1939. Apostolic administrator of Istanbul from 1955 to 1978.

[3]Gaston Pasty, S.J. (1902–1988), French, ordained in 1934. Superior of the Jesuit residence in Istanbul from 1946 to 1982, he also assumed various other ministries: teaching, spiritual direction.

[4]Enrique Pla y Deniel (1876–1968), Spanish, ordained in 1900. Archbishop of Toledo from 1941 to 1968, he was created cardinal in 1946. Member of the Board of Presidency until his resignation in 1963.

[5]Aston Chichester, S.J. (1878–1962), British, ordained in 1913. Archbishop of Salisbury (present-day Zimbabwe), then titular archbishop.

the Latin liturgy into vernacular languages in the course of the centuries, authorized by Rome, often published in Rome, by the Vatican
press: Slavonic (again under Pius IX), Croatian, Slovene (under Benedict XV),[6] Syriac, etc., and so, no obstacle in principle.

Cardinal Gracias[7] (Bombay). – For a long time now, in the mission
countries, we have been calling for the adaptation of the liturgy, "quasi
voces clamantes in deserto". "Nunc, gaudium magnum ... Opus est fes-
tinare lente, non tamen tam lente ut dici possit: 'Sicut erat in principio
et nunc et semper, etc.'[8] – How do we reconcile nos. 21 and 22 with
each other?" – No. 24: valde gratum; however, an emendatio,[9] already
demanded by many people. – No. 22, l. 15: add "majores" to "aptationes",[10] and at ll. 19–20, instead of "Conferentiae episcopali a sancta Sede
facultas tribuitur", say: "Conferentiae episcopali facultas tribuitur".[11] –
No. 41, on the vernacular language: too restrictive; this is not only for
the instruction of the faithful, but for their active participation. – Gracias
joined Card. Léger. He responded to those who extol Latin only and
to those who fear confusion. He does not like the word "concedere".[12]
On concelebration: this morning we had a beautiful example, so beautiful that many of us perhaps felt the desire to change rites and become
Greek ... – I dare to recommend strongly that the schema be accepted.

Cardinal Bea. Only two remarks: (1) De coordinandis et conjungen-
dis[13] certain analogous parts coming from various commissions: liturgy,
missions, Eastern churches, the Secretariat for Unity. Let a mixed commission be formed, and, according to what the Board of Presidency
decides, either have that commission make an entire constitution in
common, or let the various commissions simply come to agreement
on the questions in the first chapter, which would hold for all rites, and
then let each commission treat the particular questions that concern it. –

---

[6] Giacomo della Chiesa (1854–1922), Italian, ordained in 1878. Elected pope in 1914.

[7] Valerian Gracias (1900–1978), Indian, ordained in 1926. Archbishop of Bombay from 1950 until his death, created cardinal in 1953.

[8] "Like the voices of those crying out in the desert" [allusion to Mt 3:3]. "Now, great joy ... It is necessary to make haste slowly, but not so slowly that one will be able to say: 'As it was in the beginning, is now, and will be forever, etc.'" [Extract from the *Gloria Patri*, said at the conclusion of every psalm.]

[9] "Altogether welcome". "Change".

[10] "Important". "Adaptations".

[11] "That this power be granted to the bishops' conference by the Holy See". "That this power be granted to the bishops' conference".

[12] "To grant" or "to concede".

[13] "On the necessity of coordinating and uniting".

(2) De novis ritibus instituendis. Quaestio nondum est matura.[14] Let no path be closed that leads to the "salus hominum, suprema lex".[15] Already, marvelous things have brought about (ecumenism); "firmiter speramus Spiritum sanctum illuminaturum[16] those who will rule God's Church; as for us, let us pray, and let us not close any door.

Card. Bacci. – Because I am a Latinist, this might not be believed, but I am very open to the necessities of the times. However:

(1) Rosmini[17] had recommended the use of vernacular languages for the Mass; his book was condemned. The popes have often ordered that in the Western Church the Mass be in Latin. Cf. Pius X[18] and again, under the current pope, the constitution "Veterum sapientia".

(2) The people will not understand any more in the vernacular than in Latin, because we are dealing here with mysterious things; and the faithful, especially the young, will be troubled by hearing "locutiones libidinosas",[19] as in the Canticle. Besides, it is enough that catechesis is in the vernacular.

(3) The Church has always forbidden the reading of Sacred Scripture without commentary, because of the danger to the faith. There is a danger if one hears it read without commentary.

(4) Danger of disputes, of nationalism, especially in bilingual (Canada, Belgium) or trilingual (Switzerland) countries, to the great detriment of the Church.

(5) For the sacraments, one could permit some parts in the vernacular language, "probante tamen Sancta Sede".[20] Matters this serious should not be left to the bishops' conferences. Otherwise, "magna diversitas et confusio",[21] as already exists today.

Card. Meyer[22] (Chicago). – He is in agreement with several of the remarks by Gracias. The schema constitutes a "norma optima"; it is a

---

[14] "On the new rites to be established. The question is premature."

[15] "Salvation of men, supreme law".

[16] "We firmly hope that the Holy Spirit will illuminate."

[17] Antonio Rosmini (1797–1855), Italian. Priest, philosopher, and theologian. In his book *Delle cinque piaghe della Santa Chiesa* (1848), immediately placed on the Index, he denounced the faithful's lack of understanding of the liturgy and saw as a remedy the elimination of Latin.

[18] The *Motu proprio* of 1903 on sacred music made clear that "la lingua propria della Chiesa romana è la latina" (the proper language of the Roman Church is Latin).

[19] "Shocking expressions".

[20] "With the approval of the Holy See, however".

[21] "Great diversity and confusion".

[22] Albert Gregory Meyer (1903–1965), American, ordained in 1926. Archbishop of Chicago from 1958 until his death, created cardinal in 1959. Member of the Board of Presidency beginning in 1963.

"via media".[23] The faithful are expecting something from the council here. – No. 34 should be made to agree more closely with no. 24. – Do not grant too much to the institutes of pastoral liturgy.

Archbishop Pierre Van Lierde, sacristan of Saint Peter's: In the first place, the connection between liturgy and spiritual life needs to be better shown. Something ought to be said about the sacristans, about the liturgies of religious orders, about the cult of the saints, relics, images. For ecumenism: it would be good if Catholics and other Christians could work together to introduce into civil life the celebration of the great Christian feasts, etc.

J. C. McQuaid,[24] archbishop of Dublin, in the name of all the bishops of Ireland: let there be added, at the end of no. 27, what was said in the encyclical *Mediator Dei* on the other means: meditatio, exercitia religiosa,[25] etc.

J. Descuffi,[26] archbishop of Izmir (Turkey): There are a number of excellent things here; attamen [but still], some remarks on no. 24. He is not against the use of Latin, but he thinks that we should greatly expand the faculties that have already been granted, "ob novum ordinem rerum historice exstantem".[27] "Dolere fas est",[28] but it is a fact of daily experience, even in the West. Now, "non desunt traditiones aut indulta"[29] for the use of vernacular languages in the sacraments; this ought to be expanded, "sine restrictione".[30] The Eastern rites allow it: Why should the Roman Church be the only one deprived of this? ... "Ut regnum Dei sit universale, et in omni lingua ... laudetur Deus".[31] Cf. Pentecost at Jerusalem: let that be an indication to us. So let us extend the powers of the bishops, for the sacraments and the Mass. We have just heard the words of the consecration chanted aloud, in vernacular language.

---

[23] "Excellent norm; it is a middle way."

[24] John Charles McQuaid, C.S.Sp. (1895–1973), Irish, ordained in 1924. Archbishop of Dublin from 1940 to 1971.

[25] "Meditation, religious exercises".

[26] Joseph Descuffi, C.M. (1884–1972), Turkish, ordained in 1907. Bishop of Izmir from 1937 to 1965.

[27] "Because of the new historical circumstances".

[28] "It is permissible to regret the fact".

[29] "There are lacking neither traditions nor indults" [permanent dispensations granted by the Holy See with regard to a canonical instruction that would otherwise be imposed on the beneficiary of the indult in question].

[30] "Without restriction".

[31] "In order that the reign of God might be universal and that God might be praised ... in every language".

"Liturgia propter homines, et non homines propter liturgiam."[32]
Today, all regions in the West are mission territory. May the time finally
come ... "ut omnis lingua confiteatur, scienter et cum rationabili obse-
quio, quia Dominus noster Jesus Christus in gloria est Dei Patris".[33]

Alex. Gonçalves do Amara[34] (Uberaba, Brazil): In chap. 1, no. 1,
"... causa instrumentalis"[35] (with reference to St. Thomas), etc. The
Mass and sacraments should be kept in Latin; the Epistle and the Gospel
in the vernacular. Cf. *Mediator Dei* and *Veterum sapientia*. We should not
confuse magisterium and ministry.

Gilbert Ramanantoanina, archbishop of Fianarantsoa. On no. 16, let
there be options for adaptation, so that all cultures can be integrated into
the Catholic community.

Adam Kozlowiecki[36] (Lusaka, Northern Rhodesia). In chap. 1, no. 3
is not clear or well organized; the first schema and *Mediator Dei* were
better. On no. 24: thanks to Cardinals Tisserant and Bea. Let the episcopal conferences have the right to introduce the vernacular "propter
rationes practicas".[37] – At no. 21 and elsewhere: "Sancta Sedes, sancta
Sedes ...";[38] it is unsettling. "Auctoritatem Petri non timeo, sed aliquando timeo Secretarium Petri."[39]

Pietro Parente, assessor of the Holy Office. "Schema verbositate et
quadam levitate laborat."[40] Bad form. Many exaggerations. Deals only
with the Latin Church. "Prooemium claudicat";[41] no formal definition
of liturgy, etc.; should be deleted. In chap. 1, no. 1, inaccuracy on the
humanity of the Word. At no. 6 (p. 161, l. 28), "qui receperunt fidem":[42]
incorrect. (In the gallery, Fr. Camelot observed that it is Parente who
is mistaken.) – Criticism of no. 11. – At no. 16, mention should be
made of the Roman pontiff. – The Holy Office has taken a number

---

[32] "The liturgy is for men, and not men for the liturgy."

[33] "Let every language proclaim, with full awareness and due respect, that Our Lord Jesus Christ
is in the glory of God the Father."

[34] Alexandre Gonçalves do Amaral (1906–2002), Brazilian, ordained in 1929. Bishop, then archbishop of Uberaba (Brazil) from 1939 to 1978.

[35] "Instrumental cause".

[36] Adam Kozlowiecki, S.J., born in 1911, Polish, ordained in 1937. Archbishop of Lusaka (Zambia) until 1969, created cardinal in 1998.

[37] "For practical reasons".

[38] "The Holy See, the Holy See ..."

[39] "I do not fear the authority of Peter, but I sometimes fear Peter's secretary."

[40] "The schema goes astray through verbosity and a certain superficiality."

[41] "The prologue is weak."

[42] "Those who have received the faith".

of measures in matters liturgical. A lot of bad things are said about the Holy Office: "Nos sumus martyres Sancti Officii"[43] (two times). If you knew, however, with what care, conscientiousness, prudence, competence, precaution we proceed! Her acts prove that the Church is not immobile, as she is accused of being. But it is necessary to proceed "cum maxima cautela",[44] while the "novatores" ...[45] – Be careful of the "pericula versionum. Lento pede procedendum, et non secundum judicium privatum, sed secundum judicium Sanctae Sedis."[46]

Dino Staffa,[47] archbishop of Caesarea (Palestine), secretary of the Congregation for Studies. In the Prooemium, l. 5, "quoquo modo"[48] should be deleted. To admit in principle the use of vernacular languages is a serious matter, for it will not be possible to stop at half-measures. There is a great risk for the faith and for discipline. – At a time when the world is moving toward unity, will the Church move in the direction of diversity? – Numerous documents reserve to the pope everything that concerns the liturgy. – "Lingua latina integre servetur in missa."[49] – Let the schema be handed over to a mixed commission that includes members of the Commission on the Faith.

Thomas Cooray[50] (Colombo, Ceylon): Latin for the clergy, etc.

Two other bishops also spoke.[51] I left a little before the end, at 12:15 P.M. Prayed for a few minutes by the corpse of Archbishop Chichester, in the parlor of the Borgo.

---

[43] "It is we who are the martyrs of the Holy Office."

[44] "With the greatest caution".

[45] "Innovators".

[46] "Dangers of translations. Let us advance at a slow pace, not according to a private judgment, but according to that of the Holy See."

[47] Dino Staffa (1906–1977), Italian, ordained in 1929. Titular archbishop of Caesarea, secretary of the Congregation for Seminaries and Universities. Created cardinal in 1967. Member of the antepreparatory commission, then, during the first session, named by the pope as a member of the Commission for Seminaries, Studies, and Catholic Education, of which he became one of the vice-presidents.

[48] "By any means".

[49] "Let Latin be preserved in full in the Mass."

[50] Thomas Cooray (1901–1988), Sri Lankan, ordained in 1929. Archbishop of Colombo from 1947 to 1976, created cardinal in 1965. Named as a member of the Commission for the Discipline of the Clergy and the Christian People during the first session.

[51] József Gawlina (1892–1964), Polish, ordained in 1921, titular archbishop, member of the Commission for Bishops and for the Government of Dioceses from the second session, and Franjo Šeper (1905–1981), Yugoslav, ordained in 1930. Archbishop of Zagreb from 1960 to 1969, created cardinal in 1965. Prefect of the Congregation for the Doctrine of the Faith from 1968 to 1981. Member of the Doctrinal Commission at the council.

Lunched with Msgr. Simon Delacroix,[52] his fellow countryman Msgr. Pfister[53] (a Roman archeologist), and three bishops: J. M. Cordeiro,[54] archbishop of Karachi; Alexandre Lubuka-Nizundu,[55] auxiliary bishop of Kikwit (in the former Belgian Congo), and one other Congolese, Bishop Nzundu,[56] a big, jovial man full of heartiness, very happy with Archbishop Kozlowiecki's remark on the "sancta Sedes" and on the "secretarium Petri",[57] finding that there are too many things in Rome that are antiquated, etc.; we chatted while walking along; he kept patting me on the back.

Next, a long visit from Fr. Hirschmann. First, the matter of Rahner: the [Jesuit Father General's] Assistant of Germany[58] explained to him that the Holy Office has given an order to Father General to ensure the censures even in Rome; thus the will of the pope would be thwarted; Fr. General cannot inform the pope about this, because the contents of his letter would be known at the Holy Office within 24 hours, etc. – Next, the council: my visitor thought that it would be a good thing after the liturgy to move on to the schema *De Ecclesiae unitate* and then to *De episcopis*; he is going to talk to Cardinal Bea about it. On the liturgy, he judges that we should not talk of concessions or adaptations: the faithful have the right to express themselves liturgically; authority, as in any well-ordered society, intervenes to regulate the exercise of that right; the liturgy is not the property of the hierarchy, etc.

Father Léon-Dufour gave a first presentation in front of the French bishops, at Saint-Louis des Français, on the Gospels; he is to give a second one. Today, Fr. Daniélou spoke to them about the theology of the episcopate. They are also calling on Fr. Congar. – Cardinal Feltin told the bishops (*secretissime*) that the pope was unhappy that communism was mentioned at the council, in discussing the message draft;

---

[52] Simon Delacroix (1901–1969), French, ordained in 1927. Professor of Ancient History at the Institut catholique of Paris, director general of the Union apostolique du clergé (Apostolic Union of the Clergy) and editor of its journal *Prêtres diocésains*. Expert at the council.

[53] Pierre Pfister (1895–1963), French, ordained in 1924. Canon of the Lateran and protonotary apostolic from 1948 to 1963. Member of the Congregation for Seminaries and Universities.

[54] Joseph Maria Cordeiro (1918–1994), Indian, ordained in 1946. Archbishop of Karachi from 1958 until his death, created cardinal in 1973. Member of the Commission for Religious beginning with the second session.

[55] Alexander Mbuka-Nzundu (1918–1985), Congolese, ordained in 1948. Auxiliary bishop of Kikwit (Congo) from 1961 to 1967.

[56] There must be some confusion here, for no other Congolese bishop of this name exists other than the one cited above.

[57] The "Holy See" and the "secretary of Peter".

[58] Piet van Gestel, S.J. (1897–1972), Dutch, ordained in 1926. Assistant of Germany since 1946.

apparently, he did not want there ever to be any political allusions. Archbishop Villot announced that the pope wished the dogmatic schemas to be discussed, not completely rejected. What worries certain bishops is the manner of discussion: practically speaking, general observations, bearing on the whole of the schema, on the substance of it, are not remembered, they do not result in any vote; only the details are voted on. Thus the assembly might easily end up adopting, through a series of amendments, a text that it would not want and that would have been profoundly criticized by the majority of speakers. (This is what I had already noted in the work of the preparatory commission.) One is more or less a prisoner of the schemas established in advance. – The Commission for the Liturgy has started to meet. Those strongly in favor of reform say that Cardinal Larraona is drowning the members of the commission in a flood of words.

Thursday, October 25, 1962. – Yesterday afternoon, on the via della Conciliazione, Bishop Nzundu and I were besieged by photographers and journalists. – This morning, a visit from François Mayeur,[1] of the *Informations catholiques internationales*. He was complaining that he knew nothing about the council except through the very unreliable indiscretions of the Italian newspapers. I am not sure that his magazine wants to give only very objective news. – The cardinal primate of Spain[2] is supposed to have written to the pope to complain that no Spaniard was elected to the Commission on the Faith; it appears that this was the result of a maneuver by Cardinal Antoniutti,[3] former nuncio to Madrid, and of his friend Ottaviani: they supposedly saw to it that the first two names proposed on certain lists were deleted, as not being sufficiently in conformity with their point of view; thus the votes of the electors were scattered.

Archbishop Jean Kozlowiecki, who yesterday morning used the phrase about "Petrus" and "secretarius Petri", is a Jesuit. The Africans are very happy. – Responded in a few words to Dr. A. R. Bachiller,[4]

October 25

[1] This actually refers to Francis Mayor.

[2] Enrique Pla y Daniel, Archbishop of Toledo.

[3] Ildebrando Antoniutti (1898–1974), Italian, ordained in 1920. Nuncio to Spain from 1953 to 1962, created cardinal in March 1962, he became prefect of the Congregation for Religious in 1963 after the death of Cardinal Valeri. He then became president of the Commission for Religious. Member of the Secretariat for Unity.

[4] Angel Rodríguez Bachiller (1901–1983), Spanish. A former Dominican missionary in the Far East, he left the priesthood in the 1930s. Involved on the republican side during the Spanish Civil War, he was imprisoned. After he was freed, he taught in Madrid.

who sent me from Madrid a pamphlet on the Reform of the Church and against priestly celibacy; he is a former Dominican.

At 1 P.M., with Fr. Daniélou, I left for the Villa Bonaparte. There were 15 or 20 guests: Cardinal Frings, Cardinal Gerlier, the German ambassador to the Vatican;[5] the bishops of Strasbourg, Metz, Châlons, Arras,[6] etc. At table, I chatted with Fr. Delos, O.P., and Pastor Hébert Roux,[7] an observer. Also saw O. Cullmann, and R. Schutz and Max Thurian, whom I will see again. Conversation with Archbishop de Furstenberg,[8] from the Secretariat of State: we spoke of Fr. K. Rahner and his great notoriety; of the council; of the pope, who gives indications concerning what he wants and makes his leanings manifest by significant gestures, but he does not press, he gives no precise orders, with the result that the pope can say one thing and "the Holy See" do the opposite, etc. – An embassy attaché, sent to Rome as supplementary staff while the council is in session, drove us back to the Borgo S. Spirito; it was Mr. Blanchard,[9] the author of a law thesis on the canonical legislation of the Irish Church; he has spent time in Ireland; he wants to see me again.

At the bookstore at Saint-Louis des Français, they tell me that my book on Teilhard is still selling well, although they do not dare put it on display in the store anymore. – Then I saw Olivier Rousseau, the editor of *Irenikon*; he was with some journalists, among whom was Henri Fesquet, of *Le Monde*; these gentlemen were complaining about the lack of information; they admire the organization of the Germans. – At the French Seminary, via Santa Chiara, I saw Msgr. Etchegaray; I told him about the desire expressed by some for livelier contacts between the French and Italian episcopates. He explained to me what he has already done in that direction. Liaisons are being established on all sides. He left

---

[5] Dr. Albert Hilger van Scherpenberg, ambassador from 1961 to 1964.

[6] Jean-Julien Weber, P.S.S.; Paul Joseph Schmitt; René-Joseph Piérard; Gérard Huyghe.

[7] Hébert Roux (1902–1980), pastor of the Reformed Church of France, he was an observer delegated by the World Presbyterian Alliance to the first two sessions, then an observer delegated by the Protestant Federation of France during the last session.

[8] Maximilien de Furstenberg (1904–1988), Belgian. At that time he had been nuncio to Portugal since April 1962. Created cardinal in 1967, he became prefect of the Congregation for the Oriental Churches in 1968.

[9] Jean Blanchard, born in 1914, French diplomat, a doctor of law, who was first secretary at the French embassy in Dublin from 1953 to 1960 and author of *Le Droit ecclésiastique contemporain d'Irlande* (Paris: Librairie générale de droit et de jurisprudence, 1958). The diplomatic yearbook, however, does not mention this mission on the occasion of the council.

me to go to the Church of the Holy Apostles, where there is to be an hour of silent prayer for the council between 6 and 7 P.M.; he was the one, together with some French bishops, who initiated this, for every Thursday. – Today, at Saint-Louis des Français, Fr. Léon-Dufour's second talk for our bishops; tomorrow, it will be Fr. Congar's turn. – Fr. Henri Rondet has just received his book on *Vatican I*[10] (Lethielleux), which he is going to distribute to some bishops. – Many are concerned about the working procedure that has been announced for the council, which permits neither the outright rejection of a schema nor a vote on the general observations.

Friday, October 26, 1962. – Msgr. Schmaus (Faculty of Theology of Munich) apparently asked X, following my talk at Santa Marta: "Why is Fr. de Lubac trying to demolish our schemas?" (I am not the only one, nor am I, by a long shot, the most ferocious of their demolishers.)

This morning, general congregation. Mass celebrated by Archbishop Paul Zoungrana[1] of Ouagadougou (Upper Volta), a White Father. Presider: Cardinal Frings.

The first to speak was Cardinal Siri: the schema contains some doctrinal propositions that have been the object of just criticism; so let it be entrusted to a mixed commission (liturgy, sacraments, faith). It is necessary to soften art. 20, on adaptations; we must stave off the danger of a multiplicity of forms and deviations; at l. 32, on the episcopal propositions, add: let everything be submitted "judicio et auctoritati Sanctae Sedis".[2] Consequently, the articles that follow need to be modified; otherwise, abuses are sure to occur. No. 24, on Latin: caute procedendum:[3] let us abide by "Veterum sapientia".

W. M. Bekkers,[4] bishop of Hertogenbosch, Holland. He will give the details to the secretariat. He noted that the majority of the objections to the schema have been made by Fathers who spoke for themselves alone, in a private capacity, whereas many of those who praised it represented

---

[10] *Vatican I, le Concile de Pie IX, la préparation, les méthodes de travail, les schémas restés en suspens* (Paris: Lethielleux, 1962).

October 26

[1] Paul Zoungrana, P.B. (1917–2000), from Burkina Faso, ordained in 1942. Archbishop of Ouagadougou from 1960 to 1965, created cardinal in 1965.

[2] "To the judgment and authority of the Holy See".

[3] "Let us proceed with caution."

[4] Willem Marinus Bekkers (1908–1966), Dutch, ordained in 1933. Bishop of Hertogenbosch from 1960 until his death. Member of the Commission for the Liturgy.

an entire episcopate. Three sorts of objections have been made, to which he wanted to respond. 1. – There are various imperfections: no doubt, but they have been exaggerated, especially from a theological point of view; let the spirit of the schema not be changed. – 2. – On the language of the liturgy: let it be noted that what the schema and the majority are asking for is only a "facultas",[5] not an obligation for all. – 3. – Against the rights to be accorded to the bishops, canon law has been invoked; but it is necessary here to make a distinction; among Catholics, there is no dispute on the right of the pope to reserve to himself certain powers; it is a completely different question here, that of the powers that the pope can also recognize in the bishops for their respective dioceses; finally, in any event, the ecumenical council, which is held with the pope and under his power, has complete authority to decide whether to recognize the right of the bishops to use this or that power presently reserved to the pope.

Bishop M.J. Flores[6] of Barbastro (Spain). Numerous details for nos. 1, 4, 5, 6. No. 9 could be clearer, and emphasis should be placed on the "pia exercitia";[7] no. 20 is good, but be careful of the risk: make mention of the pope; no. 24: we should mistrust those who dare everything; beware, here as everywhere, of the "intolerantia auctoritatis",[8] beware of troublemakers. Flores applied the prayer of Saint Isidore recited at the beginning of every session: that we not let ourselves be diverted from truth and justice by love for our national languages. The Ecclesia must be "una in fide, una in liturgia, una in caritate".[9]

Auxiliary Bishop Ancel (Lyon). Everything in the schema responds to the pastoral aim of the council, following the desire of the pope. Two remarks. 1. – De liturgiis orientalibus,[10] a few words should be introduced at the end of the Prooemium; unity is not in uniformity, it is in faith in the same revelation. – 2. – Adaptations are necessary in the missions, but elsewhere also; everywhere, pervasive naturalism and materialism hinder the understanding of the rites, especially among the working class: "Adjuro vos, qui curam animarum non habetis,

---

[5] "Option".

[6] Jaime Flores Martin (1906–1974), Spanish, ordained in 1930. Bishop of Barbastro from 1960 to 1970.

[7] "Pious exercises".

[8] "Lack of tolerance for authority".

[9] "One in faith, one in liturgy, one in charity".

[10] "On the Eastern liturgies".

miseremini fratrum vestrorum, etc."[11] – At no. 22, an addition to the title was proposed; at ll. 14–15: this is not sufficient.

Bishop J. Hervas y Benet (Spain). Remove the note on p. 155. Number the Prooemium as well, as in the other schemas. P. 157, ll. 25ff.: keep the statement of principle; ll. 29–30: it would be good for the council to declare explicitly here its great esteem for all the Catholic rites, so that the members of the Eastern Churches do not have the impression of being treated as second-class Catholics. As for Latin, take a "via media": apply to other cultures the principles that "Veterum sapientia" applies to the Latin culture. Give more scope to the use of vernacular languages. Let these rights be given, not to isolated bishops, but to episcopal conferences; will these have a strictly legislative function? It is still difficult to say. In any case, next have recourse to the Holy See. With this moderamen,[12] no. 24 is good.

Bishop Luigi Carli[13] of Segni (Italy): P. 163, l. 16 (no. 11): an exaggeration; the liturgy is not "principal discipline". – p. 164: add an article making clear that only the pope can abrogate the approved books and asking for the promulgation of a liturgical code. – p. 167, ll. 18–19: all judgment must be left to the pope alone; otherwise, there will be variations and disagreements within the same regions, since the bishops are not bound by their episcopal conference. (Carli took this opportunity to protest against those who, by their distinctions, have shown their mistrust "erga Sanctam Sedem").[14] – P. 169, ll. 6–7: explain further or delete. – P. 169, the last part of no. 33: say that this applies to the churches of religious orders.

Christopher Butler, O.S.B., abbot of Downside, president of the Benedictine Congregation of England: In the Prooemium, p. 157, ll. 25–26, add: "neque in aliis suis actis neque in praesenti constitutione";[15] for the pope has declared that the council will not define anything. A new dogma should not be defined unless absolutely necessary: now such is not the case; and that would put one more obstacle in the way of unity, which is one of the (future) goals of the council.

---

[11] "I implore you, you who do not have souls in your charge, to have pity on your brothers."

[12] "Mitigation".

[13] Luigi Carli (1914–1986), Italian, ordained in 1937. Bishop of Segni from 1957 to 1973. Member of the Commission for Bishops and the Government of Dioceses. He was, with Geraldo de Proença Sigaud and Marcel Lefebvre, one of the organizers of the *Coetus internationalis patrum*, which represented the minority party of the council.

[14] "Toward the Holy See".

[15] "Neither in its other acts nor in the present constitution".

A bishop from Vietnam:[16] pp. 157–58, add that these usages must be "ad mentem sacrae traditionis recogniti".[17]

The auxiliary of Burgos[18] (Spain): no. 3, p. 160, the comments of the priest are not always the words of Christ. P. 162, no. 9: specify the spiritual exercises. P. 167, no. 24: without Latin, the Mass will be even less understood. The Fathers at Trent had to react against variety; "fructus ex historia capiamus."[19]

Costantini,[20] a Franciscan bishop: vernacular languages are constantly changing. Comments in the vernacular are sufficient. And the liturgy in the vernacular languages will not suffice to bring back our separated brothers.

La Ravoire,[21] bishop of Krishnagar (India): Latin must remain the official language of the Latin Church, but the question of liturgical usage is something else. On that, the schema is "nimis timidum".[22] Latin is a "medium ad finem, sc. bonum animarum";[23] it is not an end. Now, bonum animarum hodie requirit linguam vernaculam.[24] A pastoral reason: for an active and conscious participation, quae est vix possibilis[25] with Latin. Some have brought up the danger of corruption: sed tutius conservabuntur a corruptione formulae, si intelliguntur a circumstantibus.[26] Even in Rome, the ancient Church used the language of the people. Moreover, firmiter speramus unionem:[27] now, non-Catholics do not use Latin; we must remove all obstacles, when it is not a matter of something necessary. – At no. 24: expand. "Judicium opportunitatis pertinet ad conferentias episcoporum, approbante Sancta Sede."[28]

---

[16] Simon Hoa Nguên-van Hien (1906–1973), Vietnamese, ordained in 1935. Bishop of Dalat (Vietnam) from 1960 until his death.

[17] "Revised in the spirit of sacred tradition".

[18] Demetrio Mansilla Reoyo (1910–1998), Spanish, ordained in 1934. Auxiliary bishop of Burgos from 1958 to 1964, then bishop of Ciudad Rodrigo.

[19] "Let us gather the fruits of history."

[20] Vittorio Maria Costantini, O.F.M. (1906–2003), Italian, ordained in 1929. Bishop of Sessa Aurunca from 1962 to 1982.

[21] Louis La Ravoire Morrow, S.D.B. (1892–1987), American, ordained in 1921. Bishop of Krishnagar (India) from 1939 to 1969.

[22] "Too timid".

[23] "A means to an end, namely, the good of souls".

[24] "The good of souls today demands the use of the vernacular."

[25] "Which is hardly possible".

[26] "But the formulas will be better preserved from alteration if they are understood by the congregation."

[27] "We firmly hope for unity."

[28] "The judgment about the appropriateness of this decision falls to the bishops' conferences, with the approval of the Holy See."

Reetz,[29] Benedictine abbot of Beuron. He is for a "usus moderatus linguae vulgaris",[30] but he would not wish Gregorian chant to be condemned to death; he does not believe it is necessary for everyone to understand everything; the other day, I only understood one word of the Greek Mass: Amen; and yet it was of spiritual benefit.

K.J. Calewaert, bishop of Gand (who was put on the Preparatory Theological Commission by mistake: in Rome, he was mistaken for another man with the same name, dead these last few years, a great specialist in liturgy):[31] Latin is the best sign of unity; in conferences, pilgrimages, international meetings, it is necessary that everyone be able to chant together the Gloria, the Credo, the Salve Regina ... The vernacular can be allowed for the sacraments.

Auxiliary Bishop Le Cordier[32] of Paris: a question: this initial note? – A testimony: nos. 22 and 24 respond to the expectations of the working-class faithful.

Dom Jean Prou,[33] Abbot of Solesmes: nos. 20 and 21 would be the dissolutio totius ordinis romani. The schema nihil dicit de consuetudinibus quae vim legis obtinuerunt, quod erat modus innovandi secundum morem et prudentiam.[34] It is to be feared that this reform, the work of periti, might be too intellectual, too abstract, and may turn out in damnum boni communis.[35] As for no. 24, it is dangerous: there is a risk of

---

[29] Benedikt Reetz, O.S.B. (1897–1964), German. Superior general of the congregation of Benedictines of Beuron from 1957 until his death, on December 28, 1964. Member of the Commission for Religious.

[30] "A moderate usage of the vernacular language".

[31] Karel Justinus Calewaert (1893–1963), Belgian, ordained in 1922, bishop of Gand from 1948 to 1963. Karel Calewaert was a member, not of the Preparatory Theological Commission, but of the Preparatory Commission for the Liturgy. The rumor that H. de Lubac reports here, and that Yves Congar also mentions (*My Journal of the Council*, trans. Mary John Ronayne and Mary Cecily Boulding [Hindmarsh: ATF Press, 2012], p. 21), is not accurate. It is true that there was someone else with the same last name, Camiel Callewaert, president of the Seminary of Bruges and a great liturgist, but he (K. Calewaert) knew Ferdinando Antonelli, a member of the Preparatory Liturgical Commission, who must have had him called to join the commission. Karel Calewaert had a great interest in liturgy and was elected a member of the conciliar Commission for the Liturgy.

[32] Jacques Le Cordier (1904–2003), French, ordained in 1928. Auxiliary bishop of Paris from 1955 to 1966. He was named under-secretary of the council at the beginning of 1965, replacing J. Villot, who became archbishop of Lyon at the death of Cardinal Gerlier.

[33] Dom Jean Prou, O.S.B. (1911–1999), French, abbot of Saint Peter's Abbey, Solesmes, from 1959 to 1992. Superior general of the Benedictine congregation of Solesmes. Member of the Commission for the Liturgy.

[34] "The total dissolution of the Roman rite. The schema says nothing about the customs that have obtained the force of law, which was a means of innovating in a prudent and permitted fashion."

[35] "To the detriment of the common good".

no longer being able to go back. It would be necessary to place strict limits on this.

Another bishop:[36] a myriad of remarks ...

Bishop Rau (?):[37] on no. 24. This is not a dogmatic question but a pastoral one, and one of extreme importance. Tempus urgenter exigit profundam renovationem liturgiae;[38] let the liturgy no longer be something that can be spoken of as the concern of only some, of priests and the learned. We must accede to the desire of the Christian people, even in Europe; they want to understand. Even when the priest addresses God, he does so in the name of the plebs christiana,[39] who should participate in it. The whole liturgy signifies the Mystery of Christ; now the sign must be understood. Moreover, Ecclesiae qua tali nulla est propria cultura. Et, ad unionem fratrum separatorum ...[40] No. 24: a wish for a mensura amplior.[41] Of course, always "actis a Sancta Sede recognitis".[42]

Del Campo y de la Bárcena[43] (Calahorra, Spain): Desideratur clara notio liturgiae;[44] ambiguities concerning the word throughout the schema. – Numerous diverse remarks. – No. 21: the episcopal conferences are constantly evolving; the problem will be treated in the schema De episcopis; in the meantime, let us not be specific about anything; find a general formula that does not close the path forward, etc. (He goes on too long; the president stops him.)

Bishop Lokuang[45] (Formosa) recalled the faculties accorded by the Holy See to the Jesuits in the seventeenth century; but the arguments over this brought the adaptation to a standstill.

Archbishop Lefebvre, superior general of the Holy Ghost Fathers, relinquished his turn to speak.

---

[36] Jesús Enciso Viana (1906–1964), Spanish, ordained in 1928. Bishop of Majorca from 1955 until his death. Member of the Commission for the Liturgy.

[37] Enrique Rau (1899–1971), Argentinian, ordained in 1922, bishop of Mar del Plata (Argentina) from 1957 to 1971. Member of the Commission for the Liturgy.

[38] "Our time urgently demands a profound renovation of the liturgy."

[39] "Christian people".

[40] "The Church is not attached to any particular culture. And, with a view to union with our separated brothers ..."

[41] "A more wide-ranging measure".

[42] "By means of acts approved by the Holy See".

[43] Abilio del Campo y de la Bárcena (1908–1980), Spanish, ordained in 1931. Bishop of Calahorra y La Calzada (Spain) from 1953 to 1976.

[44] "A clear idea of the liturgy is desired."

[45] Stanislas Lokuang (1911–2004), Chinese, ordained in 1936. Bishop of Tainan (Taiwan), from 1961 to 1966. Member, then vice-president of the Commission for the Missions.

A Brazilian bishop:[46] p. 166, ll. 7–8, delete the reference to canon law: the councils meet for new laws. Let there be confidence in the Catholic sense and prudence of the bishops. No. 24: let all of the Mass of the Catechumens be in the vernacular.

Bishop Borromeo[47] (Italy): let Latin be kept, even for the sacraments.

This afternoon, a meeting at the *Civiltà cattolica*, with the editors of the Jesuit journals, in the office of Fr. Tucci. Cordial atmosphere. Numerous small pieces of news, perhaps too small. An examination of the procedures that would be useful so as to avoid wasting time, etc. – Returned to the Borgo. A visit from Mr. Jean Grootaers,[48] editor in chief of the Flemish Catholic journal *De Maand*. He has visited a certain number of bishops and theologians before returning tomorrow to Brussels.

At 4:30 P.M., funeral Mass for Archbishop Chichester, at the Gesù.

Saturday, October 27, 1962. – At 8:30 A.M., Father Moubarac came to introduce me to his Polish friend, a journalist who has come for the council, Casimir Morawski.[1]

At Saint Peter's, Mass by the archbishop of Mexico.[2] Today's president: Cardinal Ruffini, who recommended brevity.

Archbishop Olaechea Loizaga[3] of Valencia (Spain): "Schema subjiciendum examini theologorum, sicut dictum fuit"[4] by the speakers from the Holy Office. Prooemium, no. 10: instead of "exercetur", say: "applicatur"[5] ("exercetur", however, is the word in the liturgy). Ll. 19–20:

[46]Clemente de Gouvea Isnard, O.S.B. (1917–1992), Brazilian, ordained in 1942. Bishop of Nova Friburgo (Brazil) from 1960 to 1992.

[47]Luigi Carlo Borromeo (1893–1975), Italian, ordained in 1918. Bishop of Pesaro (Italy) from 1952 to 1975. Member of the Commission for Religious.

[48]Jan Grootaers, born in 1921, Belgian, chief librarian of the Belgian parliament, chronicler of the council for the journals *Irénikon* and *De Maand*, secretary general of the "Rencontres internationales des Informateurs religieux" (founded in 1961 with a view to Vatican II), professor at the theology faculty of the Katholieke Universiteit Leuven from 1966 to 1987, author of numerous works on Vatican II.

October 27

[1]Casimir Marawski, Polish journalist accredited at the council for the newspaper *Zaiprzeciw*.

[2]Miguel Darió Miranda y Gómez (1895–1986), Mexican, ordained in 1918. Archbishop of Mexico City from 1956 to 1977, president of CELAM from 1958 to 1963. Created cardinal in 1969. Member of the Commission for Bishops and the Government of Dioceses.

[3]Marcelino Olaechea Loizaga, O.S.B. (1889–1972), Spanish, ordained in 1915. Archbishop of Valencia from 1946 to 1966. Member of the Commission on Seminaries, Studies, and Catholic Education.

[4]"The schema should be submitted to the examination of theologians, as has been said."

[5]"Is exercised", "is applied" [concerning the work of redemption].

the texts quoted from St. Paul are not ad rem. – Chap. 1, no. 3, p. 160: various types of presence, which should be distinguished. – p. 162: make this clearer. – p. 163, nos. 11–12: exaggerations. – Delete ll. 30–34, etc.

Da Cunha Marelim[6] (Brazil): p. 166, no. 21, ll. 3–5, delete the mention of the Ordinaries, keep the reference to the national episcopal conferences. No. 22, ll. 15–17: should be changed, in accordance with no. 21. – p. 167, l. 16: say: "national" episcopal conferences. – P. 169, no. 32, l. 17: add that offices in the churches near the place where the bishop preaches are forbidden.

Eugène D'Souza,[7] archbishop of Nagpur (India): no. 21 gives broad powers, and no. 22 takes them back; however, the system whereby we ask Rome for everything has practical drawbacks. In Rome, one has a harder time judging regional cases; the real periti are on site; the best judges are the bishops, assisted by their consultors. This text in no. 22 says nothing: we already have the right to make proposals to the Holy See. – "Nonne episcopi in missionibus jam aetatem habent?"[8] They will be the first to "frenum imponere",[9] if need be. So let them be granted the "facultas statuendi aptationes".[10] Let us decide on a time limit, after which it will be necessary to have the judgment of the Holy See. "Concilium largius se praebeat erga conferentias episcopales".[11]

Garcia de Sierra y Méndez,[12] archbishop of Pario, coadjutor of Oviedo: let us not fall into liturgism. Let greater mention be made of secret prayer in cubiculo, of pietas privata,[13] as the encyclical *Mediator Dei* does. There are multiple forms of piety; Pius XII, sanctae memoriae,[14] spoke about them. Ne simus renovandae liturgiae specie decepti.[15] Scripture ceaselessly recommends piety; cf. the example of the saints.

---

[6] Luís Gonzaga da Cunha Marelim, C.M. (1904–1991), Brazilian, ordained in 1927. Bishop of Caxias do Maranhão from 1941 to 1981.

[7] Eugène D'Souza, M.S.F.S. (1917–2003), Indian, ordained in 1944. Bishop, then archbishop of Nagpur (India) from 1951 to 1963, then archbishop of Bhopal from 1963 to 1994. Member of the Commission for the Missions, elected during the second session of the council.

[8] "Are the bishops in the missions not yet adults?"

[9] "To put on the brakes".

[10] "Right to determine the adaptations".

[11] "Let the council show itself more open with respect to the bishops' conferences."

[12] Segundo Garcia de Sierra y Méndez (1908–1998), Spanish, ordained in 1931. Coadjutor of the archbishop of Oviedo from 1959 to 1964, titular archbishop of Parium (Pario, in Italian). He was named archbishop of Burgos in February 1964.

[13] "In one's room, private piety".

[14] "Of sainted memory".

[15] "Let us not allow ourselves to be fooled by the appearance of a liturgy to be renewed."

Tantum unum argumentum proponam, brevitatis causa ...[16] (A conclusion in 6 parts, the last divided into 3 points).

F. Marty,[17] archbishop of Reims. (1) There should be mention made of the Holy Spirit, too absent in this schema. – (2) Nos. 5 and 6: it is not said that all liturgy of the Church must be a missionary call. – (3) No. 22: "Insinuari videtur concessio, accidentaliter, ex necessitate. Atqui, semper parata esse debet Ecclesia ad evanglizandos homines. P. 26: in omnibus regionibus vita liturgica praebere debet alimentum spiritui missionario Ecclesiae."[18]

Cyrille[19] ... in Armenia: History of the Armenian rite, the antiquity of which is underrated. (The president recalls him to the subject.) Do not impose on the Eastern Churches certain modifications that would differentiate their rites from those of their Orthodox fellow countrymen.

Anicet Fernández, O.P.,[20] master general: Major concordia esset si duae quaestiones distinguerentur: (a) major libertas in usu linguarum vernacularum: resp.: affirmative; – (b) utrum omnes sacerdotes debeant cognoscere linguam latinam: affirmative, nam: lingua latina possidet (jus a longo tempore) – est lingua officialis – in lingua latina continentur immensi thesauri sapientiae christianae.[21]

H. Jeny,[22] auxiliary bishop of Cambrai. P. 160, no. 2, l. 11, delete "sacramenta administrantur",[23] which, having been added, breaks the

---

[16] "I am going to give only one argument, for the sake of brevity."

[17] François Marty (1904–1994), French, ordained in 1930. Archbishop of Reims from 1960 to 1968, created cardinal in 1969. Consultor to the Preparatory Commission for Studies and Seminaries. In the first session, he was elected a member of the Commission for the Discipline of the Clergy and the Christian People.

[18] "A concession seems to be accidentally implied, out of necessity. Yet the Church must always be ready to evangelize men. In every land, the liturgical life must nourish the missionary spirit of the Church."

[19] Cirillo Giovanni Zohrabian, O.F.M. Cap. (1881–1972), Turkish, ordained in 1904. Titular bishop.

[20] Aniceto Fernández, O.P. (1895–1981), Spanish. Master General of the Dominicans from 1962 to 1974. He was named as a member of the Doctrinal Commission by the pope during the first session.

[21] "There would be greater agreement if two questions had been distinguished: (a) a greater freedom in the use of vernacular languages. Response: yes. (b) Must all priests know Latin? Yes, because: Latin is in place (and has been so for a long time already), it is the official language, immense treasures of Christian wisdom are contained in the Latin language."

[22] Henry Jenny (1904–1982), French, ordained in 1927. Auxiliary bishop of Cambrai from 1959 to 1965. Member of the Preparatory Commission for the Liturgy. Member of the Commission for the Liturgy.

[23] "The sacraments are administered."

unity of the paragraph. No. 3, l. 21, delete "et explicantur".[24] P. 161, no. 5, l. 10, delete: "in suo centro, quod est divinum Eucharistiae sacrificium".[25] No. 6, l. 29, add: "in aqua et Spiritu sancto".[26] P. 165, no. 19: let the text of the commission be restored. – "Poetica verba? Sed tota Scriptura est poetica",[27] etc.; and the Fathers of the Church ... "Attendatur ne sub specie verae doctrinae"[28] we do not do away with the biblical and traditional life-blood ... – P. 167, no. 25: add something on catechesis, which is still, proh dolor! abstracta et scholaris.[29]

Marcus Gregorius McGrath,[30] auxiliary bishop of Panama. The Prooemium, ll. 26ff., is not theological enough; there are some inaccuracies in the schema; it should be revised by the periti who are theologians. However, it would be pointless to send it back to the Commission de Fide;[31] it is not the same situation here as it was at Trent or at the First Vatican Council: each commission is endowed with experts in various fields. – De lingua latina:[32] the reasons for the use of vernacular languages need to be better explained, so as not to give the impression that we are only dealing here with exceptional cases. – The appellation of "novatores",[33] thrown out yesterday, is an insult; the pope himself has exhorted us to a "renovatio".[34] Moreover, if there is legitimate progress in dogma, then this holds a fortiori in practical matters as well. The bishops' wishes have been approved by the pope, and now the council is gathered to work on this renewal. The code of canon law recognizes the supreme power of the council united under the authority of the pope.

Zacharias Rolim de Moura,[35] bishop of Cajaserias (?), Brazil. – Diverse details. We must avoid the multiplication of local rites. A speech in

---

[24] "And explained".

[25] "In its center, which is the divine sacrifice of the Eucharist".

[26] "By water and the Holy Spirit".

[27] "Poetic expressions? But all of Scripture is poetic."

[28] "Take care that, under the guise of true doctrine".

[29] "Alas! abstract and unimaginative".

[30] Marcos Gregorio McGrath, C.S.C. (1924–2000), Panamanian. Auxiliary bishop of Panama City from 1961 to 1964, then bishop of Santiago de Veraguas (Panama). He was elected as a member of the Doctrinal Commission during the first session.

[31] This is referring to the Doctrinal Commission.

[32] "On Latin".

[33] "Innovators".

[34] "Renewal".

[35] Zacarias Rolim de Moura (1914–1992), Brazilian, ordained in 1937. Bishop of Cajazeiras (Brazil) from 1953 to 1990.

defense of Latin. Let there be no excessive innovations or exaggerations against the venerabiles traditiones.[36]

Jorge Kemerer,[37] bishop of Posadas (Argentina). He spoke in the name of 20 bishops. Generatim, optimum schema, omnino conforme cum sana traditione et doctrina Ecclesiae.[38] Let the corrections that are to be made go in the same pastoral direction. – Add a no. 4 to article 5. At article 24, necessarium videtur dicere: "statuere". – Concilium maxima gaudet auctoritate;[39] all the rest is good for enlightening us, but not binding us. – Latin, bond of unity? But the Eastern Catholics are certainly in the unity of the Church. The unity is threefold: "regiminis, veritatis, caritatis";[40] it does not depend on one language. Fons unitatis est Spiritus sanctus, qui obstaculum superavit et superabit, non lingua unica, sed illustratione mentis et amoris.[41]

Umbertus Mozzoni (?),[42] Argentinian: against the stipendia[43] and the appearance of commerce.

Pierre Arikata Kobayashi,[44] bishop of Sendai, in the name of all the Japanese bishops, insistently recommended the schema. He asked for an "amplior usus linguae vernaculae"; it is of a "speciale momentum pro Japonia".[45] Uniformity is not necessary for the oeconomia salutis.[46] Is the unity around the pope so weak that it must collapse without exterior uniformity? God has laid out a path proper to every people. – For the episcopal conferences, at no. 24, instead of "proponere", put "statuere, actis a Sancta Sede recognitis".[47] (Applause.)

---

[36] "Venerable traditions".

[37] Jorge Kemerer, S.V.D. (1908–1998), Argentinian, ordained in 1932. Bishop of Posadas (Argentina) from 1957 to 1986.

[38] "In general, an excellent schema, in complete conformity with sound tradition and doctrine of the Church".

[39] "It seems necessary to say 'establish'. The council possesses the greatest authority."

[40] "Of government, of truth, of charity".

[41] "The source of unity is the Holy Spirit, who has overcome and will overcome the obstacle, not by a single unique language, but by the illumination of spirit and heart."

[42] This was in reality Alberto Devoto (1918–1984), Argentinian, ordained in 1942. Bishop of Goya (Argentina) from 1961 to 1984.

[43] Fees for Masses.

[44] Petro Arikata Kobayashi (1909–1999), Japanese, ordained in 1935. Bishop of Sendai from 1954 to 1976.

[45] "A broader use of the vernacular language; this is of particular importance for Japan."

[46] "Economy of salvation".

[47] "Instead of 'propose', put 'establish, by decisions approved by the Holy See'."

Hyacinthe Thiandoum,[48] archbishop of Dakar, spoke in the name of all Africa, Madagascar, and the Isles. He asked that "occidental" be replaced by "Roman" and explained why. Everyone considers that it is of "maximi momenti, ipsum celebrantem directe uti posse lingua vernacula in iis missae partibus in quibus alloquitur fideles."[49] We do not want to exclude Latin. But let the episcopal conferences decide in different cases.

Antoine Pildáin y Zapiáin,[50] bishop of the Canary Islands (Spain). No. 31 is very good, praesertim in eo quod in re pecuniae insistit;[51] we must do away with the stipendia, the classes of marriage and funeral services, etc. Do not humiliate the poor or disappoint them; it is a gravissima quaestio justitiae socialis, ecclesiasticae et liturgicae.[52] (A little old man, thin and energetic, very insistent; he is applauded.) Correct the last words of no. 31. Think of the "Beati pauperes". But: (1) Toto coelo differt practica nostra a littera et spiritu evangelii;[53] (2) Today: cf. the epistle of James[54] and Bossuet's sermon on the eminent dignity of the poor;[55] (3) This whole system of classes is a great injustice. (More applause. The president, Ruffini, intervened to say that from now on there was to be no more applause.)

Joseph Melas,[56] bishop of Nuoro (Italy). Let Latin be preserved and recommended, ut ex omni lingua et natione ... latine loquantur.[57] Do not scandalize the faithful by innovations.

A Franciscan missionary bishop (India).[58] Against the use of vernacular languages. Besides, most of the time, one does not hear the priest: so what does it matter whether he speaks in Latin or in another

---

[48] Hyacinthe Thiandoum (1921–2004), Senegalese, ordained in 1949. Archbishop of Dakar from 1962 to 2000. Created cardinal in 1976.

[49] "Of the highest importance, that the celebrant himself might be able to employ the vernacular language in those parts of the Mass in which he addresses the faithful".

[50] Antonio Pildáin y Zapiáin (1890–1973), Spanish, ordained in 1913. Bishop of the Canary Islands from 1936 to 1966.

[51] "Particularly in the part that deals with money".

[52] "Very serious question of social, ecclesiastic, and liturgical justice".

[53] "Blessed are the poor" [Mt 5:3]. (1) Our practice differs completely from the letter and the spirit of the Gospel."

[54] "Let the lowly brother boast in his exaltation" [Jas 1:9].

[55] Sermon sur l'éminente dignité des Pauvres dans l'Église (1659), by Jacques-Bénigne Bossuet (1627–1704), French orator and bishop of Meaux.

[56] Giuseppe Melas (1901–1970), Italian, ordained in 1926. Bishop of Nuoro (Italy) from 1947 until his death.

[57] "So that people of all languages and all nations might speak Latin".

[58] Albert Conrad De Vito, O.F.M. Cap. (1904–1970), Italian, ordained in 1927. Bishop of Lucknow from 1946 until his death.

language? The divine mysteries are diminished by the use of vernacular languages.

Joseph Schoiswohl,[59] bishop of Seckau (Austria). He submitted his text to the secretariat. A simple remark: let the bishops take advantage of Sundays to go and see how church services are done in the parishes of Rome, *sicut ego feci* ...[60]

A Brazilian bishop.[61] This council offers us an opportunity, unique in our century, that we must not miss. Let the vernacular languages be permitted, so as to come to the aid of men affected by materialism and atheism. Latin is not the bond of unity. *Bonus et malus homo utuntur eadem lingua. Caritas est unicum vinculum inter homines.*[62] Every people has the right to praise God in its own language. *Quam primum*,[63] let us put the experts to work. And now, let us hasten to vote on the schema.

Another Brazilian.[64] Experience shows that great confusion has arisen in the last few years. *Hodie lingua, cras aliud* ...[65] And the laity claim to know better than the clergy. There is no one who is incapable of understanding the Latin Mass, after some explanation. The silence of the faithful better shows the sacred character of the priest. Let us not grant anything to the bishops' conferences: the bishop is master in his diocese; *nullum moderamen, nulla juridictio inter episcopum et Romanum Pontificem.*[66] (One person applauded.)

Thomas William Muldoon[67] (Australia). He gave up his turn to speak. He asked the Board of Presidency to close the discussion of the Prooemium and chapter 1. Let the text of the interventions already planned be sent to the secretariat, if need be.

Cardinal Ruffini answered that he did not have the right to prevent anyone from speaking; but he recommended that the suggestion just made be taken into consideration.

---

[59] Josef Schoiswohl (1901–1991), Austrian, ordained in 1924. Bishop of Seckau (Austria) from 1954 to 1969.

[60] "As I have done myself".

[61] In reality, this was a German missionary, Charles Weber, S.V.D. (1886–1970), ordained in 1910. Bishop of Ichow (China) from 1946 to 1970.

[62] "The good man and the bad man use the same language. Charity is the only bond between people."

[63] "As soon as possible".

[64] Carlos Eduardo de Sabóia Bandeira Melo.

[65] "Today the language, tomorrow something else ..."

[66] "No intermediate body, no jurisdiction between the bishop and the Roman Pontiff".

[67] Thomas William Muldoon (1917–1986), Australian, ordained in 1941. Auxiliary bishop of Sydney from 1960 to 1982. Member of the Commission for the Discipline of the Sacraments.

Joseph Carraro,[68] bishop of Verona (Italy), proposed a reconciliation between the two views. He laid out some guiding principles. Let us bring together the vota pastoralia and the exigentia unitatis et doctrinae.[69] – Remarks on nos. 7–9. – Praise of St. Pius X.[70]

Charles Ferrero de Cavallerleone,[71] archbishop of Trebizond, an Italian. He recommended great prudence. He complained that, in 1955, the reading of the Passion during Holy Week was shortened; it is a great doctrinal injury: we no longer read the institution of the Eucharist, etc. Let the Fathers restore it.

A Benedictine abbot:[72] praise for the encyclical *Mediator Dei*.

Eleven speakers passed on their turn to speak. There are still about thirty expected for Monday. The cardinal president asked them to pass or to be brief. The council Fathers will send a message to John XXIII for the anniversary of his election.[73]

Meeting adjourned at half past noon.

Had lunch at the Ursulines' (not federated), who have a small boarding school for girls here in Rome, with Father René Laurentin, who recently published a book on the stakes of the council.[74] He gave me some details on the Liturgical Commission, etc.

Fr. Camelot is very happy with the talk that F. Congar gave yesterday at the French Seminary, on tradition.

They tell me (I suppose it was a joke) that the moderate Italian bishops, in a conciliatory spirit, would gladly accept, for the conciliar commissions, an equal division of votes: fifty-fifty; half Italians, half foreigners. – A thick notebook of remarks printed "sub secreto",[75] on the doctrinal schemas, was loaned to me for a brief time.

At 4 P.M., in the large parlor of Santa Marta's, a continuation of last Saturday's conversation with the French bishops on the doctrinal

---

[68] Giuseppe Carraro (1899–1980), Italian, ordained in 1923. Bishop of Verona from 1958 to 1978. Member of the Commission for Seminaries, Studies, and Catholic Education.

[69] "Pastoral wishes and the demand of unity and doctrine".

[70] Giuseppe Melchiorre Sarto (1835–1914), Italian, ordained in 1858. Elected pope in 1903, beatified in 1951, and canonized in 1954.

[71] Carlo Alberto Ferrero de Cavallerleone (1903–1969), Italian, ordained in 1928. Archbishop in charge of the Italian military from 1944 to 1969.

[72] Cesar Gerardo Vielmo Guerra, O.S.M. (not Benedictine) (1914–1963), Italian, ordained in 1937. Apostolic vicar of Aysén (Chile) from 1960 until his death.

[73] John XXIII was elected pope on October 28, 1958.

[74] *L'Enjeu du Concile* (Paris: Éd. du Seuil, 1962).

[75] "Under secrecy".

schemas I and II. Many more people than the first time: about 150; some bishops from Africa and elsewhere joined the French group; ten or so young priests or seminarians. I announced that today it would be the bishops' turn to talk, to raise objections or ask questions; but first, some preliminary remarks: my criticisms are not inspired by personal theories – I recognize some good elements in the schemas – I felt obliged in good conscience to show a certain severity – I refuse to dissociate the pastoral and the doctrinal, etc. – Then they spoke of the link between Scripture and tradition; the chapter de Deo;[76] of the positive text that would be desirable; of the response to be brought to men of today by the council; of Father Teilhard; chap. V of the Epistle to the Romans; of polygenism; of the patchwork method used in drafting the schemas; of the necessity of putting the person of Our Lord Jesus Christ at the center of everything; of the overly scholastic and purely Latin character of the texts; etc. Among the interventions, I noted those of Veuillot, de Provenchères,[77] Cazaux, Maziers, Stourm,[78] Lebrun,[79] Puech, Barthe, Lallier, Béjot ...[80] Archbishop Garrone kept quiet. As on the other day, Archbishop Guerry was absent. Two or three times, interventions by Bishop Philippe, O.P.: as a "Roman", he defended (with moderation) the point of view of the Theological Commission, toning down what I had said. He raised one objection: he did not understand why I criticized the passage saying that it is the place of the magisterium "judicare ... et enucleare ..."[81] I responded, among other things: one could not refuse to Saint Thomas any role in the enucleatio[82] of doctrine; but he was not part of the teaching Church ... – Archbishop Dubois, who was on the Theological Commission, was not there (archbishop of Besançon). – I said nothing about the more serious reproaches that one could legitimately address to the commission.

[76] "On God".

[77] Charles de Provenchères (1904–1984), French, ordained in 1928. Archbishop of Aix-en-Provence from 1945 to 1978. Member of the Preparatory Commission for the Discipline of the Clergy and the Christian People. Member of the Commission for Eastern Churches beginning with the second session.

[78] René-Louis Stourm (1904–1990), French, ordained in 1928. Bishop of Amiens from 1951, he was named archbishop of Sens in October 1962. Member of the Commission for the Lay Apostolate, named by the pope during the first session.

[79] Lucien Lebrun (1896–1985), French, ordained in 1923. Bishop of Autun from 1940 to 1966.

[80] Georges Béjot (1896–1987), French, ordained in 1925. Auxiliary bishop of Reims from 1955 to 1971.

[81] "Judge and explain in depth".

[82] "Explanation".

At 6 P.M., a brief conversation with Bishop Charles de la Brousse and Bishop Vial, two men from Lyon. – Bishop Gay[83] of Basse-Terre and Pointe-à-Pitre (Guadeloupe) came to greet me. He had presented his thesis at the Theology Faculty of Lyon in 1931.

Fr. G. Martelet was at Santa Marta's. He drove me back to the Borgo. He recently gave a doctrinal presentation in front of the Marist bishops (fifteen or so). He has just received permission from Fourvière to extend his stay in Rome.

Some German bishops, aided by Fr. Karl Rahner, have set forth their views on the schema that would be a desirable replacement for the doctrinal schemas. They had invited Cardinal Siri and Cardinal Montini to attend. Siri appeared to be very much opposed; Montini, somewhat reserved.

This morning, before the general congregation, in the experts' gallery, I greeted Msgr. Schmaus (Munich) and explained to him my position on the schemas.

Sunday, October 28, 1962. – This morning, rest; read Fr. Louis Bouyer's book, *Le rite et l'homme*. Visit from Fr. Dehergne,[1] who would like me to ask Cardinal Bea to intervene against false relics. – At noon, the pope recited the Angelus from his window and gave a short speech on the 4th anniversary of his election.

In the afternoon, visited the Basilica of Santi Quattro Coronati (the Four Crowned Martyrs), St. Clement, St. Peter in Chains. At the Maronite college, saw Fr. Khalifé, who was composing some observations on the first two doctrinal schemas; he would like to have his patriarch (Meouchi) present them at the council; they are more or less the same as mine. Visited for a few moments His Beatitude Patriarch Paul Meouchi, who offered me coffee. – Vain attempt to meet with Fr. Congar. – At the Biblical Institute, Fr. S. Lyonnet gave me some copies of the pamphlet written by the Institute in response to Spadafora's[2] criticisms.

---

[83] Jean Gay, C.S.Sp. (1901–1977), French, ordained in 1925. Bishop of Basse-Terre from 1945 to 1968. His thesis in theology was dedicated to Father Francis Libermann, who restored the Congregation of the Holy Ghost in the nineteenth century.

October 28

[1] Joseph Dehergne, S.J. (1903–1990), French, ordained in 1934. Up until 1951 he was a missionary in China, where he taught history and French. Next he worked as the librarian and archivist of the Jesuit Province of Paris while doing research on the Jesuit missions in China.

[2] *Une nouvelle attaque contre l'exégèse catholique et l'Institut biblique,* 15 p.

Fr. Rondet brought Archbishop Dalmais and Fr. Rouquette to Father L. de Peretti, superior general of the Canons Regular of the I. C. at Monte Verde.

An incredible fact, but confirmed, it seems; it was Fr. Khalifé who related it to me. He supposedly had it from the very mouth of Cardinal Bea's secretary. Some time ago, some articles appeared in the Communist newspapers against the personal secretary of John XXIII, Msgr. Capovilla: immorality, secret apartments kept for that purpose. The pope, upset, wanted a thorough investigation into the origin of this campaign. Fanfani[3] is supposed to have put his counter-espionage police on the trail and to have come in person to report the findings to the pope: apparently everything had its origin with three *minutanti* of the Holy Office. The story goes that Cardinal Bea was present at the conversation between John XXIII and Fanfani. The pope did not want to create a scandal: the 3 *minutanti* were soon transferred, and everything was hushed up. – What is this about, really? – Msgr. Capovilla has a lot of influence with John XXIII.

Archbishop Dante, grand master of ceremonies, was not elected to the Liturgical Commission, nor was he named by the pope to complete it. Many consider that a scandal. Fr. Dezza[4] himself, a serious, prudent man, who scarcely speaks to me, pointed it out to me. But there is an effort being made to bring it about and even a hope that he might be named secretary of the commission. That would be rather curious; for he criticized the schema in twelve points, which seems to have been well received by a great number of Fathers, and the proposed amendments, of which he should theoretically have taken account, are most often opposed to his.

Monday, October 29, 1962. – The October 28 edition of the *Espresso* has a long article on the council. Title: "Verso la nuova teologia".[1] The article talks about the "program of the new theology", its condemnation in 1950 by *Humani generis*, its partial return in 1960 when Congar and Lubac were named as consultors, although they rank lower than

---

[3] Amintore Fanfani (1908–1999), Italian politician, of the Christian Democratic party. He was prime minister from July 1960 to June 1963.

[4] Paolo Dezza, S.J. (1901–1999), Italian, ordained in 1928. Professor at the Bellarmino. Expert at the council.

October 29

[1] Carlo Falconi, "Prevalgono i padri conciliari favorevoli al rinnovamento: Verso la nuova teologia", *L'Espresso*, October 28, 1962.

simple old-school types like Piolanti and Parente, etc. It also says that my book on Teilhard has been censored; and that, despite that, I was called with Daniélou as an expert to the council, and that Chenu is the theologian of a Malagasy archbishop. The article ends with a long quotation from Parente's speech at the Lateran in 1960 and the threats that it contained: as one can see, it concludes, a great battle is brewing. – Articles like this are well designed to create a battlefield atmosphere, if not within the council, at least around it, in public opinion, and to distort everything.

This morning, at 8:15 A.M., a visit from a young American priest of the Congregation of the Holy Cross, sent to invite me to give a lecture at their college. I will go this very evening.

Arriving at St. Peter's, I encountered once again the good, large, jovial Bishop Mbuka-Nzundu of the former Belgian Congo; then Archbishop Blanchet; Bishop Courbe,[2] whose foot I stepped on, stopped me, and we chatted: he explained to me the tendencies of the council as he saw them being formed, with his customary moderation. At the gallery of the periti, spoke with Msgr. Onclin,[3] professor of canon law at Louvain. I made room for Fr. Charles Boyer beside me, but I did not succeed in getting him to talk.

Going back down, in the right-hand nave, I was accosted by an American bishop, a missionary in Burma. He told me that he made great use of my book *Aspects du Bouddhisme*,[4] in its English translation. I also said hello to the good, intelligent, and jovial Bishop Wright of Pittsburgh, USA, who was a member of the Preparatory Theological Commission.

The Mass was celebrated by Archbishop Yamaguchi[5] of Nagasaki. The president would be Cardinal Caggiano,[6] archbishop of Buenos Aires. Archbishop Felici gave the names of the Fathers named by the

---

[2] Stanislas Courbe (1886–1971), French, ordained in 1915. Auxiliary bishop of Paris from 1943 to 1968.

[3] Willy Onclin (1905–1989), Belgian, professor of canon law at the University of Louvain. An expert at the council, he participated in, among other things, the drafting of the decree *Christus Dominus* on the pastoral responsibility of the bishops. In 1965, he was named assistant secretary of the Papal Commission for the Revision of the [1917] Code of Canon Law.

[4] H. de Lubac, *Aspects du bouddhisme* (Paris: Éd. du Seuil, 1951), trans. George Lamb as *Aspects of Buddhism* (New York: Sheed and Ward, 1954).

[5] Paul Aijirô Yamaguchi (1894–1976), Japanese, ordained in 1923. Bishop, then archbishop, of Nagasaki from 1937 to 1968.

[6] Antonio Caggiano (1889–1979), Argentinian, ordained in 1912. Created cardinal in 1946, archbishop of Buenos Aires from 1959 to 1975. Member of the Board of Presidency.

pope to the various commissions. There are 9 per commission, and not 8 as we had expected. I noted, on the Commission for Doctrine: Cardinal Browne, O.P., Irish, former master general; Father Fernández, O.P., Spanish, master general; Archbishop Parente; – on the Liturgy: Archbishop Dante. The rumor is going around that it was to make room for the latter that the number of new names was raised from 8 to 9, the Commission for the Liturgy having already been filled.

The interventions resumed on the Prooemium and chap. 1 of the Liturgy. The president implored that no one speak any more on what has already been said, particularly on Latin. (The warning would do little good.)

Bishop Antonio Santin[7] of Trieste Italian: p. 165, l. 31, and p. 166, l. 10, delete "praesertim":[8] thus, it will only be a question of mission countries. De lingua latina aliquod novi:[9] there is no piety or dignity in a liturgy in the vernacular language. – The doctrinal part should be better written. – "Non amore novi procedamus!",[10] etc.

Joseph Battaglia,[11] bishop of Faenza (Italy): Miror, in toto hoc schemate, nihil de B.M. Virgine, Socia Christi. Silentium gravissimum.[12] For the adaptations, let the bishops' conferences meet by nations, not simply regions, even if there are various languages; let the minorities, the émigrés not be treated as foreigners. – At no. 24, lingua latina "diligenter et cum amore servetur. – S. Pontifex luculenter demonstravit nexum inter Ecclesiam et linguam latinam."[13] All the children of the Church must hear the voice of their Mother, the same voice. Latin, sign of unity. Adjuro vos …[14]

A bishop from China:[15] p. 161, add something on communion.

---

[7] Antonio Santin (1895–1981), Italian, ordained in 1918. Bishop, then archbishop, of Trieste from 1938 to 1975.

[8] "Especially".

[9] "Something new concerning Latin".

[10] "Let us not proceed from a love of novelty!"

[11] Giuseppe Battaglia (1890–1984), Italian, ordained in 1914. Bishop of Faenza (Italy) from 1944 to 1976.

[12] "I am surprised that nothing is said, anywhere in this schema, on the Blessed Virgin Mary, Associate of Christ. This is an extremely serious omission."

[13] "Let Latin be preserved zealously and with love. The Supreme Pontiff has amply demonstrated the link between the Church and Latin."

[14] "I implore you …"

[15] Federico Melendro Gutiérrez, S.J. (1889–1978), Spanish, ordained in 1922. Archbishop of Anking (China) from 1946 until his death.

Bishop Franić of Split (Yugoslavia). We are Westerners; but our Mass is completely in Old Church Slavonic. It is the Roman rite, translated by Cyril and Methodius,[16] and for more than a thousand years now always approved by the popes. Our missal is printed at the Vatican. The sacraments are given in lingua vernacula.[17] Let no one come to contest our practice, just when we are in such great difficulties. And let no one add an obstacle to union. We ask this in the name of the eight Yugoslav bishops present here. Thanks to Cardinal Tisserant for his intervention. Let us celebrate once here a Mass in Old Church Slavonic (applause).

Archbishop Enrico Nicodemo[18] of Bari (Italy). Non humanae sapientiae verbis, sed ad custodiendum depositum fidei recurramus.[19] The end of the liturgy is the glory of God. The desire for the salvation of souls, which must not be set against it, must not make us lose sight of the periculum fidei et unitatis; ergo, non sine magna cautela . . .[20] Moreover, Christus non omnibus fidelibus sed tantum apostolis et eorum successoribus dedit depositum fidei et gratiae . . .[21] If the faithful read for themselves, there is a danger of subjective interpretation. Christ said to Peter: "Confirma fratres tuos."[22] Petrus nos illuminat, nos dirigit, nobis succurrit . . .[23] Now he recommended Latin to us.

A bishop from East Germany.[24] In our country there are atheist liturgies, socialist marriages, etc., ceremonies for the education of the young. The sacra liturgia[25] is the only remedy left for us. So, no. 24 is very good; but it ought to go farther. Let there be added to it what the preparatory commission had planned. Adaptatio est quaestio de vita vel morte.[26]

---

[16]Brothers who, in the ninth century, translated the Gospels into Slavonic. They are considered the founders of the Slavic Church.

[17]"In the vernacular language".

[18]Enrico Nicodemo (1906–1973), Italian, ordained in 1928. Archbishop of Bari from 1952 until his death. Member of the Commission for the Discipline of the Clergy and the Christian People.

[19]"Let us not have recourse to words of human wisdom [1 Cor 2:13], but to the deposit of faith, which must be preserved."

[20]"Danger for faith and unity; so, not without great caution . . ."

[21]"Christ gave the deposit of faith and grace, not to all the faithful, but only to the apostles and their successors."

[22]Lk 22:32: "Ego autem rogavi pro te ut non deficiat fides tua: et tu aliquando conversus confirma fratres tuos." (But I have prayed for you that your own faith may not fail; and when you have turned again, strengthen your brethren.)

[23]"Peter illuminates us, gives us direction, helps us."

[24]Otto Spülbeck (1904–1970), German, ordained in 1930. Bishop of Meissen from 1958 until his death. Member of the Commission for the Liturgy.

[25]"Sacred liturgy".

[26]"Adaptation is a question of life or death."

A bishop from Paraguay.[27] Various details. No. 15, p. 164, is not worthy of the council, etc.

A Spanish titular bishop[28] (Garcia?); observations on details.

A Coptic bishop[29] (Egypt). Among us as well, the old Coptic is not understood. But we have the vernacular language as well. Our liturgical books are bilingual. The Latin Church could imitate us. All of the dialogue parts are in the vernacular language.

A Brazilian bishop.[30] It is necessary to introduce the vernacular a little more; let this be permitted, sed nulli implacabiliter impositum.[31] In the solemn offices, lingua latina adhibenda, ut officialis.[32] Do not improvise, call on the periti in lingua et in doctrina.[33] Do not abandon the exterior traditions, even in the vestments. For the sacraments, the vernacular. Delete the exorcisms from the rite of baptism, etc. (He was stammering. He is, they tell me, a convert, ordained and consecrated late in life; he does not have a diocese.)

A Spaniard:[34] no contradiction between *Veterum sapientia*, which speaks about clerics and their studies, and liturgical adaptation, a pastoral matter. Besides, the Holy See, guardian of the tradition, has granted a number of exceptions. Via media. Sedulo clerus a populo secernendus.[35] – There is no coherence in what is said about episcopal conferences; let the text be unified.

F. Simons,[36] bishop of Indore (India). Most priests have a poor knowledge of Latin. There is no need for Latin at large meetings: simultaneous translation. Even in correspondence with the Holy See, the vernacular languages are used more and more. Everywhere one finds oneself obliged to translate the Acts of the Holy See. In seminaries and universities, Latin is insufficient and of little use. The study of the sources is a matter for

---

[27] Felipe Santiago Benítez Avalos, born in 1926, Paraguayan, ordained in 1952. Auxiliary bishop of Asunción from 1961 to 1965.

[28] Fidel García Martínez.

[29] Alexandros Scandar (1895–1964), Egyptian, ordained in 1922. Coptic-Catholic bishop of Assiut (Egypt) from 1947 until his death.

[30] Salomão Ferraz (1880–1969), Brazilian, ordained in 1945. Titular bishop.

[31] "But not imposed in an implacable manner".

[32] "Latin must be employed, as the official language."

[33] "Experts in language and doctrine".

[34] Pablo Barrachina Estevan, born in 1912, Spanish, ordained in 1941. Bishop of Orihuela-Alicante from 1954 to 1989.

[35] "The clergy must be carefully distinguished from the people."

[36] Franz Simons, S.V.D. (1908–2002), Dutch, ordained in 1932. Bishop of Indore in India from 1952 to 1971.

only a small number of specialists. Quin unitatem foveat, lingua latina facta est principium divisionis:[37] between priests and faithful, Easterners and Westerners, etc. Ideo, p. 167, "lingua latina solis philosophiae et theologiae professoribus servetur."[38]

Titular Archbishop Jules Kandela.[39] We have changed into another language the Syriac language spoken by Jesus and his Mother and, thus, venerable above all others. Having become unintelligible, it was better to sacrifice it than to harm the good of souls. We are not asking that Latin be despised but that we see the practical necessities.

An Italian bishop.[40] A lack of theological precision; *Mediator Dei* was better. P. 162, ll. 28–29, active participation is not sufficient; piety is necessary. – Without doubt Latin non est de essentia fidei, sed: una fides, unum baptisma, una liturgia. To say "catholicus sum" is to say "civis romanus sum."[41] Let the West preserve Latin . . .

Another Italian, a Carmelite.[42] By way of example, I point out two omissions: nothing on Our Lady of Mount Carmel, illa salutifera populi christiani devotio;[43] nothing on St. Joseph, the patron of the council! In the missal and the calendar, too many omissions. (The president recalled him to the subject. He concluded.) Let the council revise the calendar.

J. B. Peruzzo, archbishop of Agrigente. Multa audivi contra sacram traditionem. Haec verba causa mihi fuerunt anxietatis et timoris.[44] Let history teach us. Si res aliqua sana fuit ab initio, bene; si fons inquinatus erat, difficillime mundatur. Atqui, origo motus liturgici:[45] it was the pagan humanists in Italy, the innovators in France in the fifteenth century. Many people followed them, who separated themselves from the Church. There is not one saint in the liturgical movement. All the saints adhered to the Latin tradition (he cited some of them). Erasmus, in the preface to his commentary on St. Matthew, said that good women had

---

[37] "Instead of promoting unity, Latin has become a principle of division."

[38] "For this reason, let Latin be preserved by professors of philosophy and theology alone."

[39] Jules Georges Kandela (1889–1980), Iraqi, ordained in 1913. Titular archbishop.

[40] Biagio D'Agostino (1896–1984), Italian, ordained in 1926. Bishop of Vallo di Luciana (Italy) from 1956 to 1974.

[41] "Is not of the essence of the faith, but: one faith, one baptism, one liturgy. To say 'I am Catholic' is to say 'I am a Roman citizen.'"

[42] Tarcisio Vincenzo Benedetti, O.C.D. (1899–1972), Italian, ordained in 1927. Bishop of Lodi (Italy) from 1952 until his death.

[43] "That salutary devotion of the Christian people".

[44] "I have heard many things against sacred tradition. Those words were for me a cause of anguish and fear."

[45] "If a thing has been sound from the beginning, it is good; if the source was polluted, it is very difficult to purify it. Well, consider the origin of the liturgical movement."

to be able to read the Gospel and understand it; but he was condemned by the University of Paris as inept and leading to error.[46] All those who want to diminish Latin always invoke the same reason: so that the people will understand and participate better. That is what the Augsburg Confession[47] demanded. Now, quid evenit? Actus separationis a Sancta Matre Ecclesia. Separatio a lingua latina, per quandam inexplicabilem rationem, fere semper, etiam cum permissu Summi Pontificis,[48] ends up in absolute separation. The popes have strongly resisted numerous entreaties: thus again Leo XII,[49] etc., who recommended Latin. Was this only advice? Precepts, rather. Discussiones contrariae liberae sunt, sed, mihi videtur, submissa voce; sed, in oboedientia S. Pontifici.[50]

Then, standing, we listened to the pope's reply to the message sent by the council for his fourth anniversary.

At eight minutes before noon, we broached the second chapter of the liturgy. The president: let no more be said about Latin, and let no one repeat himself!

Cardinal Spellman. Maxima prudentia et circumspectio est necessaria. – De liturgismo exaggerato vitando. – no. 27: cur ordinem missae recognoscere? – Attendamus, ne minuatur reverentia erga SS. Sacramentum. Beware of magna confusio![51] – Let the powers of the Ordinaries be extended, etc.

Cardinal Ruffini: P. 175, ll. 14–15, "restituat" est nimis rigida forma dicendi, injuriosa pro Sancta Sede.[52] – P. 176, no. 42, Communion

---

[46]Didier Erasmus (1469–1536), Dutch humanist. In the preface to his translation of the New Testament, he wrote: "I would like the humblest women to read the Gospels, the epistles of Paul." Erasmus was condemned by the Sorbonne in 1527, under pressure from Noël Béda.

[47]Profession of faith written by Philip Melanchthon in 1530, presenting the fundamental articles of the Lutheran doctrine and developing the points that were the most debated with the Catholic Church. In its article 24, *On the Mass*, it clearly states: "We have made hardly any changes to the public ceremonies of the Mass, except that in a few places we sing some canticles in German along with Latin chants, in order to instruct and train the people, since all the ceremonies must serve principally for the instruction of the people in what is necessary for them to know concerning Christ."

[48]"What was the outcome? An act of separation from Holy Mother Church. The abandonment of Latin, for some inexplicable reason, almost always, even with the permission of the Supreme Pontiff."

[49]Annibale della Genga (1760–1829), Italian, pope from 1823 to 1829. The encyclical *Ubi primum* of May 1824 states: "To allow holy Bibles in the vernacular language, wholesale and without distinction, would, on account of human rashness, cause more harm than good" (article 19).

[50]"Discussions in the opposite sense are free, but, in my opinion, in a whisper and in obedience to the Supreme Pontiff."

[51]"Very great prudence and circumspection are necessary. We must avoid a liturgical mania. Why revise the ritual of the Mass? Let us be careful not to diminish respect toward the Blessed Sacrament. Beware of great confusion."

[52]" 'Restore' is too rigid an expression, insulting to the Holy See."

under both species: Martin V, at Constance, rejected that;[53] it figures among the errors of Martin Luther; the Council of Trent again in 1562, and its canon: anathema sit![54] Now, the grave reasons invoked then are even more pressing today. – P. 176: we ought not to permit concelebration, except, perhaps, in certain very rare cases.

Card. Léger. No. 44 on concelebration, placet. However, what is said under b is said badly. It is necessary to give positive reasons; this is not a stopgap, for the sake simply of convenience. Say, at l. 19, "ex eo quod, natura sua, concelebratio pietatem sacerdotis fovet et unitatem Ecclesiae demonstrat",[55] etc. We must here put back the preparatory commission's text, which had been approved by the Central Commission. (The change was evidently made here, I am told, by Card. Cicognani.)

As I went out, around 12:30, I exchanged a few words with Fr. Congar.

The members of the Secretariat for Unity, now a conciliar commission, will vote within the commission even if they are not bishops.

Yesterday, Cardinal Tisserant drove a few cardinals to Frascati. He probably already knew the composition of the commissions. I was told that he protested to the pope against Cardinal Ottaviani, who supposedly ensured for himself more than a third of the votes in each commission so as to control the council. An unverifiable rumor. In any case, the French bishops appear unhappy.

Brief conversation, in St. Peter's Square, with Archbishop Veuillot.

It seems that Saturday, around 11 in the morning, someone was distributing to journalists a press release on the session of the council. It only talked about the praise of Latin. The journalists pointed out that the session was still going on. The man behind this clumsy little maneuver was supposedly Archbishop Dante.

This afternoon, a meeting with Frs. Grillmeier and Hirschmann. (For a brief time Frs. Chenu, Rondet, and Lucas also came.) According to Fr. Hirschmann, one can see rather well what governed the pope's

---

[53] Oddone Colonna (1368–1431), Italian, pope from 1417 until 1431. His election put an end to the great schism of the West. The decree *Cum in nonnullis* (June 15, 1415) of the Council of Constance (1414–1418), confirmed by Martin V in 1425, stipulated that "even if in the early Church this sacrament [the Eucharist] was received by the faithful under both species, nevertheless it would afterward be received by the celebrants under both species and by the laity under the species of bread alone.... This custom ... must be considered a law that it is not permitted to deny or change as one pleases without the authorization of the Church".

[54] "Let it be anathema!"

[55] "Thus, by its very nature, concelebration fosters the piety of the priest and shows the unity of the Church."

choices for the commissions. He wanted to make a place for the "Curia", too much "forgotten" by the bishops, especially for the secretaries of the Roman congregations; to introduce some religious superiors; to balance nationalities so as to satisfy the small countries; to ensure a continuity with the preconciliar commissions. Certain personal influences were also at work. The "conservative" tendency was accentuated.

For the liturgical schema, it seems that Cardinal Siri (Genoa) and the Spaniards wish to have a via media prevail. – In the Board of Presidency, they are supposedly hesitating between three schemas, to follow the one on liturgy: a dogmatic schema – the schema *De Ecclesia* – the schema *De spectaculis*.[56]

There are supposedly two Latin texts of the pope's speech at the opening of the council (plus the Italian version, which differs from both of them). At the Secretariat of State, apparently, the first text, inspired in part by Cardinal Bea, was thought to be too "progressive", and the pope had to retreat a little. Once again, a rumor that it would be difficult to check.

It would be desirable, Frs. Hirschmann and Grillmeier think, for the periti to furnish the Fathers with objective reports on the principal questions to be treated. The Notes for the schemas are in this regard totally insufficient. In the same way, the facts set forth in the interventions of the Fathers are in general more like arguments chosen for a thesis than solid documentation. A small meeting is foreseen to organize this work; some Dutchmen are the driving force behind this. Will they really want us to gather information in an objective way?

Met Bishop McGrath, from Panama, very friendly.

Fr. Jean Daniélou saw Archbishop Garrone this evening, who seems a little discouraged by the composition of the Doctrinal Commission. Since our arrival in Rome, Archbishop Garrone has not been in touch with me.

Tuesday, October 30, 1962. – At 8:25 A.M., left the house just at the same time as Fr. Abellan;[1] impossible to approach him. Via della Conciliazione, I met Dom Vagaggini, O.S.B., from Saint Anselm; yesterday afternoon, he told me, Cardinal Larraona gathered privatim a certain

---

[56]"On shows". [This refers to the schema prepared by the Secretariat for the Instruments of Social Communication, on the press, cinema, and radio and television.]

October 30

[1]Pedro Maria Abellan, S.J. (1905–2000), Spanish, ordained in 1934. Rector of the Gregorian from 1951 to 1957, professor of theology in the same university from 1947 to 1963, he was then named Procurator General of the Society of Jesus, an office he held until 1989.

number of bishops and experts, mainly Spanish, to entreat them to defend the Holy See and the piety of the faithful valiantly against the maneuvering of the Franco-Germans. He also spoke to me about the article in *L'Espresso*, written by a priest[2] who left the Church, well-informed and intelligent. – In the gallery, I was seated beside Fr. Häring, a Redemptorist. He told me that Archbishop Staffa, after the promulgation of the Constitution *Veterum sapientia*, is supposed to have exclaimed: "We have won a victory more important than that of Saint Leo over Attila!"[3] Fr. Häring, a German, has little sympathy for what appears to him to smell of Roman imperialism; in his view, some in Rome think before all else of consolidating their power, no longer through material means, as in former days, but thanks to the centralization of the Church and Latin culture. He is also of the opinion that Cardinal Larraona lacks judgment; that Fr. Tromp hopes to conquer on the dogmatic front, while knowing full well that his schemas do not go in the direction of the objectives of John XXIII. As for the Curia, it has recently made some tactical errors, it speaks with arrogance but, at the same time, with nervousness; that, still according to Häring, is a pathological sign, which must give us hope. – During this time, in the opposite gallery, I noticed Frs. Gagnebet and Daniélou in an animated discussion. Fr. Balić, O.F.M., continues to give me the cold shoulder, since I showed some reservations toward his mariological drafts, which are too loose.

Fr. Gagnebet was saying to Father Daniélou that, at the Commission for the Liturgy, Larraona formed a subcommittee for doctrine and summoned to it as experts the theologians of the Holy Office. In a few days, Fr. Tromp has to organize the work of the Doctrinal Commission with Card. Ottaviani. The presidents of the other commissions could proceed in the same way as Larraona, with the result that the handful of men in Ottaviani's confidence would rule in the commissions, and the Holy Office would make the council.

After the Mass and the usual rites, Cardinal Alfrink,[4] who was presiding, gave the floor to Cardinal Godfrey, archbishop of London: It is

---

[2] Carlo Falconi (1915–1998), Italian, ordained in 1938, he left the priesthood in 1949. He devoted himself to journalism and the study of Catholicism.

[3] Leo (ca. 400–461) was elected pope under the name of Leo I in 440. In 452, he was given the responsibility of persuading Attila, who had reappeared in the north of the Italian peninsula, not to invade Rome.

[4] Bernard Jan Alfrink (1900–1987), Dutch, ordained in 1924. Archbishop of Utrecht from 1955 to 1975, created cardinal in 1960. Member of the Board of Presidency.

difficult to make the offices longer; so, at nos. 39 and 40, add: "ubi com-
mode fieri poterit".[5] No. 42: not too much of the vernacular language;
risk of error in matters of faith; and if the choice is left to the bishops,
erit maxima confusio;[6] practical drawbacks ... Nos. 44ff. : strictly limit
the cases of concelebration; even then, anceps maneo.[7] The faithful will
not be content with it; they will think they are not getting their money's
worth.

Cardinal Gracias. – He asked for the floor for two reasons: (1) Ratio
liturgica.[8] The manner in which we are proceeding is not logical; it is
impossible to decide many of the points, as long as the principal question of chap. 1 is not settled. At no. 44, give more positive reasons; add:
"exempli gratia".[9] – 2) Will we, the 42 bishops of India, remain at the
council, or will we rejoin our people? As Nehru[10] said, today it is a
question of life or death for India. I am taking this opportunity to ask all
of you to pray for the safety of our country and for the Catholic Church
in our country.[11]

Card. José Bueno y Monreal[12] (Seville): nothing in the schema on the
time of Masses, etc.

Card. Alfrink. On no. 42, "sub utraque specie":[13] he will say nothing about the theological, historical, practical, hygienic aspects, he
will only speak of the aspectu biblico.[14] Cf. the Gospel: Bibite ex eo
omnes.[15] – Manducate et bibite.[16] – We know of course that under
one species alone sacramentum non est incompletum in sua essentia;
tamen est incompletum in sua externa forma; secundum intentionem

[5] "Where this can take place easily".
[6] "There will be great confusion."
[7] "I remain skeptical."
[8] "Liturgical reason".
[9] "For example".
[10] Jawâharlâl Nehru (1899–1964), Indian statesman. After struggling against British colonization, he became prime minister in 1947 and held that office until his death.
[11] India at that time had to face an escalation of its border conflict with China. The Chinese army had in fact crossed the border on October 20, 1962, and did not withdraw until one month later.
[12] José María Bueno y Monreal (1904–1987), Spanish, ordained in 1927. Archbishop of Seville from 1957 to 1982, created cardinal in 1958. Vice-president of the Commission for Bishops and the Government of Dioceses.
[13] "Under both species".
[14] "About the biblical aspect".
[15] "Drink of it, all of you" [Mt 26:27].
[16] "Eat and drink."

Domini: manet quodammodo incompletum,[17] even if one has very good reasons for so deciding. The schema desires only that the complete form be more frequent; non semper, sed pro certis casibus a Sancta Sede bene determinatis.[18] All abuses are guarded against by the text of this no. 42.

Card. Ottaviani. – no. 37: Si oportet sic recognoscere Ordinem Missae, quid manebit? Haec res sanctissima non debet mutari at every generation. – No. 42: Miror;[19] this proposal had been rejected by the Central Commission; it had been requested that the Martyrology be revised; everyone had approved; now, there is no longer any question of that in the schema. – If the practice of Communion under both species was necessary, it should have been instituted everywhere; and what does "remoto fidei periculo"[20] signify? No. 44: There is an appeal to the authority of Pius XII; but there is no mention of his speech to the international liturgy congress,[21] where he said: "the Church has the grave duty to maintain firmly the unconditional usage of Latin, sine ulla remissione.[22] – On concelebration: be careful of theatrical ceremonies! One seems to believe that one gives greater thanks to God this way than by individual Masses; in *Mediator Dei,* the pope reproved the doctrine of those who scorned private Masses. Some maintain that one can concelebrate in silence: that is a confusion, indeed, a doctrinal confusion, and is condemned; and missa concelebrata privat fideles a missis privatis;[23] and then there is the question of honorariums.

(Cardinal Alfrink, the president, stopped him: "Habe me excusatum ...[24] – He had been talking for 15 minutes. – There was applause. – Archbishop Villot would later tell Fr. Rondet that it was he, as undersecretary, who had alerted Alfrink.)

---

[17] "The sacrament is not incomplete in its essence; however, it is incomplete in its exterior form; according to the intention of the Lord: it remains in some way incomplete."

[18] "Not always, but for certain occasions carefully determined by the Holy See".

[19] "If we must revise the ritual of the Mass in this way, what will remain of it? This very holy matter must not be changed at every generation. No. 42: I am surprised."

[20] "The danger for the faith having been removed".

[21] At the International Congress of Pastoral Liturgy at Assisi (September 1956), Pius XII declared: "It would nevertheless be superfluous to recall one more time that the Church has grave reasons for firmly maintaining the unconditional obligation in the Latin rite for the priest celebrant to use the Latin language."

[22] "Without any relaxation".

[23] "The concelebrated Mass deprives the faithful of private Masses."

[24] "Please excuse me."

Card. Bea – P. 175: the Council of Trent was "accuratius et clarius"[25] on this point. It would be necessary to show more clearly the sacrificial nature of the death. Symbolum would be more accurate than exemplar,[26] etc. The homily must be not only recommended but required. The prayers of the faithful that follow will be a worthwhile replacement for the non-liturgical Leonine[27] prayers. Before the *De episcopis*, we cannot rule on the episcopal conferences. It is better to explain the positive reasons for concelebration. – Sub utraque specie: the Council of Trent made clear that it would be permissible to change the usage; other authorities as well: thus Pius IV,[28] two years afterward, granted the chalice to the German regions, etc. There is nothing here contrary to doctrine or authority. Other examples. – Omnino placet no. 42; add "auditis conferentiis episcoporum".[29]

Card. Browne. – In the introduction, it would be better to recall, with St. Thomas, that the Eucharist is a memorial, the representation of the death of Christ, the sacrament of Christus passus[30] ... L. 9: cf. *Mediator Dei*; let there be no liturgism. Ll. 9–10: this leaves the impression that the essence of the Mass would be incomplete without Communion when it says "mensa tam verbi quam corporis",[31] etc.

Archbishop Florit of Florence. Nihil habetur de aspectu sacrificii.[32] – No. 39, l. 26: Omnino praecipitur[33] when there is a large crowd of people; in ceteris casibus, valde commendatur.[34] – There is nothing on the preparation for Mass. – No. 42: that would entail great practical difficulties. No. 43: two questions are mixed together. The precept is satisfied by arriving before the offertory.

Bishop Melendro of Anking, China (expatriate). No. 39: add formulas showing the unity and universality of the Church.

Bishop Pereira[35] in Mozambique: restrict no. 42, etc.

---

[25] "More exact and more accurate".

[26] "Symbol would be more accurate than model."

[27] This refers to prayers said while kneeling at the end of private Masses, starting from the nineteenth century (Leo XIII).

[28] Giovanni Angelo de Medici (1499–1565), Italian. Elected pope in 1559.

[29] "I completely approve of no. 42; add: 'after having listened to the bishops' conferences'."

[30] "Christ who suffered".

[31] "The table, as much of the word of God as of his body".

[32] "Nothing is said on the sacrificial aspect."

[33] "To be completely dropped".

[34] "In the other cases, it is very much recommended."

[35] Custódio Alvim Pereira (1915–2006), Portuguese, ordained in 1937. Archbishop of Lourenço Marques (Mozambique) from 1962 to 1974.

Bishop Lo-Kuang of Taiwan, China: on no. 38 . . .

Msgr. Paulus Rusch,[36] Administrator of Innsbruck: his pastoral experience shows him the joy of the people and their presence in large numbers at a renewed liturgy.

Bishop Dwyer[37] of Leeds (England): no. 37 is not clear. If every nation can change things, "non erit recognitio, sed potius destructio".[38]

Archbishop Trindade Salguerio[39] of Evora (Portugal): We could easily go in corruptionem . . .[40]

Bishop Zazinovic[41] in Yugoslavia spoke about the readings and sermons. No. 42: to be restricted.

Bishop Arattukulam[42] of Alleppey, India.

McQuaid, archbishop of Dublin, in the name of the Irish bishops: against Communion under both species. – The piety of the faithful is better served by individual Masses.

Another Indian bishop[43] laid stress on the homily.

Helmsing,[44] bishop of Kansas City, USA, passed on his turn to speak.

Adrianus Ddungu,[45] bishop of Masaka (Uganda): Difficulty with the eucharistic fast for priests who must say several Masses; aqua parum juvat.[46]

Very Reverend Fr. Kleiner,[47] abbot general of the Cistercians, in the name of all the Cistercian abbots and various Benedictines: placet quod

---

[36] Paulus Rusch (1903–1986), German, ordained in 1933. Apostolic administrator of Innsbruck (Austria) from 1938, then bishop of Innsbruck from 1964 to 1980. Member of the Commission for the Discipline of the Clergy and the Christian People.

[37] Georges Dwyer (1908–1987), British, ordained in 1932. Bishop of Leeds from 1957 to 1965. Member of the Preparatory Commission for Bishops and the Government of Dioceses, then a member of the same conciliar commission.

[38] "There will not be a revision but, rather, a destruction."

[39] Emanuele Trindade Salgueiro (1898–1965), Portuguese, ordained in 1921. Archbishop of Evora (Portugal) from 1955 until his death. Member of the Commission for the Discipline of the Clergy and the Christian People.

[40] "Toward corruption".

[41] Karmelo Zazinović (1914–1997), Yugoslav, ordained in 1937. Auxiliary bishop of Krk (Croatia).

[42] Michael Arattukulam (1910–1995), Indian, ordained in 1937. Bishop of Alleppey (India) from 1952 to 1984.

[43] Angelo Fernandes (1913–2000), Indian, ordained in 1937. Coadjutor archbishop of Delhi from 1959 to 1967. Member of the Commission for Bishops and the Government of Dioceses.

[44] Charles Helmsing (1908–1993), American, ordained in 1933. Bishop of Kansas City from 1962 to 1977. Member of the Secretariat for Unity starting from the second session.

[45] Adrian Kivumbi Ddungu, born in 1923, Ugandan, ordained in 1952. Bishop of Masaka (Uganda) from 1961 to 1998.

[46] "Water is not much help." [Before the council, the fast was required for celebrating the Mass. However, the priest was allowed to drink water, which did not break the fast.]

[47] Sighard Karl Kleiner (1904–1995), Austrian, ordained in 1928. Abbot General of the Cistercians from 1953 to 1985. Member of the Commission for Religious.

dixit card. Léger.[48] Example of the monks: each attends and participates
in the monastic Mass in accordance with his station. The schema only
asks for permission, which only those pastors who judge it good will
use.

Bishop Stein[49] of Trier: for the "mensa verbi Dei",[50] he referred to
Card. Bea.

Sansierra,[51] Argentinian bishop, in the name of many others; he began
"Eminentissimi, etc. – et observatores". No. 42: good. No. 43, add "et
in concilio oecumenico"[52] (laughter and applause).

At 1 P.M., Enrico Castelli[53] came to get me. Lunched at his place (1, via
Lagrange) with Father R. Pannikar,[54] Fr. Scrima[55] (Rumanian), a Dutch
Franciscan[56] from the Antonianum (prof. of philosophy), whom I had
seen in Paris and who is the theologian of a bishop from his country. We
chatted about Castelli's next conference, on hermeneutics and tradition.
After lunch, two philosophers came, Biancho and Balbo.[57] Castelli said
to me: with Ottaviani, one could come to some agreement, if he did
not have his two evil geniuses, Parente and Piolanti, with him. The
latter, he told me (it was no doubt the speech that someone else had
summarized, attributing it to Parente), supposedly declared in a public
conference on the council: the Holy Church, instructed by the history
of the First Vatican Council and its consequences, wished to avoid what
happened at that time; the Church had left to one side some heterodox

[48]"I endorse what Cardinal Léger has said."

[49]Bernhard Stein (1904–1993), German, ordained in 1929. Auxiliary bishop of Trèves from 1944
to 1967. Member of the Commission for Religious starting from the second session.

[50]"Table of the Word of God".

[51]Ildefonso Maria Sansierra Robla, O.F.M. Cap. (1910–1980), Argentinian, ordained in 1936.
Auxiliary bishop of San Juan de Cuyo (Argentina), from 1962 to 1966.

[52]"Eminences, etc., – and observers"; "and in an ecumenical council".

[53]Enrico Castelli (1900–1977), Italian. Professor of philosophy at La Sapienza university, he was
also director of the Institute for Philosophical Studies, attached to the same university, which organized international meetings dedicated to the philosophy of religion.

[54]Raimon Panikkar, born in 1918, of Spanish origin. Priest, philosopher, and theologian, his
work was especially widely disseminated after the council, interested particularly in intercultural
and interreligious dialogue.

[55]André Scrima (1925–2000), Romanian. Monk, philosopher, and theologian particularly interested in ecumenism. During the first two sessions, thanks to his good relations with Athenagoras, he
was the official messenger to Constantinople. When he became archimandrite of the patriarchate of
Constantinople, he was named, during the last two sessions, the delegated observer of the patriarchate of Constantinople and representative of the patriarch Athenagoras at the council.

[56]Perhaps Levinus Schuwer, O.F.M., Dutch.

[57]Felice Balbo (1913–1964), Italian philosopher.

theologians, who caused a schism: so it was with Döllinger;[58] today, worried about an analogous heterodoxy, she has called these theologians to Rome, in order to do all she can to retain them in her maternal bosom. Then he apparently named Congar, Daniélou, Rahner, and de Lubac. – We talked about the intellectual situation in Rome. Castelli is concerned over the lack of religious philosophy in Italy and is striving to remedy that. Everyone seems to be well-informed about council matters, the incidents at the sessions, etc. The Franciscan told me that Cardinal Alfrink is pessimistic; it seems to him that between the two principal tendencies there is not only opposition but no possibility of mutual understanding. The composition of the commissions, following the choices of John XXIII, is said to have saddened those who desire a renewal.

I returned to the Borgo in the company of Fr. Scrima, who, summoned by Patriarch Athenagoras, is going to leave for Constantinople. He was there when we learned the news about the envoys sent from Moscow to the council; he told me all about it. He will be in Rome again for a few days in January. He asked me, before we went our separate ways, to show him the Holy Office. He is a great admirer of John XXIII.

Despite wishes and rumors to the contrary, it seems that the council will not start up again in January, but only after Easter. One of the reasons would seem to be that it is impossible to heat Saint Peter's adequately enough to permit a large number of old men to remain sitting there for almost four hours at a stretch.

The Fr. Superior of Florence, Dall'Olio,[59] came to ask me to stop in Florence in December. He wants me to give a talk on Teilhard. There is, it appears, a Teilhard de Chardin Society in Florence, with which he is in touch. He spoke to me also about the group from *Testimonianze*, headed by Fr. Balducci.

I was called to the parlor by a German,[60] who spoke French badly. An art historian, he has just published a book on El Greco. He has been in Rome for two years, working on a book about Michelangelo. He has

---

[58] Johann von Döllinger (1799–1890), German. A priest, he was a vigorous adversary of ultramontanism. He opposed the *Syllabus* and rejected the dogma of papal infallibility in 1870. He was excommunicated in 1871.

[59] Alessandro Dall'Olio, S.J. (1919–1983), Italian. Superior of Florence.

[60] This must have been Karl Ipser, author of *El Greco* (Berlin: Klinkhardt & Biermann, 1960) and of *Michelangelo, der Künstler-Prophet der Kirche* (Augsburg: Kraft, 1963).

discovered, with some excitement, that Michelangelo's intention was very much the same as Teilhard's! He set this out in a preface that he had translated for me by one of his friends, a religious who is, he told me, a peritus at the council; he got me to read the translation and then gave it to me. Overjoyed, he cried out: "Oh! it is an extraordinary thing to find myself thus face to face with a man who knew Teilhard well!" He asked me his height, etc. He also said to me: "He had a fine head, he was a man of the Germanic race; I have studied these things"; and, to pay me a compliment: "You, too, I see, you are of Germanic descent!" But, I said to him timidly, Michelangelo ... "Oh! he was an exceptional man; he was not Mediterranean", etc.

I missed Fr. Martelet. Fr. Léon-Dufour, who had been expected, was not able to come, since he had an appointment with Card. Tisserant before leaving Rome this evening.

At 6:15 P.M., two young Fathers of the Holy Cross, an American and a Canadian, came to get me, to drive me to their College, on via Aurelia Antica. A very fraternal welcome. In the front row, four bishops, the superior general,[61] etc. About fifty theology students. I spoke to them about the trinary structure of the Credo. At 7:30, a meal with the community of theologians. The auxiliary bishop of Panama, Bishop Marc-Gregoire McGrath, joined us. There were six of us at the central table; the bishop said to me: our four companions are the secretaries of four bishops; so, no secrets! And the whole time, we spoke with great freedom about the council. Bishop McGrath reminded me that he had come to see me in Paris, in the autumn of 1950, when he was still a student and a young professor. After dinner, for more than an hour, questions from the young Fathers: on the faith, on its relation to science, on Teilhard, on working methods, etc. "Speak openly", Bishop McGrath had told them, "there are almost no bishops here, there is only the young people's bishop." Afterward he drove me back to the Borgo; he is a member of the Doctrinal Commission, and he told me that he will call on me for help.

Wednesday, October 31, 1962. – Yesterday, they gave out Vatican stamps to us. Today, each of the Fathers received a medal; they will give them out to the periti later.

---

[61] Germain-Marie Lalande, C.S.C. (1911–1996), Canadian. Superior general of the Congregation of the Holy Cross from 1962 to 1974.

On the way to Saint Peter's, I said hello to Fr. Ab.,[1] preparing to chat with him; a quick nod of the head without looking at me, and he hurried on. Is this perhaps a sign in him of the combination of Romanism and his Hispanic character? – Met Canon Martimort (Toulouse), always ready to fight for the defense of the schema on the liturgy, on which he worked actively. Canon Boulard[2] joined us. At Saint Peter's, I greeted Msgr. Dumont, O.P.[3] (of Istina), Fr. Balić, who still gives me the cold shoulder, etc., the archbishop of Pakistan,[4] with whom I lunched at Msgr. Delacroix's place. – The Mass was celebrated according to the Dominican rite by Archbishop Lemieux, O.P.,[5] of Quebec City. At his seat, Cardinal Rugambwa was magnificent as always. Archbishop Villot brought in the Gospel. (Horribly extravagant surplices on the altar servers.) – Cardinal Tisserant was presiding. – Archbishop Villot would say to me on leaving that he is striving to bring it about that the presidents of the commissions will not get a vote in their commissions; this is to restore balance a little. – They say that the next schema to be discussed will be *De fontibus revelationis*. Cardinal Bea, they also say, is supposed to have an alternative draft all ready that is rather good.

Cardinal Lercaro (Bologna) spoke first. He strongly recommended no. 40: prayers of the faithful replacing the "oremus",[6] which no longer signifies anything. No. 43, on the obligation of the Mass, an exhortation to pastors and the faithful so that they might better understand the importance of the first part.

Card. König. At no. 37, restore the commission's original text, which explains and justifies the requested recognition.[7] Nos. 42 and 44: K. joins Card. Bea and Alfrink; he cited the example of the Orientals; this is not

---

October 31

[1] Father Abellan.

[2] Fernand Boulard (1898–1978), French. Priest, specialist in religious sociology, teacher at the Institut catholique of Paris. Member of the Preparatory Commission for Bishops and the Government of Dioceses, named as an expert to the council during the first session.

[3] Christophe-Jean Dumont, O.P. (1897–1991), French. Superior of Istina, a center for ecumenical research founded by the Dominicans in 1923. Since 1954, this center has published a journal, *Istina*. Consultor to the Secretariat for Unity. Expert at the council.

[4] J.M. Cordeiro.

[5] Marie-Joseph Lemieux, O.P. (1902–1984), Canadian, ordained in 1928. Archbishop of Ottawa from 1953 to 1966. Member of the Commission for Bishops and the Government of Dioceses.

[6] "Let us pray."

[7] "Revision".

the time to reject them. The text obliges no one; sed, ne claudatur janua a concilio![8] etc.

Bishop Placide Cambiaghi[9] (Cremona). There should be a proper preface for the feast of Corpus Christi. Homilia praecipienda[10] for every Sunday and feast day in the public churches, including those of religious orders. – Reserve Communion "sub utraque specie" for the ordination of priests. – No. 44; Libenter accipitur quaedam ampliatio[11] for concelebration around the bishop, but with conditions; around a priest: doubts.

A Polish bishop[12] (?) at no. 39, "commendatur"[13] is not sufficient; this would not go as far as the current canon law. The homily must always be given, nisi ex dispositione Ordinarii. – No. 42: magna practica difficultas, etiam pro sacerdotibus in missa ordinationis.[14] There would be involuntary acts of profanation. Therefore, omnino omitti debet.[15]

A Spanish bishop.[16] No change should be made to the Mass without very grave reasons. The Last Supper was a Mass of ordination. See the decrees of the popes. Fidei periculum, et irreverentiae periculum,[17] very real. The social customs of the Orientals toto coelo differunt[18] from Western customs. The reasons given for concelebration are of no value.

Bishop Jean Nueir,[19] Coptic (Egypt) "… et carissimi observatores".[20] He asks for the possibility of using leavened or unleavened bread for the two rites, etc.

---

[8] "But let the door not be closed by the council!"

[9] Placido Maria Cambiaghi (1900–1987), Italian, ordained in 1924. Bishop of Crema (Italy) from 1953 to 1963, then of Novara (Italy) from February 1963 to 1971.

[10] "Body of Christ. Homily to be required".

[11] "Let a certain extension be willingly accepted."

[12] Franciszek Jop (1897–1976), Polish, ordained in 1920. Auxiliary bishop of Sandomierz (Poland) from 1945 to 1972, member of the Commission for the Liturgy.

[13] "Recommendation".

[14] "Except by arrangement with the Ordinary. No. 42: great practical difficulty, even for priests during the Mass of ordination".

[15] "It must absolutely be omitted."

[16] Ramón Iglesias Navarri (1889–1972), Spanish, ordained in 1912. Bishop of Urgel (Spain) from 1942 to 1969.

[17] "Danger for the faith and danger of a lack of respect".

[18] "Differ completely".

[19] Youhanna Nueir, O.F.M. (1914–1995), Egyptian, ordained in 1943. Auxiliary bishop of Luxor (Coptic) from 1955 to 1965, then bishop of Assiut (Coptic) from 1965 to 1990.

[20] "And very dear observers".

Bishop A. N. Jubany,[21] of Ortosia di Feniora (Spain). No. 42: the council does not intend to "repristinare"[22] the usage anterior to the fifteenth century; no one is asking for that. Besides, one will recall that the concession granted by Pius IV had to be revoked as early as the following year, due to unpleasant consequences. The drafting of this no. is not accuratissima.[23] – We can restore concelebration in some cases, such as the Mass for the taking of religious vows; let everything be made precise in the ritual. The reasons given sunt valde indigentes.[24] There is a real risk of doctrinal error. Saint Thomas responded to those who, even at that time, were demanding it. However, the speaker is not totally against ... (the president stopped him).

Another bishop.[25] Sub utraque specie: placet ut janua reaperiatur, non est obligatio.[26] In my diocese, there is no question of it; but each of us must think of the whole Church. Atqui, expedit ut porta in concilio aperiatur. Cardinalis Alfrink optime exposuit quaestionem.[27] If there were strong reasons against it, the practice would have to be forbidden to the Eastern Churches. – De concelebratione[28] ... (He also went on too long; the president stopped him.)

Albert Devoto, bishop of Goya (Argentina). He spoke in the name of a group of bishops. At No. 37, add some general directions. Simplify the rites: for example, not so many signs of the cross. – Censeo stipendia abolenda esse.[29]

Laurent Satoshi Nagae,[30] bishop of Urawa (Japan). No. 41: "nonnullis cantibus"[31] is not clear. In regions where the roots of the languages

---

[21] Narciso Jubany Arnau (1913–1996), Spanish, ordained in 1939. Auxiliary bishop of Barcelona from 1955 to 1964, then bishop of Gerona from February 1964, created cardinal in 1973. Consultor to the Preparatory Commission for Bishops and the Government of Dioceses, then a member of the same conciliar commission.

[22] "Bring back into force".

[23] "Very accurate".

[24] "Are very insufficient".

[25] João Batista Przyklenk, M.S.F. (1916–1984), German, ordained in 1940. Bishop of Januária (Brazil) from 1962 to 1976.

[26] "Communion under both species: I approve that the door should be open again, it is not an obligation."

[27] "So it is desirable that the door be open to the council. Cardinal Alfrink has presented the question very well."

[28] "On concelebration ...".

[29] "I propose that the stipends be abolished."

[30] Laurent Satoshi Nagae (1913–1998), Japanese, ordained in 1938. Bishop of Urawa (Japan) from 1957 to 1979. Member of the Commission for the Discipline of the Clergy and the Christian People beginning with the fourth session.

[31] "Certain chants".

are not Latin, it is necessary that all chants be in the vernacular language; the prayers also, not just the oratio communis.[32]

Paul-Jean Hallinan (?),[33] bishop of Atlanta, USA, in the name of a number of American bishops: we accept the adaptations, ad vere fructuosam participationem fidelium.[34] Often our faithful have an excessive individualism; the liturgy must educate them. Vere publica esse debet: ad hunc finem, intelligi debet. Optat Sanctus Pater ut novas vias aperiamus;[35] let every person, even those not instructed, understand. Ecclesia omnium mater alma est.[36] And, this conforms to the ecumenical spirit.

Lorenz Jäger (Germany). No. 42: the very decree of Trent shows the council's power to change a usage. Do not extend it too far; however, marriage Masses (for the two spouses); new converts, etc. In each case, give the reasons. The Church has always permitted it for the Eastern Churches. Hodie non jam adest periculum fidei. Erit aliquod caritatis exemplum pro fratribus separatis.[37] This would be in the spirit of the pope.

A bishop from Brazil.[38] P. 176, n. 42, l. 11, delete "tum laicis".[39] No. 43: talk about the celebratio versus populum;[40] reserve it for cases allowed by the Ordinary.

Bishop Weber of Strasbourg. No. 42: The restitutio sic definita[41] conforms to the vota of numerous bishops. No danger to the faith. The liberty of the bishops remains intact. This practice corresponds better to the Gospel. Ratio oecumenica: passus ad reconciliationem. Rationes pastorales:[42] this rite would illustrate for the faithful the value of the priesthood in its relation to the sacrifice of the Mass, etc.; it would exalt the sacrament of marriage.

Arthur Elchinger, coadjutor bishop of Strasbourg. No. 44: contra concelebrationem audivimus multas objectiones.[43] However, it was

---

[32] "Common prayer".

[33] Paul John Hallinan (1911–1968), American, ordained in 1937. Bishop of Atlanta from 1962 until his death. Member of the Commission for the Liturgy.

[34] "In view of a truly fruitful participation of the faithful".

[35] "It must be truly public: for that, it must be understood. The Holy Father wishes us to open new paths."

[36] "The Church is the nurturing mother of all."

[37] "Today, the danger for the faith does not exist. This will be an example of charity for the separated brothers."

[38] Luís Gonzaga da Cunha Marelim.

[39] "Also for the laity".

[40] "Celebration facing the people".

[41] "The reinstatement so defined".

[42] "Ecumenical reason: a step toward reconciliation. Pastoral reasons".

[43] "We have heard numerous objections against concelebration."

advocated by Pius XII.[44] Remarks on this no. were passed on to the secretariat. – No. 37: needs to be clarified. Let the text of the preparatory commission, which was very clear, be restored: one saw there that this is not a revolution, but an evolution that is sana et prudens.[45] – The religious desires and expectations of young people: we must not disappoint them. Young people are not receptive to the reasons of those who confuse divine tradition and human traditions, the mystery of Christ and the obscurity of rites that are not understood. Our excessive conservatism is a scandal to them, leads them to reject religion, etc. (Applause. In my gallery, several were unhappy; in particular, an American Franciscan of Irish origin and another religious, a Spaniard, I think.)

Joseph Khoury, bishop of Tyre of the Maronites. "... et carissimi observatores".[46] (In my gallery, there was some shrugging of shoulders.) He praised the chapter, but found the no. on concelebration too limited. No. 26 sets forth a good principle; no. 44 makes too timid an application of it. One used to say that concelebration is praeferenda;[47] now it is no more than tolerated, in rare cases. Cf. what Saint Augustine and Saint Ignatius of Antioch said: the Mass, "actus presbyterii".[48] In former days there was never more than one altar in the Church. It is for private Masses that the permission of the bishop is required. The drawbacks and scandal of simultaneous private Masses. The religious have all things in common, except for the mensa Domini![49] – He proposed a new text, deleting no. 45: thus it will not be a matter of simply tolerating it; it will be more in conformity with St. Thomas and the mind of John XXIII. (The president stopped him.)

Melchite Archbishop N. Edelby. Adhaereo toto corde.[50] – No. 42: the intention of Christ is clear: "bibite ex eo omnes";[51] so the apostles understood it. Haec est praxis evangelica, genuina, apostolica, normalis, non concessio nec privilegium nec exceptio.[52] There are, however,

---

[44] The speaker is making reference here to the speech of Pius XII of September 22, 1956, at the conclusion of the First International Congress on Pastoral Liturgy in Assisi.

[45] "A sound and prudent evolution".

[46] "And very dear observers".

[47] "To be preferred".

[48] "Act of the presbyterium" [all the priests of the same diocese around their bishop].

[49] "Table of the Lord!"

[50] "I wholeheartedly support".

[51] "Drink of this all of you."

[52] "It is the evangelical, original, apostolic, normal practice, not a concession, a privilege, or an exception."

practical reasons, in certain cases, for the use of the species of bread alone, even in the East. But that is a res mere disciplinaris. Decursu temporis, mutari potest. Si fieri possit, melius est servare usum apostolorum.[53] The reasons why the Western Church moved away little by little from the original usage are psychological and practical, not doctrinal. Those who are totally opposed to returning to it are affected by a double "complex": they do not want the Church to appear to contradict herself or for her to seem to concede anything to our separated brethren. But we need to be able to overcome these complexes. Nulla est verecundia si Ecclesia mutat disciplinam,[54] when nothing exerts any pressure on her from outside. And, incolumi prorsus fide catholica, nulla est verecundia[55] in moving closer to the practice of non-Catholics on one point. Practical difficulties exist, but they must not be overestimated. We Byzantines manage it well. Sacerdos tingit hostiam sacram in vino consecrato, etc. – Moderatio.[56] He does not ask for a mass introduction of the practice. Sed non occludatur via![57] One only asks that the Holy See might concede in certain cases ... (The president stops him).

Juan Carlos Aramburu,[58] archbishop of Tucuman (Argentina). On the time of Mass and the eucharistic fast, etc., he asks for some practical permissions. – No. 42: some difficulties in the application; and if it is granted to priests, the laity will demand it. Risk of contagion. Delete "laicis".[59]

A Chinese bishop[60] (Formosa?). Several people are trying to introduce some beautiful novelties. Canon missae idem debet remanere ubique terrarum, etiam quoad linguam, exceptis Pater noster et Agnus Dei. Ante et post canonem,[61] preserve the ceremonies, but in various languages. If some bishop or priest wants to introduce other prayers or ceremonies, let it be outside of the Mass. One could shorten the

---

[53] "A purely disciplinary matter. In the course of time, that can change. If it is possible, it is better to preserve the usage of the apostles."

[54] "There is no shame in the Church modifying her discipline."

[55] "And the Catholic faith remaining absolutely intact, there is no shame."

[56] "The priest dips the sacred host in the consecrated wine, etc. Moderation."

[57] "But let the path not be closed!"

[58] Juan Carlos Aramburu (1912–2004), Argentinian, ordained in 1934. Bishop, then archbishop, of Tucumán (Argentina) from 1953 to 1967. Created cardinal in 1976.

[59] "Laity".

[60] Petrus Pao-Zin Tou (1911–1986), Chinese, ordained in 1937. Bishop of Hsinchu (Taiwan) from 1961 to 1983.

[61] "The canon of the Mass must remain the same everywhere on the earth, even in what concerns the language, with the exception of the Our Father and the Lamb of God. Before and after the canon".

beginning of the Mass a little and lengthen the end, for example, by moving the Gloria to the end.

Charles-Marie Himmer,[62] bishop of Tournai (Belgium). Homilia, "pars liturgiae", omnino placet.[63] Already the Council of Trent was insisting on that. From St. Justin up to *Mediator Dei* and the code of canon law, there has been talk about it. Reintroductio precum publicarum: optime;[64] it is very traditional. It was in Rome that St. Prosper of Aquitaine wrote his famous formula: "Lex supplicandi, sc. in oratione communi fidelium, legem statuat credenda"[65] ... Delete the orationes imperatas[66] and the Leonine prayers. – In the name of several bishops of Belgium, Austria, etc., he asked for an attenuation of the eucharistic fast, for both priests and the faithful.

Bishop Jean Van Cauwelaert[67] of Inongo (Congo). Someone has asked that "paschale convivium"[68] be removed from the Prooemium. But Saint Paul said: "Pascha nostrum immolatus est Christus."[69] And the whole of tradition. And St. Thomas: "Novum Pascha novae legis"[70] (Against Ottaviani). – Concelebratio:[71] all of Africa approves of it, all the more so because it conforms to the communitarian spirit of our peoples, and they will understand the Church's unity better by this means than by abstract explanations. Moreover, this will be a great consolation and spiritual support for our priests, usually so alone. – 260 bishops of Africa, Madagascar, and the Isles earnestly ask that what Cardinal Léger proposed be approved. – Another remark, a general one. There has been talk of "novationes".[72] When a great "conventus episcopalis"[73] like this one asks for some "innovatio",[74] one must think that it is an indication

---

[62] Charles-Marie Himmer (1902–1994), Belgian, ordained in 1926. Bishop of Tournai from 1948 to 1977. Member of the Commission for Bishops from the fourth session on, he was one of the architects of the group "Jesus, the Church and the Poor".

[63] "I completely approve of the homily as part of the liturgy."

[64] "Reintroduction of the prayers of the faithful: very good".

[65] "The manner of praying, particularly in the common prayer of the faithful, forms the manner of believing."

[66] "Compulsory prayers".

[67] Jan van Cauwelaert, C.I.C.M., born in 1914, Belgian, ordained in 1939. Bishop of Inongo (Congo) from 1959 to 1967. Member of the Commission for the Discipline of the Sacraments.

[68] "Paschal banquet".

[69] "Christ, our Paschal Lamb, has been sacrificed" [1 Cor 5:7].

[70] "The new law's new oblation". [Excerpt from the chant *Lauda Sion* by Saint Thomas Aquinas.]

[71] "Concelebration".

[72] "Novelties".

[73] "Episcopal assembly".

[74] "Innovation".

of the Holy Spirit. We do not have the right to stifle the Spirit. Besides, no one is being placed under any obligation. But let us not be guided by human prudence, etc. "Spiritus aperiat Ecclesiam omnibus populis",[75] etc. (Applause.)

Bishop Cyrille Zohrabian, Armenian: Eliminate the last Gospel; at the end of the Mass, let the people chant: "Deo gratias."

Bishop Boudon of Mende:[76] Let Communion under the species of wine be granted to the sick and dying who can no longer take anything but liquids.

Bishop de Vito of Lucknow (India): No concelebration in meetings of priests. On the time of Mass: the Lord placed no restrictions, and today restrictions are no longer necessary. Let the faithful be able to receive Communion at all the Masses they attend. – On Communion in the absence of any priest.

Joseph Melas, bishop of Nuoro (Italy): Communion "sub utraque specie etiam laicis"[77] has many drawbacks and no advantages. – Let priests each separately be able to celebrate Mass on Holy Thursday, etc.

This afternoon, I saw Fr. Congar in his room at the Angelicum. He has written a general Prooemium for the dogmatic part of the council; this text has been approved in principle by the small group that had assigned him the task. He has had invitations to speak from all sides. But he has the impression (as I do) that the French bishops have little desire to consult him methodically and to work with him. Every night he writes his journal of the council. He writes a news column on the council every two weeks for the *Informations catholiques internationales*. – Fr. Cottier, O.P.,[78] from Geneva, is the theologian of Archbishop de Provenchères (Aix). Fr. Karl Rahner invited Fr. Labourdette, O.P., to join the group of theologians who are trying to work out some texts.

The German theologians (conciliar and private experts) are all getting together once a week. I believe the Spanish are doing the same. Both groups are organically linked with their bishops. There is nothing comparable for the French.

---

[75] "Let the Spirit open the Church to all peoples."

[76] In actual fact it was Pierre Boillon (1911–1996), French, ordained in 1935. Coadjutor of Verdun from 1962, he became bishop of Verdun in August 1963 and continued until 1986.

[77] "Under both species, for the laity as well".

[78] Georges Cottier, O.P., born in 1922, Swiss. Professor of philosophy in Geneva then Fribourg, prior of the Saint Thomas Center in Geneva, secretary of the journal *Nova et vetera* founded and edited by Charles Journet. Created cardinal in 2003. Expert at the council from the fourth session on.

At the Gregorian, I saw Fr. O. Philip and Fr. D. Mollat. Fr. Guy de Broglie was greatly delighted to learn that Cardinal Ottaviani's speech had been cut off. Fr. É. Pin drove me back to the Borgo S. Spirito.

Received from Fr. Alfred de Soras the text of the lecture he gave on October 4 at Yaoundé on Vatican II.

This evening, a visit from Jean Goss-Mayr,[79] a Catholic pacifist, who is preparing some texts to submit to the council. He has been in contact with Ottaviani, Parente, and Tromp for a long time. He would like to get me to work on his draft of a conciliar constitution. I declined.

Three articles by Jean Daujat on Teilhard have appeared in *France Catholique*. A fourth is announced. They are rather favorable and on many points prove me right. – Received today from Fr. G. Salet[80] (Fourvière) an excerpt from the *Quinzaine religieuse de la Savoie* (Chambéry): an article by E. V. on "the Monitum of the Holy Office relative to the works of Father Teilhard de Chardin"; very moderate, and even favorable to Teilhard; he protests against the defamatory libels; recommends my book.

At the Angelicum, at the moment I was giving my name to the porter, a big, young, good Neapolitan priest who was passing by made a great demonstration of joy and friendship toward me; we kissed each other's hands, etc.

All Saints' Day 1962. – In the morning, a conversation with Fr. Grillmeier on our theological difficulties over the last fifteen years. – A visit from Father Gajáry,[1] theology tutor at the Germanic College. – An invitation from the Belgian College for next Monday.

In the afternoon, left for Naples, with Archbishop Dalmais, Bishop Véniat, Frs. Rondet and Martelet. Arrived at the Jesuit residence in Naples at night and in the rain; our places had been taken by another group; however, the superior found us rooms. – Friday, in Pompei; there we had the chance to meet Don Francesco Tortora,[2] a specialist. –

---

[79]Jean Goss (1912–1991), French. President of the International Movement of Reconciliation, he was an activist for non-violence. His wife has recounted their struggle: *Oser le combat non violent: Aux côtés de Jean Goss* (Paris: Éd. du Cerf, 1998).

[80]Gaston Salet, S.J. (1891–1966), French, ordained in 1922. He taught theology at the scholasticate of Fourvière starting from 1929 and provided sermons that were much admired from 1940 on.
November 1, All Saint's Day

[1]Aladár Gajáry, born in 1925, Hungarian priest. Tutor in theology from 1958 to 1964, then professor of theology at Chur (Switzerland).

[2]Francesco Tortora (1915–2004), Italian, ordained in 1940. Professor of letters, for a long time responsible for the work of the prelature of Pompei, he launched in 1953 the crusade of the Rosary.

The Neapolitan churches: an extraordinary place held by the cult of relics and pious images. In the streets of the old city, every shop has a picture or a statue or a whole little shrine, with lamps, flowers, surrounded by cans of sardines or garlands of sausages, etc. – A visit, in the cathedral, to the chapel of Saint Januarius. – In the parlor of the residence, I saw an issue of the Bulletin of the Jesuits of Southern Italy that contained an Italian translation of an article by Fr. Le Blond on Teilhard and on my book. – Saturday morning, November 3, at the Museum of Naples, visited not long ago by Father Teilhard, who, on exiting, sent a postcard to his friend Father Breuil[3] (or Father Gaudefroy?) with only these words: "How great the Ancients were!" – I rested while the others went to Herculaneum. – Sunday the 4th, at the scholasticate in Posilipo; a charming welcome from the rector and professors. I said a few words to the seminarians; Fr. Martelet spoke after me, then, for a longer time, Archbishop Dalmais. Returned to Rome in the evening. I found there an issue of *France-Forum*, October 1962, with "Teilhard Contested" by M. de Gandillac, C. Cuénot, and Étienne Borne.[4]

Monday, November 5, 1962. – Between 8:30 and 9 A.M., a conversation with Fr. Häring in the gallery of Saint Peter's. He told me that the Belgian bishop[1] who had spoken the other day in the name of 260 African bishops had received a letter from the president of their group, telling him that he was basically in agreement with him, but that he would have liked him to take a more dispassionate tone. This was Fr. Häring's opinion as well: the bishops, he told me, will only take back their ascendancy over the Curia by means of good humor and respect. He also thinks that by insisting on the discussion of the dogmatic schemas, the partisans of the Holy Office are hastening their own defeat. – Archbishop Garrone has just invited Fr. Häring to give one of the upcoming talks at Saint-Louis des Français. I have heard that Msgr. Spadafora has replied to the Response of the Biblical Institute and that his Reply is already circulating among the bishops.

---

[3] Henri Breuil (1877–1961), French. Priest, prehistorian, ethnologist, and archeologist, he was a professor at the Collège de France from 1929 to 1947.

[4] Maurice de Gandillac (1906–2006), French, was a philosopher, professor at the Sorbonne. Claude Cuénot was a specialist on Teilhard de Chardin; among other things, he had published in 1958 *Pierre de Chardin: Les Grandes Étapes de son évolution.* Étienne Borne (1907–1993), French, was a philosopher. He contributed to several journals, including *La Vie intellectuelle* and *Esprit.*
November 5
[1] Jan van Cauwelaert.

Mass according to the Antiochian rite of the Maronites, celebrated by Archbishop Khoury. The president today is Cardinal Liénart. Archbishop Felici gave the names of the Administrative Tribunal (3 cardinals, 1 archbishop, 6 bishops). He entreated the council Fathers "iterum atque iterum"[2] to be brief, not to repeat themselves, to group their interventions. The president seconded this entreaty.

Cardinal Confalonieri.[3] – In response to certain expressions of surprise, he explained how the preparatory commission functioned. The text established by it was submitted to the Central Commission. The latter voted on whether or not it was advisable to submit the questions to the pope. In November 1961, it passed the text to the subcommission "de schematibus emendandis";[4] that subcommission studied all the observations made by the Central Commission and transmitted them to the cardinal president of the original commission, in order to come to an agreement on the observations to be accepted or rejected. Next the cardinals of the subcommission de Schematibus emendandis did their work; when there was disagreement among the various observations issued by the Central Commission, they chose prudently. They held several sessions for that purpose, out of which emerged the current schema. It is that one only that we must now discuss; it was signed by the cardinal secretary of state. – It has been said that, contrary to the unanimous opinion of the Central Commission, the schema says nothing about revising the martyrology; those who say that have not read carefully; it clearly says: "Libri liturgici recognoscantur";[5] now the martyrology is a liturgical book. (That last remark was a response to Cardinal Ottaviani.)

Card. J. McIntyre (Los Angeles). Everything is fine with us. P. 175 introduces some doctrinal confusions. On Latin, "S. Pontifex locutus est."[6] – Dixi.

An apostolic vicar from the Philippines.[7] – Principia fundamentalia proponere vellem.[8] There have been numerous changes in the rites in the

---

[2] "Again and again".

[3] Carlo Confalonieri (1893–1986), Italian, ordained in 1916. Created cardinal in 1958. Secretary of the Congregation of the Consistory, he became pro-prefect of that body in 1965, then prefect in 1967. Member of the Central Preparatory Commission, president of the subcommission for amendments. He was a member of the Coordinating Commission.

[4] "The schemas to be amended".

[5] "Let the liturgical books be revised."

[6] "The Supreme Pontiff has spoken."

[7] Wilhelm Josef Duschak, S.V.D. (1903–1997), German. Apostolic vicar of Calapan (Philippines) from 1951 to 1973.

[8] "I would like to put forward the fundamental principles."

course of the centuries. If we want to reform, let us refer back to the first institution. I will not say anything against Latin or against any other rite. But, such as it is, does our Latin rite permit the active participation of the faithful? It is necessary that all of the Mass of the Catechumens at least be in the vernacular language. Christ celebrated coram populo, alta voce, lingua vernacula. Dixit: Exemplum dedi vobis,[9] etc. Our separated brothers will never accept our rite in its current state. There is nothing reckless in following the precept and example of the Lord. This council must be a council of unity. If we have faith, God will give the fruit. Nothing is impossible for him.

Étienne László,[10] bishop of Eisenstadt (Austria). He handed in his text to the secretariat. Tantum aliqua verba ad no. 37.[11] It is not a question here of something new: for many years, there have been numerous acts of the Holy See in this direction: cf. the A.A.S.;[12] even in matters that have to do with the Mass; and the decree on the Easter feasts, talking about a return to the "original splendor", etc. Moreover: respectus biblicus – pastoralis sollicitudo – postulata multorum episcoporum ...[13] The time has come for an "instauratio generalis".[14] The pope is asking for this; if the council fails on this point, it will not have fulfilled its duty. We must exercise "fortitudo apostolica",[15] as the Holy Father gave us an example right here in his inaugural speech.

Carlo Ferrari,[16] bishop of Monopoli (Italy). – P. 175, we should add the doctrinal principle underlying the active participation of the faithful. There should be a Mass magis communitati accommodata,[17] between a private Mass and a solemn Mass; etc.

Armand Farès, archbishop of Catanzaro and Squillace (Italy). Be mindful of the Council of Trent. At no. 37, do not exaggerate active participation. Ne tangatur canon missae; cf. Trent: canon est ab omni errore purum.[18] – No. 39 ... – No. 40: compose a form for various

---

[9] "Facing the people, aloud, in the vernacular. He said: 'I have given you an example'" [Jn 13:15].

[10] Stefan László (1913–1995), Austrian, ordained in 1936. Bishop of Eisenstadt (Austria) from 1960 to 1992. Member of the Commission for the Lay Apostolate beginning with the first session.

[11] "Only a few words on no. 37".

[12] Acta Apostolica Sedis.

[13] "Respect for the Bible, pastoral solicitude, demands of numerous bishops ..."

[14] "General renewal".

[15] "Apostolic courage".

[16] Carlo Ferrari (1910–1992), Italian, ordained in 1935. Bishop of Monopoli (Italy) from 1952 to 1986.

[17] "More adapted to the congregation".

[18] "Let the canon of the Mass not be touched; cf. Trent: the canon is pure of all error."

circumstances. No. 42: no; we must not arouse the miratio populi,[19] etc.
– No. 44: good for monks. The title: "concelebratio sacramentalis"[20] is
bad: the sacrament is already common, since everyone communicates . . .

Sabóia Bandeira, bishop of Palmas (Brazil). P. 177: omnino debet
remanere sicuti est.[21] The Latin rite is the rite of the first century; it is
the rite of Catholic truth; if we touch that, everyone will propose his
own change, etc.

Another Brazilian[22] gave up his turn to speak.

Albert Cousineau,[23] bishop of Cap-Haïtien (Haiti). Concelebration:
very good; that will do more good than a great deal of catechesis. No. 37:
mention Saint Joseph in the liturgy every time there is a reference to the
Blessed Virgin.

Bishop Jenny, auxiliary of Cambrai. No. 37 is maximi momenti.
Aliqui interrogant: cur? et quomodo? Respondeo: Si verba obscura sunt,
hoc accidit post declarationem suppressam, quae necessaria erat ad intel-
ligentiam. Pastores, una cum peritis, approbaverant eam.[24] It relates to
the following passages: shorten the prayers at the foot of the altar; – better
distinguish the two parts of the Mass, even by their location (ambo –
altar); – fewer oscula altaris, signa cruces,[25] etc.; – at the offertory, let
the populi participatio magis appareat; – oratio super oblata clara voce
fiat;[26] – during the canon, let the principal prayers be said clara voce,[27] so
that the people can respond: Amen; – fractio hostiae et pax melius ordi-
nentur; – formula ad communionem sit brevior (Corpus Xti – Amen);[28]
let the Mass end with the blessing and the dismissal. Restore the solemn
Mass with deacon. Missa pontificalis simpliciori ritu celebretur.[29] – The
new text proposed for this no. was submitted to the secretariat.

---

[19] "Astonishment of the people".

[20] "Sacramental concelebration".

[21] "It must absolutely remain as it is."

[22] João Batista da Mota e Albuquerque (1909–1984), Brazilian, ordained in 1933. Archbishop of Vitória (Brazil) from 1958 to 1984.

[23] Albert Cousineau, C.S.C. (1895–1974), Canadian, ordained in 1918. Archbishop of Cap-Haïtien (Haiti) from 1953 to 1974.

[24] "No. 37 is of very great importance. Some are wondering: Why? And how? I answer: if the words are obscure, it is due to the removal of a statement that was necessary for understanding. Pastors, together with experts, had approved it."

[25] "Kisses of the altar, signs of the cross".

[26] "The participation of the people be more apparent; let the prayer over the offerings be said aloud."

[27] "Aloud".

[28] "Let the breaking of the host and the peace be better linked; let the formula for Communion be briefer (the Body of Christ – Amen)."

[29] "Let the pontifical Mass be celebrated according to a simpler rite."

Archbishop Perraudin[30] of Kabgayi (Rwanda). Insert in the Ordo romanus[31] some readings from the holy books for the catechumenate. No. 42: Optamus ut deleantur verba "sublato fidei periculo".[32] No. 44: join Card. Léger; concelebratio restituatur secundum modum Commissionis praeparatoriae.[33]

Paul Barrachina, bishop of Alicante (Spain). No. 37 is ambiguous: Will it be necessary to change everything? Our Mass today has the same structure as it had in the time of Saint Justin. Neither should we change the other parts of the liturgy. Maxima prudentia,[34] etc.

Augustin Lopes de Moura,[35] bishop of Porto-Allegre (Portugal). At no. 38: everything is fine already.

Most Reverend Gut,[36] abbot primate of the Benedictines, in the name of numerous monastic orders. At no. 44, restituatur textus propositus commissioni centrali.[37] At no. 42, let the cases be rare and carefully determined (four cases; he proposes a text for each one); let us add: "firmo decreto concilii Tridentini".[38]

Archbishop Yü Pin[39] of Nanjing in exile: vernacular language even for the canon – except in private Masses: the language of the priest is Latin.

Bishop Bekkers of Bois-le-Duc (Holland), in the name of a whole group. Communion under both species: it is the true tradition, etc. Moreover, concelebration: the true nature of the sacrament of Holy

---

[30] André Perraudin, P.B. (1914–2003), Swiss, ordained in 1939. Archbishop of Kabgayi (Rwanda) from 1959 to 1989.

[31] "Roman ritual".

[32] "We desire that the following words be eliminated: 'the danger for the faith having been removed'." [This number (42), devoted to Communion under both species, stipulated that "Communion under both species can be granted, the danger for the faith having been removed, to the clergy and religious as well as the laity, in cases carefully determined by the Holy See, as for example in an ordination Mass, in accordance with the judgment of the bishops."]

[33] "Let concelebration be reestablished in accordance with the provision of the Preparatory Commission."

[34] "Very great prudence".

[35] Agostinho Lopes de Moura, C.S.Sp. (1911–1989), Portuguese, ordained in 1934. Bishop of Portalegre (Portugal) from 1952 to 1978.

[36] Benno Gut, O.S.B. (1897–1970), Swiss, ordained in 1921. Abbot primate of the Benedictines from 1959 to 1967, created cardinal in 1967. Prefect of the Congregation for Rites from 1967 to 1969, then of the Congregation for Divine Worship from 1969 until his death. Member of the Doctrinal Commission named by the pope.

[37] "Let the text proposed by the central commission be restored."

[38] "The decree of the Council of Trent remaining in force".

[39] Paul Yü Pin (1901–1978), Chinese, ordained in 1928. Archbishop of Nanjing (China) from 1946 until his death, created cardinal in 1969. Elected member of the Commission for the Lay Apostolate during the first session of the council.

Orders, etc. Delete "sublato fidei periculo".[40] – He turned in the rest of his remarks to the Secretariat.

Bishop Vicuña[41] of Chillan (Brazil). Distinguish better the two parts of the Mass (ambo – altar). 25 episcopi, cum nostro cardinali, vehementer optant et enixus postulant[42] that the council allow the use of the vernacular. Ex toto corde adhaereo[43] to the opinions expressed in this sense. We have been gathered together by the pope to study the renewals that are appropriate for our times. Cf. Cardinal Bea: let us not close the doors. Let us recall the "misereor super turbam".[44] (Applause.)

Paul Seitz,[45] bishop of Kontum (Vietnam). Full support for nos. 42 and 44. Latin, private Masses, etc., all that causes people to say that our religion is foreign; so, not only is all this an obstacle to evangelization, but our own faithful are turning back to their ancestral rites.

Joseph Pont y Gol,[46] bishop of Segorbe, Spain. At no. 41, aliquid addendum in fine: quam plurimum.[47] For the vernacular languages, when there are several of these, let the Ordinaries settle the matter.

Auxiliary Bishop Muldoon of Sydney, Australia. In the Prooemium to chap. 2, let the theologians clearly explain to us the dogmatic foundations; the current text "congeries est confusa conceptuum",[48] etc. Let the connection between the Mass and the sacrifice of the Cross be shown: cf. Trent. Theologice, omnino non placet.[49] Be careful of the word "repraesentatio",[50] which today evokes an idea that is too weak (he proposed a different text). In the second paragraph, "una cum sacerdote offerendo", delenda;[51] this too closely resembles the error condemned

---

[40]"The danger for the faith having been removed".

[41]Eladio Vicuña Aránguiz, born in 1911, Chilean, ordained in 1934. Bishop of Chillán (Chile, not Brazil) from 1955 to 1974.

[42]"Twenty-five bishops, with our cardinal, energetically wish and demand with all their strength".

[43]"I wholeheartedly join".

[44]"I have compassion on the crowd" [Mk 8:2].

[45]Paul Seitz, M.E.P. (1906–1984), French, ordained in 1937. Bishop of Kon Tum (Vietnam) from 1960 to 1975.

[46]José Pont y Gol (1907–1995), Spanish, ordained in 1931. Bishop of Segorbe (Spain) from 1951 to 1970.

[47]"Something to add at the end: as much as possible".

[48]"A confused heap of concepts".

[49]"Theologically, I do not at all approve it."

[50]"Representation".

[51]"'Conjointly with the officiating priest' should be deleted."

by Pius XII;[52] say, "ita cum sacerdote ut per sacerdotem ...". At no. 42: Nimis nimisque generatim rem proponit;[53] etc.

Georges Xenopulos, S.J.,[54] bishop of Syra (Greece): Communion under both species: periculum saltem irreverentiae, pro laicis;[55] three ways of doing this: each has its drawbacks ... (The president's bell stops him; there is applause.)

Bishop Théas[56] of Tarbes: with regard to concelebration, "tota mente et toto corde adhaereo. Novum argumentum, ex experientia:[57] the throngs of priests at Lourdes. (A practical reason and a spiritual reason.) Let the faithful be able to communicate at the Easter Vigil and on Easter Sunday.

Archbishop Mosquera Corral[58] of Guayaquil (Ecuador). Attenta penuria sacerdotum in missionibus,[59] let there be permission to celebrate two Masses on the same weekday, etc.

Archbishop Modrego y Casaus[60] of Barcelona (Spain). Make provision for a series of readings and homilies over four years; let no church, even those of religious orders, be exempt. If the homily is well done, no need for the vernacular language at Mass. No. 42: omitto – nihilominus quaedam dicam ...[61] (There is laughter.) Even if the cases are rare, there is danger for the faith: the faithful will believe that Communion under both species has a higher power. – De concelebratione nihil dicam[62] (he

---

[52] This refers to the encyclical *Mediator Dei* of November 1947, devoted to the sacred liturgy. Indeed, it states that it is an error to consider that "the people are possessed of a true priestly power, while the priest only acts in virtue of an office committed to him by the community. Wherefore, they [those who advocate such ideas] look on the Eucharistic sacrifice as a 'concelebration', in the literal sense of that term, and consider it more fitting that priests should 'concelebrate' with the people present than that they should offer the sacrifice privately when the people are absent" [*Mediator Dei*, no. 83].

[53] "'At this point with the priest as through the priest'. At no. 42: it presents the matter in far too general a fashion."

[54] Georges Xenopulos, S.J. (1898–1980), Greek, ordained in 1926. Bishop of Syros and Melos (Greece) from 1947 to 1974.

[55] "At least a danger of irreverence, on the part of the laity".

[56] Pierre Théas (1894–1977), French, ordained in 1920. Bishop of Tarbes and Lourdes from 1947 to 1970.

[57] "I support it with my whole mind and heart. A new argument, from experience".

[58] Cesar Antonio Mosquera Corral (1896–1971), Ecuadorean, ordained in 1921. Archbishop of Guayaquil (Ecuador) from 1956 to 1969.

[59] "Have regard for the lack of priests in the missions."

[60] Gregorio Modrego y Casáus (1890–1972), Spanish, ordained in 1914. Bishop, then archbishop, of Barcelona from 1942 to 1967. Member of the Commission for Seminaries, Studies, and Catholic Education, named by the pope during the first session.

[61] "I pass, except to say a few things."

[62] "I will not say anything about concelebration."

spoke about it nevertheless): there will be a shortage of priests for Mass, for confessions, etc. (The president: Satis – Tempus elapsum.[63] – More laughter.)

Archbishop d'Avack of Camerino (Italy). He joins Bea, etc.

That afternoon, at 4:30, I was in the parish hall of Santa Maria in Traspontina (via Traspontina), where the African group holds its meetings. Lecture to the Francophone African bishops by Father Martelet: what a dogmatic schema should be, according to the method of understanding of the faith marked out at Vatican I (analogia naturalis – nexus mysteriorum inter se et cum fine ultimo).[64] The 3rd point will be the subject of a later talk. The need for a synthesizing schema, in which the Christian mystery is not diminished in favor of natural truths and which has Jesus Christ as its center.

It is Archbishop Zoa, president of the group from Equatorial Africa, who organizes these conferences, gives information, advice, etc. At the end of the conference, the presidents of each of the 9 African groups are invited to gather in the small neighboring hall. – On the afternoon of November 7, there will be a lecture by Fr. Congar here; on the 10th, the continuation of Fr. Martelet's talk; on the 18th, a conference by Küng, in French. Archbishop Zoa announced a conference for the Anglophone group. – Some questions were posed to Fr. Martelet, who has been followed with great attention and sympathy. – I returned home with Archbishop Sartre, who is very unhappy that he has still not received the first volume of the schemas.

At 6:30 P.M., at the Belgian College, via del Quirinale, between St. Andrew's and the Four Fountains. About twenty-five students, philosophers, and theologians, with their rector.[65] I gave them a commentary on the "Credo in Deum".[66] After dinner, various questions. The rector drove me back in his car. He promised to send me a copy of the draft of the doctrinal schema prepared by Fr. Karl Rahner and a few others, gathered around Bishop Volk.[67] He told me that Msgr. Cerfaux had

[63] "Enough. Time has elapsed."

[64] "Natural analogy. The connection of the mysteries among themselves and with the ultimate end": see the constitution Dei Filius, chap. 4: Faith and Reason.

[65] Albert Prignon (1919–2000), Belgian, ordained in 1942. Rector of the Belgian College from 1962 to 1972.

[66] "I believe in God."

[67] Almost as soon as they arrived in Rome, the German bishops, around Cardinal Frings, Bishop Volk, and Karl Rahner, sought to substitute a new schema for those of the Theological Commission. This draft document was written by K. Rahner and Joseph Ratzinger.

given a talk to the bishops here at the Belgian college on the chapters of the schema *De fontibus* that concern the Bible.

Tuesday, November 6. – On the via della Conciliazione, I saw a bishop in full violet garb, busy fixing his car, which had broken down. – Arrival of some fifty buses, unloading their violet cargo onto Saint Peter's Square. – Upon entering, an Eastern bishop said to me, laughing, that I was going to be arrested at the door as a danger to the council. Inside the basilica, I greeted some of the observers. Oscar Cullmann introduced me to the Waldensian pastor of Rome, at whose home he was staying. Schutz and Thurian invited me for Friday evening. Thurian told me that he sees from time to time, opposite him, Cardinals Marella and Döpfner having a good laugh together. Also met Archbishop Dupuy[1] (Albi), formerly from Lyon, and Archbishop Dubois (Besançon), who had made a written intervention. In the peritis' gallery, my neighbor told me that they would soon be distributing the schema on the relations between bishops and religious; it is, he told me, "the schema that all the bishops are waiting for". It is certain, in any case, that several French bishops had scarcely any other idea, on the eve of the council, than to demand the elimination or the weakening of the "exemption".[2] – Cardinal Montini up until now has played a rather unobtrusive role; someone said to me: "he is papabile, he cannot compromise himself."

The president for today is Cardinal Tappouni.

Bishop Žak[3] of S. Polten (Austria). Non solum caritas, sed etiam veritas urget nos.[4] Cf. Card. Alfrink. Some criticisms have been made here: ad quid istae exagerationes inserviunt? Non sumus homines revolutionis.[5] We are carrying out our duty, ad mentem Summi Pontificis.[6] Let no. 42 be accepted, while deleting the three words: "sublato fidei periculo".[7] (Applause.)

November 6

[1] Claude Dupuy (1901–1989), French, ordained in 1926. Archbishop of Albi (France) from 1961 to 1974.

[2] This concerns the provision according to which "Religious are attached to the Supreme Pontiff or other ecclesiastical authority and withdrawn from the jurisdiction of bishops", as is indicated by the Vatican II decree *Christus Dominus*, which, moreover, gives a more detailed explanation.

[3] Franz Žak (1917–2004), Austrian, ordained in 1947. Bishop of Sankt Pölten (Austria) from 1961 to 1991.

[4] "Not only charity, but also truth urges us on."

[5] "What is the point of these exaggerations? We are not revolutionaries."

[6] "In the spirit of the Supreme Pontiff".

[7] "The danger for the faith having been removed".

Francesco Zauner,[8] bishop of Linz (Austria). With respect to con-celebration, restore the original text. Let no one treat us as innovators or modernists or as young people. The pope is more than 80 years old; in the commissions, there are many elderly bishops; the pope wanted a truly ecumenical council; this council has been prepared with great care; there have already been three deaths among those who worked out the schema on the liturgy; the text has passed through diverse com-missions. – Plurimum valet argumentum ex experientia.[9] Now, a good many experiments have been made for some time. Ex fructibus bonis arborem bonam cognoscere possumus.[10] Some have invoked a text from Exodus to exhort us not to change anything; my conclusion is the exact opposite: depone tua calceamenta, id est, rejice impedimenta[11] (some applause).

Jules G. Kandela, auxiliary archbishop of Antioch of the Syrians. On the reservation and adoration of the Blessed Sacrament; on the rates of Mass stipends, which have become very insufficient: they are owed to the priest as a matter of distributive justice. Let the Eastern Churches be able to celebrate three Masses on All Souls' Day.

Antoine Pildáin y Zapiáin, bishop of the Canary Islands. Prayers of the faithful: for princes, and nothing for the people! for those who are in sublimitate positi,[12] and not for the poor! I fear that our council might be for many people a deceptio amarissima,[13] and even a scandal. The social problems ...

The president: "Satis!" Then Archbishop Felici announced that the pope has conceded to the Board of Presidency the right to propose to the Fathers that a discussion that is dragging on too long be closed. The Fathers will vote by sitting or standing. If this measure is accepted, those who would still want to intervene will submit their text to the Secre-tariat. Everyone applauded. Immediately, Cardinal Tappouni proposed to close the discussion on the 2nd chapter; almost everyone stood up. Then he asked: let those who are opposed stand up now. No one got up. We laughed.

---

[8] Franz Zauner (1904–1994), Austrian, ordained in 1931. Bishop of Linz (Austria) from 1956 to 1980. Member of the Commission for the Liturgy.

[9] "An argument drawn from experience is worth a great deal."

[10] "We can recognize a good tree by its good fruits" [reference to Mt 7:16–20].

[11] "Remove your sandals [Ex 3:5], that is to say, cast off the fetters."

[12] "In high positions".

[13] "Very bitter disappointment".

So we made a start on the 3rd chapter: De sacramentis et sacramentalibus.[14]

Cardinal Ruffini. Nonnulla emendanda sunt. Inconsulte simul tractatur de sacramentis et de sacramentalibus.[15] P. 179, ll. 6–7: that only applies to sacraments; ll. 11–13 and 15–17, should be modified. P. 180, no. 59: Permirum mihi est quod ibi proponitur.[16] No. 60: this is contrary to Trent and canon law; the "solatium spirituale"[17] is an insufficient reason to repeat the sacrament of Extreme Unction. P. 182, l. 14: I am not opposed to all adaptation, but it should be truly useful.

Card. Cento.[18] No. 62, ll. 5–6 and 17–19: recte, bene;[19] but add something. Let the man and the woman be equally blessed (rings).

Card. Browne. P. 181, no. 56, add: "in quantum opus sit".[20] No. 57: why change the name of Extreme Unction?[21] It has been established by the councils and by the Tridentine confession of faith. Let us call on some experts for help, not to change the schema, but to improve it.

F. Hengsbach,[22] bishop of Essen (Germany). For chapter 3 in general, there is need for a mixed commission. In order to make the necessary connections, let us finally be given the other schemas. A number of the faithful have expressed wishes on the subject of confirmation and the apostolate of the laity; for this reason also, let us be given the schemas without delay. – Bring together, in the schema, the rites of baptism and confirmation.

Bishop Arneric[23] of Šibenik, Yugoslavia. Prooemium, p. 179, ll. 22–23: this is insulting to the Church. No. 47: concedatur facultas transferendi

---

[14] "On sacraments and sacramentals". [Sacramentals are religious signs that are instituted by the Church and that act in virtue of the subordinate sanctifying power that belongs to the prayer of the Church (ex opere operantis Ecclesiae).]

[15] "Some things need to be amended. To treat of sacraments and sacramentals at the same time is not wise."

[16] "What is presented here is very surprising to me."

[17] "Spiritual consolation".

[18] Fernando Cento (1883–1973), Italian, ordained in 1905, created cardinal in 1958. Major Penitentiary of the Apostolic Penitentiary from 1962 to 1967. President of the Preparatory Commission, then of the conciliar Commission for the Lay Apostolate.

[19] "Right, good".

[20] "For as much as there is need".

[21] It was a matter of preferring the name "anointing of the sick".

[22] Franz Hengsbach (1910–1991), German, ordained in 1937. Bishop of Essen from 1957 to 1991, created cardinal in 1988. Member of the Commission for the Lay Apostolate.

[23] Josip Arneric (1912–1994), Yugoslav, ordained in 1936. Bishop of Šibenik from 1961 to 1986.

rituale romanum in linguas vernaculas.[24] No. 51: let the parents receive the sacraments of penance and Eucharist for their child's baptism. No. 56: good; but let this be brief and simple. No. 62, etc.: let the bishops' conferences only ever be able to propose matters to the Holy See; for in certain countries they have no liberty and could be forced into regrettable decisions. Vitetur periculum fidei – et etiam confusio.[25]

Bishop Capozi[26] (Franciscan) of Taiwan, expelled from China. The schema says several times "actuosa";[27] it would be better to say: "interior et spiritualis".[28] No. 48, on the catechumenate, placet; but let us add that there can be no baptism before sufficient instruction, etc. Let bishops, like cardinals, have authority ubique terrarum.[29] No. 57, on Extreme Unction: let the faithful be well instructed. No. 63: our current practice, in the case of marriage, is partialis et odiosa pro feminis.[30]

Adam Kozlowiecki, archbishop of Lusaka, Northern Rhodesia. Why not reconsider the question of laypeople conferring the sacramentals when there are no priests? – There is also the question of the Christianization of local rites.

Bishop Pham Ngoc Chi[31] of Quinhen, Vietnam. No. 47: the ceremonies are too long and too complicated. So add: Vitanda nimia prolixitas,[32] etc.

Bishop Maziers at Saint Stephen's. Occasio est ut melius explicetur indoles socialis catholicismi, aspectus ecclesiasticus rituum. Multi ex fidelibus quaerunt in Ecclesia unice quae sua sunt.[33] (He reviewed each sacrament, saying how it must be explained.) So, p. 179: "... per sanctificationem membrorum Corporis Christi, etc."[34] (A deplorable accent, as is true of most Frenchmen, so that many did not understand [his Latin] and gave up trying to follow what he was saying.)

---

[24] "Let the option of transposing the Roman ritual into vernacular languages be granted."

[25] "Let us avoid a danger to the faith, and even confusion."

[26] Dominic Capozi, O.F.M. (1899–1991), Italian, ordained in 1926. Archbishop of Taiwan (China) from 1946.

[27] "Active".

[28] "Interior and spiritual".

[29] "Everywhere in the world".

[30] "Biased and odious for women".

[31] Pierre Pham-ngoc-Chi (1909–1988), Vietnamese, ordained in 1933. Bishop of Quy Nhon (Vietnam) from 1960 to 1963, then of Da Nang (Vietnam) until his death.

[32] "Excessive prolixity should be avoided."

[33] "This is the opportunity to explain better the social character of Catholicism, the ecclesial aspect of the rites. Numerous are those among the faithful who are only looking in the Church for the things that interest them."

[34] "Through the sanctification of the members of the Body of Christ".

Archbishop Plaza[35] of Plata, Argentina: I will not talk about this, I will not talk about that, etc. (The president stopped him twice.)

Bishop Lebrún[36] of Valencia in Venezuela: on no. 52, ordo baptismi.[37]

Archbishop Jules Botero[38] of Medellín, Colombia. No. 55: in our regions, confirmation is given to infants; so it is necessary to make provision for two ordines confirmandi,[39] as for baptism. It would be good to designate precisely the matter and the form of confirmation, as Pius XII did for Holy Orders.[40] No. 59: let the formula be neither too brief nor too long. No. 57: bene. No. 60: optime.[41] No. 65: these rites of clothing with the religious habit are sometimes more solemn than the consecrations of bishops! Nos. 66–67: eliminate the different classes for funerals.

Bishop Pailloux[42] of Fort Roosebury, Northern Rhodesia. (I could not hear him.)

This afternoon, at 4:30, a meeting with the Madagascar bishops at Saint Chrysogonus, the home of the Trinitarian Fathers. Archbishop Jean Wolff[43] of Diego-Suarez, presided. Msgr. Pirozzi, apostolic delegate, was present. Archbishop Wolff gave various explanations: (1) The African secretariat, grouping 299 bishops, has now been organized; Cardinal Rugambwa is president; Archbishop J.B. Zoa (Yaoundé) and Bishop Joseph Blomjous[44] (Mwanza) are secretaries; 9 episcopal conferences are grouped together within it, etc. – (2) Contacts have been established with CELAM, the secretariat of Latin America, which groups together around 650 bishops and includes 5 specialized commissions to deal with

---

[35] Antonio Plaza (1909–1987), Argentinian, ordained in 1934. Archbishop of La Plata (Argentina) from 1955 to 1985.

[36] José Lebrún Moratinos (1919–2001), Venezuelan, ordained in 1943. Bishop of Valencia (Venezuela) from 1962 to 1972, created cardinal in 1983.

[37] "The rite of baptism".

[38] Tulio Botero Salazar, C.M. (1904–1981), Colombian, ordained in 1931. Archbishop of Medellín (Colombia) from 1957 to 1979. Member of the Commission for Seminaries, Studies, and Catholic Education.

[39] "Confirmation rites".

[40] This is in reference to the apostolic constitution Sacramentum ordinis of Pius XII issued in November 1947.

[41] "No. 57: good. No. 60: very good."

[42] René Pailloux, P.B. (1902–1988), French, ordained in 1928. Bishop of Fort Rosebery (Northern Rhodesia, now Zambia) from 1961 to 1971.

[43] Jean Wolff, C.S.Sp. (1905–1990), French, ordained in 1928. Archbishop of Diégo-Suarez (Madagascar) from 1958 to 1967.

[44] Joseph Blomjous, P.B. (1908–1992), Dutch, ordained in 1934. Bishop of Mwanza (Tanzania) from 1953 to 1965. Member of the Commission for the Lay Apostolate.

the Roman congregations; for the 2nd session of the council, the permanent secretariat of CELAM will move to Rome. – (3) Two motions have already been made to the council's Board of Presidency by the African secretariat: (a) the wish that priority be given to the discussion of the schema on the Church; Cardinal Tisserant has let it be known orally that there is no chance of that; – (b) (October 26): that interventions be grouped, etc., in order to lose less time; CELAM has imitated Africa; there has been a good result, as was seen this morning in session; the Fathers desired it, the pope as well, but he wished the initiative to come from the Fathers. – (4) A draft is being studied that would allow the procurators of absent bishops to attend the sessions and vote. – (5) The African secretariat is in the process of establishing 11 commissions, each made up of 9 or 10 members, for the study of the schemas prepared by the preconciliar and conciliar commissions. A list was distributed: Archbishop Duval[45] (Algiers) and Archbishop Gilbert Ramanantoanina have been designated for the Doctrinal Commission. – (6) On the lecture series; divided into two sections (French and English language); place: via Traspontina. Next talk: the 7th, Congar on tradition; the 9th, Martelet on the doctrinal schemas, continued; the 12th, Häring on Moral Doctrine; the 16th, Küng on the collegiality of the episcopate and the episcopal conferences.

Bishop Rolland[46] next gave a brief report on the African Commission for the Liturgy, which was the first to be formed. Great reserve toward adopting local rites; restraint recommended; avoid folklore. On funeral services without priests; it would be inopportune to make a special intervention with a view to introducing a ritual, since customs differ so much from one country to the next, and even within one diocese.

Then I spoke on the first two dogmatic schemas. Some friendly interventions. Fathers Anselmo and Greco were there. – Returned home by way of Santa Maria in Trastevere.

Wednesday, November 7. – Arrived at Saint Peter's with Canon Martimort (Toulouse); he said to me: "Things are looking up ... I keep wondering what will cause us to slip and miss our goal." Taking a walk

---

[45]Léon-Étienne Duval (1903–1996), French, ordained in 1926. Archbishop of Algiers (Algeria) from 1954 to 1988, created cardinal in February 1965.

[46]Claude Rolland, M.S. (1910–1973), French, ordained in 1936. Bishop of Antsirabe (Madagascar) from 1955 to 1973.

around inside the basilica, I met Msgr. Schauf, the German expert in canon law, very "Roman", who gave me an article he had written. I greeted Bishop Maziers and thanked him for the intervention he made yesterday. Chatted with some other French bishops: de Bazelaire,[1] Jauffrès,[2] Vial; I hope that the expected success with regard to the Liturgy will not lull them to sleep: the discussion to follow, on the doctrinal schemas, will be very important. In the gallery, I was with Mr. Martimort and Canon Boulard; beside me was Fr. Antonelli, who behaves with a certain lack of consideration; one has the sense that he is at home here.

President: Cardinal N. Gilroy (Sydney). An announcement was made that, after the discussion of chap. 3 in process, then of chap. 4, chapters 5–8 of the Liturgy will be discussed together. Then we will pass on to *De fontibus revelationis*.

Bishop Pierre Rougé,[3] coadjutor of Nîmes. He replied to the objections made yesterday on art. 57 concerning the sacrament of the sick. It conforms, he said, to the spirit of the Council of Trent (cf. its "praesertim");[4] it is the traditio evangelica and the praxis primitivae Ecclesiae;[5] it is the sense of the prayers that accompany the anointing; finally experientia pastoralis[6] shows that the name and the practice of these last centuries have turned the faithful away from this sacrament. – Art. 59: it is desirable that the texts indicate the value of suffering associated with Christ the Redeemer; etc.

Bishop Angelini[7] (?, Italy). Full agreement with nos. 57–60. Let us be able to confer the sacrament before a serious operation; let us anoint just the forehead and hands.

November 7

[1] Louis de Bazelaire de Ruppierre (1893–1981), French, ordained in 1916. Archbishop of Chambéry (France) from 1947 to 1966. Member of the Preparatory Commission for Studies and Seminaries.

[2] Auguste Jauffrès (1886–1972), French, ordained in 1908. Bishop of Tarentaise from 1944 to 1961, then titular bishop.

[3] Pierre Rougé (1910–1977), French, ordained in 1932. Coadjutor of Nîmes from 1959 to 1963, then bishop of Nîmes until 1977.

[4] "Especially". [The Council of Trent stipulated that "this anointing is to be administered to the sick, especially (*praesertim*) to those who are so dangerously ill that they seem near to death": DH 1698.]

[5] "Evangelical tradition and the practice of the early Church".

[6] "Pastoral experience".

[7] Fiorenzo Angelini, born in 1916, Italian, ordained in 1940. Bishop and general chaplain of the men's branch of Catholic Action, appointed by Blessed Pope John Paul II as national chaplain of the Italian Catholic Doctors' Association. Created cardinal in 1991.

Bishop Wilhelm Kempf (Limburg, Germany). At no. 57: the new name does not indicate one of the aims of this sacrament: it is "ad gloriam resurrectionis";[8] that also is a source of "consolationis, non timoris".[9]

Bishop Clément Isnard, O.S.B., of New Fribourg, Brazil. – No. 55: placet, intra missam; "et renovatio promissionum baptismi optime introducitur ut pars sacramenti".[10] The objections made yesterday have no value. No. 65: placet juxta modum;[11] add one word: "ut ... quidam *integri* ritus[12] ..." for there is nothing that needs to be changed in the Benedictine clothing ceremony.

José-Ildefonse Sansierra, Argentina. He is in agreement with the schema on the whole. No. 55: more than the renewal of the baptismal promises is necessary: a "professio fidei erga Christum et Ecclesiam".[13] Nos. 62–63: the action of the spouses in the sacrament needs to be more clearly seen ... No. 66: our funerals nimis sapiunt tristitiam paganorum;[14] let us, "prudenter et paulatim, sed efficaciter",[15] discard the black vestments ...

Louis Faveri,[16] bishop of Tivoli (Italy). No. 58: good. No. 59, let us exhort to submit always to the divine will. No. 60: placet.

Ant. Mistrorigo,[17] bishop of Treviso (Italy): Rites of baptism and confirmation: "aliqua supprimenda".[18] He talked about the water used for baptism, the godparents, etc. (That was Faveri's intervention; the one above was Mistrorigo's.)

Aurelio del Pino Gómez,[19] bishop of Lerida (Spain)? The first sentence of the Prooemium of chap. 3 is wrong, it confuses sacraments and sacramentals. The 3rd sentence needs to be corrected, etc.

---

[8] "Directed toward the glory of the resurrection".

[9] "A sign of consolation, not of fear".

[10] "I approve, during Mass; and a renewal of the baptismal promises is introduced very well as part of the sacrament."

[11] "I approve with amendments".

[12] "Certain rites in their entirety".

[13] "Profession of faith with regard to Christ and the Church".

[14] "Smacks too much of the sadness of the pagans".

[15] "Prudently and gradually, but in an efficacious manner".

[16] Luigi Faveri (1891–1967), Italian, ordained in 1920. Bishop of Tivoli from 1950 until his death.

[17] Antonio Mistrorigo, born in 1912, Italian, ordained in 1935. Bishop of Treviso from 1955 to 1988.

[18] "Certain things should be deleted."

[19] Aurelio del Pino Gómez (1888–1971), Spanish, ordained in 1913. Bishop of Lérida from 1947 to 1967.

Joseph Sibomana,[20] bishop of Ruhengeri (Rwanda). All the bishops of Africa, Madagascar, and the Isles, grati et laetantes salutant textum numeri 49, etc. Let the textus integer[21] be approved. He based this on Pius XI.

F. Peralta y Ballabriga,[22] bishop of Vitoria (Spain). No. 66: Major simplicitas in exsequiis,[23] so that one priest alone might be able to perform the service; let this be more intelligible; let all worldly elements be deleted; let the Pascal mystery of death be expressed in it, let there be a variety of readings, etc.

Adrien Djajasepoetra,[24] archbishop of Djakarta (Indonesia): " ... et carissimi fratres observatores".[25] At the Prooemium of chap. 3, p. 179, l. 22, this direct, negative argument is not sufficient; it is a question of renovare et adaptare circumstantiis hodiernis.[26] No. 48: let the catechumenate be not only instruction but an initiation into Christian life. No. 55: on the age for confirmation ... – "Ex corde et unanimiter laudamus schema."[27]

Willem Bekkers, bishop of Bois-le-Duc (Holland). Laudo caput. It is a restauratio.[28] It also proceeds from sound anthropological principles. The sacramental signs have been chosen from among the natural signs common to all. In their choice there must be an amplissima libertas;[29] only the bishops' conferences are able to judge in this matter.

Charles Wojtyła,[30] auxiliary bishop of Kraków (Poland). Valde opportunum et necessarium.[31] P. 179, l. 7, add an exhortation to pastors to combine Christian instruction with the administration of the sacraments.

---

[20]Joseph Sibomana (1915–1999), Rwandan, ordained in 1940. Bishop of Ruhengeri (Rwanda) from 1961 to 1992.

[21]"Gratefully and gladly welcome the text of number 49, etc. Let the entire text".

[22]Francisco Peralta y Ballabriga (1911–2006), Spanish, ordained in 1936. Bishop of Vitoria (Spain) from 1955 to 1978.

[23]"Greater simplicity in funeral services".

[24]Adrianus Djajasepoetra, S.J. (1894–1979), Indonesian, ordained in 1928. Archbishop of Djakarta from 1961 to 1970.

[25]"And very dear brother observers".

[26]"Renewing and adapting to today's circumstances".

[27]"We praise the schema wholeheartedly and unanimously."

[28]"I praise the chapter. It is a return to the sources."

[29]"A very broad freedom".

[30]Karol Wojtyła (1920–2005), Polish, ordained in 1946. Auxiliary bishop of Kraków from 1958 to 1964, then archbishop of Kraków from January 1964 to October 1978. Created cardinal in 1967. He was elected pope under the name John Paul II on October 16, 1978.

[31]"Very timely and necessary".

Nos. 48 to 50: accentuate the meaning of "initiatio christiana";[32] add a few words to no. 51 to show the necessity of an initiation after the baptism of a child.

Guillaume Van Bekkum,[33] bishop of Ruteng (Indonesia): apply to this chapter, for the faithful, the same principles as for concelebration; that is very useful for the Ecclesiae noviter erectae[34] and conforms to the communitarian sense of our populations. The path will be open: optandum[35] that we embark on it resolutely. Let the rites, to the full extent that ecclesiastical law allows, be adapted; let the role of Christ be emphasized everywhere in order to remove all danger or suspicion of magic; this will be a return to the purior antiqua traditio romana.[36] Some fear diversity; but Saint Ambrose already affirmed it in principle, in communion with Rome. – And Rome and Milan were not so far apart ...

Bishop D'Souza of X, in India. No. 47, pp. 179–80: optime; but what exactly is meant? Which bishops' conferences will be excluded from the powers recognized here? For see nos. 21 and 22, where it is a question of mission countries. See also no. 62. If all bishops' conferences enjoy these powers, and if these powers are extended to all rites, optime! Certain current rites no longer have any significance for our people; an adaptation is necessary. Quaestio maximi momenti.[37] It is absurd to pronounce very beautiful texts in an unintelligible language, and there is in this the danger of an appearance of magic, as in other religions. All the formulas of the sacraments must be understood. It is deplorable that some among us are still so attached to outdated forms, for the dominatio linguae latinae; they forget that sacramenta sunt propter homines.[38] While taking care to set limits, let our episcopal conferences be granted ampliores facultates.[39] Certainly, to repeat words pronounced here, non timemus Petrum, non timemus proximos ejus adjutores[40] – but we fear the bureaucracy, we fear certain minutanti who, on their own authority,

---

[32] "Christian initiation".

[33] Willem van Bekkum, S.V.D. (1910–1998), Dutch, ordained in 1935. Bishop of Ruteng (Indonesia) from 1961 to 1972. Member of the Preparatory Commission for the Liturgy, then member of the same conciliar commission.

[34] "Newly established Churches".

[35] "It is to be wished."

[36] "The purer, ancient Roman tradition".

[37] "The question is of very great importance."

[38] "Domination of Latin; they forget that the sacraments are for men."

[39] "Broader powers".

[40] "We do not fear Peter, we do not fear his closest collaborators."

with a stroke of the pen, without knowing anything about what is at stake, cancel projects that have been worked on for a long time in our episcopal conferences. (Applause.)

Auxiliary Bishop Mendoza[41] from Peru. Penuria sacerdotum in multis regionibus; unde,[42] simplify absolution, etc.

Auxiliary Bishop André Wronka,[43] from Poland. In the introduction to the chapter, let the relation of the faithful to Christ be indicated. "Mysterium paschale": optime; an expression at the same time intellectualis et vitalis.[44] P. 179, ll. 22–24: delete "non sine fidelium detrimento".[45] No. 47: let the appendices to the ritual be incorporated into the ritual itself. No. 55: add something; let there be a dialogue between the bishop and the candidate for confirmation; have the latter recite the Credo and the Pater Noster, etc. Let there be only one sign of the cross for the trinitarian formula. Let the age of the confirmation candidates be fixed.

Bishop Joseph Malula[46] (former Belgian Congo). The African bishops beato animo approbant nos. 47, 64 et alios.[47] These nos. correspond perfectly to the wishes of the last popes. They establish the principle of diversitas in unitate.[48] Cf. the Epiphany, etc. (Applause.)

Bishop Romo[49] of Torreira, Mexico. (1) On the Eucharist ... (The president interrupted him: that is not ad rem). (2) Confirmation: simplify the rite.

Bishop García[50] Spain. No. 60, p. 181: quaestio non liturgica, sed doctrinalis; ergo,[51] if the council does not intend to define anything, let this paragraph be deleted. The doctrine here does not conform to

---

[41] Alcides Mendoza Castro (1928–2003), Peruvian, ordained in 1951. Auxiliary bishop of Abancay (Peru), he became bishop of Abancay in December 1962 and remained so until 1967.

[42] "A scarcity of priests in numerous regions; hence".

[43] Andrzej Wronka (1897–1974), Polish, ordained in 1923. Auxiliary bishop of Wrocław from 1957 to 1974.

[44] "'Paschal mystery': very good; an expression both intellectual and at the same time vital."

[45] "Not without harm for the faithful".

[46] Joseph-Albert Malula (1917–1989), Congolese, ordained in 1946. Auxiliary bishop of Leopoldville [now Kinshasa] from 1946 to 1964, then archbishop of Leopoldville-Kinshasa from July 1964 until his death. Created cardinal in 1969. Member of the Commission for the Liturgy.

[47] "Approve with happiness nos. 47, 64 and other numbers".

[48] "Diversity in unity".

[49] Fernando Romo Gutierrez, born in 1915, Mexican, ordained in 1940. Bishop of Torreón (Mexico) from 1958 to 1990.

[50] Fidel García Martínez.

[51] "It is not a liturgical question, but a doctrinal one; therefore".

the doctrine of St. Thomas, Trent, the Roman ritual, the Codex juris canonici.[52]

Archbishop Émile Tagle Covarrubias[53] of Valparaiso (Chile). No. 57: bene. No. 59: we must be able to simplify in certain circumstances. On the use of the vernacular: optime.

We moved on to the examination of chap. IV, De officio divino.[54]

Card. Frings (Cologne). 1. In the translation of the psalms let us preserve the Latin of the Fathers. Remaneat textus Vulgatae[55] as long as it agrees with the Hebrew; where it departs from it, let us refer to St. Jerome's translation juxta Hebraeos;[56] if that is unsatisfactory, let it be translated into the language of the Holy Fathers. Example: the efforts of Fr. Weber, O.S.B.[57] – Haec est unica via ad restituendam unitatem in recitandis psalmis.[58] – 2. (?) – 3. Restituatur rythmus inter psalmos et lectiones;[59] not too many psalms one right after the other. Let us be allowed to anticipate Matins and Lauds. – 4. In the name of the conference of all German-speaking bishops: dolendum[60] that people no longer know Latin; the Church can do nothing about it; therefore, it is necessary to free the young clergy from a burden that is too heavy: let the episcopal conferences be able to permit the vernacular language. (Applause, especially from the rows of the young bishops.)

Card. Ruffini (Palermo). P. 186, no. 69: praise of the psalms, according to St. Athanasius and St. Thomas. However, omit those in which an imperfect revelation is expressed (on death; or the deprecatory psalms), especially if they are read in the vernacular. No. 74: publica oratio Ecclesiae est solius sacerdotis.[61]

---

[52] "Code of canon law".

[53] Emilio Tagle Covarrubias (1907–1991), Chilean, ordained in 1930. Archbishop of Valparaíso (Chile) from 1961 to 1983.

[54] "On the divine office".

[55] "Let the text of the Vulgate remain."

[56] "According to the Hebrews". [This refers to a translation of the psalter by Saint Jerome, a little before A.D. 395.]

[57] Dom Robert Weber, O.S.B. (1904–1980), French, a monk of Saint-Maurice and Saint-Maur of Clairvaux, a monastery of the Congregation of Solesmes, on which Saint Jerome Abbey in Rome depends, charged with producing a critical edition of the Vulgate. He is the author in particular of *Le Psautier romain et les autres anciens psautiers latins*, Collectanea Biblica Latina (St. Jerome Abbey–Vatican Bookstore, 1953).

[58] "This is the only way to restore unity in the recitation of the psalms."

[59] "Let there be a balance between the psalms and the readings."

[60] "It is regrettable".

[61] "The public prayer of the Church is a matter for the priest alone."

Card. Valeri.[62] Pp. 185–86, no. 68: not coherent. – Agrees with Frings. No. 71: beware of making the office longer; Augustine already found the Milanese readings too long. No. 73: neque hic neque alibi,[63] we must not go outside the measure of moral obligations; let us only impose the recitation under pain of mortal sin for the substantial parts (Lauds and Vespers). Example of the Eastern Church.

Card. Quiroga y Palacios,[64] archbishop of Santiago de Compostela. On the composition and distribution of the hours of the office.

Card. Léger, archbishop of Montreal. Now, it is a question of our pastoral concern for our priests. 1. De obligatione recitandi officium:[65] let there be a strict obligation only for Lauds (in the morning), Vespers (afternoon), a period of lectio divina[66] (about ten minutes, at any time). The principle of the schema only applies to monks, only in part to priests in active ministry, etc. – 2. No. 77: let priests be able to use the vernacular language: so many priests do not know the Scriptures and the Fathers that they read every day in Latin! (Applause.)

Last evening, the cardinals of the Board of Presidency still did not know which schema would be chosen to follow the one on the Liturgy.

One bishop, I was told, had himself photographed in Saint Peter's talking at the microphone, no doubt to show the members of his diocese his active participation in the council.

A witticism of Cardinal Tisserant. There are in Saint Peter's, the catholici (Italians), the fratres uniti (all the others), and finally the fratres separati[67] (observers).

Fr. Rondet is writing a report summarizing the pope's instructions concerning the council; Fr. Daniélou asked him for it for Archbishop Garrone.

At 4:30 P.M., in the hall at the via Traspontina, lecture by Fr. Congar on tradition, in front of the African bishops. The meeting was organized

---

[62] Valerio Valeri (1883–1963), Italian, ordained in 1907, created cardinal in 1953. Nuncio in France from 1936 to 1944. Prefect of the Congregation for Religious from 1953 until his death. President of the Preparatory Commission for Religious, then of the same conciliar Commission for Religious.

[63] "Neither here nor elsewhere".

[64] Fernando Quiroga y Palacios (1900–1971), Spanish, ordained in 1922, created cardinal in 1953. Archbishop of Santiago de Compostela from 1949 to 1971. Vice-president of the Commission for Eastern Churches.

[65] "On the obligation of reciting the office".

[66] "Meditative reading of the Bible".

[67] "Catholics" – "united brothers" – "separated brothers".

by Archbishop Zoa (Cameroon) and Archbishop Gantin[68] (Dahomey). Yesterday, in the same room, Fr. Daniélou gave a talk for the Anglophone Africans. A good speech by Congar. A few objections, without any ill will, from some missionary bishops who vaguely recalled their textbook. At the end, a small impromptu meeting around Archbishop Zoa; besides Congar, Frs. Chenu and Martelet were there. There was talk of the doctrinal schema prepared by Fr. Rahner; the German bishops hope to have it substituted for the official schemas, but that is very probably an illusion. It would, however, be necessary to have a text ready to put forward at the proper time if the criticisms of the Fathers were numerous and strong enough to get the text under discussion rejected. So it is desirable that the text prepared by Rahner be reviewed by some bishops and theologians, so as not to appear to be the work of a single man, and a controversial man at that. Archbishop Zoa and Fr. Martelet went to see Fr. Rahner at the Germanicum to put this request to him. I went out with Frs. Congar and Chenu. The latter proved to be timid and suspicious: he regretted the fact that Fr. Labourdette had attended the meeting in which the plan for Rahner's schema was decided; he asked me for some clarifications on the Preparatory Theological Commission, on such and such a theologian, etc.

Louis Massignon[69] has just died. Fr. Daniélou received a telegram from Fr. Giuliani,[70] asking him for a few pages on him for the next issue of *Études*.

After dinner, a visit from Fr. Martelet. With Archbishop Zoa, he saw Fr. Rahner. The latter seemed to have understood the situation. Instead of immediately having numerous copies of his work printed, he is going to do a reduced print run and distribute it to a few people for examination and correction. I will receive a copy. Fr. Martelet, who is on very good terms with Cardinal Liénart, will bring him a copy and consult him on the course to follow.

---

[68] Bernard Gantin, born in 1922, Beninese, ordained in 1951. Archbishop of Cotonou (present-day Benin) from 1960 to 1971, created cardinal in 1977. Prefect of the Congregation for Bishops from 1984 to 1998. Member of the Commission for the Discipline of the Clergy and the Christian People beginning with the second session.

[69] Louis Massignon (1883–1962), French, Orientalist, professor at the Collège de France and the École des hautes études until 1954. Founder of the Comité chrétien d'entente France-Islam, he sought to promote Islamic-Christian dialogue.

[70] Maurice Giuliani, S.J. (1916–2003), French. Creator of the journal *Christus* in 1954, a journal devoted to spirituality. He was an architect of the development of Ignatian spirituality. Assistant of France from July 1965 to 1972.

I now have in my hands the "Animadversiones in Primam Seriem schematum ..." [71] by Father Schillebeeckx, O.P.: 47 large pages. He had the help of Father Smulders, S.J., for the chapter on original sin.

The November 1 issue of *L'Osservatore Romano* contains an article by Card. Cento, "Il vero Volto della Chiesa",[72] which concludes by repeating a phrase already used to good advantage by Fr. Charles Boyer in an article on Christian unity: "Incessu patuit dea: è impossibile sottrarsi al fascino del divino che irradia dal suo volto."[73]

In the same issue, a report on the 11th General Congregation, in French: "The Fathers repeated on many occasions their desire to facilitate the participation of the faithful in the sacrifice of the Mass, to develop an awareness of a priesthood common to all the faithful by virtue of the character conferred on them by baptism and confirmation." And again, in English: "... an awareness of a priesthood common to all, etc."; in German: "... allgemeinen Priestertum";[74] in Spanish: "la conciencia de un sacerdocio comun a todos en virtud del caracter ..."[75] But, in Italian: "... la consapevolezza degli obblighi comuni a tutti i fideli in virtu del carattere del Battesimo, etc."[76]

This morning, on exiting Saint Peter's, I had met Archbishop Zoa, sitting in the small car belonging to the priors of Taizé. "I had not seen you dressed in violet before." – "Yes, up until now, you might have taken me for a seminarian!" Spoken with his hearty laugh. We laughed as well, R. Schutz, M. Thurian, and I.

In the afternoon, I saw Fr. Jean Lucas. He told me that he would have more news about the council and its surroundings if he were willing to pay; for there exists a mercenary attitude among some of the Vatican's personnel. This evening, he is going to broadcast an intervention made by Patriarch Maximos, which has already been published in some paper, I no longer remember which.

---

[71] "Observations on the first series of schemas". [About two thousand copies of this text, which put forward the weak points of the preparatory schemas, were distributed, with the unofficial approval of the Dutch bishops.]

[72] "The true face of the Church".

[73] "Her gait reveals the goddess [Virgil, *Aeneid*, I, v. 603]: it is impossible to escape the fascination of the divine that shines forth from her face."

[74] "A common priesthood".

[75] "The awareness of a priesthood common to all in virtue of the character ..."

[76] "The awareness of the duties common to all the faithful in virtue of the character of baptism".

Thursday, November 8, 1962. – This morning, I went to the Hotel Picadilly behind St. John Lateran, where Bishop Seitz and his secretary, Fr. Jacques Dournes,[1] are staying, to study with them the first two doctrinal schemas. I stayed to have lunch at the hotel, where I saw various bishops from the Far East (Chinese, Vietnamese, etc.). Bishop Seitz told me that there has been no attempt made among them to get organized. A certain number were formerly students at the Propaganda, where they took Archbishop Parente's courses; some of them were saying, during the first days of the council: "Archbishop Parente is the one who will make the council."

In the afternoon, a conversation about the council with Fr. Anselmo, S.J., former provincial of Sicily, a missionary in Madagascar, where he teaches theology; he is the theologian of the archbishop of Tananarive.[2] At 6 P.M., I went with Fr. Martelet to the Church of the Twelve Apostles, for the hour of prayer organized by some French bishops and Msgr. Etchegaray. First, passed by the Biblical Institute, where I found Archbishop Veuillot in Fr. S. Lyonnet's room.

Bishop Charue[3] of Namur has offered to intervene vigorously to defend the exegetes in the debate on the schema *De fontibus*.

Father Congar wrote today to Archbishop Garrone to express his astonishment that the French episcopate seem to want to ignore the theologians named as experts by the Holy See.

In *L'Osservatore,* the October 24 issue, Father Lio, O.F.M., a moral theologian at the Antonianum, one of the principal authors of the moral schemas of the Preparatory Theological Commission, wrote: "To disregard the doctrine de fide et de moribus,[4] which demanded such great effort in the course of preparing for the council, would be not only to fail to keep the promises made by the pope, ... but it would also be to fail in what the world is waiting for today, after the council Fathers'

November 8

[1] Jacques Dournes, M.E.P. (1922–1993), French, ordained in 1945. Missionary to Vietnam, he became a renowned specialist in the ethnology of Southeast Asia. Secretary and personal expert of Bishop Seitz of Kon Tum (Vietnam) at the council.

[2] Jérôme Louis Rakotomalala (1913–1975), Malagasy, ordained in 1943. Archbishop of Tananarive (now Antananarivo) (Madagascar) from 1960 until his death, created cardinal in 1969. Member of the Commission for Bishops and the Government of Dioceses.

[3] André Charue (1898–1977), Belgian, ordained in 1922. Bishop of Namur from 1941 to 1974. Elected member of the Doctrinal Commission at the time of the first session. He became its vice-president at the end of the second session.

[4] "On faith and morals".

solemn message." – Someone pointed out to me that the work of Fr. Lio is weak and that the world is not particularly waiting for it.

In the trolleybus this morning I met Archbishop Élie Zoghby of the Greek-Melchite patriarchate in Egypt. He had wanted to chat. He knew Fr. Robert Clément, S.J.,[5] well (the nephew of Father Paul Couturier).[6] He was struck by the sympathy that sprang up very quickly between the old Eastern Church and the young Christianities of black Africa. He invited me to have lunch with him someday soon.

Friday, November 9, 1962. – A few encounters this morning in St. Peter's: Bishop Renard (Versailles), who asked me to help him (especially, I believe, with the Latin) in an intervention he wants to make against the first two chapters of the *De deposito fidei*; – Bishop Huyghe (Arras), determined to do everything possible to have the two dogmatic schemas completely rejected; – Bishop Cazaux (Luçon), who proved very cordial. A Brazilian bishop, whose name I do not know, stopped me as I went along and spoke to me with complete trust.

In the gallery, I was between Father Balić and Father Tavard, A.A.,[1] a former student of mine from Lyon. Since Wednesday, Fr. Balić has started smiling again; he recounted to me this morning how he succeeded in having Father René Laurentin, who had come as a journalist, registered among the periti. Father Tavard talked to me about the sessions of the Secretariat for Unity and about Cardinal Bea. – At the "Exeant omnes",[2] as on every morning, a patrol of Swiss guards, with halberds held out in front of them. – In a little while, Fr. Balić will go to the bar, telling me: "I'm going to the 3rd Vatican Council."[3]

---

[5] Robert Clément, S.J. (1918–1994), French, ordained in 1949. He had teaching responsibilities in several educational establishments, in Egypt, then in Lebanon.

[6] Paul Couturier (1881–1953), French, ordained in 1906. Very dedicated to ecumenism, he was behind the first meeting for Unity at Lyon in 1933, the forerunner of the Week of Prayer for Christian Unity. He was also the founder of the Dombes group [a group of Roman Catholic and Protestant theologians that meets regularly].

November 9

[1] Georges Tavard, A.A., born in 1922, French, ordained in 1947. Professor of theology in the United States. Expert at the council, consultor to the Secretariat for Unity, he worked particularly in the area of ecumenism.

[2] "Let all go out".

[3] Two food and beverage outlets had been set up: one in the sacristy of the chapel of the Blessed Sacrament, the other near the passage between the choir chapel and the sacristy.

Cardinal Manuel Gonçalves Cerejeira,[4] patriarch of Lisbon: Necesse est equilibrium reperire inter obligationes sacerdotum, orationem propriam et liturgicam, actionem pastoralem. The breviary: adaptari debet hodiernis conditionibus, etiam circa structuram. Prout jacet, vitae verae concretae sacerdotis non bene accommodatur. Quaestio magni ponderis. In general law, lingua latina a clericis servari debet, quia in officio sacerdos est tanquam vox Ecclesiae.[5] – As for the obligation, determine the concrete cases in which a dispensation can be granted.

Cardinal Spellman (New York): permit the choice between Latin and the vernacular.

Cardinal Étienne Wyszyński[6] (Warsaw). Let the emendatio[7] not go too far: Servanda sunt monumenta antiquissimae traditionis. Quaedam sunt obsoleta; sed ...[8] Devoted admiration for the Roman breviary, even among those outside the Church. Praebet oratori sacro elementa pretiosa ... Fovet unionem sacerdotis cum Ecclesia.[9] It contains the principal Christian truths. Finally, and most importantly, it constitutes a very strong bond for the whole Mystical Body. – One does not have time for it? That is insulting to so many good priests; and for others, the shortest prayer would still be too burdensome. – Lingua latina conservanda videtur in breviario.[10] A number of beautiful texts cannot be well translated. If we yield on this point, priests will lose the habit of Latin to an even greater degree. In the name of the 64 Polish bishops: let us refrain from shortening the breviary too much (some applause) and let us keep the Latin.

Cardinal William Godfrey, archbishop of Westminster. – Some people exaggerate the onus sacerdotum in opere pastorali.[11] I have

---

[4] Manuel Gonçalves Cerejeira (1888–1977), Portuguese, ordained in 1911, created cardinal in 1929. Patriarch of Lisbon from 1929 to 1977. Member of the Commission for the Missions.

[5] "It is necessary to find a balance once again between the priest's obligations, his personal and liturgical prayer, his pastoral action. The breviary must be adapted to today's conditions, even in its structure. As it is, it is not well adapted to the real, practical life of the priest. This is a question of great importance. In general law, Latin must be retained by the clerics, for in the office the priest is, so to speak, the voice of the Church."

[6] Stefan Wyszyński (1901–1981), Polish, ordained in 1924, created cardinal in 1953. Archbishop of Gniezno and of Warsaw from 1948 until his death. Member of the Board of Presidency of the council. Member of the Secretariat for Extraordinary Affairs.

[7] "The change".

[8] "We must preserve these monuments of the most ancient tradition. Certain ones are obsolete, but ..."

[9] "It provides precious elements for the preacher. It fosters the union of the priest with the Church."

[10] "It seems that Latin must be retained in the breviary."

[11] "The burden of priests in pastoral work".

been a parish priest; I see a large number of priests; I have never met any who have told me that they no longer have time for the breviary. Do not legislate universally for a few exceptional cases. Be careful of the haeresis bonorum operum.[12] Work must be subordinate to prayer. The breviary has already been made lighter. It must remain the essentiale nutrimentum nostri laboris.[13] – If, in some regions, Latin is no longer much used or esteemed, that is not a reason for abandoning its use in the office: on the contrary, we must make an effort to restore it. Do not give a signum debilitates.[14] – In our cathedral, the office is recited or chanted every day; our work is not neglected because of that. No ulteriores abreviationes: jam generose concessae sunt;[15]; and cf. *Veterum Sapientia*. – Liceat mihi rem satis miram narrare:[16] while we were debating here whether or not to abandon Latin, the Anglican Church, gathered together these last few days in meetings, were extending usum linguae latinae in caeremoniis. Vix risum tenemus, cardinales, in concilio.[17]

Card. Lefebvre[18] (Bourges). Let the obligation of saying the breviary be once again firmly declared. In order that priests might fulfill it libenter et fideliter,[19] let us set forth the reasons for this serious precept. Page 185, the principal end of the office is very well expressed; but it is necessary to stress this, for a good number of priests do not see well enough how important the recitation of the office is for their ministry and their sanctification. We must clearly state two principles: a. "Sine me nihil potestis facere". Nullam exceptionem hoc principium admittit; atqui, nullae preces efficaciores officio, ex opere operantis Ecclesiae.[20] Fons mirabilis gratiarum ad fecundandum ministerium . . . – b. Officium praebet textus Scripturae et Patrum . . . – Diversae aptationes, ut suavius et fructuosius recitari possit . . . Tunc, levis apparebit

---

[12] "Heresy of good works".

[13] "The essential nourishment of our work".

[14] "A sign of weakness".

[15] "No further abridgements: they have already been generously conceded."

[16] "Let me be permitted to recount something rather surprising."

[17] "The use of Latin in their ceremonies. We have a difficult time refraining from laughing, cardinals, at the council."

[18] Joseph Lefebvre.

[19] "Willingly and faithfully".

[20] This expression applies to the religious signs instituted by the Church to signify that they act in virtue of the sanctifying subordinate power that belongs to the prayer of the Church, and not *ex opere operato*, which designates the mode of action of the sacraments and signifies that they have efficacy, as divine acts, by the virtue that is proper to themselves, that which God has conferred on them in Christ.

obligatio.[21] It will be seen that the authority that imposes it is in the image of the authority of God, quae est Caritas.[22]

Card. Döpfner (Munich). He proposed aliquas emendationes,[23] while approving the chapter. Nos. 68, 76, and 77: restore the commission's text, indicating that the bishops' conferences will be able to rule on the language. Cardinals Frings and Léger have spoken very well. We all desire Latin to remain; we are working for that end; volumus Veterum Sapientia in praxim ducere. But ... in multis regionibus[24] the young men come to us without knowing a word of Latin; I am not exaggerating. If we impose Latin on them, the number of priests, already insufficient, will be reduced by half. Already several acts of the Holy See have started the necessary evolution; nil mirum si concilium procedit in eadem via.[25] We value unity; but there is also a kind of variety that is good and necessary in the body of the Church. The episcopal conferences must not be simple "conventus";[26] let them exercise the rights that the council will confer on them. There is nothing dangerous in that: their decrees will only have authority once they have been confirmed by the pope. This will not be the introduction of a new authority between the bishops and the Holy See. Döpfner, in conclusion, entreated certain bishops not to think only of the situation in their own territory, but to have regard for the needs of the universal Church (applause).

Card. Albert G. Meyer (Chicago). On no. 77: res magni momenti pro vita spirituali sacerdotum.[27] Let us permit the vernacular language for the private recitation of the office. Let the council concede this, not only because of the ignorance of Latin, but majoris pietatis causa[28] (applause).

Card. J. Santos Rufino (Manila, Philippines). Officium, honor et onus;[29] it is too heavy for many. So, at p. 187, no. 73, distinguish between priests in active ministry and the others; make provisions for some relief for the first group.

---

[21] "a. 'Apart from me you can do nothing' [Jn 15:5]. This principle admits of no exception; however, no prayer is more effective than the prayer of the office, ex opere operantis Ecclesiae. It is a marvelous source of graces to enrich ministry ... b. The office furnishes texts from Scripture and the Fathers ... Various adaptations, in order that it might be able to be recited in a more agreeable and fruitful manner ... Then, the obligation will seem light."

[22] "Which is love".

[23] "Some amendments".

[24] "We would like to put Veterum Sapientia into practice. But ... in numerous regions".

[25] "There is nothing surprising if the council advances down this same path."

[26] "Gatherings".

[27] "A very important thing for the spiritual life of priests".

[28] "For the sake of greater piety".

[29] "The office, honor, and burden".

Card. Enrique Pla y Deniel (Toledo).[30] No. 73, ll. 3–4: this does not agree with no. 72 b. – At no. 73, ll. 6 and 10, graviora notanda.[31] What does "capitula residentialia"[32] mean? Add, at l. 10: "... saltem partem officii, judicio Ordinarii loci."[33] No. 76: do not do away with all the "horae minors".[34]

Card. Ant. Bacci. He proposed a reform of the breviary; this had already been called for by Vatican I, but had hardly been put into effect. – 1. In the readings, there is only 1/5 of the New Testament, and in the Old Testament, few from the wisdom books; give a better proportion. – 2. Delete the deprecatory psalms, etc. (nearly a third). – 3. Versio psalmorum:[35] the new version departs too much from the Vulgate; data fuit ad experimentum;[36] we must return to the lingua christiana. – 4. Lectiones historicae:[37] not enough has been done to rid them of legends. – 5. Lectiones SS. Patrum: subtilitates rhetoricae et cavillationes,[38] should be deleted. – Name a commission for this reform. Support for no. 77: lingua latina;[39] liturgical Latin is easy; the bishops have a serious obligation to take the necessary measures. (He spoke in a modest, soft tone, very different from the affected and almost arrogant tone of his intervention at the beginning of the council.)

Card. Aug. Bea. – Let the council give only some normae generales.[40] The schema enters into too many particular details (so, for example, nos. 70, 71, 79 ...). Some clear indications have already been given, which the council does not have to repeat. For the version of the psalms, see the fine work of Fr. Weber, O.S.B. It is all the more necessary to restrict ourselves to a broad outline, since we are an ecumenical council, not only a Latin council. There are breviaries other than the Roman one, about which our schema speaks almost uniquely. – The cardinal enumerated the few principles that should be set down. – Let us talk also about the relation between personal and public prayer. Let the rest be sent back to the competent authorities from the various rites. Let

---

[30] It was not Cardinal Pla y Deniel but Juan Landázuri Ricketts who spoke.

[31] "Some rather serious things should be noted."

[32] "Residential chapters".

[33] "At least a part of the office, according to the judgment of the local Ordinary".

[34] "Little hours".

[35] "Version of the psalms".

[36] "It has been tested."

[37] "Christian language. 4. Historical readings".

[38] "Readings from the Fathers: rhetorical niceties and subtleties".

[39] "Latin".

[40] "General rules".

us remember the survey instituted by Pius XII on the recitation of the office: as much as the bishops agreed on the necessity of a reform, they differed just as much in their opinion about the particularities.[41] We will not come to any greater agreement here. We should not discuss this any more; and let the Constitution not speak about it (applause).

Card. Ans. Albareda, O.S.B. [42] – On nos. 69 (revision of the Latin of the psalms), 70 (revision of the hymns), 71: a profound critical revision is necessary; delete all the legends.

A bishop from the USA.[43] – P. 185: in the name of numerous priests ubique terrarum,[44] let them be allowed to recite the office in the vernacular (cf. Spellman and Meyer). The breviary would not be published in vernacular language without the approval of the Holy See: so, there is no risk of error. Whatever we might wish and whatever we do, ubique terrarum a good number of priests do not know and are no longer able to know Latin.

Bishop A. S. Méndez (Cuernavaca, Mexico). (Various remarks).

Archbishop Weber (Strasbourg). He spoke in the name of 25 years experience as a seminary rector and numerous times preaching spiritual exercises. Praise for the divine office. Dolendum est[45] that a good number of priests dispense with it, in whole or in part. (1) Let the council recall the grave and salutary obligation (according to the norms of moral theology). – (2) Abbreviations and adaptations are necessary (e.g., as in Easter week). – (3) Produce bilingual editions; let the Ordinaries be allowed to give indults for recitation in the vernacular language. – (4) Let the new editions be definitive; prepared with care by a commission of bishops and experts or, better, by the commission that Cardinal Bea suggested. Res valde urget.[46]

Bishop Franić (Split, Yugoslavia). Let us not shorten the office any more. Let us also talk about private prayer. Nos. 73 and 77: Adhaereo ex toto corde.[47] Keep the Latin. The wisdom of 77 c.

---

[41] The Sacred Congregation for Rites had consulted the episcopate in May 1956 on revising the breviary. The bishops responded that they were in agreement on the necessity for a reform, but they differed in the details.

[42] Joaquín Anselmo María Albareda y Ramoneda, O.S.B. (1892–1966), Spanish, ordained in 1915, created cardinal in 1962. Titular archbishop. Member of the Commission for the Liturgy.

[43] William Connare (1911–1995), American, ordained in 1936. Bishop of Greensburg (Pennsylvania) from 1960 to 1987.

[44] "Everywhere in the world".

[45] "It is regrettable".

[46] "It is a very urgent matter."

[47] "I wholeheartedly support".

Bishop Jacobus Romeijn.[48] Simplify Matins. Delete the psalms and hymns that are scarcely intelligible. Reduce the readings from the Old Testament, etc. Let the office for the dead be in the vernacular language.

Bishop Reed (USA).[49] Difficulties with the current form of the breviary. P. 187, no. 73 b: soften.

An Argentinian,[50] in the name of the bishops of Argentina, Paraguay, and Uruguay. Support the position of Cardinals Frings and Léger. The difficulties will remain if the breviary keeps its current structure. Non minus sed melius generaliter volunt orare sacerdotes.[51] Let the breviary of priests in active ministry no longer be the monastic breviary. Let communal recitation be recommended, when this is possible. Let the council give bishops the right to grant certain dispensations.

An archbishop from China.[52] On nos. 69 and 71, numerous details.

Toward noon; the secretary general announced the 100th birthday of Archbishop Carinci,[53] former secretary of the Congregation for Rites; the assembly stood up in his honor and addressed a telegram to him.

Friday afternoon, at 3:30, a visit from Father Daly,[54] professor at the University (or the Seminary) of Belfast, Ireland. He came to consult me on *De fontibus* and *De deposito fidei*. He is alarmed by the spirit of these documents, and most particularly by the chapter on creation and evolution. He fears that the English bishops, out of an instinct for security, might accept these schemas. He wants to come back and see me. A clear, sound mind.

At 4:30 P.M., at the Traspontina, the second part of Father Martelet's talk. About 70 bishops were present. The connection between the mysteries and our ultimate end: he took the example of sin, original and actual. Man created in Christ. At the end, he sketched out in broad

---

[48] It was really James Corboy, S.J. (1916–2004), Irish, ordained in 1948. Bishop of Monza (Zambia) from 1962 to 1991.

[49] It was in fact Francis Reh (1911–1994), American, ordained in 1935. Bishop of Charleston from 1962 to September 1964, the date on which he became rector of the American College. Member of the Commission for the Discipline of the Sacraments.

[50] Antonio María Aguirre (1908–1987), Argentinian, ordained in 1943. Bishop of San Isidro from 1957 to 1985.

[51] "Priests generally want to pray, not less, but better."

[52] Archbishop Melendro.

[53] Alfonso Carinci (1862–1963), Italian, ordained in 1885. Titular archbishop, secretary of the Congregation for Rites from 1945 to 1959. He had participated as an altar boy at Vatican I.

[54] Cahal B. Daly (1917–1996), British, ordained in 1941. Professor of philosophy at Queen's University in Belfast. Personal expert of an Irish bishop, he was an expert at the council starting from the third session. Created cardinal in 1991.

outline what he thought the conciliar constitution should be. He was so passionate that he got them to listen, although the details were difficult to follow. Various questions showed that he was well enough understood. Friendly discussion, at the end, with Archbishop Luc Sangaré of Bamako (Mali) on creation "in the Word" or "in Christ".

I went next to the Biblical Institute, to see Father Stanislas Lyonnet, who showed me the report written by Fr. Smulders (Maastricht) for the use of the Dutch bishops on the schema *De fontibus*: a schema "unworthy of a council", "penitus rejiciendum".[55] This report is very well done. Fr. Lyonnet told me that the Spadafora's pamphlet against the Biblical Institute has been translated into French. He also told me that if Cardinal Ottaviani has not been coming to the council these last few days, it is by way of protest, because Cardinal Alfrink has refused to apologize to him for having bluntly interrupted him the other day.

At 7:30 P.M., at the Taizé Brothers' place. They have rented a small apartment right in the center of Rome, on the via del Plebiscito, across from the Palazzo di Venezia. They entertain there for lunch and dinner a number of bishops and theologians. Brothers Schutz and Thurian gave a lecture this afternoon in front of numerous bishops of CELAM (Latin America) with Cardinal Silva Henriquez, archbishop of Santiago, Chile, presiding: they are greatly touched by the welcome they have received. The cardinal, whose presence intimidated them a little, wept, it seems. They are supposed to speak one day soon to the bishops of Argentina, who could not attend today because they had another meeting. I was in their chapel, attending the Brothers' office (there are four of them); then, a meal. Numerous details on their different stays in Rome, the disappointing exchanges organized by Fr. Charles Boyer at the Gregorian, etc.; on the council also, on the cardinals they observe during the sessions: there are those who sleep, those who are always impassive, those who are having fun, those who seem unhappy at the presence of the observers ... Roger Schutz told me that five cardinals went to ask the pope to order Cardinal Alfrink to apologize to Card. Ottaviani; but the pope did not want to interfere. He spoke to me about Cardinal Montini, who treats them with great affection. When I said to him that Montini seems to want to keep a low profile, he answered me: "He is papabile."

---

[55] "It should be totally rejected."

General André Metz[56] sent me the text of an article that he is proposing to the *Archives de philosophie*: personal memories of Fr. Teilhard.

Saturday, November 10, 1962. – At the entrance of Saint Peter's, I was stopped by a missionary bishop from Indonesia, English-speaking, it seemed to me, who spoke to me with great affection, thanked me for my books, told me that one must often suffer in the Church, and embraced me. In the gallery, I found a place for Father Laurentin, who arrived at the same time as I did; he is very happy to find himself now on the inside of the council. Beside him was Father Boyer, always silent, and who would end up sleeping a good while. My other neighbor was Fr. Labourdette; we exchanged a few reflections that were in agreement. Father Congar confirmed to me that he had written to Archbishop Garrone: he seems especially surprised by the fact that the French bishops are scarcely concerned at all about uniting their efforts with those of the other episcopates; he told me that if things do not change, he will leave soon, so as not to waste any more of his time. Seated behind me was the young Msgr. Lafortune[1] from Montreal, Cardinal Léger's secretary; he loaned me the text of Léger's remarks on the schema *De fontibus* (they are the work, I believe, of another young Canadian,[2] a professor at the Major Seminary of Montreal, brought to Rome by the cardinal). – At 9:02 a.m., our centenarian bishop arrived; we all applauded him. Mass was said by the archbishop of Braga;[3] the rite included some unique details; I retained this beautiful formula, from the beginning of the priest's prayers before Communion: "Domine Jesu Christe, qui es vera pax et vera concordia, fac nos pacificari in hac sancta hora."[4]

---

[56]Jules Eugène André Metz (1891–1968), French, a graduate of the École polytechnique, he was particularly interested in the sciences and the philosophy of science.
November 10
[1]Pierre Lafortune (1926–1984), Canadian, ordained in 1951. Theologian and canonist in training, chancellor of the archbishop of Montreal, he was the personal expert of Cardinal Léger and was named an expert to the council during the first intersession.
[2]This must be André Naud, P.S.S. (1925–2002), Canadian, ordained in 1950. Professor of philosophy at the Seminary of Philosophy in Montreal from 1962 to 1964. Personal expert of Cardinal Léger. Expert at the council beginning with the second session. He had prepared several reports in Montreal during the summer.
[3]Antonio Benedetto Martins Júnior (1881–1963), Portuguese, ordained in 1903. Archbishop of Braga (Portugal) from 1932 until his death.
[4]"Lord Jesus Christ, you who are true peace and true concord, make us peaceful in this holy hour."

Cardinal Ruffini was presiding. He gave a piece of advice: let there be no applause. He addressed himself especially, laying stress on this, to the back rows,[5] "who could not have heard very well". It is improper to applaud, he said, for several reasons. It could provoke murmurs in the opposite sense and create factions. Then, with a certain vehemence, he complained of those who, in the assembly, are lacking in respect for the members of the Roman Curia, who are the immediate, faithful, and devoted collaborators of the Holy Father, etc. We listened to him in silence. Everyone understood that he had prepared this reprimand with his friend Ottaviani. An archbishop I met that afternoon would tell me that his two neighbors, Italians, were saying to each other: "He has no right to talk like that." At half past noon, on the via della Conciliazione, Msgr. Noirot[6] would talk to me about the incident as something that he knew in advance was bound to happen.

Bishop Martin Jaime Flores of Barbastro (Spain) gave his assent to Cardinal Wyszyński. He extolled the importance of the office, made a speech in praise of prayer: "Oratio est labor pastoralis."[7] Generalities.

Auxiliary Bishop Martinez Fidel García from Spain proposed an addition to no. 71 a: "tam in officio quam in missa, praesertim ex Novo Testamento".[8]

Auxiliary Bishop Vielmo[9] from Chile. We must distinguish three kinds of Roman breviaries: monastic, common, pastoral; the last is for the use of priests in the most active days of their ministry. – Corrections that need to be supplied in the current breviary.

Very Reverend Jean Prou, Abbot of Solesmes. He spoke in the name of various monastic orders. A brief history of the attempts made to correct the Latin of the psalms. Let us adopt the christiana latinitas.[10] At no. 69, ll. 16–17, add: "... et laboriose prosecutum ... necnon totius traditionis linguae Ecclesiae."[11] Delete the deprecatory psalms? No, but

---

[5] These rows were occupied by the youngest bishops, by reason of precedence.
[6] Marcel Noirot (1915–1996), French, ordained in 1938. Professor at the Pontifical Institute of Sacred Music in Rome since 1957.
[7] "Prayer is a pastoral work."
[8] "As much in the office as in the Mass, especially of the New Testament".
[9] Cesar Gerardo Vielmo Guerra.
[10] "Christian Latinity".
[11] "And the work to continue, taking into account the whole tradition of the language of the Church" [concerning the revision of the psalms].

understand them in their spiritual sense; otherwise, it would be necessary to delete also a similar passage in the Apocalypse (cf. the common of martyrs). At no. 71 a, minus placet[12] the reduction of the readings from the Old Testament. If there is a longer reading during the Mass from the epistles and gospels, the balance will be established.

Auxiliary Bishop Joseph Reuss of Mainz. He spoke about the residential chapters; the nuns who understand nothing in Latin. Let the clerics have the office in the vernacular language, generaliter,[13] and not by special permission. Otherwise, it will be merely mechanical and tedious repetition, not spiritual prayer, and their spiritual life will not be nourished. On the matter of obligation: cf. Cardinal Léger and alii Patres.[14] What is necessary: Lauds, Vespers, and about 20 minutes of reading.

Bishop René Piérard[15] of Châlons-sur-Marne. Necessity of reminding about the obligation of the office. Many priests today are overwhelmed with work; hence the necessity of shortening the breviary. He proposed some adjustments. He asked that the bishops be able to determine the conditions for exceptions, etc.

Archbishop Raphaël García y García de Castro[16] of Grenada (Spain). No. 73: What does "infirmitas humanae naturae" mean? – Quod pejus est,[17] the schema minimizes the value of personal prayer. – No. 73, 3 b: should be deleted, etc.

Archbishop Michel Gonzi[18] of Malta: We are reducing too much the obligations of the chapters...

Bishop Stephen?[19] USA. P. 188, no. 77: add: d. let the vernacular language be permitted. The "separated brothers" give us a good example here (he has numerous contacts with them). In order to acquire familiarity with the sacred texts, with a view to preaching, it is necessary to read them for oneself in the same language.

---

[12] "I approve less".

[13] "Generally".

[14] "Other [council] Fathers".

[15] René Piérard (1899–1994), French, ordained in 1923. Bishop of Châlons-sur-Marne from 1948 to 1973.

[16] Rafael García y García de Castro (1895–1974), Spanish, ordained in 1919. Archbishop of Grenada from 1953 until his death.

[17] "'Weakness of human nature'? What is worse".

[18] Michael Gonzi (1885–1984), Maltese, ordained in 1908. Bishop of Malta from 1943 to 1976.

[19] Stephen A. Leven (1905–1983), American, ordained in 1928. Auxiliary bishop of San Antonio from 1955 to 1969. Member of the Secretariat for Unity beginning with the second session.

Archbishop Garrone of Toulouse. Episcopal anxiety. It seems at first sacrilegious to change anything in an office so venerable, but, on the other hand, we cannot close our eyes to the grave difficulties that disturb the conscience of many priests. Gaudeo,[20] that several here do not feel this anxiety in their own case; fortunatos nimium![21] Sed, venerabiles Fratres,[22] when you cast your votes, think of the others. Petitio nostra non venit ex amore novitatis, sed traditionis Ecclesiae,[23] etc. He, too, has a whole program worked out. Matutinum pro monachis tantum valet.[24] Let the reading be done in the vernacular language. As for the rest, remittatur ad conferentias episcopales. Nullo modo sum rerum novarum cupidus. Testis est mihi Deus.[25]

Bishop Joseph Mc (USA):[26] lingua vernacula[27] for private recitation.

Bishop Émile Guano[28] of Livorno traced out some general principles. He wants us to continue to recite all the psalms each week. Directions for correcting the Latin of the psalms.

Very Reverend Fr. Anicet Fernández, master general O.P. At Matins, three psalms; four reasons for this. The readings can be done in the vernacular language, and, for nuns, the whole office. But priests must recite in Latin. Major caritas quam nimia indulgentia.[29] (A speech in 8 points).

Bishop Luigi Carli of Segni. Do not shorten the breviary: it should rather be augmented. Against an activismus exaggeratus.[30] We will have to say, with Saint Bernard: occupationes illas maledictas.[31] If we reduce

---

[20] "I rejoice".

[21] "Too happy!" [An allusion to Virgil's *Georgics*, II, 458: "*O fortunatos nimium sua si bona norint!*", too happy if they could but know their blessedness!]

[22] "But, Venerable Brothers".

[23] "Our request does not come from a love of novelty but from the tradition of the Church."

[24] "Matins is only obligatory for monks."

[25] "Let it be referred to the bishops' conferences. I am in no way avid for new things. God is my witness."

[26] Joseph Marling, C.PP.S. (1904–1979), American, ordained in 1929. Bishop of Jefferson City from 1956 to 1969.

[27] "Vernacular language".

[28] Emilio Guano (1900–1970), Italian, ordained in 1922. Bishop of Livorno (Leghorn) from 1962 until his death. Member of the Commission for the Lay Apostolate appointed by the pope at the end of the first session.

[29] "It is more a matter of greater charity than one of excessive indulgence."

[30] "Exaggerated activism".

[31] "These cursed occupations". [Saint Bernard, *De Consideratione ad Eugenium papam*, bk. 1. This was written for Pope Eugene III, a Cistercian. His pontificate was from 1145 to 1153.]

the breviary, hoc erit mirum, fere scandalosum pro toto populo chris-tiano.[32] There followed a full-scale assault on the use of the vernacular.

Archbishop Yago[33] of Abidjan (Côte d'Ivoire). In the name of all the West African bishops and many other Africans, he stood behind Cardinals Frings and Léger. Some say that there is plenty of time to recite one's office; but we see here many bishops reciting it during Mass, which is scarcely an edifying practice. (All this was very well said).

There followed a bishop from Spain,[34] who made various detailed remarks; then Bishop Victor Costantini of Sessa Aurunca (Italy), against the vernacular.

Cardinal Ruffini, president, next proposed that we stop the discus-sion of chap. IV. Almost everyone stood up to approve the motion. Some who were not paying attention remained seated; their neighbors made them get up. We started on the examination of chaps. V–VIII, per modum unius.[35]

Cardinal Spellman: no reason to change the calendar.

Melchite Archbishop Philippe Nabaa[36] of Beirut: de festo paschali.[37] The necessity of having the same date for this as the Orthodox. Let a mixed commission be created, catholicorum et a-catholicorum.[38] We could propose, for example, the 2nd Sunday of April for everyone. This would be one obstacle to unity removed, and it would already be the unity of all those who believe in Christ for the celebration of Christ's Resurrection. (I saw Fr. Boyer make a vague gesture of disapproval.)

Archbishop Antonio Jose Plaza of La Plata (Argentina). Remarks on sacred art. Images of Our Lady of Mount Carmel.

Bishop Pierre Čule (?)[39] of Mostar (Yugoslavia). Sermon full of ardor on Our Lady of Mount Carmel and on Saint Joseph, who should be

---

[32] "It will be shocking, almost a scandal for the whole Christian people."

[33] Bernard Yago (1916–1997), a native of Côte d'Ivoire, ordained in 1947. Archbishop of Abi-djan from 1960 until 1994, created cardinal in 1983. Named as a member of the Commission for the Missions during the first session.

[34] José Souto Vizoso (1893–1973), Spanish, ordained in 1916. Bishop of Palencia (Spain) from 1949 to 1970.

[35] "As a single whole".

[36] Philippe Nabaa (1907–1967), Lebanese, ordained in 1931. Melchite archbishop of Beirut from 1948 until his death. Under-secretary of the council.

[37] "On the Paschal feast".

[38] "Of Catholics and non-Catholics".

[39] Petar Čule (1898–1985), Yugoslav, ordained in 1925. Bishop of Mostar from 1942 to 1980. Member of the Commission for Bishops and the Government of Dioceses from 1964.

introduced into the canon of the Mass and proclaimed the greatest of the saints, etc. (The cardinal president stopped him. Next came an Italian,[40] another one,[41] and that was the end.)

Going out of Saint Peter's, exchanged some news with Dom Olivier Rousseau and Fr. Antoine Wenger. Entering the Curia, I found Archbishop Philippe Nabaa there, who took me in his car to "Salvator Mundi", behind the Janiculum hill, where Patriarch Maximos was expecting me. Maximos asked that I be left alone with him; then he showed me an absurd text exalting the pope and making him the equal of God; he asked me what theological grade I would give to this text; I answered that it was too absurd to merit being graded theologically; he replied that what made the thing so serious was that the text did not come from some pious author without any authority but from an important figure – who is even said to be, he told me (but he had not yet been able to verify this), on the Doctrinal Commission of the council; if that is verified, he is determined to intervene in the council. That, he said to me, is blasphemous, and the Orthodox are continually reproaching us for things like this; they make any union absolutely impossible. I had the impression that he was getting a little too upset.

Around 1:30, lunch. At the patriarch's table, there was also his secretary and two bishops: Bishop Georges Hakim of Nazareth and Oreste Kéramé, whose birthday we were celebrating. At the neighboring tables were some Austrian and American bishops, with a few secretaries; among them, Archbishop Edelby – After lunch, recreation with the patriarch; Archbishop Edelby joined us. Little anecdotes, cheerfulness. Maximos IV told me the story of how three Melchite bishops came one day to Rome to complain to Leo XIII about their patriarch, who had become unbearable. The pope insisted on having specific complaints; at first the bishops could not come up with anything that the pope judged to be very serious; then one of them, after all sorts of delays, said: "He sometimes says something bad about Your Holiness" (another version, spiced up a little: "His faith is not pure, he goes so far sometimes as to doubt the primacy of Your Holiness"). Then Leo XIII said, laughing, "Oh! but all of you do that just as much, in the

---

[40] Antonio Tedde (1906–1982), Italian, ordained in 1929. Bishop of Ales and Terralba (Italy) from 1948 until his death.

[41] Rafael González Moralejo (1918–2004), Spanish, ordained in 1945. Auxiliary bishop of Valencia from 1958 to 1969.

East!" And he dismissed them, adding: "You are the ones who elected him, live with the consequences of your action." And Maximos burst out laughing.

Oreste Kéramé then took me to an upstairs floor to see two young American priests: one, Reverend Raymond W. Lessard,[42] is a secretary prelate of a bishop; the other is a student who is preparing a thesis in ecumenical theology under the direction of Fr. Witte (Gregorian). We chatted freely; some book signing; a photo on the terrace.

Back at the Borgo S. Spirito, I studied the Votum of Cardinal Léger on the schema *De fontibus* that his secretary, Msgr. Lafortune, had given me. – Visit from Father Jorge Mejía, professor of Sacred Scripture at the Theology Faculty of Buenos-Aires, editor of the journal *Criterio*, the theologian of the Argentinian bishops; together we studied the schema *De fontibus*, with a view to interventions. – Visit from Father L. de Peretti, who gave me various bits of information on the Canadian bishops.

Sunday, November 11, 1962. – A few days ago, an article by Cardinal Siri, in an Italian newspaper, traced out a program for the doctrinal work of the council – in some ways similar to that of Archbishop Parente and Fr. Lio.

I wrote a few observations on Cardinal Léger's Votum. A Canadian theologian, Father Primeau,[1] secretary of Archbishop Maurice Baudoux of Saint Boniface,[2] came to pick them up.

Archbishop Veuillot is working with Fr. Stanislas Lyonnet.*[3]

Father Durocher,[4] Bursar General, passed on to me a magazine article that was sent to him from the USA: *Letter from the Vatican*, by "Xavier

---

[42] Raymond William Lessard, born in 1930, American, ordained in 1956. From 1960 to 1962, he was the secretary in Rome of Cardinal Aloysius Muench. After the death of the cardinal, he became assistant superior of the North American College in Rome. At the council, he was the personal consultor of Leo Dworschak, Bishop of Fargo (United States). Expert at the council.

November 11

[1] Pierre Primeau, P.S.S., Canadian, ordained in 1958. Professor of theology at the major seminary in Saint Boniface. The personal theologian of Archbishop Baudoux at the council, however, was Antoine Hacault (1926–2000), born in Belgium, ordained in 1951. Professor of theology at the major seminary in Saint Boniface until 1964, then auxiliary bishop of Saint Boniface from July 1964 until 1972. Expert during the first two sessions.

[2] Maurice Baudoux (1902–1988), born in Belgium, ordained in 1929. Archbishop of Saint Boniface (Canada) from 1955 to 1974. Member of the Commission for Eastern Churches.

[3] *This sentence has been crossed out.

[4] Romulus Durocher, S.J. (1889–1967), Canadian, ordained in 1924. Bursar General of the Society of Jesus and of the Curia from 1945 to 1967.

Rynne".[5] It is a study on the situation of the Church in the course of the last few years, the work of John XXIII, the council, the American bishops. "Many responsible French and German Catholics believe that the time has come to break the stranglehold on ecclesiastical thought and operations exercised by the self-perpetuating clique of Roman Curial officials, who, as heads and administrators of the various Congregations that make up the Curia, dictate Roman Catholic policy and, to a large extent, control the Pope himself." Information on the June debates: Card. Ottaviani having the letter (in Italian translation) of the Dutch episcopate suppressed;[6] Cardinals Döpfner, König, and Liénart siding with Card. Alfrink. An enumeration of all Archbishop Parente's charges, which make him seem like a sort of dictator. The French, German, and American theologians, excluded from the preparatory commissions or named only as consultors. Details on the offensive led by Msgr. Romeo, with the support of the Lateran, against the Biblical Institute, so as to present John XXIII with a fait accompli. The pope assured the rector of the Biblical Institute of his confidence; he made Cardinal Pizzardo[7] write to Cardinal Bea in order to deny any responsibility on the part of the Congregation for Seminaries and Universities (of which Romeo is a member), etc. The general of the Jesuits took a strong stand. Cardinal Ruffini's positions are contrary to those of the encyclical *Divino afflante*. On the Italian mentality: "The function of the theologian is to preserve Catholic doctrine from the least taint of change or error"; the axiom: "No heresy has ever been born in Italy." Methods of the Italian seminaries. Reduction of the teaching of Christ to some logical concepts. The Curia's insistence on Latin. The great unknown element for the council is the North American episcopate: numerous, considered in Europe to be without theological culture; most of them were formed in Rome; they have adopted the conservative attitude of their schoolmasters; "they could easily render an aggiornamento of the Church impossible." Some

---

[5] Xavier Rynne, C.Ss.R. (1914–2002), American, pseudonym of Francis X. Murphy. Professor of patristics and missiology at the Alphonsian Academy in Rome. He published articles on the council in the *New Yorker*. Expert at the council.

[6] This letter, *De bisschoppen van Nederland over het Concilie*, was intended to arouse the interest of the faithful and to serve as a guide for a more in-depth study. The Italian translation, *Il Concilio Vaticano II: il contributo dei fedeli: Lettera pastorale dell'episcopato olandese* (Turin: L.D.C., 1962), was withdrawn from sale because it was judged too inaccurate and liable to provoke misinterpretations.

[7] Giuseppe Pizzardo (1877–1970), Italian, ordained in 1903, created cardinal in 1937. Prefect of the Congregation for Seminaries and Universities from 1939 to 1968. President of the Preparatory Commission for Studies and Seminaries, then president of the conciliar Commission for Seminaries, Studies, and Catholic Education.

views on the history of the councils. – (The American Fathers here are trying to find out who could be the author of this article, certainly well informed – although dramatizing things in a one-sided manner.)

At 11 A.M., Mass at Saint-Louis des Français. All of our bishops were present. Archbishop Ferrand[8] of Tours, gave a banal sermon on charity. It seems that anything that might resemble a patriotic sentiment scares our bishops. In the cloister, hand shakes. Cordial words from Bishop Théas, etc. I saw Bishop Collini again, whom I knew in Lyon; I had already seen him eleven years ago in Tunis.

At 12:30, I was at the Gregorian. I went to greet the rector[9] and Fr. Jarlot, who was celebrating his 50th year as a Jesuit. I was beside Fr. René Arnou. He reported to me the words of a prelate of the Secretariat of State, whom he sees on a regular basis: the pope would seem to be disposed to receive favorably a request from the cardinals that he put an end to the campaign against the Biblical Institute and restore Frs. Lyonnet and Zerwick to their teaching posts,[10] etc. In the afternoon, a conversation with Fr. Gathier, librarian, former missionary in Madura; he is very busy these days with the Indian bishops, who feel a little lost in Rome. Cardinal Gracias has gone back to India.

The Italian newspapers are relating the already old news about Cardinal Alfrink cutting off Cardinal Ottaviani's speech; they say that Ottaviani will not return until he has received an apology.

At 6:30 P.M., at the Germanic College. Conversation with Cardinal Döpfner. He seems to be taking to heart the plan to speak to the pope about the Biblical Institute affair. He is not the one, however, who would make the request, for he has just had an audience with John XXIII. Next we spoke about the two theological schemas; I gave him various details on the preparatory commission. He does not understand French well; sometimes we spoke in Latin, or Father Gajáry, present at the conversation, served as interpreter. – At table, I was beside the rector[11] and the bishop of Luxembourg.[12] A period of recreation with bishops and priests; chatted with Msgr. Willebrands, Dutch, secretary of

---

[8] Louis Ferrand (1906–2003), French, ordained in 1929. Archbishop of Tours from 1956 to 1980.

[9] Pablo Muñoz-Vega.

[10] These two professors of the Biblical Institute had been among the persons most strongly attacked by A. Romeo. They were suspended from their teaching responsibilities at the request of the Holy Office at the end of the academic year 1961–1962.

[11] Friedrich Buuck, S.J. (1909–1981).

[12] Léon Lommel (1893–1978), Luxembourger, ordained in 1919. Bishop of Luxembourg from 1956 to 1971. Member of the Commission for the Discipline of the Clergy and the Christian People.

the Secretariat for Unity. I next gave a talk to the students of the Germanicum; I recounted some memories of Frs. de Grandmaison, Lebreton, Huby,[13] Teilhard de Chardin.

Fr. Daniélou passed on to Archbishop Garrone the long Note written by Father Rondet, quoting all the characteristic texts of the pope on the desirable orientation of the council.

Monday, November 12, 1962. – On entering Saint Peter's, I was called over by Bishop Villepelet[1] (Nantes), who gave me some news about his nephew. We exchanged a few words on the dogmatic schemas; he appears to me to be convinced of their poor quality. Melchite Archbishop Tawil[2] invited me to have lunch on Thursday, to speak to a small group of bishops. At the entrance to my gallery, a Capuchin was waiting for me: he wanted the complete reference for a text from Claudel that he is quoting from the Italian edition of my *Méditation sur l'Église* (*Splendor of the Church*); he is the pope's preacher. – Saw a few observers next: O. Cullmann told me that when the speakers in the council are boring, at least he is getting a Latin lesson; I thanked Schutz and Thurian. Two secretaries have been added to the Secretariat for Unity, assigned to look after the observers. – In the gallery, Msgr. Rodhain[3] told me that Cardinal Richaud[4] wrote to the pope to criticize the doctrinal schemas. In these last few days, a good share of new periti (or those comparable) have been allowed across the triple barricade to attend the sessions. – Mass in Slavonic by a Yugoslav bishop.

Cardinal Antoine Caggiano (Buenos Aires) was presiding. Archbishop Felici announced that the pope will preside over the final session on December 8. On the 9th, there will be a canonization. The 2nd session

---

[13]Joseph Huby, S.J. (1878–1948), French, ordained in 1910. A disciple of Léonce de Grandmaison, he was H. de Lubac's professor of theology at Hastings. Father de Lubac found in him a true master. He also taught exegesis at Fourvière, then he dedicated himself to editing the journal *Études* and to the intellectual and spiritual apostolate.

November 12

[1]Jean-Joseph Villepelet (1892–1982), French, ordained in 1916. Bishop of Nantes from 1936 to 1966.

[2]Joseph Tawil (1913–1999), Syrian, ordained in 1936. Patriarchal vicar of the Melchites of Damas from 1960 to 1969.

[3]Jean Rodhain (1900–1977), French priest, secretary general of Le Secours catholique, which he founded in 1946. Expert at the council.

[4]Paul-Marie Richaud (1887–1968), French, ordained in 1913, created cardinal in 1958. Archbishop of Bordeaux from 1950 until his death. Member of the Central Preparatory Commission. During the council, he was a member of the Technical and Organizational Commission.

will start on the 4th Sunday after Easter (May 12, 1963) and will end on June 29.[5] In the meantime, the commissions will be working. – On the last four chapters of the Liturgy schema, many have asked to speak.

Card. Jaime de Barros Câmara, archbishop of São Sebastião (Brazil) on sacred music. Let those in seminaries and religious novitiates be well formed in Gregorian chant, etc.

Card. Feltin: De festo paschali.[6] Let it be on a fixed day, e.g., on the first Sunday in April. Debemus recognoscere institutiones nostras.[7] Soon the feast of Easter might not be observed any longer if we do not take the initiative: and a fixed day will be more convenient for everybody. (No allusion, it seems to me, to Orthodoxy). Supports the idea of a mixed commission as proposed yesterday, etc.

Card. Laurean Rugambwa (Bukoba, Tanganyika). De musica sacra.[8] Who will decide what is suitable or not? The liturgical commissions will not be able to do so without periti from every region. Debemus modos africanos componere,[9] etc.

A Sicilian bishop (?).[10] On the reform of the calendar (art. 82). Let every year start on a Sunday. Let one week be added every 5th or 6th year, etc. Everyone will be happy: the Eastern churches, the separated brothers, Hebrews, Muslims, the laity. All sorts of advantages, etc. (Long-winded.)

A bishop from China (?).[11] De veneratione martyrum in Ecclesia.[12] Let us restore in the churches the pious images that have been removed from them; especially the images of the Sacred Heart, etc.

A bishop from the USA,[13] on no. 84: let a certain feast be extended to the whole Church.

A Polish bishop:[14] on the calendar. Cardinal Feltin is right, however ... Let a plan be submitted by the Church to the U.N. Let each month have 28 days, etc. Let Christmas be set on December 22, etc.

---

[5] The second session would actually open on September 29, 1963, and close on December 4.

[6] "On the feast of Easter".

[7] "We must reform our institutions."

[8] "On sacred music".

[9] "We must compose some African music."

[10] Corrado Bafile (1903–2005), Italian, ordained in 1936. Nuncio in Germany from 1960 to 1975, created cardinal in 1976. Prefect of the Congregation for the Causes of the Saints from 1976 to 1980.

[11] F. Melendro.

[12] "On the veneration of martyrs in the Church".

[13] J. Marling.

[14] Antonio Baraniak, S.D.B. (1904–1977), Polish, ordained in 1930. Archbishop of Poznan from 1957 until his death. Member of the Commission for Eastern Churches.

Another bishop (?)[15] spoke about nos. 81 and 84. Let us admit exceptions for certain saints. On the calendar, the schema is not coherent. We must have one calendar, as we have one language, Latin.

Maronite Archbishop Khoury of Tyre. De anno liturgico. 1. Mirum, nihil dici de diebus liturgicis;[16] the liturgical day has always been, in the East and in the West, de vespere ad vesperam;[17] it must not change: this is what the divine office presupposes, and it conforms to social usages; this can be very practical for Sundays (Masses on Saturday evening). – 2. no. 83: restore a true Lent. – 3. no. 85: a fixed date for Easter is desirable: but it is necessary to take into account the difficulties for everyone; so establish a status quaestionis,[18] and immediately undertake negotiations with our separated brothers, so that the council might be able to make a ruling, to the great joy of all.

Bishop Victor Reed[19] of Oklahoma City (USA): On no. 81: let there be greater variety in the readings for Sundays, etc. Let the votive Masses be more specialized; for example, in the Mass of the Holy Spirit, let the prayers vary according to the type of ceremony, etc.

A Coptic bishop:[20] on some details of the liturgical calendar (I did not understand him).

Bishop Antonio Iannucci[21] of Penne-Pescara (Italy). On transferring the feast of St. Thomas the Apostle and some other feasts from the octave of Christmas. Institute feasts of the childhood and youth of Jesus. The last Sunday of October, the dedication of St. John Lateran, should be moved to a different date, etc. All these changes will show the vitality of the Church.

Bishop Russell Joseph McVinney[22] of Providence (USA). No. 83 is ambiguous. On penitential practices, the Paschal fast, bishops give dispensations too easily.

---

[15]Sebastião Soares de Resende (1906–1967), Portuguese, ordained in 1928. Bishop of Beira (Mozambique) from 1943 until his death.

[16]"On the liturgical year. 1. It is surprising that nothing is said about the liturgical days."

[17]"From the evening to the following evening".

[18]"State of the question".

[19]Victor Reed (1905–1971), American, ordained in 1929. Bishop of Oklahoma City from 1958 until his death.

[20]C. Zohrabian, who was not a Coptic, but of the Armenian rite.

[21]Antonio Iannucci, born in 1914, ordained in 1938. Bishop of Penne and Pescara from 1959 to 1990.

[22]Russell Joseph McVinney (1898–1971), American, ordained in 1924. Bishop of Providence (United States) from 1948 to 1971.

A Spanish bishop.[23] Nos. 81 and 84: very good; but let there not be constant repetitions on the weekdays. Vary the readings from Holy Scripture.

A bishop from Vietnam.[24] A good number of feasts in the Roman liturgy are pagan feasts that have been Christianized: the Purification, etc. Recently, May 1 became the feast of St. Joseph. In the missions, let us be able to proceed in the same way, for the feasts that have been customary from time immemorial, etc. — No. 84: Let us be able to celebrate the dies natalis[25] of martyrs in the dioceses where they were martyred. — No. 83: We no longer do enough preaching on penitence, omnis temporis, praesertim Quadragesimae.[26] — No. 84: let bishops be able to allow feast days, change the days, etc., for the consolation of the faithful. — Chap. VI: let us eliminate the maniple and the amice,[27] useless.

Bishop J. Léonard Raymond[28] of Allahabad (India). General principles. No. 85: in our country, it is too hot in April to celebrate Easter; etc., etc.

Archbishop M. Castellano[29] of Siena, O.P. (?) — On Easter. At no. 86 it is not enough to say: "non obstat". Create a commission. — Make a single chapter out of chaps. 6 and 8. Nos. 87 and 91: again the episcopal conferences, and still nothing on the provincial councils. Let us vote on the episcopal conferences before voting on the liturgy. No. 89: let this be clarified.

Archbishop Pierre Ngo-dinh-Thuc[30] of Hué (Vietnam). In the name of the bishops of Vietnam. This schema proposes so many innovations that nothing of the Roman ritual will remain; this could be very harmful.

---

[23] Lorenzo Bereciartúa y Balerdi (1895–1968), Spanish, ordained in 1919. Bishop of Sigüenza-Guadalajara (Spain) from 1955 to 1963, then of San Sebastián until his death.

[24] Simon Hoa-Nguên-van Hien.

[25] "Birthday" [the day of their martyrdom is the day of their birth into eternal life].

[26] "At every liturgical season, especially Lent".

[27] These are liturgical vestments.

[28] Leonard Joseph Raymond (1899–1974), Indian, ordained in 1926. Bishop of Allahabad (India) from 1947 to January 1964, then archbishop of Nagpur (India) until his death. Member of the Secretariat for Unity starting from 1964.

[29] Ismaele Mario Castellano, O.P. (1913–2007), Italian, ordained in 1942. Archbishop of Siena from 1961 to 1989. Member of the Commission for the Lay Apostolate.

[30] Pierre Martin Ngô-dinh-Thuc (1897–1984), Vietnamese, ordained in 1925. Archbishop of Hué (Vietnam) from 1960 to 1968. He was named a member of the Commission for the Missions during the first session. After the council, he ordained some bishops on his own initiative and was excommunicated by Paul VI.

De aspectu sociali, multi Patres exagerant:[31] among us, for a long time, this social aspect has been very intensive; but we still value individual piety. So much freedom requested for adaptations! In this, too, there is danger. Latin has always been the language of a minority: so the situation is not new: it has brought about unity; it must do so still. Let the pope, aided by the Roman congregations, determine everything. Without the Congregation of the Propaganda, we, the bishops of Vietnam, but also of other places, Africa, Madagascar, and the Isles, would not be in this assembly.

A bishop from Chile,[32] in the name of numerous bishops of South America: on the necessity of poverty. Renounce all "vanitas";[33] vestments should be simpler. We must be Ecclesia docens, non verbo tantum, sed re.[34]

An Italian bishop.[35] On chaps. 6–7–8. A history of the measures taken by the popes. The absurdities of sacred art in Gallia.[36] We can accept greater simplicity in the vestments. For sacred music, write a code. Fix some norms for sacred art.

Bishop Paul Gouyon[37] of Bayonne. Evangelical poverty. Simplify the vestments, even the liturgical ones, etc. (He strongly accentuated his words, almost always on the wrong syllable: exprimère, voluèrit, exprimītur, etc.) – (Two other French bishops had given up their turn to speak so that he could speak in the name of the three of them; but he confined himself to his own individual agenda, which caused some displeasure).

At 2:30 P.M., a visit from Rev. Fr. Laurent Volken,[38] Swiss, rector of the Collegio Salettino. He is busy working on ecumenism and is going to

[31] "On the social aspect, a number of Fathers are exaggerating."

[32] Manuel Larrain Errázuriz (1900–1966), Chilean, ordained in 1927, Bishop of Talca from 1939 until his death. Member of the Preparatory Commission for the Lay Apostolate, then of the same conciliar commission. He was one of the founders of CELAM and its president from 1963 until his death.

[33] "Vanity".

[34] "We must be the teaching Church, not only by words, but also by actions."

[35] Primo Gasbarri (1911–1989), Italian, ordained in 1933. Auxiliary bishop of Velletri from 1953 to 1964, then apostolic administrator of Grosseto from 1964 to 1970.

[36] "In France".

[37] Paul Gouyon (1910–2000), French, ordained in 1937. Bishop of Bayonne from 1957 to 1963. He was named coadjutor of Rennes in September 1963 and became archbishop of Rennes in September 1964. Created cardinal in 1969. Member of the Secretariat for Unity beginning with the second session.

[38] Laurenz Volken, M.S. (1914–2002), Swiss, ordained in 1941. Professor of theology, rector of the Salesian College in Rome from 1961 to 1964.

publish a book; he came to talk to me about the question of the members of the Church. He finds the position of Father Tromp "horrible". He has close ties with Taizé, etc.

A visit from the young Father Ceccon, S.J., [39] who was at Vals[40] last year and has come here to do three years of social studies at the Gregorian before going to South America. (He is a Savoyard, of Italian origin.)

At 4:30 P.M., via Traspontina, Father B. Häring's talk on moral theology: about 60 African bishops and some others were there. He spoke for an hour and a half. About a dozen black bishops were present. He took as his starting point a quote from Claudel: "We love Jesus Christ, the Church; no one will make us love morality."[41] He asked: "Would our schemas make us love the Church and her moral teaching?" Four criteria: The evangelical spirit – the primacy of charity – the orientation toward unity – following the aims of the council as defined by John XXIII. – A patient and comprehensive dialogue is necessary with the men of today (cf. existentialism, etc.). – A response to Marxist collectivism and to the call of the African sense of community. – Unity through Christ – but, in our schemas, it is the complete opposite. – Some questions were posed to the lecturer about how to replace them. Archbishop Duval of Algiers presided. Archbishop Zoa gave some advice.

I returned to the Borgo under a torrential downpour with Father Jullien,[42] professor of moral theology, the theologian of Bishop Fauvel of Quimper. He showed me the first circular issued by a study group constituted under the direction of Bishop Himmer (Tournai) and Bishop Hakim (Galilee, Israel), on "Jesus, the Church and the poor". He wondered if right now was a good time to get a petition under way in this sense, etc. We discussed it. The matter does not seem to me to be very serious. Next we spoke about the French bishops: we find them to be generally a little lax, not much concerned about doctrine, and not much concerned about effective action. He told me that he wants to meet with me again.

---

[39] Mario Ceccon, born in 1936, French, was a member of the Society of Jesus from 1957 to 1968.

[40] A Jesuit scholasticate.

[41] "And certainly we love Jesus Christ, but nothing on earth will make us love morality", an excerpt from the poem "Sainte Thérèse" from the collection *Feuilles de saints* (1925).

[42] Jacques Jullien, born in 1929, French, ordained in 1954. Professor of moral theology at Quimper from 1957 to 1969, he became, after the council, bishop of Beauvais, then archbishop of Rennes.

Father Martelet arrived around 7 P.M., coming from the French Seminary, where he spoke in front of 60 French bishops. Archbishop Guerry, who was presiding, appeared enthusiastic; the others were of the same mind. Only one small objection from Bishop Ancel. They wanted to have copies made of his text: he answered that it had already been done by another group of bishops. He is supposed to resume on Friday, at Saint-Louis des Français; Archbishop Garrone will be there; he sent him an objection in writing, after having read his text: Vatican I, he told him, did not think particularly of Christ in speaking about the "nexus"[43] of the mysteries.

Fr. Karl Rahner has finished writing his draft. Two thousand copies of his text have been mimeographed. Father Daniélou brought me one. De revelatione Dei et hominis in Jesu Christo facta. Three chapters: I. De vocatione hominis divina. – II. De occulta Dei in generis humani historia praesentia. – III. De revelata praesentia Dei in praedicatione Ecclesiae.[44] – A Prooemium follows, which he was advised to put at the beginning. – The initial note: "Quia impossibile apparet, Concilium omnia schemata tractare et de eis votare posse, necesse videtur alia omittere, alia abbreviare et inter se conjungere. Qua propter praesides conferentiarum episcopalium Austriae, Belgii, Galliae, Germaniae, Hollandiae, sequens compendium materiae priorum duorum schematum, et quidem in tono magis positivo et pastorali, prout fundamentum disceptationis proponere audent."[45]

Cardinal Döpfner said to me last evening: "What Cardinal Ottaviani has come out with for us at the council, one would reprimand severely if it came from a first-year theology student."

In places, Rahner's schema proposes to assert what is condemned as an error by the official schemas (namely: Jesus Christ, unity of all revealed truths). How will an imbroglio like this be resolved?

---

[43] "Bond". [The nexus mysteriorum designates the unity and internal coherence of the truths of the faith. Chapter 4 of the constitution Dei Filius (1870) specifies: "When reason, enlightened by faith, seeks carefully, piously, and soberly, it achieves by the gift of God a certain very fruitful understanding of the mysteries, whether by analogy with the things it knows naturally or from the connections that link the mysteries with one another (mysteriorum ipsorum nexu inter se) and with the final end of man."]

[44] "On the Revelation of God and man made in Jesus Christ. I. On the divine vocation of man. II. On the hidden presence of God in the history of mankind. III. On the revealed presence of God in the preaching of the Church".

[45] "Since it appears impossible that the council will be able to deal with all the schemas and vote on them, it seems necessary to abandon some of them, to abridge others, and to combine them. This is why the presidents of the bishops' conferences of Austria, Belgium, France, Germany, the Netherlands dare to propose the following summary of the two previous schemas as a basis for discussion, one that would have a more positive and pastoral tone."

Bishop Maziers asked me this morning to come and see him soon, to help him prepare an intervention he is planning on eschatology.

Tuesday, November 13, 1962. – At Saint Peter's, met Archbishop Pierre Veuillot, who asked me to come to Paris in April, to speak to the congress of the Fédération des étudiants catholiques (Federation of Catholic Students). – Bishop Charles de la Brousse (Dijon) spoke to me about Father Martelet's talk yesterday; some bishops, he said, do not understand that Christ's role goes beyond satisfaction for sin; to speak about Christ with regard to our supernatural end, is that not to develop a theology of a particular school, in fact, the theology of the "school of Lyon"? The bishop of Dijon expressed to me his astonishment at such a misunderstanding (but it reveals the distrust sown in the minds of our bishops by the events of 1950). Bishop Vial, however, would come to see me in the gallery to tell me his great satisfaction with that lecture of Martelet's.

Also met Bishop Griffiths, auxiliary of New York, a member of the doctrinal commission (as he was of the preparatory commission), which, he told to me, is supposed to meet this afternoon for the first time. Bishop McGrath, a member of this same commission, has not yet been invited. So it seems there is some disorder in the secretariat of the council. – Canon Martimort told me that, for the Liturgy, everything is going well now; after having held things up for a long time, Cardinal Larraona last evening had the work begin, and even sped it up; he must have received an order from the pope. – Msgr. Lafortune handed me the draft, revised, of Cardinal Léger's intervention on the schema *De deposito fidei* and his criticisms of various chapters. Canon Martimort told me as well, without indicating to me his source, that Fr. Tromp did not want the periti to be admitted inside the Doctrinal Commission.

The president of the day: Cardinal Alfrink. "De mandato consilii praesidentiae: Patres velint orationes suas coercere",[1] in order to keep to the emendationes propositas[2] (advice that was to be largely ignored). Let people submit their texts to the secretariat, with a detailed summary; petitions without a summary will not be studied.

Archbishop Joseph Urtasun of Avignon: on no. 89. (1) Missa pontificalis simplicior reddatur; minuantur honores externi. – (2) Episcopi

---

November 13

[1] "By a mandate of the Board of Presidency: let the Fathers please shorten their interventions."

[2] "Proposed amendments".

habeant pro sua opportunitate jus celebrandi missam cantatam ritu minus solemni.[3]

Titular Archbishop Aloisius Alonso,[4] Spanish. On no. 104: the "new iconoclasts". One no longer wants to put the image of the Virgin in a place of honor; one no longer wants any image of St. Joseph. The new usage is even invading Spain and Spanish America. If this number is approved by vote, all the bishops risk being treated as iconoclasts by the Christian people. Images of the saints are important for spirituality. Let the bishops remedy this new evil.

Bishop Antonio Fustella[5] of Todi (Italy). Let the council Fathers themselves actively participate in the liturgy. At the upcoming Mass on December 8, let them all chant the Credo and the Sanctus.

Msgr. César D'Amato,[6] Abbot of St. Paul Outside the Walls. Nos. 91–94: distinguere oportet cantum popularem liturgicum et cantum religiosum liturgicum.[7] In point of fact, the first is left to a choir; it is unfortunate. Praise for Gregorian chant; it is impossible to adapt it to languages other than Latin, in the same way as one cannot change an architecture, etc. Let the bishops not show such little regard for cantors, etc.

Bishop Luis Hernandez Almarcha[8] of León (Spain). No. 99: do not allow ancient works of art to be destroyed. Revere and preserve ecclesiastical traditions. Guard our treasures. Found institutes of sacred art and practical schools.

The Abbot of the Olivetans.[9] De sacra supellectile.[10] In our regions, no scandal; on the contrary, populus christianus videt cum magna laetitia[11] everything that contributes to the splendor of the ceremonies. Jesus,

---

[3] "1. Let the pontifical Mass be made simpler; let the external gestures of honor be reduced. 2. Let the bishops have the right, for their personal convenience, to celebrate the missa cantata according to a less solemn rite."

[4] Luigi Alonso Muñoyerro (1888–1968), Spanish, ordained in 1912. Archbishop of the Spanish armed forces from 1950 until his death.

[5] Antonio Fustella (1913–1986), Italian, ordained in 1937. Bishop of Todi (Italy) from 1960 to 1967.

[6] Cesario D'Amato, O.S.B. (1904–2000), Italian, ordained in 1928. Abbot of Saint Paul Outside the Walls (Rome) from 1955 to 1964. Member of the Commission for the Liturgy.

[7] "We must distinguish popular liturgical singing and religious liturgical singing."

[8] Luis Almarcha Hernández (1887–1974), Spanish, ordained in 1910. Bishop of León from 1944 to 1970.

[9] Pietro Romualdo Zilianti, O.S.B. (1901–1970), Italian, ordained in 1924. Abbot of the Olivetans from 1946 until his death.

[10] "On sacred furnishings".

[11] "The Christian people regard with great joy".

who was poor in his private life, received ointment on his feet. Cf.
Saint Thomas, Prima Secundae, q. 102, art. 5, ad. 10 m. And the holy
Curé of Ars.[12] The Church has always loved beautiful churches, etc. We
must preserve our sacred patrimony, see to it that sacred objects do not
become secular possessions.

The Abbot of the Canons Regular of the Lateran,[13] on no. 89, p. 194:
the regular abbots are frustrated by this measure. Six reasons for not
depriving these abbots of their right. Propter splendorem cultus divini,[14]
do not suppress the usus pontificalium.[15] – He claimed to speak in the
name of several canons regular and even of the Benedictine and Cistercian abbots. (These demands were difficult to hear.)

The floor was then given to Cardinal Amleto Cicognani, secretary of
state. He announced that the Holy Father, complying with the council's
wishes, has deigned to decide that Saint Joseph's name would be inserted
into the canon of the Mass, at the "Communicantes", immediately after
the name of the Blessed Virgin. This will begin on December 8.

Archbishop Henrique Trindade[16] of Botucatu, Brazil: "... et fratres
observatores".[17] On the Prooemium of chap. 6, lines 7 to 18: "humana
vanitas";[18] yes, alas! To be sure, the liturgy is not the essential point
of the council, and the vestments are not the essential point of the liturgy; nevertheless, they have their importance. Remember that true
beauty lies in simplicity; it is compatible with austerity and poverty.
Remember also the demands of our times. This Prooemium is therefore
very timely. Some say that we must conduct ourselves "juxta liturgicam
traditionem";[19] but where and when do we find it? Which period will
be on this point "summe legitima"?[20] The temporal princes have disappeared, but, proh dolor! the Church preserves princely baubles. The
legitimate tradition is the antiquissima et genuina liturgia;[21] that is, the

---

[12] Jean-Marie Vianney (1786–1859), French, ordained in 1815. Parish priest of the village of Ars
in the Dombes region of France, canonized in 1925.

[13] Joseph Soetemans, Belgian, Abbot General of the Canons Regular of the Congregation of the
Holy Savior of the Lateran.

[14] "For the splendor of the divine worship".

[15] "The use of the pontifical insignia".

[16] Henrique Golland Trindade, O.F.M. (1897–1974), Brazilian, ordained in 1926. Bishop, then
archbishop, of Botucatu (Brazil) from 1948 to 1968.

[17] "And brother observers".

[18] "Human vanity".

[19] "According to the liturgical tradition".

[20] "The most legitimate".

[21] "The most ancient, original liturgy".

life of Christ, consummata in cruce.[22] For a serious reform, nunc est tempus opportunum. Humilis, sed firmissima petitio mea.[23] All of us are acquainted with the social situation, the aversio a luxu et ostentatione. Reducantur res ad antiquam formam. Parcite mihi, venerabiles Patres, ultimo fratri vestro.[24] (He is a Franciscan bishop.)

Bishop Casimir Kowalski[25] of Chelmno (Poland). No. 88, l. 32, is unclear. Let the bishops' conferences not have legislative power. Maneat salva structura Ecclesiae monarchica.[26] – On chap. 7: Just as the complete life is the vita mixta,[27] so also the complete liturgy is mixta, allowing for Gregorian chant and vernacular hymns. – Chap. 8: Let the council inaugurate a new period for chant and sacred art.

Bishop Paul Yoshigoro Taguchi[28] of Osaka (Japan). Vestments that are simpler and closer to local usage. Certain external factors create obstacles to evangelization. Have consideration for aetatis nostrae conditionibus.[29] Make sure that any adaptations, in art, etc., be authentic.

A Polish titular bishop.[30] No. 89 is very good. P. 159, l. 1 instead of "exercitationes", put "opera".[31] In the name of all the Polish bishops and their primate: there are too many particular details in the schemas; let the principles be revised and clarified by the men competent to do so. Lingua latina magni pretii est;[32] it must remain; it is linked to the birth of our nation; the first history of Poland is in Latin, etc. (The president brings him back to the subject at hand.) Against the growth of the powers of the episcopal conferences.

Bishop Pierre Canisius Van Lierde, sacristan of Saint Peter's. De musica sacra. No. 91: If we allow two liturgical chants, magnum

---

[22] "Consummated on the Cross".

[23] "The moment has now come. My request is humble, but very firm."

[24] "Aversion with regard to luxury and ostentation. Let matters be brought back to the ancient form. Venerable Fathers, spare me, the least of your brothers."

[25] Kazimierz J. Kowalski (1896–1972), Polish, ordained in 1922. Bishop of Chelmno from 1946 until his death.

[26] "Let the monarchical structure of the Church remain intact."

[27] "Mixed life". [This is a reference to Saint Augustine, who judged that this combination of a contemplative and an active life was the best form of life.]

[28] Paul Yoshigoro Taguchi (1902–1978), Japanese, ordained in 1928. Bishop, then archbishop, of Osaka from 1941 until his death. Created cardinal in 1973. Member of the Commission for the Discipline of the Sacraments.

[29] "The conditions of our time".

[30] Franciszek Jop.

[31] "Exercises, works".

[32] "Latin is of great value."

periculum erit pro Ecclesia.[33] Praise of Gregorian chant; impossible to chant it with words in the vernacular. We must make allowances for both kinds: Gregorian chant – popular singing. We must also prepare a new kind of liturgical chant, as close as possible to Gregorian. – No. 91, l. 28: "insuper", and not "proinde",[34] etc.

Bishop Wilhelm Kempf of Limburg (Germany). De musica sacra. Addendum at no. 94; cf. the Cologne congress,[35] etc.

Bishop André Sapelak,[36] Argentinian. Chap. 5, nos. 85–86, on the calendar; do not propose a new calendar; that would be very dangerous.

Bishop Paul Seitz of Kontum (Vietnam) of the Foreign Missions of Paris. In the name of the Episcopal Conference of Vietnam. De arte sacra: bene; attamen:[37] (1) Let it be well shown that sacred art is a part of the liturgy; let us reject any "indigna simulatio",[38] etc. – (2) Sacred music is a part of sacred art, so no special chapter; at no. 94, do not encourage polyphony to such a degree. – (3) P. 201 note, cite other sources as well: the councils of Nicaea and Constantinople. – Let Christ alone (on the cross) dominate the altar. Do not multiply images. – Our churches should be the house of all the people, especially the poor.

Bishop Hermann Volk of Mainz. On popular singing. No. 94: support for Cardinal Fring's position. But that is not sufficient. Necessity of the vernacular language.

Archbishop Maurice Baudoux of Saint Boniface (Canada), recommended simplicity.

Bishop Paul Cheng[39] (Formosa), O.S.B.: Let the council authorize bishops to transfer a feast to the nearest Sunday, etc. – No. 99: have great respect for the art of all peoples.

Archbishop Michel Miranda y Gómez of Mexico City. De musica sacra. Finis pastoralis recte adhibendus, secus …[40] Now, cf. Piux X, followed by Pius XI and Pius XII. This schema stops all progress so far

---

[33] "There will be a great danger for the Church."

[34] "Moreover" and not "consequently".

[35] This refers to the International Congress of Sacred Music held in Cologne in 1961.

[36] Andrés Sapelak, S.D.B., born in 1919, Polish, ordained in 1949. Auxiliary bishop of Argentina for the faithful of the Eastern Rites from 1961 to 1968, then appointed archiepiscopal exarch for the Ukrainians in Argentina. Member of the conciliar Commission for Eastern Churches.

[37] "On sacred art: good; and yet".

[38] "Unworthy simulation, pretense".

[39] Joseph Cheng Tien-Siang, O.P., Chinese, ordained in 1952. Bishop of Kaohsiung (Taiwan) from 1961 until his death.

[40] "The pastoral aim must be applied with discernment, according to …"

realized; it makes us take a step backward. And what will our faithful say if they learn that sacred music has been relegated by the council to the end of the schema, in a chapter that is so meager and of a spirit so reactionary?

Bishop José Lopez Ortiz, O.S.B.,[41] of Tui-Vigo. (He did not seem to me to put forward anything very clear.)

Bishop Jean Pohlschneider[42] of Aix-la-Chapelle. On no. 83. (1) Let us make mention of the necessary spirit of self-abnegation on the priest's part, in imitation of Jesus Christ. Let us preach, as a replacement for the fasting that cannot be restored, certain other privations during Lent (e.g., movies, etc.). Without the example of the priest, it is useless to exhort the faithful. "Si quis vult post me venire ..."[43] "Spiritus paenitentiae et abnegationis, in pastoribus primum"[44] ...

The president, Card. Alfrink, proposed that "cum hoc optimo oratore, disceptatio schematis liturgiae concludatur".[45] They voted. Everyone stood up. That was the end.

As I left Saint Peter's, Bishop Pourchet[46] of Saint-Flour said to me that he wants to see me so that I can help him draft an intervention. On the square, Archbishop Villot gave me information about the Board of Presidency meeting that took place last evening. They seemed at first to have decided to admit the principle of having a vote, after the interventions on the schema De fontibus as a whole, to see whether the council would move on to the examination of chapters or if it would reject the schema. Cardinal Ruffini proved to be very unhappy with this procedure. It seems that this morning everything is in question.

In the bus, with a group of bishops. We are going to the Casa Pallotti, via dei Perinarii, near the Tiber, the boarding house where Archbishop Zoa is staying. At 1 P.M., a meeting with Archbishops Zoa and Wolff and Bishop Blomjous, another bishop from South Africa and Frs. Greco and Martelet. Examination of the motions that the Africans want to present to the council: 1st/ that the vote on the schema on the Liturgy take place before the end of the session; 2nd/ that the following schemas

[41] José López Ortiz, O.S.A. (1898–1992), Spanish, ordained in 1922. Bishop of Tui-Vigo (Spain) from 1944 to 1969.

[42] Johannes Pohlschneider (1899–1981), German, ordained in 1924, bishop of Aix-la-Chapelle from 1954 to 1974.

[43] "If any man would come after me" [Mt 16:24].

[44] "A spirit of penitence and self-abnegation, first of all among the pastors ..."

[45] "We conclude the discussion of the schema on the liturgy with this excellent speaker."

[46] Maurice Pourchet (1906–2004), French, ordained in 1931. Bishop of Saint-Flour from 1960 to 1982.

be printed and distributed as much as possible before December 8: it is a question of good sense and trust. – Then we planned some interventions, for the next few days, on the schema *De fontibus*; provisional designation of some names [to make these interventions]. – Next we all had lunch together.

I went with Fr. Martelet to the French Seminary, via Sta Chiara, to see the Sisters who are making copies of his lecture. Conversation with Card. Lefebvre, archbishop of Bourges; we spoke about G. Soulages,[47] a man of his diocese, a teacher at the high school in Châteauroux and a devotee of Teilhard, who has just written me a long letter. I went next to the Borgo S. Spirito to let Archbishop Sartre know that he has been named by the African bishops as a possible speaker, and I brought him to the via Traspontina. There, while the two great halls were occupied by two speakers, one speaking to the Anglophones and the other to the Francophones, we held a little meeting: Archbishop Sartre, Archbishop Michel Bernard[48] (of Brazzaville), Fr. Greco, Fr. Martelet, Fr. van Cauwelaert[49] (cousin of the bishop of Inongo), and myself. The remarks to be presented on the schema *De fontibus* were divided into three sections, in view of three interventions: (1) The pastoral point of view and remarks on the schema as a whole; (2) The exegetical problem; (3) The doctrinal problem. We next went successively to the Anglophones and to the Francophones, to fill them in, summarize for them the theme of the planned interventions, receive their suggestions, and finally ask for their agreement – which was given.

Before returning home, conversation with the secretary of the bishop of Mans, who is at the same time the theologian of Archbishop Gantin of Cotonou (Dahomey). We talked about Rahner's schema, which was distributed to various people in the course of the day. Archbishop Duval joined us. He had just seen this schema and made a rather severe assessment of it. On one point or another, I noticed that he had read too quickly, and we discussed the subject for a while. One objection

---

[47] Gérard Soulages (1912–2005), French, professor of philosophy at Châteauroux. In 1972 he formed the group "Fidélité et ouverture" (Fidelity and openness), which refers in particular to the work of H. de Lubac and Charles Journet.

[48] Michel Bernard, C.S.Sp. (1911–1993), French, ordained in 1938. Archbishop of Brazzaville from 1955 to 1964, he became archbishop of Nouakchott (Mauritania) in 1965 and remained so until 1973.

[49] Frans van Cauwelaert, O.S.B. (1906–1986), Belgian, ordained in 1931. At the time he was the spiritual assistant of the Byelorussian students at the Catholic university of Louvain. He was involved in the ecumenical movement with the Eastern Churches. Bishop Jan van Cauwelaert had asked his cousin to help him during the first session to prepare his interventions on the liturgy.

remained for him: it is the same one that a number of bishops make, when presented with an idea set out from a personal viewpoint: "These are theses of one school." The objection is no doubt a little better founded in this case than in the case of Martelet's conference.

Card. Ottaviani had returned to the council this morning.

Fr. Daniélou has prepared some texts to replace or patch up the doctrinal schemas. Fr. Congar, they tell me, found this patch-up insufficient.

This evening, Fr. Grillmeier (Frankfurt) was pessimistic. He was already wondering if it would not be good to encourage some journalist to write articles on this subject: Is the council going to fail? – Bishop Volk is supposedly more optimistic. This afternoon, a new meeting was held around him. Msgr. Schmaus (Theology Faculty at Munich) and Msgr. Schauf, the canon law expert and friend of Tromp, were present, which bothered Grillmeier. Father Smulders (Maastricht, Holland), who was not informed about what Schmaus and Schauf represent, kept asking questions that Grillmeier and others had to dodge.

For numerous bishops, this council is the occasion of a sort of "third year"[50] in theology. They are taking part in it with good grace, some even with a kind of naïve eagerness. None of them, however, is willing to accept the direction of an Instructor.

Wednesday, November 14, 1962. – This morning, the 19th General Congregation, a historic session.

I met Archbishop Duval of Algiers, to whom I apologized for the brusqueness with which I had argued with him for a moment yesterday. Bishop Barthe showed me the summary of an intervention he is proposing to make on the schema *De fontibus*; I found it a little weak, and I told him so; he answered that it would be clearer in the oral intervention. Canon René Laurentin gave me a copy of the criticisms he had written and had printed on the *De fontibus*; his work contains a brief history of the schema's composition. Msgr. Lafortune told me about the collaboration he had obtained to help Cardinal Léger.

After the votive Mass of Saint Joseph, chanting of the Credo during the enthronement of the Gospel. – Cardinal Tisserant was presiding.

"Velint omnes audire."[1] A double vote was proposed to the assembly: (1) Upon examination, the council approves the criteria directiva

---

[50] Among the Jesuits, this refers to the third year of novitiate, which ends the cycle of formation.
November 14
[1] "Let all please listen."

schematis de sacra Liturgia,[2] etc. – (2) Let the emendationes propositae[3] be examined immediately by the commission, to be submitted for the approval of the Fathers. The vote is to be finished at 11 A.M. In the meantime, let everyone remain seated.

The floor was given to Cardinal Ottaviani. He first asked for an explanation on the double vote that had just been announced. Then he spoke about the schema *De fontibus*. Four points: 1. Circumferuntur quaedam schemata quae essent substituenda schemati officiali. Hoc non videtur congruere cum dispositione canonis X. juris canonici.[4] Nor does this show respect for the Supreme Pontiff. Anyone can propose corrections; but let us discuss the true schema. – 2. People would like a pastoral tone. Sed dico: primum munus, munus fundamentale concilii oecumenici est doctrinale: "Docete omnes gentes".[5] Afterward, the style will be polished, to give it a pastoral expression. But let this not be like a homily, non ad modum praedicationis.[6] There is a stylus conciliaris,[7] to which we must adhere. – 3. Facta est quaedam observatio . . .[8] But, let us not listen to a new school. – 4. Spero fore ut debitam considerationem habeatis[9] for the two years of preparation, the wisdom of the commission's members, who have come ex universo orbe,[10] bishops with pastoral concerns and theologians diversarum scholarum,[11] as well as for the work of the Central Commission, and then of the subcommission for amendments.

Because of his weak eyesight, Card. Ottaviani declared that he would have his report read by someone else, Msgr. Garofalo (rector of the College of the Propaganda, a biblical scholar). Tueri ac promovere doctrinam catholicam est primum munus concilii oecumenici. Debet esse integra, non imminuta non distorta, doctrina catholica.[12] It is not a

---

[2] "The guiding criteria of the schema on the sacred liturgy".

[3] "Proposed amendments".

[4] "Some schemas have been circulated for the purpose of being substituted for the official schema. This does not seem to be in accordance with the provisions of canon X of canon law." [The canon invoked is canon 222.]

[5] "But I say: the first task, the fundamental task of the ecumenical council is doctrinal; 'Make disciples of all nations'" [Mt 28:19].

[6] "In the style of preaching".

[7] "Conciliar style".

[8] "A certain observation has been made . . ."

[9] "I hope that you will have due consideration."

[10] "From the whole world".

[11] "From various schools".

[12] "To protect and promote the Catholic doctrine is the first task of the ecumenical council. Catholic doctrine must be whole and complete, not weakened, not deformed."

matter of making homilies. We must not give up refuting errors, whatever form they take. The doctrinal schemas have been written according to the wishes of the bishops. There is consonantia[13] between them, the bishops' wishes and the desires of the pope. Some words on the history of the commission (a very official history). Rapid presentation of the five chapters: the first chapter was written in such a manner as to respond better to the current mode of thinking (!). The second was drawn from the teachings of the last popes. The third was conceived "ut praecaveantur excessus".[14] In the fourth, ea tantum ponuntur, quae nostro tempore in discrimen vacantur. Urget.[15] – The fifth chapter is an exhortation to go back ad fontes, attenta tamen Ecclesiae doctrina, etc. The studium divini verbi[16] cannot be purely scientific.

Schema est dogmaticum, non disciplinare. Debet per saecula vigere. Sunt irreformabilia decreta. Unde genus loquendi, quod vigere semper possit.[17] There is also an ecumenical interest, so that our separated brothers cognoscant quam clarissime doctrinam catholicam.[18] It contains nothing that could be disputed in the schools (!). Veritatem solemniter ab erroribus defendere, pertinet ad concilium.[19] No one can maintain that this is contrary to the pope's discourse. There is, finally, a pastoral interest: custodia et defensio doctrinae maxime ad munus pastorale pertinet ... Vos estis testes et judices fidei.[20]

Cardinal Achille Liénart (Lille). – Praesens doctrinale decretum mihi non placet. In toto suo tenore, prorsus inadaequatum materiae quam debet tractare.[21] – (1) "Two sources":[22] divus Fons omittitur, profundior,

---

[13] "Agreement".

[14] "To guard against excesses".

[15] "Only those things are presented that are in jeopardy in our times. This is urgent."

[16] "To the sources, taking account, however, of the doctrine of the Church. The study of the word of God".

[17] "The schema is dogmatic, not disciplinary. It must remain valid throughout the centuries. The decrees are irreformable. Hence the language employed, which can always remain valid."

[18] "Might know the Catholic doctrine as clearly as possible".

[19] "It is the responsibility of the council solemnly to defend truth from errors."

[20] "The preservation and defense of doctrine is at the heart of pastoral duty ... You are the witnesses and the judges of the faith."

[21] "I do not like the present doctrinal decree. In all of its content, it is totally inadequate for the matter with which it must deal."

[22] This refers to the idea of two sources of revelation. The schema identified two distinct sources: Scripture and tradition, which corresponded to a theme inherited from the anti-Protestant arguments against the idea of sola scriptura. This conception was criticized by some Fathers who insisted on the one and only source: the Word of God.

unicus, sc. Verbum Dei. Cf. the Council of Trent (he read the text); essentialis Fons.[23] – (2) Modus est nimis prorsus scolasticus.[24] Such a style, in the face of God's marvelous gift to men! Dignum et justum fuisset,[25] to celebrate the Verbum Dei in front of our separated brothers, who venerate and love it as much as we do. Vivus sermo Dei et efficax,[26] etc. Cf. Vatican I, c. 3. – (3) There is here a series of condemnations rather than an ostensio veritatis.[27] – (4) Absence of a chapter on revelation. Everything is contained in divino Verbo;[28] the Holy Spirit will explain it: that is the principle of tradition. – Non in dissertationibus scholasticis fundatur fides nostra. Enixe peto ut schema recognoscatur penitus.[29]

Card. Jos. Frings. Schema non placet. (1) The two doctrinal schemas are bad. The first pastoral duty is doctrine, but how? ita ut alliciantur homines,[30] or even though they be driven away? At Vatican I, they rejected a schema that was too professorial, and it was replaced. Non auditur in hoc schemate vox Matris et Magistrae, sed vox nec aedificans nec vivificans;[31] and cf. John XXIII. – (2) In this schema there are two fundamental doctrines: a. De duobus fontibus. Hic modus loquendi est recens; non invenitur in Patribus, nec apud scolasticos (non est in sancto Thoma), nec in conciliis;[32] it is the fruit of the historicism of the 19th century. In ordine cognitionis, possunt dici duo fontes, sed in ordine essendi, unus est fons. De hoc unico fonte, valde dolendum est quod nihil sit in schemate.[33] And from the very first lines, by these "two sources", our separated brethren will be offended, a new gap will be created.

---

[23] "The divine source has been omitted, the deeper, unique source, that is, the Word of God. The essential source."

[24] "The style is much too scholastic."

[25] "It would have been fitting and just".

[26] "The word of God is living and active."

[27] "Presentation of the truth".

[28] "In the Divine Word".

[29] "Our faith is not founded on scholastic dissertations. I ask with all my strength that the schema be entirely revised."

[30] "In such a way as to attract men".

[31] "One does not hear in this schema the voice of a Mother and Teacher, but a voice that is neither edifying nor vivifying." [The reference here is to the encyclical of John XXIII, *Mater et magistra*, of May 1961.]

[32] "a. On the two sources. This manner of speaking is recent; it is not found in the Fathers or in the scholastics (it is not in Saint Thomas) or in the councils."

[33] "In the order of knowledge, one can speak of two sources, but in the order of being, the source is unique. Concerning this unique source, it is greatly to be regretted that there is nothing in the schema."

– b. De inerrantia Scripturae. Doctrina nimis rigida, appropinquans ad doctrinam inspirationis verbalis.[34] The schema is against scientific work, etc. On this subject there are two opinions in the process of being debated: non est mos conciliorum dirimere discussiones;[35] one school of thought must not anathematize the other. Necesse erit sine dubio damnare opiniones falsas[36] – but no more. – 3) Nec placet nimia amplitudo schematis.[37] With all the others, it imposes an impossible task on the council. It is necessary to omit, abridge, merge sections. Let the first two schemas be combined into one, reduced to a quarter. That is what was done in the text Cardinal Ottaviani[38] mentioned. In order that the council might be able to accomplish its work within a reasonable time frame.

Cardinal Ruffini. – Non est cur dicam hoc schema esse summi momenti, supremi momenti; est quasi centrum nostri concilii ... Mihi universum placet.[39] It would be imprudent to reject a schema that was so carefully examined by eminent men from every nation. The schemas have been approved by the Sovereign Pontiff; the book that contains them bears the signature of Card. Cicognani. And what would happen if the substituted schema was also rejected? We would have to create a third one, etc. So let us discuss the official schema. Perficiatur et compleatur.[40]

Card. Siri (Genoa). (1) Quamvis debeat emendationibus quibusdam perfici; utile, imo necessarium schema apparet. Sufficit ad discussionem.[41] – (2) There was the modernist heresy; since its condemnation, the consequences continue ... – (3) A number of the faithful and pastors are grieved by seeing that the dignitas, valor, certitudo divinarum Scripturarum[42] are not safeguarded. – (4) Sunt quaedam, circa Traditionem et Scripturam,[43] the declaration of which is debated in the schools of

---

[34] "b. On the inerrancy of Scripture. The doctrine is too rigid, approaching the doctrine of literal inspiration."

[35] "It is not the tradition of the councils to resolve disputed questions."

[36] "It will no doubt be necessary to condemn false opinions."

[37] "Nor do I approve of the excessive length of the schema."

[38] An allusion to the Rahner-Ratzinger schema.

[39] "There is no need for me to say that this schema is of the greatest importance, of supreme importance; it is, in a manner of speaking, the center of our council ... I entirely approve it."

[40] "Let it be improved and completed."

[41] "Although it must be improved by some amendments, the schema is useful and even necessary. It suffices as a basis for discussion."

[42] "The dignity, the value, the certitude of the divine Scriptures".

[43] "There are certain points, concerning tradition and Scripture".

Catholic thought. On this point, I heard yesterday some Italian bishops: they noted two things: a. there is not an aequa proportio between Traditio et Scriptura,[44] the part relating to the first is too brief; b. sometimes, one cannot see clearly how theological criteria for the interpretation of Scripture prevail over scientific criteria.

Card. Quiroga y Palacios (Santiago de Compostela, Spain). The Holy Father sent this schema to us acceptandum.[45] It continues the work of Trent and Vatican I. It is brief and excellent. There is a means for reconciling opposed opinions: some clarifications are needed on certain points; avoid condemning Catholic schools of thought, but ... – Certain expressions must be revised in order that our separated brethren might better understand. Revise also, arctius,[46] the no. on the historicity of the Gospels.

Card. Léger. – Post maturam considerationem – tota praesens constitutio recognoscatur. Est mens ejus Ecclesiam nullo modo adjuvans. – (1) Realiter imprudens est decidere (sic) cum tanta certitudine de quaestionibus disputatis; for example, on the relations inter Scripturam et Traditionem. – (2) Valde nocet Ecclesiae tractare cum diffidentia de Scriptura et de investigationibus scientificis exegetarum;[47] a danger of injustice toward our exegetes. – (3) Hoc est contrarium spiritui renovationis Joannis XXIII.[48] One does not base a constitution on the fear of error, etc. – (4) It is one school alone that wishes to substitute itself for the others. – Recognoscatur ergo schema a theologis et exegetis diversarum scholarum. Ad exponendas omnes divitias Scripturarum, et in mente habendo desiderium fratrum separatorum.[49]

Card. König (Vienna). This schema contains various doctrines that should not be promoted by a council: a. on Scripture and tradition; b. on inerrancy: plus dicit quam potest concilium;[50] cf. literary genres,

---

[44] "An equitable proportion between tradition and Scripture".

[45] "To be accepted".

[46] "More closely".

[47] "After mature reflection – let all of the present constitution be revised. Its spirit in no way helps the Church. (1) It is truly imprudent to decide disputed questions with such certitude; for example, on the relationship between Scripture and tradition. (2) It harms the Church a great deal to treat Scripture and the scientific investigations of the exegetes with distrust."

[48] "This is contrary to the spirit of renewal of John XXIII."

[49] "Therefore let the schema be revised by theologians and exegetes from different schools. In order to set forth all the riches of the Scriptures, having in mind the desire of our separated brethren."

[50] "It says more than a council can say."

etc., and compare with the encyclical *Divino afflante*; c. What theological notes? There are too many. – Nondum placet.[51]

Card. Alfrink. Legens et studens hoc schema (sic), non potui non cogitare ea quae Summus Pontifex in allocutione sua dixit, 11 Oct.[52] – This schema repeats textbook pages. It has not profited from recent theological studies, which would be of a very great importance from the point of view of unity, which is so dear to the Holy Father's heart. The author has not taken account of the pontifical directives. Hoc dico, cognoscens mentem papae.[53] Let us have a schema brevius, emendatum, aut, si possibile est, novum schema.[54] Emin. Ruffini (qui fuit meus magister[55] in a course in Assyriology) habeat me excusatum:[56] in discussing as we are now, we are doing what the pope wanted us to do.

Card. J. Suenens (Brussels). On the two schemas. Primum schema non placet.[57] (S. agreed with the opinions of the cardinals who had just spoken against the schema.) Schemata quae sequuntur adhuc minus placent.[58] Although not as bad, they would be too long. All the Fathers – or in any case many of them – are troubled by the slowness of the modus progrediendi aut potius non progrediendi.[59] Another way must be found. Here is one proposed way: a. Immediately after the discussion of a schema in genere, votandum erit de acceptabilitate schematis ut sic;[60] reason: many Fathers speak, but during this time the council is silent; etc. b. Emendationes circa particularia remittantur scripto;[61] let the commission study them immediately, and patefaciat suam opinionem.[62] – c. Let the various commissions work on abridging their schemas before even proposing them to the Fathers. d. Let the postconciliar commissions be constituted immediately after the voting on each schema, in order to deal with the practical details: certain decrees of Vatican I are still today waiting to be implemented!

---

[51] "I do not yet approve it."

[52] "In reading and studying this schema, I cannot help but think about what the Supreme Pontiff said in his speech of October 11."

[53] "I say this knowing the mind of the pope."

[54] "Shorter schema, amended, or, if possible, a new schema".

[55] "Who was my teacher".

[56] "Let His Eminence Cardinal Ruffini excuse me."

[57] "I do not approve the first schema."

[58] "And I approve even less the schemas that follow."

[59] "Of the manner of progressing or, rather, not progressing".

[60] "In general, we will have to vote on accepting the schema as it is."

[61] "Let the amendments concerning particular points be submitted in writing."

[62] "Make known its opinion".

– e. The publication of names in the papers perhaps incites some orators to speak; therefore let the names of the speakers not be published each day; or, instead, let the list of all those who intervened either orally or in writing be published. – f. Finally, leave out empty artificial formulas: "Eminentissimi, etc.": we will save time, and this will be more evangelical. (Applause.)

Card. Joseph E. Ritter, archbishop of Saint Louis (USA). Schema rejiciendum est; aliud proponatur. – 1. Evidenti utilitate caret;[63] this goes especially for the repetition of things already known. – 2. Abundat ambiguitas;[64] everything is arranged so that one can see the preferences of the writers, but without anything clear or specific. – 3. Totum schema spiritu negativo et pessimismo laborat;[65] it casts doubt and suspicion on the work of our exegetes, who on the contrary have the right to expect sustentationem[66] from the council. On those matters where solutions are not ready, let the council keep silent. Such texts as these are likely to destroy unity in the Church and encourage suspicions everywhere. I fear that they might foster distrust with regard to Scripture, potius quam amorem et reverentiam.[67]

Card. A. Bea. – I know how many eminent men worked on this schema for a long time; eo magis doleo, dicere debere: non placet. 1. Non respondet scopo a Summo Pontifice Concilio proposito: ne fusius repetantur, etc.[68] (There followed various quotations from the pope.) Omnino caret indole pastorali. (Doctrina est fundamentum, sed non est res.) Non habet prae oculis homines modernos, sed potius scholas theologicas.[69] Certain paragraphs take aim at unum solum theologum, qui fortasse una vice aliquid erroneum dixit.[70] The style is too scholastic; even in Latin, it is possible to speak clearly without using

---

[63] "The schema should be rejected; let another one be proposed. 1. It lacks any evident usefulness."

[64] "Ambiguity abounds."

[65] "The whole schema suffers from a negative spirit, from pessimism."

[66] "Support".

[67] "Rather than love and respect".

[68] "It is all the more painful for me to have to say that I do not approve it. 1. It does not correspond to the aim proposed for the council by the Supreme Pontiff: that things not be repeated at length." [These last words are taken from a passage of *Gaudet Mater Ecclesia* in which John XXIII announced that the principal task of the council is not the discussion of particular points of fundamental doctrine by the repetition of the teaching of the Fathers and theologians.]

[69] "It completely lacks any pastoral character. (Doctrine is the foundation, but it is not in itself pastoral.) It has before its eyes, not modern men, but, rather, theological schools."

[70] "A single theologian, who perhaps once said something erroneous".

scholastic terminology. – 2. Nihil dicitur de facto revelationis.[71] Almost nothing is said about the importance of Scripture. What is lacking here is not a sermon, it is a doctrinal presentation. – 3. The schemas claim to have decided on a number of points that are debated among Catholics: on the evangelists, on the Vulgate, etc., praesertim de natura inspirationis.[72] Personal inspiration is opposed to collective inspiration: now, perhaps one or two authors have said what is here rejected, but that is not the question. – 4. Quaestio oecumenica nullatenus consideratur ... – 5. Multum loquitur schema de exegetis;[73] but it does not have a word of respect for their labor. It casts suspicion on them; it leads to fear of error everywhere, without going deeply into any problem. – Ergo schema omnino profunde recognoscatur, ut sit brevius, magis clarum, minus ambiguum, magis pastorale et oecumenicum.[74]

Maximos IV Saigh, Melchite patriarch. – Venerable Fathers. I will give you some overall advice, guided by pastoral and ecumenical considerations. In this schema, everything is envisaged from an angle that is limited, negative, contentious. Does it respond to the wishes of the bishops and of the Catholic universities? It was drawn up, rather, to resolve the questions debated among the theological schools. The council must stay out of these disputes. It is useless to bring forth decrees on the sources of revelation: no danger truly threatens the Church today on that subject. The declarations that are proposed to us could stop the harmonious development of dogma. On Scripture and tradition, on the interpretation of the biblical texts, let us institute research and peaceful discussion among specialists. We do not yet have the necessary elements to decide certain questions, the discussion of which has not sufficiently matured. Some parts of the schema give the traditional teaching, but in a negative, polemical form that condemns. Today we need to have an exposition of salvation history that is dispassionate, positive, rich. Finally, the schema makes no effort to prepare paths toward unity but, rather, blocks them. It hardens even more the outdated positions of the Counter-Reformation and of anti-modernism. Let the council reject this schema. The world expects that from us. Dixi.

---

[71] "Nothing is said about the fact of revelation."

[72] "Especially on the nature of inspiration".

[73] "4. The ecumenical question is in no way taken into consideration ... 5. The schema talks a great deal about exegetes."

[74] "Therefore the schema should be very profoundly revised, in order to make it briefer, clearer, less ambiguous, more pastoral and ecumenical."

Archbishop Felici then announced that the schema *De Ecclesia*[75] would be distributed in a few days. Next the president reported the result of the vote on the Liturgy:[76] 2,215 votes cast; majority: 1,476. Placet: 2,162. Non placet: 46. Invalid ballots: 7.

An archbishop from Indonesia.[77] Cum modestia, sed simul cum claritate, in the name of all the bishops of Indonesia, dico schema ita displicere, ut nisi funditus emendetur, rejiciendum sit. Plura sunt superflua.[78] There are some polemical condemnations, taking aim at several Catholic authors bonae famae;[79] this is contrary to the usage of Trent and Vatican I. Nova obstacula movet in colloquio cum fratribus separatis,[80] etc. (I have a copy of the mimeographed text of this intervention; the wording of it is due, I believe, to Fr. Smulders.)

A 2nd bishop from Indonesia[81] spoke in the same sense. Is this schema likely to achieve the aims of the council juxta mentem S. Pontificis?[82] He enumerated these aims and showed how the schema ran counter to them. The same must be said of the other doctrinal schemas.

Archbishop Casimir Morcillo Gonzalez of Saragossa. There is much to criticize in the schema; however, also much to preserve. He responded to the principal criticisms, with some concessions; the speaker proposed a sort of compromise.

Going out of Saint Peter's, I saw Archbishop Staffa (secretary of the congregation for seminaries) and Msgr. Spadafora (professor of Sacred Scripture at the Lateran, author of the pamphlet against the Biblical Institute) exchange gestures of distress. – An expression of Bishop Rupp (of Monaco), an adversary of the liturgical constitution, was reported to

---

[75] "On the Church".

[76] This refers to the vote on the proposals communicated at the beginning of the general congregation.

[77] Gabriel Manek, S.V.D. (1913–1989), Indonesian, ordained in 1941. Archbishop of Endeh (Indonesia) from 1961 to 1968. Member of the Secretariat for Unity beginning in 1964.

[78] "With modesty, but at the same time with clarity, in the name of all the bishops of Indonesia, I say that the schema is so unsatisfactory that it must be rejected or at least be radically amended. Several points are unnecessary."

[79] "Of good repute".

[80] "It will create new obstacles to the dialogue with the separated brothers."

[81] Albert Soegijapranata, S.J. (1895–1963), Indonesian, ordained in 1931. Archbishop of Semarang (Indonesia) from 1961 until his death. Member of the Commission for the Missions.

[82] "In accordance with the mind of the Supreme Pontiff?"

me, concerning the bishops who had just approved it: "All those gull-
ible fools ...". – Cardinal Ottaviani, unhappy (as he said in the session)
about the draft of the schema written by Rahner, is supposed to have
asked the pope to have Rahner driven from Rome, as a "perturbator";[83]
unverifiable rumor.

At 4 P.M., meeting at Saint Chrysogonus, home of the Trinitarians, for
the bishops of Madagascar. Archbishop Wolff informed them of the
three African interventions planned and prepared on the schema *De
fontibus*. Father Greco, secretary, spoke about the two African motions
presented today to the Board of Presidency (cf. Tuesday, November 13).
I continued the examination of the schema *De deposito fidei*; I finished
with a summary in ten points on the theme: "Diminutae sunt veritates
a filiis hominum",[84] and with an examination of the Prooemium of the
1st constitution.

At 6 P.M., under a torrential rain, in the midst of cars that were splash-
ing me, I strode along the via Giulia, transformed into a stream, to get
to the Circolo Romano, where I had been invited to a reception in
honor of the observers. A welcome from the president (who at present
is the Belgian ambassador[85] to the Holy See) and from M. Veronese.[86]
A speech by the president, then by an Armenian Orthodox.[87] Chatted
with various people, in particular the good Bishop Cassien, rector of the
Saint-Serge Institute in Paris, etc. Father Rahner was there. Fr. Delos,
O.P. (ecclesiastical consultor to our embassy to the Holy See), confided to me his concern: How are we going to get out of the dogmatic
impasse? Will we be able to agree on another text, if only as a simple
starting point? What will the commission do? etc. – Returned to the
Borgo in the company of Fr. Rondet.

Thursday, November 15, 1962. – *Le Monde* of November 11–12 has
a sensationalist article on two famous cardinals absent from the council:

---

[83] "Troublemaker".

[84] "The faithful have vanished from among the sons of men" [Ps 11:2].

[85] Prosper Poswick (1906–1992), ambassador from 1957 to 1968. His journal was published: *Un
journal du Concile: Vatican II vu par un diplomate belge* (Paris: F. X. de Guibert, 2005).

[86] He must be referring to Vittorino Veronese (1910–1986), Italian. A lawyer, former president
of Italian Catholic Action, director of UNESCO from 1958 to 1961, he was a lay auditor at the
council beginning with the second session, then a consultor to the Secretariat for Nonbelievers.

[87] This was the archimandrite Karekin Sarkissian (1932–1999), Armenian. Ordained a deacon of
the Armenian Apostolic Church in 1949, he then became a monk, taking the name Karekin, in
1952.

Cardinal Cushing[1] (Boston), who has left for his diocese and supposedly declared on leaving Rome that he was tired of hearing people go on forever about the merits of the Latin language – and Cardinal Ottaviani, who is giving the council the cold shoulder after the president was applauded for interrupting his speech.

Il Tempo of the 14th: "... Mentrè è poco probabile che la discussione venga rimandata, la critica che Padri francesi, tedeschi ed olandesi muovono alla Commissione Teologica preparatoria è di non aver sufficientemente interpellato i consultori della Commissione stessa e principalmente il Padre Gesuita de Luback e il Padre Domenicano Congar. A detta dei Padri francesi i due consultori sarebbero stati esclusi dalle reunioni della Commissione preparatoria e lo schema da esaminare stamani sarebbe stato concordato dei membri della Commissione senza riferimento ai consultori, etc."[2]

I am told that in the intervention he made yesterday at the council Cardinal Bea stated that he had written to the Preparatory Theological Commission several times on the question of Sacred Scripture and had received no response, or only dilatory responses.[3] (This is possible; I did not hear everything yesterday.)

This morning, at 9, young Father Biot, O.P.[4] (son of Dr. René Biot, of Lyon), came to ask me to speak to a group of young Italian intellectuals about Father Teilhard de Chardin. He spoke to them recently on ecumenism. – Then, visit from Father Motte,[5] a missionary in Vietnam, in Rome for a few days; he talked to me about the Vietnamese bishops.

At 10 A.M., Bishop Maurice Pourchet (Saint-Flour) arrived. He read me the draft of his intervention on the schema *De fontibus*. He looks at the matter from the point of view of exegesis. His presentation is good; it has been approved by Bishop Volk (Mainz). I advised him to be clearer

---

November 15

[1] Richard J. Cushing (1895–1970), American, ordained in 1921. Archbishop of Boston from 1944 to 1970, created cardinal in 1958.

[2] "While there is little chance that the discussion might be postponed, the criticism that the French, German, and Dutch Fathers are voicing with regard to the Preparatory Theological Commission is that the commission did not sufficiently call upon the consultors of the commission itself, and especially the Jesuit priest de Luback [sic] and the Dominican priest Congar. According to the French Fathers, the two consultors were excluded from the Preparatory Commission meetings and the schema that is supposed to be studied this morning was written solely by the members of the commission, without having been referred to the consultors."

[3] Cardinal Bea, who spoke on November 14, said nothing on this subject. See *AS*, I, 3, 48–52.

[4] François Biot (Marie-Irénée in religion), O.P. (1923–1995), French, ordained in 1949. Consultor to the Saint Dominic Center, he took part in the council as the expert of Bishop Jacq.

[5] Jean Motte, S.J. (1902–1970), French, a missionary in China, then in Vietnam.

in his conclusion. He informed me about the meeting of the French bishops that took place yesterday afternoon, at Saint-Louis des Français. They had a secret vote on the subject of *De fontibus*: 85 requested its rejection; about 35 requested a profound revision; 3 requested that it be discussed. To the surprise of Bishop Pourchet, two bishops, among the most representative, then intervened to ask that we not judge with passion and that we adopt a more moderate attitude.

Frs. Daniélou, Congar, and Labourdette have worked together to propose some new paragraphs.

Met Father Salaverri, S.J., from Comillas, who is staying at the Curia. Up until now I had not spoken much with him. He told me that a good number of bishops are a priori against whatever Ottaviani proposes and that there is something excessive in that. I explained to him why, in my opinion, a good number of bishops, who have no a priori at all, have become exasperated by the way the cardinal and the Holy Office have been proceeding for some time now and again in the first few days of the council. Hence their distrust and the ill humor of some of them.

There is talk that Archbishop Garrone will remain in Rome between the two sessions to work in the Doctrinal Commission. An auxiliary would be named for Toulouse. People are also saying that he will soon be made a cardinal.

At noon, Oreste Kéramé came to get me. We went to a boarding house behind the Porta San Pancrazio where some Melchite bishops are lodging, in response to an invitation from Bishop Joseph Tawil, secretary of Patriarch Maximos. My long-standing friendship with Oreste Kéramé (novitiate in common[6] at St.-Leonard's-on-Sea, 1913–1914) assured me of a warm welcome. Naturally, they recounted to me some stories concerning their disagreements with the Latin hierarchy in the East. They gave as an example a Latin-rite priest in Jordan, a monk, who, in order to have one more family in his rite, exhorted a young woman (Latin-rite) to make her fiance, a Greek Catholic, convert to Orthodoxy, so that he would be able to marry them in the Latin Church, etc. Besides Bishop Tawil, there were three other bishops there, one of whom was the archbishop of Jordan, Michel Assaf.[7] These good bishops, outraged, had left the consistory that took place this morning. All the bishops were asked to vote, by placet or non placet, on the three canonizations

---

[6] Oreste Kéramé had been ordained as a priest of the Society of Jesus, which he left in 1945 to return to the Melchite Patriarchate.

[7] Mikhayl Assaf (1887–1970), Syrian, ordained in 1912. Melchite archbishop of Petra (Jordan) from 1948 until his death.

(or beatifications) that are to take place on December 9 and that have already been announced.[8] When one of them said to his neighbor, an Italian bishop, that he knew nothing about these three causes, the bishop answered him: "Oh! I am used to that; I always vote placet." What made our Melchites even more indignant than this empty and insincere ceremony was the presentation of the palliums, with the long prostrations in front of the pope and the oaths against heretics and schismatics: "They dared to invite representatives of the Protestant Reformation to come to Rome in order to hear these insults!" Their wrath was all the stronger in that the Armenian patriarch[9] had agreed to receive the pallium. This kneeling, this kissing of feet, were, they said, disgraceful for a patriarch; in the East we never allow such gestures, they are disgraceful for any man. They also disliked the ceremony of obedience that the cardinals performed. They pitied John XXIII, a pope so good and so simple, for being obliged to submit to these absurd rites. A poor old cardinal, approaching the throne, evidently fell, tripped up by his train; "fortunately, after a dozen of these, the pope said that it was enough, and he dispensed the others."

Cardinal Ottaviani has spread all over Rome the report he gave yesterday morning. A hundred copies of it came to the Hotel Caesar Augustus, where our two bishops from Chad (Dalmais, Véniat) are staying.

At 4 P.M., with Fr. Rondet, visit to Fr. Lyonnet (Biblical Institute). We exchanged news. Fr. Lyonnet insisted that I write some coherent remarks on the essential deficiencies of the two dogmatic schemas, from the doctrinal point of view. He will have need of them, he told me.

At 5:30, at the French center at Saint-Louis (basement hall), a lecture by Archbishop Blanchet (rector of the Institut catholique of Paris) on Pascal. Chatted with some bishops, in particular Bishop Ménager,[10] who is very actively opposed to the first schema but is hesitant about purely and simply rejecting it. Saw Fr. Rouquette (*Études*), Dom Olivier Rousseau (Chevetogne), etc. Also saw a young academic, André Cantin,[11] who is preparing a thesis on Saint Peter Damian; he is supposed to come

---

[8] The canonizations were of Pierre Julien Eymard, Antonio Pucci, and Francesco Da Camporosso.

[9] Ignace Pierre XVI Batanian (1899–1979), born in Turkey, ordained in 1921. Armenian patriarch of Cilicia (Lebanon) from September 1962 to 1976. Member of the Commission for Eastern Churches.

[10] Jacques Ménager (1912–1998), French, ordained in 1936. Bishop of Meaux from 1961 to 1973. Member of the Commission for the Lay Apostolate.

[11] André Cantin, born in 1929, French, holder of an advanced degree in philosophy. He produced a number of works on medieval philosophy.

and see me in a few days. Bishop André Jacquemin[12] of Bayeux is very opposed to the schema; he told me that yesterday, at the assembly of French bishops, Card. Lefebvre and Archbishop Guerry preached moderation; they recommended the adoption of the schema as a foundation, imagining that it should give rise to serious criticism. Fr. Daniélou, who attended this meeting, would tell me later that Archbishop Weber was of the same opinion.

Father Robert (?), secretary of Father de Peretti (Sup. Gen. of the Canons Regular of the Immaculate Conception), told me that he had guessed as early as Tuesday evening the direction the council session would take on Wednesday because on Tuesday morning, for a whole hour, Msgr. Piolanti had indulged in a violent diatribe in front of his students at the Lateran, saying for example that every day at the council one could hear modernist speeches, etc., and that if some of his students did not accept his judgment, they were fools and henceforth they had only to go join the fools at the Gregorian ...

At 7:30 P.M., returned to the Borgo with Fr. Rondet. Read the tendentious report in the *Tempo*: supposedly the bishops and cardinals opposed to the schema were only the "trans-Alpines", motivated by practical necessity, obliged as they are to come to terms with the Protestants.

At 8 P.M., visit from Fr. Martelet, who spent the afternoon at the via Santa Chiara (the French Seminary) correcting the text of his lecture, as it had to be typed up. He informed me about the meeting of a certain number of representatives from various episcopal conferences on the afternoon of the 13th, at the "Domus Mariae" (behind the villa Tarpenia). Represented there were the conferences of: Germany – the Philippines – South America (CELAM) – Japan – India – France – Mexico   Burma – Ceylon – Spain – Italy – Canada – all of Africa. Some bishops had brought a secretary (for the French bishops: Msgr. Etchegaray; for west Africa: Fr. Martelet). There was a message from Bishop Câmara:[13] 1. A petition has been organized for a more efficient agenda (the next morning, Card. Suenens endorsed it at the council); 2. We ask that *De Ecclesia* have priority in the second session and that an order be

---

[12] André Jacquemin (1902–1975), French, ordained in 1926. Bishop of Bayeux from 1954 to 1969.

[13] Helder Pessoa Câmara (1909–1999), Brazilian, ordained in 1931. Auxiliary bishop of Rio de Janeiro from 1952 to 1964, he was appointed archbishop of Olinda and Recife in March 1964. Member of the Commission for the Lay Apostolate beginning with the second session. He was actively involved in particular with the group "Jesus, the Church and the Poor".

indicated for what follows; 3. The constitution *De laicis*[14] should be integrated within *De Ecclesia*. – Archbishop Veuillot next proposed an insistent request: that the bishops might be allowed, in the interval between the two sessions, to send in their remarks on the schemas and that the commissions might consequently set to work immediately. – Next it was announced that Cardinal Bea was requesting a mixed commission, charged with drafting the new schema that would replace *De fontibus*. And each group said, in a few words, through its representative, what its intention was on the subject of this schema. Spain: it is the Holy Father's schema; it must be accepted. – Italy (Castelli): it is inopportune and illegitimate to give an opinion for the episcopal conference; each will decide for himself. – Japan: the schema is worthless; how do we get it rejected? – France (Veuillot): we hope that there will be a vote after the discussion on the whole of it; the schema is bad. – India: unanimously against the schema. – Mexico: doubts; various opinions; but quite against it. – Germany: firmly against. – Burma: divided. – All of Africa: firmly against. – Ceylon: it is important not to close the paths for exegesis; therefore, against. – The Philippines: against. – CELAM: against. – Canada: divided.

Bishop Himmer, representative of Belgium, was absent. He let it be known through Bishop Larraín[15] (of Rancagua, Chile) that there are already 50 signatures on an episcopal petition: that the council concern itself with the exercise of social justice and charity, the apostolate to the poor, hunger, peace; that a special secretariat be created for this end within the council.

For the schema on the Liturgy, there are, they say, 1200 emendationes to examine. The overly impatient bishops do not seem to see the complexity of such a task.

Someone said to me: the French bishops cultivate two virtues: one natural, namely, prudence; the other supernatural, charity. That harms to some degree the firmness of their judgments and the effectiveness of their action. – Fr. Daniélou told me this evening that, after having listened to the conferences for a month as if attending an academic meeting, our French bishops have decided to put themselves to work; they are organizing focused study groups and are appealing to exegetes

---

[14] "On the laity".

[15] Eduardo Larraín Cordovez (1890–1970), Chilean, ordained in 1913. Bishop of Rancagua (Chile) from 1938 to 1970. It seems more likely, however, that it was Manuel Larraín Errázuriz.

and theologians for help. Fr. Daniélou pressed me with questions about anthropology, etc.; matters that correspond more or less with chapters 2, 3, and 7 of the schema *De deposito fidei*.

At the last meeting of German-language bishops, Cardinal Döpfner offered to denounce in front of the council the irregularities that are said to have tainted the Central Commission's work. Apparently he received a big round of applause; Cardinal Bea, who was present, expressed to him his agreement.

I was told that yesterday, on leaving Saint Peter's, Cardinal Ruffini was supposed to have said out loud, talking to himself: "Why didn't they say all that earlier?" – Some other cardinals apparently said to each other, on leaving: "Well, at least now we know for whom we are voting!" (thinking of the next conclave). – It has been remarked, however, that certain papabili are keeping quiet. – I repeated this afternoon to some bishops something Fr. René Arnou said Sunday at the Gregorian: "If the bishops understood how much power they currently have and that the pope expects them to use it!"

At Saint-Louis des Français, I also met Dom Frénaud, of Solesmes, who was accompanying his abbot, Dom Prou, a member of the council. Greeting him, I cheerfully made an allusion to the articles he had written fifteen years ago, railing against me. He answered me in all seriousness: "But since then, you have written some fine things." Thus each of us stood his ground.

Father Daniélou wants to write to Cardinal Liénart to suggest a process for voting: let the vote on the schema *De fontibus* as a whole, if we can succeed in having it take place before moving on to an examination of the individual articles, be worded something like this: "Do you approve the spirit of the schema, etc.?" He hopes that in this way a certain number of bishops, who would not have dared simply to reject the schema, will vote no.

Another anecdote recounted at noon by Archbishop Assaf. Since he has been in Rome, he has not succeeded in penetrating the Propaganda to deal with some urgent matters there. He ended up writing to the secretary of the Congregation, more or less in these terms: "During the five weeks I have been here, I have not been able to see you: in the morning, I am at the council; in the afternoon, I find the door of the Congregation closed. Thursday, there will be no general congregation; so I will come to you in the morning." But, around 11 A.M., immediately upon leaving the Consistory, he hurried to the Spanish Square: the door of the Congregation was closed, even the heavy outer door. – Fr. Kéramé in this connection related to us the following joke. Someone said to a monsignor of the Congregation: "So, in the afternoon, it seems that you don't do anything? – Excuse me, Excellency, that is a mistake: in the afternoon, we are not there; it is in the morning that we do not do anything."

Friday, November 16, 1962. – Father Renard[1] (Belgian) told me, on leaving breakfast: "Yesterday, I saw an Italian bishop; he said to me: Some Italian bishops are saying among themselves: We used to think that some bishops from the other side of the mountains were Protestants; but now, we have seen for ourselves and know that there are a lot of them!"

On entering Saint Peter's, I saw Bishop Ménager, then Father Lécuyer (C.S.Sp.), both of them very hostile to the schema under discussion. Met Msgr. Lafortune, to whom I returned the observations he had prepared on *De deposito fidei*. – Armenian Mass, celebrated by Archbishop Layek[2] of Aleppo; the thurible had small bells on it; beautiful chant at the Consecration.

"Audiant omnes":[3] they are going to distribute the first corrections made by the Liturgical Commission; they relate to the Prooemium, divided into four points. The suffragatio[4] will take place tomorrow morning. (Fr. Jungmann (Innsbruck) would tell me this evening that he is rather happy with them.)

The president was Cardinal Liénart. He said: "Haec discussio est maximi momenti. Ideo convenit ut omnium sententias audiamus, etsi diversas, fraterno animo, et in mente meditemur coram Domino."[5]

Eugène Tisserant, decanus.[6] We noted the day before yesterday some contentious expressions directed toward exegetes. Pius XII had read numerous biblical works and journals in Germany; he subsequently kept himself up to date; hence his acts on the subject of Sacred Scripture. He wanted to give some general principles for the interpretation of Genesis, then ... (a history of his acts); finally, once again new progress. Ne

---

November 16

[1] Louis Renard, S.J. (1903–2000), Belgian, ordained in 1932. He was called to Rome in 1962 by Father Janssens to collaborate on the preparation for the Thirty-First General Congregation.

[2] Georges Layek (1922–1983), Syrian, ordained in 1945. Armenian archbishop of Aleppo from 1959 until his death.

[3] "Let all listen."

[4] "The vote".

[5] "This discussion is of very great importance. For that reason, it is fitting that we listen to the opinion of everyone, even those opposed, in a fraternal spirit and that we meditate on them in the presence of the Lord."

[6] "Dean" [of the Sacred College].

cassum faciatis laborem Pii XII.[7] (In this way Tisserant pointed out that the schema is a reaction against the encyclical *Divino afflante*.)

Card. Cerejeira (Lisbon). Recognoscatur schema ut melius sit.[8] It is not bad, however. One can only base pastoral and ecumenical actions on the truth. Ne simus minuentes veritatis integritatem. Si non praedicamus Jesum Christum, nihil amplius habemus praedicandum.[9] This schema is presented to us by so many learned and wise men ... Debeo meam dolorosam observationem patefacere:[10] our debates have been disseminated in the newspapers. (He reminded everyone of the obligation of secrecy, the safeguard of liberty.)

Card. de Barros Câmara. This schema has very great importance: everything depends on it. We must therefore study it and discuss it before thinking of rejecting it. If we must start a discussion, why set out from any other text than the official one? Let everyone be heard. (Against Suenens).

Card. McIntyre (Los Angeles, USA). Let it be shortened, but in its substance be kept. A number of things are taught today in seminaries and Faculties that the Church has not approved. So people expect from the council clear declarations. There has been too much talk of pastoral concerns: the essential thing, for pastors, is to guide the faithful, priests, and especially young clerics. Let this be done now. The schema brings some useful clarifications. Let us not scorn the work of so many eminent men. Let us weigh our responsibility, gathered cum Petro et sub Petro.[11] We must guide the Christian people tute et indubitanter.[12] Obedience and humility are necessary in order to keep the doctrine without ambiguity. Servare debemus quod traditum est, contra doctrinas varias et peregrinas,[13] etc. (Quotation from the Letter to the Hebrews). "Quod ubique, quod semper, quod ab omnibus ...":[14] there is Catholicism. Dixi.

---

[7] "Do not make the work of Pius XII pointless."

[8] "Let the schema be revised so that it might be better."

[9] "Let us not weaken the integrity of the truth. If we do not preach Jesus Christ, we no longer have anything to preach."

[10] "I must confide to you my sad observation."

[11] "With Peter and under Peter".

[12] "Safely and sheltered from doubt".

[13] "We must preserve what has been handed down, against all kinds of strange teachings" [Heb 13:9].

[14] An excerpt from the *Commonitorium* by Vincent of Lerins (fifth century). For the author, this maxim was supposed to serve as a guide to answer the question, "What must a Christian do when a part of the Church separates herself from communion with the rest?" Only admit as Catholic what has been believed everywhere, always, and by everyone.

?[15] – The gravity that a vote of "non placet" would have. It would then be necessary to substitute another schema. But the reasons are not sufficient. The schema was written by a commission that brought together eminent men from every region; it has been reviewed by the Central Commission, corrected by the subcommission "de emendandis",[16] finally put forward by the pope: it would be a huge responsibility to reject it. – Some say that we must not speak of two sources: but quite to the contrary it is necessary to speak of that; we do not have the right to cast doubt on that: it is the teaching of the Council of Trent, etc. The question cannot be disputed among Catholics; our separated brothers know this well. At the Central Commission, we were concerned solely with the complete truth, and that is what we ask here every morning in the prayer "Adsumus": ut in nullo deviemus a vero.[17] Let us study the texts of Trent and Vatican I. – In *De deposito fidei* also, we can make corrections here and there, to achieve a better expression; but let the doctrina integra[18] still remain! We must be silent about nothing of the deposit of faith through opportunism. – The schema placet juxta modum. It is a little lacking in the modus pastoralis.[19] Our preaching is often superficial, because our studies are not intense enough. We must reform, work harder, deepen the doctrine.

Card. Jos. Lefebvre (Bourges). Constitutiones de fide et de moribus minime respondent textibus Summi Pontificis. Doctrina saepe praesentatur modo negativo, et in forma nimis scolastica.[20] They do not incite minds to receive the truth with gladness. Salvo merito[21] of those who composed them, it is necessary to submit them to a profound revision in order to complete them.

Card. Rufinus Santos (Manila). Let us be able to examine and correct the schema freely. The objections that have been made against it are not valid. Our duty is to declare doctrine. "Pastoralis"[22] is an adjective; the doctrine is the substance. Certa, integra, sana, incorrupta sit doctrina.[23]

---

[15] A. Caggiano.

[16] "For amendments".

[17] "In order that we might not deviate in any way from the truth".

[18] "The complete doctrine".

[19] "The pastoral manner".

[20] "The constitutions on faith and morals correspond very little with the texts of the Supreme Pontiff. The doctrine is often presented in a negative way and in a form that is too scholastic."

[21] "While recognizing the merit".

[22] "Pastoral".

[23] "Let the doctrine be certain, complete, sound, uncorrupted."

Afterward, we will write pastoral letters; inveniantur tunc formulae accuratae, non nimis scolares et solemnes.[24] – People have spoken about adapting to the conditiones hodiernae:[25] but the truth is immutable; it is not a ceremony or a simple method. Doctrina ipsa sacra, heri, hodie et in saecula; nulla adaptatione nec reformatione indiget.[26] – Again, it has been said: this schema settles disputed questions; but why should it not do so? There have always been opposing views: the councils resolve them by deciding on the truth. – Dixi.

Card. Jean Urbani, patriarch of Venice. – Nonnullis indiget correctionibus, sed placet.[27] For some time, these questions have been studied and debated, not always with charity and truthfulness. In the seminaries, they expect from the council a decision that is firm, clear, precise. Quae dicuntur in schemate sunt valde utilia, bene respondent necessitatibus hujus temporis, etsi aliquando modo nimis scolastico.[28] Let us set aside matters that can be legitimately disputed: let our exegetes be praised and paternally advised. Clariori modo doctrina de traditione ponatur[29] – as well as the connection between the magisterium and Scripture. Let the Doctrinal Commission be assigned this revision.

Card. Raoul Silva Henriquez (Santiago, Chile). In the name of all the bishops of Latin America, especially of Chile: the indoles pastoralis[30] is lacking. All the schemas must be pastoral and of an ecumenical spirit. Nunc autem, sufficienter patet[31] that this schema is completely lacking in that regard. It seeks to promote a single school of thought: not only will it not serve unity in the Church, it will provoke arguments among Catholics. Sapit professoralem deformationem, ut hodie dicitur.[32] It defends doctrine rather than showing it to be the path of salvation. The Council of Trent itself often had a mind to act through exhortation. – "Veritas liberabit vos": but we need an apta veritatis propositio, ad alios alliciendos et Regnum Dei et justitiam ejus amandam.[33] It does not

---

[24] "Let precise formulas be found at that time that are not too much like school formulas or too solemn."

[25] "Conditions of today".

[26] "Sacred doctrine itself, yesterday, today, and for all ages: it needs no adaptation or reform."

[27] "This schema needs some corrections, but I approve it."

[28] "What is said in the schema is very useful and responds well to the necessities of this time, although sometimes in a manner that is too scholastic."

[29] "Let the doctrine on tradition be affirmed in a clearer way."

[30] "The pastoral character".

[31] "But now, it is sufficiently clear."

[32] "It has a flavor of professorial distortion, as is said today."

[33] "'The truth will set you free' [Jn 8:32]: but there must be a presentation of the truth adapted to attract others and make them love the Kingdom of God and its justice."

suffice to define doctrine strictly: it is necessary to proclaim the saving evangelical truth amabiliter.[34] Let the schema assume vestem paternam et pastoralem.[35] – It contains certain questions, such as inerrancy, etc., that should be sent back for discussion to the periti, brought together in a commission that reflects a variety of views.

Card. Michael Browne, O.P. – (He sought some agreement). Placet quoad substantiam.[36] Ten objections have been made to the schema. Certain corrections will be easy. On tradition, Trent and Vatican I taught the two sources; they speak explicitly of tradition. Magisterium ordinare hodiernum de illa loquitur, specialiter encyclica *Humani generis*: "Divinae revelationis fontes".[37] Saint Thomas also speaks about tradition in several passages (In *Sent.*; *Summa*).[38] As for the separated brethren, we have no other desire than to explain the Catholic doctrine to them with charity and to receive them into the Church.

Archbishop Armando Farès of Catanzaro (Italy). The schema is the work of successive commissions, it figures in a book signed by Cardinal Cicognani ... The Council of Trent legislated "ad coercenda petulantia ingenia".[39] Three centuries later, the Vatican Council once again took up the subject "De fontibus revelationis et de interpretatione Scripturae".[40] Rationalism had gotten worse, "praesertim in re biblica".[41] The popes had to intervene, "sive ad coercendum audaciam novatorum, sive, etc.",[42] cf. Leo XIII, Benedict XV,[43] Pius XII (*Divino afflante, Humani generis*) ... Hodie tempus est dicendi quid ab omnibus sentiendum sit;[44] how to study Scripture so as to protect, defend, and proclaim the faith; how, under the guidance of the Church, the faithful will be able to advance. Non solum conveniens, sed necessarium est, tractare de hac materia, sine ambiguitate neque timore. Deus est Veritas. Lumen Christi ab Ecclesia defenditur et omnibus ostenditur.[45] Let this schema,

---

[34] "With kindness".

[35] "A paternal and pastoral appearance".

[36] "I approve the schema in its substance."

[37] "Today's ordinary magisterium talks about this, especially in the encyclical *Humani generis*: 'the sources of divine revelation'" [see paragraph 8 of the encyclical].

[38] *Scriptum super sententiis* and *Summa theologiae*, two works of Saint Thomas Aquinas.

[39] "In order to restrain impassioned spirits".

[40] "On the sources of revelation and the interpretation of Scripture".

[41] "Especially in biblical matters".

[42] "Either to restrain the audacity of innovators or, etc.".

[43] *Providentissimus Deus* (1893) and *Spiritus Paraclitus* (1920), respectively.

[44] "It is time today to say what all must hold."

[45] "Not only is it fitting, it is necessary to treat of this matter, without ambiguity or fear. God is Truth. The Light of Christ is defended and shown to all by the Church."

so well prepared, "sit, ut est, basis hujus discussionis. Possunt partes quaedam emendari".[46] Develop the teaching on tradition. Speak a little more about the pastoral use of Scripture, sed semper modo digno concilii.[47]

Archbishop Alfred Bengsch (Berlin). Non placet. It cannot even be corrected. Its "intentio"[48] cannot satisfy us. Its modus loquendi[49] is such that the faithful would not recognize their mother in it, but only a harsh magistra. "Contradicit saltem ex parte verbis papae"[50] saying that the council will not condemn. It rejects the doctrines of men unknown outside of a small circle of specialists. The Council of Trent was more flexible and more reserved. Discussion among theologians, under the vigilant control of the ordinary magisterium, is a good thing. – I speak also in the name of my experience. In East Germany, as in many other countries, there is an imminent danger of materialism. The faithful expect from us help and consolation. This was a superb opportunity: to speak to them about the revelation of Christ, open wide for them the "divinus thesaurus",[51] explain to them as well how the Redeemer can reach great numbers of men who have not outwardly received the good news, etc. But, on all of this, nothing or almost nothing in the schema. – It adds new obstacles to union. There are those who tell our faithful that the Christian faith is no longer anything more than an antiquity, something that belongs in a museum; they speak to them in a completely different language that seems new and stirring. This schema is made to support that kind of talk. – The Gospel of Christ, that is the good news: it must be proclaimed, and there indeed is the munus concilii ... – Ergo, ex conscientia mea dicere debeo: non placet.[52]

Bishop Arthur Tabera[53] of Albacete (Spain). Schema praebet fundamentum solidum discussionis.[54] The difficulties are not insurmountable.

---

[46] "Be, as it is, the basis for this discussion. Certain parts of it can be amended."

[47] "But always in a manner worthy of a council".

[48] "Intention".

[49] "Mode of expression".

[50] "Teacher. It contradicts, at least in part, the words of the pope."

[51] "Divine treasure".

[52] "Task of the council. Therefore, in good conscience, I must say that I do not approve this schema."

[53] Arturo Tabera Araoz, C.M.F. (1903–1975), Spanish, ordained in 1928. Bishop of Albacete (Spain) from 1950 to 1968, created cardinal in 1969. Prefect of the Congregation for Divine Worship from 1971 until 1973, then of the Congregation for Religious from 1973 until his death. Member of the Commission for Religious.

[54] "The schema presents a solid foundation for discussion."

It has been well worked out: the dogmatic and Catholic content of it is good. Eximiae qualitates. Nihil proponit novum, sed ut noviter appareat doctrina. Semper habet oculos versos ad magisterium.[55] It is neither as inelegant nor as scholastic as some have said. Our separated brothers demand of us that we conceal nothing of the Catholic faith. Testes Dei fideles sine simulatione nos exhibeamus. "Maledicta sit caritas, quae servatur in jactura fidei."[56] – Some criteria for the corrections to be discussed: do not propose anything that is the subject of serious debate; doctrina proponatur suaviter sed sincere.[57]

Bishop Joseph Reuss, German. Non placet. Evidentissima argumenta allata sunt contra.[58] It is difficult to discuss theological questions deeply here, attamen diligens et accurata discussio absolute necessaria est. Plurimi Patres conciliares hoc non possunt:[59] that would take a number of years. Ideo, votum propono, ut concilium decernat vel a papa petat, ut antea locutio sit in concilio de Verbo Dei revelato – de Ecclesia – de Episcopis – de unitate Ecclesiae.[60] These schemas are ready; they would be very useful and very important. We could if need be relinquere confidenter[61] the current schema for a future time.

Bishop Joseph X.,[62] Italy. – Let the first two schemas be combined into one. Many things in them can be corrected. Let us distinguish the questions that have the greatest interest today. Usus valde modicus fiat damnationum. Non sumus functionarii, ... sed patres et pastores et fratres.[63] – No. 28 addresses itself ad exegetas catholicos;[64] let us insert something on the importance of scientific work. New problems are always

---

[55] "Outstanding qualities. It proposes nothing new, but in such a way as to make the doctrine appear in a new light. It always has its eyes turned toward the magisterium."

[56] "Let us prove to be true witnesses of God without pretense. 'Cursed be charity that would be preserved to the detriment of the faith!'" [A reference to Luther, *Commentary on the Epistle to the Galatians*.]

[57] "Let the doctrine be presented in a pleasant but sincere manner."

[58] "Very obvious arguments have been brought against this schema."

[59] "And yet a diligent and careful discussion is absolutely necessary. Most of the council Fathers are not able to do this."

[60] "For this reason, I propose a vote, that the council might decide, or ask the pope, that we discuss in council, before this schema, *De Verbo Dei revelato* (On the Revealed Word of God), *De Ecclesia* (On the Church), *De episcopis* (On Bishops), *De unitate Ecclesiae* (On the Unity of the Church)."

[61] "Confidently postpone".

[62] Joseph Gargitter (1917–1991), Italian, ordained in 1942. Bishop of Bressanone (Brixen) from 1952 to 1986. Member of the Commission for Bishops and the Government of Dioceses.

[63] "Let us make a very restrained use of condemnations. We are not bureaucrats ..., but fathers, pastors, and brothers."

[64] "To Catholic exegetes".

arising: do not discourage those who study them and thus render a great
service to the Church, etc. Libertas investigationis teneatur a magisterio;[65] otherwise, along with error, we stop the progress and expression of
the truth. Let us foster technical discussions, even with the a–catholici.[66]
Finally, let us publicly express the Church's gratitude.

Bishop Simon Nguyen-Krin-Dien[67] of Cantho (Vietnam). The
introductory declaration[68] was well received. Cf. Pentecost: "Facta hac
voce, convenit multitudo",[69] etc. Let that continue. We must present to
the world Jesus Christ the Savior, doctor, brother, with all his doctrine,
sub lingua nativa, omnibus acceptabili. Atqui hoc desideratur in his schematibus,[70] etc. "Vos autem nolite vocari Rabbi, etc."[71] (The president
stopped him.)

Bishop Joseph Battaglia of Faenza (Italy). Nolo celare admirationem
et tristitiam meam[72] on hearing the schema criticized. Argumenta sunt
fallacia et inania;[73] a schema so well prepared, by so many eminent men,
proposed by the pope, etc. It is said that it does not speak de Verbo Dei,
sed de Scriptura et Traditione.[74] It is said that it uses new terminology:
but "traditio"[75] is a traditional word! It is said that it does not conform
to what the pope has said on the pastoral aim of the council: sed papa
commendat quoque doctrinam Ecclesiae![76] It is said that it is not ecumenical enough: but there is nothing more ecumenical than the truth; it
is so "ipsa sua natura".[77] Some find it too scholastic: but that is a merit.
It is said as well that Vatican I has already dealt with this subject: but it
is good to explain it. Some find fault with it for condemning certain
opinions; but surely that is the Church's duty. – I am like Daniel in the
lions' den; but I say nonetheless: Placet. – Let a Prooemium be added;
let some corrections and additions be made.

---

[65] "Let freedom of research be supported by the magisterium."

[66] "Non-Catholics".

[67] Simon Hoa Nguên-van Hien, in reality bishop of Dalat.

[68] This refers to the Message of the Council to All Mankind, October 20, 1962.

[69] "And at this sound the multitude came together" [Acts 2:6].

[70] "In the native language, comprehensible to all. And yet, this is much in demand in these
schemas."

[71] "But you are not to be called rabbi" [Mt 23:8].

[72] "I do not wish to conceal my surprise and my sadness."

[73] "The arguments are false and empty."

[74] "About the Word of God, but about Scripture and tradition".

[75] "Tradition".

[76] "But the pope also emphasizes the Church's doctrine."

[77] "By its very nature".

Archbishop Guerry (Cambrai), de consensu omnium episcoporum Galliae. Tollenda sunt quaedam,[78] that are perilous, ambiguous, etc. It is not at all a question, as some have claimed, of sacrificing doctrine. This opposition between doctrinal and pastoral necessities is false. There is an aequivocatio about the word adaptare.[79] In one sense, it signifies to accommodate, compromise: crimen esset.[80] But in another sense, it is about an adaptatio praesentationis doctrinae,[81] so that evangelical truth might shine. The schema lacks first of all a synthesis. It must have a Prooemium. Next it is necessary, as the pope has asked, to adapt the presentation of the schemas. For 3 reasons: Catholics are in a new civilization; non-Catholics must be instructed modo persuasivo et intelligibili: eis afferamus verbum salutis;[82] for that we need profundior doctrinae cognitio;[83] finally, think of the central object of doctrine: instaurare omnia in Christo. Christus venit non ut damnaret, sed ut mundum salvum faceret, etc. – Conclusio: We must have a visio generalis primi schematis.[84] (The speech, too eloquent, resembled at times a fervorino[85] in front of a typical Catholic Action audience. No precise information. Moreover, it seemed to some, especially the Italian bishops, like a disavowal on the part of the French episcopate of Cardinal Liénart. The weak conclusion, which failed to indicate any path, has encouraged the partisans of the schema. Many French bishops were dismayed. I heard quite a bit of talk about it, and on Saturday morning Archbishop Dupuy of Albi, confirmed that to me.)

Archbishop Ermenegildo Florit of Florence. Gaudemus de libertate loquendi.[86] But let us preserve charity. Valde discrepamus inter nos,[87] but only on method. A scholastic method, always approved by the Church, is securior;[88] in establishing texts, it is necessary to distrust religious emotion. Nor is a historical method without dangers. We absolutely must

---

[78] "In the name of the bishops of France. Certain points should be removed."

[79] "Equivocation about the word 'adapt'".

[80] "It would be a crime".

[81] "An adaptation of the doctrine's presentation".

[82] "In a persuasive and intelligible manner: let us bring them the word of salvation."

[83] "A deeper knowledge of doctrine".

[84] "To restore all things in Christ [Eph 1:10 and the motto of Pius X]. Christ did not come to condemn but to bring salvation to the world, etc. Conclusion: we need an overall vision of the first schema." [This last sentence does not appear in Archbishop Guerry's speech.]

[85] A brief speech, especially one of religious character, intended to stir up fervor.

[86] "We rejoice in freedom of speech."

[87] "We differ a great deal among ourselves."

[88] "Safer".

invenire synthesim altiorem.[89] No method that leads to subjectivism or existentialist angst ... – On tradition, one can refer back to the Council of Trent. The word tradition itself is not merely scholastic: it is already biblical (St. Paul) and patristic. The schema is admirable. Ecclesia jure divino est magistra filiorum suorum. Sapit pessimismum?[90] Then let it be pointed out, in the discussion of the chapters, ubi jacet anguis ille. Ambiguitates?[91] Let them be clarified. Cf. no. 22 ... Proh dolor! etiam plures auctores catholici nimis indulgent opinioni[92] of the critics who contest the historicity of the Gospels. If we yield on that point, the whole value of revelation is undermined.

A Mexican bishop.[93] On the style of the first schema and of the second. Everyone accepts both Scripture and tradition. But is it necessary to adopt a new terminology that dates from the last century? There lies the problem. Recognoscatur schema, etiam ante disceptationem particularem.[94] We could send it back to the Biblical Commission.

Rev. Christopher Butler, O.S.B., Abbot of Downside, superior general of the Benedictine Congregation of England. – Non sum Episcopus. Sed fui exegeta. Habeo proprium interesse in re biblica ... Pro conscientia mea assentior iis qui dixerunt schema non placere, iis qui negaverunt schema respondere intentioni S. Pontificis. Quantum intelligo, vult Pater noster concilium aliquod spei et boni nuntium ad mundum afferre.[95] When there is no heresy within the Church, there is no need to intervene; when there are only "domestic" disagreements, why display them coram universis hominibus,[96] and so offend aliquos bonos et doctos catholicos, quorum nomina et studia ignorantur, exceptis perpaucis? Assentior etiam eis qui dicunt quod quaestio de Traditione et ejus relatione ad Scripturam non bene tractata sit in schemate. Nemo negat doctrinam Tridentini et Vaticani I, necnon magisterii ordinarii praesentis; sed

---

[89] "Find a higher synthesis".

[90] "The Church is, by divine right, the teacher of her children. Does this smack of pessimism?"

[91] "Where that snake of pessimism is to be found. Ambiguities?"

[92] "Alas! Several Catholic authors try too hard to please."

[93] José Alba Palacios (1909–1997), Mexican, ordained in 1932. Bishop of Tehuantepec from 1959 to 1970.

[94] "Let the schema be revised, even before the discussion of its chapters."

[95] "I am not a bishop. But I have been an exegete. I have a particular interest in the biblical question. In conscience, I give my assent to those who have said that they do not approve the schema, those who have affirmed that the schema does not correspond to the intention of the Supreme Pontiff. As far as I understand him, our Father wants the council to bring a message of hope and good news to the world."

[96] "Before the world".

multis, et nobis, haec videntur sufficere. Quaestio tractata in hoc schemate est disputata inter catholicos optimae notae.[97] Let the council not
deal with it. – De inspiratione et inerrantia:[98] if we only want to repeat
the teaching of the preceding councils and the ordinary magisterium,
let us employ their expressions (e.g., as in *Divino afflante Spiritu*). Sed
ulterius schema progreditur. Invadit campum ubi sunt quaestiones dis-
putatae. Vere periculosum est si quaestiones tales velut transitorie deci-
damus in concilio oecumenico. – Dixerunt complures hodie: quamvis
corrigendum sit schema, tamen est apte fundamentum. Sed, revera, non
laborat solum aliqualiter superficialibus spinis, quae possent evelli; ipsum
schema non est aptum. Est summi, gravissimi momenti, quod concilium
ortum inveniat quasi unanimitatem in proponenda doctrina Ecclesiae.
Atqui, multi sunt inter nos qui non possunt dicere: placet, etiam si corrigatur. Ideo, necessarium omnino est ut fiat coetus inter eos qui possunt
approbare et alios.[99] Let them seek a way forward. If they are unable to
find one, it will be necessary to draft another schema so that some unanimity might emerge in this first constitution of our council.

   End of the session.

A Father from Saint Jerome, a peritus, drove me and Fr. Daniélou to
the abbey, along with Bishop Jean-Théodore Suhr, former prior of Saint
Jerome, now bishop of Copenhagen. The Very Reverend Father Salmon
welcomed us. Dom Jean Leclercq has just returned to Rome, after a
preaching and lecture tour in the USA. Two young priests were there,
who had recently defended their theses: one on St. Bruno of Segni,[100]
the other on Gottfried of Admont. Very cheerful conversation. The

---

[97] "Some good and learned Catholics, whose names and work are not known except to a small
number. I agree also with those who say that the question of tradition and its relation to Scripture
is not well treated in the schema. No one denies the doctrine of Trent or of Vatican I or of the
current ordinary magisterium; but for many, and for us, that seems to suffice. The question treated
in this schema is disputed among Catholics of good repute."

[98] "On inspiration and inerrancy".

[99] "But the schema goes farther. It enters into fields where the questions are under debate. It is
very dangerous if we decide, in an ecumenical council, such questions, as it were, in passing. Several
have said today: although the schema needs correcting, it constitutes a good foundation. But, to tell
the truth, it does not suffer only from some superficial thorns that can be plucked out; the schema
itself is not appropriate. It is of a very great and a very serious importance that the council, having
begun, find a kind of unanimity in the presentation of the Church's doctrine. And there are many
among us who cannot say: *placet*, even if the schema is corrected. For this reason, it is absolutely
necessary that a group be constituted, with those who can approve it and the others."

[100] Réginald Grégoire.

bishop and the Fathers are all opposed to the schema *De fontibus*. Dom Leclercq drove me back. I showed him the interior of Saint Peter's, open in the afternoon to visitors (who must leave everything they have in the cloakroom).

At 4:30 P.M., lecture by Hans Küng, who is a professor at Tubingen, on the collegiality of the episcopate and ecclesiastical decentralization. He spoke with a juvenile audacity; it was strange to hear that sort of thing resounding in Rome. I would have preferred a little more calm and interiority. – Talked with Archbishop Gantin of Cotonou (Dahomey). Returned home with Bishop Samuel Gaumain[101] of Moundou (Chad), who had consecrated Paul Dalmais as bishop; he spoke to me with harshness, and at the same time with concern, about the schema under discussion and the maneuvers of some "curialists". – At 7 P.M., a visit from R. Panikkar, who has been in Rome for two years, as chaplain of the university students (I got to know him when he was chaplain of the students at Salamanca). We chatted about India, the thought of J.-A. Cuttat, his works in preparation, etc. He informed me that Cardinal Ottaviani had recently telephoned Cardinal Wyszyński to offer his best wishes for the feast of Saint Stanislas (feast celebrated by the pope at the Church of Saint Andrew at the Quirinal) and to ask him to get the Polish bishops to vote in favor of his schema. Cardinal W. apparently answered: a. I do not have authority over them for that, they are free; b. I believe that a good number of them are rather against it.

There are apparently five experts officially joined to the Commission for Doctrine. Four names were indicated to me: Tromp, secretary; Msgr. Fenton; Fr. Lio; Msgr. Schauf. – It is always the same small group.

Saturday, November 17, 1962. – This morning, I took a seat in the corner gallery, near the baldachino, under the statue of Saint Andrew, across from the observers' gallery, next to the tiers of cardinals. From there, one can look along the row of the Ten of the Board of Presidency, one can see the secretariat's table, the one for the stenographers and other employees, etc.

President: Cardinal Norman Gilroy, archbishop of Sydney. Archbishop Felici read out the Emendationes made to the Prooemium of the liturgical schema. Then Cardinal Lercaro read a long report on the

---

[101] Samuel Gaumain, O.F.M. Cap., born in 1915, French. Bishop of Moundou from 1959 to 1974.

work of the commission. In passing, he pointed out that one Father had complained indignantly that the Blessed Virgin was not named in the schema: if this Father had read more carefully, he would have seen that she was named twice in it. Two subcommissions, theological and juridical, have approved the work. – It was announced that four ballots were going to be distributed, in order to vote on this Prooemium in four successive stages, in the course of the session. Utatur stylo magnetico.[1] – And we passed on to *De fontibus*.

Cardinal Carlos de la Torre[2] (Quito, Ecuador). Jam clare, praeclare ostensum fuit[3] that the schema must not be rejected. Placet juxta modum. (The cardinal is very old. – He was speaking, I was told, against the cardinal from Chile.)[4]

Cardinal José Garibi y Rivera[5] (Guadalajara, Mexico). Let us take an example from Trent, which first condemned errors, then passed on to pastoral reform. Pius XII himself, concerning Holy Scripture, marked out some clear limits against error and excess. Some have not respected them. Plura proponuntur[6] that destroy the authority of Scripture and pervert the truth. They put at risk the historicity of the actions and words of Christ, they speak against the apostolic tradition. All the councils have profited from the work of theologians to put an end to debates and to formulate doctrinal definitions. The Fathers will be able to make emendationes, sed schema placet.[7]

Cardinal Döpfner (Munich), in the name of the German bishops. He had to present animadversiones quasdam.[8] He would have to say something quite different from what had been repeated here on the preparation of the schema. In particular, he contested Cardinal Ottaviani's report, according to which one could believe that everything went perfectly at the Theological Commission and the Central Commission.

November 17

[1] "Let the magnetic stylus be used."

[2] Carlos María de la Torre (1873–1968), Ecuadorian, ordained in 1896. Archbishop of Quito from 1933 to 1967, created cardinal in 1953.

[3] "It has already been shown clearly and very distinctly".

[4] Raúl Silva Henriquez, who spoke the day before.

[5] José Garibi y Rivera (1899–1972), Mexican, ordained in 1912. Archbishop of Guadalajara from 1936 to 1969, created cardinal in 1958.

[6] "Several things have been proposed."

[7] "Amendments, but I approve the schema."

[8] "Some observations".

E contra, dubia gravissima[9] were put forward by a great number at the Central Commission; they wanted the whole schema to be rejected. As for the Theological Commission, what has been said about it is inaccurate. Atqui, iterum atque iterum, I must first of all say that it was under an influxus nimis unilateralis.[10] Next, they rejected several times the proposals made by Cardinal Bea concerning a mixed commission (or they did not even respond to him at all). They refused to invite certain competent exegetes. After the criticisms made by the Central Commission, very few corrections were made; the schema has remained substantially unchanged, etc. – His de causis, etc. Necesse est ut loquamur aperte et libere. Nul impedimentum[11] comes from the Supreme Pontiff: he himself made clear that the schemas have been submitted to us to be either adopted or corrected "or even rejected". Remanet nobis opus judicandi, an debeat schema rejici, an non.[12] I earnestly ask Cardinal Ottaviani that some periti named by the pope might study the difficulties raised; let periti from various schools of thought be invited to the commission, etc. And let us examine with care the proposals made by the Secretariat for Unity. Potius supprimatur aliquod schema, quam, etc.[13]

Card. Luis Concha,[14] archbishop of Bogotá (Colombia). This schema is presented to us by the Holy Father. Despite what has been said, I cannot change my opinion. Accurate, exacte atque opportune est confectum.[15] Nothing is more apt to satisfy our separated brothers than to propose to them the truth, such as it is in the schema. The doctrine on tradition that it presents is already in Trent and Vatican I, but it is good to recall it as the schema does. The style is scholastic? Sed hoc est in laudem schematis.[16] It is scholasticism that preserves truth in the Church. The schema shows very well the link between Scripture and tradition. Prout jacet, disceptationi tradatur.[17] Nothing prevents asking for corrections, as was done for the liturgy. But the authority of the Supreme Pontiff does not permit us to reject it.

---

[9] "On the contrary, very serious criticisms".

[10] "And, again and again, I must first of all say that it was under an influence that was too one-sided."

[11] "For these reasons, etc. It is necessary that we speak openly and freely. No impediment".

[12] "The task remains for us to judge whether the schema ought to be rejected or not."

[13] "Let some schema be eliminated rather than, etc."

[14] Luis Concha Córdoba (1891–1975), Colombian, ordained in 1916. Archbishop of Bogotá from 1959 to 1972, created cardinal in 1961.

[15] "It has been prepared carefully, with exactness, and in an opportune fashion."

[16] "But that is to the credit of the schema."

[17] "Such as it is presented, let it be given over for discussion."

Card. Antonio Bacci. The schema has been given to us not to be rejected but to be discussed. It has been prepared in the Theological Commission, reviewed by the Central Commission, approved by it. In these commissions, named by the pope, are found bishops and theologians primi ordinis. Valde est opportunum[18] to judge on the questions with which it deals. The world expects that, etc.

Bishop Schmitt of Metz. An appeal has often been made to Trent and to Vatican I. But all you need do is read: the text of Trent clearly has "fontem", in the singular, and the Fathers at Trent rejected the "partim-partim"[19] that had been proposed to them. Vatican I did not say anything more about two sources. These two councils fulfilled their task; it is necessary now to illustrate another aspect of the truth. After the mostly negative propositions of Vatican I, we need a more positive language, which emphasizes the traditional doctrine. Therefore I will propose three guiding principles for this:

1. – Tota revelatio consistit in persona Christi, qui est Ipse locutio Dei ad homines et revelatio Dei.[20] Christ is not only a legatus altissimus;[21] the whole of his life, death, Resurrection is divina revelatio.[22] From Pentecost until the end of the world, the Church will never cease to search the Depths of the Mystery of Christ. It cannot be said that the teachings of the apostles added anything to it: they are commentaries on Christ. – 2. – Revelatio christiana est evangelium.[23] There is a danger of reducing the Christian faith to an ideology if one does not see that it is faith in the Good News, in an oeconomia salutis. – 3. – Hoc evangelium salutis maxime respondet necessitatibus hodiernis. Venite, et credite nobiscum in Evangelium.[24] We must not show men "truths", but Christ himself, who is the Truth, Savior, and Judge

---

[18] "Of the first rank. It is very opportune."

[19] The Decree on the Reception of the Sacred Books and Traditions (1546) stipulates that truth and norms of conduct "are contained in the written books and unwritten traditions that have come down to us, having been received by the apostles from the mouth of Christ himself or from the apostles by the dictation of the Holy Spirit." Now, the council Fathers at Trent had rejected an earlier formula that had the word partim (partly) before the mention of Scripture and before that of traditions. This rejection emphasizes that Scripture forms a single whole with the totality of tradition and cannot be opposed to it.

[20] "All revelation consists in the person of Christ, who is himself the word of God to men and the revelation of God."

[21] "Very high-ranking envoy".

[22] "Divine revelation".

[23] "The Christian revelation is the Gospel."

[24] "Economy of salvation. This Gospel of salvation responds completely to today's needs. Come, and believe with us in the Gospel."

of the living and the dead. Fides christiana est aliquid amplius quam adhaesio intellectualis aliquibus veritatibus.[25] – Without that, there is no true evangelization.

Cardinal Ottaviani requested the floor, in order to respond to the criticisms expressed by Card. Döpfner. – The latter has just spoken, non ex mala intentione, sed ex deficientia informationis. Peto quaedam animadvertere. Non est verum quod[26] ... (this formula recurs three times). It is not true that the Preparatory Theological Commission was one-sided: it included theologians with various views; the Gregorian and the Lateran were represented on it (Tromp, Dhanis, Piolanti! ...). It is not true that exegetes were not sufficiently listened to there, since the Biblical Commission (Cerfaux) and even the Biblical Institute were there (Vogt, the rector, imposed in the end by the pope, and only a consultor). I did not say that there had been no opposition in the Central Commission, but if we did not take account of their remarks, it is because they were a minority. Besides, all the criticisms made in the Central Commission were examined by the Theological Commission (?).[27]

Archbishop P. Parente. Audivi pro et contra. Mirum non est.[28] But the schema such as we have it is one thing, its history is another. Substantia schematis: sana doctrina.[29] I propose, in order to know if we approve it, that we vote on its guiding principles. (He then stated these principles, worded in such a manner that everyone had to accept them.) Afterward we will be able, if we so wish, to give it a formam gratiorem et magis pastoralem.[30] – It has been said that Trent and Vatican I had spoken of *one* source. But why should our council not have the right to explain a little further? Non satis est dicere Scripturam esse tanquam unicum fontem[31] (no one has said that). Besides, at Trent, one solitary Father objected to the "partim-partim".[32] Since Trent, all theologians have held two sources. Dogmas not contained in Scripture have been defined. Before Scripture, tradition existed. The Fathers

---

[25] "The Christian faith is greater than an intellectual adherence to some truths."

[26] "Not from bad intent, but from a lack of information. I ask that attention be paid to certain points. It is not true that ..."

[27] Criticisms were indeed addressed to the Theological Commission, but it was essentially Father Tromp who saw to the task of responding to them.

[28] "I have heard the pros and cons. It is not surprising."

[29] "The substance of the schema: sound doctrine."

[30] "A more accessible and pastoral form".

[31] "It is not sufficient to say that Scripture is, so to speak, the unique source."

[32] "Partly, partly".

spoke about apostolic oral traditions. (As he exceeded the time limit, the president stopped him; but he insisted and was allowed to develop his conclusions.)

A Yugoslavian bishop.[33] – We must affirm two sources; we must affirm the whole truth. Traditio est prior tempore et extensione revelationis pars.[34] Let the first chapter be entitled: De traditione. Let us discuss it and correct it. Let us make ample provision for tradition. Let the two chapters on the Old and New Testaments be merged into one.

Cardinal Frings asked for the floor. He responded to a criticism that Archbishop Parente had just addressed to him. No one doubts, he said, that divine doctrine includes Scripture and tradition. But I said: in ordine essendi est unicus Fons, revelatio divina, sicut docet Tridentinum; ex hoc unico fonte duo rivuli emanant.[35] I had not expressly named Scripture and tradition at the time, but it was clear.

Bishop Francis Simons of Indore (India). He proposed a general principle of inerrantia. – Vitemus speciem quamdam vanae gloriae loquendo de magisterio.[36] Let us not be arrogant.

Bishop Charue of Namur. Card. Suenens explained why he felt obliged to say: non placet. All of the bishops of Belgium and the Belgian missionary bishops and the bishops of the Congo go along with his opinion. Dolemus quod duo prima schemata non exhibent de revelatione Christi positivam, patristicam, biblicam, oecumenicam expositionem. Eo magis dolemus,[37] because so much recent work permitted that. Instanter petimus[38] that the questions treated in the schema ex integro et omnino aliter rescribantur. – Indubie necessarium est auctoritatem declarare doctrinam, monere, damnare,[39] repress errors and take precautions against dangers, vigilare,[40] etc.: that is the task of the Holy

---

[33] Pavao Butorac (1888–1966), Yugoslav, ordained in 1910. Bishop of Dubrovnik from 1950 until his death.

[34] "Tradition is the part of revelation that is the first with respect to time and extension."

[35] "In the order of being, there is one unique source, divine revelation, as Trent taught; from this unique source flow two streams." [Cardinal Frings was inspired for his intervention by a note from J. Ratzinger. See the De Smedt collection, 608.]

[36] "On inerrancy. Let us avoid a certain appearance of vainglory when speaking about the magisterium."

[37] "We regret that the first two schemas do not present a positive, patristic, biblical, and ecumenical exposition on the revelation of Christ. We regret it all the more".

[38] "We insistently ask".

[39] "Be totally rewritten, and in a totally different way. It is without any doubt necessary for authority to express doctrine, give warnings, condemn."

[40] "Be vigilant".

Office or the Biblical Commission. Concilium autem oecumenicum non est Sanctum Officium. Declarationes conciliares sunt firma regula docendi.[41] Not so many condemnations! And, ne vituperentur homines eximii. – Caute procedatur in quaestionibus quae graviter coaetaneos nostros sollicitant,[42] and that cannot be disposed of quickly. Let us recommend prudence, let us remember the rule of faith, certainly; but the council does not have to descend ad concretas applicationes.[43] We do not have to deny the problems that, velimus nolimus, exsistunt; debent prudenter investigari, non imprudenter negari.[44] – Among certain Fathers, there is a serious confusion regarding this schema. If they want to inform themselves, let them read the booklet by Bishop Weber of Strasbourg: "Current Directions in Exegetical Studies".[45] Attendite ad conditionem eorum qui debent[46] unite Catholic doctrine and scientific studies. Think of the Galileo Affair and other more recent examples. Consider that imprudent declarations could become a very heavy weight for the Church usque in saeculum.[47] If there are evils, the remedy is not in putting a stop to work, sed in fovenda scientia una cum fidelitate et obedientia erga Ecclesiam Dei.[48] Look at the University of Louvain. Jean Rivière[49] was able to write that if modernism has been almost nonexistent in Belgium, it is to the credit of the University of Louvain. Let our council take as its model the Council of Jerusalem.[50] Just as John XXIII is reminiscent of Peter: when the first council gathered, it did not want to impede the Gentiles from entering the Church: so it should be with us, erga fratres separatos et omnes gentes. Ne quid

---

[41] "But the ecumenical council is not the Holy Office. Conciliar declarations are firm rules for teaching doctrine."

[42] "Let eminent men not be rebuked. Let us proceed with caution in questions that gravely trouble our contemporaries."

[43] "To concrete applications".

[44] "Whether we like it or not, exist; they must be prudently investigated, not imprudently denied."

[45] J.J. Weber, "Orientations actuelles des études exégétiques sur la vie du Christ", *Bulletin ecclésiastique du diocèse de Strasbourg*, October 1–15, 1962. This article was distributed at the time of the council by the Biblical Institute.

[46] "Pay attention to the situation of those who must".

[47] "For centuries to come".

[48] "But in the promotion of science, in fidelity and obedience to the Church of God".

[49] Jean Rivière (1878–1946), French, ordained in 1901. Professor in the theology faculty of Strasbourg. He had published *Le Modernisme dans l'Église, étude d'histoire religieuse contemporain* (Paris: Letouzey et Ané, 1929).

[50] A gathering of the apostles that met in the middle of the first century to determine whether Christians who had converted from paganism had to observe the Jewish law. See Acts 15:1–29.

imponamus quod non esset omnino necessarium! Spiritum amaris declarationibus non extinguamus![51]

Bishop Angel Temiño Saiz[52] of Orense (Spain). Do not confuse a conciliar declaration with preaching. It is necessary for the conciliar texts to be very precise: it is up to preachers to make use of them. The scholastic form is very precious. Plurimae emendationes faciendae;[53] let us not adopt what are simply theological opinions, but "tantum doctrina certa".[54] The schema says nothing about the "traditio vitalis"[55] and the "sensus fidelium",[56] so important. – Summatim:[57] the pastoral goal is best achieved by doctrinal precision; this is also what is most useful for a dialogue with our separated brothers. Ergo, schema retinendum et emendandum.[58] Many of the disagreements are perhaps more in verbis quam in re.[59]

Archbishop Jean-Baptiste Zoa of Yaoundé. In the name of numerous bishops of Africa. He said he was in substantial agreement with those who have spoken against the schema, notably Cardinals Bea, Frings, Léger, etc. He submitted some written details to the secretariat. Conclusio communis: schema omnino non placet; remittendum est commissioni ut renovetur. – Nunc, nomine proprio:[60] I support the proposition made yesterday by Dom Butler: a. – The doctrinal declarations of the council must obtain a moral unanimity. b. – Let our positions not be distorted: we all accept tradition! etc. We accept all of the teaching of Trent and Vatican I. c. – Let periti be chosen who represent the various schools of thought, and let them draw up a new text that would be presented to us by the Theological Commission.

---

[51] "Toward the separated brothers and all peoples. Let us not impose what is not totally necessary! Let us not extinguish the Spirit with shrill declarations!"

[52] Angel Temiño Saíz (1910–1991), Spanish, ordained in 1934. Bishop of Ourense (Spain) from 1952 to 1987. Member of the Commission for the Discipline of the Clergy and the Christian People.

[53] "A very great number of amendments to be made".

[54] "Only doctrine that is certain".

[55] "Living tradition".

[56] "Sense of the faith of the faithful". [This designates the gift that the community of the faithful has received, inasmuch as they constitute an undivided whole, of not erring in matters of faith. See *Lumen gentium*, chap. 2, par. 12.]

[57] "In summary".

[58] "Therefore, the schema should be retained and amended."

[59] "Of form rather than substance".

[60] "Common conclusion: the schema is not at all satisfactory; it should be sent back to the commission to be redone. Now, in my own name".

Bishop Maurice Pourchet of Saint-Flour. – An appeal has often been made to our responsibility. When it comes to doctrine, declarations are very serious. Alligant fideles, etiam quantum ad mentem internam.[61] Consequently, be careful. A number of theological conclusions appeared to be certain, closely related to the faith, and were taught for a long time by the ordinary magisterium – and had to be abandoned. The very title of the first chapter is intended to inhibit a theological discussion on the exact meaning of the decree of Trent. Let us leave the discussion free. No one here scorns tradition! Argumenta allata contra eos qui dicunt "unus fons", salva reverentia, non sunt ad rem. Controversia inter theologos adhuc viget. Theologia post-tridentina multis videtur passa spiritu timoris et oppositionis negativae protestantibus qui decebant "Sola Scriptura".[62] Now, the two adverse positions have moved closer together. Let us not go on to ruin the work that has been accomplished. Certainly, we must not diminish the truth through irenicism; but neither must we exaggerate or make imprudent statements. – De exegetis, Bishop Charue locutus est egregie.[63] – If we accept this schema as our basis, there will be interminable arguments on every paragraph, every line. Ideo, assentior propositioni Domini Butler.[64]

Bishop Georges Hakim of Akka (Palestine Israel). Join the position of the critics. The schema must be not merely amended but recast. – He wanted to ensure that a voice from the East and its patristic tradition be heard. These schemas are foreign, in their composition, their structure, their perspectives, their conceptualization, to that tradition. They completely ignore Eastern catechesis and theology. They monopolize the universal faith in aid of a particular theology. One does not see in them the Mystery of Christ, the economy of salvation unfolding in history. Theological explanations must not be detached from Scripture and the Fathers. One must not lose sight of the concrete character of the Word of God, of which the Church is the authentic place. Any disjunction between Scripture and tradition will be judged by many as an act of violence against the fundamental unity of revelation and the channels that transmit it to us. We have here an exclusive

---

[61] "They bind the faithful, even in their interior consent."

[62] "The arguments brought against those who say 'a unique source', despite the respect I owe them, are not *ad rem*. Controversy among theologians still exists up to the present day. Post-Tridentine theology seems to many to suffer from a spirit of fear and negative opposition toward the Protestants who were saying: 'Sola Scriptura' (Scripture alone)."

[63] "On the exegetes, Bishop Charue has spoken very well."

[64] "For this reason, I agree with the proposal of Dom Butler."

fruit of scholasticism, a very incomplete product of the tradition of the Church. – Some examples; in particular: the Paschal mystery is a totality, including death and Resurrection; it is not completely expressed by the idea of satisfaction. – Nurtured by the authentic tradition of the Church, I feel foreign to these schemas, and I deeply understand the criticisms against them.

Bishop Jacinto Argaya Goicoechea of Mondoñedo-Ferrol (Spain). It would be necessary to know exactly the theological value of what is being proposed to us in these schemas, etc.

A bishop from Australia.[65] In the name of the bishops of Australia, etc., in union with Cardinal Gilroy: Schema placet, quamvis perfectibile. Dilucide exponit veritatem.[66] The reasons brought against it are not sufficient. It is "secundum mentem Summi Pontificis. Perficiatur, ut veritas nostrae fidei, etc."[67]

The secretary general (Felici) then announced the results of the four successive votes on the liturgical Prooemium. For: 2,181, 2,175, 2,175, and 2,191 votes; against: 14, 26, 21, and 10. The Prooemium was adopted.

At the solemn assembly for the beginning of the term at the Gregorian, there were 32 cardinals; at the corresponding event at the Lateran, a few days earlier, there had been 31. This sort of thing is noted and seriously talked about, as much among rebellious spirits as among conformists. The Gregorian scored a point.

Today, the 17th, at 2 P.M., a visit from Father Moubarac, who arrived flanked by two Poles, some friends of his, he told me. They are in contact, they told me, with their bishops here. One of them is a journalist;[68] he sent me quite a questionnaire. The conversation was rather banal. I only told them things that were incontestable and that had no connection to the non-religious news.

At 3, meeting with Fr. Amiot, P.S.S.,[69] at Saint-Louis des Français. He has written, for Bishop Courbe, some remarks on the first schema,

---

[65] In actual fact, it was Julio Rosales y Ras (1906–1983), Filipino, ordained in 1929. Archbishop of Cebu (Philippines) from 1949 to 1982, created cardinal in 1969. Member of the Commission for the Discipline of the Clergy and the Christian People. He spoke in the name of the bishops of the Philippines, not of Australia.

[66] "I approve the schema, although it needs perfecting. It presents the truth in a very clear way."

[67] "In accordance with the mind of the Supreme Pontiff. Let it be improved, so that the truth of our faith ..."

[68] Casimir Morawski.

[69] François Amiot, P.S.S. (1889–1971), French. He taught Sacred Scripture and Church history.

and he consulted me on that subject. We talked. This old, honest Sulpi-cian is shocked by what he sees of intrigue and audacity among a certain number of "Romans".

At 4, still at Saint-Louis, in the small parlor, conversation with Dom Olivier Rousseau, accompanied by Father Giuseppe Dossetti[70] and his friend, a layman, professor of church history, Giuseppe Alberigo.[71] Both of them know Cardinal Montini well; both from Bologna, they are friends of Card. Lercaro. They are greatly interested in the council and would like to see its continuity assured, from one session to the next, by a permanent committee. They are writing a proposal on this that Cardinal Lercaro would put forward to the conciliar Commission for Extraordinary Affairs. Alberigo is the one who has just published the book *Conciliorum oecumenicorum Decreta*, prepared by the Centro di Doc-umentazione, Istituto per le Scienze Religiose, Bologna.

There were, I was told, three cardinals: Léger, Montini, and Lercaro, who went to see the pope, the other day, to let him know about the stagnation of the Liturgical Commission and ask him to speed things up. Which was done immediately.

At 7 P.M., I arrived at the Canadian College (Via delle Quatro Fon-tane), where I had an appointment with Msgr. Lafortune. We had dinner together in a small restaurant very close by. Next, a visit to Cardinal Léger. A simple and open welcome. We spoke about the council, the incidents of that morning. I gave the cardinal a certain number of details on the Preparatory Theological Commission. He seemed to be rather worried, because the pope is sometimes paradoxi-cal, does not follow the council closely, does not always have pleasant choices to make. He (the cardinal) judges the people around Cardinal Ottaviani at the Holy Office harshly. Ottaviani is not a bad man, quite the contrary; but he is fixed in an attitude that those who surround and flatter him support; and he needs them. Harshness also toward Msgr. Garofalo, who has reached his present position, he told me,

[70] Giuseppe Dossetti (1913–1996), Italian. A jurist and statesman, he was ordained in 1959. He was the founder of the monastic community *Piccola Famiglia dell'Annunziata* and of the documenta-tion center in Bologna. At the council, he was the expert of G. Lercaro and an expert at the council beginning with the third session.

[71] Giuseppe Alberigo (1926–2007), Italian. Jurist and historian, director of the documentation center of the Institute for Religious Sciences in Bologna. He edited the *Conciliorum oecumenicorum decreta* (Bologna: Herder, 1962), and he edited an important *Storia del Concilio Vaticano II*, 5 vols. (Bologna, 1995–2001). The French edition was published by Éd. du Cerf the English edition by Orbis Books.

by cribbing his examinations and who, superficial intellectually, is a man of insignificant schemes; etc. Next we talked about Saint-Sulpice, Lyon, G. Villepelet,[72] etc. – After having made clear my situation with respect to the council, the cardinal got up, went to his desk to get a large notebook, came back and sat down across from me, and read out to me the notes he had taken on the spot during the first meeting of the Doctrinal Commission, Wednesday afternoon.[73] The meeting was a stormy one. Card. Ottaviani was presiding; Fr. Sébastien Tromp was beside him. Everything began with a long diatribe, harsh, haughty, violent, by Fr. Tromp, directed at all those who were criticizing the schema: a retort to each of the bishops who had sent animadversiones[74] before the opening of the council, as they had been asked to do (in particular, a reply to Card. Gerlier, archbishop of Lyon); a reply to those who had just spoken at the council; an indictment of the theologians who had dared to compose criticisms (such criticisms, he was saying, written in English, are the work of a Frenchman,[75] etc.); an indignant condemnation of some theologians as traitors and trouble-makers (allusion to Fr. Rahner), etc. – When Tromp had finished, Card. Léger requested the floor; he said: I thought I was coming to the meeting of a commission working in the service of the council; I did not think I was being summoned before a tribunal. I am neither a haereticus nor a traditor.[76] But I insist on remaining entirely free to speak according to my conscience. If I cannot be free here, I would prefer to tender my resignation. – Encouraged by these words, two or three members[77] of the commission supported Léger, albeit timidly. One of them was Archbishop Garrone (Toulouse). The archbishop of Agrigento, the elderly G.-B. Peruzzo, became indignant at these protests. My visit with Card. Léger lasted a good hour. Msgr. Lafortune drove me back to the Borgo S. Spirito.

---

[72] Georges Villepelet, P.S.S. (1906–1975), French, ordained in 1929. Superior of the University Seminary of Lyon from 1945 to 1961, then director and superior of La Solitude (novitiate) from 1961 to 1973.

[73] In actuality, the meeting took place on Tuesday, November 13.

[74] "Remarks".

[75] In fact, this refers to the document by E. Schillebeeckx, who criticized the first schemas. His remarks had indeed been translated into Latin and English. According to Tromp's journal for the date of November 13, 1962, it was Archbishop Parente, however, not Tromp himself, who spoke about this document. As for Tromp, he had given a relatio on the dogmatic schemas and on the observations sent by the Fathers. ASV, Conc. Vat. II, 789–91.

[76] "Neither a heretic nor a traitor".

[77] According to Tromp's journal, these were Archbishop Garrone and Bishop Schröffer.

De Emendatione schematis constitutionis de Ecclesia, fasc. I (1962), p. 5: Ad Observationes generales circa capita I et II (Sub secreto).[78] (The fascicle has just come out).

1. – Constitutio de Ecclesia ex mandato Summi Pontificis redacta est a Commissione theologica, quae secundum ejusdem Pontificis placita, sola est competens in rebus dogmaticis. Quare si aliae Commissiones attingere debent quaestiones doctrinales theologicas, subsunt revisioni Commissionis theologicae. Eadem de causa Commissio theologica non constituit cum aliis commissionibus Commissiones mixtas quae dicuntur: commissio enim mixta supponit competentiam ex utraque parte in eamdem materiam, ut facilius accidit in disciplinaribus. Si igitur Commissio theologica non admittere potest Commissiones mixtas cum aliis Commissionibus quae studii causa sunt erectae, multo minus cum Secretariatibus, quorum finis non est studium."[79]

"... Commissio theologica composita est ex 60 personis ex diversis regionibus, ritibus, scholis theologicis; cum tendentiis diversis non solum conservativis, sed etiam progressivis; et dum alii magis considerant partem positivam, alii attendunt ad partem speculativam, moralem, juridicam, mysticam, oecumenicam. Quare difficulter in Commissione centrali aliquid ordinis doctrinalis dicitur, quod non multum amplius in Commissione theologica disputatum sit"[80] (pp. 5–6).

The first of these two texts is rather arrogant; the second only states an "official" view of the truth.

Ibid. – "... Hac in re numquam possumus satisfacere fratribus separatis. Nam si negamus eos esse membra Corporis Christi quod est

---

[78] "On the amendment of the schema of the constitution on the Church, fascicle I (1962), p. 5: General observations concerning chapters 1 and 2." [This is the response written by a small committee of the Theological Commission composed of Tromp, Gagnebet, and Schauf to the criticisms of the Central Commission on the schema *de Ecclesia*.]

[79] "The Constitution on the Church, by mandate of the Supreme Pontiff, has been composed by the Theological Commission, which, according to the wishes of the pope himself, is alone competent in dogmatic matters. This is why, if the other commissions have to touch upon doctrinal theological questions, they are subject to revision by the Theological Commission. For this same reason, the Theological Commission has not formed with the other commissions any mixed commissions, of which there has been talk: for a mixed commission presupposes a competence of two parties in the same matter, as can easily happen in questions of discipline. If, therefore, the Theological Commission cannot admit mixed commissions with other commissions, which have been established for the purpose of study, it can do so even less with the secretariats, whose aim is not study."

[80] "The Theological Commission has been composed of sixty persons from different regions, rites, and theological schools; with different tendencies, not only conservative, but also progressive; and while some examine more the positive part, others concentrate on the speculative, moral, juridical, mystical, ecumenical part. This is why it is difficult to deal with a doctrinal point in the Central Commission that has not been more fully debated in the Theological Commission."

Ecclesia, scandalizantur; et si dicimus eos esse membra Ecclesiae Catholicae Romanae, quae est Corpus Christi, scandalizantur adhuc vehementius"[81] (p. 10).

"Sanctus Petrus pro gubernio externo Ecclesiae post ascensionem Christi, sese habet ad Apostolos sicut antea sese habuit ad Apostolos ipse Dominus" [82] (p. 11).

"(Hodie) ne scandalizemus fratres separatos, verba 'schisma' et 'haeresis' absolute sunt *tabu* (cf. the remarks of Döpfner and Bea) ... Jure rogari potest num hoc sit mens S. Pauli et S. Joannis, immo Christi Domini, qui dixit (Mt 18:17): "Si Ecclesiam non audierit, sit tibi ethnicus et publicanus." Etiam fideles scandalizari possunt, et hodie scandalizantur"[83] (p. 11).

Commissio centralis "caret tum competentia juridica, tum practica. Nam nulla gaudet auctoritate doctrinali, et in ea quidem est maxima libertas criticae, attamen seria replicatio ad objectiones est impossibilis." (On the whole series of questions that have just been enumerated), "Commissio theologica post continuas disputationes venit ad Conclusiones, a quibus ipsa nullo modo recedere potest"[84] (p. 12).

"... de Corpore illo mystico-juridico-sociali ..."[85] (p. 15).

"Commissio theologica putat non esse accedendum ad votum Emin-morum Döpfner et Alfrink, dicendi nempe Christum Ecclesiam non solum aedificasse super Petrum, sed etiam super collegium apostolorum. Etenim non necessario omnia dicenda sunt; prae aliis Christus aedificavit Ecclesiam *super seipsum*. Deinde omnino alio modo Christus aedificavit Ecclesiam super Petrum quam super Collegium apostolicum.

---

[81] "On this matter, we can never satisfy the separated brothers. For if we deny that they are members of the Body of Christ, which is the Church, they are scandalized; and if we say that they are members of the Roman Catholic Church, which is the Body of Christ, they are even more highly scandalized."

[82] "After the Ascension of Christ, Saint Peter, as far as the exterior government of the Church was concerned, occupied the same place with regard to the apostles as the Lord himself had previously done with regard to the apostles."

[83] "Today, in order not to scandalize our separated brothers, the words 'schism' and 'heresy' are absolutely taboo ... It could justly be asked whether this is consonant with the mind of Saint Paul and Saint John, or even that of Christ our Lord, who said: 'If [the offender] refuses to listen even to the church, let him be to you as a Gentile and a tax collector' (Mt 18:17). The faithful can also be scandalized, and are scandalized today."

[84] "The Central Commission lacks both juridical and practical competence. In reality, it enjoys no doctrinal authority; within it, there is the greatest freedom for criticism, yet a serious response to the objections is impossible. The Theological Commission, after coninuous debates, has come to conclusions on which it can in no way yield."

[85] "Concerning that mystical-juridical-social body".

Nam ... Christus eamdem super Petrum aedificavit, non formaliter ut Apostolum, sed ut Vicarium sui ..."[86] (pp. 18–19).

"Certum est in Constitutionibus aliarum Commissionum res dogmaticas tractari non posse, nisi revideantur a Commissione theologica, quae hac in re nihil revidendum accepit"[87] (p. 30).

"Quando Episcopi loquuntur de semetipsis, id modo modesto et simplici faciant, maxime nunc quando in multis locis sparguntur voces Episcopos Romam venturos, ut sua jura contra centralismum Romanum vindicent"[88] (p. 31).

"Commissio theologica revisoria"[89] (p. 39).

Sunday, November 18, 1962. – I was invited to the "Mater Dei" boarding house by Bishop Volk of Mainz. There were about 18 of us: 6 German bishops (Schröffer,[1] bishop of Eichstätt; H. Schäufele,[2] from Freiburg, Volk, from Mainz; P. Rusch, from Innsbruck, etc.); 4 French bishops (Garrone, Elchinger, Pourchet, and the auxiliary of Lille);[3] theologians from Germany, France, Belgium, Holland ...

Bishop Volk: This is an absolutely private meeting, to examine freely among ourselves how we can get out of this impasse. There are various misunderstandings within the council. Three in particular. 1. On the word "pastoral": it is not a question of using pastoral perspectives as

---

[86]"The Theological Commission thinks that it cannot agree with the *votum* of their Eminences Döpfner and Alfrink when they say (do they not?) that the Church of Christ was built not only on Peter but also on the college of apostles. Indeed, it is not necessary to say everything; Christ built the Church above all *on himself.* Then, in an altogether different way, Christ built the Church on Peter, rather than on the college of apostles. Indeed,... Christ built the Church on Peter, not as an apostle, but as his Vicar."

[87]"It is certain that dogmatic questions cannot be treated in the constitutions of the other commissions unless they are revised by the Theological Commission, which has received nothing to revise in this area."

[88]"When the bishops speak about themselves, let them do so in a simple and humble manner, especially now that in numerous places rumors are spreading that the bishops have come to Rome to demand their rights against Roman centralism."

[89]"The revisory Theological Commission".

November 18

[1]Joseph Schröffer (1903–1983), German, ordained in 1928. Bishop of Eichstätt from 1948 to 1967, he became secretary of the Congregation for Seminaries and Universities from 1967 to 1976 and was created cardinal in 1976. Member of the Preparatory Theological Commission, then of the Doctrinal Commission.

[2]Herman Josef Schäufele (1906–1972), German, ordained in 1931. Bishop of Freiburg from 1958 until his death. Member of the Commission for Bishops and the Government of Dioceses.

[3]Henri Dupont (1896–1972), French, ordained in 1923. Auxiliary bishop of Lille from 1951 until his death.

a pretext for diminishing doctrinal density and fullness. – 2. On scholasticism: To criticize a language that is too scholastic in a conciliar text is not to find fault with scholasticism as science; we must nonetheless insert into the schema certain elements of the faith that cannot be translated into the language of the Schools and that are nevertheless doctrinally necessary. – 3. On the ecumenical aspect: the impression could be given that there might be a willingness to dilute the doctrine to make it acceptable; no; on the contrary, we want to express the totality of Catholic doctrine, of which there are important elements among our separated brothers. We want to reclaim the totality of the Catholic patrimony. The Eastern Churches and the Protestants have been led to go more deeply into certain elements than we have. – The Board of Presidency met yesterday evening; what decisions will they have made? – Let those who are members devote themselves to clearing up the misunderstandings that I have just indicated, in a language that is more objective than emotional.

Archbishop Garrone: yes, we must clear up misunderstandings as much as possible, and Bishop Volk has pointed out very well the principal ones. But let us see them clearly, without minimizing them. They are deeply rooted. Example: when someone says that pastoral concerns get in the way of the integrity of the doctrine, that points to a certain conception of doctrine. Let us be more precise: for some, doctrine consists essentially of formulas. Everything that we might desire as being rooted in the Bible or of vital significance appears to them to be something merely added on externally. For some, indeed, the events recounted in the Gospels seem to have no other reason for being other than to generate ideas.

The bishop of Innsbruck:[4] We must realize the difference in the objectives intended by the authors of the schema – and by the others. Our aim is not one particular school or theory: we want to bring the Catholic response to the men of today.

Bishop Elchinger: What did the preparatory commission have as its objective?

Bishop Schröffer: the Theological Commission was bound by a more rigorous secrecy than the others. So let everything that is going to be said remain secret.

Elchinger: Is it true that that commission was asked to recapitulate the teachings of the ordinary magisterium for the last fifty years?

[4] Paulus Rusch.

Schröffer: It was said that the Holy Father had signed the daily agenda for the commission. So it received the themes to be dealt with but not a ban on dealing with others.

Msgr. Philips (prof. at Louvain): The list of proposed subjects was a summary of what the Holy Office considers current, widespread errors. Hence its disparate character. On the other hand, the texts have been prepared by authors of the same frame of mind; it was impossible afterward to change the perspective. The instructions of the pope: "no condemnations", was understood to mean simply: no formulas of anathema. – There are, between the two groups that confront each other now, a divergence, not only in their way of doing theology, but in their way of understanding the faith. However, there is hope. Let us try to understand the others in the same way as we try to understand non-Catholics.

Karl Rahner: It is necessary to know the thinking of the Theological Commission. It seems that they now want to make of these schemas one vast dogmatic definition.

Schröffer: In the preparatory commission, I posed that question. Many people were worried. I received a response that was official, firm, categorical: we work as in the past; it will be up to the theologians to examine the theological qualifications; the only definitions of faith will be those that the Church very explicitly presents as such. Then, in the conciliar commission, in September, the question was posed again, in writing; for, without norms for reaching conclusions, there was a risk of still more serious confusion. Again a firm response: these chapters are not definitions; it will be up to the theologians to clarify them. Such was the response of Father Tromp.

Father Häring: The small group that has directed everything is of the persuasion that it must achieve its ends by employing power. Hence the choice of subcommissions Cf. certain lies told by Ottaviani yesterday morning. We must ask that Fathers Lyonnet and Zerwick be restored to their teaching positions at the Biblical Institute: that today is a symbolic point that will decide many things.

Father K. Rahner: It is said that after the criticisms made by the Central Commission, when the text was returned, the Holy Office, on its own authority, eliminated a good number of amendments. That is inadmissible. For the Holy Office is under the authority of the council, and not the other way round.

Philips: the observations of the Central Commission were transmitted to Cardinal Ottaviani, and Father Tromp was given the task of responding to them in the name of the Theological Commission, but without consulting the members. For most of the criticisms, this amounted to a total rejection. – Similarly, we had never seen as a commission the chapter "De novissimis". – Similarly, it was on opening the printed volume that we first saw polygenism declared to be "contra fidem catholicam":[5] no one had ever said that to us ...

Ego:[6] My testimony agrees with that of Msgr. Philips. Also, while endorsing the analysis of the situation he has just made and sharing his wishes, I am a little less optimistic than he is. With a number of bishops, one can hope to overcome misunderstandings and opposition. But with a small leading group the hope is less: for they are fixed in their attitude of being supreme judges.

Philips: However, on the other hand, there is great astonishment. So those in this small group are disposed, I think, to make concessions. We have scored a point, by shaking their assurance. They must resign themselves to seek a compromise.

Elchinger: Let us arrive at some practical conclusions. The duty of charity cannot induce us to sidestep the truth. – In our boarding house, there is a group of Italian bishops. We had entered into relations with them. Out of ten, nine had agreed to sign a proposal that I had drawn up ... Now, since the meeting of the Italian episcopate around Cardinal Siri, it is impossible to meet with them. It is as if they were hounded, and we, "vitandi".[7]

Volk: If the discussion has not been free enough in the course of the preparatory commission, now, in the general congregation, we can speak.

Rahner (a long intervention): we must indeed realize the situation. Either the schema will be rejected, and then it will be necessary for the commission to prepare a new one; in that circumstance, we will have to bring to it a positive collaboration, not aiming too high, in order to arrive at least at a compromise. We should be the last to want to impose our ideas. – Or else, if the current schema is accepted as a basis for discussion, it will be necessary to take it article by article, line by line, word by word, in order to bring about profound changes. Even if we do not succeed in correcting everything, it will perhaps not be catastrophic.

---

[5] "Contrary to the Catholic faith".

[6] "Me".

[7] "To be shunned" [a reference to the canonical expression applied to those who have been excommunicated *vitandi*].

With this schema more than the second,[8] there are possible arrangements. But let us determine wisely the precise points on which we must say: "Non possumus".[9] Consent to crawl, to swallow any affront, in order to wage absolute battle over some points. Prepare ammunition for that. Spread studies among the council Fathers, furnish them with materials, explanations.

Elchinger: Never has Father Rahner shown himself more conciliatory!

Rahner: Of course, I am a Christian. But I wish with all my heart for the rejection of the schema. However, in the contrary case, we must not lose courage. We must spare the Holy Father a situation that would be too painful; determine the three essential points on which no concession is possible.

Philips. – In the second eventuality, Msgr. Cerfaux would be willing to work with us.

Daniélou. – In either situation, the same fundamental questions will have to be dealt with. I propose a method of working: on each essential point, form a small team of theologians or exegetes (of divergent views, but without calling on those with whom it is impossible to collaborate), who would compose a text and would submit it to a commission of bishops. This text could then be utilized, in one manner or another, according to circumstances. We must not have each person working independently, with no coordination.

(There followed a dialogue, in which I intervened with some others, on the practical manner of organizing this type of work.)

Garrone: Would it be good to ask that the study of the schema be done "viribus unitis utriusque commissionis"[10] (= of the Doctrinal Commission and the Secretariat for Unity)?

Rahner: It would be good to complete Archbishop Garrone's proposition by another, which would not introduce anything new. Let the right of the president to call on periti be also the right of each member to bring his own peritus. Certain periti of merit have already left Rome because they were not being employed. Bishop Paul Rusch (Innsbruck) has already presented this wish on behalf of the German episcopate.

Rusch (Innsbruck): The cardinal from Vienna (König) has just told me that there has not yet been a response on this subject; but he will insist on being accompanied by Fr. Rahner.

---

[8] This refers to the *De Fontibus* and the *De Deposito fidei*, respectively.

[9] "We cannot" [a reference to the response of Peter and John to the high priests and elders, who wanted to forbid them from preaching the Gospel (Acts 4:20)].

[10] "By the united forces of the two commissions".

Rahner: In any case, let the theologians work outside of the commissions to prepare solid texts.

Grillmeier: That is what others are doing. I saw, coming out of a small room, Fr. Tromp, Msgr. Fenton, and two or three others, who had just been working together.

Volk: They have the right to hold private meetings, and so do we.

Elchinger: I think that there should be an intervention made, difficult no doubt, but necessary: let it be said that we really must work together, in the service of the council and in such a way as to encourage worthy theologians and exegetes. Following on Döpfner's intervention, this would be a new shock.

Schäufele (Freiburg): Cardinal Ottaviani has emphasized the very open composition of his commission, the different schools represented, the unanimity obtained, etc.

Eichstätt:[11] He wants at all costs to prevent the rejection of the schema. But the rules of the council are there.

Innsbruck: One of the speakers at the council ought to pose this question to the president clearly: Yes or no, is this a matter of definitions of the faith, texts claiming to be imposed in the very name of the faith? If Cardinal Ottaviani says: yes, let a member of the Central Commission remark: How is it that the two commissions, Preparatory Theological and Central, were told the opposite?

Mainz:[12] In the first schema, the fifth chapter would be the easiest to accept. Others would need to be summarized. What is essentially lacking is an exposition, longer and truer, on revelation. We must also consider the situation of the believer in the world and how he will react to it: that also is important for doctrine.

Daniélou: We could get together with some theologians this afternoon; for example, at the Gregorian, before the reception that is supposed to take place there. Between 4 and 5 P.M., we could try to organize the work.

Ratzinger: One thing is essential: let us make sure that periti of diverse tendencies are heard within the commission. Without that, there will be no real and sincere work.

Mainz: It is also essential that the bishops who are members of the Doctrinal Commission be in close contact with the theologians who are doing the work.

---

[11] Joseph Schröffer.
[12] Hermann Volk.

Semmelroth:[13] We should also try to get a modification of the rules: that the periti really be able to intervene within the commission; otherwise, they will be useless there.

Eichstätt: A request on that subject is underway: when three members of the commission request that a theologian be heard, that he be given the floor.

Innsbruck: I am happy with Archbishop Garrone's very realistic proposition that the schema be worked on in a mixed commission (doctrinal, and Secretariat for Unity). That can be done without changing the rules.

Mainz: I am not very optimistic. Several times already the Secretariat has wanted to make contact with the Theological Commission; the president of the commission has refused.

Eichstätt: In that commission (preparatory), I myself, for the questions concerning the problem of ecumenism, asked for a collaboration with the Secretariat. I was told: there can be no question of that.

Mainz: Who would agree to intervene in the general congregation, to ask for what Bishop Schäufele has suggested?

Grillmeier: And let us also not forget, either, in taking and organizing our notes, to prepare the future history of the council: Already Msgr. Jedin,[14] here in Rome, is taking an active interest in that.

It has been confirmed to me that the report introducing the discussion of the schema De fontibus had been prepared by Fr. Tromp. But it was, they said, so violent that the evening before, Cardinal Ottaviani decided to discard it and write another one during the night.

At 2:30 P.M., visit from Bishop Paul Seitz, accompanied by his theologian, Father Dournes, both of them from the Foreign Missions. They submitted to me two drafts prepared for the intervention Bishop Seitz will make tomorrow. I chose the one by the theologian; the bishop abandoned his own draft with good grace. I proposed some cuts and various corrections.

At 4 P.M., meeting of the theologians who had gotten together that morning, in a parlor of the Biblical Institute. Fr. Daniélou, who had taken the initiative on this, proposed a division into small groups among which he would distribute the work. I am to specialize in the critical examination of the texts that I have seen drafted.

---

[13] Otto Semmelroth, S.J. (1912–1979), German, ordained in 1939. Professor of dogmatics at the Jesuit scholasticate of Frankfurt. Expert at the council beginning with the third session.

[14] Hubert Jedin (1900–1980), German, professor of Church history at the university of Bonn. He had written the history of the Council of Trent. Expert at the council.

At 5 P.M., reception at the Gregorian. Numerous guests present, Romans and non-Romans. Chatted with many of them. A photo was taken of me with Father Gagnebet, of the Angelicum and the Holy Office.

At 7 P.M., with Father Congar, we went to see Bishop Elchinger, who had invited us. He is staying at a hotel with Bishops Schmitt (Metz), Flusin[15] (Saint-Claude), the auxiliary of Lille,[16] and another French bishop. Elchinger, Congar, and I continued the morning conversation. Dined with the bishops. Then, a brief conversation with the American and Italian bishops who were staying at that hotel. Chatted with the bishop of Mantua,[17] – Virgil's homeland. Bishop Flusin drove us back in his car. The auxiliary of Lille reminded me that he had come to see me long ago, in Lyon, when he was a student; he told me that he was pondering an intervention at the council. These bishops seem not to appreciate very much certain behavior by Card. Ottaviani.

Monday, November 19, 1962. – Chatted, on Saint Peter's Square, with Canon Thils,[1] from Louvain, who told me that Cardinal Döpfner did not want to use all of his documents "in order not to cause too painful a spectacle". Met Bishop Courbe in Saint Peter's; he was wondering how we will get out of this impasse, and he appeared harsh, in his always nuanced manner, toward the Theological Commission. Father Khalifé, S.J., from Beirut, told me that the Maronite patriarch,[2] whose theologian he is, did not wish to intervene in the debate or to let another Maronite bishop intervene. I took a seat in the corner gallery, to the left of the row of cardinals, beside Father Congar. I saw Cardinal Gracias (Bombay), who has been back from India for two days, pass by. We also greeted Bishop Hakim. Before Mass, I saw Cardinals Frings, Alfrink, and Döpfner conferring. I gave Msgr. Lafortune back the fascicle he loaned me the day before yesterday (remarks on the criticisms

---

[15] Claude Flusin (1911–1979), French, ordained in 1937. Bishop of Saint-Claude from 1948 to 1975.

[16] Henri Dupont.

[17] Antonio Poma (1910–1985), Italian, ordained in 1933. Bishop of Mantua from 1954 to 1968. Created cardinal in 1969. Member of the Doctrinal Commission starting with the second session.

November 19

[1] Gustave Thils (1909–2000), Belgian, professor of fundamental theology at the Catholic university of Louvain, he was engaged in the ecumenical movement. Member of the Secretariat for Unity and an expert at the council.

[2] Pierre Paul Meouchi.

of the Central Commission concerning the schema *De Ecclesia*). Father Congar gave me the conciliar *Prooemium* draft that he has written and had reproduced.

Cardinal De Arriba[3] (Tarragona, Spain): We must proceed to the discussion of the articles. The arguments for its prior rejection are not good. "Opportunissimum est uti forma scolastica contra errores. Multi loquuntur hodie in detrimentum auctoritatis Sacrae Scripturae. Scriptura debet intelligi ad mentem Ecclesiae."[4] Let us remember the Monita and other Acts of the Biblical Commission, the Holy Office, etc., on the perils and deviations in biblical matters. People are talking here of pastoral concerns: that is good; but before all else, truth. We can add a Prooemium, make some corrections, etc. – He implored the council: "ut simus unum, approbando schema nobis datum a S. Pontifice."[5] A hymn to the necessity of truth. Invocation of the Blessed Virgin and St. Joseph.

Cardinal Norman Gilroy (Sydney): The schema is good, but everyone desires a better presentation. "Oportet ut tolerantiam habeamus erga alias sententias non erroneas. Amice contendere debemus",[6] so that we can come to an agreement. – He made some practical propositions. He reminded us that we are dealing with a dogmatic constitution, which must have universal value and transcend time. He repeated the argument about its very careful preparation, made by eminent men from all over, etc. "Ergo schema dignum est quod a nobis sincere consideretur."[7] Besides, we have the right to reject it or approve it.

Card. Valérien Gracias (Bombay). He apologized for having been absent. – Let us get a constitution that is brief, clear, adapted to current needs, that can truly help us in our task as pastors. Must we conserve substantially the present schema or reject it en bloc? I propose a via media. The discussion of the schema as it is would be interminable. It has been composed by eminent men, etc., yes: "sed, ob graves rationes,

---

[3] Benjamín de Arriba y Castro (1886–1973), Spanish, ordained in 1912. Archbishop of Tarragona from 1949 to 1970, created cardinal in 1953.

[4] "It is very opportune to use the scholastic form against errors. Many are speaking today to the detriment of the authority of Sacred Scripture. Scripture must be understood according to the interpretation of the Church."

[5] "Let us be united in approving the schema that the Supreme Pontiff has given us."

[6] "We must be tolerant toward other opinions not marred by error. We must discuss as friends."

[7] "Hence this schema merits to be given honest consideration by us."

recondendum est. Nulla spes enim apparet"[8] that it will obtain a sufficient number of votes. It would be better to seek a solution immediately rather than try to rewrite it article by article. I do not say: "non placet", because that expression is harsh; but I say: "non satisfacit".[9] Therefore let us draft a new schema, as happened at Vatican I, with Fathers and theologians of various tendencies. "Summus Pontifex ipse approbavit schema, sed"[10] in the sense that he offered it for our discussion "vel admittendo, vel rejiciendo, vel corrigendo".[11] "In necessariis unitas, in dubiis libertas, in omnibus caritas."[12] We will be able to demonstrate this to the observers. The members of the Preparatory Theological Commission did not have the charism that the Holy Spirit gives to the council. So let us write a schema that all can approve.

Card. Albert G. Meyer (Chicago): "In concilio, duae sententiae oppositae."[13] The schema does not agree with the goal of the council set forth by the Holy Father: hence the concern on the part of many among us. The Holy Spirit is promised to us, but that does not dispense us from proceeding "caute et studiose",[14] etc. – He joined in the very wise propositions of Dom Butler and Cardinal Gracias. "Atqui, stante hoc schemate, numquam unanimitas obtineri poterit. Res maximi momenti";[15] we must be able to show the world our unanimity. Card. Bea made some very wise remarks in this regard. So let us draft a new schema, retaining everything from this one that can help achieve our objective, "cooperantibus theologis et exegetis variarum nationum et tendentiarum".[16] Let us express in it the Church's confidence in her exegetes; let us remind these exegetes of the obligation to conform to the interpretations given by the magisterium; let us take up again the directives given by Pius XII.

Card. Juan Landázuri Ricketts (Lima, Peru): The schema is very good. It is "scholastic": but is that a fault or a good quality? On certain

---

[8] "But for grave reasons, it should be set aside. For in fact, no hope appears."

[9] "It is not satisfactory."

[10] "The Supreme Pontiff himself has approved this schema, but".

[11] "Either to be accepted or rejected or corrected".

[12] "In necessary matters, unity; in doubtful ones, liberty; in all things, charity." [A maxim often attributed to Saint Augustine, although that is uncertain.]

[13] "In the council, there are two contrary opinions."

[14] "Prudently and diligently".

[15] "And, as the schema now stands, unanimity can never be obtained. The matter is of very great importance."

[16] "With the collaboration of theologians and exegetes of various nations and viewpoints".

secondary points, we could argue without end. Some say that it does not have an "indoles pastoralis":[17] but it is not necessary that this indoles[18] appear in every line. – "Unitas fontis, aut duplicitas? Revelatio unica, per duo media. Card. Frings claro modo hoc expressit, distinguendo ordinem essendi et ordinem cognoscendi."[19] But one could also call "fontes" the "duo tramites".[20] In this way, an agreement is possible. For that, change the title. – Some have argued also over the appropriateness of settling questions that do not appear to have fully matured; but that is not a reason to reject the whole schema. Placet juxta modum. Let us stop the general discussion (or let us stop after the general discussion?).[21]

Card. Laurent Rugambwa (Bukoba, Tanganyika): The schema (and the others) will be contested "in ipsa sua substantia et in ipsis suis principiis".[22] The same arguments will always be repeated on both sides. Now, in matters of dogma, a simple majority is not sufficient: it is necessary to obtain more than two-thirds. "Hoc non est tantum optabile, sed necessarium. Propterea propono":[23] let us ask the Holy Father to defer the subject to a later examination; let theologians and exegetes work at redoing the schema. Let us pass on immediately to the study of a non-dogmatic schema.

Msgr. ... (New Caledonia):[24] "Jam argumenta varia sunt plene exposita et apparent plene opposita. Tantum afferam unum argumentum, magni momenti. Capitulum tertium separat doctrinam de Christo et factum Christi (cf. elsewhere as well, and in the De deposito, chap. 4). Nonne est revelatio in Christo Jesu? etc. Sunt objecta fidei facta Christi, quorum testes sunt Apostoli."[25] It does not give Christ the place that falls to him in Scriptura et in Traditione.[26] Let us omit in this schema everything that it is not necessary to repeat. Let us make use of the preceding

---

[17] "A pastoral character".

[18] "This character".

[19] "One or two sources? There is a unique revelation, by two paths. Cardinal Frings explained that clearly by distinguishing the order of being and the order of knowledge."

[20] "Sources", the "two paths".

[21] He wished to stop the general discussion of the schema. See AS, I, 3, 170–71.

[22] "In its very substance and in its very principles".

[23] "This is not only desirable, it is necessary. For that reason, I propose".

[24] Pierre Martin.

[25] "Various arguments have already been fully presented and appear to be completely opposed. I will only put forward one argument, of great importance. The third chapter separates the doctrine on Christ and the actions of Christ. Is not revelation constituted by Jesus Christ? There are actions of Christ that are objects of faith and whose witnesses are the apostles."

[26] "In Scripture and in tradition".

councils and other ecclesiastical texts, which expressed themselves much better than the present schema. Let us make a single constitution out of the material in schemas 1 and 2. And let this new text "aperte nuntiet Christum".[27]

Bishop Luis E. Henríquez Jimenez[28] (Venezuela): In the name of the Episcopal Conference of Venezuela: "Schema non admittatur."[29] Let the commission work, listening to the Biblical Commission, on producing a new schema. The present schema wants to dismiss the opinions of numerous excellent theologians. It must express only "fidem universalem Ecclesiae".[30] Let us compare the encyclical "Providentissimus"[31] with "Divino afflante" or similar decrees of the Biblical Commission: one will see that opinions change, that progress is achieved: we must not stop this movement. We must not read Scripture solely according to the magisterium, but, as the magisterium teaches, according to the whole of tradition. – The pope leaves us free. Without doubt, he proposes the matter to us, but he does not impose the form on us. Cardinal Döpfner has shown this well. Stress has been laid on the distinguished knowledge of the schema's writers: but that is not the question. Let us discuss another topic while waiting for the new schema.

(Fr. Congar spoke in my ear: A few days ago I gave a conference to the bishops of Venezuela; so sometimes the work serves a purpose.)

Bishop Griffiths, auxiliary of New York (who was a member of the preparatory commission): "Post tot oratores sapientiores, elegantiores, etc., possumus dicere: Domine, tota nocte laboravimus, et nihil cepimus. Tamen, in tuo nomine etc."[32] – We all agree that we want to speak the truth and find the best means of presenting it. But immediately after that differences arise. We must get out of this. Clerus et fideles[33] would be troubled by these disagreements: the more so because the biblical controversy, a very serious matter, is rampant everywhere, inside and

---

[27] "Openly proclaim Christ".

[28] Luis E. Henríquez Jiménez (1913–1991), Venezuelan, ordained in 1937. Auxiliary bishop of Caracas from 1962 to 1972. Member of the Doctrinal Commission beginning with the second session.

[29] "The schema cannot be accepted."

[30] "The universal faith of the Church".

[31] The encyclical *Providentissimus Deus* of Leo XIII, promulgated on November 18, 1893, on the study of Sacred Scripture.

[32] "After so many speakers, so wise, so distinguished, etc., we can say: Lord, we have worked all night, and we have caught nothing. But, in your name, etc." [An allusion to Lk 5:5.]

[33] "Priests and faithful".

outside the Church; we cannot escape the world's notice. "Schema est exponendum, abbreviandum, corrigendum."[34] Keep what is good in it. "Recognoscere".[35] Let each side make its positions clear. Let us follow a via media. It is necessary that we arrive at "etsi minima, saltem sana et pura",[36] to give to the clergy and the people. For ecumenism, cf. Cardinal Bea.

Bishop Émile De Smedt[37] (Bruges), in the name of the Secretariat for Unity: "In schematis discussione",[38] the question of the ecumenical point of view has come up several times. Perhaps it would be good for to the Fathers to hear "in quo praecise consistat oecumenicitas, quid requiratur in doctrina et stylo schematis",[39] in order better to serve the cause of unity. – All Christians concur in that they all believe in Christ. "Sed, quomodo? Discordia."[40] This discord is contrary to the will of God. When will it cease? In the course of the centuries, "utraque pars"[41] thought that it would suffice to set out its own doctrine, in its own language. Proceeding in this fashion, not only have we not obtained unity, not only have we failed to come to an understanding, "sed creverunt praejudicia, suspiciones, etc. Unde, nova methodus":[42] ecumenism. Its characteristic: "cura non solum de veritate, sed de modo quo doctrina exponenda est, ut possit intellegi clare et exacte."[43] Ecumenical dialogue "non est deliberatio, nec tractatio, nec certamen; sed, ex utraque parte, serena et lucida testificatio de propria fide. Atqui, volente Summo Pontifice",[44] the ecumenical spirit must preside at our council. But to compose schemas in an ecumenical style is not a simple matter. We have to display the full and unabridged Catholic truth, "nullo modo trunca nec confusa. Non loquimur ut decipiantur alii!"[45] So it is necessary to fulfill

---

[34] "The schema should be put forward, abridged, corrected."

[35] "Revise".

[36] "Something, even if it is very short, at least sound and pure".

[37] Emiel Jozef De Smedt (1909–1995), Belgian, ordained in 1933. Bishop of Bruges from 1952 to 1984. Member of the Secretariat for Unity. He was the relator for the schema on religious liberty.

[38] "In the discussion of the schema".

[39] "In what, precisely, this ecumenical character consists, what it requires in terms of the doctrine and the style of the schema".

[40] "But, how? There is discord."

[41] "Each party".

[42] "But prejudices and suspicions have increased. Hence, a new method."

[43] "A concern not only for truth but also for the manner in which the doctrine must be presented, so that it might be understood clearly and precisely".

[44] "Is neither a debate nor a negotiation nor a contest; but, on both sides, a serene and lucid testimony of each one's own faith. So, in accordance with the desire of the Supreme Pontiff".

[45] "In no way truncated or confused. We must not speak so as to mislead others!"

at one and the same time "multas conditiones".[46] We can distinguish nine of these; I will only indicate a few of them. "Scire debemus quid sit hodierna doctrina orthodoxorum et protestantium; in quo nobiscum concordent et e contra quid non sit satis explicitum in doctrina catholica; quid non sit aliis christianis intelligibile. Exempli gratia, aliquis pure rationalis modus loquendi, pro Orthodoxis",[47] who are nurtured by Scripture and the Fathers. – The Holy Father has summoned specialists to the Secretariat for Unity; he wants the secretariat to help the council, especially its Doctrinal Commission. "Propter rationes de quibus mihi non est judicandum, noluit Commissio theologica"[48] (it has rejected all collaboration, every offer of service); that is why the secretariat has had to work alone. "Nunc, humiliter rogamus ut velint Patres examinare an sufficienter examinata sit nova methodus. – Conclusio: Munus accepimus laborandi ut dialogus feliciter procedat in hoc concilio. Hoc schema notabiliter deficit in oecumenicitate. Non constituit progressum, sed regressum; non adjutorium, sed impedimentum, immo nocumentum. Hora est providentialis, sed hora est gravis."[49] If the schemas are not rewritten "alio modo in commissione",[50] we will have lost "magnam, immensam spem".[51] We will have acted against the ardent desire of the Holy Father. – The speaker implored the Fathers to work "ad fraternam unionem".[52] (Applause.)

Bishop David De Sousa[53] of Funchal (Portugal): He proposed various improvements and a new article. He was surprised that some were extolling the Vulgate and not the original text. "Nova versio latina praeparetur",[54] etc.

---

[46] "Numerous conditions".

[47] "We must know what is the current doctrine of the Orthodox and of the Protestants, on what they agree with us, and, on the contrary, what is not explicit enough in the Catholic doctrine; what is not comprehensible to other Christians. For example, for the Orthodox, a certain purely rational manner of speaking."

[48] "For reasons it is not my part to judge, the Theological Commission has refused".

[49] "Now, we humbly ask that the Fathers be willing to examine whether this new method has been sufficiently examined. Conclusion: we have been given the task of working to ensure that the dialogue proceeds successfully in this council. This schema is notably lacking in ecumenicity. It constitutes regress, not progress; it is not a help, but a hindrance, even a harm. The hour is providential, but the hour is grave."

[50] "In a different way in commission".

[51] "A great, immense hope".

[52] "With a view to fraternal unity".

[53] David de Sousa, O.F.M. (1911–2006), Portuguese, ordained in 1937. Bishop of Funchal from 1957 to 1965, then archbishop of Evora until 1981.

[54] "Let a new Latin version be prepared."

Archbishop Garrone of Toulouse: Praise for De Smedt's intervention. The objective of this schema causes us some anxiety. Each one of us is ready, "juvante gratia Dei, vitam suam ponere tam pro fratribus, quam pro uno verbo quod procedit de ore Dei. Sollicitudo omnium gentium, sollicitudo veritatis":[55] there is no opposition between the two. "Verbum hoc non est nostrum, sed Dei."[56] But how do we reach the proposed end? We cannot treat these questions "januis clausis";[57] the whole world is listening to us, and it is necessary that it understand us. The form of the schema is too scholastic; it is necessary that we say: "*Hodie* ad vos verbum Dei annuntiatur"[58] ... Three suggestions: "1. Prooemium detur de revelatione. – 2. Recognoscatur schema ut respondeat desideriis Patrum."[59] – 3. For certain points that demand technical discussion, "ad commissionem res referatur";[60] but let the two commissions, "de doctrina et de unitate, ad hoc opus convenient".[61]

An Italian bishop:[62] We need to add something on the magisterium; say that, in teaching and in condemning, it fulfills its pastoral office.

A Spaniard[63] ...?

An American, USA:[64] "Schema est summi valoris. Pastoralis est scopus concilii; sed nihil plus pastorale quam hoc schema."[65] Entitle it De Verbo Dei.[66] Have it revised by the Secretariat for Unity. Not a single council before this one has been first of all pastoral: this is the first. Dom Butler is right: we need, for the revision, a "coetus bipartitus".[67] Those who are charged with making the schema more pastoral do not understand that in the same sense as those who are giving them the task. At

---

[55] "With the help of the grace of God, to give his life as much for his brothers as for one word that comes from the mouth of God [see Mt 4:4]. Concern for all peoples, concern for the truth".

[56] "This word is not ours but God's."

[57] "Behind closed doors".

[58] "*Today*, the word of God is announced to you."

[59] "1. Let there be a prooemium on revelation. 2. Let the schema be revised so that it corresponds to the desires of the Fathers."

[60] "Let the matter be referred to a commission."

[61] "The Doctrinal and the one for Unity, join together for this work".

[62] Giuseppe D'Avack.

[63] Aurelio Del Pino Gómez.

[64] In fact, it was Denis E. Hurley, O.M.I (1915–2004), a South African (not an American), ordained in 1939. Archbishop of Durban from 1951 to 1992. Member of the Commission for Seminaries, Studies, and Catholic Education.

[65] "The schema is of very great value. The aim of the council is pastoral; but there is nothing more pastoral than this schema."

[66] "On the Word of God".

[67] "Bipartisan group".

the Central Commission, "clamabamus in deserto."[68] We were lacking someone to direct the debates, recall the goal of the council, etc.; we lacked a head. (Cardinal Ruffini made gestures of great impatience or disagreement ...). "Profundum est discrimen de interpretatione finis Concilii. Res dirimenda est."[69] Let the pope establish a commission for that. Review, shorten, reform the schemas. In this way the original sin that has tainted the preparation of the council will be atoned for.

Bishop Joseph Ruotolo[70] of Ugento (Italy). There are two opinions. I hold to the first: let us discuss the articles of the schema immediately. However, I do not reject all the arguments of the other party. "Ad obtinendam unanimitatem, inveniri debet honorabilis quaedam compositio."[71] This is very desirable, and it is possible. "Conficiatur aliquod Prooemium",[72] which would apply to all the doctrinal schemas, indeed, to the whole council, in which salvation history would be summarized. Create for this purpose a coetus[73] of Fathers from both parties. And while that is going on, let us move on to a discussion of the articles. That will not present as many drawbacks as some fear. Some have spoken to us about anxieties: by bringing their opposing views into confrontation, the Fathers will be satisfied in the end; otherwise ... Conclusion: All have spoken well of the Holy Father; this shows to everyone, and especially to our separated brothers, that he is the sole vinculum unitatis.[74]

Bishop Alfred Ancel (auxiliary of Lyon): He supported the position of Butler, Pourchet, Zoa. I add something that should help in obtaining moral unanimity. No path appears to be open. However, let us not exaggerate the difficulty. "Maneamus in doctrina fideles et in sollicitudine pastorali."[75] A practical solution is more difficult to find. It is impossible for the schema "ordinario modo emendatum"[76] to please everyone, and if the pope wanted to propose for our discussion a new schema, there would be no hope that this new schema would gather the necessary

---

[68] "We were crying out in the desert."

[69] "There is a deep rift on the interpretation of the council's aim. It is a matter that must be resolved."

[70] Giuseppe Ruotolo (1898–1970), Italian, ordained in 1922. Bishop of Ugento-Santa Maria di Leuca from 1937 to 1968.

[71] "To reach unanimity, an honorable compromise must be found."

[72] "Let a prooemium be prepared."

[73] "Group".

[74] "Bond of unity".

[75] "Let us remain faithful in doctrine and in pastoral concern."

[76] "Corrected in the usual manner".

two-thirds of the votes, either. – The renovatio textus[77] cannot be done by those who drafted it. Let us not imagine a miracle, but let us unite our good wills. I propose a solution while waiting for someone to present a better one, if one can be found. I support Archbishop Garrone, with one addition: 1. In concilio, specialiter quando de re dogmatica agitur, non debent esse victores et victi, sed omnia debent declarari cum unanimitate morali.[78] – 2. De facto, the Theological Commission has put in an enormous effort; to reject its texts purely and simply would be neither just nor opportune; therefore we should keep all the parts of it that everyone can accept. – 3. Textus reficiatur ita ut respondeat diversis exigentiis, in primis pastoralibus, etc.; ergo, stante commissione theological,[79] let new periti be designated by the pope to study the text. – 4. Let us hold a vote to open a path forward.

Bishop Paul-Léon Seitz of Kontum (Vietnam): A number of things in the schema are not satisfactory; inerrancy, inspiration, the Vulgate. The Old and New Testaments are not linked together; "inerrantia in re profana; ambiguitates".[80] The schema condemns works and incites suspicion. The unity of the faith will not be kept safe by always saying: "duce magisterio",[81] if we do not also say that the magisterium is subject to Scripture and tradition. "Mens qua hoc schema concipitur revelat aperte defensivum complexum, qui Concilio dedecet."[82] A handbook will not suffice for us, nor do we have to canonize opinions that we might soon need to retract. It is impossible to amend the schema. "Oportet primum in suffragium ire."[83]

Immediately after the meeting was adjourned, the cardinals on the Board of Presidency gathered around their table. They were joined by Card. Cicognani, secretary of state. We would learn in the course of that day that they decided to propose an end to the general discussion and hold a vote on a formula, the terms of which we will no doubt find out tomorrow morning.

---

[77] "Revision of the text".

[78] "1. In the council, especially when it is a matter of a question of dogma, there must not be conquerors and conquered, but everything must be declared with moral unanimity."

[79] "3. Let the text be redone in such a manner that it responds to the diverse demands, first of all pastoral, etc.; then, the Theological Commission remaining in place".

[80] "Inerrancy in the secular matters; ambiguities".

[81] "Under the leadership of the magisterium".

[82] "The spirit with which this schema was conceived overtly reveals a defensive complex, which ill befits the council."

[83] "We must first of all proceed to a vote."

At 12:55 P.M., the Assistant[84] had a picture taken of the two of us in front of the house by a photographer from *Match*. – At 2:30 P.M., a visit from a Mexican Benedictine, the theologian of a bishop, accompanied by Henri Fesquet (*Le Monde*) and a journalist from *Informations catholiques internationales*. – At 3 P.M., visit from three young Spanish theologians; they showed me the remarks they had written on the schema *De fontibus*; they told me that most of the Spanish theologians who have come to Rome are of their opinion but that their bishops are following instead another group, more limited, that includes Fr. Salaverri. – At 5 P.M., visit from Father . . . , S.J., the secretary of a Japanese bishop;[85] he came to talk to me about Buddhism. The Japanese bishops, he told me, are always thinking about their return home; they are counting the days; they are a little surprised to see some episcopates working in common, etc.

At 6:30 P.M., Santa Chiara.[86] A seminarian came to get me at the porter's lodge and led me into a small room, where a dozen seminarians were gathered. On a table, some questions had been placed in advance, especially concerning Father Teilhard. At 7:30 they went for dinner. I would have gone with them but was told to wait for the bishops (all the French bishops had a papal audience that evening). I did not see, nor would I see, any of the directors of the seminary. At 8:30, arrival of the bishops; I was placed between Bishop Puech and Archbishop Garrone; across from me: Cardinals Roques[87] and Lefebvre. Uninteresting conversation. Next saw for a few moments Bishop Cazaux (Luçon) and Bishop Théas (Tarbes). Driven back to the Borgo by Msgr. Loizeau,[88] the theologian of Bishop Cazaux, who was also chauffeuring Bishop de la Chanonie[89] (Clermont). The latter, when I made mention of Teilhard, a native of Clermont, assumed a somber air and was silent; I sensed that I should let the matter drop.

---

[84] Bernard de Gorostarzu.

[85] No doubt Paul Pfister, S.J. (1906–1994), German, ordained in 1930. Professor in the Theology Faculty of Sophia University in Japan, run by the Jesuits. The theologian of Cardinal Doi, expert at the council beginning with the second session.

[86] This refers to the French Seminary in Rome, on via Santa Chiara.

[87] Clément Roques (1880–1964), French, ordained in 1904. Archbishop of Rennes from 1940 until his death, created cardinal in 1946.

[88] Eugène Loizeau (1907–1964), theologian and secretary of bishop Cazaux. A specialist on family matters, he was named as an expert to the council during the first session. However, he never had the title of Monsignor.

[89] Pierre Abel Louis Chappot de la Chanonie (1898–1990), French, ordained in 1925. Bishop of Clermont from 1953 to 1974.

Tuesday, November 20, 1962. – Canon Martimort is unhappy: the
Latinists at the Secretariat of State are holding up the texts of the corrected schema on the liturgy; they are invoking the order received from
the pope to put everything in good Latin. – I spoke to Fr. Congar
about the draft of the Prooemium that he has written.[1] – Msgr. Lafortune recounted a joke to me that is going around: A ship, which has as
passengers Ottaviani, Ruffini, and Siri, has just gone down in a storm;
someone asks: Who was saved? One would have to respond: The Holy
Church.

President of the day: Cardinal Frings.

Archbishop Georges Cabana[2] of Sherbrooke (Canada): I have many
separated brothers in my diocese. "Expectant veritatem non nebu-
losam."[3] – He recalled *Humani generis*, its warnings, its condemnation
of those "falso irenismo indulgentes".[4] Let the "integra veritas, absque
ulla corruptione" be proclaimed. "In schemate bene exponitur doctrina
secundum normas encycl. Humani generis."[5] So let us move on "quam-
primum"[6] to the articles.

Bishop Bernard Echeverria Ruiz of Ambato (Ecuador): "Usque nunc
perfecta concordia non obtinetur."[7] We all know that, in these last few
years, there have spread, even into our institutions of higher learning, nonnullae opiniones quas Mater Ecclesia numquam approbavit,
specialiter circa Novum Testamentum.[8] According to these views, a
good number of things in the O.T. are not historical and a good number of things in the N.T. are not "stricte historicae";[9] some speak of
the "communitas christiana",[10] etc. Instead of holding firmly to the

---

[1] This preamble was supposed to serve as an introduction to the conciliar texts.
[2] Georges Cabana (1894–1986), Canadian, ordained in 1918. Archbishop of Sherbrooke from
1952 to 1967.
[3] "They are expecting a truth that is not obscure."
[4] "People inclined to a false irenicism".
[5] "The complete truth, without any corruption. In the schema, the doctrine is well presented,
in accordance with the norms of the encyclical *Humani generis*."
[6] "As soon as possible".
[7] "Up until now, a perfect agreement has not been obtained."
[8] "Some opinions that our Mother the Church has never approved, especially concerning the
New Testament".
  A. Old Testament.
  B. New Testament.
[9] "Strictly historical".
[10] "Christian community".

dogma, "dogma accommodatur scientiae".[11] Many errors are taught by non-Catholics and many Catholics "proni sunt"[12] to accept them. "Munus Concilii nostri est claudendi viam his erroribus. Depositum fidei debemus, ante omnia, integrum servare."[13] Even in our presence, some declare opinions contrary to the faith: so we are breaking our own unity, under the pretext of seeking unity with others. The Theological Commission had these scandals in view. How to remedy the situation? "Attendendo ad Ecclesiae magisterium, ad Summi Pontificis doctrinam".[14] By recalling what has always been taught. Pius XII had given directives in *Divino afflante Spiritu*, but he subsequently found himself constrained to write *Humani generis*. In addition, we have had, since then, the speech of John XXIII to the Biblical Institute and the decrees of the Holy Office.[15] "Commissio theologica praeparatoria nihil aliud ante oculos habuit, quam has normas. Nihil novum in hoc schemate, est doctrina traditionalis, etc.[16] ... (The president interrupted him.)

(Fr. Labourdette, O.P., who was beside me, said to me: "He has called the Biblical Institute into question; I think your General will intervene.")

Titular Bishop Fidel García Martinez, (Spain): There are two opposing positions here. Those who dislike the schema find a certain foundation in the pope's speech opening the council. All the Fathers agree that we must profess the whole of our doctrine. But is it necessary to condemn certain debated opinions? Instead of interminable discussions article by article, let a commission be formed, truly representative of diverse opinions; let the Biblical Commission and the Secretariat for Unity be

---

[11] "Dogma is accommodated to science."

[12] "Are inclined".

[13] "The task of our council is to close the road to these errors. Before everything else, we must preserve the deposit of faith intact, in its fullness."

[14] "By paying attention to the magisterium of the Church, to the doctrine of the Supreme Pontiff".

[15] This is a reference to the speech of John XXIII on the occasion of the fiftieth anniversary of the Biblical Institute. John XXIII asked for "prudentiam et sobrietatem" (prudence and temperance) from those doing research in biblical studies. The Monitum from the Holy Office in question is from June 1961. It judged as dangerous the theses "quae in discrimen adducunt germanam veritatem historicam et objectivam" (that put at risk the genuine historical and objective truth) of Holy Scripture, not only the Old Testament, but also the New Testament, "etiam quoad dicta et facta Christi" (even including the words and actions of Christ).

[16] "The Preparatory Theological Commission had nothing else before its eyes than these norms. Nothing new in this schema, it is the traditional doctrine, etc."

represented. "Adhuc erunt aliquae difficultates, sed valde minuentur."[17] While waiting, let us discuss the schema *De Ecclesiae unitate*.

Bishop Michel Klepacz[18] of Lodz (Poland): It is necessary to write a vast prooemium. "Scriptura et Traditio non sunt nisi fontes cognitionis."[19] The influence of inspiration concerns not only the intelligence. "Extollenda est efficacitas Scripturae."[20] Many excellent works of exegesis and theology have appeared in recent years. To recognize the differences owing to the personalities of the four evangelists is not to deny the historicity of the Gospels. Our exegetes defend this historicity by showing that they were conceived inside the Church. Take care then not to discourage them. And let us have regard for the tradition of the Eastern Churches. (The president: Tempus finitum est.)[21]

Archbishop Enrico Nicodemo of Bari (Italy); Two principal questions: "1. – Utrum schema sit a nobis discutiendum an rejiciendum."[22] For a rejection to be justified, the schema would have to be substantially in error. A new schema has been circulated: that is an evident danger. The Theological Commission alone is competent. Let us discuss the schema, "ad solvendum difficultates nostras per nosmetipsos."[23] – 2. The progress of doctrine does not consist in watering it down. The faith progresses "in eodem sensu, in eodem genere, in eadem doctrina".[24] Our sole master is Christ; it is not the exegetes. We respect learned men, but we believe in the Holy Spirit. A new presentation is desired? No! Let the account be clear and without compromise, so as to enlighten all men, within the Church and outside the Church. "Sic erit Concilium enixe pastorale."[25]

Card. Frings: "In nomine consilii praesidentiae, propositio magni momenti".[26] (The text was read by Archbishop Felici.) "Progrediendum esset mox ad disceptationem de singulis capitibus schematis. Sed"[27]

---

[17] "There will still be some difficulties, but they will be greatly reduced."

[18] Michal Klepacz (1893–1967), Polish, ordained in 1916. Bishop of Łódz from 1946 until his death. Member of the Commission for Seminaries, Studies, and Catholic Education.

[19] "Scripture and tradition are only sources of knowledge."

[20] "The power of Scripture must be extolled."

[21] "Time has run out."

[22] "Whether the schema should be debated by us or rejected?"

[23] "In order to resolve our difficulties ourselves".

[24] "In the same direction, in the same kind, in the same doctrine".

[25] "Thus the council will be eminently pastoral."

[26] "In the name of the Board of Presidency, a proposal of great importance".

[27] "We should soon come to a discussion of the schema's chapters, one by one. But".

since some Fathers think that this is not timely, it has seemed to the Board of Presidency that it would be good to get the Fathers' votes on this matter. "An disceptatio interrupenda sit?"[28] Let those who so wish respond: Placet. Le those who are of the opposite opinion and want the discussion to continue respond: Non placet. – Cardinal Frings, as far as I have understood, expressed reservations about this way of presenting the vote, but he nevertheless declared that he supported the proposition; he would vote: Placet. – After some time, during which the vote was explained in various languages, Card. Ruffini got up and declared: "If the assembly says that 'placet interruptio',[29] it will never see the schema again." – A rather long time afterward, Archbishop Felici announced: "Multi Patres rogant explicationes. Placet = interruptio sine die. Non placet: continuatur disceptatio."[30] If some Fathers have made a mistake, let them cast a new ballot. – Still later, the votes having been cast, Cardinal Frings would make the remark that the vote agreeing to the interruption ("placet") did not inevitably mean the total and definitive abandonment of a schema *De fontibus*. (Some bishops would tell me that afternoon that their neighbors, hearing this clarification, subsequently regretted their votes of "non placet").

While waiting for the result of the vote, the general discussion continued.

Archbishop Geraldo de Proença Sigaud[31] of Diamantina (Brazil): "Schema placet, ad emendationes faciendas."[32] It is well written and timely; it opposes current errors. Rationalism and modernism are everywhere. The situation is very grave. The errors denounced by *Humani generis* are not dead, they still have their venom. They have even penetrated the Church: the Holy Father's distress. Some Catholics deny the historical merit of the Scriptures: for example, the earthly paradise, the Patriarchs; some compare their accounts to the Song of Roland! Jonah, his shipwreck ... And even the New Testament ..., etc. It is absolutely necessary that the council decide these fundamental questions infallibly ... (The president: "Tempus finitum est.")

---

[28] "Should the discussion be broken off?"

[29] "It approves the interruption of the discussion."

[30] "Many Fathers are asking for explanations. *Placet* = interruption *sine die* [for an indefinite period]. *Non Placet*: let the discussion continue."

[31] Geraldo de Proença Sigaud, S.V.D. (1909–1999), Brazilian, ordained in 1932. Archbishop of Diamantina (Brazil) from 1960 to 1980. He was one of the founders of the Coetus internationalis Patrum.

[32] "I approve the schema, in order to make corrections."

Bishop Pablo Barrachina[33] of Orihuela-Alicante (Spain): "Non placet. Redolet tritam formam scolasticam, etc. Breviter propono temperamentum";[34] a reference made to Ancel, etc. There would be interminable discussions. Therefore let the council produce only one, positive doctrinal exposition with a biblical, patristic, liturgical style. Let us recall Trent and Vatican I. Let us proclaim the necessity for the faithful of a vital contact with Scripture. Let us praise the labor of the exegetes. That would be dogmatic, pastoral, ecumenical, and would agree with the Holy Father's directions.

Bishop Luigi Carli of Segni (Italy): We must immediately discuss the articles. I support the compromise proposed yesterday. In the face of everything that has happened in this chamber since then, I am anceps.[35] Juridical considerations against the rejection. One could in this way reject all the rules of the council. There is nothing, in the article of the rules defining the method of discussion, that makes provision for such an eventuality. So this would be an irregular vote. "Schema istud est in possessione. Suffragatio esset nulla."[36] – He will lodge a complaint with the Tribunal.

Bishop Victor Costantini, of Sessa Aurunca (Italy): One could wish that the declarations had a more positive style: but it is the duty of pastors to protect the faithful against errors. However, let us defer until Vatican III anything that is still uncertain.

The Very Reverend Father A. Fernández, O.P., master general: "Pauca dicam de caractere pastorali et oecumenico."[37] Let us rejoice over the spirit of the two camps: "ex utraque parte, boni pastores sumus. Sed postea ..."[38] Cardinal Santos has explained well that 'pastoral' is an adjective and that the substantive is the doctrine. "Primum veritas, veritas clara: tale est praecipuum munus pastorale. Doctrina conciliaris non est unius diei vel aetatis";[39] if one wants it to be pastoral for the current times, "ad vesperam evanescit".[40] Given the choice between an

---

[33] Actually, it was Antonio Quarracino (1923–1998), born in Italy, ordained in 1945. Bishop of Nueve de Julio (Argentina) from 1962 to 1968, created cardinal in 1991.

[34] "I do not approve the schema. It has the odor of the usual scholastic form. I briefly propose a moderation."

[35] "Uncertain".

[36] "This schema is on the agenda. The vote should be null and void."

[37] "I will say a few things about the pastoral and ecumenical character."

[38] "On each side, we are good pastors. But thereafter ..."

[39] "In the first place, the truth, the clear truth: such is the principal pastoral duty. The doctrine of the council is not of a single day or era."

[40] "It is outdated by that evening."

exposition that is purely pastoral and a clear and exact doctrinal exposition, choose the second.

A titular bishop from Italy:[41] "Nolite timere, breviter loquar."[42] We are told: "abstinendum est ab omni exageratione, et":[43] it is one particular school that has written this schema. But, no! etc. Tradition contains many things that are not in Scripture, etc. "Schema placet."

Archbishop Jean Ferro[44] of Reggio Calabria (Italy): "Schema approbandum, cum aliquibus emendationibus."[45] It responds to the wishes of pastors. (He then read a paper that seemed to be almost, or exactly, the one that Cardinal Ottaviani had had distributed last evening; he must have been chosen for his good voice.) "Ne erubescere Evangelii videamur. Integritas veritatis, immutabilis. Veritas a Deo venit et ad Deum tendit ..."[46] Without truth, there is nothing else: neither revelation nor redemption nor human life nor justice nor peace, etc. Cf. the encyclical *Ad Petri cathedram*[47] and Pius XII, *Humani generis*. It is necessary to quell errors. "Sunt quaedam schemata, quae circumferuntur: piae meditationes";[48] these are in the realm of apologetics and rhetoric; subjectiva. "Veritas autem Domini manet in aeternum."[49] The whole Catholic world is praying for us to be faithful in preserving in full the deposit of faith. "Cum Petro et sub Petro".[50]

Bishop F. Franić, Yugoslavian: "Placet juxta modum, remanentibus substantia et stylo. Positive res exponere modo pastorali? dialogus oecumenicus? Sed hic latet quaedam aequivocatio."[51] We are not a council of unity but of interior reform. "Debemus errores clare indicare, ne fideles incidant in laqueum diaboli."[52] We must confine ourselves to what are undoubtedly errors, but it is very necessary to protect the faithful against

---

[41] Giulio Barbetta (1890–1976), Italian, ordained in 1915. Titular bishop.
[42] "Do not fear, I will speak briefly."
[43] "We must abstain from all exaggeration."
[44] Giovanni Ferro, C.R.S. (1901–1992), Italian, ordained in 1925. Archbishop of Reggio Calabria from 1950 to 1977.
[45] "The schema should be approved, with some corrections."
[46] "Let us not seem to blush at the Gospel. The complete, immutable truth. Truth comes from God and tends toward God."
[47] Encyclical of John XXIII of June 29, 1959, "on truth, unity, and peace in the spirit of charity".
[48] "Certain schemas are circulating: pious meditations."
[49] "Subjective". "But the truth of the Lord abides for eternity" [Ps 117(116)].
[50] "With Peter and under Peter".
[51] "I approve, with amendments. Let the substance and the style remain. Set forth the matter in a positive fashion, in a pastoral fashion? Ecumenical dialogue? But there is a certain equivocation here."
[52] "We must clearly indicate errors, so that the faithful do not fall into the snares of the devil."

them by clearly pointing these out to them, especially for the sake
of those who are most exposed. "Schema nullo modo est alienum a men-
talitate Orientalium":[53] the proof of this is that the great Eastern councils
of former times condemned errors. "Sunt hodie errores, de sancto angelo
annuntiante Mariae, etc."[54] Let a pastoral Prooemium be written.

The secretary general (Felici) announced that the result of the vote
would be given tomorrow; if necessary, "Erit secunda suffragatio."[55] If
need be, we will then deal with the schema *De instrumentis communicationis socialis*. – While waiting, we will pass on to the examination of the
first chapter of *De fontibus*.

Cardinal Tisserant: "Non deest confusio in primo capite."[56] Art. 1: cf.
farther on, art. 4, a different description. – Art. 2, "episcopi et apostoli":
"justane est ista assimilatio? et videntur apostoli inferiores esse episcopis. – Art. 3: de ministerio, etc. – Art. 4: "tanquam duplici fonte"; verba
desunt in Vaticano I ad quem remittitur." – Art. 5: "Traditio etc.",[57]
but there are many things on that subject in Scripture itself. – Art. 6:
"Habitudo inter",[58] etc.

Cardinal Ruffini: Why not declare first of all what revelation is and
its importance for us? – P. 9, l. 3: "Quid significat hoc? Œconomia non
est revelatio. Quidem hodie non dubitant dicere 'revelatio realis'!" –
"Longe transcendit antiquum testamentum?"[59] No: the two Testaments
are equally the Word of God to men. – De duplici fonte:[60] some are
playing word games when they say that Trent accepted only a single
source; we must affirm two sources, "sicut docetur in scholis catholicis a
pluribus saeculis. Traditio est antiquior et clarior Scriptura. Duo hi fontes
sunt regulae fidei remotae; sed regula proxima est magisterium. Magisterium non est regula regulata a sacra Scriptura, ut quidam proponent."[61]

---

[53] "The schema is in no way foreign to the mentality of the Eastern Churches."

[54] "There are errors today concerning the annunciation of the holy angel to Mary, etc."

[55] "There will be a second vote."

[56] "There is no lack of confusion in the first chapter."

[57] "Article 2, 'bishops and apostles': is this comparison correct? and the apostles seem to be inferior to the bishops. Art. 3: on ministry, etc. Art. 4: 'as on the subject of the two sources'; these words
are not found in Vatican I, to which reference is made. Art. 5: Tradition, etc."

[58] "The relation between".

[59] "What does that mean? Economy is not revelation. Certain people do not hesitate today to say
'real revelation'! It (the New Testament) far surpasses the Old Testament?"

[60] "On the two sources".

[61] "As has been taught in schools of Catholic thought for several centuries. Tradition is older and
clearer than Scripture. These two sources are the remote rules of faith, but the nearest rule is the
magisterium. The magisterium is not a rule regulated by Sacred Scripture, as some are proposing."

Bishop Vincenzo (Italy):[62] One point only: on the apostolic tradition and the interpretation of Scripture. This is very timely. Cf. *Humani generis*. "Debemus confirmare"[63] its teaching; "debemus inculcare fidelibus"[64] that in matters of faith and morals it is necessary to hold the meaning of Scripture that the Church holds.

At the end of the session, the result of the vote was obtained, and Archbishop Felici announced it. Those present: 2,200 and some; for sending it back: 1,368; for moving to an immediate discussion of the articles: 800 and some.[65] As the necessary two-thirds majority was not reached for sending the schema back, we will continue tomorrow with the discussion of its articles.

There was a great deal of commentary on this vote. Many found it illogical. Some wondered why the result had been announced so quickly: Was it to present the assembly with a fait accompli? Or was it, to the contrary, the Board of Presidency that wanted the immediate announcement so that objections could be organized right away? In the course of the day, I heard both hypotheses. Several remarked that if the same question had been posed in the reverse sense, the two-thirds majority would have been needed to continue the discussion. Others, and they are numerous, are talking about the ambiguity that put some bishops in an awkward position, of the pressure exerted on some others by Ruffini's intervention (discretely supported by the "sine die" of Felici). One bishop told me that his two neighbors, reassured by Frings' last clarification, went to the voting booth to change their ballots. Around 5 P.M., I was told that Cardinals Liénart and Bea met together and that the subject of their conversation was a step to take regarding this vote. At 9 P.M., the superior general of the Marists[66] and the bishops assembled around him would tell me of their displeasure.

At 3 P.M., a working meeting on the first chapter of the *De fontibus*, and especially on tradition, in a room in the Angelicum. There were fifteen of us, half bishops, half theologians. We talked about 3 or 4

---

[62] Vincenzo M. Jacono (1898–1993), Italian, ordained in 1921. Titular bishop.

[63] "We must confirm".

[64] "We must instill in the faithful".

[65] The exact figures were, respectively, 2,209; 1,368; 822; and 19 invalid ballots.

[66] Joseph Buckley, S.M. (1905–1981), American, ordained in 1931. Superior general from 1961 to 1969.

possible interventions that were allocated and whose terms were out-
lined. Father Congar was at the helm. Each of us freely expressed his
opinion. Frs. Labourdette and Camelot, O.P., were there. Among the
bishops, Bishop Pourchet (Saint-Flour). At 4:30, it was decided that the
next meeting would be on Friday. Fr. Congar told us that it would not
be at the Angelicum; the master general[67] had just forbidden all private
meetings on the premises. They say that he was sensitive to a complaint
by Card. Ottaviani, who is afraid of "seditious" meetings. Moreover,
Father Tromp has stated that a widespread schema in English had a
Frenchman as its author, and he let it be understood that this Frenchman
was Congar; in fact, it is only a matter of some critical remarks on the
official schemas, written by a Dutchman and translated into English.[68]

At 5 P.M., at the Biblical Institute, I said to Father Lyonnet that it
would be a good idea for our Father General to intervene to shield the
Biblical Institute, manifestly targeted by several.

At 5:30, saw Fr. Donatien Mollat at the Gregorian. He told me
that, upon returning from St. Peter's at 1 P.M., Fr. Dhanis did not hide
his satisfaction over the fact that the two-thirds majority had not been
attained.

At 6:30, Fr. Maurice Villain came to get me and drove me to the
Marist Fathers' place, in Monteverde Nuovo. Fr. Lyonnet was invited,
as well as some others, including Father Küng. A pleasant evening. The
missionary bishops from Oceania were especially interested in the current discussion, since they do not know if they will be able to return
for the other sessions. Their Father General, an American, reminded
me that he had written to me long ago and that we had carried on a
discussion via correspondence on the subject of the supernatural; I have
no recollection of that. Bishops Darmancier and Martin, S.M., reported
to me that from this morning a new peritus would be admitted to the
council, in the person of Jean Guitton.[69]

L'Osservatore Romano, Nov. 21, 1962 (the evening of Nov. 20):
"Given the result of the vote, announced a little before the work of the

[67]A. Fernández.

[68]This document, which did indeed express criticisms of De fontibus and De deposito fidei, was
the work of E. Schillebeeckx. As we have seen, this declaration was made by Archbishop Parente,
not by S. Tromp.

[69]Jean Guitton (1901–1999), French philosopher, member of the Académie française. He was
personally invited to the council and sat, during the first session, in the gallery of non-Catholic
observers, then, starting with the second session, among the lay auditors of the council. However,
he was not, properly speaking, an expert.

assembly ended, the examination of the chapters of the schema under discussion will proceed in the coming days."

The Assistant of France[70] saw some Italian bishops yesterday, who told him that I had been crossed off the list of periti.

November 21, 1962. – An American bishop is supposed to have voted yesterday for the continuation of the discussion, because, he said, he had prepared a good intervention that would have demolished three chapters of the schema! – An Anglo-Saxon bishop, a supporter of the schema, is supposed to have exclaimed: "All is saved, except for honor!"[1]

This morning, upon entering Saint Peter's, Father Häring told me that we have to have a great deal of hope so as to honor God and have confidence in the sense of justice that animates John XXIII. – A Father, the substitute of the Latin American Assistancy,[2] said to me last evening: "I went to see the Fathers coming out of the council, and they seemed upset." This morning, before Mass, they were agitated; groups of them everywhere, talking in loud voices; they were late taking their places in the tiers. – Beautiful Ruthenian Mass, with concelebration, although a little theatrical at times.

Cardinal Ruffini was presiding. He announced a message from the secretary general. Archbishop Felici then read a rather long text. This is what I understood and remembered of it, in summary: "De mandato Cardinalis de negotiis est: ... Scrutinium hesterno die habitum visum est quasdam sollicitudines tribuisse ..."[3] (1) This vote was not without some bending of the rules ... ; (2) Various factors suggest that we will come up against great difficulties in the discussion. Therefore it is necessary that the schema be better explained. "Augustus Pontifex, ratione habita de istis causis, etc., statuit rem commissioni dare";[4] this commission will be composed mostly of members of the Theological Commission and the Secretariat for Unity; its task will be to revise the schema. – Today,

---

[70] Bernard de Gorostarzu.

November 21

[1] An allusion to "all is lost save honor", the words of Francis I after the defeat at Pavia in 1525.

[2] The Substitute of the Assistancy of northern Latin America was A. Ernestus Bravo, S.J., and the one for southern Latin America was Zeno Etges, S.J.

[3] "By mandate of the cardinal of the Secretariat for Extraordinary Affairs [A. Cicognani]: yesterday's ballot seems to have given rise to some anxiety ..."

[4] "The Supreme Pontiff, taking account of these reasons, etc., has decided to hand the matter over to a commission."

we will finish the discussion of chapter I and on Friday move on to the schema *De instrumentis* ...

Bishop Émile Guano (Livorno, Italy): "In exordio quodam fusius recolantur sequentia puncta: 1. Deus hominibus loquitur per suum Verbum, praesertim Verbum caro factum. – 2. Christus, Verbum caro factum, est imago et vox Patris, unicus Magister et unica via ad Patrem; loquitur per sua verba et facta et gesta, immo per suam personam. – 3. Deus Verbum suum loquitur non aliquibus, sed toti generi humano, jam a prophetis, etc., et transmittitur Verbum Ecclesiae, ut omnibus hominibus illud tradat. – 4. Haec traditio Verbi pluribus modis fit; privilegiatum locum obtinet sacra Scriptura, utpote inspirata.[5] Not everything in it is explicit; however ... – 5. Our council wants to show men the path of salvation, life, peace, and God's friendship with men; it wants to tell them that man, having become in Jesus Christ the Son of God, etc. – 6. "Tota vita christiana, tota vita Ecclesiae, de Verbo Dei emanat, etc."[6] – On the magisterium of the Church, "in servitium ipsius Verbi Dei".[7] Hence the necessity for exegetes and theologians working under the leadership of the Church.

Bishop Édouard Martinez[8] (Spain): "Nonnullas observationes. 1. Introductio generalis desideratur",[9] saying why these questions are being treated and in what spirit: "concilium alloquitur homines nostri temporis; Ecclesia, quae est magistra, est etiam mater. Oportet etiam criterium exprimere, per quod omnis ambiguitas tollatur ... – 2. Titulus non est apprime aptus: non adaequate comprehendit capitis materiam";[10] and it

---

[5] "In the introduction, let the following points be recalled more fully: 1. God speaks to men through his Word, especially the Word made flesh. 2. Christ, the Word made flesh, is the image and the voice of the Father, the one and only teacher and the only way to the Father; he speaks through his words, actions, and gestures, through his own person. God addresses his Word, not to some, but to all humanity, initially through the prophets, etc., and the Word was transmitted to the Church so that she could transmit it to all people. 4. This transmission of the Word is done in several ways; Holy Scripture, because it is inspired, retains a privileged place."

[6] "All Christian life, the whole life of the Church, flows from the Word of God."

[7] "In the service of the Word of God itself".

[8] Eduardo Martinez González (1897–1979), Spanish, ordained in 1923. Bishop of Zamora (Spain) from 1950 to 1970.

[9] "Some observations. 1. A general introduction is desirable."

[10] "The council addresses itself to men of our time; the Church, which is a teacher, is also a mother. So it must express a criterion that will remove all ambiguity ... 2. The title is not at all appropriate: it does not adequately encompass the material of the chapter."

cuts off a discussion that must be left open; the encyclical *Humani generis* did not do that, and the terminology of the councils does not support it. "Non fontes, sed potius deposita vocari possunt Scriptura et Traditio, in quibus continetur objective revelatio."[11] And in the current text there is an "offendiculum ..." − 3. De facto revelationis:[12] this is not only the statement of a doctrine, "sed communicatio personalis Dei hominibus".[13] − 4. No. 1 should be written differently; "nimis est abstractum".[14] A style must be employed that is proper to councils, which is not one of exhortation, but neither is it one of scholarly abstraction. Cf. Heb. chap. 4; make mention also of the Holy Spirit. (He proposed, at the end, a new draft.)

Dom Chr. Butler, O.S.B.: "Venerabiles Fratres".[15] I propose "aliquas emendationes",[16] in the hope that they will be useful, "etiamsi revisio aliqua major jam fiat. Assentio ad ea quae dixit card. Ruffini de proemio ponendo circa revelationem, et toto corde assentio ad ea quae dicta sunt hodie mane. Ratio generalis haec est. Satis obvium est nunc, forsan, hoc schema ... non adaequate obtinere posse consensum scholarum catholicarum. Unicae scholae placet, sed non aliis",[17] that are of an equal Catholic orthodoxy. "Praeterea",[18] it is not written in such a way as to please the Eastern Churches. It is not only a question of some propositions that need changing or of a certain pastoral mellowness that needs to be introduced. The question concerns the whole aim and content of the schema. "Meo quidem judicio, et spero etiam multorum, schema tangit quaestiones legitime disputatas, et quarum solutio nondum est matura."[19] It is thus advisable to exclude from it, "per emendationes, omne quod restringit legitimam libertatem scholarum. Sic debemus agere, non

---

[11] "Scripture and tradition cannot be called sources, but rather deposits, in which revelation is objectively contained."

[12] "'An obstacle' ... On the fact of revelation".

[13] "The personal communication of God to men".

[14] "It is too abstract."

[15] "Venerable Brothers".

[16] "Some corrections".

[17] "Even if a more significant revision was already made. I approve what was said by Cardinal Ruffini about the prooemium that should be introduced concerning revelation, and I wholeheartedly give my assent to what was said this morning. Here is the general reason. It is, perhaps, now rather evident that this schema ... cannot adequately achieve the consensus of the Catholic schools of thought. It suits one particular school, but not the others."

[18] "Moreover".

[19] "According to my own opinion at least, and I hope, according to many others, the schema broaches questions that are legitimately disputed and whose solution has not yet had time to ripen."

ut substituamus sententias alterius scholae, sed ut omnes scholae possint consentire. Igitur",[20] I am transmitting to the commission a certain number of emendationes. – "Titulus constitutionis mutetur in, ex gr, De revelatione et transmissione ejus".[21] Likewise, the title of chapter 1: De traditione et sacra Scriptura,[22] etc. – P. 9, no. 2, "oportet affirmare quod Christus Dominus per ipsam suam vitam manifestat revelationem Dei; ratio: Verbum caro factum est, Christus *est* Verbum Dei. – De exegetis catholicis fuerunt dicta, heri, in hac aula, quaedam valde injuriosa, et plena suspicione de earum fidelitate, ne dicam de sana doctrina et fide eorum. De his, vere indignor",[23] and I insist on defending the Jesuit Fathers of the Biblical Institute and the Dominican Fathers of the *Revue biblique*, and many others, who were my teachers and who are my friends . . . (The president, Ruffini, interrupted him in the middle of the sentence.)

Auxiliary Bishop Vito Chang Tso-huan,[24] (residing in Germany): ". . . et observatores dilectissimi".[25] What has been said on the schema "mihi consolationi est".[26] But he would like to see at least a brief note on original revelation and the will for universal salvation. It would be offensive to God and absurd to say that God has little regard for the salvation of other peoples. All souls have been redeemed by the Blood of Christ: "ne sinatis veritatem istam longius latere".[27] The Old Testament is not rejected by the Church: Why would the Church reject the proto-revelation for the sake of paganism? Cf. St. Paul. God has manifested himself to men . . . (Ruffini: "Velis concludere, quia a nemine negatur protorevelatio.")[28]

Archbishop Maximos Hermaniuk (Ruthenian Catholic Church of Canada): "Ad majorem explicationem catholicae doctrinae, etc. Ipse

---

[20] "By means of amendments, everything that might restrain the legitimate freedom of the schools. We must do so, not in order to substitute the opinions of another school, but so that all schools might be able to agree. Accordingly".

[21] "Let the title of the constitution be changed, to, for example, 'On Revelation and Its Transmission'."

[22] "On Tradition and Sacred Scripture".

[23] "It must be affirmed that Christ our Lord manifests the revelation of God by his very life; the reason: Christ, the Word made flesh, *is* the Word of God. Some remarks were made yesterday, in this hall, concerning Catholic exegetes that were very insulting, full of suspicions regarding their fidelity and even their orthodoxy and their faith. I am very indignant at these accusations."

[24] Vito Chang Tso-huan (1903–1982), Chinese, ordained in 1930. Titular bishop.

[25] "And highly esteemed observers".

[26] "Is a consolation for me".

[27] "Do not allow this truth to be hidden any longer."

[28] "Please conclude, for no one denies the protorevelation."

titulus non placet; indicat tantum duplicem modum transmissionis et conservationis; nihil dicit de origine, id est de Deo loquente. Unicus Fons, Deus. Dicatur ergo: De revelatione divina. – No. 3, ll. 15–18: hoc est verum, sed non omnino ... – No. 4, l. 37: ad fideliter custodiendum; addatur: et interpretandum."[29] – Page 11, l. 3: there is too much separation put between Scripture and tradition; "est una doctrina, duplici modo transmissa. Claritatis causa",[30] if the schema insists on speaking of two sources, let it make clear that it is not a question of the origin, "tantum est duplex modus ..."[31]

Bishop J. Rupp (Monaco): "Confiteor quod nomine proprio loquor",[32] I cannot speak in the name of the entire episcopate of Monaco! – "Tria placent in schemate: clare distinguitur inter traditionem et magisterium; clare enuntiatur, inter elementa quae constituunt traditionem, praxis Ecclesiae, quam hodie multi, etiam theologi, sat parum curant; germana est natura theologiae, quae est scientia (cf. verba sancti Thomae): pastores egent normis praecisis",[33] the liberty of souls would be hurt if one were to overstep the bounds through lack of precise information. – "Sed: modus loquendi (style) longe differt a Tridentino et Vaticano primo. Aliqua asserta sunt minus certa. Pg. 10, dicitur quod 'doctrinam (episcopi) semper praedicatione tradiderunt': at, ni fallor, multi episcopi erraverunt in fide; humiles simus. Pg. 10, no. 4, l. 23: Scriptura, si sumitur sensu non mere litterali sed plenario, radicem fere omnium continet."[34] We should distinguish carefully between divine tradition and ecclesiastical traditions. No. 6 is not sufficient; a darkening of the faith is not unthinkable, etc. – Cf. the praxis Ecclesiae,[35] etc.

---

[29] "For a greater explanation of Catholic doctrine. The title itself is not appropriate; it indicates only a twofold mode of transmission and preservation; it says nothing about the origin, that is, about God who addresses us. There is only one source: God. So let it be called: On Divine Revelation. No. 3, ll. 15–18: this is true, but not entirely ... No. 4, l. 37: for faithfully preserving ..., let us add: and interpreting."

[30] "There is one doctrine, handed down in a twofold manner. For the sake of clarity".

[31] "Only of the twofold mode ..."

[32] "I confess that I am speaking in my own name".

[33] "I approve three things in the schema: it clearly distinguishes between tradition and the magisterium; it clearly sets forth, among the elements that constitute tradition, the practice of the Church, with which many today, even theologians, concern themselves rather little; the nature of theology is specific, it is a science (cf. the words of Saint Thomas): pastors have need of precise norms."

[34] "But: the manner of expression differs greatly from Trent and Vatican I. Some assertions are not certain enough. On page 10, it is said that '(the bishops) always transmit doctrine by preaching', but, if I am not mistaken, many bishops have made errors in matters of faith; let us be humble. Page 10, no. 4, l. 23: Scripture, if it is taken in a sense that is not purely literal, but in a fuller sense, contains the root of almost everything."

[35] "The Church's practice".

Archbishop François Marty (Reims): Nos. 4–5–6: set all of this "in mysterio Ecclesiae".[36] (A whole exposition, a little oratorical, without sufficient details.)

Auxiliary Bishop Aloisius Henríquez Jimenez of Caracas (Venezuela): "Titulus non placet. Duplex testimonium unius revelationis, sed Fons unicus (Trent), Evangelium … No. 4: germana mens Tridentini disputatur."[37] – Do not simply repeat Trent, but explain it in an ecumenical sense. – Against the "solum modo":[38] even for the Assumption, the magisterium tells us of at least a foundation in Scripture. The whole schema supposes that revelation consists entirely in verbal formulas. Let no. 5 be written "modo clariore".[39] The magisterium must receive Scripture and tradition "reverenter",[40] etc.

A Spanish bishop:[41] "Circa contextum generalem et quasdam expressiones."[42] Certain questions are debated today whose answers have not yet fully matured. We must proclaim the truth "integre, complete, precise";[43] but then it is appropriate to give an "adaequatum qualificationem theologicam"[44] and to set out the doctrine in the spirit indicated by the Holy Father. – There is a certain confusion in the use of the term "tradition" and other analogous words, etc.

Archbishop François Šeper of Zagreb (Yugoslavia): Caput primum non placet. Praecipua ratio: descriptio traditionis respicit tantum praedicationem oralem. Nimis restricitive loquitur." There is also "fides fidelium, et praxis Ecclesiae".[45] – Do not forget, either, that the apostles had in their hands the books of the Old Testament. Do not neglect the role of the faithful and of theologians in the Church.

Coadjutor Archbishop Veuillot of Paris. No. 1, p. 9: "De revelatione Veteris et Novi Testamenti: necessarium est amplius tractare in initio

---

[36] "In the mystery of the Church".

[37] "I do not approve the title. There is a twofold testimony of one revelation, but one unique source (Trent), the Gospel … No. 4: the authentic spirit of Trent is questioned."

[38] "In one way only".

[39] "More clearly".

[40] "Reverently".

[41] Pedro Cantero Cuadrado (1902–1978), Spanish, ordained in 1926. Bishop of Huelva from 1953 to May 1964, then archbishop of Saragossa until 1977. Member of the Secretariat for Unity beginning with the second session.

[42] "Concerning the general context and some expressions".

[43] "Purely, completely, precisely".

[44] "Adequate theological qualification".

[45] "I do not approve the first chapter. Principal reason: the description of tradition takes into consideration only oral preaching. This is speaking in too restrictive a fashion. There is also the faith of the faithful and the practice of the Church."

de hac revelatione. Emendationem praecisam proponere volo, ut sub-
stituatur Prooemium vel caput quoddam. 1. Valde conveniens est, de
revelatione loqui priusquam de transmissione ejus tractetur. Et esset apta
introductio ad omnia schemata doctrinalia. − 2. Adhaesio ad revelationem et Verbum Dei est communis radix fidei apud omnes christianos";[46]
in this way we would say something that unites before going into differences. − 3. "Quaestio est gravis sub aspectu pastorali."[47] Pastors have
to transmit doctrine, not theories disputed among theologians. Many
people, in a large city like Paris, have a false notion of religion and are
not acquainted with the true idea of Christian revelation. "In Filio suo,
Verbo incarnato, Pater se perfecte manifestavit."[48] − As it is not useful
to speak twice about the same thing, let us eliminate, in the following
schema, the chapter on revelation. Here is the place where it must be
treated. − I am submitting a compendium to the secretariat.

Archbishop Laurent Jäger, Paderborn (Germany). It is not simply a
question of changing words: "debet inveniri alius modus loquendi. −
No. 4: recognoscatur".[49] Take up again the formula of Trent; "unicus
fons quasi duplici rivulo nobis transmittitur, etc."[50] − Rewrite nos. 5 and
6. "Omnes fideles non parvam habent partem in conservandis et expli-
candis libris",[51] etc.

Auxiliary Bishop Raphaël Gonzalez Moralejo of Valencia (Spain):
"Quasi in deserto loquimur ..."[52] (an allusion to the fact that, at that
moment, the tiers were half-empty). Let us change the title, e.g.: "De
deposito revelationis."[53] There is an objection to talking about two
sources. Let us produce a prologue, speaking about the need to present
to the world "salutiferam veritatem",[54] proclaiming that the merciful

[46] "On the revelation of the Old and New Testaments: it is necessary to treat of this revelation
in a broader fashion, at the beginning. I want to propose a precise amendment, in order that the
prooemium or one chapter might be replaced. 1. It is very fitting to speak about revelation before
treating of its transmission. And this would be an appropriate introduction to all the doctrinal
schemas. 2. Adhesion to revelation and the Word of God is the common root of the faith among
all Christians."

[47] "The question is important from a pastoral point of view."
[48] "In his Son, the Word incarnate, the Father manifested himself perfectly."
[49] "Another mode of expression must be found. No. 4: needs to be revised."
[50] "A single source is transmitted to us through, as it were, a twofold river."
[51] "All the faithful have an important role in the preservation and explanation of the holy books."
[52] "We are speaking almost in the desert." [Numerous Fathers had in fact left their tiers to gather
in the side naves, having little interest in the analysis of a text that was no longer on the agenda in
its present form and anxious to exchange their views on the pope's decision.]
[53] "On the deposit of revelation".
[54] "The truth that brings salvation".

God has spoken to us through his Son, emphasizing the eminently salvific character of divine revelation. Explain the idea of revelation. – Page 9, l. 7: "clare indicetur subordinatio revelationis per Apostolos relate ad revelationem per Filium."[55] – L. 21: "doctrinam Christi",[56] ambiguous expression; it is not only the doctrine declared by Christ, but also concerning him: "Ipse Christus est objectum revelationis";[57] and it is not a question only of his teaching, but also of the "facta salutaria".[58] Revelation is thus not only "locutio verbalis".[59] – P. 10, ll. 14–15: delete this allusion to the magisterium, of which nothing has yet been said. – Nos. 3 and 4: "funditus reformentur"; no "duplex fons".[60] There is no need to change Trent or to close off theological discussions or to put a new obstacle in the way of unity. Let a sub-commission be formed, including members from the commissions "de doctrina" and "de Ecclesia orientali",[61] as well as from the Secretariat for Unity, etc.

An Italian bishop:[62] Gratitude toward the pope. – "Clare determinetur sensus hujus vocis: 'fons revelationis'."[63] Among theologians there are opposing views on the role of the magisterium. Distinguish more clearly two meanings of the word tradition. The schema has nothing on lived tradition (liturgy, etc.). Let us encourage translations of Scripture into all languages. (The president: remain on chap. I.)

A Polish bishop:[64] Brief dissertation on the word "fons". "Duo fontes proprie non sunt."[65] Do not confuse the media and the origo.[66]

Bishop Ubaldo Cibrián Fernández[67] of Bida (Bolivia). (As far as I understood, he was making a plea for two sources.)

---

[55] "Let it be clearly indicated that the revelation through the apostles holds a subordinate place relative to the revelation through the Son."

[56] "The doctrine of Christ".

[57] "Christ himself is the object of revelation."

[58] "The actions that have brought salvation".

[59] "A verbal locution".

[60] "To be redone completely; no twofold source".

[61] "On doctrine and on the Oriental Church".

[62] Costantino M. Attilio Barneschi, O.S.M. (1892–1965), Italian, ordained in 1919. Bishop of Manzini (Swaziland) from 1939 until his death.

[63] "Let the sense of this expression be clearly determined: 'source of revelation'."

[64] This bishop was none other than K. Wojtyła.

[65] "'Source'. Properly speaking, there are not two sources."

[66] "Means and origin".

[67] Ubaldo Evaristo Cibrián Fernández (1906–1965), Spanish, ordained in 1929. Titular bishop, prelate *nullius* of Corocoro (Bolivia) from 1953 until his death.

Card. Ruffini: All those who had asked for the floor have had their say. "Sic clauditur disceptatio de schemate *De fontibus revelationis.*"[68]

According to Don Carlo Colombo (Milan), who told this to Fr. J. Jungmann, it was Cardinal Meyer (Chicago) who went to see the pope and obtained the decision from him.

An article by Fr. Daniélou on exegesis in *France catholique.* The article had been written for *L'Osservatore Romano,* which rejected it. – The information on the council written by Parias[69] in the *France catholique* is partly taken from Father Gagnebet.

An amusing story that the Fathers are recounting. Three bishops, in a taxi, are speaking in Latin on the merits of Latin. When they reach their destination, the taxi driver tells them in Latin that he has understood everything. The three bishops marvel at this use of Latin for social interactions. – But tell us, how is it that you speak Latin so well? – Oh! I was a professor at the Biblical Institute, until I was dismissed; I have to earn a living somehow.

This afternoon, a conference for about thirty bishops and theologians from South America, mostly Argentinians; I showed them how the schema *De deposito fidei* in reality gives attenuated truths. The meeting was organized by Father Jorge Mejía, a professor at the Theology Faculty in Buenos Aires.

During this time, the African bishops were holding their first plenary session. I heard about it from Father Rondet. Opening address by Cardinal Rugambwa, surrounded by the 9 presidents of the 9 groups. A report by Archbishop Zoa, etc. The meeting, well organized, was full of energy. Fr. Greco, the secretary, indicated the motions presented to the council and gave some information; for the three linguistic groups (English, French, Portuguese), various pieces of advice. Archbishop Zoa said that, yesterday, a bishop brought to his attention the fact that the African bishops were letting themselves be guided too much by one particular nation; he answered him that they were Africans, from diverse and independent nations, and that they had no time to waste on such pettiness.

Thursday, November 22, 1962. – It was Archbishop Parente who was reproaching Archbishop Zoa for letting himself be influenced by a

---

[68] "So the discussion of the schema 'On the Sources of Revelation' is closed."

[69] Louis-Henri Parias (1913–1997), French. A writer and journalist, he also edited several historical works.

certain nation (France) and a certain theological school. He replied that Africa included millions of inhabitants, among whom there are many pagans, Muslims, etc., and many Protestants – and many Catholics (the smallest number); that, faced with such a situation, the African bishops were not wasting their time by entering into quarrels among schools of theology.

According to what Msgr. Willebrands said last evening to Father Daniélou, the dispute was so acrimonious the day before yesterday between Cardinals Ottaviani and Bea that one can no longer imagine seeing them together in the new mixed commission. One wonders how this commission is going to be constituted.

The French bishops appear to be very interested in the schema on the means of communication that is going to be discussed; they are zealously preparing interventions.

When (if this actually happened) someone complained to the pope about Fr. Karl Rahner, seeking to have him expelled from Rome, the pope is supposed to have responded: if he has done something wrong, let him sort it out with his bishop. (But how could anyone know that?)

A visit from Fr. Brown,[1] Sulpician, professor of Sacred Scripture in Baltimore, author of a thesis on the "sensus plenior". He came to Rome for the council with a bishop. He told me that several American bishops have changed their opinions since the beginning and are proving to be more tolerant. The apostolic delegate[2] has exerted pressure on them, these last few years, in the fundamentalist direction. Here, they are keeping a little too much to themselves in their hotels. Fr. Brown regrets that they have not had closer contacts with the bishops and theologians from other countries.

According to Archbishop Sartre, the secretary of state signed a decree on November 20 establishing that if three bishops, in a commission, ask to hear from a peritus, the commission must listen to him. For the dogmatic schemas, if they have to be restudied in a mixed commission, this decree loses some of its importance.

An American bishop, whom I met in the company of Oreste Kéramé, confirmed to me that, the day before the Holy Father's decision, Cardinal

---

November 22

[1] Raymond Edward Brown, P.S.S. (1928–1998), American, ordained in 1953. Exegete, professor at Saint Mary's Seminary (Baltimore), author of *The Sensus Plenior of Sacred Scripture* (Baltimore: Saint Mary's University, 1955). Member of the Pontifical Biblical Commission beginning in 1972.

[2] E. Vagnozzi.

Meyer (Chicago) appeared to be very troubled; he kept saying he feared the decisive influence of the Ottaviani-Ruffini-Siri trio.

At 4 P.M., at the book club at Saint-Louis of the French. Around 5 P.M., at the Gregorian, for the thesis defense of Father Norbert Lohfink, S.J.,[3] German (Biblical Institute thesis). Cardinal Pizzardo was presiding, with Fr. Vogt, rector of the Biblical Institute beside him, as well as the examiners: Frs. Moran (American), Alonso-Schökel (Spanish), and de la Potterie (Belgian). In the front row, numerous cardinals. Card. Gerlier (Lyon), completely exhausted, had insisted on coming; he left the hall in the middle of the session. Numerous rows of bishops. On the left, Father General and the Assistants. Ceremonious atmosphere, as usual in Rome, but serious enough. In his opening speech, Fr. Vogt (Swiss) said that his Institute wishes to promote through biblical studies, "doctrinam integram, non diminutam neque distortam"[4] – those were the very words, if I remember correctly, of Cardinal Ottaviani or Archbishop Parente at the council. Father Alonso-Schökel had the candidate explain a case of inspiration of several authors, and it seemed that this was also an allusion to a theory that the schema *De fontibus* rejected.

The names of Cardinals Léger and Bea are being mentioned for the famous mixed commission.

Friday, November 23, 1962. – Everyone this morning is bandying about the names of the cardinals who could become members of the mixed commission to revise *De fontibus* (and perhaps all of the doctrinal schemas): Ottaviani, Browne, Bea, Frings, Meyer, Lefebvre ... – Bishop Véniat expressed surprise in my presence that certain French bishops appear harsh toward Father K. Rahner's schema.[1] – For my part, I surprised the excellent Bishop Maziers (St.-Étienne) by telling him that I did not have much hope for Cardinal Lefebvre, mild and conciliatory as he is, when faced with an Ottaviani.

---

[3] Norbert Lohfink, S.J., born in 1928, German, ordained in 1956. His thesis focuses on chaps. 5–11 of the Book of Deuteronomy. Starting from 1962, he taught exegesis at the Jesuit college of theology Sankt Georgen in Frankfurt.

[4] "The full doctrine, neither attenuated nor corrupted." [Father de Lubac is making reference here to Cardinal Ottaviani's report on *De fontibus*, given on November 14, 1962.]

November 23

[1] This refers to the Rahner-Ratzinger schema, an alternative to the schema *De fontibus*, supported by the presidents of the bishops' conferences of Austria, Belgium, France, Germany, and the Netherlands.

This morning we began the examination of the schema *De instru-mentis communicationis socialis*. President of the day: Card. Ant. Caggiano, archbishop of Buenos Aires. Cardinal Cento said a few words and then yielded the floor to the "relator",[2] Archbishop Stourm. The report was too long, without great interest. A spirit of resignation with little clear insight: "Mundus, nobis luce Evangelii irradiendus, non amplius sicut Media Aetate fiebat, jure meritoque, theologicis disputationibus atten-dit. Jam desivit, proh dolor! talis aetas ..."[3] Thus he seems to confuse the empty disputes of the schools with the proclamation of the Chris-tian faith. The last page was read with this bombastic tone of false elo-quence, which is characteristic of our French bishops and which irritates or amuses all the others.

Cardinal Spellman intervened, as did Card. Ruffini (the schema is too long) and some other bishops. A Canadian[4] took advantage of the opportunity to say that the Holy See should make use of progress in order to inform the bishops of its decisions more rapidly, decisions they now too often learn from their faithful. (Like many others, I was not very interested in the speakers this morning.) In the side naves of Saint Peter's this morning there was a crowd; Archbishop Veuillot, whom I met there, said to me: "This morning, it is a concilium lateranense."[5] Also met Max Thurian, Father Khalifé (Beirut), Bishop Vial, etc. Con-versations. Caught sight of Jean Guitton.

At 1 P.M., Piazza Adriana, lunched with Archbishop Élie Zoghby, a Melchite from Egypt, who had with him a Lebanese monk and a lay friend, the proprietor of a business in the Bekaa Valley. Another guest: a Canadian bishop. The latter told me that Archbishop G. Cabana, who spoke the other day at the council, is the leader of the opposition to Cardinal Léger; that appears to be only a small group of 4 or 5 bishops.

Yesterday the press apparently published a declaration signed by three Ukrainian bishops from the United States, protesting, I am told, against the presence in Rome of two envoys from Moscow, while a Ukrainian archbishop has been deported to Siberia.[6]

---

[2] "Relator".

[3] "The world, which must be irradiated with the light of the Gospel, is no longer interested in theological disputes, as it was, with good reason, in the Middle Ages. Alas, such an age has already come to an end!"

[4] Albert Sanschagrin, O.M.I, born in 1911, Canadian, ordained in 1936. Auxiliary bishop of Amos (Canada) from 1957 to 1967.

[5] A "lateran council", i.e., in the side aisles. – TRANS.

[6] This declaration, made by fifteen Ukrainian bishops, at first intended for the council Fathers only, was nevertheless published by *Il Giornale d'Italia* (November 21, 1962). It recalled in partic-

Archbishop Zoa recounted to me in more detail the reproaches that Archbishop Parente, his former professor at the Propaganda, had addressed to him and the response that he had given to him.

An article in *Témoignage chrétien* relates that "250 black bishops" (!) rejected the schema *De fontibus*. It also reports that "some texts were already in circulation, one attributed to Fr. de Lubac, the other to Fr. Rahner" (!) Oh, the newspapers!

At 4 P.M., a visit from Fr. G. Martelet, who brought me a flood of news. He took me along to the talk that Father Boulard was giving to the African bishops, then to Oscar Cullmann's press conference on the council observers. During this time, Father Rondet was taking part in a working meeting with some bishops and theologians at Saint-Louis des Français.

The schemas *De Ecclesia* and *De B. Maria Virgine* were finally distributed this morning.

One of the "assignatores"[7] of the conciliar assembly would like to translate the complete edition of my *Paradoxes* into Italian. He told me that the translation of the *Nouveaux Paradoxes* is very bad. He was saying to me this morning, with regard to the pope's recent intervention: "I am just about the only one among us (= the assignatores) to be happy about it."

Saturday, November 24, 1962. – A few days ago, Father Gagnebet was saying to Fr. Congar that we should protest in the press against the false information according to which we could not freely express ourselves in the Preparatory Theological Commission. I have not seen any news reports of that sort. In any case, any possible "protest" should be carefully nuanced . . .

At Saint Peter's, this morning, exchanged a few words with Jean Guitton. A longer conversation with Fr. Raes; he has the impression that the council is getting bogged down. Too many schemas, all of them too long, and the mode of discussion too slow. In passing, Msgr. Garofalo greeted me and asked in friendly manner if I was not chosen to join the mixed commission as a peritus. Fr. Hirschmann (Frankfurt), always well informed, told me how that commission was composed and what

---

ular the detention in Siberia of Josyf Slipyj (1892–1984), Ukrainian, ordained in 1917; archbishop metropolitan of Lvov (USSR) from 1944 until his death. Arrested in 1945, he was imprisoned and sent to forced labor in Siberia.

[7] Seminarians or young priests who showed the Fathers to their places *in aula* and distributed attendance sheets and voting ballots.

instructions it had received from the pope; its first session is supposed to take place tomorrow. The two presidents, Ottaviani and Bea, will have a lot of trouble getting along.

President of the day: Card. Bernard Alfrink. Archbishop Felici read out a telegram to be sent by the council to the Holy Father on the occasion of his birthday;[1] it talks about what he is doing "in gloriam Sponsae Dei".[2]

Card. Wyszyński: It is necessary to recall the importance of preaching the Gospel on the radio; many people will never hear it any other way. Let Vatican radio and the other Catholic stations read the Gospel in every language.

Card. W. Godfrey (Westminster). He doubted the timeliness of such a conciliar schema. A separate document would be better. If however we decide to include it, let it be reduced to a "forma multo brevior".[3] It points out principles so evident that they do not lend themselves to discussion. Some detailed remarks; so, at nos. 80–81: the faithful can be disappointed by the official Catholic press; and if they only read the Catholic papers and magazines of their own country, they risk closing themselves off in a narrow world, since these publications are too often strictly local.

Card. Léger (Montreal). – "Timeo ne huic schemati sufficiens sollicitudo praebeatur."[4] It would be necessary to make "magnas emendationes"[5] to it. More than other constitutions, this one will be read and commented on by Catholics and by others. "Digna est igitur consideratione accurata."[6] – Three remarks: 1. Schema valde abbrevietur, etiam in parte doctrinali.[7] – 2. Let the spirit of it be changed: "modus est nimis juridicus";[8] it speaks of the rights and functions of the Church: it would be better to speak of her pastoral solicitude to come to the help of men. – 3. "Mens negativa afficit ipsam doctrinam":[9] cf. nos. 13 and 14, where, in talking very competently of the power of the information

---

November 24

[1] John XXIII was born on November 25, 1881.
[2] "For the glory of the Bride of God".
[3] "Much shorter form".
[4] "I fear that insufficient attention is being paid to this schema."
[5] "Important amendments".
[6] "Therefore it is deserving of careful consideration."
[7] "1. The schema needs to be seriously abridged, also in the doctrinal part."
[8] "The style is too legalistic."
[9] "3. A negative spirit affects the doctrine itself."

media, it scarcely does more than point out the dangers. "Ne praevaleant in christiana doctrina timor et negativa consideratio."[10] – Conclusion: it is difficult to continue the discussion until the schema has been abridged by the competent commission; let laypeople bring their experience to the task.

Card. Suenens (Malines). "Schema non est doctrinale, sed pastorale."[11] In a doctrinal text, each word must be submitted to criticism; "schema autem pastorale non exigit eamdem methodum".[12] Therefore, simply determine some methodological principles. I think everyone, or almost everyone, finds the text too long. It is good, however, and deals with an important subject. So it could be given a general approval, and then the complete document would be an act of the ordinary magisterium. – Three other remarks: 1. At no. 21, it should be recalled that information that touches on private life must be excluded; call for legislation on this point – and let there be an ordo[13] for those who give the information, as there exists an ordo avocatorum and an ordo medicorum.[14] – "2. Passivitas fidelium est maxime damnosa."[15] Let us educate them so that they might play an active role, found associations, etc. Lamenting on the evil of the times serves no purpose. – 3. Religious news is for the most part superficial and extrinsic (ceremonies, blessing of bells, etc.). It should above all be concerned with fundamental matters of faith and Christian life. To this end, a certain theology of the news is necessary. Let the "laici scriptores"[16] understand their duty here.

Card. Bea: Omnino consentio[17] what Card. Ruffini has said. "Insistendum adeo non est in jure et officio Ecclesiae interveniendi in his rebus, sed magis in magno servitio et beneficio quod Ecclesia praestare potest omnibus hominibus bonae voluntatis."[18] To her own children, the Church must stress that an image does not suffice; there is a danger that educators will not accomplish their full task: they must learn to listen

---

[10] "Let fear and a negative consideration not prevail in Christian doctrine."

[11] "The schema is not doctrinal, but pastoral."

[12] "But a pastoral schema does not require the same method."

[13] "Order".

[14] "Order of lawyers, order of doctors".

[15] "2. The passivity of the faithful is very harmful."

[16] "Laymen who are writers".

[17] "I altogether approve".

[18] "We must not insist so much on the right and the duty of the Church to intervene in this matter, but more on the great service the Church can render and the benefit that she can provide to all men of goodwill."

and to reflect or education by means of images will be totally superficial. Usefulness of the new media to make Catholic doctrine known to
all people. Catholics can collaborate with all other Christians to act on
public opinion; their union can be a powerful force; this is especially a
matter for the laity. Collaboration can be extended "omnibus hominibus qui habent bonam voluntatem et in Deum credunt."[19] Take great
care that the technical and material aspect does not get the upper hand.
Finally, one addition: it is very urgent that the Holy See have a rather
powerful communication medium.

Bishop Jacques Ménager (Meaux). "Exponitur jus Ecclesiae docendi
et moderandi: talis proclamatio non plene sufficit."[20] The question must
not be studied "sub solo aspectu juris".[21] Make an appeal to the activity
of laypeople organized among themselves, aware of their mission, determined to be witnesses of Christ and of the Church.

Archbishop Perraudin of Kabgayi (Rwanda). The bishops of Africa,
Madagascar, and the Isles thank the writers of the schema. "Instantissime
declarare desiderant"[22] how strongly they feel about this question. "In
genere schema placet. Tamen, non satis actuosum nec novum."[23] It is
not enough to warn of the dangers or to exhort to positive action. It is
necessary that the Church herself produce programs and, if possible, create radio stations. Even in Africa, the press, radio, television are making
rapid progress. Help us to equip ourselves; alone, we will not be able to
do anything. With you, the Church in Africa will be able to accomplish
a great deal. "Sine mora ulla incipiendum est. Necessitas quam maxime
urget."[24]

Bishop Alexandre Renard of Versailles. Our world is ruled by public
opinion. It would be a sin of omission not to use the new means at our
disposal. "Atqui, nobis deest structura apostolica ad publicam opinionem
informandam, etc."[25] Everything should not be standardized, however:
"timeo hominem unius methodi, etc."[26]

Etc., etc. (I heard little of what the subsequent speakers said.)

---

[19] "To all men of goodwill and who believe in God".

[20] "The right of the Church to teach and to moderate is set forth: such a proclamation is not altogether sufficient."

[21] "Solely under the aspect of right".

[22] "They wish to declare very insistently".

[23] "I approve the schema in general. However, it is not current enough or new enough."

[24] "This needs to be put into effect without delay. It is an extremely pressing necessity."

[25] "And yet, we lack an apostolic institution for forming public opinion."

[26] "I fear the man of one method." [A reference to the adage of Saint Thomas Aquinas: "Timeo hominem unius libri" (I fear the man of one book).]

Bishop Gouyon, of Bayonne insisted a little too much on the very grave responsibility of all the faithful to read the Catholic newspapers (!).

In Saint Peter's, I met an Anglo-Saxon bishop from South Africa, Bishop D. E. Hurley. He approached me and said to me in French: "Well, Father, look how this new theology has had its success at the council!" And we exchanged a few words.

In the November 23 issue of *Time* magazine, an article on the trials of Card. Ottaviani: "The Cardinal's Setback" (p. 58). In it the remark of an Irish bishop is quoted: "We have had a mistaken idea that Cardinal Ottaviani represents the Holy See. We'll have to revise our definition of what the Holy See is."

In *L'Osservatore*, following the protest of the Ukrainian bishops in exile, there appeared a "Clarification from the Secretariat for the Unity of Christians": "Il segretariato ... tiene a precisare che tutti gli Osservatori-Delegati sono stati invitati del medesimo Segretariato, che è stato di accoglierli. – Tutti, senza eccezione, hanno manifestato uno spirito sinceramente religioso e ecumenico. Il Segretariato è dolente, pertanto, di quanto è stato pubblicato in contrasto allo spirito che ha animato i tali contatti avviati e in atto con gli Osservatori-Delegati. Il Segretario non più fare altro che dissociarsene."[27]

At 4 P.M., with Fr. Henri Rondet, I went to the French Seminary. A conversation with Father Pierre Haubtmann. Saw Cardinal Lefebvre for a few minutes. On the way back, we visited a few churches.

We learned in the afternoon that the mixed commission has been formed. Even the periti have been named; but the list has not been published.

Sunday, November 25, 1962. – Archbishop Jean Villot, well placed to observe what is going on due to his functions in the secretariat of the council, has heard a number of diverse reflections. Some are bemoaning the pope's advanced age, his good heart, his lack of scientific knowledge, all of which launch him into disturbing ventures. Some express doubts

---

[27] "The Secretariat is anxious to make clear that all the observers-delegates have been invited by this same Secretariat, which has welcomed them. All of them, without exception, have shown a sincerely religious and ecumenical spirit. Consequently, the Secretariat regrets what has been published, in contrast to the spirit that has animated the contacts, past and present, with the observers-delegates. The Secretariat cannot do otherwise than to dissociate itself from [what was published]."

concerning the quality of his faith. In the circles of the Curia, there is fear that the bishops might demand a little more authority for themselves. There are also some impatient bishops.

I read this morning a manuscript work by Father Dournes (Foreign Missions) on the tribes that he is evangelizing in Vietnam, in the diocese of Kontum.

Visit from Father Martelet. He saw Cardinal Liénart yesterday. The cardinal talked to him about the mixed commission. It is supposed to prepare a schema *De revelatione*, which would replace the first two dogmatic schemas (*De fontibus, De deposito*); but it is still not very clear. Liénart is very glad of the presence of Cardinal Lefebvre, more a dogmatician than he. He is planning to intervene one day soon on *De Ecclesiae unitate* and on *De Beata Maria*.

Father Salaverri addresses some amusing observations to me from time to time (we are together at the Curia) about the observers, whose presence in Rome I gather does not please him.

This morning, with various bishops and various Protestants, Fr. Daniélou spoke on a French-language radio broadcast about the ecumenical problem: a dialogue with O. Cullmann on tradition. – I declined to speak on an Italian-language program.

A conversation this afternoon with Giuseppe Alberigo (the principal author of the compendium "Conciliorum oecumenicorum decreta"), who is a professor of Church history at the University of Florence and director of the Documentation Center, Institute for Religious Sciences, in Bologna. He is in close contact, along with his friend Don Giuseppe Dossetti, with Cardinal Lercaro. Both of them, Alberigo and Dossetti, know Cardinal Montini very well, from their student days in Rome, and keep in contact with him. Alberigo brought me a draft entitled: "Provvedimenti in vista dell'intervallo tra la prima e la seconda sessione del Concilio."[1] I made a few observations. This text, revised and accompanied with a Latin translation, would be submitted to the pope by Archbishop Dell'Acqua,[2] who is on friendly terms with Don Dossetti; a certain number of cardinals and bishops would also receive a copy. It is

November 25

[1] "Provisions in view of the interval between the first and second sessions of the council" [Suenens collection, 619].

[2] Angelo Dell'Acqua (1903–1972), Italian, ordained in 1928. Substitute of the Secretariat of State for Ordinary Affairs from 1952 to 1967, created cardinal in 1967. President of the Prefecture for the Economic Affairs of the Holy See from 1967 to 1968. Vicar General of Rome in 1968. Member of the Commission for the Discipline of the Sacraments.

a plan to reduce the program of the council and to assure a continuous presence in Rome between the sessions.

Monday, November 26, 1962 (27th General Congregation). – On St. Peter's Square, I was stopped by Father Paul Poupard (from the Secretariat of State). He is worried. He reported to me something that Fr. Seb. Tromp had said to a friend: "They have rejected our constitution; but the one that we will give them will be its twin sister." He is also worried about what could happen in Rome during the time between the two sessions. If the council does not prevail, he told me, the system will be worse than it was before; Tromp will go out strengthened by the struggle. – Entering Saint Peter's, I met Bishop Th. J. Suhr of Copenhagen, who also expressed to me his anxiety and appeared saddened by some curialist maneuvers: "There is nothing humane in that", he said to me. – Near the confessionals, Bishop Elchinger stopped me: he seemed anxious for a conciliar body that would ensure the link between the two sessions. The pope is alleged to want everything finished by June 29, 1963. – After Mass, chatted briefly with Fr. Congar, very tired, seated in the former chapel of the Blessed Sacrament.

Archbishop Felici made some announcements "ex mandato Praesidis"[1] (today, Card. Tisserant). Starting on December 1, there will be a general congregation every day except Sunday. On December 8, "solemne sacrum",[2] with the pope presiding. – "Expleta discussione de Instrumentis communicationis socialis, tractabitur decretum 'Ut unum sint', quasi praeludium alterius Constitutionis ... Multi Patres rogaverunt ut tractetur Constitutio de Ecclesia. Quapropter, incipiet postea relatio et discussio de Ecclesia. Constitutio de beata Maria Virgine, cum sit pars constitutionis de Ecclesia, cum eadem constitutione tractabitur."[3] – So let the Fathers register as soon as possible for the discussion of De Ecclesia. On the unity of the Church, there are other schemas; we will examine today only the first of these documents.

Continuation of the discussion of De instrumentis ... :

November 26

[1] "On the mandate of the President".

[2] "Solemn Mass".

[3] "When the discussion on the Instruments of Social Communication has been finished, the decree Ut unum sint will be taken up, as a prelude to another constitution ... Many Fathers have asked that we take up the constitution De Ecclesia. Because of this, we will next begin the report and the discussion of De Ecclesia. The constitution on the Blessed Virgin Mary, as part of the constitution De Ecclesia, will be discussed together with it."

Bishop Luigi Civardi[4] of Tespia (Italy). "Schema bonum, utile, opportunum. Res pastoralis summi momenti."[5] Two remarks: "1. Circa officium et jus Ecclesiae. Hoc jus evidens est",[6] but it is affirmed only with respect to ideas, instruction; we must also affirm it in the area of recreation and relaxation. "Ecclesia habet quamdam potestatem etiam in re oblectamenti."[7] Now, too many of the faithful, overcome by laicism, question this authority. It is therefore opportune to affirm it in very explicit terms. — 2. My personal experience, as a member of the Italian cinema commission, shows me the effect films have for deforming consciences and corrupting morals. Christian film schools must be established. "Est in hoc lacrimosa penuria."[8]

Bishop Josef Freundorfer[9] of Augsburg (Germany). The world today is divided, there are a plurality of religions and ideologies; the Church lives in a state of spiritual diaspora. She neither can nor wants to impose her doctrine by force. So it serves no purpose to make the demand for her rights resound everywhere. But society has an essential need, in order to live, of some moral laws recognized by all. In our pluralist society, Catholics can play a dual role: they must first choose, out of everything that is proposed to them, what is compatible with their faith; then they must cooperate with non-Catholics of goodwill; experience shows that this cooperation is often a very effective force for good.

Archbishop Léon Duval of Algiers. The missionary aspect of the question. These new means of communication permit an explicit preaching of the Gospel; they can also prepare the way for this preaching by getting men interested in all the great human problems. In this it is necessary to cooperate with all men of goodwill. Many problems cannot be resolved by Christians alone. The Catholic press: very good; but it is not always possible; there too, collaboration is necessary. "Dilatentur spatio caritatis" (St. Augustine).[10]

Bishop Santos Moro[11] (Spain)?

---

[4] Luigi Civardi (1886–1971), Italian, ordained in 1911. Titular bishop of Thespiae. A great specialist on Catholic Action, he was the first Assistant of the ACLI (Catholic Association of Italian Workers). Member of the Commission for the Lay Apostolate.

[5] "The schema is good, useful, timely. It is a pastoral matter of very great importance."

[6] "Concerning the duty and the right of the Church. This right is evident."

[7] "The Church has a certain authority also in matters of relaxation."

[8] "This is sadly lacking."

[9] In actuality, it was Joseph Höffner (1906–1987), German, ordained in 1932. Bishop of Münster from 1962 to 1969. Created cardinal in 1969. Member of the Commission for Seminaries, Studies, and Catholic Education.

[10] "Let more room be given to charity." [Saint Augustine, *Sermon LXIX*, 1.]

[11] Santos Moro Briz (1888–1980), Spanish, ordained in 1911. Bishop of Avila from 1935 to 1968.

Bishop Kempf (Germany)?

A bishop from Rhodesia:[12] Against the "detractationes"[13] by the publication of offenses, etc. – On laypeople: they have rights: cf. what Cardinals Léger and Bea have said. We must not say: "Ecclesia et laici",[14]
for the laity are members of the Church, but, rather: "hierarchia et laici.
Nescio utrum abbreviatio sit sine damno possibilis."[15] – Delete, two
times, the word "rudiores".[16]

Archbishop Émile Tagle of Valparaiso (Chile). The schema is too
long. Film corporations. If we wish to have any effectiveness, unite the
efforts of all our countries, etc.

Bishop Sébastien Soares de Resende of Beira (Mozambique). On nos.
66, 68, and 83. A union of forces is needed; this is urgent. I propose
something concrete and practical: an international Catholic organization, an information agency, etc.; supported by a financial institution. –
Standardize missionary publications.

Bishop Aurelius Del Pino Gómez of Lerida (Spain). He is happy
about the substantial unanimity obtained by the schema. We must proclaim above all the "certissimum Ecclesiae jus".[17] The Church has this
right owing to her origin: her apologists were the first to employ such
means; and it conforms to the Word made flesh, etc. Such instruments
are subject by right to the Church, which alone is the Way, the "Magistra infallibilis".[18] If our exhortations are not heard, we will leave that to
the judgment of God. – In extolling these means of information, let us
not forget more important means: penance, spiritual exercises, the Mass,
etc. – Let laypeople work "sub sacerdotum prudenti tutela".[19] – He
strenuously insisted on the principle: De malo nulla libertas;[20] God, as
perfect freedom, cannot do evil, etc.

Bishop Abdul Ahad Sana[21] of Alquoch (Iraq). He spoke in French and
apologized for that. – The schema is good; only a few remarks. We are
on new ground here, a field of action par excellence. To speak of rights,

[12] A. Kozlowiecki.
[13] "Calumnies".
[14] "The Church and the laity".
[15] "The hierarchy and the laity. I do not know if it is possible to shorten it without harm."
[16] "Uncultivated".
[17] "The most certain right of the Church".
[18] "Infallible teacher".
[19] "Under the prudent direction of the priests".
[20] "No liberty comes from evil."
[21] Abdul-Ahad Sana (1922–2007), Iraqi, ordained in 1947. Chaldean bishop of Alquoch (Iraq)
from 1960 to 2001.

to give directives is insufficient. We must give the means of practical action, etc. Improvements to be desired for Vatican radio: programs, and technical aspects.

Bishop Alexandre Fernández[22] of San Cristobal (Venezuela), in the name of the episcopal conferences of Venezuela. "Omnia probanda et laudanda."[23] However, let it be shortened. Determine the rights of the Church, civil society, the laity. Recall the dignitas personae humanae,[24] so often damaged.

Bishop Francis Simons of Indore (India). One remark only, of great practical importance. We cannot forget this: people object to us that the Church always and everywhere demands her rights but that she neglects the rights of others when she is powerful. This persistent suspicion would be effectively removed by a solemn declaration of the council on the right of every person to follow his conscience, even when it errs. The world, jure merito,[25] expects that from us. Reject any anxiety on that subject. The Church has progressed throughout the centuries without depending on recognized rights, without protection. "Malum in bono vincitur."[26] We are not able nor are we always supposed to prevent all evils ...

(For these last interventions, those absent had become very numerous, and there was a loud, confused noise of conversations coming from the lower side-aisles. The president asked the Fathers to return to their seats.)

Bishop Juan Pedro Zarranz y Pueyo,[27] of Plasencia (Spain). "Schema magnopere placet. Urgentissimae necessitatis est."[28] – There followed a violent diatribe against the evil effects of the cinema, etc., which destroy personal conscience and morals. Too little is said about this. "Explicitior declaratio hac in re desideratur. Dignitas, integritas et jura personae humanae solemniter et explicite proclamentur."[29]

---

[22] Alejandro Fernández Feo-Tinoco (1908–1987), Venezuelan, ordained in 1931. Bishop of San Crisóbal from 1952 to 1984.

[23] "Everything should be approved and praised."

[24] "Dignity of the human person".

[25] "And justly so".

[26] "Evil is conquered in the good."

[27] Juan Pedro Zarranz y Pueyo (1903–1973), Spanish, ordained in 1925. Bishop of Plasencia from 1946 until his death.

[28] "I strongly approve the schema. It is of a very urgent necessity."

[29] "A more explicit declaration is desirable on this matter. The dignity, integrity, and rights of the human person should be proclaimed solemnly and explicitly."

The secretary general: "Cum materia Constitutionis satis illustrata et enucleata videatur, Emin. cardinalis Praeses proponit: An placeat a disceptatione cessare."[30]

Voting was by sitting or standing. Everyone stood up.

"Schema *De Ecclesiae unitate*: 'Opus Redemptionis etc.' Relator:[31] Card. A. Cicognani, secretary of state." – Of the various schemas prepared by the Eastern Commission, this is the only one submitted for discussion, "ut vox attollatur Orientis amica in concilio oecumenico"[32] ... Our connection in Christ with the Eastern Churches. "Olim uniti omnes eramus. Hodie, eadem fides",[33] except on a few points, especially on the "Petra super quam aedificatur Ecclesia".[34] The concern for reunion is something we share with them. The venerable patriarchs of the Eastern Churches and other bishops of various rites are present at this council – and there are observers. "Urget quam maxime sollicitudo unionis. Fuerunt olim gravissimae difficultates",[35] and as the centuries passed, "rationes diverse cogitandi et sentiendi creverunt. Germana doctrina catholica tenenda est"[36] but with the concern of being well understood by our separated brothers. There has often been talk of union, but it bore no fruit. For a long time, how much has been written, how many prayers! The council brings a hope. (Here, Card. Cicognani spoke about the Secretariat for Unity, then about the Eastern Christians: I did not understand in exactly what sense.) Our schema wishes to point out the paths and the means to unity, so as to remove suspicions, prejudices, etc. Nothing concerning the old disputes. "Laboremus ad unitatem in veritate et caritate Christi",[37] following the spirit of the council declared by the Holy Father.

---

[30] "Since the matter of the constitution seems to have been sufficiently clarified and analyzed, His Eminence the Cardinal President proposes: Do you agree to close the discussion?"

[31] "Schema on the unity of the Church: 'The Work of Redemption, etc.' Relator".

[32] "In order that a friendly voice from the East might be brought to the ecumenical council".

[33] "Formerly we were all united. Today, the same faith".

[34] "Rock on which the Church was built." [A quotation from Origen, in reference to Matthew 16:18, repeated by Saint Thomas Aquinas in the *Catena aurea in quattuor Evangelia: Expositio in Matthaeum* (chap. 16, lectio 3), a compilation of commentaries from the Fathers of the Church.]

[35] "The concern for union is extremely urgent. Very serious difficulties existed formerly."

[36] "Ways of thinking and perceiving developed in different directions. We must hold to authentic Catholic doctrine."

[37] "Let us work toward unity in the truth and charity of Christ."

Father Athanase Welykyj,[38] Basilian: The schema aims to respond to the wishes of numerous bishops. It deals only with the Orthodox. The Eastern Commission had to occupy itself with a number of other questions, summarized in a disciplinary decree, which will be discussed later. Since the opening of the council, more than 60 Fathers sent observations. – We do not speak of our Protestant brothers: this was not within our competence; the theologians of the Secretariat for Unity are concerned with that. We do not say "de unitate Ecclesiae"[39] from a doctrinal point of view, but a social one. We had to avoid in our expressions "omnem speciem proselytismi".[40] The schema contains three parts: 1. Nos. 1 to 12, De unitate theologica,[41] with special attention to the difficulties of the Eastern Churches; "nil mirandum"[42] if we often had recourse to Scripture and if we avoided scholastic terms. However, "ne dicetur nos obnubilare integram veritatem catholicam"[43] ... Instead of "separati",[44] we say "dissidentes",[45] a word less harsh, for in fact there has not been a clear and formal separation. – 2. Nos. 13 to 47, "de mediis reconciliationis, sensu latissimo sumptae".[46] Some means are ancient; others are new; cf. nos. 31 and 35. "Quaedam solemnior declaratio concilii de libertate ritus et disciplinae."[47] – 3. Nos. 48 to 52: "Media sensu stricto[48] ..." –The Fathers will have to say "an placeat schema in genere – quaenam in particulari emendanda sint".[49]

Cardinal Liénart. – Many timely principles. "Dolendum tamen est, quod in forma et quoad rem sint aliqui graves defectus. – In forma: nimis auctoritative loquitur."[50] The more certain our Church is that she is in

---

[38] Athanasius G. Welykyj, O.S.B.M. (1918–1982), Ukrainian, ordained in 1946. Expert at the council during the first session, he became superior general of the Basilians of Saint Josaphat from 1963 to 1976. Secretary of the Commission for Eastern Churches.

[39] "On the unity of the Church".

[40] "Every form of proselytism".

[41] "On theological unity".

[42] "There is nothing surprising".

[43] "Let it not be said that we are obscuring the full Catholic truth."

[44] "Separated".

[45] "Dissenting".

[46] "On the means of reconciliation, taken in a very broad sense".

[47] "A more solemn declaration from the council on the liberty of rites and disciplines".

[48] "The means in the strict sense".

[49] "If the schema is pleasing in general, and what are the points in particular that need amending."

[50] "It is regrettable, however, that in its form and also in its content there are grave defects. In its form: it speaks in a manner that is too authoritarian."

the right, the more she must feel an obligation to talk with the others, not auctoritativo modo,[51] but through a true dialogue. – Quoad rem:[52] The schema deals, in the singular, with the Eastern Church: "atqui, non est una Ecclesia orientalis sed sunt plures".[53] That is a factual and a psychological error. "Neque curat schema de protestantibus, nec de anglicana ecclesia":[54] yet these are Christian Churches. One cannot deal with unity without thinking of all the baptized. "Hoc altum silentium"[55] would lead one to believe that we do not care about them. "Instanter igitur rogo"[56] that everything be treated in the schema. Consequently, "recognoscatur".[57]

Card. Ruffini. "Plurima, paucis forsan exceptis, maxime laudanda."[58] In almost everything, the Eastern Churches have the same faith as we do. But, difficulties: It is hard to see why this schema is separate from the dogmatic constitution De Ecclesia. – In the first part several passages can be misinterpreted. There is a lack of theological precision in places. A danger that we might lead people to believe that "Ecclesiam sola formatam esse caritate."[59] Baptism does not suffice to make one a member of the Church, etc. – This is not a "pars Ecclesiae", it is a "pars christianorum quae se subtraxit";[60] "Ecclesia numquam in seipsa habet maculam neque rugam".[61] – To say: "Ecclesiam invisibilem et caelestem"[62] is equivocal: and could be taken in a disjunctive sense. – Page 251: to be sure, we have also made mistakes; but we have not been "in aliam partem"[63] ...

Card. Bacci. "Placet ad modum". Two criticisms. 1. On the introduction and the title. "De unitate instauranda": "sed unitas jam habetur; est nota Ecclesiae indefectibilis. Cf. S. Thomas. Contra errores Graecorum. Œcumenismus est optima res, sed veritas plena, sincera, integra sit; nulla

---

[51] "In an authoritarian manner".

[52] "As far as the content is concerned".

[53] "But there is not one single Eastern Church, but several."

[54] "The schema does not concern itself with the Protestants or with the Anglican Church."

[55] "This profound silence".

[56] "Therefore I ask insistently".

[57] "Let it be revised."

[58] "A very great number of points, with the exception of a few, perhaps, should be highly praised."

[59] "The Church is constituted by charity alone."

[60] "Part of the Church, it is a part of the Christian people who have dissociated themselves."

[61] "The Church never has in herself either stain or wrinkle."

[62] "The invisible and celestial Church".

[63] "In another camp ..."

incertitudo, nulla discordia inter nos, nulla ambiguitas sit."[64] Cf. the schema *De Ecclesia*. Otherwise, we will foster indifferentism and inter-confessionalism. Say: "De omnium christianorum unitate procuranda", or: "De omnibus christianis ad unum Christi ovile revocandis".[65] – 2. Let the Secretariat for Unity continue its work.

Card. Browne. I believed that this concerned all separated Christians. And we have not yet studied the schema *De Ecclesia*. It is necessary first to have the simplex veritas, with the consideratio theologica. Otherwise, "non via recta".[66] So let our disceptatio[67] not be definitive. It will be necessary to adapt it to the schema *De Ecclesia* and to deal with all the separated brothers.

While leaving, spoke quickly with a few bishops. Two Copts approached me and spoke to me amiably in French. Started a conversation with Bishop Philippe, O.P.,[68] but we were interrupted before I could explain to him what I wanted (a clarification on the Theological Commission). – Next I met Dom Olivier Rousseau (from Chevetogne). Some journalists stopped me; one of them asked me what I thought of Fr. Rahner; I protested against their false dichotomies: conservative-liberal, etc.

This afternoon, various talks: Jean Guitton (to the Africans), Msgr. Cerfaux, etc. There were also working groups.

Father Hamer, O.P., peritus on the mixed commission, spoke to me about the first meeting, which took place yesterday. Card. Ottaviani was the one presiding, as he has been a cardinal longer than Bea. The rejected schema was nonetheless kept as a working basis. Card. Bea kept a low profile. Card. Liénart thought he was obliged to speak in Latin and stammered. Subcommissions are going to be formed. Msgr. Fenton is a peritus. Ottaviani talked a lot; he seems disposed to drown any effort toward a true revision.

---

[64] "On the unity to be established: but there is already unity, it is a note of the indefectible Church. Cf. Saint Thomas, *Against the Errors of the Greeks*. Ecumenism is an excellent thing, but let the truth be full, sincere, complete; let there be no uncertainty, no discord among us, no ambiguity."

[65] "On the unity of all Christians that needs to be procured" or "On calling all Christians back to the one fold of Christ".

[66] "Simple truth, with the theological consideration. Otherwise, the way will not be straight."

[67] "Discussion".

[68] Paul Philippe.

At 3 p.m., at the Biblical Institute, I took part in a study meeting with Congar, Labourdette, R. Laurentin, etc., and several French bishops, including Bishop Pourchet. The subject was the Marian schema. Laurentin, who was directing the meeting, explained the text. We studied it. The principal author is Fr. Balić, O.F.M. Several have criticized the tendency of the schema, which goes in the direction of the devotional ultramontanism prevailing since Pius IX (the pope and the Virgin, the Infallibilis and the Immaculata:[69] on the pope, it puts one in mind of the "Rerum Pius tenax vigor"[70] and other similar formulas). The schema takes up, concerning the Virgin, the idea of "jura maternal",[71] etc. – We composed the draft of a brief introduction that would link the schema with the one on the Church; no. 1 would then be shortened. – Next we talked about the draft composed by Msgr. Philips (Louvain),[72] in view of a new schema *De Ecclesia*. It consists of almost the same elements as the old one, but with a dynamic internal order: "Quid sit Ecclesia"[73] – Of what is she composed; hierarchy, faithful, religious life. – Doctrinal life of the Church, authority and obedience; the duty of discipleship. – Relations with the other Christians, with the earthly city. Cardinal Suenens would support this draft. The chapter on the Virgin could serve as an epilogue or crowning finish. – We examined this draft paragraph by paragraph.

At 5 p.m., at the Gesù. A talk in front of the seminarians who understand French; answered questions. Subjects broached: The credo – Theology and apostolate – Fr. Teilhard de Chardin – The life of a peritus in Rome, etc. – An Italian seminarian asked me how it happens that, if Fr. Teilhard is such as I said, the Communists are translating him into Italian.

On my return, conversation with Dr. Joseph Ratzinger. The news of the first meeting of the mixed commission dismayed him. He thinks that the orientation of this commission, dominated as it is by the Ottaviani-Tromp-Parente trio, with their experts, like Fenton, in no way corresponds to the desires of the council. We will see ...

---

[69] "The Infallible and the Immaculate".

[70] By analogy with "Rerum Deus tenax vigor", a hymn taken from the office of None in the Roman breviary. [Rerum Pius tenax vigor = literally, Pius, tenacious strength of creation. – Trans.]

[71] "Maternal rights".

[72] From the first week of the council, the bishops of Belgium, and particularly Cardinal Suenens, had asked G. Philips to draft an alternative schema to the official schema *De Ecclesia*.

[73] "What is the Church".

Fr. Daniélou took part in a meeting at which the course to follow with respect to the schema *De Ecclesia* was studied. Some would be disposed to accept it "juxta modum", while demanding profound changes; others replied that such a demand would be unrealistic: a schema that is not rejected compels recognition, and nothing more than the correction of details can be obtained. There is a hope that several cardinals will speak out firmly on the subject. But Father Gagnebet, O.P., one of the authors of *De Ecclesia*, would insist that a schema prepared by the Theological Commission not be rejected yet again.

Fr. Rondet showed me this evening, in the November 24 issue of *La Croix*, an article by Jean Pélissier, Roman correspondent for the council: "Summary of Recent Work". The article talks about a schema put into circulation and attributed to Fr. Rahner, concerning which there were complaints at the council. I know Pélissier, an excellent man; I wrote to him: ". . . I regret that you did not add (no doubt because you did not know) that this schema was proposed as a basis for discussion by the "Praesides Conferentiarum episcopalium Austriae, Belgii, Galliae, Germaniae, Hollandiae".[74] So this was not simply a private initiative . . .

Tuesday, November 27, 1962 (28th General Cong.). – People everywhere are saying that on December 11, John XXIII will go into hospital for a prostate operation.

A lot of attention has been paid to an article in the magazine *Borghese* on (against) the personal secretary of the pope, Msgr. Capovilla, "A Powerful Monsignor". The article is thought to have been inspired by Card. Ottaviani. The same for three very recent articles (Saturday, Sunday, and Monday) in *Corriere della Sera*[1] that call the pope a modernist. Father R. Rouquette, who has read them, spoke to me about them.

At Saint Peter's this morning, I told Bishop Seitz (Kontum, Vietnam) of my initial satisfaction with what I had read (I have not yet finished) of Fr. Dournes' work on his missionary life. I proposed to Roger Schutz and Max Thurian that they invite Dom Jean Leclercq, whose acquaintance they have not yet made, to visit them one day. Bishop McGrath (Cerici,

---

[74] "Presidents of the Austrian, Belgian, French, German, Dutch bishops' conferences".
November 27
[1] This refers to the articles by Indro Montanelli that appeared on November 24, 25, and 26, 1962.

Panama)[2] told me, and Father Weigel[3] as well, of his bad impression of the start of the mixed commission. Fr. Kerrigan, O.F.M.,[4] a peritus on this commission, told me of his desire for reconciliation; but he seems to me to have little awareness of the fundamental problems. Canon Thils (Louvain), also a peritus, would tell me that afternoon that he admired the skill of Card. Ottaviani as a "debater". There will be, I am told, 5 subcommissions, each with a cardinal presiding.[5]

Cardinal Liénart was presiding this morning. – Archbishop Felici: "Audiant omnes. Cum plures episcopi postulaverint a SS Domino"[6] that the council not recommence, next year, until September, the Holy Father received on November 26 the Cardinal President for External Affairs[7] and has ruled "secundam periodum initium habere die 8 septembre 1963".[8] – "Suffragium fiet hodie de propositione distributa heri, *De instrumentis* . . . , per placet et non placet",[9] polling to close at 10:30 A.M.

We continued the examination of the schema *De Ecclesiae unitate.*

Archbishop Felici read, on behalf of the Eastern Commission, a declaration in 3 points, intended to forestall objections, avoid confusion and any waste of time:

1. Bene titulus mutari posset,[10] so that it can be clearly seen that this concerns only the Eastern Churches.

2. The doctrinal part does not aim to affirm or to establish the constitution of the Church but only to provide the necessary base for indicating the means of promoting unity: thus, there is no competition with the dogmatic schema.

3. Everything is addressed to all the sons of the Catholic Church.

---

[2] M. G. McGrath, auxiliary bishop of Panama, was titular bishop of Caeciri.

[3] Gustave Weigel, S.J. (1906–1964), American, ordained in 1933. Professor of theology in the United States, he had been a teacher and dean of the theology faculty of Santiago, Chile, from 1942 to 1948. Consultor to the Secretariat for Unity.

[4] Alexander Kerrigan, O.F.M. (1911–1986), Irish, ordained in 1934. Exegete, consultor to the Pontifical Biblical Commission, he taught at the Antonianum. Consultor to the Preparatory Theological Commission, he was named an expert in 1962.

[5] They were each assigned one chapter of the schema: relations between Scripture and tradition; inspiration, inerrancy, and literary composition of Scripture; Old Testament; New Testament; Scripture in the Church.

[6] "Let all listen. As numerous bishops have expressed the wish to the Holy Father".

[7] This refers to A. Cicognani, president of the Secretariat for Extraordinary Affairs.

[8] "That the second period would commence on September 8, 1963".

[9] "We will vote today on the proposal distributed yesterday on the instruments of social communication by *placet* or *non placet.*"

[10] "The title could well be changed."

Card. Jérôme de Barros Câmara (Brazil). "Mihi placet adhaerere"[11] what the cardinals said yesterday. "Bene tenendum est dogma, ne videamur irenismo favere."[12] A sincere account of our doctrine must be given, or nothing. "Inter media psychologica":[13] maintain charity in regard to free opinions, etc. In the Litanies, separate the prayers for errant Christians from the ones for those without faith. – The majority of dissidents, in Brazil and no doubt also elsewhere, do not know the differences between themselves and the Catholics; it is not necessary to insist on the canonical requirements for receiving them into the Church.

Patriarch Maximos IV. – Venerable Brothers. This schema concerns us, Eastern Catholics, in an accessory manner. I will only make some general remarks. My brothers in the episcopate will give a more detailed analysis. This schema, though needing radical revision on certain points and emendationes on others, can constitute a basis for worthwhile discussion.

1. On the introduction, especially nos. 5 to 12: theological truths are expressed here in such a way as to antagonize the Eastern Churches; the benevolent tone in no way changes this. The schema affirms Roman authority exclusively. It shows bias in its division of historical responsibilities. The Eastern Church was the first to be born from Christ and the apostles; she was subsequently built up by the Greek and Eastern Fathers; she owes to the Roman See neither her origin nor her organization nor her thought nor anything that constitutes her in a concrete way. Our great saints are not second-class Catholics due to the fact that they are not Roman. It is necessary to speak first of all of the collegiality of the apostolate in the Church, then of the papacy as its central basis. This is an important point. It would be deadly to forget it.

2. – There has been a lack of collaboration. Hence three distinct schemas: one from the Eastern Commission, one from the Theological Commission, one from the Secretariat for Unity. We have an Arab proverb that says; "When many hands get to work in the kitchen, the food burns." Let us be presented with a single text, drafted by a mixed commission. A matter of cohesion and of time.

3. – The schema talks only about the means of uniting with the Eastern Churches. That could be made into a particular chapter in a single

---

[11] "It pleases me to support".
[12] "We must hold fast to the dogma, lest we seem to foster irenicism."
[13] "Among the psychological means".

schema on ecumenism, our Eastern Brothers having the right to a special place. The union of the Churches is for us a serious and vital problem; the schism of the Church is for us a wound that still bleeds. Hence our very great concern, the goal for which we strive – my wish to be the redeeming victim ... We need to unite with them as much as they need to unite with us. The time has come to forget our old quarrels, into which human concerns have entered more than dogmatic ones. The time has come, "ut ad rem tandem deducamus ultimum votum Domini, ut unum sint".[14]

Bishop Hakim then read a Latin translation of the patriarch's intervention.

Archbishop Primo Principi,[15] Secretary of the Fabric of St. Peter ... "Dilecti observatories".[16] Almost all the arguments in this schema are found in the schema *De Ecclesia*. Several passages are borrowed from Leo XIII;[17] but the initiatives of Leo XIII ended in an "infelix excessus".[18] Soloviev[19] and others have said: "There are no essential differences, and good faith suffices; our two Churches have the same preaching and the same liturgy", and they feared that recognition of Roman primacy would bring with it other obligations. Instructed by history, let us be careful. Incorporate everything into the treatise on the Church. – He supported the principle of a "commissio instauranda"[20] to deal with the problems of unity.

Bishop Antoine Pawlowski[21] of Włocławek (Poland). Some good things are said on the Eastern rites, especially on their relations and their evolution. But let us be distrustful of falsus irenismus.[22] A citation from *Humani generis*. The schema positively exalts irenicism, without marking out limits for it; this is dangerous. Likewise, it does not insist enough on

---

[14] "That we might finally realize the last wish of the Lord: that they might be one."

[15] Primo Principi (1894–1975), Italian, ordained in 1918. Titular archbishop, steward, and secretary of the Fabric of Saint Peter from 1952 to 1969.

[16] "Esteemed observers".

[17] The schema cites several writings of Leo XIII: the apostolic letters *Orientalium dignitas* and *Praeclara gratulationis* (1894), and the encyclical letters *Adiutricem populi* (1895) and *Divinum illud* (1897).

[18] "Unfortunate excess".

[19] Vladimir Soloviev (1853–1900), Russian philosopher. He pleaded for the union of the Roman Catholic Church and the Orthodox Church.

[20] "Commission to be established".

[21] Antoni Pawlowski (1903–1968), Polish, ordained in 1926. Bishop of Włocławek from 1950 until his death.

[22] "False irenicism".

conversions. Today Catholics, especially among the historians, exaggerate the faults of the Latins, etc. Conclusion: Pray to the Virgin, fautrix
unitatis,[23] that all might return to the Roman Church.

Melchite Archbishop Philippe Nabaa, (Beirut). "Schema in sua forma
mihi nonnisi juxta modum placet. Facile amputari et emendari potest et
debet."[24] It is good not to talk about all the separated brothers together.
But "hoc schema silet de mediis efficacioribus";[25] there is only a quick,
vague allusion to them at no. 38. We must proceed "in caritate ad veritatem. Unio immediate haberi nequit."[26] A new spirit must first appear.
For that, collaboration on all human levels with non-Catholic Christians
is needed. "Festa communia in eadem die celebrare."[27] Lighten or even
eliminate the laws against communicatio in sacris.[28] For mixed marriages, restore the situation in force before the Oriental code.[29] – The
schema describes union as a "reditus ad domum derelictam":[30] this is
offensive and is not correct for all. We must assume part of the responsibility. "Ipsi catholici habent obligationem redeundi ad fratres separatos
ad loquendum cum eis, etc."[31] Nos. 25–26–27 recall the declarations
of Paul V[32] and other popes; these are solemn promises; we must apply
them, recognize the privileges of the patriarchs, the real powers of the
bishops and provincial councils, etc.

Archbishop Joseph Parecattil[33] of Ernakulam (India). "In genere
placet." Certain expressions show a good intention, but the Eastern rites
have no need of this sort of praise; they are not an ornamentum, they
are "partes integrales Ecclesiae universalis",[34] of apostolic origin. – For

---

[23] "Promoter of unity".

[24] "The schema in its present form will satisfy me only if corrections are made. We can easily and
we must remove certain things and amend it."

[25] "This schema says nothing about more effective means."

[26] "In charity toward the truth. Union cannot be obtained immediately."

[27] "Celebrate the common feasts on the same day."

[28] Participation of a Christian in the acts of worship of another Christian Church; this participation can be active or passive, according to whether an active participation is brought to the exercise
of the worship or whether it is a matter of simply being present.

[29] The Latin code of canon law was promulgated in 1917, but the Eastern code, which concerns
the Eastern Churches united to Rome, was done so only in piecemeal fashion. Composed from
1935 to 1948, it was promulgated only in parts and was still incomplete at the date of the council.

[30] "Return to the house they deserted".

[31] "Catholics themselves have the obligation to turn back toward their separated brothers by
speaking to them, etc."

[32] Camillo Borghese (1552–1621), Italian. Elected pope in 1605.

[33] Joseph Parecattil (1912–1987), Indian, ordained in 1939. Archbishop of Ernakulam (India)
from 1956 to 1984. Created cardinal in 1969. Member of the Commission for Eastern Churches.

[34] "Ornament; they are integral parts of the universal Church."

nos. 23–24, cautiously leave the matter up to pastoral necessities and the true desires of the faithful. – Nos. 38ff.: "media practica. Aliud remedium proponam, magni momenti, praesertim in India":[35] in every case where they are sufficiently numerous, let our faithful and their pastors have their churches in the big cities. – Let us institute mixed episcopal conferences (Catholics and non-Catholics), "saltem aliquoties, v.g., semel in anno, in unaquaque regione".[36] We are putting that into practice in India, for example, with the problem of educating children.

Ukrainian Archbishop André Sapelak from Argentina. Certain paragraphs concern all the separated brothers. – "Tempora jam matura videntur."[37] The beneficial role of John XXIII. "Schema quam proxime exprimit mentem S. Pontificis."[38] It might be verbose; but the fault is not serious. There are still a number of obstacles to union, described at no. 13; have recourse to the Virgin, solemnly declare her the Patroness of unity, with St. John Nepomucene as the second patron.

Ukrainian Archbishop Ambroise Senyshyn[39] of Philadelphia (USA). "In genere placet." Let it be a corollary of the constitution *De Ecclesia*. In that way repetitions will be avoided. Omit nos. 1–8, which talk about matters treated ex professo in *De Ecclesia*. On the other hand, remove chap. 10, de unione,[40] from the schema *De Ecclesia*. – Potior pars agit, et quidem laudabiliter, de mediis unionis; sed nihil de communicatione in sacris; regulae actuales sunt nimis rigidae"[41] – the same as for Protestants: that is not logical.

A. Vuccino,[42] A.A., Greek archbishop of the Latin rite. Many thanks to those who have worked from three sides. But why, "circa unicum scopum? Defectus cooperationis".[43] So many significant faults could have been avoided by a common effort. "Utquid perditio haec temporis tam pretiosi?"[44] Let us merge the three prepared schemas into one, under the one title: *De Ecclesiae unitate*. Sic novum efficiatur schema,

---

[35] "Practical means. I will propose another remedy, of great importance, especially in India."
[36] "At least sometimes, for example, once a year, in each region".
[37] "The times now seem ripe."
[38] "The schema expresses as closely as possible the mind of the Supreme Pontiff."
[39] Ambrozij Andrew Senyshyn, O.S.B.M. (1903–1976), Ukrainian, ordained in 1931. Ukrainian archbishop of Philadelphia from 1961 until his death. Member of the Commission for Eastern Churches.
[40] "On union".
[41] "The largest part deals, and, in fact, in praiseworthy fashion, with the means of union; but there is nothing on the *communicatio in sacris*; the current rules are too rigid."
[42] Antonio Gregorio Vuccino, A.A. (1891–1968), Greek, ordained in 1918. Titular archbishop.
[43] "Around a single goal? A lack of cooperation".
[44] "Why this waste of very precious time?"

digne coronatum cum Maria, fautrix unitatis. – Nos. 1–11: "tribus primis exceptis, exponitur aspectus Ecclesiae mere juridicus, seu structura ejus socialis. Omnia ista necessaria quidem, sed solum sicut media ad finem, ad aedificationem corporis Christi."[45] All of that is ineffective for opening the door. "Non tantum non juvat, sed potius impedimentum fert ad dialogum."[46] Vuccino called on his own experience. In our post-Tridentine Latin world, we no longer speak of anything but Roman authority. Let us consult the Gospel a little more. The true office of a pastor is diaconia, service. "Non ad dominationem exercendam institutus est Primatus."[47] It was founded on charity, for charity. "Caritas in Ecclesia omnia regit, etiam potestatem juridicam, etc."[48]

The secretary general then announced the result of the vote on the schema De instrumentis. Number of votes cast: 2,160. Placet: 2,138. Non placet: 15. Invalid ballots: 7.

Coadjutor Bishop Doroteo Fernández y Fernández[49] of Badajoz (Spain). "... et carissimi observatores". He praised the broadness of heart shown by the authors of the schema. "Quoddam tamen habeo contra ipsum. Non clara distinctio fit circa naturam rerum: dogmatica cum non dogmaticis miscentur."[50] Every word should be weighed. Examples of ill-advised formulas. – The principles are eternal. It is dangerous to say: "Duae Ecclesiae"[51] (no. 7, etc.): there are not several Churches; etc. "Humilis ex parte nostra confessio";[52] but the Church is not our Church, she is God's Church.

Melchite Archbishop Neophytos Edelby. On nos. 1–11. "Fateri debeo":[53] the body of the schema deserves much praise, but not this

---

[45] "On the unity of the Church. In this way a new schema will be produced, justly crowned with Mary, promoter of unity. Nos. 1–11: the first three numbers excepted, this presents a purely juridical aspect of the Church, or her social structure. All of that is certainly necessary, but only as means to the end, to the building up of the body of Christ."

[46] "Not only is this not any help, but, rather, it is an obstacle to dialogue."

[47] "The primacy was not instituted for exercising domination."

[48] "Charity governs everything in the Church, including the juridical power."

[49] Doroteo Fernández y Fernández (1913–1989), Spanish, ordained in 1937. Coadjutor bishop of Badajoz from 1962 to 1971.

[50] "However, I have a reproach to make against it. A clear distinction is not made on the nature of things: dogmatic points are mixed with points that are not dogmatic."

[51] "Two Churches".

[52] "A humble confession on our part".

[53] "I must acknowledge".

doctrinal introduction, "incompleta, et saepe minus recta".[54] – 1–5: "Textus selecti ex Sacra Scriptura; optime dicuntur";[55] but they are out of place in a practical treatise that aims at unity. And these texts are not elucidated enough for any theological principles to be drawn from them. "E contra",[56] nos. 6–11 contain the principles for such a treatise. Sed, me dolet declarare has paragraphos minime placere; funditus recognosci debent, in spiritu, historia, doctrina. – 1. Spiritus qui insinuatur longe distat a spiritu vere oecumenico, a spiritu veritatis in caritate et claritate. Animositatem redolet erga orientales."[57] Example: it is said that all the Eastern Churches that are separated from Rome allow the interference of civil authorities, etc. – 2. Historically speaking, this is incorrect and unjust. It speaks as if the Eastern Churches had removed themselves from Roman authority malo animo.[58] It does not sufficiently show the shared responsibilities. And it is not true that the popes have always sought unity: "saepe plura fecerunt catholici, sicut non-catholici, contra unionem, et omnes egent misericordia Dei. – 3. Doctrina theologica non est omnino secura nec profunda. Levi animo agitantur quaestiones gravissimae",[59] and it supplies no solid response to them. Thus, at no. 6, "nihil de collegialitate episcoporum".[60] At no. 7, "unitas non fundatur nisi in submissione; non est erronea haec doctrina, sed vere incompleta. Vincula unitatis excedunt relationem inter pastores et subditos."[61] I ask pardon of the venerable bishop who has just spoken, but a very great number of times the Romani Pontifices[62] themselves have addressed the Orthodox Christians as Churches, "plus quam centies".[63] – The schema further says "christianos separatos privari multis mediis salutis";[64]

---

[54] "Incomplete and often inaccurate".

[55] "Texts chosen from Sacred Scripture: they are very good."

[56] "On the contrary".

[57] "But it pains me to say that these paragraphs please me very little; they must be revised thoroughly, in their spirit, in their historical and doctrinal point of view. 1. The spirit that is implied is far distant from the truly ecumenical spirit, from the spirit of truth in charity and clarity. It manifests animosity toward the Eastern Churches."

[58] "With evil intent".

[59] "Often, as many Catholics as non-Catholics did many things against union, and all have need of God's mercy. 3. The theological doctrine is not altogether certain or profound. Some very grave matters are discussed superficially."

[60] "Nothing on the collegiality of the bishops".

[61] "Unity is founded only on submission; this doctrine is not erroneous but is very incomplete. The bonds of unity go beyond the relation between pastors and subjects."

[62] "Roman Pontiffs".

[63] "More than a hundred times".

[64] "The separated Christians are deprived of numerous means of salvation."

392 VATICAN COUNCIL NOTEBOOKS I

it seems even to be doubtful of their salvation: there are exaggerations here. – "Conclusio: haec introductio, nec necessaria, nec utilis, nec bene redacta."[65] Let the rest of the schema be made into a chapter in a treatise on ecumenism.

Archbishop Élie Zoghby (Melchite, Egypt). (He spoke in French). The Eastern Church has never been a part, as the Protestants were, of the Latin Church. She is a sister Church. She is a Church at the source. Founded by the apostles, she was born before the others. She developed her discipline and her liturgy without the contribution of the West. Her doctrine is fundamentally the same as that of the Latin Church, but assimilated and lived differently. Her witnesses are the Greek Fathers. There are here two geniuses, two inspirations both going back to the living Source, Christ. So the separation cannot be explained merely as the result of a sudden impulse ... The genius of each of the two Churches has different and often irreducible properties. The same mysteries, the same feasts, are envisaged in different ways; for example, the dogmas of the Trinity and the Incarnation, the feasts of the Annunciation, of the Nativity, of the Epiphany ... The unity is one of different personalities. On the one hand, collegiality; on the other, centralization. What makes the situation difficult is that, in fact, the Catholic Church is Latin in her great majority, and likewise the Eastern Church is Orthodox in her great majority. The Catholic Church has evolved, but in one direction only. One can see it in this hall: the patriarchs are in the shadow of the great platform from whence shines the purple of the cardinals, who are today the ornament of the Church but who did not exist in former times.[66] The patriarchs cannot allow their Churches to be dissolved in Latinism. They are preserving the patrimony of the Eastern Fathers. – It has been said that this council is not a council of unity. No doubt. But as long as disunity reigns, no council can fail to be interested in unity. When the Catholic Church is decentralized, an important step will have been taken toward this unity.

Bishop Sergio Méndez of Cuernavaca (Mexico). 1. "Valde dolendus defectus coordinationis, unde tria schemata, a tribus commissionibus!"[67] And how can we discuss in depth the material in this schema

---

[65] "Conclusion: this introduction is neither necessary nor useful nor well written."

[66] At that time the Eastern Patriarchs were seated, in order of precedence, behind the cardinals. A new place was allocated to them in the *aula* starting from October 1963.

[67] "A very regrettable lack of coordination, so that the result is three schemas from three commissions!"

before having seen the other two? – 2. The other non-Catholics have been forgotten; it is not always clear of which group the schema is talking, Eastern Catholics or Eastern non-Catholics. It does not tell us what is meant by this Eastern Church, "directe ab Apostolis orta et a Patribus ordinata".[68] It proposes some means of union and ignores the Eastern Catholics! And there is nothing in it either on the collegial powers of the bishops or on "communicatio in sacris". – 3. Some other defects. When speaking to the Orthodox, "sensu pastorali caret, juridismum redolet; est monologus, non dialogus."[69] A long exhortation, in a paternal and fraternal tone; but does it seek individual conversions or unity? – Conclusion. Let us produce a single schema, with several chapters, "viribus unitis. Iterum redigatur."[70] In it, let the relation between papal authority and episcopal authority be explained. Let it not be too Latin; let ample space for the Eastern Churches be made. Let it be proclaimed that the Catholic Church, without rejecting individual conversions, does not directly seek them in this dialogue. Let the documents of the ordinary magisterium not be quoted. – Finally, "Ante nostram secundam sessionem, optimum esset"[71] if the bishops elected some of their number, for example, one out of ten, to form a permanent delegation, so as to examine the work done here by the commissions. It is not enough that each bishop deal with this from his own country. Let a simultaneous translation be organized. Let there be frequent colloquia, "peritis consultis".[72]

Bishop Felix Romero[73] of Jaèn (Spain). – "Schema majori perfectione donari potest. Placet mutatio tituli. Brevis introductio ponenda",[74] to indicate the pastoral character of the decree. Set down the dual principle of unity and diversity. Express the intention of creating another schema for the other separated brothers. The idea of the Church is not very coherent, etc. Do not let it be believed that the necessity for authority in the Church is based solely on human considerations.

---

[68] "Drawing its origin directly from the apostles and given its structure by the Fathers".

[69] "The schema lacks pastoral understanding, it suggests legalism; it is a monologue, not a dialogue."

[70] "By uniting our forces. Let it be written again."

[71] "Before our second session, it would be very good".

[72] "With consultation of the *periti*".

[73] Felix Romero Menjibar (1901–1974), Spanish, ordained in 1926. Bishop of Jaèn from 1954 to 1970.

[74] "The schema can be greatly perfected. I approve the change of title. A brief introduction should be composed."

Rev. Fr. Athanase Hage,[75] superior general of the Basilian Order. "Omnino placet":[76] moderation, simplicity, etc. "In particularibus, nonnullae emendationes."[77] Nos. 1–4: doctrine that is in the schema *De Ecclesia*; repetition – and diversity of conception. Put this schema back in the *De Ecclesia*. "Valde prolixum videtur: examples. Aliquae formulae, male sonant fratribus separatis (no. 7, ll. 20–21; no. 22; no. 27; no. 34; no. 49)."[78] Find a better title, etc.

On exiting the Basilica, Dom Olivier Rousseau told me that he had collaborated on the intervention made by Maximos. – Saw Jean Pélissier, from *La Croix*; he said that an article by Fr. Wenger, published before his, had indicated episcopal support for Rahner's schema. Also saw Fr. Jean Lucas, who took me in his car, together with a Canadian priest, on a tour of the Vatican gardens.

Lunched, at 1:30 P.M., with Msgr. Noirot, a priest from St.-Claude, former professor of canon law at the Faculties of Lyon, together with Msgr.[79] ..., a canon from Sens, professor of canon law in Paris and Fr. Robert Rouquette. Msgr. Noirot gave us various details on the current Roman milieu. He showed us, in the little basilica where he is a canon (at the entrance of the Corso, Piazza del Popolo) the altar where John XXIII was ordained a priest, at the same time as Buonaiuti[80] (hence the insinuation in the *Corriere della Sera* article, saying that the pope in his youth was a disciple of Buonaiuti, who was later excommunicated vitandus).[81]

In the afternoon, a visit from a Spanish priest, a professor of Sacred Scripture, Father J.M. González Ruiz,[82] the author of several books. He was sent to me by a Spanish publisher (Manuel Sanmiguel, Ediciones Guadarrama, Madrid), who would like to translate my book on Teilhard for his series "Cristianismo y Hombre actual",[83] which already

[75] Athanasios Hage (1898–1972), Lebanese, ordained in 1929. Superior general of the Order of Melchite Basilians of Saint John the Baptist (Chouerites) from 1961 to 1967.

[76] "I completely approve".

[77] "On some particular points, a few emendations".

[78] "It seems very prolix. Some formulas offend the ears of our separated brothers."

[79] Jacques Denis.

[80] Ernesto Buonaiuti (1881–1946), Catholic priest and theologian, professor of Church history. Accused of modernism, he was excommunicated in 1926.

[81] "Vitandus" means, literally, "to be shunned"; a grave form of excommunication. – TRANS.

[82] José María González Ruiz (1916–2005), Spanish priest and author of works focusing on Saint Paul as well as on Marxism, among others.

[83] "Christianity and Contemporary Man".

includes works by such authors as Guardini,[84] Balthasar,[85] Daniélou, Hildebrand,[86] Casel,[87] Rahner, Semmelroth, Lortz,[88] Gilson,[89] etc. He gave me some information, perhaps biased, on the Spanish bishops and theologians, the intellectual and religious situation in his country, the relationship with politics, etc.

Afterward saw Fr. Stanislas Lyonnet for a few moments; he was his usual optimistic self.

Late in the afternoon, conversation with Fr. ..., S.J., a Mexican, who has come for the council. He questioned me for a long time on the preparation for the council, then on the old Fourvière business, etc. He knew in advance about the intervention made this morning by the bishop of Cuernavaca. The Mexican bishops, he told me, had arrived in Rome without knowing anything about the situation or the theological quarrels. He had organized various talks for them; he got Fr. Alonso-Schökel and some others from the Biblical Institute to come and then, from the Lateran, Msgr. Spadafora. The bishops asked questions. After the other lectures, Spadafora proved to be so weak, so inconsistent in his criticisms that the bishops have gotten over their fears. Cardinal José Garibi y Rivera wanted to speak in their name (in an integrist sense), but they were opposed.

Wednesday, November 28, 1962 (29th General Congregation). – Ethiopian rite Mass, with strange chants and small bells; 5 officiants and 3 acolytes; enthronement of the Gospel with chanting accompanied by drum beats and rhythmic hand clapping. This African celebration in Saint Peter's was very picturesque.

---

[84] Romano Guardini (1885–1968), German priest, theologian, and philosopher. He was involved in the liturgical movement and in the Catholic youth movement Quickborn. Expert at the council beginning with the second session.

[85] Hans Urs von Balthasar (1905–1988), Swiss, ordained in 1939. He is one of the principal theologians of the twentieth century. He was a close friend of H. de Lubac, whom he had known at Fourvière and whose work he translated into German. He left the Society of Jesus in 1950, while remaining a priest, in order to collaborate more closely with Adrienne von Speyr in the Community of Saint John. Created cardinal in 1988, he died before the consistory.

[86] Dietrich von Hildebrand (1889–1977), German philosopher and theologian of the first rank, a student of Husserl. He was a convert to Catholicism.

[87] Johannes Casel (Odo in religion), O.S.B. (1886–1948), German, ordained in 1911. A monk of Maria Laach Abbey, he was a specialist in the liturgy.

[88] Joseph Lortz (1887–1975), Luxembourger, Catholic priest, expert on Church history. He is famous for his Histoire de l'Église (History of the Church) and his writings on the Reformation.

[89] Étienne Gilson (1884–1978), French philosopher, specialist in medieval philosophy, member of the Académie française. He carried on an intellectual friendship with H. de Lubac, of whose writings on the supernatural he had approved.

President: Cardinal Ignace Tappouni, patriarch of the Syrians of Antioch. The Emendationes to chap. 1 of the Liturgy were distributed; they are to be submitted to a vote on Friday morning.

Card. Tappouni. – "Schematis finis non est expositio dogmatica circa Ecclesiae constitutionem. Ejus finis est exponere mentem Ecclesiae catholicae erga orientales dissidentes, simulque indicare media ad unionem. Habemus in communi cum Orientalibus dissidentibus multa, quae Protestantes non habent. – Observatio quoad modum loquendi: una est Ecclesia catholica; patrimonium ejus est commune et communicabile. – Schema placet, ratione habita emendationum particularium."[1]

Card. Spellman. "Secundum doctrinam catholicam, Ecclesia fundata est super Petrum."[2] Moreover, the great diversity that exists demands all the more this unity "cum Petro et sub Petro".[3] The obstacles are immense: hence, before all else, supernatural means, prayer. "Apud Deum omnia possibilia sunt."[4] Pray to the Blessed Virgin. – "Caveant, ne, falso quodam irenismo ducti, doctrinam catholicam quodammodo accomodent doctrinae dissidentium. Caveant ne sensus catholicus obscuretur."[5] He spoke about the "schismatici", the "Ecclesiae schismaticae".[6] – Schema placet.

Card. Alfredo Ottaviani. "Schema propositum in suo complexu placet"[7] with corrections. He praised Tappouni and Spellman. "Inveniatur via"[8] to join the two schemas (on the Eastern Churches and the part of De Ecclesia on the Protestants) into a single schema, with different chapters. – It is almost ridiculous, added Ottaviani, to want to start the examination now of a schema (De Ecclesia) that is 80 pages long. It is absurd to say: we will deal with one part of it, and we will continue

---

November 28

[1] "The aim of the schema is not a dogmatic presentation on the constitution of the Church. Its aim is to set forth the mind of the Catholic Church with regard to the dissenting Eastern Churches and, at the same time, to indicate the means toward union. We have many things in common with the dissenting Eastern Churches that the Protestants do not have. An observation as to the manner of expression: the Catholic Church is one; her patrimony is common and can be shared. I approve the schema, with the reservation that some particular points be amended."

[2] "According to Catholic doctrine, the Church is founded on Peter."

[3] "With Peter and under Peter".

[4] "With God, all things are possible" [Mt 19:26 and Mk 10:27].

[5] "Let them beware lest, guided by a false irenicism, they adapt Catholic doctrine in some manner to suit the doctrine of the dissidents. Let them take care not to obscure the Catholic sense."

[6] "Schismatics", the "schismatic Churches".

[7] "I approve the proposed schema on the whole."

[8] "Let a way be found."

in September 1963 with the rest. So, I make the following proposition: "statim transeatur ad schema B. Mariae Virginis."[9] This is what had been decided, up until Sunday. I have even received a letter from the (president?) that assured me of this. "Miror quod tam cito transferemur in alium propositum. Optima occasio esset, spectaculum dare concordiae filiorum in discertando de Matre. Concordia etiam esset cum separatis Orientalibus. Optimum esset videre familiam christianam unitam coram Matre sua. Hoc ergo peto, ut statim, feria sexta, incipiatur examen schematis de B. Maria Virgine."[10] It would be a very fine thing to be able to proclaim this constitution for the feast of December 8. "Peto votum singulorum Patrum."[11] I appeal to the French Fathers, who have in their land "the venerated shrine of Our Lady of Lourdes" (he said this in French); I appeal to the Americans, who also have venerated shrines of the Virgin, etc.; I appeal to all nations, I appeal to the missionaries, I appeal to the Eastern Fathers, I appeal praesertim[12] to all those who have a special love for the Blessed Virgin. Let us remember the words of Scripture, which could with some adaptation be said of the Virgin: "Qui elucidant me, vitam aeternam habebunt."[13] (Some applause.)[14]

His Beatitude Paul II Cheikho, Chaldean patriarch of Babylon. – "... Amabiles fratres observatores".[15] Before the discussion, I thought: "Valde mihi placet. Nunc quoque, valde mihi placet. Nihil in eo inveni quod non perfecte concordet cum doctrina catholica, nihil quod sit tanquam spinosum fratribus nostris separatis. Est vera instructio ad nos catholicos, ut queramus unionem. Monet nos de incapacitate nostra mediis naturalibus. Monet nos ut methodum doctrinalem, pastoralem et oecumenicam adhibeamus; postea veniunt media theologica, liturgica, canonica ..., et ad vitandos defectus, offert nobis alia media, sc.,

---

[9] "Let us pass on immediately to the schema on the Blessed Virgin Mary."

[10] "I am surprised that we are passing on to another subject so quickly. This would be a very good opportunity to give a show of agreement of sons speaking about their Mother. Concord would exist as well with the separated Eastern Churches. It would be very good to see the Christian family united before its Mother. I therefore ask that, on Friday, the examination of the schema on the Blessed Virgin Mary begin immediately."

[11] "I appeal to the wish of each one of the Fathers."

[12] "Especially".

[13] "They that explain me shall have life everlasting" [Sir 24:31; this verse is in the Vulgate, but not in the NRSV, Catholic Edition. – TRANS.].

[14] A. Ottaviani received a letter from Archbishop Felici, Secretary General of the council, dated November 28, 1962, indicating to him that the agenda would not be changed. See AS, VI, I, 322–23.

[15] "Amiable brother observers".

psychologica et practica. – Sanctus Paulus se omnia omnibus fecit, attamen omnibus gentibus fidem suam praedicavit. – Votum aliquod Concilio propono: ut Patres hujus S. Concilii componant aliquam orationem, quae ab omnibus qui nomine christiano gloriantur recitari poterit, pro unione omnium in Christo credentium.[16] And let this prayer be recited in the schools, so that all Christian children might be introduced to the problems of unity. (Applause.)

Bishop Joseph Tawil, Melchite (Damas). Prima conditio viae ad unitatem,[17] is to liberate ourselves from all human impediments. I propose some emendationes to add to those that were proposed yesterday. Page 253, l. 20 (no. 7): "verbum 'coetus' falsum est: Ecclesiae orientales, etiam separatae, nomen Ecclesiae, non coetus, accipiunt." Cf. "documenta pontificalia ipsa in notis allata".[18] One could call them simply "Orthodoxi", "secundum usum receptum".[19] Why change the traditional designations? – Never were the Eastern Churches, before the separation, considered to be a part of the Western patriarchate. – The schema talks about an "error multo perniciosior",[20] concerning the right recognized by the separated Churches of the civil authority to meddle in their affairs: this insulting passage must be omitted. – At p. 259, no. 27, l. 31, and p. 266 ..., with regard to the preservation of the liturgies, a reservation is expressed concerning things that could be opposed to recta fides and to boni mores: "candide fateor, me numquam aliquid vidisse in liturgiis Orientis, quod opponatur bonis moribus",[21] and all the doctrine comes from the Fathers, who constitute a norm for the universal Church. – No. 52: "ut tandem, etc." "Hoc est absolute deficiens respectu oecumenico";[22] it seems to be saying that the Eastern Churches did not have

---

[16] "The schema pleases me greatly. Now, also, I highly approve of it. I have found nothing in it that does not agree perfectly with Catholic doctrine, nothing that could be prickly, so to speak, for our separated brothers. It is a true education addressed to us, Catholics, so that we might seek union. It warns us of our incapacity through natural means. It exhorts us to adhere to a doctrinal, pastoral, and ecumenical method; next come the theological, liturgical, canonical means ..., and in order to avoid any lack, it offers us other means, that is, psychological and practical ones. Saint Paul made himself all things to all, and yet he preached his faith to all peoples. I propose a wish to the council: that the Fathers of this holy council compose a prayer that could be recited by all those who glory in the name of Christian, for the union of all those who believe in Christ."

[17] "The first condition on the path toward unity".

[18] "The word 'congregation' is false: the Eastern Churches, even the separated ones, are called Churches and not congregations. Cf. the pontifical documents themselves, indicated in the notes."

[19] "'Orthodox', in conformity with the received usage".

[20] "Very dangerous error".

[21] "Right faith and good morals. I candidly confess that I have never seen anything in the Eastern liturgies that might be opposed to good morals."

[22] "In order that at last, etc. It is absolutely lacking in ecumenical consideration."

any fixed status before their union with Rome. " 'Status provisorius' falsum sonum reddit."[23] The Eastern Catholic Churches "sunt quoddam speculum",[24] in which the Orthodox Churches gaze at what they would be, once united; and yet, etc. – Conclusion: the schema needs to be thoroughly revised. "Quaestio valde actualis et urgens."[25] We need a mixed commission.

Bishop Jean Velasco (China).[26] "Mens schematis omnino placet. Attamen:[27] 1. Change something in the order of exposition; 2. Be wary of "falsus irenismus,[28] etc." (Bishop Velasco is the exiled bishop of Hsiamen.)

Archbishop Marcelin Olaechea Loizaga of Valencia (Spain). Explanations on the connection between the Ecclesia caelestis and the Ecclesia terrestris.[29] Some find the schema to be without enough mellowness, sometimes containing "rudior sermo";[30] some would like "reticere quod ad papam spectat".[31] (I did not understand exactly what he had in mind; he seemed rather to reject these criticisms). He went on too long.

Joseph Khoury, Maronite Archbishop of Beirut. – In the name of my brothers the Maronite bishops, of a Church that has always been united to Rome and has always worked for unity. "Nititur schema aliquibus propositis quae sunt discutienda."[32] – 1. The relations between East and West are increasingly close; our separated brothers live both in the West and in the East. – 2. This decree does not even concern all the Eastern Churches; it is rather a decree "pro Graecis. Plures sunt Ecclesiae in Oriente:[33] cf. Card. Liénart." Several of these Churches, heirs of ancient patriarchates, have always been very different from the Byzantine Church. – 3. The Eastern Fathers do not represent the patrimony of some particular Churches; they are the legacy of the entire Catholic Church. Athanasius and Cyril were from Alexandria; John Chrysostom and Gregory of Nazianzus came from Antioch and did not have much success in Constantinople; Basil and Gregory of Nyssa had

---

[23] " 'Provisional status' has a false ring to it."

[24] "Are a sort of mirror".

[25] "It is a very current and urgent question."

[26] Juan Bautista Velasco Díaz, O.P. (1911–1985), Spanish, ordained in 1935. Bishop of Hsiamen in China from 1948 to 1983.

[27] "I completely approve of the spirit of the schema. However".

[28] "False irenicism".

[29] "Heavenly Church and the earthly Church".

[30] "Rather indelicate language".

[31] "To keep silent about matters relating to the pope".

[32] "The schema relies on some propositions that are debatable."

[33] "For the Greeks. There are several Churches in the East."

no connection with Byzantium. – 4. People here have exaggerated in saying that the East owes nothing to Rome, in saying that the East and the West are, so to speak, two completely different worlds. "Liceat nobis a sic dictis valde discrepare. Nec Oriens nec Occidens, sed nova creatura in Christo. Unus eget altero, etc.[34] – 5. Pro tota Ecclesia catholica optetur: renovatio liturgica, amor Scripturae et Patrum, affirmatio episcopatus collegialis cum Petro et sub Petro, aliqua decentralisatio, applicatio in Occidente valorum conservatorum in Oriente, deductio in praxim doctrinae Patrum de Ecclesiis orientalibus, reductio mentis nimis juridicae et nimis exclusive administrationis. – Schema silet de omnibus his punctis, necessariis ad parandam unionem."[35] – Let there be a single schema de unione,[36] and let it be incorporated into the schema *De Ecclesia*. (Applause.)

Bishop Michel Darmancier, vicarius apostolicus insularum Wallis et Futuna in Oceania.[37] – "Schema sinceram erga fratres separatos caritatem exprimit, etc. Caritati tamen accedere debet humilitas ac, si res ferat, paenitentiae spiritus."[38] Cf. the intervention of Bishop De Smedt, "de qua grato animo memores sumus omnes".[39] With regard to the Eastern Churches, some historical examples should be recalled. – 1. No. 7, l. 10, "legimus: 'Proh dolor! Lamentatur Mater Ecclesia divisiones, etc.' Certe lamentatur, sed quare aperte non fatetur esse pro sua parte ad schismatum originem, saltem indirecte propriis infirmitatibus contulisse? Melius esset si cum Adriano VI[40] confiteremur divisionem Deum permisisse, propter peccata hominum et praesertim sacerdotum et praelatorum."[41]

---

[34] "Allow us to disagree strongly with what has been said here. Neither East nor West, but a new creation in Christ [2 Cor 5:17]. One has need of the other."

[35] "For the whole Catholic Church, the following are wished: a liturgical renewal, love of Scripture and of the Fathers of the Church, affirmation of the collegial episcopate, with and under Peter, a certain decentralization, the application in the West of the values preserved in the East, a putting into practice of the doctrine of the Fathers coming from the Eastern Churches, the reduction of a spirit that is too legalistic and too exclusively administrative. The schema is silent about all these points, necessary for the preparation of union."

[36] "On union".

[37] "Apostolic Vicar of the islands of Wallis and Futuna in the South Pacific".

[38] "The schema expresses a sincere charity toward the separated brothers, etc. But humility and, if necessary, a spirit of penitence must be joined to charity."

[39] "Which we all remember, in a spirit of gratitude".

[40] Pope from 1522 to 1523, he acknowledged that the Church of Rome was guilty of abuses and that that justified some criticism, but, in spite of the mission entrusted to the nuncio Chieregati at the diet of Nuremberg (January 1523), he did not manage to convince Martin Luther.

[41] "1. No. 7, l. 10, we read 'Alas! Our Mother the Church deplores divisions, etc.' Certainly she deplores them, but why not openly acknowledge that she had her part in the origin of the schisms

– 2. No. 11, ll. 32–35: "Ecclesia catholica ... numquam ab opere cessavit laborandi ad unionem." "Quis fratrum orthodoxorum his verbis assentire poterit? Pluries enim ... legati vel procuratores Ecclesiae romanae improbe et dominandi studio cum Orientalibus egerunt: sic cardinalis Humbert cum Michaele Cerulario.[42] – 3. Bene refert schema ad Leonem XIII, encycl. Orientalium dignitas;[43] sed in gravissimis rebus haec encyclica interdum violatur, etc. Duo exempla recentia: a. Jus canonicum orientale, in 'De personis', jura Patriarchis non tribuit; b. recens immixtio Sancti officii in res liturgicas orientales (decretum feliciter a papa revocatum).[44] – 4. No. 27, ll. 34–36: Ecclesia latina conatur corrigere opinionem quod Latini velint jura Orientalium minuere: bene; sed illa intentio ad effectum non perveniet, nisi Concilium solemnem actum posuerit ..."[45] – Conclusion. Cf. the spirit of humility of the Gospel, as John XXIII has recommended instanter.[46] In consideration of which, "schemati libenter assentiam. Sed aliunde, stupens reperi in schemate De Ecclesia caput quoddam 'de oecumenismo' cujus inspiratio a principiis praesentis schematis prorsus discrepat. Ad quam contradictionem solvendam",[47] etc., send all the material related to ecumenism to the Secretariat for Unity. (Bishop Darmancier, a Marist, was supplied with material for his intervention by his confrere Fr. Maurice Villain.)

---

and that she contributed to them, at least indirectly, through her own weaknesses? It would be better to confess with Adrian VI that God has permitted the division because of the sins of men, and especially of priests and prelates."

[42] "2. No. 11, ll. 32–35: 'The Catholic Church ... has never ceased to work toward union.' Who, among our Orthodox brothers, will be able to give their assent to these words? Indeed, several legates and procurators of the Roman Church have treated the Eastern Churches badly, with a will to domination: so it was with Cardinal Humbert and Michael Cerularius." [In 1054, Cardinal Humbert, one of the envoys of Pope Leo IX to Constantinople, ignored the Patriarch Michael Cerularius in order, finally, to lodge a bull of excommunication against him, in July. The Patriarch in his turn excommunicated the pope's legates.]

[43] Apostolic letter "on the Eastern Churches" of Leo XIII, November 30, 1894.

[44] "The schema rightly refers to Leo XIII and the encyclical *Orientalium dignitas*, but in some very serious matters this encyclical has sometimes been violated. Two recent examples: a. the Oriental canon law, in the *De personis*, grants no rights to the patriarchs. b. The recent interference of the Holy Office in the domain of the Eastern liturgy (a decree fortunately revoked by the pope)." [This refers to a decree forbidding the use, in America, of English in the liturgy.]

[45] "4. No. 27, ll. 34–36: the Latin Church undertakes to correct the opinion according to which the Latins want to reduce the rights of the Eastern Churches: good; but this intention will not become effective unless the council lays down a solemn act."

[46] "Earnestly".

[47] "I will approve the schema with pleasure. But, on the other hand, I have discovered to my astonishment in the schema *De Ecclesia* a chapter "On ecumenism" whose inspiration differs totally from the principles of this schema. In order to resolve this contradiction".

Bishop Dominique Dinh-Duc-Tru[48] of Thai-Binh (Vietnam). "... et observatores dilecti". To avoid repetitions, confusions, suspicions on the part of the Protestants, Anglicans, and others, I propose that everything be treated in a single constitution. A few general principles will suffice, "enuntiata modo christiano, fraterno et humano".[49] Cf. Liénart. – Coordinate the biblical citations.

Bishop Tarancón[50] of Solsona (Spain). "Schema admodum pastorale. Eximia caritas. Sed prior pars[51] overlaps with the schema De Ecclesia; it engenders a periculum erroris,[52] it is open to minimalist interpretations and more serious errors. Some examples ... The Church is a visible society, and a perfect society ... We need to provide some juridical clarifications.

Archbishop Reginald Addazi[53] of Trani and Barletta (Italy). Incorporate the schema into De Ecclesia. "Titulus: 'De Ecclesiarum unione', ut fratres separati reveniant ad domum Patris. Nimis prolixum."[54] Certain passages amount to a pastoralis homilia.[55] On that subject, permit me to say this: several times, certain council Fathers have called for a pastoral style, have seemed to scorn scholasticism, doctrine: "sed docere veritatem ut est in se, est munus pastorale per excellentiam. Debet teneri integra doctrina catholica,[56] etc." (He puts a scholastic exposition, scholastic doctrine, Catholic truth all in entirely the same category.) A bad definition of the Church. It is scandalous to claim that the Church herself had something to do with the schism of the Eastern Churches. "Redeant fratres separati":[57] we will receive them with charity.

---

[48] In fact, it was Dominique Hoàng-văn-Doàn, O.P. (1912–1974), Vietnamese, ordained in 1939. Titular bishop, he became bishop of Quinhon (Vietnam) in January 1964.

[49] "Expressed in a Christian, fraternal, and humane fashion".

[50] Vicente Enrique y Tarancón (1907–1994), Spanish, ordained in 1929. Bishop of Solsona from 1945, he was named archbishop of Oviedo in April 1964 and created cardinal in 1969. Member of the Commission for the Discipline of the Clergy and the Christian People.

[51] "The schema is quite pastoral. It is written with great charity. But the first part".

[52] "A risk of error".

[53] Reginaldo G. M. Addazi, O.P. (1899–1975), Italian, ordained in 1926. Archbishop of Trani and Barletta from 1947 to 1971.

[54] "Title: 'On the union of the Churches', in order that the separated brothers might return to the house of the Father. Too prolix."

[55] "Pastoral homily".

[56] "But to teach the truth as it is in itself is a pastoral task par excellence. The full Catholic doctrine must be upheld."

[57] "Let the separated brothers return."

Bishop Alexandre Scandar of Assiut (Egypt). We must all work for unity, to remove this scandal of the division of Christians. But let this be through reason enlightened by faith. I was not born Catholic. After converting, I worked for 40 years in Egypt for union with the Apostolic See. Fidelity to the ancient rites is necessary. I am ready to yield my seat to my brother Orthodox bishop who is in the same city as I am. But the reality is this: among the Orthodox, there is no unity or even fraternity. Some reject several Catholic dogmas: Purgatory, etc. We do not need to return, as they would like, to an earlier age: the eleventh, or even the fifth century. The Church is life, dynamism, evolution, progress. Charity, yes; "sed intacta manente veritate pro qua parati sumus dare vitam nostram".[58] Let us pray that our Lord will enlighten their minds.

Bishop Joseph Köstner[59] of Gurk (Austria). – Page 262, no. 35 (or 45), change the language, so that the council does not appear to be making political allusions. Adopt a "modus positivus loquendi, v.g.: ad astruendam fidem, ad defendendum patrimonium civilisationis christianae,[60] etc."

Auxiliary Bishop Alfred Ancel of Lyon. – "De necessitate humilitatis et abnegationis ad fovendam unitatem, vellem aliqua addere, ut melius intelligatur quid sit haec humilitas. Nequaquam est renuntiatio vel minima veritati; neque sub respectu fidei, neque sub respectu historiae. Sed oportet intelligere nos non esse dominos veritatis, sed servos, etc. Unde non sufficit gloriari quia veritas semper in Ecclesia inconcussa permanet, sed potius debemus humiliari nos, de hoc quod secundum veritatem non ambulavimus. Humilitas numquam obstat amori Ecclesiae. Absit qui diceret malum de Ecclesia, sed absit qui nollet fateri peccata filiorum ejus. – Opus unitatis ex parte nostra absque vera et operosa humilitate fieri non potest. Rejicienda est humilitas ficta, neque sufficit humilitas quae, quamvis sincera, etc. Debemus coram Deo et hominibus confiteri nos ignorantia, defectibus, etiam culpis nostris, partim esse reos divisionis. Et non sufficit dicere defectus eorum qui nos praecesserunt: debemus confiteri etiam nostros, et non tantum in genere, sed in particulari enuntiare. – Humilitati adjungi debet abnegatio. Requiritur etenim ut

---

[58] "But while preserving intact the truth for which we are ready to give up our lives".

[59] Josef Köstner (1906–1982), Austrian, ordained in 1931. Bishop of Gurk from 1945 to 1981. He is alluding to no. 35.

[60] "A positive manner of speaking, for example: to protect the faith, to defend the patrimony of Christian civilization, etc."

defectus de medio tollantur."[61] For this, generous and persevering efforts are necessary. We must abandon certain human traditions that, de facto, prevent union. Without that, all discussions will be useless. "Erit argumentorum pugna non erit pax. Cf. St. Paul: 'Si esca scandalizat fratrem meum, etc.' Ergo salvo jure veritatis, ad omnia relinquenda parati esse debemus, ut unio sit possibilis, etc. Nullo modo fratres judicabimus, sed nosmetipsos, ne a Christo judicemur ... – Soli Deo gratias agimus."[62] (Applause.)

Melchite Archbishop Michel Assaf of Petra (Jordan) (in French). Venerable council Fathers. This schema is one of the most important. It corresponds to the essential thought of John XXIII, who has already been called the pope of unity. I agree with my patriarch Maximos IV and all of the Greek-Melchite-Catholic episcopate; we approve of it on the whole. I will suggest a few amendments, especially in paragraphs 25–26, concerning liturgical means. – In nos. 23 and 26, stress is laid on the desire to respect the Eastern rites; but each time a reservation is added, offensive and unwarranted: provided that there is nothing in them contrary to the faith or to morals ... But those who are familiar with these rites know very well that they contain nothing of that kind. We must delete this reservation, even if it does reproduce the words of Paul V, pronounced in other circumstances. – No. 24 solemnly affirms,

---

[61] "On the necessity of humility and self-abnegation in order to foster unity, I would like to add something, in order that it might be better understood what this humility is. It is by no means the renunciation of even the smallest truth, either from the standpoint of faith or from the standpoint of history. But it is necessary to understand that we are not the masters of the truth but its servants, etc. Hence, it does not suffice to glory in the fact that the truth abides forever unshakeable in the Church, but rather we must humble ourselves, for we have not always behaved in accordance with the truth. Humility never stands in the way of the Church's love. Let anyone who would speak ill of the Church be far from us, but let anyone who would not be willing to acknowledge the sins of her sons be far from us as well. The work of unity cannot be accomplished without a real and active humility on our part. False humility must be rejected, nor does that humility, however sincere, suffice, which, etc. We must confess before God and men that through our ignorance, our failings and faults, we are in part responsible for the division. And it is not sufficient to say that they are the failings of our predecessors; we must confess that they are ours as well and declare them not only in a general fashion, but in particular. Self-abnegation must be joined to humility. Indeed, this is required in order to make the failures disappear."

[62] "There will be a battle of arguments; there will not be peace. Cf. Saint Paul: 'If food is a cause of their falling', etc. [1 Cor 8:13 in the NRSV, Catholic Edition. A literal translation of the verse in the Vulgate would be: 'If food scandalizes my brother' – TRANS.]. Therefore, while maintaining the rights of truth, we must be prepared to relinquish everything in order that union might be possible, etc. We will not judge our brothers in any way, but we will judge ourselves, so that we might not be judged by Christ. We give thanks to God alone."

at ll. 34–35, that the Eastern Churches will never be forced to abandon
their own rites. But on this point there is a whole, painful history. Many
of those in the Eastern Churches have been forced to pass over to the
Latin rite. And there is a moral constraint, often more effective than the
physical one. The Roman Church sincerely condemns all the schemes
that seek to Latinize the Eastern Catholics; she forbids their Latiniza-
tion, reserving to the Apostolic See the right to authorize the change
to the Latin rite. But in fact these things happen as if the Holy See had
no power to stop them ... The reasons that make me keep silent about
specific examples will be understood. – No. 25 insinuates that reforms
or innovations can be usefully introduced. This is a reminder of what
Leo XIII said in the encyclical *Orientalium dignitas*. But let us reread the
context. Our Church has no intention of introducing innovations in
the rite without the agreement of our Orthodox brothers. – Again at
no. 25: it is stressed, in order to reassure the Eastern Churches: they will
find in the Catholic Church their own home. A beautiful, ecumenical
declaration, and obvious besides. What is less obvious is the actual reality in our Eastern countries. What a situation, where we act and speak
as if the Catholic Church was the sole Latin Church! I deliberately
refrain from explaining what I mean. Let our intentions be followed
by effects. We rely on the collaboration of everyone, with the grace of
God.

Bishop George Dwyer of Leeds (England). – To whom is this schema
addressed? If it is addressed to the Orthodox Churches, it is necessary
to start with what they can understand, in order to bring them around
to us. This is an elementary pedagogical principle. "In mentem audi-
toris intrare necesse est",[63] even if we think he is mistaken. We must
at least understand the position of the other person and his reasoning.
For us, "Ecclesia romana est mater et magistra amatissima."[64] But the
Eastern Orthodox Churches have not received their faith from Rome;
Rome was only their sister. It is therefore useless and contraindicated
to start by talking about the primacy of Peter. We ought not to start
with no. 5, but with no. 10 and what follows. In the same way, we
must accentuate the points we have in common with the Orthodox,
cite the testimonia Patrum,[65] not speak right away about the need to

---

[63] "It is necessary to enter into the spirit of the listener."
[64] "The Roman Church is the well-beloved Mother and Teacher."
[65] "Testimony of the Fathers".

submit: "in fine potius".[66] So, change the order, and quote the Eastern Fathers. Otherwise the Orthodox, after the first few sentences, will stop reading, and we will have wasted our time. – With regard to wasted time: we seem also to forget the millions and millions of people who suffer from physical and spiritual hunger. "Quid juvat de duplici fonte revelationis loqui",[67] when the source of charity is dried up? "Quid juvat de lingua latina discutere",[68] when we say nothing that people can understand and that responds to their expectations? After two months of work, very few results. If we carry on like this, "valde timeo quod totus mundus de nobis non dico rideat, sed doleat, dicens: non sunt serii. Dixi."[69]

It was a quarter past noon; Archbishop Felici announced that the Board of Presidency would deliberate on Card. Ottaviani's proposal.

While I was leaving, Bishop Martin, S.M.,[70] brought me the duplicated text of Darmancier's intervention.

Immediately after the session, inside Saint Peter's itself, some subcommissions of the mixed commission for the schema *De revelatione* were formed. The subcommission for the New Testament has Ruffini and Liénart as presidents. Its experts are: Lattanzi (Lateran), Garofalo (Propaganda), Hamer, O.P. The latter, judging himself not very competent in exegesis, spoke about Fr. Daniélou to Cardinal Liénart, who hesitated, not knowing whether he had the right to accept him. They discussed the matter; his right to do so was recognized; he accepted Daniélou. But for his part, Msgr. Willebrands, in the name of the Secretariat for Unity, had designated an exegete (a rather dull fellow, I am told, the idea being to avoid bringing into the commission or subcommissions any expert that Card. Ottaviani might not like). Finally, by chance coming face to face with Fr. Daniélou, Cardinal Bea accepted him.

Msgr. Romeo very recently gave a talk to the journalists on the organization of the Curia. He complained that some journalists were claiming to do theology without knowing anything about it. Someone asked him to give some examples. Romeo: "Mr. Fesquet is one." It was Fesquet who had asked the question.

---

[66] "At the end, rather".

[67] "What is the good of talking about a double source of revelation?"

[68] "What good is it to discuss Latin".

[69] "I greatly fear that the whole world, I do not say will laugh at us, but will be saddened, saying: they are not serious. I have had my say."

[70] Pierre Martin.

The title of an article in the Saturday, Nov. 24, 1962, issue of *Corriere della Sera*: "Restituendo liberta all'episcopato il Papa ha renunciato all'assolutismo",[71] by Indro Montanelli. "... It is not difficult to see how the idea of the council had been suggested to the pope. The clergy of Bergamo ... have never had much love for Rome and have remained tainted with modernism. We do not intend to say by this that the pope is a modernist or has a modernist tendency. However, if our information is correct, the young priest Roncalli had as his professor of theology Buonaiuti, the great herald of modernism. It was [Buonaiuti], we are told, who assisted him at his first Mass. Nothing permits us to say that the student showed solidarity with his teacher, later excommunicated, or that he shared his ideas. He had a humane sympathy for him; whereas he never had any such feelings for Pius X, who excommunicated him; and although the Church canonized this pope, etc. Buonaiuti was Roman, but he had converts especially in Northern Italy ... The young Roncalli must have breathed a little of this air, and that continued when he became the secretary of the Bishop of Bergamo, Bishop Radini Tedeschi,[72] ... who had close connections with Buonaiuti and the modernists..."

Toward evening, Fr. Daniélou brought me news about one of the 5 subcommissions of the mixed commission, the one to which he was named this morning as an expert. The first meeting had just taken place. Everything went rather well. The five subcommissions are supposed to work quickly, so that the commission can hold a meeting and adopt some guidelines before December 8.

Also saw Father Martelet, who came from the Gregorian, where he had worked all day in the library on the schema *De B. Maria Virgine*. He is staying in regular contact with Cardinal Liénart.

Archbishop de Provenchères has just said this evening to Fr. Daniélou that the proposal made by Card. Ottaviani this morning has been rejected by the Board of Presidency. He had received the news from Card. Liénart. It is said that, this morning, Card. Tisserant appeared shocked by Ottaviani's nerve.

---

[71] "In giving liberty back to the episcopate, the pope has renounced absolutism."

[72] Giacomo Radini Tedeschi (1857–1914), Italian, ordained in 1879. Bishop of Bergamo from 1905 to 1914. He had to face suspicions of modernism. A. G. Roncalli was his secretary from 1905 to 1914.

The beauty of Saint Peter's, this evening, in the dark, under the thunderstorm, seen from our windows.

Thursday, November 29, 1962. – Cardinal Montini's silence has been noticeable. But it is known that he is the only one of the cardinals whom the pope invited to stay at the Vatican. It is known (or at least it is said) that John XXIII wanted to have him nearby to follow everything closely and inform him himself in confidence. (Cf. Msgr. Noirot.)

Archbishop Dalmais (of Fort-Lamy) came this morning to the Borgo. He has prepared, with Archbishop Zoa (Yaoundé), a text that will be submitted in the morning to the Board of Presidency against Ottaviani's proposition. He thinks it is an error to want to deal with the Blessed Virgin outside of any ecclesiological reference and that a hasty discussion on the Blessed Virgin might cause a good number of arguments instead of manifesting unity. In South America, it appears that an enormous number of Masses have been offered to obtain the definition of Mary as mediatrix. – Archbishop Garrone spoke harshly to Archbishop Dalmais about Rahner's schema on revelation; I explained to Archbishop D. some of the reasons for this harshness. – The African bishops who have a large Muslim population in their territory are gathering here this morning, around Bishop Mercier (Sahara) and Archbishop Dalmais; they want to form a sort of research group that would work together during the time of the council and no doubt afterward.

Yesterday afternoon, conference given by Msgr. Dumont, O.P., to the Africans. He seemed, I was told, a little discouraged, observing that the most obvious and elementary things concerning ecumenism, relations with the Eastern Churches, etc., were poorly received by many.

At 11 A.M., Archbishop Zoa's press conference on the Church in Africa and the means of communication. He started by explaining the drums. It went very well. Numerous questions. Saw the young Father ..., a Maronite; we spoke about the disagreements among the Eastern Churches. Also saw Father Paul Gauthier (Nazareth); he gave me his booklet on "Jesus, the Church and the Poor: Nazarene Reflections for the Council"; it is sponsored by his bishop, Archbishop Hakim (Melchite Archbishop of Acre and all of Galilee) and Bishop Himmer of Tournai.

Father Tucci, editor of *Civiltà cattolica*, gave me some rather precise news about the pope's health. So now I understand the contradictory rumors heard over the last two days. The doctor would like the pope to cease walking constantly when he goes anywhere, but he has not succeeded in stopping him.

Mario Rossi,[1] the former president of Italian Catholic Youth, is organizing a conference in the parish hall of Saint Mary of the People for
Sunday, December 1, at 6 P.M.; according to the program he has already
distributed, I am supposed to speak on "Interesse scientifico e religioso di
Teilhard de Chardin".[2] He assured me that the organizers have obtained
express authorization from some important Roman Monsignor or other,
as well as from the Secretariat of State. Archbishop Dell'Acqua would
appear to be completely happy with the speaker and the topic.

Msgr. Spada (?),[3] president of the Italian Catholic Press, wanted me to
write an article on the council. I declined.

Today I finished reading the printed booklet (by Father Moubarac):
Reflections on the structures of Catholicism in the Arab world in connection with the universal Church.

This afternoon, the lead article in *L'Osservatore Romano* was devoted
to the health of the pope, who is suffering, the article said, from a
"gastro-pathia".

At the Procure of Saint Sulpice, on the street of the Four Fountains,
a conversation with Father Francis Deniau,[4] who is preparing a thesis in
patristics, to be defended at the Angelicum: interpretation of some verses
of the Epistle to the Ephesians in Origen, Chrysostom, Theodoret,
Theodore of Mopsuestia. He is very enthusiastic over his discovery of
Origen. One of his fellow students is preparing a thesis on the Image
of God in William of Saint Thierry.[5] – Caught sight of Msgr. Girard
and Cardinal Gerlier, who invited me for next Tuesday. – Met Bishop
Louis-Jean Guyot[6] of Coutances, who stopped me to talk to me about
the council. He told me he had just had lunch with Cardinal Tisserant,
who had been hard on Ottaviani. He told me that many bishops, since
the beginning of the council, have discovered here a number of things

---

November 29
    [1] Mario Vittorio Rossi (1925–1976), Italian doctor, president of the Gioventù Italiana de Azione
Cattolica (Italian Youth of Catholic Action) from 1952 to 1954.
    [2] The scientific and religious interests of Teilhard de Chardin.
    [3] Andrea Spada (1908–2004), Italian priest, member of the Preparatory Secretariat for the Press
and Entertainment, expert at the council. He was one of the founders of the Unione cattolica
stampa italiana (Italian Catholic Press Union), created in 1959, but its president was Raimondo
Manzini.
    [4] Francis Deniau, born in 1936, French, ordained in 1961. Cardinal Feltin had sent him for two
years of study in Rome. Current bishop of Nevers.
    [5] Jacques Lefur, P.S.S., French.
    [6] Louis-Jean Guyot (1905–1988), French, ordained in 1932. Bishop of Coutances from 1950 to
1966. Created cardinal in 1973.

they had not suspected. He was very happy that Ottaviani's proposal had been rejected; the chapter on the Blessed Virgin, he thought, can only be studied within the framework of ecclesiology.

At the Gregorian, Fr. Donatien Mollat told me that Fr. Sébastien Tromp, according to the Dutch priests who approached him, remains unwavering: from his point of view, the council Fathers know nothing; he is the one who has the truth, and the truth will triumph. According to Fr. Mollat, one of the old cardinals of the Curia (Ciriaci?),[7] appalled at what is being said at the council, believes that the Church is in very grave danger. – Father Pin appeared rather worked-up, as a result of a pamphlet that has just been distributed to the council Fathers. This pamphlet claims to indicate the proposals formulated last year at the International Pastoral Congress that met at Fribourg; now, according to Father Pin, these proposals were falsified, and he intends to prove it. The Congress had been held under the auspices of the Congregation of the Consistory.

Back at the Borgo S. Spirito, I saw Fr. Greco, secretary of the African bishops. He set out for me the proposal that these bishops want to issue for the work of the commissions in the months to come; I informed him of the initiative of Cardinals Lercaro and Villot,[8] so that they could coordinate their efforts.

Received a letter from Dr. Denys Gorce. He is indignant over what *La Pensée catholique* wrote about Teilhard. "It is truly cheap integrism, from which I completely dissociate myself." Next he spoke to me about the domination of Cardinal Ottaviani, whom he rejoiced to see shaken today. "I have just lost my brother, a Benedictine abbot, who, on the basis of vile reports with no foundation, rotted for six years in the jails of that strange tribunal before which one is not even entitled to present one's own defense and which constitutes, as I wrote to the Holy Father, a serious wrinkle on the face of the Church. My brother has just died of a tumor contracted as a result of the ill treatment he suffered. The only consolation in all this is that the Holy Office has always

---

[7] Pietro Ciriaci (1885–1966), Italian, ordained in 1909, created cardinal in 1953. Prefect of the Congregation of the council from 1954 until his death and president of the Commission for the Discipline of the Clergy and the Christian People.

[8] Jean Villot was not yet a cardinal at that time; in fact he was only created cardinal in February 1965. Father de Lubac mentioned, in the journal entry for November 17, the plan of Don Dossetti and G. Alberigo, anxious to have Cardinal Lercaro bring forward their proposal for the continuation of work during the intersession.

been, throughout history, the anvil on which the Lord has forged his saints ..." I know nothing about this affair and its circumstances.*9

Father Daniélou worked this afternoon with Bishop Charue and Msgr. Cerfaux to prepare the text of the chapter on the New Testament; he foresees a difficult meeting on Monday at his subcommission. – Jean Guitton seems to be getting most of his information from Fr. Ch. Boyer, something that worries Fr. Daniélou a little.

At 7:30 P.M., meeting at the Mascherino Street home of Mr. Gawronski, a Pole, organized by Father Moubarac. Present: Moubarac, Daniélou, Archbishop de Provenchères (Aix), Father Colson,[10] Fr. Pin, Fathers Laurentin and Denis.[11] Exchanged views on the episcopate, collegiality, etc. Not much of any substance. Mr. Gawronski told me that the Polish bishops are keeping to themselves; he supposes that, for various reasons, they have received advice to this effect from Cardinal Wysz.[12] – He wanted to introduce me to Mr. Zaminski,[13] a writer and playwright, who has become an unofficial diplomat, having at the same time, he told me, the confidence of Rome, Cardinal Wyszyński, and the Polish government; but he was not able to come.

Friday, November 30, 1962 (30th General Congregation). – On the steps of the Basilica, a bishop I do not know came up to me and said: "Yesterday, the Board of Presidency decided to stick to the prescribed order of the day; but some might fear that Card. Ottaviani went to see the pope last night and appealed to his feelings as he tried to do with us." Here is a sign of that feverish climate of struggle that the repeated efforts of Card. Ottaviani have fueled, efforts that work against the ends he expects from them. – Inside, I met Archbishop Hermaniuk of the Ruthenians in Canada; he asked me my impressions and gave me his. He was a member of the Preparatory Theological Commission. I was never given any idea, he told me, of the offers from the Secretariat for Unity,

---

9*This whole paragraph has been crossed out, and there are question marks in the margin.

[10]Jean Colson (1913–1977), French, ordained in 1938. Professor of history of the origins of Christianity at the Catholic university of Angers, he was also a director of charity-related studies at Secours catholique in Paris. At the council, he was the personal expert of the bishop of Saint-Dié.

[11]Henri Denis, born in 1921, French, ordained in 1951. Professor at the Saint Irenaeus Seminary in Lyon, he became, in 1964, episcopal vicar of his diocese. Having come to Rome as the secretary of Cardinal Gerlier, he was named an expert at the end of the first session.

[12]S. Wyszyński.

[13]There seems to be some confusion with regard to this name. Perhaps he meant Jerzy Zawieyski (1902–1969), Catholic playwright and essayist.

etc. He, too, had harsh words for the methods of Ottaviani, Tromp, and some others. He does not believe that mental attitudes have matured enough to draw up a satisfactory constitution on the Church. He hopes instead that some practical measures, for example on the episcopal conferences, will prepare the ground. He would like to see these measures carefully weighed, in such a manner as to prevent any excess, any abuse; without that, he told me, there would soon be a retreat. He is not satisfied with the schema *De Ecclesia.* – Next saw Father Oreste Kéramé again, accompanied by the two young American priests I saw him with the other day on the Janiculum hill. – Met Fr. Martelet, arriving with his two cardinals, Liénart and Feltin, whose briefcase he was carrying. Archbishop Villot has taken him under his wing.

The president is Card. Spellman. Bishop André Charue said Mass. – Father Congar brought me his book *Sacerdoce et Laïcat*[1] (*Priesthood and Laity*), which has just come out in Rome.

The secretary general announced that Cardinal Ottaviani's proposal, despite all its merits, had not been accepted. He then announced that today there would be a vote on the first nine emendationes of the first chapter of the Liturgy. He gave some explanations in connection with this. Then Bishop Martin[2] of Nicolet (Canada) read his Relatio[3] of the Liturgical Commission's work: it had not judged it necessary to revise everything; certain suggestions were set aside; "aliud est genus encyclicarum, aliud genus constitutionis conciliaris".[4] Detailed remarks. Explanation of all the corrections of any importance. Today a vote on only nine of these is requested.

Next the discussion of the schema *De unitate Ecclesiae* was resumed.

Card. Wyszyński. "Schema generaliter bonum; optime distinguitur a schemate de Ecclesia."[5] It needs a certain breadth. Let us proclaim the urgency of unity. In our time, concern about Christian unity is in the heart of all. The question is of interest to all Churches and confessions, especially the Christians who bear witness to Christ. The materialism

November 30

[1] Y. M. Congar, *Sacerdoce et laïcat devant leurs tâches d'évangélisation et de civilisation* (Paris: Éd. du Cerf, 1962).

[2] Joseph Albert Martin (1913–1990), born in the United States, ordained in 1939. Bishop of Nicolet from 1950 to 1989. Member of the Commission for the Liturgy.

3. "Report".

[4] "The style of encyclicals is one thing, the style of a conciliar constitution is something else."

[5] "The schema is, in general, good; it is very well distinguished from the schema on the Church."

of daily life is more dangerous than doctrinal materialism. We admire all the Orthodox Christians who confess their faith in the midst of persecutions. Since the day when the encyclical de Corpore mystico[6] was promulgated, Catholic doctrine has rejected individualism; it goes back to the sources, to Saint Paul, to the Fathers of the Church; "atqui hoc fovet unionem".[7] There is already unity among us in the Mystical Body through grace and the sacraments, etc. – Some difficulties. The matter is divided into three schemas: hence repetitions; but that requires only some rather easy corrections. It would be a good idea to change the title: De schismate? or de Orientalibus?[8] As for practical means, we must let these be determined by the bishops. "Amamus, maxime aestimamus Orientales";[9] we study their great doctors, who are also ours. "Schema mihi maxime placet, tanquam osculum unitatis et pacis."[10]

Card. Bea. "De origine et fine hujus schematis."[11] It was produced to convey the council's veneration for the Eastern Churches, because of their close proximity to the Latin Church ... However, this schema also contains things similar to those treated by the other documents on ecumenism. The doctrine can only be discussed in depth in connection with chapter 11 of the schema De Ecclesia. We will have to talk then about the "communio in sacris", the patriarchates, etc. Uniting all our forces, we hope to arrive at a comprehensive decree that will apply to all our very dear separated brothers, showing them our desire for unity and calling for their cooperation toward this end. – "Schema propositum in genere valde placet. No. 15, oratio pro unitate";[12] our secretariat has worked on that. No. 17: it is not only a question of a means; the necessity of giving the example of a truly Christian life. – "Bene distinguere oportet doctrinam et modum proponendi doctrinam";[13] cf. what the pope has said on this subject; "res summi momenti".[14] – For

---

[6] Mystici Corporis, of Pius XII, in 1943.

[7] "This fosters union."

[8] "On the schism? or On the Eastern Churches?"

[9] "We love, we greatly esteem the Eastern Churches."

[10] "I completely approve of the schema, as a sort of kiss of unity and peace."

[11] "On the origin and aim of this schema".

[12] "I highly approve the proposed schema. No. 15: prayer for unity".

[13] "It is necessary to distinguish carefully between the doctrine and the manner of presenting the doctrine."

[14] "A very important matter".

collaboration in various spheres, do not speak "modo nimis defen-
sivo".[15] – Even certain doctrinal aspects concerning the unity of the
Church can be touched on in a practical decree. – Some uncertainty
has been expressed regarding the persons to whom the text is addressed:
first, to the whole Catholic Church; but also to our non-Catholic brothers. Pay careful attention, then, to the language. It is addressed to all
Christians and, finally, "quodammodo, omnibus hominibus".[16] The
style must be in accordance with that. – Allusion has been made to
Leo XIII: his work was stopped by his death; John XXIII has taken it
up again, founding the secretariat, which will henceforth contain two
sections, for the Protestants and for the Eastern Churches.

(It was explained to me that if Bea's intervention had been some-
what lacking in clarity, it was because he was anxious not to displease
Cicognani, the secretary of state, who is president of the Eastern
Commission.)

I did not hear Archbishop Trindade of Evora (Portugal); Archbishop
Hermaniuk of the Ruthenians of Canada, who asked for the creation of
two mixed commissions: Catholic-Orthodox and Catholic-Protestant;
Bishop Saba Youakim,[17] one of the Melchites from Lebanon. I heard
the end of the intervention by Bishop Franić (Yugoslavia), which was a
criticism of "progressive" Christians.

Bishop Vaz das Neves[18] of Braganza (Portugal). There is too much
talk about external unity, not enough about internal unity. It is necessary
that the separated brothers be attracted by the great current of charity in
the Catholic Church. (Pious, judicious, but lacking in vigor.)

The Very Rev. Fr. Augustin Sépinski, O.F.M.,[19] I liked the schema
before the council, and I like it even more today. The doctrinal articles
should be kept: it is good to show non-Catholics our doctrine. Nearly
60 experts, half of whom are of the Eastern rite, worked on this. Find

---

[15] "In an excessively defensive fashion".

[16] "In a certain way, to all people".

[17] In actuality, it was Eftimios Youakim, B.S. (1886–1972), Lebanese, ordained in 1912. Melchite
Bishop of Zahleh (Lebanon) and of the Bekaa Valley from 1926 until his death. Superior general of
the Salvatorian Basilian Order.

[18] Abílio Augusto Vaz das Neves (1884–1980), Portuguese, ordained in 1919. Bishop of Braganza
and Miranda from 1938 to February 1965.

[19] Augustin Joseph Sépinski, O.F.M. (1900–1978), French, ordained in 1924. Minister general of
the Franciscans from 1952 to 1965, then apostolic delegate to Jerusalem and Palestine from October
1965. Member of the Commission for Religious.

a better title, for example, "De Christianorum unitate".[20] On p. 253, lines 31–34 should be deleted for psychological reasons. Page 254, l. 20, and elsewhere, instead of "dissidentes", say "separati", or "non catholici": this "dissidentes"[21] has a bad ring to it. – Page 259, ll. 15–21, "constructio ut jacet est obscura";[22] the original text was clearer. – Page 264, l. 29: say "concilium" rather than "congregatio".[23] – Page 267, no. 52: this is not sufficiently clear.

Archbishop D. Hayek,[24] Aleppo of the Syrians. "Placet in genere." I will only speak about our Syrian brothers. They venerate the pope, even though separated. The schema could come at the conclusion of *De Ecclesia*, under the title: *De Ecclesiis orientalibus*,[25] in the plural. Page 254, ll. 3ff.: this is good; but elsewhere this is expressed differently. – Why, among the supernatural means, has the Eucharist been forgotten, sacrament of unity par excellence? – Let the norms that govern the return to the Church be required only for those who have performed schismatic acts; for the others, a simpler formula must suffice. – Eliminate certain "verba dura et acerba"[26] that even today can be found in our books, even liturgical and canonical ones.

Archbishop John Heenan[27] of Liverpool. – De facto, it is perhaps more difficult to speak of the Eastern Churches than of the Protestants, because they are closer to us. – The virtue of humility is essential, on both sides. The persecutions of Hitler brought Catholics and Protestants together in several countries; perhaps a similar situation will bring Catholics and Orthodox together. The efforts of John XXIII. He can say: "Quid facere debui, et non feci?"[28] – It is very unfortunate that we do not have any observers from Athens or Constantinople. – It would be better to shorten the schema: let it be a simple declaration of charity, in such a way that none could doubt our desire, etc. – It is sad to note

---

[20] "On the unity of Christians".

[21] "Dissidents" – "separated" – "non-Catholics" – "dissidents".

[22] "The text, as it is, is obscure."

[23] "Assembly rather than congregation".

[24] Denys Antoine Hayek (1910–2007), Syrian, ordained in 1933. Syrian archbishop of Aleppo from 1959 to 1968. Member of the Commission for Bishops and the Government of Dioceses.

[25] "On the Eastern Churches".

[26] "Harsh and bitter words".

[27] John Heenan (1905–1975), British, ordained in 1930. Archbishop of Liverpool from 1957 to 1963, then of Westminster from 1963 until his death. Created cardinal in 1965. Member of the Secretariat for Unity.

[28] "What more was there to do, that I have not done?" [A reference to Is 5:4.]

that there is nothing on the Anglicans or the Protestants, who have responded with so much eagerness to the Holy Father's invitation. More and more, there are strong bonds of charity between us. And the observers have been able to see that we enjoy the freedom of the children of God under the authority of the pope. – Let us pray that all Christians, after the council, feel closer to each other and, what is still more important, closer to Christ. (Some applause.)

Bishop Alexandre Olalia[29] of Lipa (Philippines). – "Laudandum et approbandum juxta modum."[30] Some corrections: delete the numerous references to Scripture, which interrupt the reading. Various nos. should be briefer, etc. Concerning certain means: do not be content with an optative mood; we need a "modus imperativus, sin minus indicativus".[31] Do not talk about two Churches, Eastern and Western. – Eliminate the Oriental Congregation.

Bishop Joseph Pont of Segorbe (Spain). – Nos. 18–19: "de facto, agitur de accommodatione".[32] – This is one of the most serious questions posed to the council; we have already encountered it in the liturgy, and it will be found again elsewhere. Let it be treated at once, and in depth. – No. 35: collaboration for the defense of the faith; "res proponitur modo negativo et aliquo modo bellico ('common front'); sapit pessimismum";[33] this is contrary to the pope's speech. – Nos. 23 and 26: the condition expressed is "dura assertio";[34] these liturgical books existed before the schism. So these numbers should be omitted, as has already been proposed, or else changed.

Bishop Rodolphe Staverman[35] of East New Guinea (Hollandia). This schema will be harmful rather than useful, as much for the Protestants, who are ignored, as for the Orthodox. It is too much of a monologue. And the Orthodox do not constitute a unity. – No. 31: We must remember that every day "unusquisque nostrorum deficit ab hac veritate et sanctitate. Laudanda est gratia Dei in Ecclesia indefectibili,

---

[29] Alejandro Olalia (1919–1973), Filipino, ordained in 1940. Bishop of Lipa (Philippines) from 1953 until his death.

[30] "The schema should be praised and approved, with corrections."

[31] "Imperative mode, less indicative".

[32] "In fact, it is a question of an adaptation."

[33] "The matter is presented in a fashion that is negative and, in a certain manner, conflictual; it has a pessimistic flavor."

[34] "A harsh assertion".

[35] Rudolf J. Staverman, O.F.M. (1915–1990), Dutch, ordained in 1940. Apostolic vicar of Hollandia (in New Guinea) from 1956 to 1971.

sed caveamus non gloriari nosmetipsos",[36] etc. – Nos. 5–6, "doctrina de munere apostolico in Ecclesia":[37] it is confused and "non consonum, immo contradictorium cum schemate de Ecclesia".[38] It is necessary to study the question of the "collegium episcopale. Numquam papa est solus, sine suo collegio."[39] Therefore let the schema *De Ecclesia* be corrected on that point.

Bishop Nicolas Elko[40] of the Ruthenians in Pittsburgh, USA (an American of Slovak origin). My experience, especially at Mount Athos, has shown me that the Orthodox agree with us on doctrine, except for the dogma of infallibility and the primacy of the pope. We need to show them Catholic discipline and unity; I have known some who have been converted on seeing this, etc. Here, the observers see very well that the pope is not a dictator, "sed servus servorum Dei";[41] they see our freedom of speech and that we do not put ourselves in danger of going to prison, etc. (Large gestures, grandiloquence. The president stopped him. There was laughter and applause.)

Coadjutor Archbishop Antoine Bukatko[42] of Belgrade (Yugoslavia). Placet. Some written remarks. He would only say one very brief word: there was applause. The secretary general proposed that the discussion be closed. Everyone stood up. – "Velint omnes sedere."[43]

He proclaimed the results of the first 5 votes on the corrections to chapter I of the Liturgy:

1. Those voting: 2,145	Placet: 2,096	Non: 41	Invalid ballots: 8
2. Those voting: 2,143	Placet: 2,103	Non: 34	Invalid ballots: 6
3. Those voting: 2,139	Placet: 1,984	Non: 150	Invalid ballots: 5
4. Those voting: 2,135	Placet: 2,113	Non: 13	Invalid ballots: 9
5. Those voting: 2,125	Placet: 2,049	Non: 66	Invalid ballots: 10

---

[36] "Each of us strays from this truth and this holiness. We must praise the grace of God in the indefectible Church, but let us take care not to glory in ourselves."

[37] "Doctrine on the apostolic ministry in the Church".

[38] "It does not agree with the schema on the Church; rather, it contradicts it."

[39] "Episcopal college. The pope is never alone, without his college."

[40] Nicholas Thomas Elko (1919–1991), American, ordained in 1934. Bishop of the Ruthenians of Pittsburgh from 1955 to 1967.

[41] "But the servant of the servants of God".

[42] Gabriel Bukatko (1913–1981), Yugoslav, ordained in 1939. Coadjutor of the archbishop of Belgrade from 1961 to 1964, then archbishop of Belgrade from March 1964 to 1980. Vice-president of the Commission for Eastern Churches.

[43] "Let all please be seated."

From an article in *La Libre Belgique*, Nov. 26, 1962, by Daniel Stiernon, A.A.:[44] "Many here have criticized the unilateralism on account of which the work of the Preparatory Theological Commission went astray. A number of the Fathers are of the opinion that the difficulties presented by the schemas coming from the Theological Commission could have been avoided if the preparation of the conciliar texts had widely benefited from the collaboration of Frs. Congar, O.P., Karl Rahner, S.J., Schillebeeckx, O.P., de Lubac, S.J., who are the principal theologians of the French, German, and Dutch languages and who today are setting the tone for the council, either as official experts or as private theologians. They enjoy such credit with the bishops of western and central Europe that the "integrist" elements are said to desire greatly their banishment from Rome and have even made appeals to this effect in high places, so far without success."

I exited Saint Peter's through the apse, in the company of Father Duprey,[45] a White Father, professor of Sacred Scripture at Saint Anne of Jerusalem, charged here by the Secretariat for Unity with looking after the observers. He invited me to lunch with him; other guests: Bishop Cassien, rector of the Saint-Serge Institute (Paris); Father André Scrima, a Romanian Orthodox monk; Father ..., an Armenian monk from Beirut,[46] delegated as an observer by the Armenian hierarch of Cilicia[47] (he was the one who read the observers' address the other day at the reception at the Circolo Romano). With the latter, we first went to the Governor's Palace, to buy some cigarettes, a commercial transaction profitable for the buyer and for the seller (tips). We left the Vatican by way of the Belvedere Court; in passing, I showed my companions the Latin inscriptions composed by Bacci for the elevator installed by Pius XII. We went to the Piazza Adrianna, opposite the Castel Sant'Angelo. Conversation about the council, the observers' various impressions,

---

[44] Daniel Stiernon, A.A., born in 1923, Belgian, ordained in 1949. Professor of Eastern theology at the Lateran, he also taught at the Urbaniana.

[45] Pierre Duprey, P.B. (1922–2007), French, ordained in 1950. Professor of dogmatic theology and history of dogma at the Saint Anne Seminary in Jerusalem. Engaged in ecumenical questions, he served officially as theologian and translator for the Orthodox observers. In 1963, he was named under-secretary of the section of the Secretariat for Unity concerned with relations with the Oriental Churches. He was secretary of the Pontifical Council for the Unity of Christians from 1983 to 1999.

[46] Karekin Sarkissian.

[47] Zareh I Payaslian, Catholicos of Cilicia from 1956 to 1963.

expectations. Father Scrima, who recently arrived from Constantinople, explained to us the great difficulties that still prevent the sending of observers, although he has not lost hope for the second session. One of these difficulties comes from the Turkish regime, which is putting a lot of obstacles in the way. – The schema that has just been discussed, *De unitate Ecclesiae*, appears to them to be a sign of goodwill but completely ineffective. And one of the guests said to me in jest: "There should not be too much stress on what was requested in the discussion on the liturgy, the reduction of gestures of honor, for that could create a new and invincible obstacle to unity." We lamented the disagreements among the Eastern Catholics of various rites. – After the meal, Bishop Cassien, always simple, modest, like a true staretz, spoke to us about Bulgakov,[48] whom he had known very well; "for several years, he was my spiritual father." "It is difficult still to see exactly what will remain of his work. He was a great man. He himself was aware of some contradictions in his thought from one book to another, and he wanted to work toward reducing them, etc." – Returned to the Borgo S. Spirito, under a magnificent sun, accompanied by Fr. André Scrima. We admired the dome of Saint Peter's. I got him to talk about Hagia Sophia, which he placed above Saint Peter's, in a class all by itself. He told me, or rather sang to me, his admiration for the Christians who conceived it as well as other churches and monasteries of the same period. I told him that I could almost pardon Justinian for the destruction of Origen's works[49] because of Hagia Sophia.

At 4:30 P.M., I was received by Father General (J. B. Janssens). Yesterday morning, he sent me a jar of honey from Sicily, through his private secretary, Fr. Van der Brempt,[50] who was saying that he had noticed my cough. (This good Father General does not know how much this shows me his affection, considering his past severity.) It was a good

---

[48] Sergej Bulgakov (1871–1944), Russian. Orthodox priest, professor of dogmatic theology at the Saint Sergius Orthodox Theological Institute in Paris from 1924.

[49] Justinian, Byzantine emperor from 527 to 565, condemned a current of Origenism in 543 and again in 553 at the Second Council of Constantinople, which brought about the destruction of a great part of Origen's works. H. de Lubac had made a particular study of Origen in *Histoire et Esprit: L'Intelligence de l'Écriture d'après Origène* (Paris: Aubier-Montaigne, 1950; republished by Éd. du Cerf, 2002); trans. Anne Englund Nash and Juvenal Merriell as *History and Spirit: The Understanding of Scripture according to Origen* (San Francisco: Ignatius Press, 2007).

[50] Georges van der Brempt, S.J. (1907–1997), Belgian, ordained in 1939. Secretary of the English Assistancy at the Jesuit Curia from 1946 to 1965.

conversation starter. He talked to me about Virgil and the bees, about
the description of ploughing in the *Georgics*, which still corresponds
exactly to what is done today in the countryside around Rome, etc. –
Then I broached my subject. I had made two copies of a summary of it.
It concerned the schema *De deposito fidei*, no. 22.[51] I explained to him
how this text had been drafted, what condemnation it intended, how it
was slanderous. I told him how much I regretted having to speak to him
about it. I had waited more than a year, always hoping that this would
not be necessary; but now I found myself forced into it. Then I spoke to
him about the preceding chapter, which contained a paragraph against
Fr. Teilhard.[52] He then took out his typewritten notes, which he had
prepared this summer for the Central Commission: my two remarks on
this paragraph were already his own. That put us completely at ease.
He told me that if need be he could have a cardinal intervene (Döpfner
or König or Alfrink ...). I answered him that I was not asking him for
anything; I only thought that it would be good for me to make things
clear to him in advance, rather than to have to defend myself, after the
fact, against a conciliar text. – He spoke to me also about a newspaper
article in which it was said that Rahner, Congar, and Holstein rejected
tradition in the name of Scripture alone; he understood very well that
this interpretation of their rejection of the "two sources" view was tendentious; I explained to him how it was entirely false, and I laid stress on
the text of the Council of Trent. On this subject he said to me that his
old professor of theology, Father De Villers[53] (whom I also got to know
in Louvain in 1930), taught him to read and interpret strictly the conciliar texts, and he was surprised to see so many bishops and theologians so
little versed in this art, etc.

At 5:30 P.M., a film was shown by the French Embassy to the Vatican:
The Trial of Joan of Arc, by Bresson.[54] – During this time, Fr. Lécuyer,

[51] This refers to no. 22 of chapter 4, on a "recens relativismi forma": "periculose etiam a vero
discedunt qui sentiunt enuntiationes et conceptus quibus veritates revelatae communicantur,
impares esse ad res divinas omnino vere significandas, etsi utique imperfecte et incomplete" (recent
form of relativism: those people depart dangerously from the truth who think that the assertions and
concepts through which revealed truths are communicated are incapable of truly expressing divine
things, even if only imperfectly and incompletely).

[52] Particularly no. 14 in chapter 3, on the "Sententiae hodiernae falsae de creatione et evolutione
mundi" (the current false opinions on the creation and evolution of the world).

[53] Auguste De Villers, S.J. (1862–1941), Belgian, ordained in 1892. Professor of dogmatic theology at the theologate of Louvain from 1907 to 1939.

[54] Robert Bresson (1901–1999), among the most important French filmmakers of the postwar
period. His style is characterized by studied elegance and clean lines.

C.S.Sp., was giving a talk to the Africans on the episcopate. (Fr. Martelet will give me an overview and criticism of it tomorrow.)

Saturday, December 1, 1962 (31st General Cong.). – Bishop Verwimp, S.J., who is staying at the General Curia, asked me what the story was with regard to the things reported by *La Libre Belgique* (cf. yesterday). I told him what I knew. He said to me that there was a lot of subterranean maneuvering going on around the council, and he did not hide from me that he did not think much of certain Italian ecclesiastics.

In Saint Peter's, conversation with Bishop Ménager (Meaux), happy that the discussion on the *De Ecclesia* is opening and concerned about the continuity of the council. – Father Gagnebet gave me some alarming news about the health of John XXIII. In Rome, he told me, it is a convention, as long as the pope is not on his deathbed, to say that he is doing well or that he is only slightly ill. He then told me that it would not be he who would read the report on the schema on the Church, but a bishop, Bishop Franić. – In passing, I greeted Father Antoine Wenger, who, in his gallery, was writing his next article for *La Croix*, as was Father Henri Denis; as he is living with the French bishops, I encouraged him to keep them well informed. In my gallery, I found myself between Fr. Charles Boyer and a Spanish-speaking Dominican and, as has been the case these past few days, facing Father General.

Cardinal Frings was presiding. The secretary general announced: "Laetissime communico Patribus"[1] that the Holy Father was feeling better and that he hoped to appear at his window to give his blessing tomorrow, Sunday. "Oremus omnes pro Pontifice nostro Joanne."[2] The pope greets and blesses all the Fathers. – From the Prefect of Ceremonies:[3] from tomorrow until December 7, the cardinals will attend wearing purple.[4] – Today voting will take place on the schema *De unitate Ecclesiae*, according to the printed form that has been distributed. New emendationes on the liturgy are going to be distributed; they will be submitted to a vote on Monday. – Results of the last 4 votes from yesterday:

December 1

[1] "I announce to the Fathers with very great joy".

[2] "Let us all pray for our Pope John."

[3] Eugène Tisserant, prefect of the Ceremonial Congregation.

[4] Because of Advent.

6. Those voting: 2,122	Placet: 2,101	Non: 15	Invalid ballots: 6
7. Those voting: 2,120	Placet: 2,004	Non: 101	Invalid ballots: 15
8. Those voting: 2,116	Placet: 2,092	Non: 19	Invalid ballots: 5
9. Those voting: 2,117	Placet: 2,097	Non: 13	Invalid ballots: 7

"Nunc, adest schema constitutionis de Ecclesia."[5]

Card. Ottaviani. – "Illud schema vobis commendo, praeparatum dili-gentissima cura a 70 membris Commissionis praeparatoriae, examinatum a Commissione centrali, et a Commissione emendationum perpensum. Summus Pontifex jussit ut illud exhiberetur vobis examinandum. Cura fuit quam maxime pastoralis, biblica";[6] so that it might be capable of being understood by everyone, "non scolasticus, sed forma quadam actualiter ab omnibus comprehendenda. – Vobis aliquam confidentiam debeo facere. Res jam a pluribus praejudicata est. Quidam jam dixerunt: 'Tolle, tolle!'[7]..." Before the schema was distributed, some were already saying that it should be rejected. However, "docet sacra Scriptura: Ubi non est auditus, non est habere sermonem."[8]

Bishop Franić. – He is going to set out the schema in summary form. The intention was to treat only the questions posed by the majority of bishops. – Chap. 1: No real distinction between the juridical and the pneumatic[9] Church, between the Roman Church and the Mystical Body. – Chap. 2, on the Members of the Church: nothing is said about what could be disputed concerning non-Catholics, "membra impro-prio modo et analogice";[10] it speaks only about the members "proprio

---

[5] "Now, we will discuss the schema of the constitution *De Ecclesia*."

[6] "I recommend this schema to you, a schema prepared with very scrupulous care by 70 mem-bers of the Preparatory Commission, examined by the Central Commission, and carefully analyzed by the Commission of Amendments. The Supreme Pontiff has ordered that it be presented to you to be examined. The greatest pastoral and biblical care has been taken."

[7] "It is not scholastic but assumes a rather current form so as to be understood by all. I must tell you a secret. The schema has already been judged in advance by many. Some have already said: 'Away with it! Away with it!'" [See Jn 19:15. Cardinal Ottaviani is making reference here to the action of Msgr. Philips, who had prepared, at the request of Cardinal Suenens, an alternative schema on the Church.]

[8] "As Holy Scripture teaches: 'Where there is no listening, it is useless to speak'" [Sir 32:6]. [The actual text of the Vulgate is: "Ubi auditus non est, non effundas sermonem." In the RSV, second Catholic edition, the closest parallel seems to be 32:4: "Where there is entertainment, do not pour out talk." – TRANS.]

[9] The Greek word for Spirit is *pneuma*; so pneumatic means: that which is related to the Holy Spirit.

[10] "Members in an improper way and by analogy".

et vero sensu".[11] The commission's members and consultors all voted, and their vote was unanimous. – Chaps. 3 and 4, De episcopate.[12] Chapter 3 settles a question that has been long debated in the schools and whose solution is now ripe: solemn decision on the sacramentality of the episcopate. Chap. 4 deals only with residential bishops, the other questions being still under debate. So nothing is said about titular bishops; nor does the schema speak about practical questions, subject to change, such as the bishops' conferences. – In the same way, chap. 5 is restricted to purely dogmatic truths, valid for all times. – Chap. 6, De Laicis:[13] here, too, "aspectus stricte dogmaticus, de sacerdotio universali christianorum".[14] – Chap. 7: "De magisterio, ordinario et extraordinario",[15] of the pope and the bishops. "Ad respondendum necessitatibus hodiernis",[16] it speaks also of the auxiliary magisterium of theologians, priests, preachers. Here, as at the end of every other chapter, we could not keep silent about certain errors. – Chap. 8. De auctoritate et obedientia in Ecclesia:[17] a very topical question. – Chap. 9. De relationibus intra Ecclesiam et Statum:[18] only general principles are given. The question of "tolerantia religiosa"[19] is supposed to be treated in a separate schema, drafted by a mixed commission. – Chap. 10: De necessitate annuntiandi evangelium omnibus; de vocatione et jure Ecclesiae. – Chap. 11: De oecumenismo, sub aspectu principiorum stricte dogmaticorum.[20] The Secretariat for Unity for its part gives some practical norms. – Everything is treated "modo positivo. Sed, non sine gravissimis rationibus",[21] we had to condemn errors and point out dangers, so that these would be very clear to all. The schema has been approved by the pope. Condemning errors is the best way to shed more light on what is true. We have worked on this schema over the course of nearly 100 meetings.

---

[11] "In the proper and true sense".

[12] "On the episcopate".

[13] "On the laity".

[14] "A strictly dogmatic aspect, on the universal priesthood of Christians".

[15] "On the magisterium, ordinary and extraordinary".

[16] "In order to respond to current needs".

[17] "On authority and obedience in the Church".

[18] "On the relations between the Church and the State".

[19] "Religious tolerance".

[20] "Chap. 10: on the necessity of announcing the Gospel to all; on the vocation and the right of the Church. Chap. 11: On ecumenism, under the aspect of strictly dogmatic principles".

[21] "In a positive way. But, not without very grave reasons".

Card. Liénart. "Gaudeo quod schema praesens a capite incipiat Corpori Christi mystico dicato."[22] Our Church is not merely a society like human societies, she is a great mystery: cf. Ephes. It is not necessary to try to explain it, but to display it, by a return to revelation. Be careful that our formulas, in wanting to surround it, do not destroy the mystery. Let the identity of the Mystical Body and the Church not be affirmed to the point of wanting to enclose the whole of the Mystical Body within the limits of the Roman Church. The grace of Christ overflows these limits, and no one is saved who is not incorporated into Christ. "Ergo multo latius extenditur Corpus mysticum."[23] On the one hand, we must not forget that there is the Church Suffering and the Church Militant; on the other, we must not forget any longer all baptized Christians. "Non potest sensu absoluto Ecclesia nostra identificari Corpori mystico. Unde peto quod articulus 7 capitis primi deleatur. Et schema penitus recognoscatur. Hoc non dico spiritu contentionis aut contradictionis, sed"[24] I am bound by the truth. "Amicus Plato magis amica veritas.[25] Dixi."

Card. Ruffini. "Placet. Doctrina vere catholica. Aliquae animadversiones ad perficiendum."[26] Omit chap. 5, "De statibus acquirendae perfectionis";[27] chap. 6, "De laicis"; chap. 11, "De oecumenismo", which is the subject of three other distinct schemas. "Incongrue tractatur de necessitate Ecclesiae ad salutem in capite secundo; melius de hoc dicendum in capite primo; hic, naturae Ecclesiae adjungatur finis Ecclesiae, unde, ejus necessitas ad salutem. Postea, loqui de necessitate evangelizandi. Ergo schema posset contrahi in septem capita. – Insuper: Ecclesia est una et unica, super Petrum a Christo fundata";[28] we cannot admit several Churches, or two. Those in the West and those in the East have

---

[22] "I am delighted that the present schema begins with a chapter devoted to the Mystical Body of Christ."

[23] "The Mystical Body is thus extended in a much broader way."

[24] "Our Church cannot be absolutely identified with the Mystical Body. I therefore ask that article 7 of the first chapter be deleted. And that the schema be entirely reworked. I do not say this in a spirit of conflict or contradiction, but".

[25] "I am a friend of Plato, but still more of the truth" [maxim attributed to Aristotle].

[26] "I approve the schema. The doctrine is truly Catholic. Some remarks to perfect it".

[27] "On the states of perfection to be acquired".

[28] "It is incongruous to treat of the necessity of the Church for salvation in the second chapter; it would be better to speak of this in the first chapter; let the end of the Church, that is to say, her necessity for salvation, be joined to the nature of the Church. Then, speak about the need to evangelize. Thus the schema could be compressed into seven chapters. Furthermore: the Church is one and unique, founded on Peter by Christ."

common principles. In chap. 4, then, we could speak, regarding the potestas jurisdictionis,[29] of the collegial episcopate and the patriarchates. –
The sinful members are not only infirm but dead.

Card. José M. Bueno y Monreal, archbishop of Seville (Spain). This
schema is very complex. I will speak only about the theological element.
It raises innumerable problems. "Multa habet laudanda, non tamen est
perfectum."[30] – I. "Ecclesia catholica est Corpus mysticum: haec est
doctrina encycl. Mystici Corporis et Humani generis![31] ... But there
is more stress placed on the social body than on the living and mystical body. Now the mystical aspect is the more fundamental. And what
value do we claim to give this constitution? It relies on the encyclicals,
id est,[32] on the ordinary magisterium; does it mean to canonize solemnly
the formulas of these two encyclicals? – 2. The schema recalls the tria
munera Christi,[33] left by him "continuanda Petro et Apostolis. Sed nihil
dicitur de tertio, i.e., sacerdotio. Lacuna haec omnino impleri debet."[34]
Regarding the rest, we will see later, in the discussion of the articles,
what should be rejected and what should be kept. – 3. It lacks a chapter
on the elements of the Church that are not of divine right but of ecclesiastical creation, etc.

Card. François König, archbishop of Vienna (Austria). I. "Schema
brevius esset redigendum",[35] so as not to cut off so many questions disputed among theologians or make other schemas redundant. – 2. The
Church transcends nations, etc. "Non multum juvabit declarare tantum jura Ecclesiae; declaretur potius munus annuntiandi Evangelium ad
omnes Gentes."[36] Speak about the nations, bring a judgment on their
traditions, their religions, etc. Demand for the Church the liberty that
all nations proclaim. – 3. "De Ecclesiae natura: non omittatur indoles
ejus stricte eschatologica,[37] etc." Show the Church's dependence on

---

[29] "Power of jurisdiction".

[30] "The schema contains many things worthy of praise; however, it is not perfect."

[31] "The Catholic Church is the Mystical Body, that is the doctrine of the encyclicals *Mystici Corporis* and *Humani generis*."

[32] "That is to say".

[33] "Three offices of Christ". [These three offices of Christ are: priest, prophet, and king, to celebrate, teach, and govern.]

[34] "To be continued by Peter and the apostles. But nothing is said about the third office, that is, the sacerdotal office. This gap absolutely must be filled."

[35] "The schema should be written in a briefer form."

[36] "It will not be a great help to declare only the rights of the Church. Rather, let the duty to announce the Gospel to all people be declared."

[37] "On the nature of the Church: let her strictly eschatological character not be forgotten."

Christ. – 4. De necessitate Ecclesiae:[38] the schema talks about this under a purely individual aspect. It should speak of its necessity for all mankind, unitas collectiva;[39] show the connection of all men to Christ, who assumed our human nature. – 5. We should add a "brevis expositio de populo Dei";[40] the priesthood and the episcopate are a means for the edification of the People of God. – Chapters 3 and 4 should be combined into a single chapter "De Hierarchia".[41] Chap. 5 should be abridged. From chapters 7 and 8 a single, briefer one should be made. – Regarding the magisterium, explain that the "indefectibilitas in fide competit toto corpori Ecclesiae".[42]

Card. Bernard J. Alfrink, archbishop of Utrecht (Holland). I leave out everything that is praiseworthy in the schema, for lack of time. – 1. "Plura tractantur, in aliis commissionibus tractata."[43] There was never any collaboration; let us finally coordinate our efforts. – 2. "Ecclesia est Corpus Christi: hoc, maxime laudandum; sed schema nimis premit sensum externum hujus imaginis."[44] It does not speak enough about the internal life of the Church; hence, in the second chapter, the doctrine concerning the members, "quae sapit minimismum".[45] – 3. "In capite quarto, mirum est tractari de episcopis residentialibus, sed non de munere episcopali."[46] All bishops have a mission in common. – 4. "In eodem capite 4°, tractatur de collegio episcopali modo nimis negativo: 'non nisi modo extraordinario exercetur haec potestas'."[47] "Quid de magisterio ordinario corporis episcoporum?"[48] There is something in chap. 7 that contradicts this chapter 4. "Omnino siletur de collegio episcoporum!"[49] – 5. Cap. nonum, Ecclesia et Status: nimis insistit in juribus Ecclesiae. Quaedam enuntianda sunt de libertate religiosa. – 6. Constitutio de B. Virgine organice conjungatur

---

[38] "On the necessity of the Church".

[39] "A collective unity".

[40] "Brief presentation on the people of God".

[41] "On the hierarchy".

[42] "Indefectibility in the faith falls within the competence of the whole body of the Church."

[43] "Many things are dealt with that have been dealt with in the other commissions."

[44] "The Church is the body of Christ: that is greatly to be praised, but the schema focuses too much on the exterior sense of this image."

[45] "That has a minimalist flavor".

[46] "3. In chapter four, it is surprising that it deals with residential bishops but not with the episcopal office."

[47] "4. In the same chapter 4, it deals with the episcopal college in a manner that is too negative: 'This power is only exercised in an extraordinary fashion.'"

[48] "What about the ordinary magisterium of the body of bishops?"

[49] "Nothing at all is said about the college of bishops!"

constitutioni de Ecclesia ... Schema reformetur ab aliqua commissione mixta, a Sancto Patre instituenda."[50]

Card. Ritter, archbishop of Saint Louis (USA). "Multa dicit, et bene, sed multa desunt."[51] It is a general fault in its method, with the result that it is not easy to compensate for it. The "tres potestates"[52] constitute only one part of the Church's activity. "Schema omnino inadaequatum."[53] Its faults are doctrinal ones. It says almost nothing about the sanctity of the Church, of which Saint Paul spoke. – The "munus servandi et exponendi depositum fidei"[54] is only in part the munus magisterii:[55] it belongs first of all to the whole Church. "Omnia membra etiam simplices fideles, partem habent in servando et etiam in exponendo depositum fidei."[56] This is the case, not by an indult of the magisterium, but by their character as Christians. – Third example: on the Church and the State. Those expecting a doctrine for our times will be disappointed; it is useless to return to an outmoded position; what is needed is to talk about religious liberty. – In the schema, "absentia de cultu Ecclesiae. Christ est vivens et operans in omnibus membris suis per Spiritum sanctum",[57] we must show that every member has his part, "secundum propriam mensuram",[58] in all the activity of the Church. – "Officium hujus concilii est suaviter, clare et adaequate indicare quid sentiat Ecclesia de seipsa. Debemus indicare quod *hodie* Ecclesia sentiat![59] ..." We cannot just return "ad conceptus partiales Tridentinos et Vaticanos";[60] we have to take account of all the work carried out since then and of new situations. – "Conclusio: Schema revideatur, recognoscatur."[61]

---

[50] "5. Chapter nine, the Church and the State, stresses the rights of the Church too much. It ought to talk about religious liberty. 6. Let the constitution on the Blessed Virgin be combined in an organic fashion with the constitution on the Church ... The schema should be reformed by a mixed commission, to be instituted by the Holy Father."

[51] "The schema talks about many things, and does it well, but many other things are lacking."

[52] This refers to the three powers of Sacred Order, Jurisdiction, and Magisterium.

[53] "The schema is completely inadequate."

[54] "The duty to serve and to expound the deposit of faith".

[55] "The duty of the magisterium".

[56] "That of the whole Church. All the members, even the simple faithful, have their role in guarding and also in expounding the deposit of faith."

[57] "An absence of the Church's worship. Christ is living and active in all his members through the Holy Spirit."

[58] "According to his own measure".

[59] "The duty of this council is to indicate gently, clearly, and adequately what the Church thinks about herself. We must indicate what the Church thinks *today*."

[60] "To the partial conceptions of Trent and Vatican I".

[61] "Conclusion: let the schema be revised and reworked."

Auxiliary Bishop Lucien Bernacki[62] of Gniezno (Poland). "Pauca dicam."[63] It lacks an essential chapter, on the Supreme Pontiff. An inexcusable omission. It is not enough to say that Vatican I spoke about this. "Haec carentia dolenda est in se, et respectu ad fratres nostros separatos. Haec veritas fundamentalis lucide exponatur."[64] The distinction that has been made between the Western and the Eastern Church is not in conformity with Christ, with the unity of the Church. Christ founded his one and only Church when he said: "Tu es Petrus,[65] etc." He said to Peter: "Duc in altum".[66] "Ne timeamus veritatem dogmatum clare evocare."[67] It is necessary to take up again the statement of the four Marks of the Church.[68] It is a traditional statement, already at the Council of Nicaea, etc. These Marks can only be applied objectively to the Roman Church, and the demonstration of this is easy. They come from Christ, etc. (The president: Satis).

The secretary general announced the result of the vote on the schema *De Ecclesiae unitate*. It was an overall approval, with the request for corrections and for it to be merged into one schema with the two texts, from *De Ecclesia*, chap. 11, and from the Secretariat for Unity.

Number of ballots cast: 2,112. – Placet: 2,068. – Non placet: 36. – Invalid ballots: 8.

Bishop De Smedt of Bruges (Belgium). "In schemate sunt qualitates reales. Progressus doctrinae apud theologos et apud fideles non sine influxu fuit in ejus redactione. Sunt aliqua profunda et vigorosa. Tamen, multi defectus, specialiter de ipsa conceptione Ecclesiae quae subest. Deficiens est in spiritu oecumenico, et aliena prorsus a modo quo doctrina a concilio praesentanda est. Ponam aliquam triplicem quaestionem: nonne schema emendendum est a quodam triumphalismo, clericalismo, juridismo? – 1. Nimium indulget illo stylo pomposo et romantico",[69]

---

[62]Lucjan Bernacki (1902–1975), Polish, ordained in 1926. Auxiliary bishop of Gniezno from 1946 until his death.

[63]"I will only say a few things."

[64]"This lack is unfortunate in itself and with regard to our separated brothers. This fundamental truth should be clearly set forth."

[65]"You are Peter" [Mt 16:18].

[66]"Put out into the deep" [Lk 5:4].

[67]"Let us not be afraid to bring out clearly the truth of the dogmas."

[68]One, holy, catholic, and apostolic.

[69]"There are in this schema some real qualities. The progress of doctrine among theologians and the faithful has not been without influence on its composition. Certain points are profound and vigorous. However, there are a number of defects, particularly on the conception of the Church

that we are accustomed to find in *L'Osservatore Romano* and in certain encyclicals. "Historia videtur esse concatenatio triumphorum militantis Ecclesiae. (Quaedam exempla ...). Puto stylum ipsum parum congruere cum statu reali populi Dei in terra, cum spiritu Evangelii: 'pusillus grex', cum mente serena Orientalium[70] ..." And the schema says nothing about religious liberty. – 2. The schema still assumes the famous pyramid: pope – bishop – priests – faithful. "Populus christianus est in basi, mere receptivus, et ultimum locum videtur occupare in Ecclesia."[71] It forgets entirely that the hierarchy is a transitory means; "in altera vita",[72] it will no longer have any purpose, for Christians will have reached the perfect age. What remains is the People of God; what passes away is the hierarchy. Fundamentally, all Christians are in the same situation: the pope is "unus ex fidelibus Christi";[73] he has need of grace, he prays, he confesses his sins, receives the sacraments, like everyone. The power of the pope and the bishops is a ministry: "ministerium verbi, gratiae, gubernationis".[74] It is when we forget this that we arrive at a sort of episcopolatry or papolatry. – 3. "Juridismus. Maternitas Ecclesiae fuit initio centrum doctrinae Ecclesiae."[75] Now this concept is not emphasized. "Omnes baptizati generantur a Matre Ecclesia; omnes fratres sunt",[76] – whether they are united or separated. Now the whole chapter "de membris"[77] is built on a "ratiocinatio a priori; sic mater non loquitur. Non solum hoc non est bona theologia, sed bona mater non potest permittere hunc modum loquendi."[78] (Applause.)

---

that underlies the schema. It is lacking in ecumenical spirit and is completely foreign to the manner in which the council must present doctrine. I will pose a threefold question: Is there not a certain triumphalism, clericalism, legalism in the schema that needs to be corrected? 1. It gives way too complacently to this pompous and romantic style." [We have here the first use of the word "triumphalism" at the council. The standard French dictionary Le Petit Robert also attributes to Bishop De Smedt the first use of this neologism in the French language.]

[70] "History seems to be a sequence of triumphs of the Church Militant. (Some examples ...) I think this style agrees very little with the real state of the People of God on earth, with the spirit of the Gospel's 'little flock' [Lk 12:32], with the serene spirit of the Eastern Churches ..."

[71] "The Christian people are at the bottom, merely receptive, and they seem to occupy the lowest place in the Church."

[72] "In the other life".

[73] "One of the faithful of Christ".

[74] "Ministry of the Word, of grace, of government".

[75] "3. Legalism. The Motherhood of the Church was in the beginning the center of the doctrine of the Church."

[76] "All of the baptized have been engendered by Mother Church; all are brothers."

[77] "On the members".

[78] "A priori reasoning: a mother does not speak like this. Not only is that not good theology, but a good mother cannot permit this manner of speaking."

Archbishop Marcel Lefebvre, superior general C.S.Sp. Since the beginning, there has been a lack of understanding among us. Some want a doctrinal exposition, others a pastoral one. And this is the case on every subject. This lack of understanding results from our method. We cannot speak at the same time to the experts and to the crowd. I therefore propose a new method: let all the commissions prepare, on each subject, two schemas; one, destined for the experts: clerics, theologians, professors, a schema that will be truly dogmatic and scholastic; the other, broader, simpler, less precise, destined for all the people ... In this way we will reach unanimity.

Bishop Arthur Elchinger, coadjutor of Strasbourg. "Aliqua praecisio circa mentem generalem hujus schematis. Etiam fideles exspectant a nobis aliquam explicationem de Mysterio Ecclesiae – et etiam illi qui non pertinent ad Ecclesiam catholicam. Pro multis, hodie, Ecclesia est potius velum et non revelatio Christi. Intentio pastoralis non est opposita intentioni doctrinali; e contra, debet animare ipsam doctrinalem expositionem."[79] Today's questions are not those of yesterday; other aspects need to be explored and set forth. We have in particular to show "quod Ecclesia non est tantum institutio, sed etiam communio. Heri, locutum fuit praesertim de papa; debemus hodie loqui etiam de episcopis, etiam titularibus"[80] (I am one of them). "Heri, de episcopo singulari; hodie, de collegio episcoporum. Heri, de hierarchia; hodie, etiam de populo christiano. Heri, de causis divisionis inter christianos; hodie, primo de communibus. Heri, ostendebatur Ecclesia salutem afferens illis qui sunt ad intra; hodie, etiam aliquo modo illis qui sunt ad extra. Debemus quoque purificare in Ecclesia modos evangelicos: Ecclesia non dominare vult, sed ministrare. – Omnia illa non sunt innovationes: reditus est ad Patres, ad Scripturam, ad integram traditionem catholicam."[81]

---

[79] "A point on the general spirit of this schema. The faithful also are expecting from us an explanation of the Mystery of the Church, even those who do not belong to the Catholic Church. For many, today, the Church is a veil rather than the revelation of Christ. The pastoral intention is not opposed to the doctrinal intention; on the contrary, it must animate the doctrinal exposition itself."

[80] "That the Church is not only an institution, but also a communion. Yesterday, one spoke especially of the pope; today we must also speak of the bishops, including the titular ones."

[81] "Yesterday, of the bishop alone; today, of the college of bishops. Yesterday, of the hierarchy; today, of the Christian people also. Yesterday, of the causes of division among Christians; today, in the first place, of the points in common. Yesterday, the Church was depicted as bringing salvation to those within her; today, in a certain way, also to those who are outside her. We must also purify in the Church the modes of action according to the Gospel [see the AS: "Ecclesia parata esse debet ad habitus agendique modos suos evangelice purificandos"]: the Church does not want to dominate but to serve. None of these things are innovations; this is a return to the Fathers, to Scripture, to the full Catholic tradition."

Archbishop of Camerino.[82] (I did not hear what he said.)

Bishop Pawlowski of Włocławek (Poland). (I only heard the end. The president stopped him. He then exclaimed: "Ultima sententia"[83] and made a fine but rather empty summation.)

Bishop Jean Van Cauwelaert of Inongo (former Belgian Congo). It is a unanimous wish that this council would show to the world the Church speaking to all men, in order to point out to them the meaning of life and of human history. Men have become aware of their unity. Technology has given them a new power, etc. But all of this is without soul. Hence the torment of modern existence. Men aspire to a unity that they can neither conceive nor achieve. The Church can reveal it to them; she can and must say to the world that this unity will be achieved through Christ and in Christ. She can and must call all men "ad fraternam communionem. Tragica est temporis nostri conditio. Sed nunc tempus acceptabile, novum Pentecostem instaurare."[84] All Christians must be summoned to the task. – "His dictis, multi episcopi, praesertim"[85] those in our Congo, "dicunt: celare non possumus, nos deceptos esse hoc schemate. Sunt in illo nonnulla elementa pulchra; sed praesentatio est nimis juridica; non dat sufficienter bonum salutis nuntium. Ecclesia sub aspectu nimis statico ostenditur; non dicitur Ecclesiam terrestrem esse in fieri, ad finem eschatologicum."[86] It must be shown that all the institutions and actions of the Church are ordered toward this goal, "ut omnes sint unum in Christo. In vanum docemus Ecclesiam catholicam esse veram Ecclesiam Christi, si non ostendimus ejus vitam et ejus finem. Mutatis mutandis",[87] show in the first community in Jerusalem the model of the Church. "Sine injuriosa invocatione juris",[88] show the necessitate of entering the Church for salvation, etc. We are deeply concerned about the absence of the missionary spirit as well as a "defectuosa doctrina de membris et de collegio episcoporum, etc. Unde, votum generale: ut Constitutio

---

[82] G. D'Avack.

[83] "One last sentence".

[84] "To fraternal communion. The condition of our time is tragic. But the time is now opportune to inaugurate a new Pentecost."

[85] "That said, a number of bishops, particularly".

[86] "They say: we cannot hide the fact that we are disappointed by this schema. It contains some beautiful elements, but the presentation is too legalistic, it does not sufficiently give the good news of salvation. The Church is shown in too static a way. It does not say that the terrestrial Church is constantly evolving toward an eschatological end."

[87] "In order that all might be one in Christ. It is in vain that we teach that the Catholic Church is the true Church of Christ if we do not show her life and her aim. *Mutatis mutandis.*"

[88] "Without an offensive invocation of the law."

de Ecclesia funditus recognoscatur, et a commissione mixta."[89] (Some applause.)

Bishop L. Carli of Segni (Italy). 1. "Plurimi episcopi"[90] are complaining about the agenda. We have neither the time nor the required books to study so long a schema. Why have we not brought up for discussion the schema on the Virgin or the one on the moral order? The pope's decision only concerned *De fontibus*; it does not prevent us from discussing right now some other dogmatic schema. – 2. There has often been exaggeration. Everything does not need to be seen in the light of the desired unity. This council must first of all concern itself with Catholics, "tractare res internas Ecclesiae catholicae. Extra justos limites se exercere non debet praeoccupatio oecumenica."[91] Some would like nothing said that is dogmatic, for example, "de historicitate evangeliorum, etc., de Traditione, de materialismo atheo, de Ecclesia militanti (quia sapit militarismum!), nec de magisterio ordinario Ecclesiae",[92] which must come before Scripture; "nec de justitia, de castitate, de judicio, etc. Debemus tamen procedere sine ullo complexu timoris et exponere veritatem integram."[93] There is a desire to adapt everything to modern ears. "Nimis indulgendo psychologismo,[94] etc.", we can only create instability. Do not carry a similar concern over "in textibus conciliariis. – Placet schema."[95] It deals with questions not yet treated in the preceding councils. It does not deal in depth with the question of the episcopal college: say more clearly that it is "sub capite suo".[96] – Does the council intend to define anything or only "sollemniter proponere? Sunt alia schemata, quantum scio,[97] etc." – Chap. 7 should be placed after the chap. *De episcopis*.

During the session, I helped an old, limping bishop back to his seat, below my gallery. He told me that he was Bishop Robert Picard de

---

[89] "Defective doctrine on the members and the college of bishops, etc. So, a general wish: that the Constitution on the Church be thoroughly revised by a mixed commission."

[90] "A very large number of bishops".

[91] "To deal with questions internal to the Catholic Church. The preoccupation with ecumenism must not be exercised outside of just limits."

[92] "On the historicity of the Gospels, on tradition, on atheistic materialism, on the Church Militant (because that smacks of militarism!), nor on the ordinary magisterium of the Church".

[93] "Nor on justice, on purity, on judgment, etc. We must, however, proceed without the least fear and set forth the complete truth."

[94] "By indulging too much in psychologizing".

[95] "In the conciliar texts. I approve the schema."

[96] "Under the authority of its head".

[97] "To propose solemnly? There are other schemas, for all I know."

la Vacquerie[98] of Orleans. He spoke to me in a friendly way about my books. He told me that he had not liked my book on Teilhard as much; he would like me to write another one, integrating Teilhard's principal ideas into classical theology. He gave me an account of how, as a military chaplain, he had organized meetings between French and German episcopates; Cardinal Frings had expressed his happiness about this in front of him within the last few days. He spoke to me about Father du Rivau,[99] whose action in Germany he greatly valued; about Cardinal von Preysing,[100] whom he loved and who, it appears, spoke to him about me with fondness (I had seen him in Berlin in 1947,[101] where we had an excellent conversation). Lastly, he told me that he wanted to retire; he felt he was now too old, even with a coadjutor.

Last night, Fr. Daniélou continued his work in the subcommission on the New Testament. He is not very happy, he told me, with what is going on in the other subcommissions, especially in the one on the Old Testament, whose revised text seems to be worse than the text that was rejected, because they have removed everything that concerned the relationship between the two Testaments. That does not interest the exegetes of a Bea-style formation, who see only the narrowly scientific aspect of biblical problems. The peritus called to this subcommission is Baum,[102] who seems to have little personality. On Scripture and tradition, neither Congar nor Rahner was called; the German Feiner,[103] chosen by Bea, so it seems, is letting himself be dominated by Parente. At least with chapter 5,[104] Bishop Volk is doing what he wants.

---

[98] Robert Picard de la Vacquerie (1883–1969), French, ordained in 1921. Bishop of Orléans from 1951 until May 1963.

[99] Jean du Rivau, S.J. (1903–1970), French, ordained in 1936. He was the chaplain at Offenburg (Baden) from 1945 to 1949, where he founded the Bureau international de liaison et de documentation (BILD). He organized meetings of French and German writers and sociologists.

[100] Konrad von Preysing (1880–1950), German, ordained in 1912. Bishop of Berlin from 1935 until his death, created cardinal in 1946, he became famous for his anti-Nazi positions.

[101] On this meeting, one can refer to H. de Lubac, *Résistance chrétienne à l'antisémitisme* (Paris: Fayard, 1988), p. 154 (a new edition was published by Éd. du Cerf, 2006); trans. by Sister Elizabeth Englund as *Christian Resistance to Antisemitism* (San Francisco: Ignatius Press, 1990), p. 145.

[102] Gregory Baum, O.S.A., born in 1923, Canadian. Named as a consultor to the Secretariat for Unity in 1960, then an expert during the first session.

[103] Johannes Feiner (1909–1985), Swiss. Professor of theology at the Diocesan Seminary of Coire from 1938 to 1962. Consultor to the Secretariat for Unity.

[104] On Holy Scripture in the Church. The reference here is to the mixed commission (Doctrinal Commission and Secretariat for Unity) charged with revising *De fontibus*.

Yesterday, while talking to me about the Central Commission, Father General was telling me that the Italian cardinals of the Curia always declare themselves in agreement with Card. Ottaviani. He was unhappy with the measure taken by the Holy Office against the Italian translation of the Dutch episcopate's Letter on the council.

At 1 P.M., lunched in a trattoria with Father Paul Gauthier and two young consecrated women who were accompanying him. We discussed the priest's booklet on "Jesus, the Church, and the Poor". He wants to produce a more sizable work for next year; although not entirely convinced by what I said to him, he assured me that he would take my remarks into account. I found him too bitter, also too simplistic, sometimes unjust, and too much dominated by a concern over propaganda.

At 3 P.M., visit from Stanislas Rostworowski,[105] Polish, who was sent to me by Mr. Gawronski. He seems to be a serious Catholic, well disposed, regretful about certain past excesses of the "Pax" movement[106] of which he is a member. I did not conceal my feelings from him. Nevertheless, he would like to bring Piasecki,[107] the director of the movement, more of a politician than he is, to see me; he is supposed to come to Rome for the last few days of this conciliar session. I strongly advised him to urge his friend to take advantage of this opportunity, outside of Poland, to go and see their cardinal[108] and clear up as much as possible any misunderstandings.

At 4 P.M. Father Martelet came to tell me about all the work he has been doing these past two days. Yesterday morning, in the right hand nave of Saint Peter's, he was laying out for Jean Guitton the broad lines of his draft on the revelation of Jesus Christ. Guitton interrupted him to say: "Be careful that you do not compromise the natural knowledge of God!"

---

[105]Stanislaw Rostworowski (1925–1984), Polish poet and writer, correspondent for Pax in Rome during the council.

[106]Originally a Polish publishing cooperative, founded in 1947 by B. Piasecki, it became a broader movement, wishing to "establish a bridge between Marxism and Catholicism". The episcopal hierarchy disavowed this movement, which the government in power was intending to use to divide the Polish Church.

[107]Boleslaw Piasecki (1915–1979), Polish. Leader of an organization of Fascist character during the Second World War, he convinced the Communists, after they seized power in Poland, of the need for an organization that could serve as a counterweight to the Catholic Church. The intimate links between Pax and the Polish government were little known, however.

[108]Stefan Wyszyński.

At 5 P.M., a visit from another Pole, Turowicz,[109] a newspaper editor from Krakow, in close contact with his archbishop.[110] He was rather severe in his opinion of *Pax*, although in moderate terms. He told me that it was his wife who had revised the Polish translation of my book *Catholicisme*[111] done by Father Szymusiak.[112] He was the one who edited the book. His impressions and judgments on the council seemed to me wise.

At 5:45, Mario Rossi came to pick me up in his car and drove me to the Agostiniana, the parish hall of St. Mary of the People, Piazza del Popolo. We started at 6:15. The room was rather small, and packed. I saw Msgr. Girard, superior general of the Sulpicians, there, and in the first row, in the center, Bishop Pietro van Lierde of Vatican City. I chatted with him for a few moments before beginning; he said to me: It will not bother you, I think, if I take some notes; it is my habit when I listen to a lecture. (I was tempted to think that I am obviously being kept under close watch in Rome; but in the end I believe that it was said without any ill intent, and already last year, Bishop van Lierde had spoken to me in a friendly way.) The title of the talk: Interesse scientifico e religioso di Teilhard de Chardin.[113] Father Augustin, the curate of the parish, said a few words of welcome. I spoke freely, without any prepared outline. I had fun discretely refuting, in this Roman hall, the principal criticism made against Teilhard in the famous article in *L'Osservatore Romano*. I was especially eager to bear witness to Teilhard's personality and religious life. Afterward, the bishop came to my table and thanked me. He posed three questions: 1. The published texts were revised, were they not? – 2. The place of freedom and of sin in Teilhard's thought. – 3. What did he say about death? I answered in a few words. The first question came, it appears, from a quarrel started by Madame de Wespin[114]

---

[109]Jerzy Turowicz (1912–1999), Polish, journalist and essayist. He was the founder and editor in chief of the weekly journal *Tygodnik Powszechny*, published in Kraków since 1945.

[110]At that time, there was no archbishop in Kraków. Archbishop Baziak, Apostolic Administrator, died in June 1962. The government then used its veto power over nominations to the principal episcopal offices and rejected one after the other the six candidates put forward by the Primate. After eighteen months of prevarications, Bishop Wojtyła became archbishop of Kraków.

[111]*Katolicyzm: Społeczne aspekty Dogmatu* (Kraków: Znak, 1961). The translation was indeed revised by Anna Turowiczowa.

[112]Jan M. Szymusiak, S.J. (1920–1987), Polish, ordained in 1950. Theologian, specialist in the Church Fathers, professor at the Catholic University of Lublin.

[113]"Teilhard de Chardin's scientific and religious interests".

[114]Dominique de Wespin (1911–2002), Belgian poet, writer, and journalist. She was involved in the creation of the Belgian Association of the Friends of Pierre Teilhard de Chardin.

(Brussels) with Miss Mortier,[115] on the basis of which some spread the rumor that the latter had revised some texts to make them orthodox. – Some brief exchanges as well with several in the audience. Then we went to dinner at Mario Rossi's home. Father Chenu was invited. We talked about the Catholic Church in Italy, the council, etc. Rossi seems intelligent to me, but a bit of an extremist and inclined to denigrate. He said that he was disappointed in Cardinal Montini, etc.

Sunday, December 2, 1962. – This morning, correspondence. At noon, the pope at his window. Romans came in great numbers to the square. Horns. The pope recited the Angelus; then he spoke. At first he could not make himself heard for all the applause and blowing of horns. He said that these last few days his life had seemed to be departing, and here it was, seeming to return; a little verse on the Blessed Virgin, to prepare for her feast on December 8; at the end, some words on the God who loves us and toward whom we are going.

At 1 P.M., lunch at the Gesù, seated between the rector and the theology tutor.[1] Conversation in Latin. The Father tutor started a discussion with me about the "two sources". A few days earlier, Fr. Rahner had come to speak to the seminarians, and he had raised some objections to him. I first explained to him that there were two different questions here; that the Council of Trent affirmed *the* Source, namely, the Gospel of Jesus Christ, and that that did not settle in advance the exact relationship between the two channels that are Scripture and tradition. Next I told him that the Council of Trent, in rejecting the "partim-partim",[2] had left the discussion on the nature of this relationship open; finally, that all the earlier tradition up to Trent held that the totality of the Christian Mystery is contained in Scripture, whose meaning is interpreted by tradition. He was not at all convinced. His great argument for the two constitutive sources is that they have been taught in the Catholic schools these last few centuries. The modern textbooks have more weight for him than anything else; – as always, because they are the only things he really knows. He identifies this thesis of his textbooks with the absolute truth of the faith. During the recreation period, he tackled me

---

[115] Jeanne Mortier (1892–1982), French, Teilhard de Chardin's assistant and legatee of his writings. She contributed to the publication of nearly all his non-scientific writings after his death.

December 2

[1] This refers to Luigi Pesce and Giovanni Lo Grasso.

[2] "Partly, partly".

next on St. Thomas and Aristotle. Augustine, he said to me, had made a synthesis of the faith and Hellenistic thought, but, "proh dolor !"[3] Aristotle did not figure in this thought. Fortunately, Saint Thomas came along. He did not want to accept what I said to him about the profound transformation that, according to Gilson, St. Thomas made Aristotelian thought undergo in order to Christianize it. A pleasant fellow, but a narrow mind, set in its ways. Someone would later tell me that they call him the Ottaviani of the Gesù.

Two young priests came outside with me and accompanied me as far as the Piazza del Risorgimento. One of the two is a French Canadian, studying at the Gregorian's Social Institute. – A bus conveyed me to Monte Mario where I was going to see Msgr. Luigi Valentini, of the Secretariat of State, whose acquaintance I had made through Fr. René Arnou. Msgr. Valentini welcomed me warmly. A simple, straightforward, intelligent, hard-working man; he has a good library, from which he showed me several books. He gave me an article that he had recently published: "Umanità e Spiritualità di Pio IX" (Fides, 1960);[4] he told me on this subject that in order not to judge Pius IX harshly, it is advisable not to suppose that he was very intelligent. According to him, it was less the death of Pius XII than the withdrawal of the support he had been given by Cardinal Pizzardo that ruined the influence of Msgr. Roche (Opus Cenaculi).[5] He believed that Card. Ottaviani had lured Msgr. Garofalo with the position of rector of the transformed Biblical Institute, which would explain Garofalo's accommodating attitude toward an integrist schema and his reading of the report to the council in Ottaviani's name. He also said to me: I will not speak about the state of the diocese of Rome, because it is too sad a subject. Before 1870, the Cardinal Vicar had temporal duties, in particular the administration of justice; he was not much of a shepherd of souls; after almost a hundred years, the mentality still has not completely changed. The Cardinal Vicar is still today the old Cardinal Micara. We talked about theological publications, etc. – He thinks that Fesquet's articles in Le Monde are very superficial and rebellious; but, on a charitable note, he hoped that the council will be for him an opportunity to improve himself. He called

---

[3] "Alas!"

[4] Luigi Valentini, Umanità e Spiritualità di Pio IX: l'anima de Mons: Masai attraverso i suoi scritti fino alla elevazione al Pontificato (TPV, 1960), 19p.

[5] Georges Roche (1910–1990), French. Founder of Opus Cenaculi, a diocesan secular institute, and a close collaborator of Cardinal Tisserant.

his neighbors over to meet me, Mr. Huber[6] and his wife; Huber, who is Swiss, is a correspondent for *La Croix* ordinarily.

At 5:30, in the company of Father Moubarac, visited an old female relation of his, of Polish and Russian origin, long settled in Rome. She reads Teilhard, who poses all sorts of religious problems for her. We spoke about Teilhard, personality, death, eternal life. Her daughter came to join us. – Around 6:30, I went for a few moments to the reception for members and experts of the council organized by the ambassadors at the Palazzo Barberini: a large official reception, in a beautiful setting. Exchanged a few words with Cardinal Marella, always friendly; he is greatly concerned about the lack of coordination in the preparation of the texts, etc.; but when I told him in a very low voice that the work of the Theological Commission had not been carried out under ideal conditions, I sensed that he wanted to avoid appearing to agree. Archbishop Garrone appeared optimistic; he has had, he told me, some rather good conversations with 6 Italian bishops, including Bishop Carli, and he thinks he has already got them to understand certain things well. I greeted Patriarch Maximos, who was accompanied by Archbishop Edelby and Oreste Kéramé. One of the bishops on the Liturgical Commission told me that the hoped-for promulgation of the first part of the constitution as early as this week is in the realm of dreams; he hopes, however, that the voting will progress. Cardinal Gerlier came up to me to make a few mischievous remarks. Msgr. Maury joined us; he is fairly happy with the work that is being done among the African bishops; he also strongly desires a continuity committee that would stimulate and direct the work of the commissions over the course of the coming months. A German prelate with whom I had conversed at the French embassy (Villa Bonaparte) spoke to me about another idea, launched by some German bishops: that the bishops, when they return to their own countries, address a collective letter to the pope to thank him; the pope would thus feel supported by the episcopate and encouraged to persevere along the line that has opened up. I informed Bishop Cazaux of this suggestion, then Cardinal Lefebvre. They both seemed to think the idea of the Germans was a good one, and they intend to talk to their French colleagues about it.

---

[6] Georges Huber (1910–2003), Swiss, journalist residing in Rome, correspondent for several foreign newspapers. Member of the Carmelite Secular Order.

Monday, December 3, 1962 (32nd General Congregation). – Inside Saint Peter's, Msgr. Dumont gave me his pamphlet (an off-print of *Istina*) on Catholics and Orthodox on the eve of the council. He confided in me his disappointment: he sees that there is a whole bloc for whom doctrine, orthodoxy, the faith are completely mixed up with the theological theses of some modern scholastic textbooks, and it is impossible to make them understand anything. He deplores the theory of dogmatic progress that is triumphing today among the theologians of this school. (This is the theory that Fr. Louis Bouyer so justly criticized recently.) – A Melchite archbishop[1] ... drew me away into a corner of the former chapel of the Blessed Sacrament to read me the text of an intervention he wanted to make tomorrow; I asked him to delete at least one sentence and to correct or clarify some others; it principally concerns, basically, the distinction between the scholastic (modern) concept of dogma and the idea of mystery. – I handed over to Jean Guitton Father Martelet's dissertation on the revelation of Christ, and to Msgr. Valentini my book on Teilhard. Two French bishops asked me if it was true that some have wanted to make me leave Rome; I told them what I knew, that is to say, nothing directly, without drawing any conclusions. – Starting today, the cardinals are in purple, because of Advent, and, because of the cold, the great purple seating area of the bishops is speckled with black spots. – In the gallery, still facing Father General, today I have as neighbors the canons Martimort and Boulard. – Malabar Mass (concelebration); short, lively chants; enthronement of the Gospel with four acolytes, symbolizing the four evangelists.

At the beginning of the session, Archbishop F. Grimshaw[2] (Birmingham) read a report on the emendationes to chap. I of the Liturgy, nos. 10–15. Two of these will be voted on in the course of the session. – Then the general discussion of *De Ecclesia* continued.

Cardinal Spellman. Mihi placet ... (I understood little of the rest.) We have not stressed enough some new realities, in particular Catholic action.

Cardinal Siri (Genoa). "Schema est bonum, quamvis perfectibile. Praebet fundamentum omnino aptum ad disceptationem ineundam. – 1. Optime praebet veritatem de Ecclesia visibili et juridica a Domino

---

December 3

[1] Philippe Nabaa, who did not make an intervention the next day, however.

[2] Francis J. Grimshaw (1901–1965), British, ordained in 1926. Archbishop of Birmingham from 1954 until his death. Member of the conciliar Commission for the Liturgy.

instituta. Corpus mysticum comprehendit totum ordinem incarnationis
... Veritas Corporis mystici eminet in hac constitutione."[3] We could
combine chapters 1 and 2, nos. 4 to 10, in order to show even more
clearly the relationship of the visible Church to the Mystical Body. "Hoc
debet esse clarum et firmum."[4] Talk of the Mystical Body must not
make us forget the necessity of adhering to the visible Church, necessary
for salvation. – 2. "Opportunum erit affirmare, saltem in capitulo de
Magisterio, veritatem de Ecclesia visibili juridice instituta."[5] This truth is
the same in the twentieth century as it was, for example, in the fourth.
"Ecclesia semper eadem et eodem modo docet."[6]

Card. James L. McIntyre, archbishop of Los Angeles (USA). "In
genere placet. Tamen: in cap. 2°, no. 9, qui sunt membra corporis
Christi sensu proprio? Quaestio est involuta et diuturne disputata; non
pertinet directe ad hoc schema."[7]

Card. Val. Gracias (Bombay, India). "Jam ultima hebdomada ..."[8]
We have made our novitiate. It is fortunate. We have heard the most
diverse opinions, attended Masses of diverse rites, such as this morning
for the Mass of St. Francis Xavier. But pay heed to what Archbishop
Heenan said to us... – The schema should be better written: let the
Theological Commission take charge of that. Examples: Chap. 10, "tota
expositio est unilateralis, et sic est valde periculosa; aliter concipiendum
et redigendum."[9] If that remains unchanged, we, the missionary bishops, will be its victims. For example, chap. 10, no. 46 (ll. 30–31): "sunt
verba provocantia. Habemus jam graves difficultates":[10] you are going
to make them worse. We are ready, with the grace of God, for martyrdom, in defense of the faith; but we do not want to provoke it by our

---

[3] "The schema is good, although it could be improved. It furnishes a foundation completely
appropriate for starting the discussion. 1. It presents very well the truth on the visible and juridical
Church established by the Lord. The Mystical Body comprises the whole order of the Incarnation
... The truth of the Mystical Body is prominent in this constitution."

[4] "This must be clear and firm."

[5] "2. It will be opportune to affirm, at least in the chapter on the magisterium, the truth on the
visible Church juridically instituted."

[6] "The Church always teaches the same doctrine and in the same way."

[7] "I approve of it in general. However: in chapter 2, no. 9, who are the members of the body of
Christ in the proper sense? The question is obscure and has long been disputed; it does not directly
pertain to this schema."

[8] "Already the last week ..."

[9] "The whole exposition is one-sided and is, therefore, very dangerous; it should be conceived
and written in a different way."

[10] "The words are provocative. We already have grave difficulties."

defiance. – "De modo veritatis praesentandi jam saepe locutum est."[11] We must not make an effort only for our separated brothers but for all the rest of mankind. Already the experience of centuries has shown the effectiveness of certain methods. What Augustine did long ago with Plato can be done with the Eastern philosophies. – "Conclusio. Pono quaestionem":[12] What response can we give, on returning to our countries, to those who question us about the council? For my part, I will say that, since we had to deal with spiritual matters, our motto was: "Festina lente";[13] that the Holy Father encouraged us to speak freely, that it is necessary to have patience, etc.; in short, "Roma est aeterna. Attamen, admiratio aliquando est signum ignorantiae."[14]

Card. Léger. "Hoc schema debet esse cardo doctrinalis Concilii Vaticani II. Liceat quasdam observationes afferre et vota. – Ex principalibus elementis eminet caput de Episcopis."[15] From a clear statement of the nature of the episcopate "multa alia pendent, specialiter de relationibus inter episcopos et curiam romanam".[16] But we only have a little time left, and the Fathers are beginning to be tired; now we are not able to study such a problem with enough care; and it must be treated in this "mens renovationis a Summo Pontifice saepe expressa".[17] We needed an experience, etsi quondam dolorosa, sed salutaris,[18] to open the way on which the council Fathers are embarking. – "Nunc, quaedam vota. 1. Ut mens renovationis",[19] so well expressed by the votes, might be assured and, "ut Concilium continuatur, oportet quamdam permanentem praesentiam concilii ponere."[20] This body will need to have a certain authority, clearly determined, that would permit it to coordinate the various projects and stimulate them, so that the schemas might be well prepared, in the spirit of the council, for next September. – 2. Let

---

[11]"On the manner of presenting the truth, much has already been said."

[12]"Conclusion. I pose a question."

[13]"Make haste slowly." [A maxim quoted by Augustus Caesar, according to Suetonius.]

[14]"Rome is eternal. And yet, admiration is sometimes a sign of ignorance."

[15]"This schema must be the center of the doctrine of Vatican Council II. Let me be permitted to bring up a few observations and wishes. Among the principal elements the chapter on the bishops stands out."

[16]"Many other things follow, in particular regarding the relations between the bishops and the Roman Curia."

[17]"Spirit of renewal often expressed by the Supreme Pontiff".

[18]"To be sure sometimes painful, but salutary".

[19]"Now, some wishes. 1. That the spirit of renewal".

[20]"That the council might continue, it is necessary that a permanent presence of the council be established."

the time that remains to us be used for voting on the Liturgy. Let the Liturgical Commission work zealously, and let us devote to the subject all the time necessary so that the first two chapters at least might be voted on and we might be able to bring back something substantial to our faithful. – Conclusion. The pope is our good arbiter. All, whatever their opinions, "bona fide procedunt".[21] We all desire to unite all men. Let all, "libenter, benigne et benevole",[22] communicate to men the call to the renewal launched by the Holy Father, the renewal that the Holy Spirit has caused the council to adopt.

Card. Döpfner. "Hoc schema est quasi centrum Concilii ... Habet optima elementa. Attamen",[23] given the demands of the subject, "non plene satisfacit. – 1. Ante omnia displicet structura".[24] It is too long and too extrinsic. No connection between the chapters. No foundation for the chapter on the episcopate (nothing on the People of God). Chap. 5, "De statibus acquirendae perfectionis",[25] is treated as if "religiosi prorsus distincti essent a laicis";[26] we ought to put it after the chapter on the laity and show how priests and laity can be called to this state. – 2. The scriptural foundation is often absent. On the institution of the Church, chap. 1, no. 2, is superficial. Regnum Dei is identified too much with Ecclesia,[27] etc. – 3. The juridical aspect, which is real, is developed to the detriment of the other aspects; the quotation from St. Paul is distorted, etc. – 4. Where is the indication of what the council intends to define and declare, of the weight it intends to give to its assertions? – Specific remarks: a. Collegium episcoporum:[28] its nature, its functions? "hoc non sufficienter apparet".[29] Cf. chap. 4, no. 6: a mere note! But this should be the foundation of all the doctrine concerning the bishops. We should show here the relationship, sub variis modis,[30] of the pontifical primacy with the college of bishops, and not define disputed questions like the origin of the bishops' authority, whether it comes from the pope or not.

---

[21] "Are working in good faith".
[22] "Willingly, with kindness and benevolence".
[23] "This schema is, so to speak, the center of the council ... It contains some very good elements. And yet ..."
[24] "It does not fully satisfy me. 1. First of all, its structure is displeasing."
[25] "On the States of Perfection to Be Acquired".
[26] "The religious were completely distinct from the laity."
[27] "Kingdom of God" and "Church".
[28] "The college of bishops".
[29] "That is not sufficiently apparent."
[30] "Under several aspects".

– b. "Semper dicitur 'potestas', 'gubernium' ":[31] this is not a biblical style; "potius loquatur de ministerio."[32] Cf. chaps. 7 and 8, which, by the way, are too long. – c. Ecclesia et Status:[33] this chapter has been improved by the Central Commission's remarks; but it should be rewritten in a completely different way. – d. On chap. 10, I agree with the criticisms made by Cardinal Gracias. – It is not only a matter of making some changes to the schema: it needs a "nova et profunda elaboratio. Non placet".[34] It is not rash to suppose that, if we say "placet ad modum", we will be obliged to discuss it article by article. So let us continue over the next few days the discussion of the whole, and then let us put it to a suffragatio: Placet, an non? [35] Next, until about February 15, the commission will work to correct it. Then, in union with other commissions (on the laity, on religious, the Secretariat for Unity), many good things that have come from the Theological Commission will be able to find their place in it.

Archbishop Boleslaw Kominek[36] (Poland, auxiliary archbishop). "In genere placet. Sed caret consideratione crucis Domini. Non datur bonus nuntius sine cruce – cum resurrectione."[37] Christ loved his Church and gave himself up for her, etc. (Ephesians). Are we afraid of suffering, as Peter was at first? Let us remember the answer of Jesus ... And why forget Col. 1: "Gaudeo in passionibus pro vobis,[38] etc.?" Today, so many Catholics are suffering for Christ, following the words of Paul and Jesus. This is the "verbum cruces":[39] in this way the Church becomes purer than through external prosperity. As in the first centuries, bishops are martyrs today. And let the Catholic laity know that their dignity as members of the Church is to be protected at great cost. So put the accent on Christ's words: "The one who does not carry his cross after me is not worthy of me."[40] Complete the schema in this sense. A simple addition

---

[31] "It always says 'power', 'government' ".

[32] "Let it rather speak about ministry."

[33] "Church and State".

[34] "A new and profound elaboration. I do not approve."

[35] "Vote: approval or not?"

[36] Boleslaw Kominek (1903–1974), Polish, ordained in 1927. Titular archbishop, residing in Wrocław, apostolic administrator of the diocese of Wrocław in 1962, created cardinal in 1973. Member of the conciliar Commission for the Lay Apostolate.

[37] "I approve in general. But it lacks a reflection on the Cross of the Lord. The good news is not given without the Cross – with the Resurrection."

[38] "Now I rejoice in my sufferings for your sake" [Col 1:24].

[39] "The word of the Cross".

[40] Mt 10:38.

will not suffice. We need to remember the Cross and exalt it throughout the Church's pilgrimage on earth. O Crux, ave, spes unica.[41]

Archbishop François Marty of Reims. Two observations: "ex fonte – ex fine. Ecclesia essentialiter est mysterium. Nimis ut institutio praesentatur. Fundamentum Ecclesiae est in Trinitate. Ecclesia est Corpus mysticum, non est simpliciter institutio."[42] No doubt, the two aspects cannot be separated. The hierarchy itself makes no sense "nisi ad mysterium referatur".[43] The college of bishops. The relation of the bishops to the faithful, who are not bound to them solely per subordinationem,[44] etc. – The will for universal salvation. – The Church and the State: their relations can only be understood "intra relationes inter Ecclesiam et mundum".[45] – Laity are not the servants of the hierarchy, etc. – Conclusion: "distributio nova".[46]

Bishop Joseph Gargitter of Bressanone (Brixen), Italy. We would like some clarifications now on the bishops, successors of the apostles, in union with the pope, called to "regere Ecclesiam Dei".[47] But we find nothing more on that subject here than in Vatican I. Through an exposition of the function of the bishops, the primacy of the pope will be confirmed and clarified. It is necessary to make clear the "jura et officia episcoporum in suis dioecesibus".[48] Cf. Pius IX to the German bishops (1871).[49] – The laity: the foundation of every apostolate. "Sacerdotium omnium christianorum est sacerdotium veri nominis, non solum improprium, ut dicitur – liceat non sit sacerdotium ministrale."[50] The

---

[41] "Hail, O Cross, our one and only hope." [Excerpt from the hymn *Vexilla regis* composed by Venantius Fortunatus, Bishop of Poitiers in the sixth century.]

[42] "[The Church must be explained] by her source and her end. The Church is essentially mystery. She is presented too much as an institution. The foundation of the Church is in the Trinity. The Church is the Mystical Body, she is not simply an institution."

[43] "If it is not put in relation to the mystery".

[44] "By a connection of subordination".

[45] "Within the relations between the Church and the world".

[46] "Conclusion: a new organization (of the chapters)".

[47] "To govern the Church of God".

[48] "The rights and duties of bishops in their dioceses".

[49] The Apostolic Letter *Mirabilis illa constantia* (1875) of Pius IX to the German bishops intended to respond to the dispatch circular of Chancellor Bismarck on the interpretation of the constitution *Pastor aeternus*. The pope approved the bishops who refuted interpretations such as: the bishops "have become, with regard to governments, the functionaries of a foreign sovereign and, in truth, a sovereign who, in virtue of his infallibility, is a perfectly absolute sovereign, more than any absolute monarch in the world."

[50] "The priesthood of all Christians is a true priesthood, and not only in an improper sense, as is said, although it is not the ministerial priesthood."

laity are not to be defined as persons dependent on the hierarchy but as members of the Mystical Body; they do not merely carry out orders; in many cases, they have their own particular competence and responsibility. Conclusion: "De episcopis et de laicis, clarius et modo positivo exponatur doctrina."[51]

Bishop G. Huyghe of Arras. "Talis est momenti hoc schema, ut dici possit Centrum Concilii."[52] So many men today do not know the Church or fight against her! Why? She seems like an enemy to them. It depends on the way we present her. The world is expecting that the Church, through this council, will tell it what she is: "Quid dicis de teipsa?"[53] Our answer will be known everywhere. Thanks to the means of communication, the situation today can no longer be as it was with other councils. Our texts will immediately go everywhere. The Church will be judged according to our texts. Now, although the schema presents some positive elements, it does not at all respond to what the world is asking. – 1. A "spiritus apertus et reipse catholicus" is necessary.[54] But the schema shows a Church folded in on herself. We are all collectively responsible for the world: during these past two months we have become keenly aware of this; there is a new spirit that must be breathed into the schema. – 2. "Spiritus missionarius; praeoccupatio de illis qui longe sunt",[55] for whom we wish to open the door of salvation … – 3. "Spiritus humilis demissionis et servitii".[56] Everywhere the schema speaks of "dominium",[57] etc.: sic plane a spiritu Christi est alienus. Auctoritas in Ecclesia est servitium.[58] Cf. Paul, on the Mystical Body: all, for the service of the members. We must not divide the members into "imperantes et obedientes":[59] the Supreme Pontiff himself "est servus servorum Dei".[60] – On the Church and the State, "quid prodest"[61] to speak about this as it was in the Middle Ages, when this is no longer

---

[51] "Conclusion: on the bishops and the laity, let the doctrine be presented more clearly and in a positive way."

[52] "This schema is of such great importance that it can be called the center of the council."

[53] "What do you say about yourself?" [See Jn 1:22.]

[54] "A spirit that is open and truly Catholic".

[55] "2. Missionary spirit: concern for those who are far off".

[56] "3. Humble spirit of self-abasement and service".

[57] "Ruling".

[58] "It is thus completely foreign to the spirit of Christ. Authority in the Church is a service."

[59] "Those who command and those who obey".

[60] "Is the servant of the servants of God".

[61] "What good is it".

nor can be any longer the case in any nation today? But we must have the ambition to be "tanquam anima mundi hujus universi". – Conclusion: "Necessaria est commissio mixta",[62] to put the spirit of the Gospel everywhere in the schema.

Archbishop Hurley of Durban (South Africa). "Non multum placet,[63] etc." We need a new generation of pastors, etc.

Titular Bishop Barbetta of Faran. An Italian (did not hear him).

Auxiliary Bishop Narcisso Jubany of Barcelona ... (He was very harsh toward the schema.) Several disputed questions are unduly settled. – Conclusion: 1. "Clare determinetur quisnam valor textuum."[64] – 2. Needs thorough correction. – 3. Delete everything that does not have complete theological certainty.

Bishop Rupp of Monaco. "Multa optima";[65] but it lacks a guiding idea. Always remember: "finis remotus concilii (unio christianorum), finis proximus (renovatio vitae internae Ecclesiae). His positis, quid valeat schema ad hunc duplicem finem? – Aliqua decentralisatio desideratur, et jam est in fieri."[66] The pendulum effect of the councils ... After Vatican I, a phase of excessive centralization; Vatican II must not go to the opposite extreme but, rather, restore balance. "Tamen, dolendum est"[67] that the schema goes too far in the direction of centralization. One and the same paragraph deals with the universal episcopate and that of the bishop in his diocese: "duae res omnino diversae".[68] – Delete the text on the assensus interior[69] owed to the magisterium. – "Non ita extollantur episcopi residentiales, ut alii ne quidem sint nominati!"[70] All of them have a potential authority over the whole of the Church. On this matter the Anglicans have preserved a fine and sound tradition. – But why are we talking? Why am I talking? Almost nothing of all that we say has any effect. Consider those long discussions on the Liturgy: what we are proposing now are miniscule corrections ...

---

[62] "So to speak, the soul of this whole world. Conclusion: a mixed commission is necessary."

[63] "I do not much like the schema."

[64] "Let us clearly determine what value is to be placed on the texts."

[65] "Many excellent things".

[66] "The remote goal of the council (the unity of Christians), the immediate goal (renewal of the internal life of the Church). That being the case, what is the value of the schema in view of that twofold goal? A certain decentralization is desired and is already in process."

[67] "However, it is unfortunate".

[68] "Two completely different things".

[69] "Interior assent".

[70] "Let the residential bishops not be put so much in the forefront that the others are not even named!"

Bishop Biagio Musto[71] of Aquino (Italy). The schema is accused of lacking any pastoral or ecumenical spirit. Now, to the contrary, it is what it must be: doctrinal, dogmatic. "Non intelligitur natura muneris pastoralis",[72] which consists above all in "doctrinam exponere, veritatem tueri, genuinam et integram veritatem".[73] We do not want this full truth, we are afraid it might give offense … Such artifices are not at all becoming for pastors of the Church. We must not reject or hide anything of the "veritas" or of "disciplina".[74] "Non reticita, vel attenuata veritas! sed absoluta sinceritas et claritas! Hoc schema, diuturna cura exaratum, a S. Pontifice approbatum, doctrinam catholicam rite praebet. Secundum quosdam, Ecclesia deberet esse ministra, et humilis: sed hoc est contra naturam Ecclesiae, quae est societas perfecta, quae habet auctoritatem ad servandum depositum, inconcussa auctoritate. Nefanda audacia: Jura Ecclesiae discutiuntur …"[75] On the pretext of science, the truthfulness of the Scriptures is attacked (a tirade against the exegetes …), etc. After the council is the time when, in our dioceses, we will have to put forward conciliar doctrine by means of pastoral writings and sermons. Let us remember Paul's exhortation to Timothy: "Erit tempus cum sanam doctrinam non sustinebunt, prurientes auribus, ad fabulas autem convertentur, etc. Tu vero vigila,[76] etc." (For a moment, from several quarters, people were laughing very loudly as a form of protest. The speaker pronounced his diatribe slowly, in a very emphatic tone. His time having run out, the president, Ruffini, said, "Tempus jam transit."[77] The bishop said a few words more and sat down amid the laughter.)

Archbishop Kozlowiecki of Lusaka (Northern Rhodesia). "Breviter loquar."[78] – 1. (He read some words of the pope.) That through the

---

[71] Biagio Musto (1905–1971), Italian, ordained in 1929. Bishop of Aquino, Sora, and Pontecorvo from 1952 until his death.

[72] "The nature of pastoral responsibility is not understood."

[73] "Expound the doctrine, safeguard the truth, the authentic and complete truth."

[74] "Truth", "discipline".

[75] "Not the truth concealed or toned down! but an absolute sincerity and clarity! This schema, written with prolonged care, approved by the Supreme Pontiff, presents Catholic doctrine in an authentic way. According to some, the Church should be humble, should be a servant, but that is contrary to the nature of the Church, which is a perfect society, which possesses authority for the purpose of preserving the deposit of faith, by an indisputable authority. A heinous audacity: the rights of the Church are brought up as a matter for debate …"

[76] "For the time is coming when people will not endure sound doctrine, but having itching ears, they will … wander into myths. As for you, always be steady" [2 Tim 4:3-4 and 2 Tim 4:5].

[77] "The time has already run out."

[78] "I will speak briefly."

council the Church might be shown to the world: Does the schema correspond to this goal? "Quoad plura fundamentalia, non. De stylo":[79] the language is complicated, with long sentences: cf. what Card. Gracias has said. (He read the first sentence of the schema): "Pro me saltem, difficilis intellectu; omnia vera sunt, sed, pro nobis minus sapientibus, possent dici modo simpliciori. Postea: necessaria esset major coordinatio cum aliis schematibus. Ideo, sicut jam R^{dmus} et Em. Alfrink, peto commissionem mixtam."[80] – 2. On the Mystical Body and its members: only the juridical aspect is set forth. Let the question be treated in a deeper fashion. – 3. "De indole eschatologica Ecclesiae, nihil!"[81] One can only love the Church, however, if one sees her in her connection to the celestial Church; and it is at that point that we must talk about the Blessed Virgin as well as the other saints. This would be a great service to render to our separated brothers, and no less to our faithful, who on this matter sin sometimes by default and sometimes by excess. – 4. "Omnino necessarium est ut modo valde explicito agamus de illa lege suprema, lege caritatis. Est lex, non consilium, ut ipse Christus dixit. Videntur aliqui loqui, ac si caritas periculosa esset veritati: haec suppositio injuriosa est,[82] etc." Cf. the schema on the moral order: nothing on charity! "Cur hic aeternus Amor divinus tam caute celatur?"[83] Christ has not proclaimed a law that is dangerous to truth. And St. Paul, on charity: without it, "nihil sum"[84] ... (Card. Ruffini: Hora ruit.)[85]

The secretary general announced the result of the two votes on the Liturgy; a strong majority in favor (10 and 52 votes against). – The session was adjourned.

On leaving, comments were exchanged concerning especially Léger's proposal (about which I spoke to Msgr. Lafortune) and the diatribe of the bishop of Aquino. Brief conversation with Bishop Vial, coadjutor of

---

[79] "On several fundamental points, no. On the style".

[80] "For me at least, it is difficult to understand; everything is true, but, for those of us who are less scholarly, this could be said more simply. Next: a greater coordination with the other schemas would be necessary. For this reason, following his Eminence Cardinal Alfrink, I ask for a mixed commission."

[81] "3. On the eschatological character of the Church: nothing!"

[82] "It is absolutely necessary that we deal in a very explicit manner with this supreme law, the law of charity. It is a law, not a counsel, as Christ himself said. Some people seem to speak as if charity could be dangerous to the truth: this supposition is offensive."

[83] "Why is this divine, eternal love concealed so cautiously?"

[84] "I am nothing" [1 Cor 13:2].

[85] "Time is running out."

Nevers. I saw my good black bishop from the former Belgian Congo[86] again, still smiling, who promised me some photographs. The auxiliary bishop of Laval,[87] who spoke to me in a friendly manner, told me that he found the schema "appalling", but then said: "Do you think it would really be advisable to vote non placet?" I returned to the Borgo S. Spirito with Father Khalifé (Beirut), and we talked about the Melchite-Maronite quarrel. For the feast of St. Francis Xavier and two jubilees, there were guests for lunch, including Fathers Martelet, Hirschmann, and Rahner. After the recreation period, conversation with Rahner. He told me that Léger's proposition had a chance of succeeding: the pope may have already charged Cardinal Döpfner to come up with a plan. But there are determined opponents: it would suffice for them to succeed in putting on the brakes for one or two days for nothing to come of it: for time is pressing. (I have the impression that, behind the scenes and with some German bishops acting as intermediaries, Rahner is playing an active, and not merely doctrinal, role.) – Next I saw Fr. Martelet, who is preparing, with Fr. Henri Rondet and Bishop Véniat, in a room adjacent to mine, an intervention that Bishop Véniat plans to make on the place of Christ and the Holy Spirit in a constitution on the Church.

In the afternoon, conversation with Dr. Joseph Ratzinger, who gave me various pieces of information on things as seen from the German point of view. – At 6 P.M., via Traspontina, with the Africans, a talk by Cardinal Bea, in the lingua vernacula[88] of the bishops, Latin. Regarding Africa, he spoke about the relations that we can have with various religions. There were questions in French and in English; answers in Latin; Msgr. Willebrands acted as interpreter. A blue booklet written by Bea on the historicity of the Gospels (60 printed pages)[89] was distributed.

At 7:30 P.M., I was in a hotel where some Maronite bishops were staying. Conversation with Bishop Doumith,[90] a former student of Frs. de Lanversin[91] and Bouillard in Beirut, and himself a former professor in the Theology Faculty of Beirut. We talked about the Doctrinal Commission, of which he is a member. He gave me numerous details. At the

---

[86] A. Mbuku-Nzundu.

[87] There was neither an auxiliary nor a coadjutor of Laval at that time.

[88] "Vernacular language".

[89] A. Bea, *La storicita dei Vangeli* (1962), 59p.

[90] Michel Doumith (1915–1989), Lebanese, ordained in 1940. Maronite bishop of Sarba (Lebanon) from 1959 until his death. Named a member of the Doctrinal Commission.

[91] Fernand de Lanversin, S.J. (1890–1968), French, ordained in 1910. Professor of dogmatic theology at Saint Joseph's University of Beirut.

first meeting, what provoked Cardinal Léger's statement were Cardinal Ottaviani's words, punctuating the long and forceful report given by Tromp. Ottaviani more or less said: It is the duty of all the members of the commission to support the proposed schema. Hence the protest of Léger, who demanded his freedom of judgment. Bishop Doumith has hardly any confidence in the possible work of the mixed commission, given the way it is already functioning. – Several of these Maronite bishops sang the praises of Fr. H. Bouillard to me, as well as those of Fr. Niel,[92] who taught in Beirut. We are fêting this evening one of the archbishops, whose name is Francis Xavier. A Melchite bishop and a Chaldean bishop were there. Also invited were Father A. Wenger and two other Assumptionists from *La Croix*. One of these latter two, recently returned from black Africa, spoke to me about the young black clergy, too often social climbers and materialistic, he told me; some anecdotes: on the day after their ordination, some of them organize a tour through the villages so that each might collect a certain sum of money from them, etc. One of the Fathers informed me about the author of the article published in *La Libre Belgique*: this Assumptionist,[93] he told me, is very serious and well-informed; he is a professor of Eastern theology at the Lateran ("not of the same mind as the clique"); his information is supposed to be very accurate.

I had had that afternoon a visit from Bishop Elchinger, who had come to question me on some points concerning the attitudes we would have to say are essential to the Christian. He took a lot of notes. We exchanged our impressions.

Tuesday, December 4, 1962 (33rd General Cong.). – Last night, I was given a paper: "Modus procedendi Summo Pontifici submittendus circa proximae sessionis praeparationem."[1] This is a printed text containing eight points. Cardinals Liénart and Villot[2] told me this morning that a Delegation of the council has been decided in principle. It would include three members of the Board of Presidency and three members

---

[92] Henri Niel, S.J. (1910–1967), French. A Hegel specialist, he was professor of theology and of the history of Greek and modern philosophy at the Institut catholique of Lyon.

[93] Daniel Stiernon.

December 4

[1] "Procedure to follow in making submissions to the Supreme Pontiff concerning the preparation of the next session".

[2] Jean Villot was in fact not created cardinal until February 1965.

from the Office of Extraordinary Affairs (not yet designated), under the direction of Cardinal Cicognani, who would be the liaison with the pope.

This morning in Saint Peter's I saw Father Gagnebet, who introduced me to Father Papin.[3] The latter seems to be one of his friends and to come often to Rome from Paris. Fr. Gagnebet is very pessimistic about the pope's health; he must have specific information. I also met a Protestant observer, a professor at Leyde, who is staying here in Rome with some nuns; these religious appear to be very well-informed and just told him that John XXIII is worse this morning. According to Fr. Gagnebet, the urologist has not left the Vatican in the past 8 days. – A Melchite archbishop came to make an appointment with me to finalize a planned intervention. – I met Father Colson, who was arriving at the council for the first time; the two of us chatted with Msgr. Prinaud, then I found a place for him near me in the gallery. Canon Philippe Delhaye soon arrived; the plainclothes police officer who watches the entrances wanted to make him leave; but I intervened, and everything worked out in the end. – The rector of the English College[4] asked me to come and give a talk at his venerable college; but I no longer had a free day. – Father Häring was smiling; he is happy with the turn that events have taken.

Mass was celebrated by Archbishop Jérôme Rakotomalala of Tananarive. He has a strong, beautiful voice, something I did not know about him. (At the meetings of the Madagascar bishops, he never opens his mouth.)

President of the day: Card. Antonio Caggiano, archbishop of Buenos Aires. A fascicle was distributed that contained the last emendationes to chap. I of the Liturgy. Archbishop Franjo Šeper of Zagreb (Yugoslavia), proposed an address to the Holy Father: the welcome given the episcopates by the pope has been a consolation for all; but we know that these last few days he has been ill; we are praying and offering the sacrifice of our consolation for his healing; let the president bring him the testimony of our filial affection.

Card. Frings. (He supported with all his heart Šeper's proposal.) – "In schemate doctrina de Ecclesia non totam traditionem catholicam esse

[3] Georges Papin (1907–1992), French, ordained in 1935. First vicar of Saint Ambrose Church (Paris) from 1955 to 1967.

[4] Gerard Tickle (1909–1994), ordained in 1934. He was rector of the English College from 1952 to 1964, the date on which he became bishop of the British armed forces.

respectam, sed tantum parvam partem: nec traditio graeca, nec antiquior traditio latina":[5] as if these were outdated. Cf. the sources to which the annotations refer: two brief citations from the Greek Fathers; almost nothing taken from the Middle Ages, either. Almost all the citations come "ex ultimis centum annis".[6] Thus, arts. 6, 7, and 8: "omnes allegationes sunt de hoc saeculo, excepta una de Innocentio III, una de S. Thoma, una de Tridentino; et similiter in omnibus capitibus. Quaero an talis modus procedendi sit rectus, sit scientificus, sit oecumenicus, sit catholicus (καθ'όλον). Non est vere catholicus. Hic defectus non tantum exteriora afficit, sed etiam doctrinam. Exempli gratia, de natura Ecclesiae militantis":[7] Saint Paul is quoted, but the interpretation that is given is: "magis juridica et sociologica quam theologica".[8] Nothing of the doctrine of the Greek Fathers, etc. on the Eucharist, bond of unity, etc. – Quaeri potest cur caput de magisterio sit plane sejunctum a capite de episcopo. Nonne episcopi sunt in Ecclesia doctores et magistri? Fere nihil invenitur de Verbo Dei quod, cum sacramentis, duas columnas facit, et portat totum Ecclesiae templum. Nihil invenitur de missione Verbi aeterni ad homines exientis a Patre – missio quae continuatur ab Ecclesia. Sed longe schema loquitur de jure, etc.: cf. caput de missionibus, ubi nihil dicitur acceptabile ab infidelibus. Schema ergo eget emendatione completa, profunda, universali; et in hoc sensu catholicitatis[9] that one has a right to demand from a conciliar constitution. (The one inspiring Cardinal Frings is, I believe, J. Ratzinger.)

Card. William Godfrey, archbishop of Westminster. "Generatim schema placet. Defectus, si sint, jam sunt indicati."[10] No need to repeat.

---

[5] "In the schema, the doctrine on the Church does not take into consideration all of Catholic tradition but only a small part: neither the Greek tradition, nor the most ancient Latin tradition."

[6] "From the last one hundred years".

[7] "All of the references are from this century, with the exception of one from Innocent III, one from Saint Thomas, one from Trent, and the same is true in all of the chapters. I wonder if such a manner of proceeding is correct, if it is scientific, if it is ecumenical, if it is Catholic. It is not really Catholic. This fault affects not only its exterior aspects but also its doctrine. For example, on the nature of the Church Militant".

[8] "More legalistic and sociological than theological".

[9] "One might wonder why the chapter on the magisterium is completely separated from the chapter on the bishop. Are the bishops not doctors and teachers in the Church? One finds practically nothing on the Word of God, which, with the sacraments, form two columns and support the entire temple of the Church. One finds nothing on the mission of the eternal Word, sent to men, proceeding from the Father, a mission continued by the Church. But the schema speaks a great deal about rights, etc.: cf. the chapter on the missions, where nothing is said that could be accepted by infidels. So the schema needs to be completely, profoundly, universally corrected, and in the direction of catholicity."

[10] "I approve the schema in a general way. The faults, if they exist, have already been indicated."

"Elegi materiam de oecumenismo, quaestionem magni momenti. Situatio apud nos (in Anglia) est tam complexa, ut vix possit intelligi quid in nostra regione christiani credunt. Olim 'catholica' significabat quod nos intelligimus, id est, Ecclesia ante reformationem, Ecclesia antiqua et hodierna. Hodie, Anglicanismus sibi vindicat hunc titulum, etc. Apud aliquos nos jam sumus romani, sine addito, et alii sunt catholici simpliciter. Unde mea perplexitas ... Omnino imprudens esset si aliquis, veniens in insulam nostram, de illa loquebatur, credens illam cognoscere ... speciatim, si falso irenismo indulgeret. Gravis error est dicere quod anglicani sunt prope nos, et hoc habet tristes consequentias."[11] It is said that we are cold men, without charity, "sine sympathia erga fratres separatos. Sed caritas patiens est, benigna est, habet tamen quoque alias qualitates: non agit perperam. Sumus patientes et sinceri, sed nolumus facere quod intelligeretur ut concessiones doctrinales vel morales ex parte Concilii. Hoc esset gravis imprudentia, ignorantia sit culpabilis vel non. Talis modus agendi esset agere perperam, quia alienus est a veritate. Haec res est seria."[12] A certain manner of acting "non est argumentum ad fratres separatos alliciendos, sed potius obstaculum. Aliqui poterunt dicere post Concilium: Nos sperabamus aliquam radicalem mutationem in re doctrinali et morali fieri ... Caute agamus, ne ex ignorantia situationis in aliis regionibus, proh dolor! avertamus fratres. Caritas sine scientia, non est vera caritas. Magna est veritas, et praevalebit."[13]

Card. Leo Suenens (Malines). "Antequam finis imponatur huic primae sessioni, proponere vellem ut Patres attente considerent quinam sit

---

[11] "I have chosen the subject of ecumenism, a question of great importance. The situation with us (in England) is so complex that one can scarcely understand what Christians believe in our country. Formerly, 'Catholic' meant what we understand it to mean, that is, the Church before the Reformation, the ancient and current Church. Today, Anglicanism lays claim to this title for itself, etc. Among some, we are now Romans, without any addition, and the others are simply Catholics. Hence my perplexity ... It would be very imprudent if someone, coming to our island, spoke about her, believing he was acquainted with her ... especially if he were overindulgent in a false irenicism. It is a serious error to say that the Anglicans are near to us; that has some unhappy consequences."

[12] "Without sympathy toward the separated brothers. But charity is patient, it is kind, yet it has other qualities also: it is not boastful [1 Cor 13:4]. We are patient and sincere, but we do not want to make what could be understood as doctrinal or moral concessions on the part of the council. This would be a serious lack of prudence, an ignorance, culpable or not. To act in such a fashion would be to boast, because it is foreign to the truth. It is a serious matter."

[13] "Is not an argument likely to attract the separated brothers but, rather, an obstacle. Some will be able to say after the council: We were hoping that a radical transformation in doctrinal and moral matters would be produced ... Let us act with caution, lest, out of ignorance of the situation in other regions, alas, we drive away our brothers. Charity without knowledge is not true charity. The truth is great, and it will prevail."

scopus primarius hujus concilii",[14] so that the work of the second session might be organized around a central scheme and so that the activity of each commission "sit actio partis in toto, omnibus concurrentibus ad eumdem finem, a nobis definiendum. Sicut Vaticanum I, et quidem feliciter, de primatu Romani Pontificis tractavit, ita Vaticanum II, ut dixit S. Pater, tractare debet de Ecclesia Christi, lumine gentium. Jam Vaticanum I de hoc locutum fuerat sed oportet hoc clarius declarari",[15] and let that guide our work. "Oportet nos omnes esse concordes, ad quaerendum"[16] a comprehensive plan, aliquam rationem ordinandi concilii. Propono: Constitutio de Ecclesia sit, 1. Ad intra – 2. Ad extra.[17]

1. "Ad intra: Quid sit Ecclesia? Mysterium Christi viventis in suo Corpore mystico."[18] This amounts to the rejection of the present schema. "Exponatur quod Ecclesia hodie progredi debeat, etc.; cf. Pius X: 'Omnia instaurare in Christo';[19] Pius XII and John XXIII. 'Euntes docete omnes gentes, baptizantes eos in nomine Patris,[20] etc.'" In this light, let everything be expressed "ad renovationem pastoralem in universo mundo. Ecclesia docens: usque ad munus catechismi; Ecclesia sanctificans":[21] the sacraments; "Ecclesia orans: in nomine Patris ..."[22]

2. "Ad extra: Sermo fiat de Ecclesia in quantum dialogum instituit cum mundo. Puncta quaedam sunt maximi momenti: a. Circa vitam ipsam personae humanae, inviolabilitatem vitae,[23] etc.; the demographic explosion, etc. b. Justitia socialis":[24] innumerable books on the De

---

[14] "Before we close this first session, I would like to propose to the Fathers that they attentively consider what the primary aim of this council is."

[15] "Be an action making up part of a whole, everything contributing toward the same end, which we have to define. Just as Vatican I dealt with the primacy of the Roman Pontiff, and in truth successfully, Vatican II, as the Holy Father has said, must treat of the Church of Christ, light for the nations. Vatican I had already spoken about this, but we must declare it more clearly."

[16] "We must all be in agreement, in order to seek".

[17] "A guiding principle to give order to the council. I propose that the Constitution on the Church be: 1. To those within. 2. To those outside."

[18] "*To those within*: What is the Church? The mystery of Christ living in his Mystical Body."

[19] "Let it be clearly set forth that the Church must go forward today, etc. Cf. Pius X: To restore all things in Christ" [motto of Pius X, see Eph 1:10].

[20] "Go therefore and make disciples of all nations, baptizing them in the name of the Father" [Mt 28:19].

[21] "For a pastoral renewal throughout the whole world. The teaching Church: the whole task of catechesis; the sanctifying Church".

[22] "The Church at prayer: in the name of the Father".

[23] "2. To the outside world: let us speak about the Church in such way as to institute a dialogue with the world. Certain points are of a great importance: a. concerning the very life of the human person, the inviolability of life, etc."

[24] "b. Social justice".

Sexto,[25] and very few on social justice; the social encyclicals, not sufficiently explained; how to define what from our abundance is owed
to the poor; the duty of rich nations toward the third world and world
hunger. – c. De ipsa evangelizatione pauperum;[26] conditions for our
witness to reach them and be received. – d. "De pace internationali et
de bello."[27]

The Church must enter into dialogue with her faithful – with our
brothers "nondum visibiliter uniti",[28] – with the world of today. Let
all this "magis directe et diffuse tractetur, etc. – Nihil dixi quod non
sit, explicite vel implicite, contentum in sermone S. Pontificis diei 11
septembris."[29] He invited us to a collective examination of conscience,
etc. – "Conclusio: 1. ut programma futurae evolutionis concilii ab ipso
concilio determinetur, sensu jam expresso ...; 2. ut sine mora commissiones revideant sua schemata secundum hanc determinationem",[30]
summarizing, and retaining only what is most important "sub aspectu
renovationis pastoralis";[31] 3. "Secretariatus formetur pro problematibus
mundi hodierni":[32] that it might be able to do as much in these problem areas as the Secretariat for Unity does in its domain, to which I am
happy, as the successor of Cardinal Mercier,[33] to pay homage. "Speramus pariter hunc novum Secretariatum viam aperturum ita ut mundus
etc., ut appareat magis ac magis via, veritas et vita."[34] (Applause. Praeses:
"Meminerint plausus non debere fieri in concilio.")[35]

---

[25] Moral treatise on the sixth commandment, "You shall not commit adultery."

[26] "On the evangelization of the poor".

[27] "d. On international peace and war".

[28] "Not yet visibly united".

[29] "Be treated more directly and in a more developed fashion. I have not said anything that was not contained, explicitly or implicitly, in the Supreme Pontiff's speech of September 11." [He is referring to a radio broadcast in which the pope recalled that the Church had to make her voice heard and spoke about the "great expectations of the ecumenical council".]

[30] "Conclusion. 1. that the program for the continuation of the council be determined by the council itself, in the sense already explained ...; 2. that, without delay, the commissions revise their schemas in accordance with this decision".

[31] "With respect to pastoral renewal".

[32] "Let a secretariat be formed for the problems of today's world."

[33] Désiré Mercier (1851–1926), Belgian, ordained in 1874. Archbishop of Malines from 1906 until his death. He was the organizer of the Malines Conversations, with a view toward a rapprochement between Anglicans and Catholics.

[34] "We also hope that this new secretariat will thus open a path so that the world might listen to and better accept the Church and so that Christ might be more and more the way, the truth, and the life [see Jn 14:6] for the men of our time." [For greater intelligibility, the translation includes words left out by Father de Lubac.]

[35] "The President: Remember that there should be no applause in the council."

Card. Bea. "Antequam ad judicium schematis accedam, praemittere vellem aliqua de ejus momento historico et pro nostro concilio."[36] The problem of the Church was posed in the 16th century, but the Council of Trent did not have time to clarify it; nor did Vatican I, except to make a beginning, on the pope. When Vatican II was announced, everywhere the great question was posed. "Urget eo magis, quod fratres nostri separati, praesertim protestantes",[37] have taken a great interest in it; for some time they have, in a way, discovered the Church. "Locum omnino centralem occupat hoc schema. Unde magna nostra responsabilitas, et pro Ecclesia ipsa, et pro mundo. Non est clausula styli, sed officium justitiae";[38] if I acknowledge first of all that "hoc schema compositum fuit magno labore et magna cura. Multi afferuntur textus ex sacra Scriptura et ex Magisterio. Plures aspectus doctrinae bene illustrantur. Tamen quaero: praebetne quod jure exspectari potest et debet?"[39]

1. Relate ad materiam. Essentialia quaedam desunt. A prima pagina, subjectum reducitur ad Ecclesiam militantem, omittendo pulcherrima et profundissima quae in fontibus habentur de Ecclesia purificanda et consummanda. Illa sunt essentialia ad intelligenda omnia in Ecclesia terrestri, quae ex illis totam suam lucem accipiunt. Finis magisterii et sacerdotii non indicatur. Quaestio de magisterio tractatur extra quaestionem naturae Ecclesiae. Fere nihil est de pluribus essentialibus. Plura sunt vel superflua, vel non habent locum in schemate dogmatico: sic res controversae inter theologos, v.g. de iis qui vere et proprie sunt membra Ecclesiae: res saltem non est satis matura, et nulla necessitas adest ut definiatur.[40]

---

[36] "Before proceeding to the judgment of the schema, I would like to put forward its historical importance and its importance for our council."

[37] "This is all the more urgent in that our separated brothers, especially the Protestants".

[38] "This schema occupies an absolutely central place. Hence our great responsibility, for the Church herself and for the world. It is not a mere formality, but a duty of justice."

[39] "This schema was composed with a great deal of effort and with great care. Numerous texts, from Holy Scripture and from the magisterium, have been cited. Several aspects of the doctrine are well explained. However, I pose this question: Does the schema offer what can and must be rightfully expected from it?"

[40] "1. Concerning the matter. Some essential points are missing. From the first page, the subject is reduced to the Church Militant, omitting very beautiful and very profound things contained in the sources, on the Church to be purified and perfected. These things are essential for understanding all things in the terrestrial Church, which receive from them all their light. The end of the magisterium and the priesthood is not indicated. The question of the magisterium is treated outside the question of the nature of the Church. There is almost nothing on several essential points. Several points are either superfluous or do not belong in a dogmatic schema; this is true for questions disputed among theologians, for example, regarding who are truly and properly members of the Church. This question at least has not yet received mature reflection, and there is no need to define it."

2. Relate ad ordinem. Jam ut dixi, cap. 7 non est in suo loco. In isto capite, statim fit sermo de Romano Pontifice, tanquam sit periculum ut ejus auctoritas non admittatur. Postea veniunt episcopi, postea tandem collegium episcoporum. E contra, ordo naturalis et biblicus debet incipere a collegio apostolorum, qui apparent primi in evangelio; postea Petrus ostendatur, ut caput illius collegii. Sic non separatim, sed ut culmen apparet, sicut vere est.[41]

De Argumentis: ex puris Sacrae Scripturae et Traditionis debent oriri. Atqui, videantur Notae, v.g. in cap. 7:[42] cf. what Card. Frings said; they almost all refer to the last hundred years. – "De modo proponendi doctrinam: Veritates insufficienter explicantur, et ideo argumenta potius offuscant quam illustrant eas. Variae metaphorae designant Ecclesiam; sed non bene explicantur et, de facto, statim veluti confugitur ad unicam metaphoram, pulcherrimam sane, sed minime exprimentem totam realitatem Ecclesiae."[43] – The quotations from Scripture, taken out of context, often prove little. – "Permultae inveniuntur exhortationes, specialiter in capite de laicis: non sunt in suo loco in constitutione dogmatica. Indoles pastoralis consistit in eligendis quaestionibus, non in praedicationibus. – Quaedam radix est horum omnium quae placere non possunt tale quale est, non respondet schema illi scopo quem Summus Pontifex constituit, et quem nostrum concilium suum fecit: omnibus hominibus exponere doctrinam de Ecclesia... Tale quale est, non placet. Nova elaboratione, profunda et solida, indiget. Dixi."[44]

---

[41] "2. Concerning the structure. As I have already said, chapter 7 is not in its proper place. In this chapter, the schema speaks immediately of the Roman Pontiff, as if there were a danger that his authority might not be recognized. Next come the bishops, then finally the college of bishops. On the contrary, the natural and biblical order should start with the college of the apostles, who appear first in the Gospel; let Peter next be presented, as head of that college. In this way he does not appear separately but as the summit, as he in fact is."

[42] "On the arguments: they must arise from the pure [sources] of Holy Scripture and tradition. And let us also look at the notes, for example, in chapter 7."

[43] "On the manner of presenting the doctrine: the truths are insufficiently explained, and for that reason, the arguments obscure them more than they clarify them. Various metaphors are used to refer to the Church, but they are not well explained, and, in fact, the schema immediately takes refuge, so to speak, in a single metaphor, indeed a very beautiful one, but expressing very incompletely the whole reality of the Church." [He is referring to the Mystical Body.]

[44] "Several exhortations are found, especially in the chapter on the laity: these do not belong in a dogmatic constitution. The pastoral character consists in the choice of questions, not in sermons. The root of all these things that one cannot approve in the present state of the schema is the fact that it does not respond to the goal that the Supreme Pontiff has given and that our council has made its own: to present the doctrine of the Church to all men. Such as it is, I do not approve the schema. It needs a new elaboration, profound and solid. I have had my say."

Card. Bacci. "Brevissime loquar, ut semper soleo."[45] He urged the Fathers not to go on about superficial matters or to give a sermon. – 1. "Dilectissimis observatoribus a nobis sejunctis, non separatis (sicut scripsi abhinc 30 annis). Liceat nobis ab illis veniam petere, si per dissensiones nostras damus illis offensam vel animi depressionem, adhuc et verbis acertioribus. Non dissentimus inter nos de doctrina catholica, sed de modo tantum[46] ... – 2. Si ergo nostrae dissensiones non in doctrina catholica versantur, sed de modo tantum, cur ad novum schema provocamus?"[47] Let us simply correct the one that exists. "Non agitur de substantia sed de forma. Peritissimi theologi paraverunt hunc textum";[48] if we reject it, another one will be put forward, then another, perhaps none of which will be satisfactory, "et sic erit error pejor priore. Valde opportunum quoad doctrinam probatur; quoad formam, remittatur commissioni theologicae",[49] composed of the best theologians the Church has.

Card. Browne, O.P. – "Non obstantibus omnibus, schema in sua substantia mihi placet. Est opus evidenter manuum peritissimarum."[50] We can perfect it, complete it, make some deletions. "Plura dicta sunt in laudem, in criticam. Placet ut agat de Ecclesia Corpore Christi mystico; thema quam maxime pastorale"[51] and very effective ecumenically. Criticisms: "natura nimis juridica? Non intelligo talem criticam sine difficultate. Sine jure in hac vita non vivitur. Caritas ipsa sine jure et sine justitia non subsistit. Pax quoque opus justitiae est. Jura Ecclesiae sunt jura ipsius Dei."[52] I do not see either how it can be said that there is

---

[45] "I will speak very briefly, as is always my custom."

[46] "1. To the very esteemed observers, distant from us and not separated (as I have been writing for thirty years now). Let us be permitted to ask their pardon if by our differences of opinion we have given them any offense or worry, and, moreover, with rather harsh words. We do not disagree among ourselves about Catholic doctrine, but only about form ..."

[47] "If, therefore, our disagreements do not have to do with Catholic doctrine, but only with form, why are we asking for a new schema?"

[48] "It is not a question of substance but of form. Excellent theologians have prepared this text."

[49] "And thus the error will be worse than before. It is very timely that the doctrine be approved; as to the form, let us send the schema back to the theological commission."

[50] "Despite everything, I approve the schema in substance. It is obviously the work of very expert hands."

[51] "Many things have been said in praise or in criticism of the schema. I approve of the fact that it treats of the Church as the Mystical Body of Christ, an eminently pastoral theme."

[52] "Its nature is too legalistic? I have difficulty understanding such a criticism. We do not live in this life without law. Charity itself does not subsist without law and without justice. Peace also is the work of justice [Is 32:17: Opus justitiae pax. Motto of Pius XII]. The laws of the Church are the laws of God himself."

no question of the People of God: Is there not a whole chapter on the laity? etc. Let no one be troubled over names: the Church Militant, Triumphant; these have a venerable tradition; just explain these terms in catechism class; they are neither worldly nor political. "Schema nunc adhuc mihi placet."[53]

Archbishop Émile Blanchet (Paris, Institut catholique). "Schema capitibus constat inter quae tam maximae sunt differentiae",[54] that one can guess the diversity of their authors. "Non vere consentiunt."[55] No unity. "Idem objectum in pluribus partibus tractatur: sic, de episcopis, etc. Unde, non habemus sufficientem et vere theologicam doctrinam de episcopatu. Atqui haec quaestio in primis exspectatur. Oportet res dispersas in unum colligere, et de natura episcopatus, etc., clare, realiter, substantialiter tractare. Saepius quam decet, datur de episcopatu et aliis rebus notio nimis exclusive juridica. Sunt canonicae notiones et exhortationes piae, potius quam vera theologia. Jus suum locum habet, et quidem necessarium, sed in primo gradu appareat evangelica virtus. – Non tractatur de vero et hodierno statu Ecclesiae."[56] Today the titular bishops make up more than one-third of the episcopal body: "atqui, ne nominantur quidem; stupenda verba: 'sive aliorum'!"[57] If the episcopate is not defined solely by territory, etc. "Theologia ergo non realis; non respondet statui Ecclesiae, et habet aliquid angustum."[58] – It appears to confuse the potestas episcopalis[59] with the particular jurisdiction received from the pope, etc. "Non est bona theologia."[60] Cf. the famous letter of Pius IX. The schema substitutes external bonds for vital bonds: this is

---

[53] "Still now, I approve the schema."

[54] "The schema is made up of chapters between which there are such very great differences."

[55] "They do not really agree."

[56] "The same subject is treated in several parts: thus, on the bishops, etc. From this follows the absence of a sufficient and truly theological doctrine on the episcopate. And this question is among the most expected. It is necessary to gather together the dispersed points and to deal with the nature of the episcopate, etc., clearly, in a real and substantial fashion. More often than is proper, the episcopate and other things are given a notion that is too exclusively legalistic. These are canonical notions and pious exhortations rather than true theology. The law has its place and is certainly necessary, but let the first place be occupied by evangelical virtue. The true and current situation of the Church is not treated."

[57] "And yet they are not even mentioned; surprising words: 'or others' ". [This refers to a passage of the schema that says "episcoporum sive residentialium sive aliorum", of bishops, whether bishops residential or others.]

[58] "Therefore, this is not a real theology; it does not correspond to the state of the Church, and it has a certain narrowness."

[59] "Authority of the bishop".

[60] "This is not good theology."

contrary to history, the nature of things, everyone's expectations. – Two remarks in conclusion: 1. "Non est bonum neque efficax toties dicere de auctoritate et juribus. De modo agitur. Sufficit ut semel, bene, firmiter dicatur. Jus tantum vindicatur ad servitium, non ad dominationem."[61] And by insisting, there is a risk of causing fastidium et iram . . .[62] 2. Take care to employ words in their true sense. Thus, "episcopus"[63] does not always signify the same thing; the same is true for "Ecclesia".[64] Texts from the O.T. are quoted speaking of the Ecclesia Dei: "nihil deducendum de hodierna Ecclesia. Vera, proba, solida theologia sanam criticam supponit."[65]

Syrian Archbishop Raphaël Rabban[66] of Kerkuk (Iraq). "Placet secundum modum. – Nescimus cur sermo de corpore Christi mystico separetur a capite de membris Ecclesiae;[67] etc., etc."

Archbishop Guerry of Cambrai. On the priesthood and the episcopate. He refers to Suenens and asks for a better order. "Votum unum Concilio proponere cupio. Nulla praesentatio est in schemate de una realitate magni momenti: de paternitate episcoporum."[68] A simple word, mentioned once in passing (patres),[69] one note tells us that this means "potestatem",[70] etc. Now, "episcopus, imago Patris".[71] Three reasons: 1. "Paternitas episcopi solidis textibus Scripturae et Patrum fundatur[72] (Paul, Ignatius of Antioch, etc.). – 2. Cohaeret cum conceptione vitali Ecclesiae";[73] by that the expression, "Holy Father" takes on its full

---

[61] "It is neither good nor efficacious to speak so often about authority and rights. It is a question of form. It suffices that this be said only once, clearly and firmly. The right is only claimed for the sake of service and not for domination."

[62] "Aversion and anger".

[63] "Bishop".

[64] "Church".

[65] "Church of God: nothing to be deduced relevant to the Church of today. A true, honest, and solid theology presupposes a sound criticism."

[66] Raphaël Rabban (1910–1967), Iraqi, ordained in 1933. Chaldean archbishop of Kirkuk (Iraq) from 1957 until his death. Member of the Secretariat for Unity.

[67] "I approve with amendments. We do not know why the passage on the Mystical Body of Christ is separated from the chapter on the members of the Church."

[68] "I wish to present a wish to the council. There is no presentation in the schema of something that is really of great importance: the fatherly role of the bishops."

[69] "Fathers".

[70] "Authority".

[71] "Bishop, image of the Father".

[72] "The fatherhood of the bishop is founded on solid texts from Scripture and the Fathers of the Church."

[73] "This coheres with a living conception of the Church."

sense. – 3. Important repercussions for the Church ... (The Latin accents were wrongly placed; he spoke in a sonorous, emotional tone; oratorical developments. My neighbors in the gallery: "He is preaching!")

Bishop Raphaël Macario,[74] assistant general of Italian Catholic Action. Almost nothing to say after so many remarks. Nevertheless, four more: 1. Schemati unitas deesse videtur.[75] No central idea. The diversity of authors and styles is easily seen. "Schema reficiendum est, ita ut commissio aliqua parva, vel saltem unus theologus reddat illi unitatem."[76] Let the idea of the Mystical Body be developed, or of the Ecclesia mater et magistra,[77] and let a single hand smooth out the whole schema. – 2. Constitutio amplissimo titulo ornatur,[78] and in fact the schema only talks about the Church Militant. So change the title; vel potius optandum est loqui de tota Ecclesia, saltem in aliquo prologo,[79] which would clearly state the aim of the constitution. Put in a clearer light what the world is expecting, what the bishops have asked for, what has been recalled this very day. – As Card. Ruffini has said, chaps. 5, 6, and 11 should be deleted. They are more disciplinary and canonical. Let the schema treat de membris Ecclesiae[80] in a better way. For chap. 11, let a single document be created, in union with the Secretariat for Unity and the Eastern Commission. – 4. Chap. 9: Let a single decree deal with religious liberty, and let agreement be reached on this with the Secretariat, etc. – No provision was made, concerning the schema on the unity of the Church, regarding who would correct and unify the three analogous documents. We must form a mixed commission, which will be charged not only with merging these three documents together, but also with doing the same for the two texts on the Church and the State and on religious liberty. – I support many of the wishes expressed by the bishops. All are asked to leave out words that would distract attention ... Before we return to our dioceses, let the various schemas be distributed to us, or at least a first batch of them. – We must believe that the rules of the council, such as they

---

[74] Raffaele Macario (1909–1993), Italian, ordained in 1932. Auxiliary bishop of Albano from 1948 to 1966.

[75] "The schema seems to lack unity."

[76] "The schema should be redone, so that a small commission, or even a single theologian, might give it this unity."

[77] "Church as Mother and Teacher".

[78] "2. The constitution is adorned with a very sweeping title."

[79] "Or rather it is desirable to speak of the whole Church, at least in a prologue."

[80] "Of the members of the Church".

are expressed in the printed regulations, should be revised; the pope has had to intervene; let that no longer be necessary from now on. Let us also find a way for the Fathers to be able to give their opinions on every proposed emendatio. – "Liceat quoque notare"[81] that electronic voting machines did not exist at the time of Vatican I. – Let us be able to vote on the emendationes that the commissions do not think worth keeping. Finally, etc.

Bishop Carlo Maccari[82] (Italy). "Schema grato animo est accipiendum."[83] It deals with very current matters, which it must proclaim solemnly. Some remarks on the chapter "De laicis". There is talk today of the promotion, or the emancipation, of the laity. "Haec verba male sonant et periculo non carent."[84] People, young people especially, could conclude from this that this is something new. Let the doctrine on the laity be treated "modo stricte dogmatico".[85] It is not only a question of new apostolic necessities; it is the consequence of their "incorporatio Corpori Christi per baptismum"[86] and their "roboratio per confirmationem".[87] Proclaim it. Also dismiss "periculosas opiniones. Modo temperato et firmo",[88] dismiss errors. (Some details.) The chapter grants too little to the laity; recent popes have granted them more. – On the definition of Catholic action.

Bishop Thomas Holland,[89] coadjutor of Portsmouth (England). "In genere confiteor, primo intuitu, schema valde placuit. Attamen",[90] after careful study, "video quod deficit a legitimis expectationibus."[91] If we are aware of any truth, it is surely that of the Roman primacy. For about 30 years, much theological work has been done concerning the Mystical Body. "Grato animo excipio"[92] that the schema takes up the idea. Worry over the future fate of the council. Some have asked that

---

[81] "Let me also be permitted to note".

[82] Carlo Maccari (1913–1997), Italian, ordained in 1936. Named bishop in 1961, assistant general of Catholic Action from 1961 to 1963, then archbishop of Mondovi from 1963 to 1968.

[83] "The schema should be accepted with a grateful spirit."

[84] "These words have a bad ring to them and are not without danger."

[85] "In a strictly dogmatic way".

[86] "Incorporation into the Body of Christ through baptism".

[87] "Fortification through confirmation".

[88] "Dangerous opinions. In a moderate and firm manner".

[89] Thomas Holland (1908–1999), British, ordained in 1933. Coadjutor of Portsmouth from 1960 to 1964, then bishop of Salford from August 1964 to 1983. Member of the Secretariat for Unity.

[90] "I must tell you that in general, on first sight, I liked the schema very much. And yet".

[91] "I see that it does not satisfy legitimate expectations."

[92] "I note with gratitude".

the schema be redone: anxius sum.[93] Is that the best course? It would be better to have two kinds of documents: a "medicamentum misericordiae"[94] for mankind as a whole, and texts that are properly doctrinal for the clergy, etc. (Praeses: "Tempus finitum est.")[95]

Bishop Albert Devoto, of Goya (Argentina). He referred to Bea's speech. The idea of the "populus Dei" ... "Exponere oportet collegialitatem episcopatus et ejus responsabilitatem in totam Ecclesiam. – De opinione publica in Ecclesia":[96] a great force, etc. – "Praesentatio Ecclesiae in sua evangelica simplicitate et paupertate, etc. – Schema ut jacet non respondet his justis expectationibus."[97]

Bishop Vairo[98] of Gravina (Italy). "Juxta modum placet. Quaedam desiderantur: 1. Amplior Ecclesiae prospectus, de Ecclesia terrestri et caelesti; cf. St. Augustine. Ecclesia terrestris et peregrinans est sicut via ad terminum; ad caelestem Jerusalem tendit."[99] Now (cf. chap. 2) it seems that only the individual end is envisaged. We must not forget the union of all those who participate in the divine life: "perfecta communio",[100] realized in the "Caelestis urbs, Jerusalem, beata pacis visio. – 2. Nexus inter Corpus mysticum et Trinitatis mysterium: cf. St. Cyprian ... – 3. Munus centrale doctrinae Corporis mystici"[101] should be better emphasized throughout the schema. – 4. "Sacerdotium stricte sumptum appellari hierarchiam, non sacerdotium ministeriale":[102] for the faithful are themselves ministers, for example, of the sacrament of marriage. – 5. Give a better indication of the relations between the Church and the State, interpreting them in accordance

---

[93] "I am worried."

[94] "Remedy of mercy".

[95] "Time has run out."

[96] "'People of God' ... We must present the collegiality of the episcopate and its responsibility for the whole Church. On public opinion in the Church".

[97] "Presentation of the Church in her simplicity and her evangelical poverty. The schema as it is does not respond to these just expectations."

[98] Giuseppe Vairo (1917–2001), Italian, ordained in 1940. Bishop of Gravina-Irsina from 1962 to 1971.

[99] "I approve with amendments. Some wishes: 1. a broader perspective on the Church, the terrestrial and the celestial Church; cf. Saint Augustine. The terrestrial and pilgrim Church is like the road toward the goal, she tends toward the heavenly Jerusalem."

[100] "Perfect communion".

[101] "Heavenly city, Jerusalem, blessed vision of peace. 2. The connection between the Mystical Body and the mystery of the Trinity: cf. Saint Cyprian ... 3. The central function of the doctrine of the Mystical Body".

[102] "The priesthood taken in the strict sense should be called hierarchy and not ministerial priesthood."

with natural law. – 6. Identity of the Mystical Body and the Church: it is real, but inadequate.

Bishop Hengsbach of Essen (Germany). "Laudo laborem. Adhaereo his quae dixerunt"[103] Liénart, Alfrink, Döpfner, Gracias, Frings ... Excessive clericalism and legalism. 1. Let us include a chapter on Jesus Christ, "caput et Dominus suae Ecclesiae: primatus Christi relate ad Ecclesiam ita pateret,[104] etc. This introductory chapter would have as its counterweight the concluding chapter on the Blessed Virgin. – 2. ... Ut funditus reformetur cap. 8, de Ecclesia et Statu: non satisfieri videtur toti doctrinae ecclesiasticae de hac re. Cf. Pius XII et auctores catholici injuste tractati ..."[105] – 3. Let the second part of chap. 6 "conjungatur cum schemate de apostolatu laicorum",[106] etc. – 4. For chaps. 6 and 8: in cap. 7 "de magisterio",[107] the schema speaks about the cooperation of the laity (no. 34, ll. 11ff.); "postulatur quod periti laici adjungantur magisterio":[108] Why not apply this request to our work in this council? "Multum nos juvare possint aliqui laici periti."[109]

Maronite Bishop Michel Doumith, of Sarba (Lebanon). We desired a schema on the episcopate, important both for Catholics and for our separated brothers. "Loco hujus optatae constitutionis, schema loquitur de Ecclesia in genere, ubi, inter alia, de episcopis agitur, et modo tam analytico, ut inde tota res obscuretur ... Frequenter invitati sumus ad bene utendum potestate, et frequenter revenit Primatus S. Pontificis. Sed potestatis descriptio est incompleta."[110] The schema does not say what the priesthood is in its relation to the priesthood of Christ and to the body of Christ. It does not show the bishop's relation to his Church. It does not say that he has an "accuratam potestatem pascendi gregem, etc. Haec descriptio analytice facta consecrat disciplinam nunc vigentem;

---

[103] "I praise the work. I support what was said by Liénart, Alfrink, ..."

[104] "Head and Lord of his Church: the primacy of Christ in relation to the Church would thus be clearly apparent."

[105] "2. Let chapter 8 on the Church and the State be entirely rewritten: it does not seem to satisfy all the ecclesiastical doctrine on the subject. Cf. Pius XII and Catholic authors unjustly treated".

[106] "Be joined with the schema on the apostolate of the laity".

[107] "On the magisterium".

[108] "It is to be wished that lay experts might be joined to the magisterium."

[109] "Some lay experts could be of great help to us."

[110] "In the place of that hoped-for constitution, the present schema speaks of the Church in general, where, among other things, there is discussion about the bishops, and that is done in so analytical a fashion that everything is obscured. We are frequently invited to make good use of our authority, and the schema frequently comes back to the primacy of the Supreme Pontiff. But the description of authority is incomplete."

non immunis est ab omni aequivocatione."[111] There is no connection between the various passages that speak of it. "Expositio est captiosa, si sumitur ut norma juris."[112] Cf. what the former discipline was, the intrinsic link between consecration and mission,[113] etc. (Here, a lesson in history and theology that set out from common ground and seemed very pertinent. – I would later congratulate Bishop Doumith. Several also expressed to me their good impression of his intervention; the author was asked to have copies made of his text so that it could be studied.)

Archbishop Joseph Descuffi, of Izmir (Turkey). (An old man with a white goatee, he has the no. 2 at the council.) (Some words of introduction to explain that the last to come might have a hard time getting people to listen ...) "Oportet venire tandem ad examen conscientiae, de mutua reverentia debita."[114] (Some criticisms have been heard that are too caustic toward some council Fathers ...) – The great question of the pope's infallibility must be considered. We hear it said continually: "Primatus non provenit ex verbis Christi, sed ex factis historicis et politicis";[115] and again, "Si Pontifex summus est infallibilis, vana evadit infallibilitas Ecclesiae; si Ecclesia est infallibilis, quid prodest infallibilitas Pontificis?" "Hoc argumentum est quod dicitur in scholis argumentum cornutum."[116] The objection is false but it brings us to the crux of the matter. We absolutely must deal with this essential point, waiting since Vatican I. Something useful on this topic is found at nos. 28 and 29 of the schema; but let this be shortened, and the essential thing "in plena luce ponatur. Loquatur de subjecto magisterii; declaretur clarius relatio inter duas infallibilitates."[117] Let us, finally, explain the famous formula "ex sese",[118] which is itself equivocal and capable of being misunderstood when taken out of context; let us replace it by something different,

---

[111] "The specific power of pasturing a flock. This description made in an analytic manner enshrines a discipline now in force; it is not exempt from all equivocation."

[112] "The presentation is deceptive if it is taken as a norm of law."

[113] "Mission".

[114] "It is necessary to come finally to an examination of conscience, on the mutual respect owed to each other."

[115] "The primacy does not come from the words of Christ but from historical and political facts."

[116] "If the Supreme Pontiff is infallible, the infallibility of the Church becomes vain; if the Church is infallible, what use is the infallibility of the pope? This argument is what one calls in the schools a sophistical argument."

[117] "Be presented in full light. Let us talk about the subject of the magisterium; let us state more clearly the relation between the two infallibilities."

[118] Reference to the constitution *Pastor aeternus* (1870), which attributed infallibility to the pope when he intervenes *ex cathedra*. For the position of Vatican II, see *Lumen gentium*, no. 25.

clearer, that leaves no doubt that the infallible pope expresses the faith of the entire Church.

There is a lot of talk these days about a Pastoral Letter written by Cardinal Montini[119] deploring the poor preparation for the council. The *Tempo* has taken some quotations from it that some have called tendentious. Some members of the Curia are making a show of saying that it is insulting to the pope. In reality, the campaign for the election of the successor of John XXIII is underway, and this is what explains certain things.

This morning, in the middle of the session, Bishop A. Mbuka-Nzundu sent an usher to ask me to meet him near Michelangelo's *Pieta*; he handed me two beautiful photos sent by the photographer from Vienna who had taken a picture of us together, a month ago, on Saint Peter's Square.

On leaving the Basilica, got into the bus that serves the Procure of Saint-Sulpice and the residence of some Yugoslavian bishops. Among the latter was Bishop Franić, whom I had not yet seen this fall; I said to him in a few words, before getting on, that there were certain things "non secundum Mattaeum"[120] in the way things were run in the Preparatory Theological Commission – resulting in certain stormy moments at the council. On the bus, chatted with Archbishop Dupuy (Albi), dead set against the maneuvers of certain members of the Roman Curia; he expressed to me his indignation over the manner in which Cardinal Pizzardo had treated Card. Gerlier a few years ago, etc. (the accumulated resentment among numerous bishops and theologians are today aggravating the conflicts that the council is causing to appear). Spoke next with Archbishop Marty (Reims) and Archbishop Villot, who appears rather optimistic. – At the Procure, at table, conversation with Msgr. Girard, superior general, Archbishop Lamy[121] of Sens, retired, Bishop Jenny ... During the recreation period, chatted with Cardinal Gerlier,

---

[119] In this letter of December 2, G. B. Montini drew up the balance sheet of the first conciliar session and did his best to respond to two criticisms current at the time: the council arrived at no conclusions, and it manifested divergences of opinions. Moreover, departing from his habitual prudence, he did not hesitate to make an inventory of the errors committed during the preparation of the council.

[120] Literally, "Not according to Matthew". The French translation of the Latin is "Pas très catholique" ("Not very Catholic"), but in English we would say something like "Not really kosher" or "Rather fishy". – TRANS.

[121] Frédéric Lamy (1887–1976), French, ordained in 1912. Archbishop of Sens from 1936 to October 1962, he then became a titular archbishop.

etc. Cardinal Liénart asked me what I was doing in Rome (no official list of periti has been published). We talked about the famous continuity committee of the council. Then, conversation with the small group of young priests who are here working on a doctorate.

At the Borgo, at 4 P.M., visit from André Cantin, a young French academic, who is preparing a thesis on Saint Peter Damian. At the moment, he is working every morning at the Vatican on some manuscripts. He finds his subject fascinating, but what interests him above all is the idea of the unity of knowledge. He explained to me how he conceived the relation between philosophy and theology in the understanding of the faith. He wants to meet with me again in January.

At 5 P.M., Stanislas Rostworowski, whom I had recently seen, brought his friend Piasecki, who arrived in Rome last night, to meet me. No political topic was broached. There was talk about the situation of Catholics in the world, of the necessity for intellectual reflection to safeguard the faith; we took up the theme of man made in the image of God, of his collaboration in the work of creation, always in the closely related thought of his supernatural end and of redemption, etc. We spoke about Father Teilhard. I stressed the necessity for each to have a trusting relationship with the bishops. They both ought to take advantage of their stay in Rome to have an interview with Cardinal Wyszyński. They acknowledged simply that they had made mistakes in the past. I told them that the moment had come to straighten things out with their bishops; they said that they had already made an appointment with the cardinal. I promised to pray for them.

At 5:30 P.M., visit from Mr. Robert Sencourt[122] (Farnborough Abbey, Hampshire), an old Englishman of 72 years, a convert from Anglicanism who had known Lord Halifax;[123] very ecumenically minded; in contact with Dom Olivier Rousseau. He knows a number of bishops from various countries and seems to me to be very well-informed on the council. A good number of American bishops, he told me, have changed a great deal in the course of these two months. He was rather hard on

---

[122] Robert Sencourt (1890–1969), British, pseudonym of Robert Esmonde Gordon George. A Catholic of Anglican origin, linked to the ecumenical movements. He was a regular visitor to Farnborough Abbey, the abbey founded on the initiative of the Empress Eugénie (wife of Louis Napoleon) to house the tombs of her husband and her son. He is the author, moreover, of works on the Emperor Napoleon III and his wife.

[123] Edward Frederick Lindley Wood (1881–1959), British statesman. He was viceroy of the Indies, minister of foreign affairs from 1938 to 1940, then ambassador to the United States. He participated in the Malines Conversations in 1926.

the English bishops, apart from a few exceptions; he sees them as being jealous of the Anglican bishops, more cultured, and of the academics. He told me a joke, in questionable taste, that is making the rounds among the American bishops: "We are leaving for nine months, and on our return we will be present at the birth of a legitimate child, but the child's conception might be immaculate." R. Sencourt is the author of diverse religious works; he is now working on a book on "Council and Reconciliation", the manuscript of which I see him carrying with him in a small suitcase.

At 6 P.M., a visit from Father Luciano Tosti and Stefano Minelli,[124] editor in chief of the Morcelliana publishing house (Brescia). They came to talk to me about a projected translation of the augmented edition of my *Paradoxes*, but there are some difficulties, because of some partial translations that have appeared from other publishers. Minelli also spoke to me again about the hoped-for translation of my Teilhard book, which is all ready in manuscript form; I could only explain to him why it was impossible.[125]

At 6:45, a visit from two seminarians from the Capranica,[126] come to question me about Teilhard. I went out with them as far as the Piazza Adriana; they left me at the door of the Vitali boarding house, where I was supposed to see Archbishop Élie Zoghby, a Melchite archbishop in Egypt. He had asked me this morning to come read and correct the draft of an intervention on the relations between the papacy and the episcopate. He was still unsure whether to speak in French or in Latin. I proposed some rather major corrections, deletions, softening. I urged him to reread it himself again so as to check every one of his expressions closely; the least exaggeration on his part could ruin the whole effect that he expects his intervention to have.

At 8 P.M., Fr. Daniélou came to tell me about the meeting of the mixed commission that he had just left. He was happy to have obtained something. The Prooemium on revelation, written by Archbishop

---

[124]Stefano Minelli (1929–2001), Italian, lawyer and publisher. He was the editor in chief of Éditions Morcelliana, founded in 1925 in Brescia by, among others, G.B. Montini, to promote a culture of Christian inspiration.

[125]On June 28, 1962, Father de Lubac was informed by his provincial that any republication or translation of *La Pensée religieuse* was forbidden. The superior general, in a letter dated August 27, 1962, wrote, however: "It was my judgment that your book served the Church, and I wanted it to be published. I have not regretted that decision."

[126]One of the seminaries in Rome. The institution was founded in the fifteenth century by Cardinal Domenico Capranica, originally for the priestly formation of the poor.

Garrone (aided by Daniélou and perhaps some others), has resisted in its essential points the attacks of Ruffini, Parente, etc. Fr. Tromp said nothing. Four chapters out of five are ready in their new draft. The chapter on tradition is not ready, its editors not having been able to reach agreement. On that note, an interminable discussion arose between Ruffini and Browne: the first wants everything to be in tradition; Browne thinks that some truths can be scriptural but not traditional; but both admit, of course, the constitutive tradition[127] and would like to insert that idea in the new text, just as it figured in the old one. The commission is supposed to work all through the next few days, including Saturday the 8th.

An intervention prepared by Archbishop de Provenchères and registered in accordance with the rules has been suppressed. Several people suspect that Archbishop Felici had it rejected because its topic was the bishops' conferences; perhaps it was simply because of the need to restrict the number of interventions, as the session is nearing its end. – Cardinal Agagianian[128] summoned Archbishop Zoa, reproached him for the work of organizing the African bishops to which he contributed, and made him take the withdrawal of subsidies by the Propaganda into consideration. – Italian newspapers have written that Card. Liénart "contests papal infallibility".

Wednesday, December 5, 1962 (34th General Cong.). – Father Durocher, Canadian, bursar general of the Society of Jesus, mentioned to me a remark by Fr. Hirschmann, with whom he had just been speaking. According to Fr. Hirschmann, Archbishop Dell'Acqua had said that John XXIII had complained, saying that what exhausted him the most was the opposition of Cardinals Ottaviani and Ruffini. Here in any case is one more indicator of the oppositions that are far from settling down.

There is a little joke about Ottaviani going around. He is supposed to have said: "I want to die soon." – "What's that, Your Eminence?" – "Yes, soon; I would like to die before the end of the council." – "But why, Your Eminence?" – "Oh! I would very much like to die a Catholic!"

---

[127] The idea of an oral tradition coming from Christ and containing truths absent from the Gospels.

[128] Gregorio Agagianian (1895–1971), Armenian, ordained in 1917. Armenian Patriarch of Cilicia from 1937 to 1962, created cardinal in 1946, prefect of the Congregation of the Propaganda from 1958 to 1970. At the council, he was president of the Commission for the Missions, a member of the Coordinating Commission and a moderator starting from the second session.

Ottaviani used to declare that the schema on the Liturgy was heretical, that it was absolutely never going to pass. Now here it is, being
passed. – In his press conference, Msgr. Romeo supposedly said that
even if an angel from heaven came and said the opposite of what he,
Romeo, affirmed, that angel could only be speaking falsehoods; for he
himself is certain that he holds the true Catholic doctrine.

Fr. Martelet yesterday evening saw Archbishop Villot and Cardinal
Liénart, who seemed to him both firm and confident.

Some words going around, supposedly expressed by some member
of the Curia: "Starting from the 10th", one said, "when they have left,
we will set everything back in order." And another one, less confident:
"We will start paying a heavy price for a quarter hour of madness." That
quarter hour is the one when the pope had the idea for the council.

This morning, on the steps of the basilica, one of the French bishops
from Madagascar stopped me to express his satisfaction: the council is
going well, he is happy. – Near the obelisk, I had just passed a bishop
in purple smoking his cigar. – A quick hello to Bishop A. Renard of
Versailles. – Inside Saint Peter's, greeted some pairs: Card. Marella and
Archbishop Weber (Strasbourg); Card. Suenens in a private conversation with Bishop Huyghe; Archbishop Garonne, who was chatting with
Fr. Daniélou. – I conversed with Bishop Volk (Mainz) on the subject of
the fifth chapter[1] of the former De fontibus; he had been able to obtain
some deep modifications and seemed happy. – Bishop Pourchet is also
optimistic; the opponents, he said to me, for the most part speak only in
their own name, and in certain cases it is easy to recognize who is pull-
ing their strings. – Father Khalifé is very happy, for the Maronite cause,
over the success achieved by Bishop Doumith. – A friendly greeting
to Max Thurian. – Handed the text of Martelet's talk over to Father
Duprey. – Dom Pierre Salmon (St. Jerome, Rome) appeared satisfied. –
Bishop Suhr (Copenhagen) gave me a Latin text from the Middle Ages
from Dom Jean Leclercq. – I thanked Msgr. Achille Glorieux for the
papers received yesterday on the apostolate of the laity. – Hello to Oreste
Kéramé. – A Melchite presented me with the work that has just arrived
in Rome: *Voix de l'Église en Orient*,[2] a collection of texts by Patriarch

---

December 5

[1] On Holy Scripture in the Church.

[2] *Voix de l'Église en Orient, voix de l'Église melchite: Choix de textes du patriarche Maximos IV et de l'épiscopat grec-melchite catholique* (Basel: Herder; Paris: Desclée De Brouwer, 1962).

Maximos IV and the Greek-Melchite-Catholic episcopate (published by Herder).

Presidency: Card. Alfrink. – Archbishop Felici announced that new emendationes to the Liturgy were going to be distributed, plus a fascicle summarizing the schemas "quae studio subjicientur in commissionibus"[3] with the idea of achieving a better unity. Today voting would take place on the emendationes proposed yesterday: eleven votes; this would continue tomorrow. A long Relatio, by Bishop Calewaert of Gand. – In the gallery, Canon Martimort told me that he is very pleased with the emendationes made to the first chap. of the Liturgy; extrinsic evidence that they are good, he told me: Archbishop Dante was against them.

The discussion of *De Ecclesia* was continued.

Card. Ruffini. – "Card. Bacci asseruit nostras discussiones non esse de doctrina, sed tantum de ratione seu modo proponendi doctrinam. Magno cum gaudio haec audivi."[4] So let us compose two schemas: one strictly dogmatic, the other pastoral, for the masses. In this way we will come back to the wish expressed by Card. Suenens: the Church ad intra et ad extra.[5] And we will reach unanimity.

Card. Montini (Milan). We must consider very diligently what Card. Suenens said to us yesterday "de fine concilii et de ordine argumentorum tractandorum".[6] We are here at the central point of the council; this schema can unify everything. "Quid est, et quid agit Ecclesia?"[7] Everyone expects that the council will set this out perspicue.[8] – "In schemate proposito, multa continentur quae probanda sint."[9] A number of points need to be explained and perfected. "Ad hunc finem, tria vota":[10]

1. I was happy about the glorification of Saint Joseph. I am even happier at the thought that we are preparing to glorify the Blessed Virgin, mother of the Church. But how much more important it is that "pie, solemniter et consulto Jesus Christus sit glorificatus! Imago Christi, mens Christi, aptius exprimi debent in ministerio et in vita mystica et morali

---

[3] "Which will be submitted for study in the commissions".

[4] "Cardinal Bacci has affirmed that our disagreements do not bear on the doctrine but only on the organization of the doctrine and the manner of presenting it. I heard that with great joy."

[5] "To those within and to those outside".

[6] "On the goal of the council and the organization of the subjects to be treated".

[7] "What is the Church, what does she do?"

[8] "Very clearly".

[9] "The proposed schema contains many things that are to be approved."

[10] "Toward that end, three wishes".

Ecclesiae. Ostendi debent relationes inter Ecclesiam et Christum, Ecclesia nihil potest ex sese, scit omnia accipere a Christo, etc. Non solum est a Christo condita, sed praesentia secreta Christi in ea"[11] supports everything, animates and promotes everything.

2. – "Secundum optatum: Doctrina episcopatus et modus quo proponatur. In schemate, expositio hujus doctrinae non est perfecte logica. Et forma est potius juridica quam theologica. Debemus exponere mentem et voluntatem Christi quoad episcopos et eorum munus in Ecclesia. Sic erit ordo procedendi: Institutio a Christo collegii apostolorum. – Successio corporis episcoporum. – Sacramentalitas episcopatus,[12] etc." Thus the connection between the bishops' authority and the Roman primacy would be better seen. In this authority, "respectus supernaturalis exhibeatur: imago Patris, imago Christi."[13]

3. – On chaps. 9 and 10 ... – "In capite 10° sunt duae res omnino diversae."[14] Let the first be incorporated in the chapter de Magisterio. – How can we make the "jus Ecclesiae praedicandi"[15] known and understood by people who do not recognize the Church's mission? We must proceed in a different fashion: "declarare hominum omnium jus ad veritatem accedendi".[16]

"Conclusio: a Commissionibus competentibus et a Secretariatu pro unitate schema recognoscatur, ita ut praebeat doctrinam congruam et aptam",[17] etc. (Applause.)

Partiarch Maximos IV. Let no one see in the criticisms anything other than a testimony to the interest taken in this text. It is the cornerstone

---

[11] "That Jesus Christ be glorified piously, solemnly, and explicitly! The image of Christ, the spirit of Christ must be expressed in a more appropriate fashion in the ministry and in the mystical and moral life of the Church. The relations between the Church and Christ must be shown; the Church can do nothing by herself, she knows that she receives everything from Christ. Not only was she founded by Christ, but the secret presence of Christ within her".

[12] "Second wish: the doctrine of the episcopate and the manner in which it is presented. In the schema, the presentation of this doctrine is not perfectly logical. And the form is more legalistic than theological. We must present the spirit and the will of Christ regarding the bishops and their task in the Church. Such would be the order to follow: institution of the college of apostles by Christ. Succession of the body of bishops. Sacramentality of the episcopate".

[13] "Let the supernatural aspect be made manifest: image of the Father, image of Christ."

[14] "In chapter 10, we find two completely different things."

[15] "The right of the Church to preach".

[16] "Proclaim the right of all people to have access to the truth."

[17] "Conclusion: that the schema be revised by the competent commissions and by the Secretariat for Unity, so as to display a coherent and fitting doctrine."

of the council. It is supposed to complete the teaching of Vatican I, so that the primacy and infallibility of the pope might appear in the general context of the hierarchical pastorate and the infallibility of the universal Church. – Chap. 1 does not correspond to sound ecumenical theology. It does not contain any errors, but it does not state the whole truth. Incomplete, it distorts the perspective on the truths that it expresses. – To compare the Church to an army arrayed for battle is not the most felicitous choice of metaphors; and it has no foundation in the Gospel. The Church is the Body of Christ living and risen, etc. – At no. 5, the foundation of unity in the Church is placed solely on the rule of some and the submission of others: that is not the whole truth; there are many relations other than that of ruler and subject. That distorts the true idea of the Church of Christ. By this insistence and this exclusivity, the thinking becomes foreign to the thinking of Christ. The schema develops a stifling legalism; the titular bishops, since they do not have a jurisdiction, are not even mentioned: this reticence is very significant. – Even more: the primacy of Peter and his successors; the unhealthy insistence on repeating this truth, as if everything were contained in this dogma, as if the pope were alone, gives a false presentation of the Church. Here as well, what the schema says in a positive manner is true, but it is not all the truth. Jesus established the apostles to pasture his flock, to govern the Church of God, in union with Peter and under the direction of Peter; cf. the texts of St. Paul, and of St. John in the Apocalypse: the twelve stones, which are the twelve apostles, the foundation of the wall of the city.[18] – We must protest against the partiality with which a certain school treats the truth, to the point of accusing the others of seeking compromises. We do not want any compromises; we want the whole and complete truth to be set forth. We ask that the whole truth be told, exactly. – What is the pontifical primacy: it is not a pale imitation of the ancient imperium; it all comes from Christ, from his Gospel, and it was instituted for service, etc. Cf. Jesus to Peter: "Do you love me? – Feed my sheep, etc."[19]

Archbishop Florit of Florence. (I could not hear him.)

Archbishop Antonio José Plaza of La Plata (Argentina). We must have humility, but not false humility, etc. "Agendum est de collegio epis-coporum – sed cavenda lata applicatio hujus doctrinae ad conferentias

---

[18] Rev 21:14.
[19] Jn 21:15–17.

episcopales nationales ..."[20] – Combine this with the schema on the Virgin, etc.

The secretary general: "Cardinalis Decanus rogat ut omnes Patres, tanquam possibile est, maneant"[21] in their seats. "Suffragatio continuator."[22]

Auxiliary Bishop Guillaume Pluta[23] from Poland. We must speak "de vita spirituali ut essentiali Ecclesiae. Pertinet ad essentiam Ecclesiae."[24] Cf. no. 5: it is good, but incomplete. On this subject there are only some obiter dicta.[25]

Bishop Pierre Fiordelli[26] of Prato (Italy). There are some very good chapters. "Sed dolendum videtur quod in toto schemate nihil sit de statu sacramentali matrimonii."[27] (There followed a lofty discourse on the status matrimonialis christianus,[28] very touching, pronounced in a soft, whimpering voice.) (Praeses: Hoc est valde utile, sed extra ordinem schematis.) – Concludo ...[29]

The secretary general announced that the pope's benediction would take place on the square at noon.

Archbishop Bernard Mels[30] of Luluabourg (Former Belgian Congo). "De natura Ecclesiae. Sperabamus fore ut",[31] etc. On the mission of the Church, which would have clarified "ejus jura et munera".[32] (The conversation of my neighbors, as occasionally happened, prevented me from hearing certain sentences.) Missio non est aliqua obligatio particularis et

---

[20] "It is necessary to treat of the college of bishops, but we must beware of a broad application of this doctrine to include the national episcopal conferences."

[21] "The cardinal dean asks that all the Fathers, as much as possible, remain."

[22] "The vote continues."

[23] Wilhelm Pluta (1910–1986), Polish, ordained in 1934. Auxiliary bishop.

[24] "Of the spiritual life as being essential to the Church. This belongs to the essence of the Church."

[25] "Things said in passing".

[26] Pietro Fiordelli (1916–2004), Italian, ordained in 1938. Bishop of Prato from 1954 to 1991. Bishop Fiordelli achieved notoriety by describing a couple in his diocese who married in a civil service as "cohabiting, public sinners" in a pastoral letter read in the churches of the diocese. The affair caused a great uproar, and Bishop Fiordelli was fined 40,000 lire in 1958.

[27] "But it is unfortunate that in the whole schema nothing is said on the sacramental status of marriage."

[28] "Christian matrimonial status".

[29] "President: that is very useful but unrelated to the matter of the schema. I conclude ..."

[30] Bernard Mels, C.I.C.M. (1908–1992), Belgian, ordained in 1933. Apostolic vicar then archbishop of Luluabourg (present-day Kananga in the Democratic Republic of the Congo) from 1949 to 1967. Member of the Commission for Religious.

[31] "On the nature of the Church. We were hoping that".

[32] "Her rights and functions".

adventitia; pertinet ad constitutionem Ecclesiae, et pertinet ad omnnes in Ecclesia. In suo statu terrestri, Ecclesia est missa[33] (a reference to Suenens and Marty). Ideo tractetur de missione Ecclesiae; omnia alia sic debent uniri et illuminari ... Dolendum, et mirum, quod apostolatus sit quasi privilegium, "speciale mandato episcoporum!"[34] Hence the ruin of the Church in a number of regions. Even in Africa, that land of Christian conquests: Islam is gaining ground there, etc.; and in the old Catholic countries we are seeing the spread of indifferentism and neo-paganism. At this rate, in a short time Catholicism will no longer be more than the religion of a few in the world. "Urgentissima quaestio":[35] How to bring the "missionem Christi ad effectum suum?"[36] It will not be by always demanding the Church's rights or even by reminding all the faithful of the duty to participate in the apostolate. "Omnino necessarium est quaerere quomodo, in praxi, procedere. Quando patria periclitatur",[37] all quarrels and all secondary questions , all privileges and noble customs are forgotten: there is a general mobilization of all the united forces. Today, "mater Ecclesia in periculo est":[38] a new unity and a new zeal are necessary. "Videamus quomodo in statu missionis restitui possit Ecclesia, non tantum"[39] to escape danger, but for the outpouring of a new Pentecost. Conclusion: "Schema recognoscendum, etc. – Adhuc unum verbum: loquor ut parvulus."[40] The oppositions among us have to be reduced through frank discussions and extraconciliar exchanges. "Sunt diffidentiae, suspiciones. Hoc est vere peccatum contra Spiritum sanctum. Oportet fieri discussio fraterna quam citius. Hoc fiat in corpore episcoporum",[41] while waiting for the next session.

---

[33] "Mission is not a particular and supplementary obligation; it pertains to the constitution of the Church and is the concern of everyone in the Church. In her terrestrial state, the Church is on a mission."

[34] "For this reason, let the mission of the Church be dealt with; everything else must in this way be brought together and illuminated. It is unfortunate and surprising that the apostolate is almost a privilege, 'particularly by the mandate of the bishops'."

[35] "A very urgent question".

[36] "The mission of Christ to its fulfillment?"

[37] "It is absolutely necessary, in practice, to plan how to proceed. When our country is in danger".

[38] "Mother Church is in danger."

[39] "Let us see how the Church can be restored to a state of mission, not only". [See L.J. Suenens, *L'Église en état de mission* (Paris: Desclée Brouwer, 1955).]

[40] "The schema should be revised, etc. One more word: I am speaking like a child" [see 1 Cor 13:11].

[41] "There is mistrust, suspicion. This is truly a sin against the Holy Spirit. As soon as possible, there must be a fraternal discussion. Let this be done within the corps of bishops."

Archbishop Felici gave the results of the following 4 votes on the emendationes to chap. I of the Liturgy:

Votes cast: 2,110	Placet: 2,087	Non: 14	Invalid ballots: 9
Votes cast: 2,114	Placet: 2,083	Non: 21	Invalid ballots: 10
Votes cast: 2,109	Placet: 2,044	Non: 50	Invalid ballots: 15
Votes cast: 2,073	Placet: 2,033	Non: 36	Invalid ballots: 4

We left Saint Peter's at five minutes to noon, so that we could recite the Angelus with the pope. The square was open to the public. It was black with people, with large purple patches. The pope spoke in a voice that appeared strong. He gave his blessing. Then he gave a short, paternal speech: rejoicing to see the whole Christian family, bishops and faithful, gathered together; and he gave his blessing again.

I got into a bus that was to take me to the residence of Bishop Fauvel. Someone had left on each seat a booklet with a blue cover, 15 printed pages long: it was Francesco Spadafora's reply to the Response of the Biblical Institute.[42] In his conclusion, he attacked Father Zerwick once again on the subject of the primacy of Peter and Father Lyonnet on Romans 5:12, etc.

During the bus ride, I chatted with Archbishop Perrin of Carthage, always good and tactful; he knows exactly what is going on with certain maneuvers of a small clan. – We arrived at the house of the Sisters of the Retreat of Angers, on the Janiculum hill, where seven or eight French bishops are staying, as well as some Italians and Chileans. Talked with Bishop Fauvel (Quimper), his auxiliary,[43] and his theologian, Father Jullien, a professor of moral theology at Quimper. Also saw a French bishop expelled from China and now settled in Liverpool; he told me that Cardinal Godfrey's intervention reflects rather precisely the mentality of the majority of English bishops. Father Jullien told me about a recent talk given by Card. Ruffini to the Brazilian bishops: expressing his fears on the orientation of the council, which was off to a bad start, in his opinion, the speaker said that we had to expect some sad things, unless, by a stroke of Providence, some great disruption intervenes to save the Church from the danger she is in. That was the day when people most feared for the life of the pope, and the bishops, it appeared, understood

[42] F. Spadafora, *Razionalismo, exegesi cattolica e magistero* (Rovigo: IPAG, 1962).

[43] Vincent Favé (1902–1997), French, ordained in 1925. Auxiliary bishop of Quimper from 1957 to 1977.

the cardinal's allusion very well. At the end of the lecture, according to someone who was present, only about twenty people applauded, a certain number of whom did so solely as a matter of courtesy.

Every week, for the last two months, the bishops who are staying here have invited some bishops from various countries; Father Jullien is the one who organizes these encounters. Today, they received the nuncio in Paris, Msgr. Bertoli,[44] whom I greeted. Also at the table were: Father Hua,[45] Father Paul Gauthier, etc. Bishop Picard de la Vacquerie (Orleans), who has a reputation for outspoken boldness, told me that he was beside himself about Card. Ottaviani's 2nd intervention; he was speaking to his neighbors about it at the end of the session, still inside the basilica, when he saw Ottaviani coming toward him on the way to the exit; then, taking a stand in front of him with his cane to block his way, he said to him: "Your Eminence, one does not speak that way to bishops! And besides, you know that during the council there is no longer any Holy Office: there are only bishops!" He also told me that the nuncio had wanted to make him an archbishop, but that Cardinal Feltin had opposed it: "He gave some reasons that had no merit, because he did not dare say the real reason: it was because he did not want to have an eminence of my sort in the meeting of archbishops."

A priest from Besançon drove me back to town with Bishop Fauvel. – At 4 P.M. visit from Fr. Martelet. At 4:30, with him and Fr. Rondet, I went to the meeting of Africans on via Traspontina: a lecture by Pastor Hébert Roux on ecumenism and the missions. Mission in modern times, marked by confessional proselytism and competition; our divisions imposed on the new Christianities of Africa. – Mission and Church: the goal is to reconcile the entire world to God; all the Church, as such, is sent. – Apostolate and unity. – The Church draws her life from the Word of God so as to announce it to the world; unity is both the condition and the goal of mission. – Practical questions. – He was asked a number of questions. Archbishop Zoa, who introduced and thanked him, talked about the Protestant Theology Faculty established in Yaoundé; if this foundation, he said, has caused some discomfort for

---

[44] Paolo Bertoli (1908–2001), Italian, ordained in 1930. Apostolic nuncio in France from 1960 to 1969, created cardinal in 1969. Prefect of the Congregation for the Causes of Saints from 1969 to 1973.

[45] Maxime Hua (1900–1983), French, ordained in 1925. Former national chaplain of the male branch of the JOC [one of the groups comprising Catholic Action in France], priest of the Mission of Paris.

those outside, at the actual location, on the contrary, it is an aid to ecumenical dialogue. He ended with the wish for the development of theological studies on African soil.

With Fr. Martelet and Pastor Roux, I set out on foot for the Palazzo Farnese; Fr. Martelet left us at the entrance. Reception by the embassy near the Quirinal. Saw Dom Sortais, Abbot General of la Trappe, and numerous French bishops. A Protestant couple (he is an embassy attaché), fervent admirers of Teilhard, expressed their happiness over the friendliness shown them by the Roman authorities (apart from the Holy Office). I spoke with some Protestant observers; Cullmann bid me good-bye; the day before yesterday he saw Card. Montini, who presented him with a memento; he is pleased to have observed that Montini knew his books well. "He has not only read my *Saint-Pierre*, about which everyone here is talking; he has read my *Christologie du N. T.*"[46]

Thursday, December 6, 1962. – Archbishop Zoa, whom I saw yesterday, confirmed and clarified what I had been told. In his interview with Card. Agagianian, he was not able to talk about matters that concerned him; the card. talked without stopping, without making any direct reproaches, but by way of insinuation; he made him understand that the work the African bishops did in organizing themselves was viewed badly here, etc. (The Apostolic Delegate in Western Africa, Msgr. Maury, fears that on the contrary, given its purely practical and episodic nature, the organization might be fragile.) Earlier, Archbishop Parente had vehemently reproached him as a traitor.

This morning, in Saint Peter's, Archbishop Philippe Nabaa, Melchite, spoke to me again about the intervention he is making tomorrow; he had greatly modified his first text; I urged him to make some new corrections, but I did not have the time to see them. – Bishop Schmitt of Metz talked to me about the assembly of French bishops held yesterday afternoon: at the meeting, he had asked why so little use was being made of the periti and other theologians. – I gave Msgr. Lafortune, for Card. Léger, a copy of Fr. Martelet's printed lecture on "The Dogmatic Schemas of Vatican II in the Light of Vatican I". – Fr. Congar told me that yesterday he saw Card. Montini, who asked him to give me his

---

[46] O. Cullman, *Saint Pierre, disciple-apôtre, martyr* (Neuchâtel-Paris: Delachaux & Niestlé, 1952), and O. Cullman, *Christologie du Nouveau Testament* (Neuchâtel-Paris: Delachaux & Niestlé, 1958).

warmest regards. The meeting that Congar had had a few days earlier with Card. Ottaviani had not been pleasant; in his judgment, Ottaviani's henchman is Parente. – Msgr. Dumont, O.P., spoke to me about a piece that appeared in the magazine *Le Monde et la Vie*: "Where Is the French Church Going?"

35th General Congregation. Mass celebrated by a black bishop, Archbishop Gantin of Cotonou (Dahomey); some seminarians sang Gregorian chant, and the crowd of bishops joined in; this gave us a rest from the motets of the Sistine Chapel Schola.

President: Card. Eugene Tisserant, decanus: "Loquitur excellentissimus archiepiscopus a Secretis."[1] Archbishop Felici: "Velint omnes attente audire. Censemus facturos esse rem gratissimam omnibus Patribus, si paucis verbis enarremus quae fecimus ad laudem Dei et decus Ecclesiae":[2] 34 general congregations, 5 schemas discussed, 33 suffragationes in schedulis.[3] 587 interventions of the Fathers, 523 others submitted in writing (in total: 1,110). "Labor hodie prosequitur. Summus Pontifex dignatus est aliquas normas statuere pro laboribus futuris."[4] – Yesterday's votes, for emendationes 5–8:

Votes cast: 2,072	Placet: 2,011	Non: 44	Invalid ballots: 17
Votes cast: 2,082	Placet: 2,016	Non: 56	Invalid ballots: 10
Votes cast: 2,079	Placet: 2,041	Non: 30	Invalid ballots: 8
Votes cast: 2,086	Placet: 1,903	Non: 38	Invalid ballots: 145

This last figure (invalid ballots, and especially blank ones) was not explained; nevertheless, as the requisite majority was greatly exceeded, it was decided not to repeat the vote. – "Hodie, suffragatio erit circa emendationes 9, 10, et 11; deinde, continuo, circa duas emendationes contentas in altero fasciculo (ad cap. I, nos. 32 et 36)."[5]

December 6

[1] "Dean. Let the most excellent archbishop secretary speak."

[2] "Let everyone please listen attentively. We are of the opinion that it would please all the Fathers very much for us to list in a few words what we have done for the praise of God and the glory of the Church."

[3] "Votes on magnetic forms".

[4] "The work continues today. The Supreme Pontiff has thought it good to establish some rules for the work to come."

[5] "Today the vote will concern amendments 9, 10, and 11; then, without interruption, the two amendments contained in the other fascicle (on chapter 1, nos. 32 and 36)."

Relatio Domini Francisci Grimshaw, arch. de Birmingham, de his emendationibus.[6]

Felici: "S. Pontifex concedit omnibus Patribus facultatem impertiendi apostolicam benedictionem in suis dioecesibus. Largitur facultatem dicendi missam quacumque hora[7] on their return voyage (and the same for their theologians, etc.)."

Card. Lercaro, archbishop of Bologna. "Ante Omnia"[8] (he stressed what Montini had said). "Requiritur doctrina de Ecclesia quae penetret ultra ordinem juridicum. Haec videtur posse esse conclusio sessionis nostrae. Debemus ostendere hominibus Ecclesiam esse sacramentum Christi viventis et inter homines operantis; mysterium Christi in Ecclesia. Hoc est maxime doctrinale, et hoc est maximae historicae actualitatis. Hodie, ostendere praecipue mysterium Christi in pauperibus: Ecclesia est praesertim Ecclesia pauperum. Omnia schemata nobis proposita vel proponenda non videntur considerare hunc aspectum essentialem mysterii Christi, a prophetis annuntiatum, ab ipsa Salvatoris Matre manifestatum, in nativitate, infantia, vita publica Christi exhibitum; apertum fundamentum Regni Dei, etc., in communitate apostolica . . . , et aspectum tandem qui sanciretur in aeternitatem . . . Quapropter nos oportet agnoscere et sollemniter proclamare hoc mysterium Christi in paupertate et in evangelizatione pauperum. Urgens in aetate nostra est. Est aetas in qua paupertas est in 2/3 mundi";[9] offensive contrast . . . It is not sufficient to make the evangelization of the poor a side matter: this must be, simpliciter,[10] the theme of our council, "plena cum

---

[6] The report of Archbishop Francis Grimshaw of Birmingham, on these amendments.

[7] "The Supreme Pontiff has granted to all the Fathers the right to give the apostolic benediction in their dioceses. He also confers the option of saying Mass at any time."

[8] "Above all".

[9] "We need a doctrine of the Church that goes beyond the legalistic order. This seems like it could be the conclusion of our session. We have to show to men that the Church is the sacrament of Christ, living and acting among men; the mystery of Christ in the Church. That is very doctrinal, and that is of very great historical relevance. Today, to show above all the mystery of Christ in the poor: the Church is especially the Church of the poor. All the schemas that have been proposed to us or that are to be proposed do not seem to take account of this essential aspect of the mystery of Christ, announced by the prophets, manifested by the Mother of the Savior herself, displayed in the nativity, the childhood, the public life of Christ; the manifest foundation of the Kingdom of God, etc., in the apostolic community . . . , and finally the aspect that is sanctioned in eternity. It is why we must recognize and solemnly proclaim this mystery of Christ in poverty and in the evangelization of the poor. This is an urgent matter for our age. It is an age in which poverty exists in two-thirds of the world."

[10] "Simply".

conformitate Evangelio",[11] etc. Hence these proposals: "1. Concilium quasi primariam partem attribuat enucleationi hujus mysterii pauperum in Ecclesia,[12] etc. – 2. Habeat aequam prioritatem dignitas pauperum in Ecclesia.[13] – 3. In omnibus schematibus habeatur connexio ontologica inter Christum in pauperibus et praesentem in actione eucharistica et in sacra hierarchia.[14] – 4. Pariter, de renovatione institutionum et methodi evangelizandi: connexio historica inter amorem hujus eminentis dignitatis et nostram propriam actionem.[15] – Concl.: Unum exemplum. Agere cum sapientia quidem et moderatione, sed absque ulla timiditate et compromissione";[16] to be able to say with Peter: "Argentum et aurum non habeo,[17] etc."; certain ornaments of the bishops "hodie praebent scandalum";[18] eliminate them, "ne divites videamur. Debet esse paupertas etiam communitatis. De re oeconomica":[19] learn to abandon outmoded institutions. "Si dociles nos praebemus in consilio divinae Providentiae, etc. Fideles Illi qui factus est pauper ut gratia sua nos ditaret."[20] (Scattered applause.)

Archbishop Felici proclaimed the rules fixed by the pope for the interval between the two sessions; "ut labores concilii prosequantur fructuose, etiam in intervallo temporis, Summus Pontifex, juxta ..., hunc ordinem statuere dignatus est et approbare",[21] in an audience granted to the secretary of state[22] on December 5: 1. "Longo temporis intervallo",[23] ... the schemas will be corrected, submitted again to examination, and perfected. This work will be done in the conciliar commissions, which will

---

[11] "In full conformity with the Gospel".

[12] "1. That the council give first place to the exposition of this mystery of the poor in the Church".

[13] "That the same priority be given to the dignity of the poor in the Church".

[14] "3. In all the schemas, let an ontological connection be made between Christ present in the poor and Christ present in the celebration of the Eucharist and in the sacred hierarchy."

[15] "4. In like manner, concerning the renewal of institutions and the method of evangelization: historical connection between the love of this eminent dignity and our own action".

[16] "Conclusion: one example only. To act with wisdom and moderation, but without any timidity or compromise".

[17] "I have no silver and gold" [Acts 3:6].

[18] "Cause a scandal today".

[19] "Lest we seem to be rich. Poverty must also be that of the community. On the economy".

[20] "If we show ourselves docile to the counsel of divine Providence, etc., we will be faithful to the One who made himself poor in order to enrich us by his grace."

[21] "In order that the work of the council might continue in a fruitful manner, also during the intersession, the Supreme Pontiff, in accordance with ..., has judged it good to establish and approve these provisions."

[22] A. Cicognani.

[23] "1. During the long intersession".

have to call upon the mixed commissions. – 2. "Finis Concilii oecum. Vat. II proprius, est ille quem S. Pater saepe declaravit",[24] recalled again in his discourse of October 11 (a long quotation). "Permulti Patres de hac re sententiam tulerunt in eodem sensu, etc. – 3. In primis opus est ut ex pluribus argumentis tractatis quaedam seligantur; ex. gratia, quae Ecclesiam, Christi fideles et omnem Christi familiam respiciunt."[25] Let us restrict ourselves to "generalia principia. Quare",[26] do not deal with what should be made the subject of future canonical provisions; leave the applications to the postconciliar documents. – [4.] "Interea, nova commissio instituetur, ad coordinandos labores. Praeses erit[27] "the secretary of state, who will keep the pope informed. "Proprium munus":[28] to coordinate the work, to follow it closely, to speak with the presidents of the various commissions about everything necessary to ensure this coordination. [This commission] will have vice-presidents, a secretary, members. Those who are able to bring some insight, even if they are from outside, will be questioned. Let the greatest possible number be able to speak freely. – 5. Once the schemas have been "recognized" and approved, they will be sent to the bishops, to the presidents of the episcopal conferences. Let the latter study them and send them back in due time, a time that will be short. – 6. The conciliar commissions, after receiving the bishops' remarks, will proceed with the emendationes, which will be ready for September. (Applause.)

Bishop Enrico Compagnone[29] of Anagni (Italy). We have been able to observe a great variety of opinions among the Fathers. Praise for those who have prepared this schema. They did not want to do something definitive; so it is not surprising that we are debating it; but we must be just toward them. We should not criticize without proposing concrete changes. There has been a great deal of criticism; but what positive

---

[24] "The proper goal of the ecumenical council Vatican II is that which the Holy Father has often stated."

[25] "A very great number of Fathers have expressed themselves in the same sense on this point. In the first place, the task is to make a selection from the many subjects discussed; for example, those things that concern the Church, the faithful, and all the family of Christ."

[26] "General principles. For that reason".

[27] "In the meantime, a new commission will be instituted, to coordinate the work. Its president will be".

[28] "Its specific task".

[29] Enrico Compagnone, O.C.D. (1908–1989), Italian, ordained in 1930. Bishop of Agnani from 1953 to 1972. Member of the Commission for Religious.

consensus within this negative consensus? "Audivimus demagogicas orationes."[30] We do not need eloquence but reason. Some are indoctrinating us like catechumens. "Res momentosae sunt. Rationem reddituri sumus. Debemus meditari et judicare. Gaudeo quia ea quae scripsi omnino consentaneae sunt his quae nobis hodie declarata sunt";[31] I am in complete agreement with the pope. (Apologia for the preparatory commissions): the pope, who was often present there, praised them; I am delighted to be in agreement with him. I want to express to our very dear observers our ardent desire that they understand the Church and return to embrace us within her maternal bosom. (Card. Tisserant: Hora est.[32] You had asked for the floor to talk about *De Ecclesia*; you have said nothing about it; you have caused us to make an examination of conscience: we thank you.)

Bishop Hervás y Benet (Juan) of Ciudad-Real (Spain). We all have the same goal: to evangelize and to preserve intact the true faith. We must not be suspicious of those who are seeking to make the Catholic faith better understood and loved by those outside: an anxious search on behalf of the mission countries, the men of today, our separated brothers. I share the anxiety of this search. We must find a way to progress in the propagation of our faith, without any false irenicism, drawing support from traditional theology. I would like to provide here a "specimen methodi, ex experientia mea; non nova, sed noviter. Schema quoad doctrinam est solidum. Aliunde, nil mirum si quibusdam defectibus laboret. Sed",[33] let us have no radicalism! "Vitentur pericula"[34] pointed out by Pius XII in his encyc. *Humani generis*, etc. "Duo ergo extrema vitanda: ex una parte, novationes quae corrumpunt doctrinam; ex altera parte, archaïsmum"[35] that is very common in seminaries and among preachers. Some are beginning to say on the outside that here in the council we are abandoning traditional theology as useless and that we want to change

---

[30] "We have heard some demagogic speeches."

[31] "These are important matters. We will have to render an account. We must meditate and judge. I rejoice because the things that I have written are absolutely in agreement with those that have been announced to us today."

[32] "The time is up."

[33] "An example of method, drawn from my experience; it is not new, but it is done in a new way. The schema, as far as its doctrine is concerned, is solid. On the other hand, there is nothing surprising if it should suffer from some defects. But".

[34] "Let us avoid the dangers."

[35] "Therefore two extremes are to be avoided: on the one hand, innovations that corrupt the doctrine; on the other, archaism."

everything. It is absolutely indispensable for us to declare that we respect it, making reference to *Pascendi*,[36] to *Divino afflante*, to *Humani generis*. Let us beware of distorting seminarians and even religious. For attaining unity among ourselves, the formula is simple: 1. "Schema approbandum",[37] even if it means that the commission revise it; 2. "Aliud schema parallelum paretur, sicut dixit heri Card. Ruffini ..."[38] (Tisserant: Tempus jam finitum est.)[39]

Bishop Sergius Méndez of Cuernavaca (Mexico). We are the judges of the faith here, we do not have to conform to textbooks. I have already corresponded with the people of my diocese: they are happy and are expecting a great deal from us. The schema contains a number of invaluable things; "sed funditus corrigatur et ante omnia, evangelice".[40] – Chap. I, no. 2, l. 22: "Tantum episcopi nominantur, et unice ut 'praepositi'. Altissimo silentio collegium episcoporum schema premit. Veritas rerum est omnino alia quam ostenditur."[41] The bishops must not appear simply as subject to the magisterium of the pope. For those who make even a cursory study of history, it is a different story. Restore to its evangelical purity the balance instituted by Jesus Christ. "Cum et sub Summo Pontifice, collegium episcoporum regit Ecclesiam, ordinarie, non tantum extraordinarie."[42] This is an indispensable point to remember for the unity between the bishops and the Curia. – Two more considerations: a. Toward those who, as sons of Abraham, do not yet believe in J. C., repudiate all antisemitism. – b. For the rest of mankind, "non pauci domestici fidei",[43] even non-Catholics, who for two centuries have been in conflict with the Church, in particular the Freemasons – who in the beginning were not anti-Christian: "ex una parte ..., ex altera parte ..."[44] Possibilities for reconciliation.

Bishop William Philbin of Down Connor[45] (Ireland). This schema is dogmatic, not mystical or missionary or ecumenical, etc. "Caveamus

---

[36] Encyclical of Pius IX of September 8, 1907, condemning modernism.

[37] "1. The schema must be approved."

[38] "Let another, parallel schema be prepared, as Cardinal Ruffini said yesterday."

[39] "Time has already run out."

[40] "Let it be completely corrected and, above all, in an evangelical fashion."

[41] "Only the bishops are named, and solely as 'leaders'. The schema maintains a profound silence on the college of bishops. The truth is completely different from what is shown."

[42] "With and under the Supreme Pontiff, the college of bishops governs the Church, ordinarily and not only extraordinarily."

[43] "Many of those closely associated with the faith".

[44] "On the one hand, on the other hand".

[45] William J. Philbin (1907–1991), Irish, ordained in 1931. Bishop of Down and Connor (Northern Ireland) from 1962 to 1982.

ne detorqueamur nostrum scopum. Debet esse constitutio theologica. Ad hunc scopum, tria principia:[46] 1. Quod ad doctrinam spectat, munus principale concilii est defendere doctrinam contra errores et impugnationes; ex. gratia, de juribus et auctoritate Ecclesiae; debemus publice vindicare haec jura, etc. Ne timidi simus![47] etc." Another example: to defend the true idea of the priesthood by distinguishing it very clearly from a certain kind of priesthood "lato sensu".[48] – 2. Outside of these cases of defense, do not enter in rebus theologicis;[49] so, on pp. 48f., do not cut short the discussions on the transmission of jurisdiction to the bishops; or, on pp. 49–50, on the obligation of the assensus interior[50] to the decisions of the ordinary magisterium. In the chapter on the Church and the State, to the contrary, the schema proceeds with great prudence. – 3. "Ubique vitemus ne videamur nos detrahere a doctrinis receptis in Ecclesia."[51] The schema never makes this mistake. However, according to certain interventions, it would seem that there are some who would like us to impose a new rule of secrecy, under the pretext of not offending one or another group, in particular our separated brothers: for example, concerning the Mystical Body and the Roman Church or concerning the members of the Church. – In summary: "secundum substantiam schema placet; sed forma est nimis longa et multa sunt minuscula, parum digna concilio."[52]

Bishop Alexandre Renard of Versailles. "De sacerdotio secundi ordinis: cur presbyteratus neglectus esset a concilio? Talis defectus attristabit multos episcopos et sacerdotes."[53] Let us work sincerely to state our common faith, without arguments. Let us state the Church's doctrine on priests: this subject does not appear in the chapter De Sacerdotio.[54] Three principles: 1. Presbyter episcopi sacerdotio participat;

---

[46] "Let us take care not to be turned aside from our goal. This must be a theological constitution. To this end, three principles".

[47] "1. In what concerns doctrine, the principal task of the council is to defend it against errors and attacks; for example, concerning the rights and authority of the Church; we must publicly demand these rights, etc. Let us not be timid!"

[48] "In the broad sense".

[49] "Into the domain of theology".

[50] "Interior assent".

[51] "Let us everywhere avoid seeming to distance ourselves from doctrines received in the Church."

[52] "I approve the schema in substance, but the form is too long, and there are many minor details unworthy of a council."

[53] "On the priesthood of the second degree: Why would the priesthood be neglected by the council? Such a lack will sadden numerous bishops and priests."

[54] "On the priesthood".

ordinatur enim non solum ad missam, sed etiam ad orationem et praedicationem. – 2. Existit sacerdotale collegium quoddam. – 3. Oratio,
quae est pastoralis actio, fit in persona Christi, sed in corpore Ecclesiae,[55] etc. Clearly distinguish the obedience owed by priests, "ex ipso
sacramento",[56] from the obedience of the laity "ex jure".[57] – "Unde,
votum":[58] that a paragraph on the priests be added.

Archbishop Armand Farès of Catanzaro (Italy). Particular reasons
"tractandi de Ecclesia: intrinsecae et extrinsicae".[59] Contemporary atheism, etc. Let us carefully distinguish two things: a doctrinal schema and
another document, pastoral, ecumenical, missionary. Let the doctrinal
schema, the one before us, which is good, be preceded by a Prooemium
on Peter, fundamentum Ecclesiae.[60]

Bishop Jean Velasco of Hsiamen (China), in exile. If something is
defined, it will be irreformable. That being the case, do we have the
right to omit or to contradict what was solemnly defined by earlier
councils? It has been said here that the pope has to be in union with the
college, but Vatican I defined "ex sese", etc.

Bishop Pablo Barrachina of Orihuela-Alicante (Spain). This schema is
of the utmost importance. "Ecclesia est mysterium."[61] This is sometimes
spoken of "minus convenienter ..."[62] Comparison with Christ, man,
and God: so, a twofold element in the Church, "sacramentum sacra-
mentorum. S. Pontifex est Christus visibilis,[63] etc." There is a mystical
aspect and a visible, social aspect: cf. St. Thomas, $1^a 2^a$. "Necesse est, in
hoc schemate, bono in multis, dare locum aspectui mystico."[64] Best to
recall also that "laici non sunt christiani secundi ordinis".[65]

Rev. Fr. Joseph Buckley, superior general of the Marists. "Quaestio
de auctoritate et obedientia."[66] The schema has not seen the underlying

---

[55] "1. The priest participates in the priesthood of the bishop; he is ordained, indeed, not only
for the Mass, but also for prayer and preaching. 2. There exists a certain priestly college. 3. Prayer,
which is a pastoral action, is made in the person of Christ but within the body of the Church, etc."

[56] "By the sacrament itself".

[57] "By law".

[58] "And so, a wish".

[59] "For discussing the Church: intrinsic and extrinsic".

[60] "Foundation of the Church".

[61] "The Church is a mystery."

[62] "In an inappropriate fashion".

[63] "Sacrament of sacraments. The Supreme Pontiff is Christ visible."

[64] "It is necessary in this schema, good in a number of points, to make room for the mystical
aspect."

[65] "Laypeople are not second-class Christians."

[66] "The question of authority and obedience".

cause or the foundation of the crisis of authority. I also reprove errors ...
However, there need to be distinctions and clarifications made. "Pro
multis catholicis, inter quos non rari religiosi, crisis non stat in obediendo
vel non obediendo. Est quaestio spectans ad rationem et methodum. –
1. Ad rationem."[67] Many think that we must start from the human person, with his responsibilities and the rights that follow from this, to
demand the spread of freedom. Obedience is a necessary virtue, "sed
non est perfectio pura (Deus est liber, non obediens)."[68] – 2. "Quoad
methodum".[69] Distinguish the various levels of authority. "Existit aliqua tendentia exhibendi omnes voluntates superioris cujusdam esse voluntatem Dei. Atqui est tantum voluntas Dei ut superiori obediatur in
genere."[70] The order given by a simple superior cannot be equated to
an order given by the pope, etc., "nec auctoritatem Ecclesiae, quae est
a Deo in Christo, auctoritati Status, quae venit ex eo quod Deus creavit
hominem socialem",[71] etc. And even ecclesiastical authority is exercised
day to day by fallible men. It is necessary to bring together the principle
of authority and the principle of autonomy: cf. Pius XI and John XXIII
("principium subsidionis*[72] officii"[73]). Uphold the "prioritas individuae
personae et conscientiae personalis".[74]

Archbishop Costantino Stella[75] of L'Aquila (Italy). I will have to be
controversial in order to respond. Some are complaining that "Ecclesia ut agmen describitur: sed est Ecclesia militans."[76] Some are complaining about clericalism: "sed Ecclesia est hierarchica; dividitur inter
Ecclesiam docentem (hierarchia) et Ecclesiam discentem (fideles)".[77] Cf.
already Ignatius of Antioch. One can distinguish: a. Christus et Petrus;[78]

---

[67] "For numerous Catholics, including numerous religious, the crisis is not in obedience or disobedience. It is a question relating to reason and method. 1. Relating to reason".

[68] "But it is not a pure perfection (God is free and not obedient)."

[69] "In what concerns method".

[70] "There is a tendency to present all the wishes of a superior as if they were the will of God. But
the will of God is only that the superior be obeyed in general."

[71] "Or the authority of the Church, which comes from God in Christ, to the authority of the
State, which comes from the fact that God has created man as a social being".

[72] *The word has been changed to "subsidiaritatis".

[73] "The principle of subsidiarity".

[74] "Priority of the individual person and the personal conscience".

[75] Costantino Stella (1900–1973), Italian, ordained in 1925. Archbishop of Aquila from 1950
until his death.

[76] "The Church is described as an army on the march, but this has to do with the Church
Militant."

[77] "But the Church is hierarchical; she is divided into the Church that teaches (the hierarchy) and
the Church that is taught (the faithful)."

[78] "Christ and Peter".

b. the bishops; c. the rest of the priesthood; d. "in ultimo ordine, plebs
fidelium, ergo, apte Ecclesia ut pyramida describitur.[79] Cf. Ephesians."
Some are complaining about the schema's legalism: but, in chap. 1, no. 5
"affirmatur Ecclesiam piam esse matrem."[80]

   Melchite Archbishop Georges Hakim of Acre and all of Galilee. Venerable Brothers, dear observers. We have all come to this council born up
by the hope that great things were going to be accomplished here, despite
our weakness and pettiness. This hope comes to us from our beloved
pope, John XXIII, etc. He has opened a new path, one that responds to
the aspirations of the world. The Church is the universal mother, and she
is most especially the Church of the poor, as John XXIII has reminded us,
as has Cardinal Lercaro just recently. The real results of the council will
only begin to be known in ten or fifteen years. It will be the council of
the 21st century. Between now and then, the population of the earth will
have doubled, and no doubt also world hunger, etc. – We would like to
find in the schemas set before us, not the texts of our textbooks of yes-
teryear, as correct as they might be, but a real response, coming from the
Church, to the real questions of today. Let us speak as John XXIII speaks,
as the Gospel speaks. That would be so reassuring! Such language would
be understood by all.*[81] My remarks only intend to make a voice from
the East heard. I will express first of all my gratitude to Cardinal Frings,
who pointed out that this schema takes no account of Eastern thought.
The Mystical Body itself is reduced here to visible realities alone. Out
of hundreds of references, five in total refer to the Greek Fathers. The
realism of Greek theology is atrophied by the legalism of this schema.
Two examples: – 1. The Church is the mystery of Christ continued, into
which one enters by means of an initiation; one penetrates farther into it
by means of the sacramental and liturgical life; it takes shape in a visible
society, with its authority, its members; but that does not exhaust the
whole of it: cf. the Catecheses of St. John Chrysostom and the work of St.
John Damascene, the first to write a comprehensive survey of theology.
The Greek Fathers did not reduce the doctrine of St. Paul on the Mystical Body to the definition of a society where obedience would suffice to
define the attitude of the faithful. It is sad to see the chapter on bishops,
where the exercise of episcopal authority is presented as an irrefutable

---

[79] "In the lowest position, the people of the faithful, so the Church is rightly described as a
pyramid".
[80] "It is affirmed that the Church is a devoted Mother."
[81] * This sentence has been crossed out.

right and nothing more, etc. – 2. The bishops are not first defined by their jurisdiction, but by the mystery of which they are the architects and strategists, as a Greek hymn from the 2nd century says. The body of bishops issues from Christ; the jurisdiction, conferred by the pope, localizes and determines a collegial function that preexists it. This collegial function is exercised in an extraordinary manner in the council, but each bishop is at all times in solidarity with the whole work of salvation entrusted to the Church. It is a grave matter to diminish or attenuate this truth. Eastern theology has never forgotten it. – Conclusion: I suggest that this schema be sent back to a commission that includes some experts in Eastern theology; they are numerous, even among our Latin brothers, to whom we owe so much. Finally, to reassure those who might be troubled, I will say that if we make an appeal to the Eastern Fathers, this is not done out of any local patriotism, but as a means of returning to the sources of the apostolic tradition. We are attached to Peter and his successors; in our regions we have the opportunity to give evidence of this, sometimes with our blood, with love and joy, etc. (Some applause.)

Archbishop Felici announced the results of the votes cast in the course of the session and: "De mandato Praesidis: Cum omnes emendationes prooemii et capitis primi approbatae sint, majoritate longe gravi, placetne Patribus crastina die procedere ad suffragationem, formula statuta, an non ?"[82] (By standing: Placet.)

1st fascicle of amendments:
   9th amendment:
      Votes cast: 2,082   Placet: 2,054   Non: 22   Invalid ballots: 6
   10th amendment:
      Votes cast: 2,078   Placet: 2,037   Non: 37   Invalid ballots: 4
   11th amendment:
      Votes cast: 2,058   Placet: 2,023   Non: 21   Invalid ballots: 4

2nd fascicle of amendments:
   1st amendment:
      Votes cast: 2,037   Placet: 1,916   Non: 115   Invalid ballots: 6
   2nd amendment:
      Votes cast: 2,014   Placet: 1,981   Non: 22   Invalid ballots: 11

---

[82] "From the mandate of the President: as all the amendments to the prooemium and the first chapter have been approved, by a large majority, are the Fathers in favor of proceeding tomorrow to a vote, according to the agreed formula or not?"

Leaving Saint Peter's, meeting with Archbishop Robert Dosseh[83] of Lomé (Togo) near the baptismal fonts. I laid out for him the matter about which Daniel de Coppet[84] had written to me (a Togolese arbitrarily incarcerated, etc.); Archbishop Dosseh promised me to deal with it (he was well acquainted with the whole affair), without offering me much hope. – Next met Fr. Rouquette and Dom Olivier Rousseau, and a Belgian priest, an advocate for the "world of hunger".

At 3 P.M., at the Borgo, six young priests, who are staying at the Procure of Saint-Sulpice, came to talk theology: tradition, the Greek Fathers, Origen, the Supernatural, Teilhard, etc. At 4:30, with two of them, I went on foot to the Biblical Institute. Father Lyonnet already knew about Msgr. Spadafora's response; I told him that another booklet, in response to the one of Cardinal Bea on the historicity of the Gospels, was supposedly already in circulation. Brief conversation with Msgr.? – At the Gregorian, met Fr. D. Mollat. At Saint-Louis des Français, a talk by André Latreille[85] on the dechristianization in France in the 19th century. At 7:20, at the Borgo, a visit from Father C. B. Daly (Belfast; an Irish theologian, peritus), who came to say good-bye; he was saddened by the intervention made this morning by his bishop, Bishop Philbin, an excellent bishop, but not very enlightened; he himself was, in general, delighted over the direction taken by the council. – At 8 P.M., saw Father Pierre Dentin.[86]

Friday, December 7, 1962. – The bishop of Constantine[1] spoke to me yesterday about our Jesuit residence in Constantine and the hope he has in its new superior, Fr. François d'Oncieu.[2] – Have seen Msgr. Felice Pirozzi, apostolic delegate to Madagascar, several times these last

---

[83] Robert Dosseh, born in 1925, Togolese, ordained in 1951. Bishop of Lomé from 1962 to 1992.

[84] Daniel de Coppet (1933–2002), French anthropologist.

[85] André Latreille (1901–1984), professor of modern history at the university of Lyon. He had a regular historical column in the newspaper Le Monde from 1945 to 1972. He was the founder of the journal Cahiers d'histoire and, in 1962, of the Centre interuniversitaire d'histoire religieuse, a historical field to which he had given a strong impetus.

[86] Pierre Dentin (1912–2000), French, ordained in 1936. Superior of the Little Seminary of Amiens beginning in 1955, he became the chaplain of the students of the diocese in 1963. He was particularly interested in ecumenism.

December 7

[1] Paul Pinier (1899–1992), French, ordained in 1922. Bishop of Constantine (Algeria) from 1954 to 1970.

[2] François d'Oncieu, S.J. (1920–2001), French, devoted the main part of his apostolate to Algeria.

few days. (I had made his acquaintance through our friend Paulus Lenz-Médoc[3] when he was at the Paris nunciature.) He would like the council to take an interest in the value of non-Christian religions. He had met with this problem when he was the Holy See's representative to the U.N.; he did not seem to have any very clear ideas on this subject, but he would like me to take an interest in it. – Fr. André Scrima (Romanian Orthodox) talked to me recently about the unsuccessful negotiations regarding the attendance of Greek Orthodox observers. I asked him if any errors had been committed on our side; not exactly, he said, the intentions were perfectly good, but there was a slight lack of psychology and imagination. When, in a delicate matter, a response from the East does not come, there should be no hesitation in writing a second time. And when someone takes a flight to Moscow to ask for observers, it would not be a bad idea to make a courtesy stop in Constantinople, either on the way there or on the way back. The fact is that the secretary of the Secretariat, Msgr. Willebrands, a good, straightforward, intelligent man, has little knowledge of Orthodoxy, and the imagination of this placid Dutchman is not very lively.

In Saint Peter's, the devotions of the bishops. Some were going to confession. Others were saying their office in the transept on the right, or, for still more peace and quiet, in the apse, protected by a barrier. There were those who were making a visit to the Blessed Sacrament, those who were visiting the chapel of Saint Pius X, those who preferred to go down into the crypt; there were the outsiders, like Archbishop Dalmais, who went to pray for a few moments in front of Michelangelo's *Pieta*.

This morning, Friday, the journalists were invited to the Mass. They were in one of the four corner galleries. In passing, I greeted Jean Pélissier, from *La Croix*, and Father Mejía (*Criterio*, Buenos Aires), to whom I gave a copy of Fr. Martelet's work. I gave another one to Father Khalifé. I met Bishop McGrath (Panama), whom I informed of my concern regarding the chapter on Scripture and tradition (chap. I), such as it has been drafted by the subcommission of the mixed commission. He appeared to me to have made up his mind not to accept such a text, bad in every respect, he told me; even if certain features that came from

[3] Paulus Lenz-Médoc (1903–1987), German Catholic intellectual, anti-Nazi, a refugee in Paris and then in Lyon during the Second World War.

the team of Tromp and Parente were deleted, it would be very much inferior to the text of Trent. – Rapid but friendly conversations with a bishop from India and several Africans. Before leaving I also greeted Bishops Maziers, Vial, Jacquot (Gap), Émile Pirolley[4] (Nancy), the coadjutor of Orléans.[5] I thanked Archbishop Gilbert Ramanantoanina, "my" archbishop,[6] who yesterday had had passed on to me the volume he had received, as had many others: *Complotto contro la Chiesa*,[7] by Maurice Pinay (Rome: Tipografia Dario Detti, 1962, 618p.); four parts: 1. Il Motore segreto del Communismo. – 2. L'occulto Potere della Massoneria. – 3. La Sinagoga di Satana. – 4. La "Quinta Colonna" ebrea nel clero;[8] this part is the longest, pp. 263 to 610.

President of the day: Card. Liénart. The pope will recite the Angelus at the microphone, and we will hear an "augustissima oratio"[9] from him. The prefect of pontifical ceremonies gave notice of the procedures and the place for tomorrow's Mass (celebrated at 10 A.M. by Card. Marella) and the ceremony the next day. Tomorrow, Gregorian chants, so that the Fathers will be able to participate (applause). A number of items were going to be distributed: the Ordo agendorum tempore quod inter conclusionem primae periodi concilii oecum et initium secundae intercedit,[10] the booklet containing the conciliar commissions and the periti (the list of the latter, at this point very much expanded), an image of St. Joseph with the new formula of the Canon. This morning the suffragatio[11] on chap. I of the Liturgy will take place, by placet, non placet, placet juxta modum: Archbishop Felici explained the meaning of 3rd third vote (juxta modum) and what it entails; he repeated his explanation twice in Latin, then had it translated into the vernacular languages, "ut intelligentia sit perfectissima".[12] – Card. Liénart then made

---

[4]Émile Pirolley (1898–1971), French, ordained in 1925. Bishop of Nancy from 1957 until his death.

[5]Guy-Marie Riobé (1911–1978), French, ordained in 1935. Coadjutor of Orléans from 1961 to May 1963, then bishop of Orléans until his death. Member of the Commission for the Missions.

[6]Before learning of his nomination as a *peritus*, Father de Lubac was supposed to leave for the council as the personal expert of this Malagasy Jesuit archbishop.

[7]"Plot against the Church".

[8]"1. The Secret Driving Force of Communism. 2. The Occult Power of Masonry. 3. The Synagogue of Satan. 4. The Jewish Fifth Column among the Clergy".

[9]"Prayer of very great nobility".

[10]"Program of what must be done between the conclusion of the first period of the ecumenical council and the start of the second".

[11]"Vote".

[12]"So that understanding would be perfect".

a brief speech: "Gratias ago Deo cum omnibus vobis,[13] etc." Then the interventions:

Emin. Dominus Franciscus Cardinal König. Those who have read the Acts of Vatican I know that, at the end of the first session, which had lasted three months, one of the Fathers exclaimed: "Domine, per totam noctem laboravimus et nihil cepimus" – nihil confecimus. Non est idem pro nobis.[14] Already a number of fruits; colloquiums and important contacts. And yesterday, great joy at the news of the "Mandatum Summi Pontificis";[15] we are very grateful to him for that. It is full of promise. The dangers that some fear are not real. Always, here, there has been "in necessariis unitas". "Etiam in disputando, unum in Domino fuimus,[16] etc."

Card. Joseph Lefebvre (Bourges). "Schema De Ecclesia: opus eximium; auctores valde laudandi sunt. Placet mihi in multis. Attamen, profunda deceptio: nihil dicit de caritate Christi qua totam Ecclesiam vivificat. Vox ipsa caritatis raro invenitur"[17] – exception made for the chapter De laicis. However, St. Paul tells us: "Christus Ecclesiam dilexit,[18] etc." (Numerous texts from Scripture, organized into a homily on charity.)

Bishop Vincent Reyes[19] of Borongan (Philippines). "Omni laude a nobis prosequendam est schema de Ecclesia, licet quaedam animadvertenda sint."[20] Some have reproached it for its military language: but the Church is militant; "Christus est dux, rex; dixit: 'Ego vici mundum'."[21] And Paul: "Qui legitime certaverit, etc." "Acies ordinata", etc. Imperium suum dedit Christus apostolis suis et eorum successoribus quando

---

[13] "I give thanks to God with all of you."

[14] "'Lord, we have worked all night long, but we have caught nothing' [See Lk 5:5], we have done nothing. It is not the same for us."

[15] "Mandate of the Holy Father". [This is in reference to the order of work decided by the pope for the intersession, announced on December 6, 1962.]

[16] "'Unity in necessary things'. Even in disagreements, we were one in the Lord."

[17] "The schema on the Church is an excellent piece of work. The authors should be highly praised. There are many things I like. And yet, one deep disappointment: the schema says nothing on the charity of Christ, through which he vivifies the whole Church. The very word charity itself is rarely found."

[18] "Christ loved the Church" [Eph 5:25].

[19] Vicente P. Reyes (1907–1983), Filipino, ordained in 1932. Bishop of Borongan (Philippines) from 1961 to 1967.

[20] "We should greatly praise the schema on the Church; nevertheless, let a few remarks be permitted to me."

[21] "Christ is the leader, the king; he said: 'I have conquered the world'" [Jn 16:33].

dixit: "Qui vos audit, me audit;[22] etc." (One of my neighbors whispered in my ear: He is a descendant of the Conquistadors!)

Archbishop de Bazelaire of Chambéry. "Schema merito affirmat auctoritatem Ecclesiae. In nostro tempore, ubi crisis est auctoritatis, haec affirmatio est valde necessaria."[23] None of us would want to deny this authority or to diminish it. But the principle is one thing, the exercise of it another. How must authority be exercised in order to have its effect? for it to be accepted willingly? "Nimis dura videtur affirmatio in schemate";[24] it is not adapted to men of our time. "Ecclesia est magistra: nemo est qui de hoc dubitet. Sed in quo sensu? Ad servitium."[25] Two things to consider: "(1) Primo et essentialiter, Ecclesia habet auctoritatem"[26] because she has the responsibility to preach to all men; (2) But also, she must be their teacher. Now, today, many would be ready to hear the authentic voice of Christ and his Church, but ... "Ecclesia non est tantum magistra: est mater."[27] Let her understand the failings of her children, the causes of these failings, of their resistance, etc. Like Christ, she has authority only in order to serve. She must act in such a way that her doctrine is freely and willingly accepted. (A short course on charitable education.)

Bishop Isaac Ghattas,[28] Coptic bishop of Thebes (Egypt). This schema has stirred up in my pastor's soul the following reflections. 1. Desiring to fix the limits of the visible Church, it progressively reduces the Mystical Body of Christ to the Church alone – then to the members submissive to this Church – then to the Roman Church. Now the visible and the invisible cannot be separated. First of all, no separation can be made between the Church Militant and the Church Triumphant; even here below we have been restored to life in Christ through baptism. – 2. The schema seems to forget that, for a number of centuries, the expression "mystical body" designated the Eucharist. That indicates to us the way by which our incorporation in the Church is effected: not by

---

[22] "'Who has competed according to the rules' [2 Tim 2:5], 'an army with banners' [Song 6:3 and 6:9 (6:10 in the NRSV)]. Christ gave his authority to his apostles and their successors when he said: 'He who hears you hears me'" [Lk 10:16].

[23] "The schema rightly affirms the authority of the Church. In our time, marked by a crisis of authority, this affirmation is very necessary."

[24] "The affirmation seems too harsh in the schema."

[25] "The Church is mistress: no one doubts that. But in what sense? For service."

[26] "First and foremost, the Church has authority."

[27] "The Church is not only a teacher, she is a mother."

[28] Isaac Ghattas (1909–1977), Egyptian, ordained in 1932. Coptic bishop of Luxor (ancient Thebes) from 1949 to 1967.

baptism alone, nor by submission to Rome alone. All those who receive in Communion the same Bread and profess (almost) the same faith as we do, how can we completely exclude them from the Mystical Body and put them on the same plane as the pagans who are extra Ecclesiam?[29] So membership in the Church should be considered in a manner that is not univocal, but analogical. – 3. The last part of chap. I: there is no longer anything but the Roman Church alone; it is the last step of this narrowing spirit. Tradition has always spoken of Churches, in the plural: of Rome, of Constantinople, of Alexandria, of Antioch, of Jerusalem ...; even today we talk about the Churches of Africa, of Japan, etc. This traditional formulation has the great merit of taking collegiality into account. The Catholic Church is the union of all these Churches with the Church of Rome. The formula of the schema is not false, but it is too narrow and not traditional. Dogma is a sacred thing; we must not abandon any of it. Now this formula is innovative: we do not have the right to adopt it. – Therefore let the schema be at the very least profoundly revised: let the unity and indivisibility of the Mystical Body, of the three parts of the Church, militant, suffering, triumphant, be stated. Let the idea of membership in the Mystical Body be conceived in an analogical fashion; the desire for precision must not win out over the necessity to preserve all of the doctrine. Finally, let the collegial aspect of the Church be clearly indicated.

Bishop Alfred Ancel, auxiliary of Lyon. "Pluries quasi oppositio facta est sive inter aspectum juridicum et aspectum spiritualem Ecclesiae, sive inter aspectum potestatis et servitii, sive inter aspectum collegialem Ecclesiae et Primatum romanum. Non sufficit dicere oppositionem esse mere apparentem; eam solvere debemus."[30] Now, we cannot reduce [this opposition] by means of pure concepts, "sed tantum per recursum ad Evangelium. – 1. Christus, verus rex transmisit potentiam suam apostolis et eorum successoribus, sed natura hujus regni est spiritualis. Verbum Dei – paupertas – virtus Spiritus sancti (cf. Lercaro: pulcherrime dixit)".[31] Gospel principles apply to ecclesiastical organization. This

---

[29] "Outside of the Church".

[30] "Several times, an opposition has been made, either between the juridical aspect and the spiritual aspect of the Church or between the aspect of authority and that of service or between the collegial aspect of the Church and the Roman primacy. It is not sufficient to say that the opposition is purely superficial; we must resolve it."

[31] "But only through recourse to the Gospel. 1. Christ, true king, passed on his authority to his apostles and their successors, but the nature of this reign is spiritual. The Word of God, poverty, virtue of the Holy Spirit (cf. Lercaro, who spoke in a very beautiful way)".

is not a spiritual exhortation: it is a matter of doctrinal principles. It must therefore be the case that the juridical organization of the Church be entirely subject to her spiritual aim. "Ergo spoliari debet ex omnibus quae sive fidelibus sive infidelibus scandalum praestant. Ita clarum fiat mysterium quod Ecclesia visibilis repraesentat.[32] – 2. On reading the Gospel, we see that there is no opposition between authority and service ... – 3. "Tandem, Evangelium clare nos docet Petrum non esse separatum a collegio apostolorum, sed in ipso collegio Petro primatum donatum esse. – Conclusio. Non solum conveniens, sed omnino necessarium est, quod major pars fiat studio Evangelii Dei."[33] It is not a question of finding there a simple illustration of our theses, "sed debemus tanquam doctrinae fontem illud recipere".[34]

Archbishop Alfred Silva,[35] of Concepción (Chile). He will say little, in order to allow others to speak. I have listened with respect to the criticisms made concerning this schema. Some of them have been very good. The Theological Commission will be able to take account of them. But on the whole, I like the schema. I join in what Cardinals Ruffini, Bacci, Browne have said. The schema is profound. Often, especially on Saturday, it has been criticized under the pretext that our council is pastoral: but the office of pastor is in the first place doctrinal, is it not? etc.

Archbishop Felici announced: "Laetissimum nuntium. Sanctus Pater ipse adveniet in aula concilii."[36] Results of the vote on the Prooemium and chap. I of the Liturgy: Votes cast: 2,118. – Placet: 1,922. – Non: 11. – J. Modum: 180. – Invalid ballots: 5. – "Ergo, caput approbatum."[37] So there is no need for those who voted juxta modum to send in their remarks.

Archbishop Eugène D'Souza Lima of Nagpur (India). There must be an invitation addressed "ad omnes homines".[38] So, another thing.

---

[32] "Therefore, she must be divested of everything that causes scandal to the faithful or to those without faith. In this way, the mystery that the visible Church represents will become clear."

[33] "Finally, the Gospel clearly teaches us that Peter is not separated from the college of apostles but that Peter has received the primacy in this college. Conclusion. It is not only appropriate, it is altogether necessary that a larger part be given to the study of the Gospel of God."

[34] "But we must receive the Gospel as the source of doctrine."

[35] Alfredo Silva Santiago (1894–1975), Chilean, ordained in 1917. Archbishop of Concepción from 1939 to 1963, then titular archbishop. Member of the Commission for Seminaries, Studies, and Catholic Education.

[36] "A very joyous piece of news. The Holy Father himself will come into the council hall."

[37] "So the chapter is approved."

[38] "To all men".

"Cur res tam juridico et scolastico modo proponitur? Oportet ut concrete agamus, pro omnibus fidelibus et iis qui foris sunt."[39] A Father asked: Why should we always keep before our eyes those who are outside? Because that is essential for the Church. Our schema could only confirm so many unbelievers in their false idea of the Church. Let us make charity show forth rather than authority alone. "Nimis partialiter tractatur de auctoritate in Ecclesia. Tractandum est quoque de statu episcoporum. Visio Ecclesiae in schemate est nimis restricta."[40] The authors of these chapters envisage the question as if we were in the 15th or 16th century, in a mind-set that is purely possessive and defensive. "Magnam partem schematis revisioni fundamentali subici debet. Insisto ut, in hac revisione, vox episcoporum in missionibus degentium non remaneat vox clamantis in deserto."[41]

Bishop Hermann Volk of Mainz. Everyone was expecting from us an exposition of the Church that would have a biblical fullness. Now the biblical foundation of the schema is slender; it should have a broader scope. Everything is deduced from the sole image of the body, and even that image is limited. It needs to be completed by recourse to other images: in the first place, that of the People of God. Certain oversights, or certain artificial additions, can be understood on the basis of this overly narrow foundation. The Church, considered in her end, is the "communitas redemptorum in gratia Christi. Ecclesia est et sacramentum et res sacramenti."[42] Greater simplicity has been requested: yes, "sed non sit simplicitas falsa",[43] which would omit essential elements. "Solum totum est vere simplex."[44] Everything must be said analogically. The entire truth cannot be expressed in a single sentence or by using a single image. The various images must complete and interpret each other. "Et cur vox 'ministerium', quae est evangelica, tam raro invenitur?

---

[39] "Why is the matter presented in so legalistic and scholastic a fashion? We must act in a concrete manner, for all the faithful and for those who are outside."

[40] "Authority in the Church is treated in too partial a manner. It is also necessary to deal with the status of the bishops. The vision of the Church in the schema is too restrictive."

[41] "A large part of the schema must be submitted to a fundamental revision. I insist that in this revision, the voice of bishops in the mission countries not remain the voice of one crying out in the wilderness."

[42] "Community of those redeemed in the grace of Christ. The Church is at the same time both sign and reality." [It is a matter here of distinguishing in the sacrament the sign (*sacramentum*) from the reality (*res sacramenti*).]

[43] "But let it not be a false simplicity".

[44] "Only the whole is truly simple."

E contra",[45] in a few lines, the word "subjici"[46] is found eleven times. The doctrine that the council intends to declare, to be authentic, must be put forward as the "bonum nuntium";[47] otherwise it will be neither pastoral nor truly doctrinal; the two things must not be separated. It is not at all a question here of concessions: quite the contrary. Let the doctrine embrace "totam realitatem ..."[48] – It would not be sufficient to correct the schema. The whole thing needs to be rewritten.

The Most Rev. Dom Christopher Butler, O.S.B., superior general of the Benedictine Congregation of England. – "Certe, summa cautela procedendum est in rebus dogmaticis. Spero nos nullum novum dogma definituros esse."[49] But we must declare what is common doctrine in the Church. "Etiamsi nihil definimus, sed tantum declaramus vel damnamus, sciamus magnam responsabilitatem nos assumpturos esse. Qualis est causa, cur tam multae objectiones allatae contra hoc schema, ac tam graves et profundae, ut requiratur vere novum aliquod schema? Illi qui tales objectiones movent, sunt homines sanae mentis et sanae orthodoxiae. Quis ex illis negat solam Ecclesiam, vel primatum Romani Pontificis, etc.? Sed, in nostro saeculo, theologia de Ecclesia aliquo modo renascitur."[50] We must have prudence, as at Trent. But who does not see that, today, renovation extends to all parts of theology? Here we have an effect of the Holy Spirit, it is a sign of the Church's life. It is the answer that the Word of God brings to our new circumstances. There is, in human terms, "aliquis progressus in novam visionem mundi historicam; omnino inconveniens esset",[51] if the Church does not succeed in Christianizing it. – In all matters theological, "opinionem meam humiliter commendare vellem: primo, teneamus, tuti, res definitas, fideliter illis adhaereamus. Postea, simus in laeta et generosa gratitudine

---

[45] "And why is the word 'ministry', which is evangelical, so rarely found? On the contrary".

[46] "Submissive".

[47] "Good news".

[48] "All of reality".

[49] "Assuredly, we must proceed with the greatest prudence in dogmatic matters. I hope that we will not define any new dogmas."

[50] "Even if we define nothing, but content ourselves with declaring or condemning, let us be aware that we will be assuming a great responsibility. Why are so many objections being brought against this schema, and such serious and profound objections, that a veritable new schema is demanded? Those who are raising these objections are men of good sense and sound orthodoxy. Who among them would deny [that the Church founded by Christ is the one and only sacramental communion] or the primacy of the Roman Pontiff, etc.? But, in our century, the theology on the Church has experienced, in a certain way, a renaissance."

[51] "A certain progress into a new historical vision of the world. It would be altogether improper".

pro renascentia theologiae in diebus nostris."[52] Let us think also that no previous council has been in our situation. We have to say to the entire world "aliquid positivum".[53] What are we to say to it, if not what the necessities of today require, that is to say, "ostendere semper salutem mundi in Christo Jesu? Missio doctrinalis Ecclesiae non est nisi Bonum Nuntium afferre",[54] with everything that this explicite and implicite[55] involves. Let us have before our eyes the world, to which we have to give a new vision of Christ our Savior. In this way the Church will truly be the humble servant of the Savior.

Dom Butler's intervention was the last. All the Fathers were requested to remain in their seats. It was five minutes to noon. Soon the Holy Father arrived by way of the left transept. The members of the Board of Presidency moved their chairs, on the left and the right. Having arrived at his throne against the high altar, John XXIII recited the Angelus, with the three Gloria Patri and the prayers customary in Rome. Then he sat down, took out his glasses and read a short speech. He was applauded, he departed, and we left the basilica.

54 speakers, Archbishop Felici said, were still registered for the general discussion of De Ecclesia, which we were not able to continue any longer; among them, Bishop Joseph Tawil (Syria) and Bishop Véniat.

According to Fr. Tucci, there is some friction between the Board of Presidency and the Secretariat for Extraordinary Affairs,[56] presided over by Card. Cicognani, whose members are Cardinals Confalonieri, Montini, Siri, Döpfner, Wyszyński, Meyer, and Suenens, with Archbishop Felici as secretary. The malcontents on the Board say that the Secretariat (which they call the "Politburo") reserves the principal decisions to itself and lets itself be guided by "diplomatic" views. Apparently, Cardinal Tisserant is also complaining about this duality for other reasons.

---

[52] "I would like humbly to offer my opinion: first, that we hold as certain the things that have been defined, let us adhere to them faithfully. Next, let us be joyful and show a generous gratitude for the rebirth of theology in our days."

[53] "Something positive".

[54] "Always to show the salvation of the world in Jesus Christ? The doctrinal mission of the Church is nothing other than to bring the Good News."

[55] "Explicitly and implicitly".

[56] The function of the Secretariat for Extraordinary Affairs, named in September 1962, was to study the proposals of the Fathers, while the Board of Presidency was charged with directing the discussions, up until the creation of moderators at the beginning of the second session. This Secretariat was eliminated at the beginning of the second session.

A new pamphlet, unsigned, dated November 1962, has just been distributed. Archbishop Sartre received a copy: "De quibusdam periculis in statu hodierno exegeos catholicae."[57] The author says that he will not cite any names, "ut attente vitemus quidquid polemicam sapit".[58] It is not a matter of simple discussions among specialists, he says, but of opinions that are spreading everywhere. "Tempore quo Pius XII f. r. mirabilem encyclicam *Divino afflante Spiritu* Ecclesiae dedit, fuerunt qui festinanter affirmarent jam exegetos nostros 'liberos' esse ut ingrederentur aperte viam criticae historico-litterariae ad Libros sanctos moderna ratione interpretandos. Brevi tamen tempore factum est ut abusus irrepserint, nam, post septem annos, ipse Pius XII in encycl. *Humani generis* debuit audaces monere,[59] etc." – "Collectio aliqua biblica 'catholica' recentissime edidit *separatim* 'Codicem sacerdotalem' Geneseos et Exodi: audacia inusitata etiam apud non catholicos."[60] – A summary of the "Formgeschichtlich"[61] method, etc. – Errors concerning the ignorance of the Son of Man, on the progressive messianic awareness of Jesus, on inerrancy, etc. – The tone of these pages is relatively moderate. The author makes clear that he only intends to challenge abuses: abuses that are serious, numerous, and widespread enough for it to be necessary for the council to establish norms for Catholic exegesis.

This afternoon, at 3 P.M., visit from Mr. Blanchard, sent by the French government to our embassy at the Vatican for the duration of the council. He has questioned various people; he had me speak, which I did without any reticence, explaining to him the theological positions, on which he had very little information. He asked me about Cardinal Montini; I get the sense that he is anxious to inform the French Foreign Office on the *papabili*.

---

[57] "On certain dangers in the current state of Catholic exegesis".

[58] "In order to avoid carefully anything polemical".

[59] "At the time when Pius XII, of blessed memory, gave the Church the admirable encyclical *Divino afflante spiritu*, there were some who quickly asserted that our exegetes were now 'free' to engage openly on the path of historico-literary criticism for interpreting the Holy Books according to modern reason. In a short time, however, abuses crept in, and, in fact, after seven years Pius XII himself had to warn those who were overly bold, in the encyclical *Humani generis*."

[60] "A 'Catholic' biblical series has very recently published *separately* the 'Priestly Code' of the Books of Genesis and Exodus: this is an audacity that is not the current practice, even among non-Catholics." [The book in question is: J. Steinmann, ed., *Code sacerdotal I: Genèse, Exode*, Connaître la Bible (Paris: Desclée de Brouwer, 1962). The Priestly Code is one of the sources of the Pentateuch. On February 14, 1962, Jean Steinmann (1911–1963), French, ordained in 1937, a vicar in Paris, was forbidden by the Holy Office to publish anything new on biblical matters.]

[61] Critical study of forms. This way of doing exegesis focuses closely on the literary genres in the Scriptures.

A journalist, Catholic, she told me, besieged me on the telephone, trying to obtain an interview; I answered that I did not have a spare minute before my departure and only expressed my hopes to her in a single sentence.

Msgr. Gouet, Secretary of the French Episcopate, has just sent a circular letter to the "experts" – no doubt following the complaint expressed the day before yesterday by Bishop Schmitt. He asked the experts to collaborate with the bishops. That seems like a joke: the letter was received on returning from the 36th and last general congregation, on the eve of my departure from Rome. It is true that our bishops say that they want to work in the interval between the two sessions. But it is really up to them to ask the periti for their collaboration, if they so wish.

At 6 P.M., at the Saint Gregory monastery, at the base of the Caelian hill, a lecture to the Swiss ecclesiastical students and the young monks of the monastery. Among other things, they asked me about Teilhard. One of them, Fr. Luigi Clerici, a priest, who had been a missionary to Japan and was preparing to become a professor of theology at the scholasticate of his congregation, drove me to the Palazzo Baldassini (via delle Copelle), where Jean Guitton was giving a talk on the council in front of the guests of the Circolo di Roma.[62] Shortly before the end, a young priest came to get me and drove me to the Venerable English College (via Monserato, near the Palazzo Farnese). We arrived there for dinner. I greeted Cardinal Godfrey and several bishops; the rector,[63] Msgr. ..., still rather young, gave me a quick tour of the premises; then we went up to the third floor. There the "literary society" of the ecclesiastical students received me. A short speech by its president, in French. I spoke in French: about the place of the Church in our faith; then (requested subject) about Teilhard. An expression of thanks, also in French, by another student. A charming reception. The rector drove me back in his car.

Fr. Martelet took care of getting my ticket for our departure. He brought me a copy of a note consisting of five densely printed pages: "The Sanctity of the Laity and the Mystery of the Church: Remarks on the Schema *De Ecclesia*, Rome, Dec. 2–6, 1962." – Fr. Daniélou attended the meeting of the mixed commission for the revision of the *De fontibus* this evening. A stormy, even dramatic meeting. Since yesterday, Fr. Rahner has been present as a peritus. They were discussing

---

[62] Circle founded in 1950, bringing together the *establishment* of the Holy See and seeking to promote international meetings and studies.

[63] Gerard Tickle.

the first chapter, drafted by subcommission no. 1.[64] Fr. Tromp laid out
its doctrine and wanted to get his wording on the truths that are not
in Scripture admitted, "praesertim"[65] the inspiration and the canon of
the Scriptures. The floor was given to Fr. Rahner, who came up to the
microphone, stood there, right next to Tromp, and expressed his point
of view. Tromp replied, insisted, supported by Ottaviani. Rahner then
asked: Do you mean to affirm that inspiration and the canon are the only
truths that Scripture does not contain, or do you intend to affirm that
there are others? In the first case, I accept your formula; in the second,
I reject it. Various interventions followed, a little confused. Fr. Feiner,
peritus designated by the Secretariat for Unity at the 1st subcommission,
kept quiet. Card. Bea ended by accepting Tromp's formula, without
seeming to see very well what it was about and so won over the votes
(or at least a certain number of them) of his Secretariat. They moved
to the vote: a majority for Tromp. Ottaviani declared that the text was
adopted. It was at that point that Bishop Charue (I think)[66] protested: in
a matter this serious, a simple majority was not sufficient. Various incidents, which I forget. Protests from Card. Léger. Ottaviani then said that
he consented to constituting a select subcommission, the presidency of
which he would entrust to Card. Browne. Card. Bea stayed out of the
matter. Then Card. Frings asked for the floor: the president (Ottaviani),
he declared, did not have the right to constitute a subcommission in that
way, as he pleases; if there is an insoluble conflict here, it will be referred
to the new commission instituted by the Holy Father, etc. Just at the
moment when they were going to leave, Bishop De Smedt (Bruges) got
up and requested the floor; for ten minutes, he protested against a letter
that he had recently received, as had all the members and periti of the
commission: a letter of denunciation, addressed to the Holy Father, that
Card. Ottaviani had had signed by some fifteen cardinals, which Card.
Cicognani had handed to him [Bishop De Smedt] with a banal note
and copies of which he had officially given to the whole commission.[67]
Five exegetes were denounced in it, including Fr. Dubarle, O.P.,[68] and

---

[64] "On the twofold source of Revelation".

[65] "Especially".

[66] In fact it was Cardinal Frings, cf. G. Alberigo, *Histoire du Concile*, 2: 417–20.

[67] This letter, dated November 24, was signed by nineteen cardinals. It judged it necessary that
the council "affirm at least certain doctrinal principles in order to guarantee the Catholic faith
against errors and deviations that have appeared almost everywhere." See *AS*, VI, 1, p. 303.

[68] André-Marie Dubarle, O.P. (1910–2002), French, ordained in 1934. Professor of exegesis at
the Dominican monastery of Le Saulchoir in Étiolles.

a priest from Bruges[69] writing under the imprimatur of Malines. Card. Ottaviani defended himself, said that all that was very legitimate, etc. They ended by dispersing.

The Jesuit provincial from Venezuela[70] came to speak to me; he thanked me for my books. – The other day, speaking at the Capranica about tradition, he was accused of heresy by one of the members of his audience.

Saturday, December 8, 1962. – At 9:15 A.M., left for Saint Peter's with Frs. Rondet and Grillmeier. The latter told us about last night's meeting of the mixed commission; he knew about it from Fr. Rahner. After winning the timid support of Bea, Ottaviani had obtained 19 votes against 16. It appears that Frings has decided to appeal this to the pope, perhaps as early as today.

At the peritis' gallery, I was beside the parish priest of Saint Vincent's Church in Lyon,[1] a friend of Archbishop Villot, who had just arrived in Rome. Chatted a moment with Fr. Balić, who was friendly and asked me to send him my remarks on the collected work that he had just edited (*De Mariologia et œcumenismo*).[2] Mass said by Card. Marella, sacristan of the basilica, with Gregorian chant; all the bishops sang. After Mass, the pope arrived with a small retinue by way of the left transept, took his seat on the throne, put on his glasses, and read a rather long speech in Latin. Three main points: the start of the council (up until now) – its continuation – the hoped-for fruits. When he entered, the "Tu es Petrus" was sung. – As we went out, we took leave of one another, whomever we chanced to encounter. A friendly wave from Bishop P. Philippe, O.P. A warm "good-bye" from Bishop Mbuka-Nzundu, etc.

Fr. Martelet saw Card. Liénart this morning before Mass. The latter told him about the hopelessly tangled situation at the mixed commission. – I encountered the former priest Boulier,[3] very happy about the

---

[69] Frans Nierynck, born in 1927, Belgian. Professor at the major seminary of Bruges, then at the Catholic university of Louvain. Specialist in New Testament exegesis.

[70] Víctor Iriarte, S.J.

December 8

[1] Jacques des Horts (1900–1976), French, parish priest of Our Lady of St. Vincent (Notre-Dame-de-Saint-Vincent) from 1956 to 1969.

[2] *De Mariologia et oecumenismo*, preface by C. Balić (Rome: International Pontifical Marian Academy, 1962).

[3] Jean Boulier (1894–1980), French, ordained in 1924 for the Society of Jesus, which he left in 1932. He was then incardinated in the diocese of Paris, but was reduced to the lay state by a decree of the Holy Office dated February 14, 1952, before being reinstated to the priesthood in 1971. Founder of the movement of the Fighters for Peace and Liberty.

council; he saw Card. Suenens, to whom he had given a draft document on the problem of peace. – Saw Father Paul Gauthier again, the man behind Card. Lercaro's intervention on the poor. I fear there is a certain lack of realism with him and a certain opportunism with some (not the majority) of those who are promoting this line of thinking. – Last night, at the English College, the rector showed me the gallery of portraits of the English cardinals; a rather fine portrait of Newman[4] that I do not believe I have ever seen reproduced. In a sitting room, a portrait of Msgr. Talbot, with the coarse and fleshy face of a self-satisfied man; I reminded the rector of what Talbot[5] said when he learned of the publication of the *Apologia*:[6] "We had succeeded in making him keep quiet, and now here he is starting up again!" – I answered Gouet's circular letter, saying that I would be at the bishops' disposal as much as possible. – I was told that a recent article in *L'Osservatore Romano* criticized Fr. Congar for having failed to keep secrecy regarding council affairs in one of his articles for the *Informations catholiques internationales*.[7]

Concerning the first session of the council and Liénart's intervention. To someone of our group who congratulated him, the cardinal replied: "I am like a jay dressed up in peacock feathers"; he had read a text, which was still only a rough draft, which was not by him (perhaps by Archbishop Garrone), which he had among other papers and which he suddenly had the idea of using, seeing that everyone was keeping quiet and that people were beginning to fill out their ballot sheets. – They tell me that Card. Liénart will be a member of the new higher commission[8] instituted by the Holy Father; without doubt Archbishop Villot as well.

At 12:30, I was received by Father General. He had summoned me to tell me that, given the situation, the increased attacks against the Biblical

---

[4] John Henry Newman (1801–1890), English. An Anglican priest, he personified the Oxford Movement. He converted to Catholicism in 1845 and was created cardinal in 1879 (He was beatified in 2010 – TRANS.) He is the author of an important and many-sided body of work: literary, historical, philosophical, theological.

[5] George Talbot (1816–1886), an Anglican who converted to Catholicism in 1842. Chamberlain of Pius IX, rector of the English College, he was a tenacious opponent of Newman until he was institutionalized in a mental hospital.

[6] J. H. Newman, *Apologia pro vita sua, Being a Reply to a Pamphlet Entitled "What, Then, Does Dr. Newman Mean"* (London: Longman, 1864).

[7] Father Congar, in his *Journal*, does not mention any such article.

[8] This refers to the Coordinating Commission, announced on December 6, charged with eliminating repetitions, shortening and bringing together schemas dealing with the same subject. Its composition was made public on December 14. A. Liénart was a member, and J. Villot attended the meetings as under-secretary of the council but was not a member.

Institute, it would perhaps not be a good idea for me to give a lecture there in January; for he knows as well that my presence in Rome is not well tolerated by the same party: "those Gentlemen", as he said to me, talking to me about the personnel of the Holy Office and indicating to me with his hand, beyond his window, the direction of their Palazzo. A very cordial conversation.

At 9 P.M.: Termini station, with Fr. Martelet. Fr. Rondet accompanied us; he is not leaving Rome until tomorrow evening. – In our couchette compartment on the train was Bishop Sauvage,[9] from Lille, the new bishop of Annecy, a former student at the Biblical Institute. He seemed determined to work hard in the coming months to prepare for the next session.

In Lyon, gave some news about the council to Fourvière, Saint Helen's College, and to the Carmelites. – On returning to Toulouse, Fr. Labourdette told Fr. Nicolas,[10] who repeated it to Msgr. de Solages: "It was an earthquake." – An article by Robert Havard de la Montagne[11] in *Aspects de la France*, December 13, 1962, was passed on to me, in which the author expressed his indignation over the fact that I had given a talk in Rome on Teilhard. – Archbishop Garrone sent from Toulouse, around December 16, a bulletin to all the French bishops, suggesting to them some practical working arrangements; I had a confidential communication on this from Fr. de Baciocchi, S.M.; his colleague Bishop Darmancier had let him read the bulletin. After his telephone interventions with Father Denis[12] (at the major seminary in Lyon) and Fr. de Baciocchi (superior of the Marist scholasticate), Fr. Martelet learned that the work was being organized among the bishops of the region; neither he nor I have been invited to participate.

On December 13, Dom Jean Leclercq, O.S.B., spoke on Italian radio after Brothers Schutz and Thurian and Bishop Suhr. He said that "the ecumenical councils of the Middle Ages had carried on an activity that was doctrinal but not dogmatic, that is to say, without definitions accompanied by condemnations. This was due neither to a lack of theologians nor to a lack of disputed or erroneous opinions (Averroism!), but to the

---

[9] Jean Sauvage (1908–1991), French, ordained in 1934. Named bishop of Annecy in September 1962, he continued in this office until 1983.

[10] Marie Joseph Nicolas, O.P. (1906–1999), French, ordained in 1932. Theologian, former provincial of the Province of Toulouse.

[11] Robert Havard de la Montagne (1877–1963), French novelist, historian, and journalist.

[12] Henri Denis.

desire to leave to the theologians the tasks that fall within their proper competence, even if it meant monitoring them in case of necessity ..."

The American weekly magazine *Time* of December 14, in its "Religion" column, has an article devoted to Fr. Karl Rahner, with a photo: "A Holy Boldness". For many, it says, the most vital location of the council was not Saint Peter's, but a room on the 4th floor of the German College, occupied by Fr. Rahner, regarded as the most profound theologian of today. The article is rather well researched.

To Dr. Denys Gorce, who had sent me the article from *Aspects de la France*: "Thank you for sending me this article, which I found most amusing. If ever one of your friends should wish some clarification on this lecture, you could tell him that I learned that I was to give it by learning that it had already been authorized, with great satisfaction, by the Secretariat of State (Archbishop Dell'Acqua); that it was presided over by Bishop Pierre Van Lierde, Ordinary of Vatican City, who took it upon himself to make some concluding remarks; that my judgments on Fr. Teilhard and his work were warmly approved by my superior general, better placed than anyone to know the opinion of the Holy Father. As for the article in *L'Osservatore* that Mr. Havard de la Montagne mentions, its author (?), who is my friend (Philippe de la Trinité), himself acknowledged to me my right to have an opinion different from his. What I found best in the article you sent me is the allusion at the end to "busybodies": a rather just comparison that I myself have often employed, in the course of these last two months, about myself."

December 30, at Fourvière, visit from Mother Jean-Paul, superior of the Dominican sisters (Veritas School, Lyon). A few days before the council, she told me, Fr. Gagnebet had written in France that everything was ready, that the council would not last long, that all the prepared texts would be approved without difficulty. She spoke to me about Bishop Philippe, O.P., who espoused the thesis of the Curia in opposition to the council; he had supposedly spoken in rather harsh terms of the "maneuver" of some men who pushed Cardinal Liénart to intervene at the beginning: a scandalous intervention, an unacceptable sign of distrust toward the Curia. In Rome, the superior general of the Dominicans invited one after another the cardinals and bishops who have houses of his Order in their diocese. The first one invited was Card. Tisserant, as dean of the Sacred College: at table, he proved to be rather harsh toward certain things concerning the Curia; almost the same was true each time with the other guests. Bishop Philippe, present each time, took this rather badly. At the last meal, the matter took a tragic turn. It was Cardinal Léger's turn, accompanied by bishops from several countries. The cardinal, encouraged by the bishops, was severe; then Bishop Philippe stood up, exclaimed his indignation, declared that he would not stay one minute longer at that table. Cardinal Léger then apparently burst out laughing, and the bishops joined in — all of this under the astounded eye of the Mother General.

1963: Between the Two Sessions of the Council

January 8, 1963. – Arrived in Rome (for the Religious Philosophy Congress organized by Enrico Castelli). I am staying at the Biblical Institute. At table, Fr. Vogt, the rector, talked to me about the address to the pope signed by 19 cardinals: the Biblical Institute has written a Note expressing the opposite opinion, distributed to several other cardinals.

January 9. – Father Alonso-Schökel spoke to me about Fr. Salaverri, who was his professor, with whom he had a long conversation here in December, etc. He also spoke to me about the keynote speech given by Archbishop Parente at the week-long conference at the Lateran in 1960 on the councils: this text, he said to me, contains the whole theory behind the current practice of his circle, and this text is heterodox. It was Father J. Alfaro (Gregorian) who drafted the intervention made by the coadjutor bishop of Barcelona.[1]

January 10. – First day of the Castelli Congress, at the University of Rome. Talks by Ricœur,[1] de Waehlens,[2] etc. A Franciscan from the Antonianum, a philosopher and friend of Castelli, told me that several of his confreres (Balić, Lio, Kerrigan, and even the rector, Damien Van den Eynde) are worried about what emerged at the council; they believe that the Church has set out on a path of "progress" that is dubious and dangerous. – Fr. Lentzen-Deis,[3] who is studying at the Biblical Institute, told me that the Germans are full of optimism and determination with regard to the future of the council. An American priest of the Institute told me that at the end of the session a few bishops from his country held a press conference here; the archbishop of San Francisco,[4] known for his arch-conservatism, apparently declared there that, although at

---

January 9

[1] This must be N. Jubany Arnau, auxiliary of Barcelona, who made an intervention on December 3.

January 10

[1] Paul Ricœur (1913–2005), professor of philosophy at the Faculty of Letters of Paris, one of the greatest French philosophers of the twentieth century.

[2] Alphonse de Waehlens (1911–1981), Belgian, professor of philosophy at the Catholic University of Louvain.

[3] Fritzleo Lentzen Deis, S.J. (1928–1993), German, ordained in 1960.

[4] Joseph McGucken (1902–1983), American, ordained in 1928. Archbishop of San Francisco from February 1962 to 1977.

first having a favorable impression of the schema *De fontibus*, he had completely changed his mind after hearing the criticisms made against it.

January 11, 1963. – This morning, at the Castelli Congress, a talk by Henri Gouhier:[1] tradition and development in the modernist crisis. This afternoon, at the Istituto storico italiano del Medio Evo;[2] about twelve of us gathered around a table; I gave an exposition on the Christian humanists and their historians (the exegesis of Lefèvre d'Étaples, G. Budé and the four senses, etc.). Objections, questions, a pleasant atmosphere. Then they got me to talk about the council. Some of them seem to fear a danger of nationalism on the part of the bishops' conferences. A curious mixture of open-mindedness, even liberalism, and a certain unconscious Italian bias.

The *New Yorker* (USA) published a long "Letter from Vatican City",[3] dated December 9, 1962, on the council: 22 columns. Praise for John XXIII. Importance of his aggiornamento. Account of the council. Naming of the "prophets of doom" criticized in the inaugural address: Ottaviani, Siri, Ruffini, Dante, Felici, Parente, Pietro Palazzini[4] (from the Congregation of the Council). – Patriarch Maximos. – The theme of a return to simplicity. – The complaints against the use of Latin; it was supposedly Felici who, despite the pope's desire, had refused to have simultaneous translation. – The schema on the Liturgy and the use of Latin: criticized by Dante and by Vagnozzi (Apostolic Delegate to the United States), who asked that it be submitted to Ottaviani's commission. – In front of a group of nuncios and apostolic delegates, Vagnozzi is reported to have pleaded with them to "save the Curia" from the machinations of the reformers. – The long discussions on the liturgy. – Ottaviani's vehement intervention: Alfrink stopped him, he continued to speak, then the power to his microphone was cut off, with the resulting applause. – The "Bar Jonah": it was the pope who apparently had the idea for a bar. The bishops meet there

---

January 11

[1] Henri Gouhier (1898–1994), French, professor of the history of religious thought at the Sorbonne. Elected in 1961 as a member of the Academy of Moral and Political Sciences.

[2] "Italian Historical Institute of the Middle Ages".

[3] This refers to the chronicles on the council by Xavier Rynne, alias Francis X. Murphy.

[4] Pietro Palazzini (1912–2000), Italian, ordained in 1934. Secretary of the Congregation of the Council from 1958 to 1969. Created cardinal in 1973, prefect of the Congregation for the Causes of Saints from 1980 to 1988. Member of the Commission for the Discipline of the Clergy and the Christian People.

with the observers. – The observers-delegates: their satisfaction. – Cullmann. – The two Russian delegates, who arrived October 12. – The protest made by the expatriate Ukrainian bishops: the secretary of state persuaded them not to make it public, but one of them passed it on to the press; Msgr. Willebrands' reply. – November 14, discussion of the schema *De fontibus* commenced. The 5 chapters; the question of the two sources; Fr. Congar's position. Frings and Liénart against the schema; Ruffini counter-attacked them. The argument about the pope's authority taken up again by Ottaviani; the text of the council rules was then read out: ". . . to be accepted, amended, or rejected" – Siri, Quiroga y Palacios, McIntyre supported the schema; Léger, König, Alfrink attacked it; Suenens also, who criticized the slowness of the debates and expressed his wish that the council would turn to the problems of the day. – A lengthy intervention, unexpected, by Ritter: "Rejiciendum est!"[5] This schema is "old-fashioned, ambiguous, pessimistic, negative, calculated to inspire a servile fear rather than love for the Bible". That had the effect of a bomb. – But the most important intervention was Bea's: everyone understood that although Bea was the one speaking, the sentiments expressed were those of John XXIII. – etc. (Accurate information, but anecdotal, and of a Manichean tendency, without anything on the actual heart of the matter.)

January 12, 1963. – Father Tucci (*Civiltà cattolica*) told me that the pope was already ill to the point of death in October 1961, much as in November 1962; the doctors fear a third crisis. Tucci is somewhat pleased with the composition of the Coordinating Commission, to which the pope is said to have given rather precise instructions. For the schema *De fontibus*, in the process of being revised, Ottaviani insisted to Cicognani that the majority vote in the mixed commission (19 votes against 16) should be definitive;[1] Cicognani refused, saying that this would be contrary to the rule that requires a two-thirds majority. Then Ottaviani asked that his

---

[5] "It should be rejected!"

January 12

[1] Recall that this formula, put to a vote on December 7, 1962, stipulated that "certain revealed truths, especially those that refer to the inspiration of various books, to their canonicity, and to their integrity, are only known and only become clear thanks to tradition." This concerns the delicate question of the connection between Scripture and tradition and of whether tradition supplies truths of law not contained in Scripture.

request be transmitted to the pope; Cicognani answered that he could not do that, it was contrary to the will of the Holy Father. It is also said that the pope gave Cicognani instructions that they keep to the subjects taken up at Trent and Vatican I. Tucci also spoke to me about the affair of the Dutch Jesuit who rose up against the Holy Office, a matter that in the course of the last month has taken on a greater scope.[2]

This morning, at the Castelli Congress, I talked about the Christian humanists of the 15th–16th centuries and the hermeneutic tradition. Then we listened to Fr. G. Fessard on the 13th rule of orthodoxy of Saint Ignatius.[3] – Lunch at the small residence of the university chaplains. Father Panikkar came with me. There were seven of us: everyone spoke or understood French; the superior: Fr. Parisi.[4]

The continuation of Xavier Rynne's article in the *New Yorker*. It was becoming evident that the majority was against the schema *De fontibus*; sending it back to the commission would not break the deadlock. Then Cardinal Rugambwa proposed that the pope be asked to postpone the discussion until the following session. The archbishop of Durban, D. E. Hurley, noted that the problem was the result of the fact that the preparatory commission had not followed the wishes of the bishops. Bishop Ancel observed that a vote one way or the other would not obtain the required two-thirds of the votes, and therefore it was necessary to appeal to the pope. On November 20, on the order of the pope (?), Felici announced that there would be a vote: "placet" to halt the discussion, "non placet" to continue it. There were 1,368 placet, 822 non placet; the

---

[2] Jan van Kilsdonk, S.J., Dutch, born in 1945. This matter started in September 1962, when Father van Kilsdonk accused the Roman Curia of "spiritual terror" and gave as an example the Monitum published following Father de Lubac's book on Teilhard. He then pleaded for a "loyal opposition". The Holy Office asked for Father van Kilsdonk's resignation as chaplain of the students of Amsterdam. After discussions between the Holy Office and Bishop van Dodewaard of Haarlem, it was decided, in January 1963, that the appropriate measures should be taken by the bishop, who decided to support Father van Kilsdonk.

[3] The eighteen rules of orthodoxy of Saint Ignatius of Loyola intend to answer this question: How can we be assured of having the thoughts and feelings of a true Catholic, agreeing in all things with the Church? The thirteenth rule specifies: "To keep right in all things, I must always be ready, faced with what I see as white, to believe that it is black, if the hierarchical Church so determines. For we believe that between Christ our Lord, who is the Bridegroom, and the Church his Bride there is one and the same Spirit who governs and directs us for the good of our souls. Indeed, it is this same Spirit and Lord who gave us the Ten Commandments who guides and governs our Holy Mother Church." For a better understanding of these rules, one can consult G. Fessard, *La Dialectique des Exercices spirituels de saint Ignace de Loyola*, 3 vols. (Aubier-Lethielleux, 1956–1978).

[4] Pio Parisi, S.J., born in 1926, Italian, ordained in 1956. Chaplain of the La Sapienza university in Rome.

needed two-thirds being 1,473. Felici announced that they would continue. Some said that the strangeness of the wording caused confusion,
and some Fathers mixed up the two votes: Ottaviani reportedly voted
"placet"! (?) The following morning, with Ruffini as president, another
dramatic announcement: the pope ordered that the schema be withdrawn and reconsidered by a mixed commission, with Bea and Ottaviani
as presidents. The "liberals" are Cardinals Frings, Liénart, Meyer; the
"traditionalists", Browne, Ruffini; in the center: J. Lefebvre. L'Osservatore Romano, which from the beginning of the council reflected the line
taken by the Curia, delayed as long as possible the announcement of
these facts. – Many wondered how a man as intelligent as Ottaviani could
have miscalculated so badly. For several years one could see the formation of a powerful party desiring a reform, and it was clear that this party
had the favor of the pope. Ottaviani must have been badly informed by
his sources: Archbishop Parente, Father Ermenegildo Lio, and the two
Americans, Msgr. Joseph Fenton (Catholic University of Washington)
and Msgr. Rudolph Bandas[5] (St. Paul, Minnesota). These men were
telling him that only a small group of French and German extremists
wanted important changes in the Church. The men who prepared this
schema with them (Tromp, Hürth, Alvarez, O.P., Ciappi, O.P., Balić,
O.F.M.) could conceive of no other way to present the Catholic faith
than by the repetition of past formulas and the condemnation of anything new. – The major fact of this session was without any doubt the
great force shown by the advocates of a renewal. That was not foreseen.
Their principal supporter in the Curia was Cardinal Bea, who before
these last two years had not shown anything extraordinary. "All my life
has been a preparation for this", he declared. The role of his Secretariat.
It collaborated with Ottaviani: this is the first time that a doctrinal matter
has been examined in this way; up until now, everything was reserved to
the Holy Office. – The BEA sign of British European Airways, everywhere in Rome; the Italians say that now a notice has been put up on
the door of the Holy Office: "Travel with BEA". – The importance
of the gathering in Rome of so many theologians. Their conferences
with the bishops. The Holy Office became alarmed: toward the middle
of November, Ottaviani asked the pope to forbid these conferences to
the Jesuits at the Biblical Institute and to drive Karl Rahner from Rome;

---

[5] Rudolph George Bandas (1896–1969), American. Theologian, priest of Saint Agnes parish in
Saint Paul (Minnesota). Expert at the council.

the pope answered that he did not want to violate the rights of the bishops; he took advantage of the opportunity to show Ottaviani the testimony of three cardinals in favor of Rahner. It is also known that the pope had the Dominican Spiazzi[6] recalled from exile and named as a member of the Preparatory Commission for the Laity. – Who are the pope's advisers? He himself is a good Church historian and a man of experience. He brought Msgr. Loris Capovilla from Venice. Cardinal Bea; also, it seems, Montini, Suenens, Léger; perhaps Alfrink, Frings, Döpfner, Liénart. He has some old friends among the conservatives: Ruffini, Pizzardo, Bacci, who are not able to see him as often as they would like, however. After all, his inaugural speech shows that the "prophets of doom" see him on a regular basis. – His illness; his various appearances at his window and in St. Peter's. – December 6, the announcement of the final arrangements; the creation of the new commission; the expressed hope that the "council by correspondence" would function well. – Despite the pope's optimism, anxiety: for the pope, besides his great charity, willingly lets things go. Now those of the conservative faction will probably never admit that times have changed for them. The very day of the pope's address "adjourning" the council, *L'Osservatore Romano* published an article by Father Lio in which the author, as if nothing had happened and omitting any reference to the inaugural discourse of the Holy Father, gave his verdict that the council was bound to condemn errors and claimed to base himself on the pope's September radio message.[7] Now in this message, the pope breathed not a word of condemnation: it was entirely a message of hope, charity, peace, service, and joy. – Ruffini and Ottaviani have also, it is said, presented a request to the pope, that all those who might have uttered heresies at the council be condemned; the petition bore the signatures of 8 cardinals. (?) – December 7; the pope's speech. There is now a great task "to accomplish in silence" ...

January 13, 1963. – Lunched at the *Civiltà*. According to Fr. Tucci, a sentence of the Christmas speech, in which the pope quoted himself,

[6]Raimondo Spiazzi, O.P. (1918–2002), Italian, ordained in 1944. Professor of fundamental theology at the Lateran University, provincial of the Province of Saint Peter Martyr from 1960. He has left a huge literary output, notably on the social doctrine of the Church and on the mariological documents of the magisterium.

[7]Message of September 11, 1962, in which the pope recalled that the Church had to make her voice heard and spoke of the "great expectations of the ecumenical council".

on the use of modern research methods, could be taken as an implicit response to the message from the 19 cardinals.[1] It is said, on the other hand, that five of these cardinals regretted and disavowed their signatures; the names Traglia[2] and Urbani are mentioned.

Fr. Charles Boyer has just published an article in *Doctor communis* to support the thesis of the "two sources". – Some people are amusing themselves here by saying that from now on, thinking of the council, Card. Bea,[3] when he prays the Confiteor, says: "Bea culpa, Bea maxima culpa!" – A meeting between Siri and Bea is reportedly being prepared; it is to Siri that the saying on "the quarter hour of extravagance" is being attributed. – Certain Roman circles are harsh toward Card. Léger; his words regarding one schema ("Everything must be redone") are interpreted as a criticism of the council itself.

When Father General asked that the Holy Office say what criticisms they had to make against Frs. Lyonnet and Zerwick, Card. Ottaviani is said to have responded that he was surprised by such a request: Fr. General ought to know that the Holy Office has never had to give reasons for its actions.

January 14, 1963. – A visit from two Franciscan students (American and Belgian), from the Antonianum, one of whom is preparing a thesis on the Mariology of Erasmus. – Talked exegesis with Fr. Meyer, S.J.,[1] who is doing a fourth year at the Biblical Institute. Dined at the Bellarmino; after the meal, conversation with the biennists.

January 15. – We have learned that Fr. Murphy,[1] editor of the biblical journal published by the American Jesuits, has just been forced to resign,

---

January 13

[1] This refers to the speech of John XXIII, in response to the wishes of the Sacred College, on December 23, 1962, in which the pope went back over his opening address at the council and recalled that *aggiornamento* has to be carried out through the methods of research and the formulations of modern thinking, all this within the bounds of a magisterium that is essentially pastoral. *La Documentation catholique*, 60, 1963, 99–102.

[2] Luigi Traglia (1895–1977), Italian, ordained in 1917, created cardinal in 1960. Pro-vicar general of Rome from 1960 until March 1965, then vicar general of Rome until 1968.

[3] Undoubtedly he meant to say Cardinal Ottaviani here. – TRANS.

January 14

[1] No doubt Benjamin F. Meyer.

January 15

[1] This name is without doubt erroneous. We have not been able to find a Father Murphy corresponding to this description.

by an order transmitted by the Apostolic Delegate. – At the Lateran, in December, Msgr. Piolanti treated in class the question: in case of a heretical pope, what is the proper thing to do?

January 16. – At noon, end of the Castelli colloquium. At 2 P.M., Termini station, to which Fr. S. Lyonnet accompanied me. Florence.

January 17. – This morning, a visit to Archbishop Florit, a member of the Doctrinal Commission of the council and of a subcommission of the mixed commission. He had received in this very place a visit from Card. Lefebvre and is in correspondence with Archbishop Guerry, to some extent also with Bishop Ancel; he knew Archbishop Veuillot and Archbishop Villot at the preparatory commission for *De episcopis*. A former student of the Biblical Institute (Bea and Vaccari), former professor at the Lateran. He is rather "conservative". We had a half-hour conversation, in French. He told me, in order to make me happy, that he had heard in Rome that my book on Teilhard was making a number of reservations (it was also an invitation to do the same here); I told him to what extent and in what sense. – Next, a visit to the Marchioness Trigona (via S. Spirito), who spoke to me for a long time about Teilhard and about Fr. Auguste Valensin, as well as about her grandson, a Jesuit in Genoa.

Lunched with the French consul general,[1] in a villa on the outskirts of the city, with the superior, Dall'Olio. From 4 to 5 P.M., a chat with the Jesuits doing their Tertianship.[2] Then, at the Palazzo Vecchio, conversation with La Pira,[3] who explained to me in a charming way what the little "Republic of Florence" was trying to accomplish – always with the approval of "the double Rome". He would like to have me give a talk in the great hall of the Palazzo Vecchio; I told him that the sociopolitical applications of the Christian faith were not directly my affair. He is a Teilhard enthusiast and talks about him everywhere with statesmen, Christian or not. We had tea at his desk. Commemorative brochures.

January 17
  [1] Christian Fouache d'Halloy, French Consul General in Florence from 1960 to 1966.
  [2] Jesuits carrying out the third year (of their novitiate), coming to the end of the formation cycle.
  [3] Giorgio La Pira (1904–1977), Italian, Christian Democrat mayor of Florence from 1951 to 1957 and from 1961 to 1965.

The three conferences that he arranged here (Féret,[4] Daniélou, Balducci) attracted a large crowd, which flowed over into the other halls: almost all were young people, students, workers as well; he gave me the text of his opening address. – At 9:15 P.M., talk on Teilhard in the hall of the Jesuit residence.

January 18, 1963. – From Florence, wrote to Father Jean Steinmann[1] regarding his book on F. von Hügel. – Turin. Francesco Coppellotti drove me to his mother's place and introduced me to some of his comrades, who pass for being communists, more or less. He has undertaken a thesis on the eschatology of the 4th Gospel, which frightens his entourage; for the moment he is reading Dodd,[2] etc. – At 6 P.M., Fr. Colli,[3] provincial of Turin, came to get me and brought me to his villa, on the slopes of the Superga hill. – On the 19th, at noon, lunched at the college; saw some students and professors; a doctor is undertaking a study on Teilhard's biology; a student wants to present a thesis in Milan on the supernatural. – At 6 P.M., at the Carignano theater, a lecture in French: the current demands of our faith; generalities, but against the humanization of the faith and in the sense of the aggiornamento of John XXIII; emphasized the difference between conservatism and traditional spirit. The coadjutor archbishop,[4] a Franciscan, declared himself satisfied; and also for the Dominican superior.[5] – Dined with various authorities in a nearby restaurant, famous for having been frequented by Cavour.[6] –

---

[4] Henri-Marie Féret, O.P. (1904–1992), French, ordained in 1928. Theologian, he had been dismissed from his teaching position at Le Saulchoir. He was prior of the monastery of Dijon and private expert of Bishop Flusin (Saint-Claude) during the council.

January 18

[1] Jean Steinmann is the author of *Friedrich von Hügel: Sa vie, son oeuvre et ses amitiés* (Paris: Montaigne, 1962). F. von Hügel, Austrian by origin and a naturalized British subject, was a philosopher of religion.

[2] Charles Harold Dodd (1884–1973), British, author of *The Interpretation of the Fourth Gospel* (Cambridge University Press, 1953), among other works.

[3] Giovanni Colli, S.J. (1913–1989), Italian, ordained in 1943. Provincial Superior in Turin from 1958 to 1964.

[4] Felicissimo Stefano Tinivella, O.F.M. (1908–1978), Italian, ordained in 1931. Coadjutor bishop of Turin from 1961 to 1965.

[5] There are two Dominican monasteries in Turin, whose superiors are Francesco Gusberti and Gusmano Ghittino.

[6] Camillo Benso, Count of Cavour (1810–1861), Italian statesman, one of the great architects of Italian unity.

Father Georges Haubtmann[7] had come. He informed me about the death, at Fourvière, of Fr. Auguste Décisier.[8]

January 20, 1963. – At St.-Jean-de-Maurienne, with Father Pierre Viallet;[1] dined that evening with Bishop Bontems.[2]

January 21. – Saint-Pierre-d'Albigny (Visitation [convent]). Chambéry (Saint Ambrose Boarding School). Visited the parents of Fr. Michel de Certeau.[1] – Lyon.

Leonardo da Vinci, at the moment when he conceived his Last Supper and the face of Christ (1495):

> Non iscoprir se libertà t'è cara
> Che il volto mio è carcere d'amore.

("Be very careful not to discover – if you love freedom – that my face is a prison of love.") (In E. Castelli, *Le démonique dans l'art*, p. 101).

Official experts of the mixed commission for the redrafting of the *De fontibus*: – from the Secretariat for Unity: Fathers Maccarrone,[2] Stakemeier,[3] Vodopivec;[4] Canons Thils and Feiner; Frs. Hamer and Baum.

---

[7] Georges Haubtmann, S.J. (1906–1991), French. A friend of Father de Lubac, he had been attached to the Jesuit University Cultural Center of Grenoble from 1948 until 1962, then at Le Châtelard, a Jesuit spiritual center in the outskirts of Lyon.

[8] Auguste Décisier, S.J. (1878–1963), French. Provincial of the Province of Lyon from 1945 to 1949.

January 20

[1] Pierre Viallet (1918–1979), French, ordained in 1944. Former professor of dogma and Sacred Scripture, he was the director of works and diocesan chaplain of the independent media branch of Catholic Action in the diocese of Maurienne from 1961 to 1970.

[2] André-Georges Bontems (1910–1988), French, ordained in 1933. Bishop of Saint-Jean-de-Maurienne from 1960 to 1966, then archbishop of Chambéry, Saint-Jean-de-Maurienne and Tarentaise until 1985.

January 21

[1] Michel de Certeau, S.J. (1925–1986), French, ordained in 1956. A specialist in the editing of spiritual texts, he also became known, starting in the late 1960s, for his researches in historical and religious epistemology.

[2] Michele Maccarrone (1910–1993), Italian priest, professor of church history at the theology faculty of the Lateran. Expert at the council and a member of the Secretariat for Unity.

[3] Eduard Stakemeier (1904–1970), German, ordained in 1929. Director of the Institut für Konfessions- und Diasporakunde (the future Institut Johann-Adam-Möhler) of Paderborn. Consultor to the Secretariat for Unity and expert at the council.

[4] Janez Vodopivec (1917–1993), Yugoslav, ordained in 1941. Professor of ecclesiology at the Urbaniana. Consultor to the Secretariat for Unity.

– from the Doctrinal Commission: Msgrs. Lattanzi and Fenton, Father Castellino;⁵ Frs. Van den Eynde, Balić, di Fonzo,⁶ Kerrigan.⁷

Sunday the 27th, with Fr. Martelet and Father Denis, prepared a talk to be given to the priests of the diocese of Lyon and for the meeting of the bishops of the region (February 4). – Gave a talk to the Sisters of the Assumption.

February 4, 1963. – Father Greco told me all sorts of things about what was going on around the 1st session of the council. – Cardinal Bea, to the Africans, regarding some versions of the Bible in various languages produced by the Protestants: "You are bishops; it is up to you to judge; if you find they are well done and without offense for the Catholic faith, you can give them the imprimatur or let it be known that you approve them. – But do not say anything to the Holy Office about what I just told you!" – The Holy Father, receiving Father Raes (and one or two other persons) at table, recounted the first days of his pontificate: each cardinal came to do him homage, offer him his service, etc.; all were perfect; then, the pope concluded mischievously, I applied to myself the words of the psalm: "Et in medio sanctorum detentio mea!"¹ – The

⁵Giorgio Castellino, S.D.B. (1903–1992), Italian, ordained in 1929. Professor of Sacred Scripture at the Pontifical Salesian Athenaeum of Turin from 1938 to 1965. Consultor to the Pontifical Biblical Commission. Expert at the council.

⁶Lorenzo Di Fonzo, O.F.M. Conv., born in 1914, Italian, ordained in 1937. Professor of Sacred Scripture and Mariology at the Pontifical Theological Faculty of Saint Bonaventure in Rome, of which he was president. Expert at the council.

⁷Five subcommissions were each reworking one chapter of the *De Fontibus*:

1. The twofold source of revelation: *presidents*: J. Frings and M. Browne. *Members*: L. Jäger, T. Holland, J. Schröffer, P. Parente. *Periti*: E. Stakemeier, D. van den Eynde, J. Feiner, M. Maccarrone, C. Balić.

2. Inspiration, inerrancy, and the literary composition of Holy Scripture: *presidents*: F. König and R. Santos. *Members*: E.J. De Smedt, J.M. Martin, F. Spanedda, G.L. Pelletier. *Periti*: G. Thils, L. Di Fonzo, S. Tromp.

3. The Old Testament: *presidents*: A.G. Meyer and J. Lefebvre. *Members*: F. Charrière, F. Barbado y Viejo, A. Scherer, B. Gut. *Periti*: G. Baum, G. Castellino, A. Kerrigan.

4. The New Testament: *presidents*: E. Ruffini and A. Liénart. *Members*: A. Charue, J. Heenan, E. Florit, F. Franić. *Periti*: S. Garofalo, J. Hamer, U. Lattanzi.

5. Holy Scripture in the Church: *presidents*: F. Quiroga y Palacios, P.É. Léger. *Members*: H. Volk, J. Griffiths, M.G. McGrath, A. Fernández. *Periti*: J. Fenton, C. Boyer.

February 4

¹"I stay in the midst of the saints!" [This is actually a reference to Ecclesiasticus: "Et in plenitudine sanctorum detentio mea", Sir 24:16.]

Malagasy archbishop of Tananarive[2] did not come to the meetings of Madagascar and African [bishops] when they discussed the doctrinal schemas. He had been a member of the Central Commission and had said nothing against the schemas; as a result, he felt offended when the bishops began to challenge them. – A text has been drafted by a group of bishops on the pope, the ecumenical council, etc. The Africans are adopting it; all the bishops have signed it; the same also for the apostolic delegates, except for one; the reason: this text does not put the Roman congregations in the same category as the pope, above the council. – A confidant of Card. Ottaviani gave Fr. Greco a package of copies of Ottaviani's printed report on De fontibus; the next day, he told Fr. Greco that several bishops were complaining that they did not have this report in hand; Greco replied that he had not been given any orders on that score.

February 7, 1963. – Thursday, at *Études* (Paris). News was given by Fr. René Marlé[1] on his return from a meeting of S.J. editors in Geneva. Card. Ottaviani has reportedly complained to Cicognani about the manner in which certain Catholic journals (above all Father Rouquette's chronicles in *Études*) are reporting on the council, are talking about the Curia and its theologians. Cicognani is said to have responded that the pope wants to leave each his freedom of expression and refuses to intervene personally in anything that touches on the council: if anyone has a complaint to make, it should be addressed to the presidency of the council. – Card. Döpfner seems to be quite happy with the work carried out in January by the conciliar commission. – Cardinal Bea seems to have come to realize what is at stake in the matter of the "two sources". He has reconsidered his moment of weakness of December 7. – It is hoped that the text of the first chapter of the former De fontibus will be rewritten in a satisfactory way. – The reports spread in the press regarding a rebuke addressed to Card. Bea by the Holy Office following his words on tolerance at the ecumenical meeting that took place in December in Rome are evidently false; what is true is that these words were sharply criticized by certain members of the Holy Office. He was

---

[2] Jérôme Louis Rakotomalala.

February 7

[1] René Marlé, S.J. (1919–1994), French. Professor of theology at the Institut catholique of Paris, an editor of the journal *Études*, he afterward devoted a great deal of effort to the catechetical movement.

reproached in particular for having abandoned the old slogan, "Truth has all the rights, error has no rights."

Saw Fr. Daniélou at *Études*. He has worked and traveled a great deal for the council for the past two months. Meetings in Paris, Lille, Angers; a trip to Belgium; correspondence; compiling and editing (as part of a group) papers printed by the Secretariat for the Episcopate and distributed sub secreto[2] to all the bishops, also sent to bishops outside the country. He thinks that *De revelatione*[3] (formerly *De fontibus*) will be able to give satisfaction; that *De Ecclesia* will be reduced and given a good orientation. There remains the problem of *De deposito fidei* and *De ordine morali*, which are intact; it will be difficult to demand a total rewrite if the big conciliar commission does not act with authority. Nevertheless, a new draft is going to be prepared in France, and Fr. Daniélou suggested to Archbishop Garrone a meeting of bishops and theologians to work on this; he wants to have me invited as well as Fr. Martelet and would also like to have the presence of a Dutchman (Schillebeeckx?)[4] and a Belgian (Thils?). – I am told, on the other hand, that, after their various labors, 80 German-language bishops have recently come together to share their drafts. – A letter from the pope, a photocopy of which Fr. Rouquette saw, is said to specify the prerogatives of the conciliar commission and to strengthen its authority.[5]

February 8, 1963. – Fr. Martelet laid out for me the report that Archbishop Villot made to the bishops and theologians assembled at La Rivette (near Lyon) on February 4, on the first meeting, in Rome, of the Coordinating Commission:

A. The 70 schemas of the preparatory commissions have already been reduced to 20 (cf. the gray fascicle): of the 6 schemas from the Theological Commission, 4 remain (*De deposito* and *De vita morali* have been set aside or their contents placed elsewhere). – The 11 schemas prepared by the Eastern Commission have been reduced to a single one, with 5 headings (gray notebook: schema 8). – Out of the 17 schemas of the commissio de disciplina cleri et populi,[1] only one remains (schema 9).

---

[2] "Under secrecy".
[3] "On revelation".
[4] E. Schillebeeckx is Belgian, not Dutch.
[5] This refers to the Letter *Mirabilis ille* to the Catholic episcopate, published on February 7, 1963, one part of which was dedicated to the Coordinating Commission.
February 8
[1] "Commission for the Discipline of the Clergy and the People".

– Of the 10 schemas in 9 opuscules from the commissio de episcopis, there are 5 left (no. 10 in the gray notebook). – The schema in 11 opuscules of the commissio de religiosis[2] is reduced to 4 opuscules (no. 11). – The schema of the commissio de apostolatu laicorum,[3] in 3 parts and 4 fascicles, now contains 3 parts and 3 fascicles (no. 12). – The commissio de sacramentis[4] had prepared 9 schemas: only one has been retained, containing 6 parts, on marriage (no. 13). – The schema on the Liturgy remains. – A schema de cura animarum[5] has been put together from bits coming from various sources (De episcopis, De ap. Laicorum, a mixed commission of bishops and religious, etc.) (no. 15). – The 2 constitutions and 3 decrees from the commissio de seminariis et studiis[6] have been reduced to 2 schemas (nos. 16 and 17). – Of the 7 schemas of decrees, in 7 opuscules, from the commissio de missionibus,[7] there is 1 schema in 2 parts left (no. 18). – Com. de instrumentis communic. soc.[8] (no. 19). – De unitate: the 4 prepared schemas are reduced to 1 (no. 20).

B. Information on the work accomplished by the Coordinating Commission at the end of January. This work focused on 18 headings, concerning all the subjects of the council (except for liturgy and instruments of social comm.). The task was divided up among seven subcommissions, each with a cardinal presiding:

> Liénart: De rev. and deposito
> Döpfner: Bishops, dioceses, religious
> Urbani: De clericis et laicis
> Spellman: De castitate et matrimonio[9]
> Suenens: De ecclesia et B. Maria
> Confalonieri: Seminaries, schools, studies, missions
> Cicognani: "Eastern Churches, ecumenism"[10]

---

[2] "Commission for Religious".

[3] "Commission for the Lay Apostolate".

[4] "Commission for the Sacraments".

[5] "On the care of souls".

[6] "Commission for Seminaries and Studies".

[7] "Commission for the Missions".

[8] "Commission for the Instruments of Social Communication".

[9] "On chastity and marriage".

[10] This distribution is based on the list of 20 schemas distributed on December 5, 1962, but on January 27, 1963, the Coordinating Commission adopted a new list, proposed by Urbani, consisting of 17 schemas, even if other schemas were sometimes placed on the agenda. In this distribution, we can add, for Döpfner the care of souls, for Urbani the means of social communication, for Spellman the liturgy, for Suenens the moral order and the social order. Suenens was also afterward put in charge of the De castitate (On Chastity).

Two tendencies very quickly came to light: one radical, in favor of reducing everything to 2 or 3 schemas (Döpfner and Liénart, it seems); the other, more conciliatory, in favor of accepting as a basis the schemas, already reduced, as found in the printed gray fascicle. The 2nd tendency prevailed. – Method adopted: After the plenary session, the subcommissions set to work: the cardinal president lays out the state of the question; there is discussion; only on the next day are concrete proposals formulated.

Opinions of the various cardinals on the subject they have been given and basic discussions:

Card. Liénart. On *De revelatione*. He reported on the last meeting of the mixed commission, on the evening of December 7. Then he proposed, like the pope, that if they could not find a better formula, they should be content with the one of Trent. *–De deposito*, as such, has disappeared; the chapter "De satisfactione Christi"[11] has been eliminated; chaps. 1, 4, 5, 7 will be reduced to general principles, in order to take a modest place in *De magisterio*. The other chapters, rewritten, will be integrated into a schema "De admirabili vocatione hominis secundum Deum",[12] a sort of Christian anthropology. The commission "vehementer exoptat"[13] that something should be done in this sense.

Card. Suenens. He thoroughly criticized the schema *De Ecclesia*. He proposed: 1. a single chapter to replace chaps. 1 and 2; this would be a chapter "De Ecclesiae mysterio",[14] in which three things would be discussed: elementum mysticum Ecclesiae; relatio inter vitam spiritualem et structuram hierarchicam; relatio Ecclesiae illis qui sunt foris bona fide.[15] – 2. A second chapter: "De institutione hierarchica Ecclesiae".[16] – There was a discussion concerning this second chapter. Confalonieri wanted it to start with the primacy of the pope; a lively debate; there was reference made to Vatican I, which started differently; Suenens won out and proposed the following plan: De institutione duodecim apostolorum – De episcopis successoribus – De episcopatu ut sacramento – De munere docendi, sanctificandi, regendi – De episcoporum corpore.[17]

---

[11] "On the satisfaction of Christ".

[12] "On the wonderful vocation of man according to God".

[13] "Strongly desires".

[14] "On the mystery of the Church".

[15] "The mystical element of the Church; the relation between the spiritual life and the hierarchical structure; the relation of the Church with those who are outside but of good faith".

[16] "On the hierarchical institution of the Church".

[17] "On the institution of the twelve apostles. On the bishops as successors. On the episcopate as sacrament. On the task of teaching, sanctifying, governing. On the body of bishops".

– Card. Döpfner asked that a 3rd chapter be added, on religious: "De statu imitationis Christi secundum praecepta evangelica, seu de statu charismatico in Ecclesia."[18] The question remained on hold. Suenens continued the exposition of his plan: Chap. 3, De laicis; chap. 4, De magisterio; chap. 5, De relatione inter Ecclesiam et Statum.[19]

Suenens posed a final problem: De ordine morali (5th schema of the Preparatory Theological Commission) is going to disappear as such, to be rewritten and placed elsewhere. But where? Discussion. Liénart thought that it fits in naturally with his draft De admirabili vocatione hominum. Suenens would like it to be incorporated in a schema De persona in societate humana.[20] Nothing was decided. For Suenens, the new schema that he indicated is only a framework; he is awaiting suggestions on how to flesh it out; it could have two parts: 1. De Ecclesia Christi;[21] 2. De praesentia Ecclesiae in mundo.[22] These 2 large parts would include all the essential matters of the council's work, with De divina revelatione as an introduction. Such is the general outline in 20 points that a confidential paper proposes. For the 2nd part, "De praesentia Ecclesiae in mundo", the pope had at first thought to create, according to Suenens, a special commission; he had given that up for two reasons: it was too late; and he wants to transform the Commissio de apostolatu laicorum[23] into a permanent Secretariat, analogous to the Secretariat for Unity; so there could be a chance of redundancy. – So who would write this 2nd part? It would be a mixed commission, made up partly of members of the Doctrinal Commission (in particular Garrone and Charue) and partly of members of the "apostolate of the laity".

Card. Spellman. The schema De castitate will be included in the schema on the religious state. De matrimonio will come in the chapter of "De praesentia Ecclesiae in mundo" devoted to the family.

De Ecclesiae unitate: there will be only one schema in 3 parts: General principles on ecumenism. – The Orthodox. – The Protestants.

Card. Urbani. De Clericis: One constitution on the clergy will contain three parts: clerical life – pastoral science – De bonis ecclesiasticis

---

[18] "On the state of the imitation of Christ according to the evangelical precepts, or the charismatic state in the Church".

[19] "On the relation between the Church and the State".

[20] "On the person in human society".

[21] "On the Church of Christ".

[22] "On the presence of the Church in the world".

[23] "Commission for the Lay Apostolate".

(and not: De beneficiis);[24] the rest will go into postconciliar decrees and into the reform of canon law. – De laicis: The doctrinal part is included in *De Ecclesia*; the rest will be incorporated into the schema on the apostolate of the laity, in three parts: Promotion of the Gospel – Actio caritativa – Actio socialis.[25]

Cardinal Döpfner. A radical, he would have liked to eliminate all the work of *Disciplina cleri et populi*[26] as well as the disciplinary decree *De episcopis* (schema 10 of the gray notebook), except for two specific questions: a. the age limit (at age 75, bishops would be at the pope's disposal; but John XXIII refused); b. the bishops' conferences (but these could be treated in the chap. of *De Ecclesia* on the bishops). – It seems, however, that a schema will be prepared on the relationship between bishops and religious. Starting from the definition of the religious life, "status charismaticus in Ecclesia",[27] Döpfner would want this schema to be composed under three headings: a. the religious vocation; b. the renewal of religious life; c. the formation of religious. A number of subsequent problems would be dealt with in the postconciliar instructions or in the reforms of canon law. The doctrine on the religious life would figure in *De Ecclesia* (v. *supra*).

On the Missions: There was discussion on whether it was necessary to maintain the current distinction between dioceses of common right and territories dependent on the Propaganda. No decision was reached.

Finally, it was decided that there will be good reason to distinguish carefully: conciliar constitutions – conciliar decrees – postconciliar documents – revision of the Code of Canon Law. – Example of the matters that will be the subject of postconciliar documents: De cura animarum – De sacrorum alumnis formandis – De studiis – De instrumentis.[28]

In *Irenikon*, vol. 35 (1962, no. 4), pp. 467–78, article by Dom Olivier Rousseau: "The 2nd Vatican Council, Ecclesiological Reflections": "… The Roman Curia is so rooted in the exercise of its functions that it has not fulfilled its role of self-effacement before the council …" Great psychological difficulty "for the functionaries accustomed to dominate everything", to understand that the bishops, "whom they ordinarily

---

[24]"On ecclesiastic goods (and not On benefices)".

[25]"Charitable action, social action".

[26]"Commission for the Discipline of the Clergy and the Christian People."

[27]"A charismatic state in the Church".

[28]"On the care of souls. On the formation of future priests. On studies. On the instruments [of social communication]".

oversee, were going to become their masters". Especially for the Holy Office: it had been "practically inserted into the Preparatory Theological Commission to the point of merging with it and eliminating from it anything not itself. What is more, it had sought ... to dominate the other commissions with which it refused to collaborate. It seemed in the end that it was the entire council it wanted to direct" ... "The pope can say what he likes, the decrees drafted in the offices constitute the official commentary ..., and the cardinals of the Curia can present their work as being what the Holy Father desires ... Although he has fundamentally upset many of the preparatory schemas, in particular those of the Theological Commission, the schemas continued to be presented imperturbably as the thought of the pope, who, they kept saying, had approved them ..." "From that point on ... it was clear that the Curia's attempt to dominate the council had failed ..."

Msgr. Joseph Fenton published not long ago three articles tending to discredit Newman: 1. "Some Newman Autobiographical Sketches and the Newman Legend" (*The American Ecclesiastical Review*, 136 [June 1957], pp. 394–410); 2. "Newman's Complaints Examined in the Light of Priestly Spirituality" (ibid., 138 [January 1958], pp. 45–65); 3. "The Newman Legend and Newman's Complaints" (ibid., 139 [August 1958], pp. 101–21). – These articles are discussed in a thesis written at the Gregorian: Antonio T. Padovano,[29] *The Cross of Christ, the Measure of the World: A Study of the Theology of the Cross in the Life and Writings of John Henry Newman* (Rome, 1962). (The faculty adviser for the thesis was Fr. Hugo de Achaval, S.J.).[30]

In the *Nouvelle Revue Théologique*, January 1963, an article by Fr. G. Dejaifve, S.J.:[31] "From One Council to the Other; Balance Sheet of the First Session"; p. 59: "Some of them (= preconciliar commissions) drew up drafts more impeccable from the doctrinal point of view than open to modern pastoral perspectives." That is the sort of thing that is commonly said. But I believe particularly that the doctrine in these

---

[29] Anthony T. Padovano, born in 1934, American, ordained in 1960. A theologian, he left the priesthood after the council and became the first president elect of Corpus, which promotes the ordination of women and men, whether single or married.

[30] Hugo de Achaval, S.J. (1909–1990), Argentinian, ordained in 1939. Spiritual director at the Latin American College in Rome from 1953 to 1965 and professor of theology at the Gregorian, a Newman specialist.

[31] Georges Dejaifve, S.J. (1913–1982), Belgian, ordained in 1944. Professor of fundamental theology and ecclesiology at the Jesuit college of theology of Eegenhoven-Louvain from 1948 to 1966, he was particularly interested in ecumenism.

schemas was poor, too modern, with integrist excesses coming from a diminished Truth.

At the Council of Constance, "speeches followed on speeches, a profound torpor took hold of everyone whenever it was a question of fundamental problems" (Fliche-Martin,[32] 14, p. 190). – At Basel, "whoever went against the sentiment of the majority exposed himself to being hounded as a 'turbator concilii'."[33] (At Vatican II, it was rather the inverse of this!)

La Documentation catholique of 2.3.63 has, one after the other, two texts: one by Archbishop Guerry of Cambrai, the other by Archbishop Florit of Florence. It is a result of their common efforts toward unifying the two episcopates, French and Italian, that is to say, rather, to supplement the Italian doctrine with some "pastoral" accommodations and extensions. – Archbishop Guerry: "We declared that we were refusing such an opposition (inside the council) ... first because the unity of the council was a higher good that all the Fathers must pursue and safeguard constantly ... The tension concerned the manner of presenting the doctrine in a totally pure and luminous way to the men of our times, a way that was pastorally effective." (Praise for the doctrine of the members of the Holy Office followed.) – From Archbishop Florit: "Rather than a confrontation of leanings and opinions, it seems to me that we must speak of an 'encounter' that enriched and delighted both sides."

February 17, 1963, Sunday. – A talk at the Congress of the French Federation of Catholic Students. Met various chaplains from just about everywhere. Lunched with Frs. Brien,[1] Biard,[2] and Petit.[3] Fr. Biard had a lot of information on the council from Bishop Huyghe (Arras) and Schmitt (Metz) as well as from Fr. Congar. In the afternoon, a long

---

[32] This refers to *L'Histoire de l'Église depuis les origines jusqu'à nos jours* (Paris: Bloud et Gay, 1935–1964); this work in several volumes was initiated by Augustin Fliche and Victor Martin.

[33] "Troublemaker of the council".

February 17

[1] André Brien (1913–1998), French, ordained in 1939. Chaplain of the École normale supérieure until 1959, then professor at the Catholic theology faculty of Strasbourg.

[2] Pierre Biard (1921–2003), French, ordained in 1945. After serving as chaplain in many different places, in 1958 he became assistant ecclesiastic of the Centre catholique des intellectuels français (CCIF) (Catholic Center of French Intellectuals), a position he held until 1966.

[3] Bernard Petit, born in 1924, French, ordained in 1954. Chaplain of the École normale supérieure from 1961 to 1966.

conversation with my two archbishops from Madagascar, Thoyer and Gilbert Ram,[4] who continue to take an active interest in the council.

February 22. – Talk on the question of the "two sources" at the ecumenical meeting at Fourvière; among the pastors, three had come from Geneva, as had Father Chavaz.[1] –Have corresponded these past few days with Msgr. Lafortune, who is in Rome with Card. Léger for the Doctrinal Commission. It is hard to reject totally the impression that among certain men of the Church in Italy, a certain concept of Rome, a certain ideology of Rome's centrality, enters in a substantial way into their Catholicism and their love of the papacy. For such people, who are naïvely conscious of forming the heart of the Church, the "transalpines", the "people from across the mountains", are more or less "outsiders". There is so visceral a memory of ancient Rome still mixed with their Catholic spirit. Cardinal Siri, gathering together the bishops of Italy, supposedly said to them that it was up to them to defend Rome and the Holy See by closing ranks in a "tortoise" formation – an old Roman military metaphor. In this attitude, moreover, there is great sincerity: it is said that many times, after certain sessions of the council, Cardinal Siri was weeping, feeling the Church endangered. Such a conception of the Church, understandable from a historical viewpoint, has its grandeur and its beauty, but the fact remains that it is not dogmatic and it does not foster a very spiritual Catholicism. And it easily provokes biased and impassioned reactions.

February 23. – Cardinal Gerlier passed on to me a copy of the desiderata formulated by the bishops of the region concerning *De Ecclesia*. They are rather good, although expressed in very general terms and without criticism of the existing texts: Is this fear of giving offense or inexperience with how the commissions work?

February 27, 1963. – Fr. Martelet showed me a letter from Bishop Elchinger. On receipt of the letter I had recently written him, he spoke to Archbishop Weber. The latter has just written to Archbishop Garonne (presently in Rome) to press him to obtain a radical revision of all of *De Ecclesia*; without that, he, "a moderate bishop", would get

---

[4] Gilbert Ramanantoanina.

February 22

[1] Edmond Chavaz (1905–2000), Swiss, ordained in 1932. Parish priest of Le Grand-Saconnex (Switzerland) from 1951 to 1977. He was involved in the ecumenical movement.

angry. – I corrected a part of the long work undertaken on *De Ecclesia* by Fr. Martelet, who would like to have it disseminated by Msgr. Gouet. – In *L'Osservatore* of February 22, a long article by Fr. Luigi Ciappi, O.P., Master of the Sacred Palace: "Pastor Ecclesiae",[1] on the magisterium of the pope. He ends with the ritual words: "... ad esaltazione dell'unità e della santità della Chiesa Cattolica ed Apostolica."[2] Always the exaltation of the earthly Church given apparently as the last end. – In *Time* magazine's January issue, an article on John XXIII, "Man of the Year"; among the photographs: "Jacqueline and John" (the pope and Mrs. Kennedy). – The February issue of *Time* announced that, among the speakers whom the Catholic University of Washington was intending to invite, four have been excluded by the vice-rector: J. C. Murray, S.J.;[3] G. Weigel, S.J. (from the Secretariat for Unity); Godfrey Diekmann, O.S.B.;[4] Hans Küng (Tubingen); it is said that it is because they would have talked too much about the council.

March 2, 1963. – I received a late, brief response from Fr. Tromp, telling me (what I knew already) that the schema *De deposito fidei* will not be presented to the council, so there was no cause for me to worry about the subject of paragraph 22. Otherwise, he added, Fr. Dhanis would be willing to change the text (for which I am grateful to him). – According to the *Informations catholiques internationales* of March 1, the Doctrinal Commission of the council, just like the preparatory commission, is supposed to have refused to participate in a mixed commission to prepare the new schema on ecumenism. Of the three texts prepared separately, the Coordinating Commission, interpreting the desires expressed at the council, has asked that they be made into a single text, written in common by members of the three groups that had drafted them. The Commissions for Eastern Churches and for Unity have agreed to collaborate (without having gotten along very well up until now, by the way), but

---

February 27

[1] "Pastor of the Church".

[2] "For the exaltation of the unity and the sanctity of the catholic and apostolic Church".

[3] John Courtney Murray, S.J. (1904–1967), American. Professor of theology at the Theologate of Woodstock (Maryland), he had to cease writing on religious liberty in 1955, on orders from Rome. Private expert of F. Spellman, he was named an expert to the council beginning with the second session.

[4] Godfrey Diekmann, O.S.B. (1908–2002), American, ordained in 1931. Professor of patrology and Church history at Saint John's Seminary in Collegeville, Minnesota. Expert at the council beginning with the second session, he was particularly interested in the liturgical movement.

the Doctrinal Commission reportedly only delegated an expert; none of its members apparently has appeared at the meetings.[1]

March 4, 1963. – From a letter from Fr. Donatien Mollat, of which Fr. R. Isaac[1] spoke to me: one evening, on returning from the mixed commission (*De revelatione*), Father Tromp reportedly went to bed and is still unwell.

April 3–5. – At Angers, at the Good Shepherd, with about fifteen bishops, meetings on conciliar theology. Bishop Mazerat[1] of Angers, presided. A cordial atmosphere. Fr. Le Guillou, O.P.,[2] spoke about the schema on moral order and on the family. Msgr. Etchegaray came, as well as Father R. Laurentin. Bishop Cazaux of Luçon, always very friendly. Chatted with Dom Prou, Abbot of Solesmes, whom I had already met in Rome (St. Jerome Abbey); very amiable. – The April 5 issue of *Time* gave an account of the recent talks given by Cardinal Bea in the United States; invited by Card. Cushing (Boston), he spoke in particular at Harvard University. *Time* also mentioned the conferences of Hans Küng, who, in Chicago, at Notre Dame, in Boston, launched a sort of radical program of reforms (suppression of the "Nihil obstat", the Index, the secrecy of the Holy Office, whose methods "offend not only against the Gospel, but against the natural law, which is often quoted", etc.). – I wrote up some remarks on the new schema "de revelatione" and sent them to Archbishop Villot.

April 23, 1963. – Bishop Ancel sent me, belatedly, the two chapters of *De Ecclesia*[1] that Archbishop Villot had twice told me were on the way. I

March 2

[1] Some members of the Doctrinal Commission did in fact go to the meetings. Even if the Doctrinal Commission was demanding control over the texts, the obstruction was also coming from the Commission for Eastern Churches: see G. Alberigo, *Histoire du concile Vatican II*, vol. 2 (Paris and Louvain: Éd. du Cerf-Peeters, 1998), pp. 510–17.

March 4

[1] Robert Isaac, S.J. (1923–1986), French. Consultor to the Provincial of Lyon.

April 3-5

[1] Henri Mazerat (1903–1986), French, ordained in 1932. Bishop of Angers from 1961 to 1974. Member of the Commission for the Discipline of the Clergy and the Christian People.

[2] Marie Joseph Le Guillou, O.P. (1920–1990), French. Theologian, former professor at Le Saulchoir (1949–1954). In 1967 he founded the Institut supérieur d'études œcuméniques at the Catholic University in Paris. Expert at the council.

April 23

[1] This is referring to a new text, based on the text prepared by Msgr. Philips, and discussed during the first intersession.

answered him this morning: "Immediately upon receiving this text, last evening, I read it. But our mail leaves at 9 A.M., so I absolutely could not find the time to write up my remarks. Besides, a text like this must be closely studied, and the poor "periti" are sometimes surrounded by so many unfavorable prejudices and so much distrust that I would not write anything on a subject of such importance without having thought it out thoroughly enough. I am only jotting down on the enclosed paper two very general remarks, etc., etc."

The Assembly of the French Clergy in 1720 recommended the reading of Holy Scripture and declared that the Church did not want to "hide this divine treasure from her children" and that she would not yield "to the communions separated from her the advantage of showing zeal and ardor for the reading of the Scriptures" (R. Mercier, 1960 thesis, p. 144).

May 11, 1963. – At La Baume.[1] Received a letter from Card. Ottaviani inviting me to the next session of the Doctrinal Commission, starting on May 15. I wrote to Father Tromp to have myself excused.[2] – *May 15.* A novice (Pasquier),[3] whose brother, an Oblate of Mary, is studying theology in Rome (Angelico), told me what his brother wrote to him: the students at the Angelicum apparently started a petition for the replacement of some professors, who this year were still taking the same hard line in their teaching, in opposition to the orientation of the council. It seems that the petition was not badly received by the rector.[4] But the general of the Dominicans[5] supposedly reprimanded the rector.

September 2, 1963. – After my recent hospital stay,[1] the provincial (Arminjon) wrote to the Assistant [to the Jesuit Father General][2] to have me exempted from attending the second session of the council.

May 11

[1] In Aix-en-Provence.

[2] Father de Lubac considered himself too tired and wrote to Father Tromp that he was "incapable of usefully undertaking this trip" (see the letter to Gaston Fessard of May 12, 1963).

[3] François Pasquier, born in 1945, French, was a Jesuit from 1962 to 1967.

[4] Raymond Sigmond, O.P., Hungarian, rector of the Angelicum until 1964. Consultor to the Preparatory Theological Commission, an expert at the council.

[5] Aniceto Fernández.

September 2

[1] H. de Lubac was hospitalized in June 1963 for appendicitis, then for a prostate operation.

[2] From March 16, 1963, the Assistant was Étienne Pillain, S.J. (1906–2004), French. He was Assistant of France in Rome from March 1963 to July 1965.

INDEX

Abdul-Ahad Sana, 377–78
Abellan, Pedro Marie, 215, 224
Achaval, Hugo de, 526
Adappur, Abraham, 131
Addazi, Reginaldo G. M., 402
Adenauer, Konrad, 168
Adriano VI, 400
Agagianian, Gregorio, 469, 478
Aguirre, Antonio María, 263
Alba Palacios, José, 314
Albareda y Ramoneda, Joaquin
    Anselmo María, 262
Alberigo, Giuseppe, 326, 374, 410
Alfaro, Juan, 57, 100, 509
Alfrink, Bernard Jan
  in October 1962 notebook, 162, 216,
    217–18, 222, 224, 226
  in November 1962 notebook, 241,
    264, 272, 273, 281, 286, 294, 329,
    337, 420
  in December 1962 notebook,
    426–27, 448, 464, 471
  in January 1963 notebook, 511, 514
Allard, Michel, 182
Almarcha Hernández, Luis, 282
Alonso Schökel, Luis, 57, 70–72, 367,
    395, 509
Alvarez, 513
Alvim Pereira, Custódio, 219
Amadouni, Garabed, 177
Ambrose, Saint, 250
Amiot, François, 325–26
Anastasius, 84, 152

NOTE: Names in parentheses are alternate
spellings used in the text.

Ancel, Alfred
  in the introduction, 36
  in October 1962 notebook, 125, 151,
    165, 166, 167, 192
  in November 1962 notebook, 280,
    345–46, 403–4
  in December 1962 notebook, 495–96
  in January 1963 notebook, 512, 516
  in April 1963 notebook, 530–31
Angelini, Fiorenzo, 247
Anselmo, 246, 256
Antonelli, Ferdinando, 140, 161, 171,
    195, 247
Antoniutti, Ildebrando, 189
Aramburu, Juan Carlos, 229
Arattukulam, Michael, 220
Araud, Régis, 62
Argaya Goicoechea, Jacinto, 177, 325
Aristotle, 437
Arminjon, Blaise, 21, 98, 125, 531
Arneric, Josip, 243–44
Arnou, René
  in November 1960 notebook, 60, 64
  in October 1961 notebook, 98
  in March 1962 notebook, 100, 120
  in October 1962 notebook, 129, 137
  in November 1962 notebook, 273,
    304
  in December 1962 notebook, 437
Arrupe, 43
Assaf, Maikhayl (Michel), 300, 304–5,
    404–5
Athanasius, Saint, 399
Athenagoras, 133, 162, 221, 222
Attila, 216
Audet, Lionel, 80
Augustin, 435–36

Butler, Christopher
  in September 1961 notebook, 84
  in October 1962 notebook, 193
  in November 1962 notebook,
    314–15, 323, 324, 339, 359–60
  in December 1962 notebook, 498–99
Butorac, Pavao, 321
Buuck, Friedrich, 273

Cabana, Georges, 348, 368
Cacheux, 67
Caggiano, Antonio (Antoine), 162, 208,
  274, 307, 368, 451
Cajetan, 106
Calewaert, Karel Justinus, 195, 471
Callewaert, Camiel, 195
Caloyera, Domenico, 182
Câmara, Helder Pessoa, 302
Cambiaghi, Placido Maria, 225
Camelot, Pierre-Thomas, 143, 175, 186,
  204, 356
Canali, Nicola, 70, 71, 101
Cantero Cuadrado, Pedro, 362
Cantin, André, 301–2, 467
Capovilla, Loris, 108, 207, 384, 514
Capozi, Dominic, 244
Capranica, Domenico, 468
Carinci, Alfonso, 263
Carli, Luigi, 193, 268, 352, 432, 438
Carraro, Giuseppe (Joseph), 204
Casel, Johannes, 395
Cassien, 133, 162, 298, 418, 419
Castellano, M. (Ismaele Mario), 277
Castelli, Alberto, 174, 303
Castelli, Enrico, 221, 222, 509, 518
Castellino, Giorgio, 519
Cavour, Count, 517
Cazaux, Antoine, 171, 205, 257, 347,
  438, 530
Ceccon, Mario, 279
Cento, Fernando, 243, 255, 368
Cerfaux, Lucien
  in March 1962 notebook, 113, 115,
    116, 120
  in November 1962 notebook,
    240–41, 320, 334, 382, 411

Certeau, Michel de, 518
Cerularius (Cerulario), Michaele, 401
Chang Tso-huan, Vito, 360
Chantraine, Georges, 21
Chappot de la Chanonie, Pierre Abel
  Louis, 347
Chappoulie, Henri, 129
Charnière, François, 65, 519
Charue, André
  in November 1962 notebook, 256,
    321, 324, 411, 412
  in December 1962 notebook, 502
  in January 1963 notebook, 519
  in February 1963 notebook, 524
Chateaubriand, 121, 148
Chavaz, Edmond, 528
Cheng Tien-Siang, Joseph, 285
Chenu, Marie-Dominique
  in the preface, 9
  in October 1962 notebook, 135, 139,
    142, 144, 161, 165, 208, 214
  in November 1962 notebook, 254
  in December 1962 notebook, 436
Chevallier, Paul, 141, 151, 158
Chichester, Aston, 182, 187, 197
Chiesa, Giacomo della. See Benedict XV
Ciappi, Mario Luigi, 86–87, 88, 90,
  106, 513, 529
Cibrián Fernández, Ubaldo Evaristo,
  364
Cicognani, Amleto Giovanni
  in October 1962 notebook, 128, 147,
    149, 156, 214
  in November 1962 notebook, 283,
    292, 346, 379, 385, 414
  in December 1962 notebook, 451,
    481, 499, 502
  in January 1963 notebook, 511–12
  in February 1963 notebook, 520, 522
Ciriaci, Pietro, 410
Civardi, Luigi, 376
Claudel, Paul, 274, 279
Clément, Robert, 257
Clement XIV, 54
Clerici, Luigi, 501
Colli, Giovanni, 517

Dubois, Marcel-Marie, 88, 205, 241
Dubois-Dumée, Jean-Pierre, 142
Dumeige, Gervais, 57, 182
Dumont, Christophe-Jean, 224, 408, 439, 479
Dupont, Henri, 330, 337
Duprey, Pierre, 418, 470
Dupuy, Claude, 241, 313, 466
Durand, Alexandre, 20
Durocher, Romulus, 271–72, 469
Duschak, Wilhelm Josef, 234–35
Duval, Léon-Étienne, 246, 279, 287–88, 376
Dworschak, Leo, 271
Dwyer, George, 220, 405–6

Echeverría Ruiz, Bernard, 177, 348–49
Edelby, Néophytos, 159, 228–29, 270, 390–92, 438
Elchinger, Léon Arthur
  in October 1962 notebook, 165, 227
  in November 1962 notebook, 330, 331, 333, 334, 335, 337, 375
  in December 1962 notebook, 430, 450
  in February 1963 notebook, 528
Elko, Nicholas Thomas (Nicolas), 417
Enciso Viana, Jesús, 196
Enrique y Tarancón, Vicente, 402
Erasmus, 212–13, 515
Etchegaray, Roger, 169, 190–91, 256, 302, 530
Etges, Zeno, 357
Eugene III, 268
Eymard, Pierre Julien, 301

Falconi, Carlo, 101, 207, 216
Fanfani, Amintore, 99, 207
Farès, Armando (Armand), 176, 235–36, 309–10, 486
Farkasfalvy, Denis, 140
Farrar, Frederic, 55
Fauvel, André, 170, 279, 476, 477
Favé, Vincent, 476
Faveri, Luigi, 248
Feiner, Johannes, 433, 502, 518, 519

Felici, Pericle
  in March 1962 notebook, 117
  in October 1962 notebook, 128, 133, 145–46, 151, 153–54, 171, 175, 208–9
  in November 1962 notebook, 234, 242, 274, 297, 316, 325, 350, 351, 354, 355, 357–58, 375, 385, 397, 406
  in December 1962 notebook, 469, 471, 476, 479, 480, 481–82, 489, 492, 496, 499
  in January 1963 notebook, 510, 512–13
Feltin, Maurice
  in October 1962 notebook, 134, 152, 161, 178, 179, 188
  in November 1962 notebook, 275, 412
  in December 1962 notebook, 477
Fenton, Joseph
  in September 1961 notebook, 81, 92–93
  in March 1962 notebook, 110, 111, 116, 118, 119, 122
  in November 1962 notebook, 316, 335, 382, 383
  in January 1963 notebook, 513, 519
  in February 1963 notebook, 526
Féret, Henri-Marie, 517
Fernandes, Angelo, 220
Fernández, Aniceto (Anicet)
  in October 1962 notebook, 199, 209
  in November 1962 notebook, 268, 352–53, 356
  in January 1963 notebook, 519
  in May 1963 notebook, 531
Fernández Feo-Tinoco, Alejandro (Alexandre), 378
Fernández y Fernández, Doroteo, 390
Ferrand, Louis, 273
Ferrari, Carlo, 235
Ferrari Toniolo, Agostino, 105–6
Ferraz, Salomâ, 211